A TEXTBOOK OF
ECONOMICS

J. L. HANSON

M.A., M.Ed. (Leeds), Ph.D., B.Sc.(Econ.) (London)

*Formerly Senior Lecturer in charge of Economics
Huddersfield College of Technology
(now Huddersfield Polytechnic)*

SEVENTH EDITION

MACDONALD AND EVANS

MACDONALD AND EVANS LTD.
Estover, Plymouth PL6 7PZ

First published 1953
Reprinted 1954
Second edition 1956
Reprinted 1957
Reprinted 1958
Reprinted 1959
Reprinted 1960
Third edition 1961
Reprinted 1962
Reprinted 1963
Reprinted 1963
Reprinted 1964
Reprinted 1965
Fourth edition 1966
Reprinted 1967
Reprinted 1968
Reprinted 1969
Fifth edition 1970
Reprinted 1971
Reprinted (with corrections) 1971
Sixth edition 1972
Reprinted 1974
Reprinted 1975
Seventh edition 1977
Reprinted 1978

©

MACDONALD AND EVANS LIMITED
1977

ISBN 0 7121 2020 3

Printed in Great Britain by Hazell Watson & Viney Ltd,
Aylesbury, Bucks

PREFACE TO THE FIRST EDITION

The tendency of professional economists at the present day—as of scientists in other fields—is to specialise in particular aspects of their subject. Students in Technical and University Colleges, however, must cover the whole subject, and if a textbook writer is to be of service to them, he must endeavour to satisfy their wide, non-specialist needs.

The present work attempts to provide a systematic course which will meet the requirements, at all levels, of the numerous professional bodies which set papers in economics, and also the needs, short of what is necessary for the final examinations, of students studying for university degrees. No university student reading for a final degree in economics, or indeed in any subject, would expect to find all his work treated within the covers of a single volume. Nevertheless, it is hoped that even they may find a textbook which ranges over the whole field of service to them by providing a foundation on which wider study can be based. The recommendations for further reading at the end of each chapter will be helpful in this respect, and should be regarded as an integral part of the course.

Appended to each chapter is a representative selection of questions on its subject-matter, taken by permission from recent examination papers. These will serve both as tests of the student's mastery of the chapter and as an indication of the type of question he is likely to meet with in the examination room. It would be well if all students attempted some of them.

It may be said, generally, that the main purpose in studying economics is to acquire knowledge of the techniques of economic analysis, and the ability to apply that knowledge to the solution of economic problems. In the words of the late Lord Keynes, economics "is a method rather than a doctrine, an apparatus of the mind, a technique of thinking which helps its possessor to draw correct conclusions." Nevertheless, the present volume is not restricted to economic theory; it discusses also some of the outstanding problems of applied economics in relation to the theory upon which their solution depends. It cannot be forgotten that economics is a social science dealing with a particular aspect of human existence: if theory is completely divorced from

vi PREFACE

reality we are left only with the dry bones of the subject. Certainly, the student must learn to use the tools of economic analysis, but he can do so only if he has factual material upon which to work. For this reason descriptions of economic institutions have been included, and more attention than is usual in a general textbook has been given to consideration of such matters as the population problem, the location of industry, the capital market, foreign exchange, transport, nationalised industries and public finance.

J.L.H.

NOTE TO THE SEVENTH EDITION

For this edition the book has been subjected to a thorough revision to take account of recent changes in economic affairs. An attempt has been made to bring examples and illustrations as nearly up-to-date as is feasible in a study prone to continual change and development. The statistics, too, have been brought up-to-date and the opportunity has been taken to add a number of questions from recent examination papers. Additional questions have been inserted in appropriate chapters to assist students taking the Ordinary National Certificate in Business Studies.

Once again my thanks are due to the many correspondents, both teachers and students, who have written to me since the book was first published offering most helpful suggestions.

Grateful acknowledgment is made to the Controller of Her Majesty's Stationery Office for allowing the use of copyright material taken from White papers and other Government publications. I also wish to thank the Senate of the University of London, the Councils of the professional bodies, and the Principals, Heads of Department or Senior Lecturers of the various Colleges listed on pp. xxxi and xxxii, for permission to reproduce questions from examination papers set by them.

1976

J.L.H.

CONTENTS

Chapter 3

FACTORS OF PRODUCTION 33

Part Three. THE ORGANISATION AND STRUCTURE OF PRODUCTION

Chapter 6

Chapter 7

PART FOUR. THE TOOLS OF ECONOMIC ANALYSIS
(continued)
(ii) The Concept of the Margin

Chapter 12

THE BASIS OF DEMAND

Chapter 13

THE BASIS OF SUPPLY: UNDER PERFECT COMPETITION

Chapter 14

THE BASIS OF SUPPLY: UNDER MONOPOLY . . 241

Chapter 15

THE BASIS OF SUPPLY: UNDER IMPERFECT COMPETITION 258

Part Five. THE NATIONAL INCOME AND ITS DISTRIBUTION

    10. Gross profit and net profit
    11. Elements of profit
    12. Causes of uncertainty
    13. Differences in profit
    14. Profit and cost of production

Part Six. BANKING AND FINANCE

Chapter 20

THE ORIGIN AND FUNCTIONS OF MONEY . 363

    I. The Origin of Money
        1. Disadvantages of barter
        2. Early forms of money

    II. Types of Money
        3. Coins
        4. Legal tender
        5. Paper money
        6. Convertible and inconvertible money
        7. Bank deposits subject to withdrawal by cheque

    III. Functions of Money
        8. Advantages of using money
        9. Functions of money

Chapter 21

THE VALUE OF MONEY 375

    I. The Price Level
        1. The value of money and the price level
        2. Changes in the value of money

    II. The Determination of the Value of Money
        3. The Quantity Theory of money
        4. Some criticisms of the Quantity Theory
        5. The money supply and the demand for money

    III. Index Numbers
        6. Measurement of changes in the value of money
        7. The problem of weighting
        8. Other problems of index numbers
        9. The index of retail prices

    IV. Inflation
        10. Effects of changes in the value of money
        11. Meanings of inflation
        12. The inflationary gap
        13. Persistent inflation
        14. Hyperinflation

Chapter 25

THE CAPITAL MARKET 451

PART SEVEN. INTERNATIONAL ECONOMICS

Chapter 26

INTERNATIONAL TRADE 467

Chapter 27

FOREIGN EXCHANGE 490

T.E.—2

Chapter 30

PUBLIC FINANCE 564

LIST OF ILLUSTRATIONS

LIST OF TABLES

EXAMINATION QUESTIONS

The following abbreviations are employed to indicate the sources of the examination questions:

RSA — Royal Society of Arts

LC Com. — London Chambers of Commerce

IT — Institute of Transport

Exp. — Institute of Export

BS — Building Societies Institute

CIS — Chartered Institute of Secretaries and Administrators

SIAA — Society of Incorporated Accountants and Auditors

AIA — Association of International Accountants

ACCA — Association of Certified and Corporate Accountants

IMTA — Institute of Municipal Treasurers and Accountants

IB — Institute of Bankers

IHA — Institute of Hospital Administrators

LGB — Local Government Board

University of London examinations:

GCE — General Certificate in Education (Advanced Level)

DPA   Diploma in Public Administration

Degree   Final B Sc (Econ.)

Ordinary National Certificate examinations:

Bolton   Bolton Technical College

Bournemouth   Bournemouth College of Technology

Chesterfield   Chesterfield College of Technology

City   City and East London College

Huddersfield   Huddersfield Technical College

NC   Northern Counties Technical Examinations Council
          (Newcastle upon Tyne)

Norwich   Norwich City College

SE London   South East London Technical College

Southampton   Southampton Technical College

UEI   Union of Educational Institutes (Birmingham)

ULCI   Union of Lancashire and Cheshire Institutes
          (Manchester)

Wales   Welsh Joint Education Committee

W London   Hammersmith and West London College

Yorks   Yorkshire and Humberside Council for Further
          Education

Part One

INTRODUCTORY

CHAPTER I

SOME PRELIMINARY IDEAS

I. THE SCOPE OF ECONOMICS

1. The subject-matter of economics

At one time books on economics always used to open with a discussion of the difficulties of giving in a concise form an adequate definition of the subject. Inadequacy of concise definition, however, is not peculiar to economics, as a glance at the definitions of other subjects of study given in any good dictionary will confirm. On account of this difficulty there seemed at one time to be almost as many definitions of the subject as there were economists, for few writers on economics appeared to be satisfied with the definitions put forward by their predecessors.

Though it may be difficult to agree upon a satisfactory, concise definition of economics, its subject-matter is beyond dispute. Almost any business transaction involves the many branches of the subject, for under modern economic conditions most people earn their living by specialising in comparatively narrow fields of activity. Specialisation, however, makes the business of production and exchange more complex. If people specialise in different kinds of work it becomes necessary for them to exchange goods and services with one another. People prefer to be paid for their services in money because money is a medium of exchange, and the use of money facilitates exchange for only a miser desires money for its own sake. Payment in money is preferred solely because money can be exchanged for food, clothing and many other things, or, if one so wished, deposited in a bank and its spending deferred until a later date. The fact that money has been paid for these things, however, hides what has really taken place—namely, that he has exchanged his own services for these various commodities. Economists used to refer to this as the "money veil."

Suppose, for example, that a man visits his tailor for the purpose of buying a new suit. This simple transaction involves almost the entire complex economic system. He is probably shown bunches of patterns, and, in itself, the very act of choosing involves an economic decision, for choice, as will be shown shortly, is fundamental to economics.

Maybe he selects a worsted cloth, woven in the West Riding of Yorkshire. Consider, then, the long chain of events that took place before the cloth reached the tailor's shop: there was the Australian sheep-farmer who sold the wool to a merchant, who arranged for its sale at the wool auctions in Melbourne or London; there was the transport of the wool from Australia to the West Riding, numerous merchants again being involved; then there were the firms that handled the commodity after it had reached Yorkshire—the scourer, the wool-comber, the spinner, the weaver—each employing many people; and finally the merchant who sold the cloth to the retailer.

This by no means exhausts the list of people who have had a share in the production of this piece of worsted cloth. Next it might be asked: how were all the various stages of production financed? The banks probably assisted the Australian sheep-farmer, the different manufacturers and possibly the merchants, too; while the risks of loss or damage to the materials in stock or in transit were covered by insurance companies, the transport itself being provided by railways, steamship companies and perhaps airlines. The risks of production were borne by the shareholders in the case of companies, or by the traders themselves if they were working on their own account. The power to drive the machinery in the mills may have been supplied by coal hewn from the earth by the miners, by electricity, or by oil. The manufacture of spinning-frames, looms and other machinery may have employed workers in the iron mines of Sweden or Cleveland, and steel-workers in many parts of Great Britain.

The making of the suit involves those engaged in the Lancashire cotton industry, who made the linings from cotton grown in the United States of America; the workers at Paisley who spun and reeled the thread with which it was sewn together; the button-makers of Birmingham, and many others. While all these people were going about their own individual tasks they had to be fed by the efforts of others who were employed in food production.

Every one of these people is engaged on some kind of economic activity that is of interest to the economist. He is not interested, however—at least, not in his professional capacity—in the technical aspect of production: how to work a particular machine, how to judge the quality of the wool, or things of that kind. These are problems for the technician. The economist, however, is interested in such questions as: Was the production at the various stages of manufacture on a large or a small scale? Was one firm responsible for several processes or only for a single process? Was the work done by hand or by machine?

The economist then endeavours to discover why one form of production was preferred to another, and what determined the size of the various firms; how much of the different commodities was produced; and why more of one was made than of another. He also wants to know how the different stages of production were financed, and if the banks were responsible for this, how they obtained the money for the purpose. He may ask further how the prices of the different raw materials and the final finished products were determined; what wages were paid to the different workers, and why some workers received more than others, and how the imports of wool, cotton, iron, etc., were paid for. All these are economic problems. It also falls within the province of economics to describe the working of the basic economic institutions, such as the banking system, and the money and capital markets.

2. Some definitions of economics

Keeping in mind the sort of questions with which economics attempts to deal, it will be of interest to consider some definitions of the subject put forward by different economists. The earliest definitions were in terms of wealth, by which was meant not only gold and silver but also all kinds of other goods—houses and public buildings, furniture, works of art and other private possessions, as well as ships, workshops, tools and the machines in use at the time for the production of goods. Adam Smith, for example, considered his work to be "an inquiry into the nature and causes of the wealth of nations," while J. S. Mill looked on economics as "the practical science of the production and distribution of wealth"—the definition adopted by the *Concise Oxford Dictionary*. Adam Smith, then, was concerned with the broader aspects of wealth, the means by which the total volume of production could be increased —an important aim of economic policy today. J. S. Mill's definition went a stage further and included problems of both production and distribution, thus covering the two main influences on the standard of living. A large part of economics, however, is now devoted to a study of problems of exchange, and Davenport emphasised this aspect of the subject when he declared economics to be "the science that treats phenomena from the standpoint of price."[1] Important as is the price mechanism, this definition gives little indication of the subject-matter of economics. A. C. Pigou defined economics in terms of welfare, thereby stressing the human as well as the material aspect of the subject,[2] regarding economics as a means of studying how to increase total

[1] H. J. Davenport: *Economics of Enterprise*, Chapter 2.
[2] A. C. Pigou: *Economics of Welfare*, Part I, Chapters 1 and 2.

production in order to raise the standard of living. Alfred Marshall's definition appears to form a link between those centred on wealth and those that stress welfare and the standard of living. First he declares somewhat vaguely that economics is "a study of mankind in the ordinary business of life," but then goes on to amplify this statement by saying that economics "examines that part of individual and social action connected with the attainment of the material requisites of well-being," so that the subject becomes "on the one side, a study of wealth; on the more important, a part of the study of man."[1] Like Pigou later, he regarded the accumulation of wealth only as a means towards raising a people's standard of living. Modern economics, however, is based on a theory of *scarcity* and *choice*, and this approach to the subject makes possible the framing of a definition in yet another form. Before this definition can be given, however, it is necessary to consider exactly what the economist means by the two terms, *scarcity* and *choice*.

II. THE BASIC PRINCIPLE OF ECONOMICS— SCARCITY AND CHOICE

3. Scarcity

To the economist all things are said to be scarce, since by "scarce" he means simply "limited in supply." In ordinary speech, however, the word "scarce" has a more restricted meaning. In the past there was always a danger of a "scarcity" of food as a result of bad harvests. To countries like Great Britain this danger may now seem very remote, but it is still present even today for people in many parts of the world. Nowadays British shops are generally well stocked with all kinds of goods, and there seem to be ample supplies of everything for everybody—for everybody, that is, who wants them and has the money with which to buy them. However, it is in such conditions as these that economists say that all goods are scarce. What is meant is that all goods are scarce relative to people's desire for them. Most people would probably like to have more of many things or goods of better quality than they possess at present: larger houses, perhaps, in which to live, better furnished with the latest labour-saving devices, such as electric washers, cookers, refrigerators; more visits to the theatre or the concert-hall; more travel; the latest models in motor cars, radios and television sets; and most women exhibit an apparently insatiable desire for clothes. People's wants are many, but the resources for

[1] A. Marshall: *Principles of Economics*, Book I, Chapter I.

making the things they want—land, labour, raw materials, factory buildings, machinery—are themselves limited in supply. There are insufficient productive resources in the world, therefore, to produce the amount of goods and services that would be required to satisfy everyone's wants fully. Consequently, to the economist all things are at all times said to be "scarce."

Although the output of all kinds of things has increased enormously during the past hundred years, goods are still scarce relative to the demand for them. However rapid may be the rate of economic progress in the future, so far as we can see, therefore, it appears to be extremely unlikely that it will ever be possible to produce any kinds of goods in unlimited quantities. With regard to services their supply is limited by the number of people who can be spared from the production of goods.

4. Choice

If, then, all things are scarce relative to the *desire* for them, and if people have many unsatisfied wants and the means exist for satisfying only some of them, obviously they cannot satisfy all of them, and therefore they must make a choice. In order to be able to enjoy some things it is necessary to do without others. If every human action was perfectly rational everyone would naturally satisfy his more pressing wants first, choosing the things he desired most and going without those he considered less desirable. There are few people, however, who have not at some time or other given way to impulse, and made a purchase they have afterwards regretted. Strictly, the economist is not concerned—that is, not concerned as an economist, though he may be vitally interested for other reasons—with the merits or demerits of the choice. An alcoholic prefers to go without all sorts of things in order to satisfy his craving for drink; at one time the scholar had to stint himself of food so that he could have more books; the traveller may deprive himself of a home in order to allow full play to his urge to see the world. All these people are making choices, enjoying one thing at the expense of another, but whether they are making good or bad choices is a matter not for economics but for ethics.

A few moments' thought is sufficient to reveal how fundamental to economic problems is this question of choice. How frequently one hears the complaint that a person has not the time to do this or that. It will generally be found, however, that this is merely an excuse for his not doing something that he dislikes. What he really means is that he prefers to do something else. "I can't find the time to attend a course of lectures on economics," says the young man who spends most evenings at a youth club and the rest at a dance-hall or viewing television. Time is "scarce," and therefore one has to choose between competing ways of spending it. Most people have little control over the amount of time required of them by their employers, but some can choose between working overtime or not; and if they choose to work overtime they forgo so much leisure. Sometimes, too, a man may be able to choose between a well-paid, but uncongenial occupation, and a more congenial one at a lower rate of pay.

The greatest amount of choice occurs, however, in the expenditure of one's income. First, one has to decide how much to spend and how much to save, and then how much to spend on such things as rent, food, clothing, holidays, etc. People often say they cannot afford to buy something when they really mean they prefer to spend their money on something else. A man may say, for example, that he cannot afford a better house although he may run an expensive motor car and take his holidays abroad. Another may say that he cannot afford books or visits to the theatre and yet he may be a member of an exclusive golf club.

Scales of preference. One of the assumptions of economics is that people always act rationally. Thus, if a person has to make a choice between one thing and another, it is assumed that he will always choose the alternative that will yield him the greater satisfaction. This implies, too, that each individual has a scale of preference, a sort of list of all his unsatisfied wants arranged in order of preference. Near the top of the scale one will expect to find what he regards as his most pressing wants, and these he may be expected to satisfy before he pays any attention to wants near the bottom of his scale. Faced, then, with the alternative of satisfying either want No. 2 or want No. 5, he would therefore satisfy No. 2. Few people have such a definite scale of unsatisfied wants, though they may be able to distinguish between their most pressing and their least pressing wants, but for the purpose of economic theory it is necessary to make the assumption that people behave rationally, it therefore being assumed that each person has his own scale of preference, on which his wants are arranged in order of relative importance to him. The ethical or moral aspect of the order of preference is not the direct concern of economics. On one person's scale a "thriller" may occupy a higher place than a play of Shakespeare's; another person may prefer a football match to a symphony concert; other people may think both these preferences ill-chosen. Economically, however, the wisdom of the choice is not important.

Opportunity-cost. Since an individual cannot satisfy all his wants, but must choose between one thing and another, the satisfaction of one want involves going without something else. Thus, the real cost of satisfying any want is the alternative that has to be forgone in order to do so. If a man is confronted by a choice between living in a larger house and running a motor car, the real cost of running the motor car, if he chooses that alternative, would be the larger house he has had to do without. In the expenditure of time, this idea of real cost is even more readily understood. If a student misses one of his lectures on economics in order to see a football match, its cost to him is the lecture on economics that he has missed. The real cost of anything, in the sense of the alternative that has to be forgone, is known as its "opportunity-cost."

5. Choice in different economic systems

Businessmen, too, are constantly being confronted with choices. In the first place, they have to decide what to produce. Then they have to decide what method of production to adopt, how much capital and labour to employ, whether to produce on a small or a large scale and so on. As already noted, the choices of individuals are not always deliberately made after alternatives have been carefully weighed. Business choices or decisions, on the other hand, are usually made only after careful consideration, since the making of a wrong decision can have very serious consequences. Whatever form an economic system may take the scarcity of productive resources makes choice essential, though how choice is made and by whom depends on whether the system is one of free enterprise, or State-planned or a combination of the two.

In a free economy consumers have a free choice as to what they buy, limited only by the amount of money they have to spend. The relative strength of consumers' demands for various commodities determines the amount of each that will be produced. Thus, for example, an increase in the demand for a commodity will stimulate an expansion of its manufacture and the industry will attract to itself the required amount of labour and other resources. Industries producing commodities for which there is a small demand will require less productive resources. In this way scarce or limited resources, which have alternative uses, are distributed among the various producers.

In a State-planned economy the State decides what shall be produced. In such an economy some choice is taken away from consumers. In a completely planned economy the State will accept entire responsibility for making all the choices—deciding what shall be produced, how much shall be produced and allocating productive resources among the various producers. In a free economy the consumer himself makes the choice; in the planned economy the choice rests with the State, acting through its planning committee.

No country in the world today has either a perfectly free economy or a completely State-planned economy. In all of them there is a public sector and a private sector. Even in those countries where individuals have the greatest freedom of choice there are some choices that must be left to the State. In State-planned economies it is easy for the State to make the choices that affect production but much more difficult to distribute among consumers the goods produced for them. Rationing of many large goods would be almost impossible other than through the price mechanism and so in any case a limited number of choices have to be left to individuals.

6. Economics as a study of the disposal of scarce goods

Since, then, wants are many and the means for satisfying them are limited, a choice has to be made as to what shall be produced and how much shall be produced. The fundamental principles of economics, therefore, are scarcity and choice. Thus, the basic problem in any type of economic system is how to allocate scarce resources among the many lines of production competing for them. This brings us to a more modern definition of economics than those considered in paragraph 2 above—"the science which studies human behaviour as a relationship between ends and scarce means which have alternative uses."[1] Thus economics justifies its name by becoming a study of a particular kind of economising—the economising of resources and their apportionment among all the industries competing for their use. The advantage of this definition is that it covers all kinds of economic activity, in the home as well as in the outside world. Unfortunately, such a definition gives little indication of the scope or subject-matter of economics. It is, in fact, a definition of economics for economists.

III. THE SOCIAL SCIENCES

7. Economics and ethics, theology and politics

The social sciences concern themselves with the study of different aspects of human behaviour, whereas the province of the physical

[1] L. Robbins: *Nature and Significance of Economic Science*, p. 16.

sciences is the study of various aspects of Man's environment, while the concern of the natural sciences is with the physical side of animal. (including human) life. The early philosophers such as Plato and Aristotle allowed their thoughts to roam over any aspect of the universe that aroused their curiosity. They recognised no clear line of demarcation between ethics, politics and economics; to them all subjects of study were only different aspects of one great comprehensive subject—philosophy.

Economic questions were touched upon by the Greek philosophers only when incidental to ethical or political problems; for example, it was on ethical grounds that Plato objected to the payment of interest on borrowed money. Similarly, Aristotle for ethical reasons condemned exchange when money was employed instead of barter. The question of value was also approached from the point of view of ethics, and discussion centred round the idea of a "just price". Plato propounded his theory of communism because he thought it was a prerequisite of the good life, and it was for exactly the same reason that Aristotle favoured private property. Medieval philosophers inherited the Greek and Roman objection to usury, but they regarded economics as subsidiary to theology. Though they taught that all men were equal before God, inequality of station was accepted, as earthly existence was regarded as merely preparatory for the after life.

Then came the Age of Mercantilism with the growth of nationalism and a great expansion of trade. Economics became the handmaid of politics to point the way towards the creation of prosperous, national states. The accumulation of wealth, previously frowned upon, acquired a degree of respectability. The State intervened to regulate trade and industry in order to promote the prosperity of the nation, and so economic matters became political questions.

8. Economics as an independent subject of study

Increasing knowledge, however, made the study of Man and his environment too vast for a single subject, and in course of time it split up into an increasing number of separate sciences. The physical and natural sciences were the first to become independent disciplines, but until quite recent times philosophy still embraced all the social sciences. One by one, however, the social sciences eventually broke away from philosophy.

It was the Industrial Revolution which completely freed economics from the other social sciences. The Industrial Revolution resulted in a vast increase in production and increasing specialisation, with its corollary of increased exchange, so that the economic system became increasingly complex. Economics shook itself free from ethics, theology and politics. The development of the doctrine of *laissez-faire*, which favoured a policy of non-interference by the State, assisted in its emancipation.

Adam Smith was the first writer to produce a work devoted purely to economics. Though published in 1776, before the Industrial Revolution was fully under way, his *Wealth of Nations* is a landmark in the development of economics as an independent subject of study. Since that time the number of writers on economics has greatly increased, until now a flood of new work is published each year. In fact, economics has now expanded to such an extent that economists now find it necessary to specialise in small branches of the subject.

9. The barriers between economics and other social sciences again breaking down

At the present time, however, there is a tendency to break down the barriers that have been built up during the past two hundred years between economics and the other social sciences—ethics, theology, politics, sociology and psychology. Not so long ago it used to be emphatically stressed that ethical or political aspects of economic problems were not the concern of the economist.

A practical problem has many different aspects—economic, social, ethical, political, legal and possibly others. All these aspects of a problem are of importance to the community but not all are matters for the economist. It is, of course, essential to isolate economic considerations in order to secure clarity of thinking; but, having done so, it is important then to discover whether the economist's solution conflicts with the findings of workers in other fields, for economic questions are often inextricably entangled with social or political implications.

Reaction to the *laissez-faire* of the nineteenth century led the State to intervene increasingly in economic affairs. Acceptance of responsibility for full employment has given the State a greater interest in economic affairs than ever before. The greater the extent of State planning, the greater is the intermingling of economics and politics.

Thus economics, once merely incidental to philosophy, has become a separate social study, but, since all such study relates to Man and his environment, it cannot be rigidly marked off from the other social sciences.

IV. PURPOSE AND METHOD

10. Economic theory

Though they can never be completely separated from one another, there are, in effect, three branches of economics: (*i*) descriptive economics, which is concerned, as the name implies, with describing the working of economic institutions; (*ii*) economic theory or principles of economics; and (*iii*) applied economics, where theory is used to assist the study of actual economic problems.

Economic theory, or pure economics, consists of a body of principles, logically built up. It provides the tools of economic analysis, but it is pursued without any thought as to whether it is likely to yield practical results or not. Theory is developed and reasoning is carried to its logical conclusion, irrespective of where this may lead. In this it is similar to other sciences, where the research worker pursued his investigations with the sole object of increasing the total of human knowledge. If there should prove to be some practical application of the theory that is something for others to develop. In pure economics it is necessary to make so many assumptions that sometimes theory seems to bear only a slight relation to fact. It is assumed, for example, that men in their economic activities always behave quite rationally, whereas most people are to some degree creatures of habit or impulse. If two exactly similar commodities were offered for sale by different shops, the price at the first shop being 5p and at the second 4p, a perfectly rational economic action would be for everybody to buy at the cheaper shop, whereas to most people it would be too much trouble to seek out the cheapest shop every time a small purchase had to be made. Economics should not be condemned as unrealistic just because such unreal assumptions are made, for without making such assumptions it would not be possible to build up a body of economic principles at all, and a scientific approach to economic problems would be impossible.

11. Economics a science

Reference has been made above to economics as a social science. Can economics, then, be regarded as a science? Subjects such as physics, chemistry, botany, etc., are easily recognised as sciences, and though the Latin word *scientia* merely means knowledge, the modern term "science" has taken on a more restricted connotation. Characteristics of a science are the observation of certain facts, the selection and classification of relevant material, and the using of these as a basis for generalisation. It then becomes possible to formulate laws which are universally true under specified conditions and which can be applied to the analysis of new situations. In this sense economics can be considered to be a science, its fundamental facts being observations from everyday life. It is sometimes said to be a positive science because it considers things as they are and not as they ought to be, though not positive in the sense that definite and infallible predictions can be made of the future consequences of current economic happenings.

In order to build up a set of economic principles, certain basic assumptions are made as in other sciences—though in the practical sciences they may be more realistic. One of the most important assumptions is that men in their economic life always act rationally. This being so, then (*i*) the businessman always aims to make the maximum amount of profit; (*ii*) people will always buy goods of the same quality in the cheapest market; and (*iii*) when a choice has to be made, an individual will always select that commodity which yields the greatest amount of satisfaction. Starting from a given hypothesis— some accepted fact of everyday experience—logical deductions are made, theories being deduced by logical reasoning. From these deductions economic laws are formulated which, like other scientific laws, merely assert what takes place when certain conditions are fulfilled. Algebraic and geometrical methods were developed because they show relationships, as for example between demand and price, without actual quantities being required.

As an alternative to the *deductive* method, some economic problems are approached on *inductive* lines—that is, a mass of data is obtained from actual experience and then used as a basis for generalisations. The inductive method has been employed in Great Britain to discover businessmen's reactions to changes in the rate of interest and to obtain information on family expenditure as a basis for the index of retail prices.

Compared with the practical sciences, economics is at a disadvantage, for the data obtained by a chemist from a succession of experiments will be more precise than that acquired from the behaviour of human beings by the research worker in the field of economics. The deductive and the inductive methods, however, are appropriate to their own fields. The method of study in economics is, therefore, scientific and so economics can be regarded, if one so wishes, as a science.

12. Why study economics?

A student embarking upon a set course of study generally asks for a reason for his having to take a particular subject only if he finds that subject distasteful. Few ask to know the use of physical training and games; many put the question, for example, in the case of history. The question seems unnecessary as regards applied economics, for it appears to be "useful" to understand economic problems. In contrast, economic theory may seem to many to be a "useless" subject. It would however, be a sufficient defence for the study of pure theory to assert that all knowledge is useful for its own sake, since there is no need for a subject to have practical application for it to be worthy of study.

It is the aim of pure economics to build up a body of principles and to furnish the economist with tools of economic analysis that will enable him not only to understand current economic problems but also to see the economic consequences of pursuing a particular line of policy. Economics should provide a training in a technique of thinking which will enable those who have acquired it to attain a clearer understanding of economic problems. Defects are to be found in any economic system or policy, and the economist should be able to say whether proposed changes are *likely* to be economically advantageous or not. Unfortunately, he cannot always say so with certainty, since the economic is only one of many aspects of actual problems; hence economists often disagree on such questions.

Against undue concentration on pure theory it may be argued that economists, of all people, should be imbued with a desire to increase the well-being of the community. Indeed, many people come to economics to seek a solution of current problems and feel a sense of disappointment when they realise the limitations of the subject. The economist cannot offer any final solution to the practical problems of everyday experience, though he may often be able to indicate the economic advantages or disadvantages of a particular policy. Moreover, a trained economist is better equipped than others to understand these problems. Professor A. C. Pigou believed economics to be worthy of study because it made it easier to institute practical measures to promote welfare—so that "statesmen may build upon the work of the economist." For, he says, "it is not in the ordinary business of life that man is most interesting, or inspiring." He concludes, therefore, that the study of economics is not worth while for its own sake but only "for the healing that knowledge may help to bring."[1]

As Sir Henry Clay has said, "Some study of economics is at once a practical necessity and a moral obligation,"[2] for economic questions touch the daily lives of everyone.

[1] A. C. Pigou: *Economics of Welfare*, p. 10.
[2] H. Clay: *Economics for the General Reader*, p. 6.

RECOMMENDATIONS FOR FURTHER READING

A. Marshall: *Principles of Economics*, Book I, Chapters 1–3.
A. C. Pigou: *Economics of Welfare*, Part I, Chapter 1.
L. C. Robbins: *The Nature and Significance of Economic Science*.
F. H. Knight: *Risk, Uncertainty and Profit*, Chapter 3.

QUESTIONS

1. "Choice is at the centre of all economic problems." Discuss this statement and indicate how far an individual has freedom of choice. (Chesterfield)

2. What is the basic economic problem facing any society? How can it be solved? (Huddersfield)

3. Consider the subject-matter of economics by reference to any three definitions of the study. (RSA)

4. What is meant by the statement that economics is a social science? (IT)

5. Give a definition of economics and give an explanation justifying your definition. (Exp.)

6. For what purposes do we study economics? Of what value is the study of economics to a secretary? (CIS)

7. Discuss the statement that modern economics is based upon a theory of scarcity and choice. (AIA)

8. Write a short essay on: "Economic laws." (IMTA)

9. Economics has been described as the science that concerns itself, on the one hand, with *scarce means* and, on the other, with *wealth*. Do you consider this to be an adequate description? In your answer carefully analyse the use of the two terms, *scarce means* and *wealth*, in this context. (IHA)

10. "The assumption of rational behaviour in modern economic theory is but a variant of the classical notion of economic man." Discuss. (Degree)

Part Two

THE PROCESS OF PRODUCTION

CHAPTER 2

PRODUCTION

I. THE PURPOSE OF PRODUCTION

1. The satisfaction of wants

The aim of all production is to satisfy people's wants. When each family had to satisfy its wants by its own efforts the extent and strength of its wants decided the activities of the group. Man's earliest wants were for food, clothing and shelter, and in early days it might take all his time and energy to provide himself with even a bare minimum of these things. With the development of civilisation people's wants multiplied, and the more wants people are able to satisfy the higher will be their standard of living. However, few people nowadays satisfy their wants directly. The use of money makes it possible for them to work for money payments, and afterwards to use the money to buy the things they desire which other people have made. Under present conditions of economic organisation a vast range of goods is produced and new commodities are constantly being introduced. People engage in production, therefore, in order to earn the means by which they will be able to satisfy their own wants, and at the same time they are helping to satisfy the wants of other people. The same people are thus at the same time both producers and consumers.

Production can take many forms. Primary production includes the extractive occupations, that is, all branches of farming, mining, quarrying and fishing, and so is concerned with the production of food-stuffs and raw materials. Secondary production comprises all kinds of manufacturing and constructive work, turning the raw materials provided by primary production into finished goods. These are the only occupations which many people would regard as productive. However, the production of a commodity is not complete until it has reached consumers—the people who actually want to use it.

2. The meaning of production

In everyday speech the word *production* is often used as if it were synonymous with *creating* something. The making or manufacture of a commodity—for example, a motor car—means no more, however, than putting together certain quantities of different kinds of materials. Even processes involving chemical action only change the form of substances, and do not actually create anything. In economics however, production is not restricted to the manufacture of commodities but also includes the provision of direct services, such as those of the lawyer, the accountant, the actor or musician, etc. Since all these people aim at satisfying other people's wants just as much as those working in a motor-car factory, their work also can be considered to be productive. When a sum of money is paid to a retailer for a purchase this really comprises a series of payments for the services of the various people involved in its production. Basically, therefore, all production consists of the provision of services.

As will be seen shortly, a larger total output is achieved when people specialise, but this makes exchange necessary, and so the extra cost of distribution must be set against the gain from specialisation. Production therefore covers the following activities: (i) changing the form of a good at any stage from the raw material to the finished product as, for example, weaving woollen yarn into cloth; (ii) changing the situation of a good as, for example, from a factory in the Midlands to a retail shop, say, in Bournemouth; (iii) changing the position of a good in time as, for example, holding stocks of goods until they are required; and (iv) the provision of some kind of service, such as retailing, banking, entertaining.

3. The volume of production and economic welfare

The purpose of production, therefore, is to increase the economic welfare of a people, that is, to raise their standard of living by enabling them to satisfy more fully a greater number of their wants. Economic welfare clearly depends in the first place on the volume of production, and consequently to expand the volume of production will generally increase economic welfare and make possible a rise in the standard of living. An expansion of the volume of production thus becomes one of the principal aims of economic policy, but this of itself will not increase the standard of living of the whole community if nearly all the additional goods and services produced go to a small section of the people. In the second place, therefore, a people's standard of living depends on how these goods and services are distributed among them, and generally the more nearly equal is this distribution, the greater will be the economic welfare of the community. This does not necessarily mean that in order to achieve the highest possible level of economic welfare the total product must be divided equally among all people, so that everyone has exactly the same income, but it does mean that extremes of very high or very low incomes should not exist side by side. In Great Britain there was a much smaller volume of production and a very much greater inequality of income in 1900 than there is today, and therefore for both these reasons economic welfare is greater and the standard of living higher at the present day than it was in 1900.

4. The planning of production

The aim of production, as already pointed out, is to satisfy people's wants. Whatever form an economic system may take, all production must be planned by someone. In a fully planned economic system it is the State, through its central planning committee, that decides what shall be produced and what portion of a country's resources shall be devoted to different lines of production. Under a system of free or private enterprise, when production is in the hands of independent firms, those things will be produced which producers believe that consumers want. Every purchase, therefore, is equivalent to a vote in favour of the continuing production of that commodity, so that production is based on past experience and anticipated future demand. Under this system an attempt is made to plan production in such a way that consumers as a whole can have that assortment of goods which they appear to prefer. In the one case, then, the State decides what shall be produced, and in the other it is the consumers themselves who decide.

Some of the worst drawbacks of private enterprise, in fact, resulted in the intervention of the State long before central planning came to be advocated. For example, the demand for gin which at one time was considered excessive because of its ill effects, was checked by taxing it heavily, while the possession of certain drugs, considered to be harmful, was made a criminal offence. During the past fifty years the State has intervened in economic affairs to an increasing extent in both Great Britain and the United States, especially since 1945. In some countries today the planning of production is entirely the responsibility of the State as, for example, the Soviet Union, China and other communist states. No country, however, now remains where unfettered private enterprise exists. Many countries have what is called a "mixed" system, in which some forms of production are undertaken by the State and some are left to private enterprise. These include Great Britain, the United States and most of the countries of Western Europe, although the proportion and form of production in the hands of the State varies very considerably between one country and another.

II. WEALTH

5. What is wealth?

Production aims, then, at producing both goods and services. Some goods are durable—for example, a church or a factory; some are wanted for immediate consumption—for example, food; and some are intermediate between these—for example, a television set or an electric washer. Services are of two main kinds: (*i*) commercial services, such as wholesaling, retailing, insurance, etc., (*ii*) direct services such as those of doctors, solicitors, teachers, etc. At any given moment there is in existence in a country, a definite quantity of goods of all types. These comprise the country's wealth at that time.

To the economist wealth is a stock of goods existing at a particular time that conform to certain requirements. Such goods must possess four qualities. In the first place, they must possess utility—that is, they must be capable of yielding satisfaction, and so they must be desirable. Secondly, before goods can be considered as wealth they must have a money value, even though they may be considered to be invaluable. Such things as the paintings in the Tate or other art galleries, the stained glass in many medieval cathedrals such as York and Canterbury, are clearly wealth, though their value in terms of money could not be calculated. Thirdly, they must be limited in supply. Fourthly, the ownership of such goods must be capable of being transferred from one person to another. This fourth condition carries with it the assumption that all wealth is owned by someone—an individual or a public body. This definition of wealth is more precise than the meaning often attached to the word in ordinary speech, and would exclude intangible things such as acquired skills. An independent craftsman—as, for example, a carpenter, could count his tools as part of his stock of wealth but not his skill in using them, since skills are not transferable. In speaking of a country's wealth, however, some people might include the quality of its labour, especially if there was a high standard of education and training. For clarity of thinking it is essential to attach precise meanings to terms, and it is therefore better to regard only tangible things as wealth.

The total national wealth of Great Britain over the years has been increasing and there is no doubt that the total wealth of this country is considerably greater today than it was fifty years ago.

6. The ownership of wealth

Three classes of ownership of wealth may be distinguished:

(i) *Personal wealth*. First there is what may be called personal wealth. This comprises personal belongings such as clothes, watches, jewellery, books, motor cars, household equipment and furniture, and the house one lives in. All these things presumably give satisfaction to their owner, or they would not have been acquired; all have a money value, all are limited in supply, and in all cases ownership is transferable from one person to another.

(ii) *Business wealth*. Secondly, there is business wealth—that is, such things as factory buildings, machinery, raw materials, railway systems, canals, roads, land. These things also possess all the attributes of wealth, although they do not yield satisfaction for their own sake. They are desired only because they can be employed in the production of other things—ultimately, personal wealth or social wealth. This kind of wealth is used as an agent of production, and, as will be seen below, economists differentiate it from other kinds of wealth by calling it land or capital.

(iii) *Social wealth*. This forms the third type of wealth. It consists of wealth owned collectively, and includes all property owned by the State or local authorities—schools, public libraries, art galleries and museums, gas and electricity undertakings, town halls, Government offices, etc. Since 1945 a number of industries have been nationalised and their assets, previously privately owned, have been added to the stock of social wealth. Some of this wealth (for example, pictures in art galleries) is similar to personal wealth, in being desirable for its own sake, but too costly for most people individually to afford; and some of it is collectively owned business wealth, as, for example, coal-mines and railways.

7. Individual and collective wealth

In calculating his personal wealth an individual would include any money he had in the bank, and the present value of any Saving Certificates, British Savings Bonds, Treasury Stock or shares in companies that he might possess. An individual is justified in doing this because he can easily turn any of these investments into money which he could then use to purchase tangible goods that form real wealth.

In calculating the total wealth of the community as a whole, however, neither money nor Government securities must be included. Money is simply a claim to goods and services, and is worthless unless these goods and services are available at the time when they are required. Government securities are generally claims to sums of money which the Government undertakes to pay to the holders at a stated future date, and the interest is paid to particular persons out of taxes collected from the whole community—that is, the interest is merely a transfer of purchasing power from one group of people to another. Further, these Government securities represent no real assets, and form part of the National Debt, most of which represents Government borrowing in the past, mainly to finance wars. On the other hand, a share in a company represents a definite fraction of the company's business wealth, but the share certificate and the actual asset itself must not both be counted. In calculating a country's wealth it is necessary too to take into account its international assets and liabilities. A foreign debt must be deducted from the total, for it can be liquidated only by the export of actual goods or services. Similarly, any debts owing to it by other nations must be added to the total.

8. The ownership of wealth and the form of the economic system

Three categories of ownership of wealth were noted above: personal, business and social. Business wealth or capital can, however, be owned by private individuals or the State. The following diagram shows the ownership of different types of wealth:

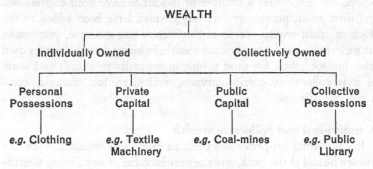

Fig. 1.—Types of Wealth.

Under a system of free enterprise (capitalism) most wealth, both personal possessions and capital, would be privately owned by individuals or groups of people. Even so, some wealth (for example, Government offices) would be collectively owned by the community as a whole. In a fully State-planned economy (communism) all business wealth would be collectively owned and probably also some durable personal goods such as houses. Private transport too might not be permitted, but people would have to be allowed to own other private personal possessions. In recent years the tendency has been for the State to acquire a greater share of wealth in capitalist economies and for individuals under communist regimes to be allowed more personal possessions. It is, however, the ownership of business capital that has given rise to different economic and political systems.

In Great Britain there is a mixed system, the State owning a number of basic industries—coal-mining, railways, gas, electricity and steel production—though most industries in this country are still carried on under private enterprise, though often subject to controls and restrictions imposed by the State. The present economic system of Great Britain, though now a mixed system, is still therefore largely based on free enterprise and private property.

9. Poverty, wealth and income

Poverty may be defined as either (i) lack of wealth, or (ii) insufficiency of income. Persons or countries therefore may be poor because they possess little wealth or because of the smallness of their incomes. Thus, the word is used in two senses. It can refer to one's stock of goods, that is, wealth, or it can refer to one's income. By income is meant a regular flow or addition to one's stock of wealth, and generally a person is considered to be poor if his income is small. Similarly, a poor country is one with a small income—that is, where the volume of production is small as an average per head of the population. Poverty, therefore, means the ability to satisfy only a small proportion of one's wants. Output per head in countries such as Great Britain has enormously increased over the past century, and what today is regarded as poverty would have been thought to be comparative affluence in the Great Britain of a hundred and fifty years ago, or by many people in other parts of the world even today. By the taxation of incomes and inherited wealth, the provision of social services and, since 1971, payments to families with low incomes, inequality of income and poverty have been considerably reduced.

III. DIVISION OF LABOUR

10. Development of division of labour

Four distinct stages can be distinguished in the development of division of labour:

(i) *Specialisation by craft.* Even under the most primitive conditions of human existence there was some division of labour: the man spent his time fighting and hunting, while the woman looked after the home and the children. When agricultural pursuits were undertaken, work on the land often devolved upon the woman, the man regarding himself primarily as a warrior. Later, in village communities, some occupations required specialists, and so we find men working as millers, black-smiths or carpenters. In the Middle Ages the number and variety of craft guilds in London, York and other cities indicates the extent of specialisation in those days—the goldsmiths, the merchant "taylors," the barber surgeons, the glovers, the mercers, the drapers, the haber-dashers, the grocers, the smiths, the bakers and many more. Masters, journeymen and apprentices were members of the same guild, for no master employed more than a few journeymen, each of whom expected to be a master himself one day.

(ii) *Specialisation by process.* This, the second stage in the division of labour, tends to be associated with the Industrial Revolution, although there was division of labour of this kind long before that. The develop-ment of the factory system led to a great extension of the principle of the division of labour, as well as to the rise and development of the capitalist system. Under the domestic system the merchant-manu-facturer financed production carried on in the homes of the workers; under the factory system there was an increasing use of capital, and this brought into existence the large-scale employer of labour. Where each stage of production is carried out by a different person, there is clearly division of labour by process, even though each process is done by hand.

(iii) *Regional specialisation.* A further extension of division of labour occurs when industries are localised in particular areas, this being known as territorial division of labour. There are many examples of this in Great Britain—the manufacture of cutlery in Sheffield, cotton goods in Lancashire, woollen goods in West Yorkshire, boots and shoes in the Northampton–Leicester district, tin-plate in South Wales—this development being mainly due to the nearness of these areas to cheap power. When division of labour is extended in this way it becomes possible for the individual firms comprising the industry to specialise in particular processes.

(iv) *International division of labour.* The final stage in the division of labour occurs when countries specialise in the production of those com-modities for which they have the greatest comparative advantage over others. For more than a hundred and fifty years most of the world's cotton cloth was manufactured in South Lancashire because during that period this commodity could be produced more cheaply there than elsewhere. Some international specialisation—for example, in the production of many raw materials—has its origin in differences of climate and geology. Although countries often put obstacles in the way of the full development of international division of labour, specialisation at every stage involves exchange and dependence on others for some things. International division of labour thus brought into being an interdependent world.

Division of labour began, then, in the dividing of the day's work among the members of the family, extended with the growth of towns to the specialisation of individual trades, and with the development of the factory system it came to mean the splitting up of production into a number of separate processes, each undertaken by a different worker. From the single firm the principle was eventually extended to the industry, for where an industry came to be concentrated in one area the individual firms could then specialise in single processes. The Lancashire cotton industry provides an excellent example of this, but this aspect of the division of labour—the localisation of industry—will be considered later. From specialisation by districts to specialisation by countries is not a big step, and international trade is based on this principle. Territorially, then, division of labour expanded from the family to the town, from town to the country, and from the country to the world.

11. Division of labour and output

The aim of division of labour is to increase output.

Adam Smith was greatly impressed by the increase in production resulting from division of labour, and he devoted the first three chapters of his book *The Wealth of Nations*[1] to a discussion of this topic. To illustrate how output is increased where division of labour is in operation he selected pin-making, which in his day involved eighteen separate operations. Without division of labour—that is, if one man performed every operation himself—a workman could produce no more than twenty pins in a day. In one small workshop that Adam Smith visited ten men were employed, and though some of them were apparently undertaking more than one operation, their total output often reached 48,000 pins per day, giving an average of 4,800 per workman, as against twenty each where there was no division of labour.

A more modern example is provided by the manufacture of motor-

[1] In full the title runs: *An Inquiry into the Nature and Causes of the Wealth of Nations.*

car engines. At one time the entire engine was assembled by one man. To speed up production Henry Ford divided the work into eighty-four operations, each performed by a different man, with the result that the total output of the eighty-four men was more than trebled.

It is perhaps necessary at this point to utter a cautionary word. The enormous expansion of production over the past two centuries has not been the result of division of labour alone. The most important influence has been the invention of new and better machines, that is, the increasing use of capital. Division of labour did, of course, make possible a greater use of machinery.

How, then, does division of labour increase output? We cannot do better than go to Adam Smith for our answer, since his analysis largely holds good today. Five reasons can be given:

(*i*) *Greater skill of the workers.* Division of labour results in workers acquiring greater skill at their jobs, for "by reducing every man's business to some simple operation, and by making this operation the sole employment of his life, necessarily increases very much the dexterity of the workman." In other words: "practice makes perfect." The constant repetition of a task makes its performance almost automatic. The importance of this sort of skill, however, has been greatly reduced as more sophisticated machinery came to be used.

(*ii*) *A saving of time.* There is a "saving of the time which is often lost in passing from one sort of work to another, for a man commonly saunters a little in turning his hand from one sort of employment to another." By keeping to a single operation, a workman can accomplish a great deal more, since he wastes less time between operations. Less time, too, is required to learn how to perform a single operation than to learn a complete trade.

(*iii*) *Employment of specialists.* The carrying out of almost any piece of work requires the performance of many separate tasks, each often needing its own particular skill. Specialisation therefore makes it possible for each workman to specialise in the work for which he has the greatest aptitude.

(*iv*) *It makes possible the use of machinery.* Adam Smith, in listing the advantages of the division of labour, was thinking of it independently of the use of machinery. It may be put forward as a further advantage of the division of labour that it made possible a greater use of machinery. Once a piece of work was reduced to mere routine, it opened the way for the employment of a machine to carry out the operation, so that output was still further increased. Though division of labour without the use of power-driven machinery is possible, yet specialisation of process is itself induced by machinery, and makes division of labour essential. Division of labour paved the way for the introduction of machinery and mass-production methods.

(*v*) *Less fatigue.* It is sometimes claimed that the worker, habituated to the repetition of simple tasks, becomes less fatigued by his work. But it is necessary for all workers to maintain the same pace if division of labour is to work smoothly, and so the fatigue of the slower workers may be increased by the effort required to keep up with the quicker. Machinery does not tire however long the day, and where it is used the workman cannot slow down, but must keep pace with it.

12. Disadvantages of division of labour

The increased output resulting from the division of labour is obtained, however, only at a certain cost, for it has brought with it its own problems. Consider some of its disadvantages:

(*i*) *Monotony of the work.* Minute specialisation of processes means that each workman performs only one small operation a great many times during each working day. His work therefore becomes very monotonous and tends to dull the intelligence. Well-meaning people are perhaps apt to over-sympathise with those who have to spend their working lives doing monotonous work. Such sympathy, however, is often wasted. Cases have been noted of workers transferred from routine tasks to work of a more varied kind calling for closer attention, and within a week asking to be allowed to return to their former, less exacting jobs.

(*ii*) *The decline of craftsmanship.* It is said, too, that with the employment of machinery the workmen ceases to be a craftsman and becomes just a tender of a machine. Though to a large extent this is true, it is also true that when all work was done by hand a good deal of it was both laborious and monotonous—as, for example, the planing by a carpenter of a large number of planks: work calling no doubt, for a certain amount of skill, but hardly to be classed as craftsmanship. Many other forms of hand work were equally laborious and monotonous and not always well done. On the other hand, looking after some modern machines entails a considerable degree of skill and intelligence, and though the quality of the work may never approach the highest standards of the craftsman, it is generally well above that of the less efficient workers by hand.

(*iii*) *Greater risk of unemployment.* Division of labour increases the complexity of production. To a greater or lesser degree the division of labour turns workers into specialists. The greater the skill required in their work—that is, the more specific the labour—the more difficult it becomes for the workers in a declining industry to obtain alternative employment. Division of labour requires the co-operation of a group of people in production, but this dependence on others increases the risk of unemployment under modern conditions of large-scale production, where goods have generally to be produced in anticipation of demand, instead of in response to direct orders, as in the days of small, independent craftsmen.

13. Division of labour necessitates exchange

When a family provided for all its wants by its own efforts it was self-supporting, and economically independent of other families. As soon as division of labour was carried to the point where men began to specialise in particular trades, it became necessary for them to exchange goods with one another. Thus, exchange is a consequence of specialisation. The carpenter, who spent all his time working in wood, had to exchange some of the things he had made with the weaver for cloth, or with the baker for bread. Specialisation and exchange make all those taking part richer, since it increases their combined output. An exchange of goods for goods is known as barter, but it is a clumsy method of exchange and to obviate it some form of money came to be used as a medium of exchange at quite an early date.

Division of labour increases output, but advantage can be taken of specialisation only if the goods produced are distributed among the people demanding them. The greater the degree of specialisation, therefore, the greater becomes the work of distribution and the larger the number of people required in commerce. Thus, to some extent the advantage of division of labour in making possible a great increase in output is offset by the extra work of distribution.

Many people are engaged in extractive industries, such as mining, quarrying, farming, fishing; many more are employed in the various branches of manufacture, in the textile, iron and steel, pottery industries, etc.; many others work at commercial occupations which assist the distribution of raw materials and the manufacture of goods, such as the retail and wholesale trades, import and export trades, transport, banking and insurance. As a result of division of labour people engaged in commercial occupations help to satisfy the wants of others indirectly. A fourth category of workers perform more direct services. Among these are doctors and dentists, lawyers and judges, teachers and parsons, civil servants and all employed in local government, in the Armed Services and police, musicians, sculptors and painters, actors, singers and entertainers of all kinds. The higher the standard of living enjoyed by a community, the larger generally will be the proportion of its people in this group. Before 1939 about 20 per cent of the working population of Britain was engaged in occupations supplying direct services; by 1975 the proportion of people in this group had increased to 28 per cent. Division of labour thus makes it possible to have large numbers of persons employed in occupations not concerned with satisfying material wants.

The principle of comparative advantage. Both the individual and the community will benefit to the greatest extent if each person specialises in that occupation in which he has the greatest comparative advantage over others. This is the principle of comparative advantage. A successful barrister may be at the same time an excellent interior decorator. Nevertheless, it will not be an economic proposition for him to decorate his own house if, in order to give himself time in which to do this work, he has to decline a valuable brief. He can earn much more as a barrister—the occupation in which he has the greatest comparative advantage over others—in the time it would take him to paint and decorate his house. Thus, he could indirectly accomplish this task of painting and decorating by working only a fraction of the time, as a barrister and paying someone else to do the work. Much work, therefore, that people do for themselves instead of employing others to do for them, is uneconomic and contrary to the principle of division of labour.

14. Division of labour is limited by the market

The extent to which division of labour can be carried is determined by the extent of the demand for the commodity. Division of labour results in an increase in total output, and the further it is taken the greater will be the output achieved. The greatest specialisation will occur, then, in the production of those commodities the cost of production of which can be reduced by division of labour and for which there is a wide market. For some things there is a very large demand if the price of the commodity is low enough, but however cheap some things became, the demand would remain small.

Therefore, as Adam Smith pointed out, division of labour is limited by the market. In a densely populated area like Greater London division of labour can be carried to greater lengths than in a thinly populated area like the Highlands of Scotland, where a man must often of necessity be a jack of all trades. The extent of the market depends also on the facilities which exist for distributing commodities from the place of production.

Division of labour was not possible therefore to any considerable extent before the middle of the eighteenth century because before that time transport facilities were generally poor. The construction of roads, canals, and railways made possible a wider distribution of manufactures, and the resulting extension of the market enabled greater specialisation of processes to be introduced.

RECOMMENDATIONS FOR FURTHER READING

A. Marshall: *Principles of Economics*, Book II, Chapters 1-3.
Adam Smith: *Wealth of Nations*, Book I, Chapters 1-3.

QUESTIONS

1. "Specialisation brings its benefits, but it also has its limitations." Discuss this statement. (NC)

2. What are the economic advantages and disadvantages of specialisation? (Wales)

3. When is division of labour uneconomic? Give examples. (RSA Inter.)

4. Describe the conditions in industry which tend to encourage minute division of labour and mention the advantages and, if any, the disadvantages of minute division of labour. (LCCom.)

5. What do you understand by the term "wealth" in economics? Discuss the relationship between wealth and welfare. (CIS)

6. Explain what is meant by "division of labour." How can the underlying principle be applied to increase production per man hour? (Exp.)

7. "Although machinery goes hand in hand with specialisation, the two things are obviously quite distinct, and each makes a separate contribution to industrial efficiency." (Cairncross.) Give a short account of the contribution to industrial efficiency of (a) specialisation and (b) machinery. (ACCA)

8. Distinguish carefully between the terms "income," "capital" and "wealth," and then show the possible relationship between them. (IHA)

9. State the main advantages that follow from the division of labour. Do the principles involved apply only to labour? (IB)

10. What is meant by the division of labour and what are its advantages? Show how the size of the market limits the degree of specialisation. (GCE)

CHAPTER 3

FACTORS OF PRODUCTION

I. THE PRODUCTIVE RESOURCES

1. Land, labour and capital

One of the principal influences on any country's total volume of production is the extent and quality of its resources of land, labour and capital. These productive resources are known as *agents* or *factors of production*, or sometimes *inputs*. The term *input* is perhaps to be preferred to *agent* or *factor* of production, for an agent implies the playing of an active role, whereas these three factors are better considered simply as resources at the disposal of the organisers of production. It is important to notice too that it is the services of the factor, rather than the factor itself, that contribute towards production.

The term *land* is used in the widest sense to include all kinds of natural (as distinct from man-made) resources: farmlands, mineral wealth, such as coal and metal ores, and fishing-grounds. Perhaps the main service of land is the provision of a site where production can take place. *Capital* comprises factory buildings, machinery, raw materials, partly finished goods, means of transport. All these things are wanted not for their own sake but solely to assist the production of other commodities. Land consists of all resources provided by Nature, whereas capital has been accumulated as a result of Man's past efforts. "In a sense," says Marshall, "there are only two agents of production, nature and man,"[1] By *labour* is meant the human effort employed in production. If land, labour and capital are considered as productive resources this emphasises their similarity rather than their differences.

Even for the most primitive method of production all three factors are required. Early Man, even in the Stone Age, made simple tools to assist him in his work. Some fruits—*e.g.* blackberries and bilberries—may grow wild, but nevertheless labour is needed to gather them and some form of capital required to transport them to consumers. In the extractive group of occupations—farming, hunting, fishing, mining, etc.—land is a predominant factor, but never to the complete exclusion of capital and labour.

[1] A. Marshall: *Principles of Economics*, IV, 1.

II. LAND

2. Does land differ from the other factors?

Formerly economists placed the factors of production in rigidly defined groups, and treated each of them as separate and distinct from the others. In particular, Ricardo and his followers considered that land differed fundamentally from the other factors. in three ways:

(*i*) Land is "*a gift of Nature*," that is, Man has done nothing to bring it into existence, whereas capital is accumulated only by the employment of labour and other factors of production.

(*ii*) Unlike the other factors of production, land is strictly *limited in quantity* even in the long period.

(*iii*) In those industries primarily dependent on land, production is subject to the *Law of Diminishing Returns*.

It can be shown without much difficulty that these alleged peculiarities of land do not entirely agree with the facts:

(*i*) The contention that land is a gift of Nature is of little economic significance. Man has certainly done nothing to bring into existence the supplies of coal in South Yorkshire, but while the coal remains underground it can serve no economic purpose. Large stocks of coal, as yet unworked, exist several thousand feet below the surface near Selby, but until mining operations have been undertaken this coal is of no use to production. One aspect of land is outside the control of Man—namely, its situation—and this is a chief characteristic of land as a factor of production. Land, too, is said to have no cost of production, for no costs were incurred to produce it, but land has sometimes been reclaimed from the sea at enormous expense. Nevertheless, Man is in no way responsible for the location in particular places of minerals such as iron ore and oil, and for agricultural production he has to accept climate as a factor beyond his control.

(*ii*) Although it must be admitted that the total area of land on the earth's surface cannot be appreciably increased, it is nevertheless not strictly true to say that the supply of land is fixed. In the Netherlands, for example, land has been reclaimed from the sea; in Great Britain the Fenlands, formerly a mere swamp, have been transformed into one of the most fertile areas in the country; in the United States great irrigation schemes, such as that at Boulder Dam, have brought into cultivation vast areas that were formerly desert.

Increasing the area under crops, as a result of improvements in farming technique, is really equivalent to an increase in the supply of land. This occurred in Great Britain in the mid-eighteenth century, when the cultivation of root crops made it possible to end the practice of leaving fallow each year one-third of all the agricultural land. Improving the fertility of existing land is also equivalent to increasing its supply, though the improvement is in fact the result of the application of more capital and labour to the land. From the standpoint of a single country, to import additional supplies of food from abroad is similar in effect to increasing the supply of land at home, though clearly, all countries cannot do this.

The total amont of land on the earth's surface can be reduced by such occurrences as coast erosion, flooding or soil erosion. Whole villages have disappeared into the sea on the Yorkshire coast; the Zuider Zee inundated a large area of the Netherlands during the thirteenth and fourteenth centuries. Soil erosion, considered by some people to be one of the most serious problems confronting the human race, has resulted in a large area of the United States, once good grassland, becoming desert. Nevertheless, even taken together, all the changes that have taken place in the land surface of the earth form a very small proportion of its total area.

(*iii*) At one period it was thought that agriculture was an industry peculiarly subject to the Law of Diminishing Returns, while manufacturing industry was carried on under conditions of increasing returns. The Law of Diminishing Returns, however, is not restricted to those forms of production in which land predominates. It can now be shown that in different circumstances both agriculture and manufacture can be subject to either diminishing or increasing returns. It can be said therefore that economically land, though it has, of course, some special features of its own, is mainly similar to, and not different from, the other factors of production.

3. The law of diminishing returns

It will be useful, however, at this stage to take a brief preliminary glance at the Law of Diminishing Returns as it applies to land. All that the law states is that after a certain point successive applications of equal amounts of resources to a given area of land produces a less than proportionate return. A simplified example will make this clear. Consider a piece of land of a size larger than one man is capable of cultivating successfully by his own efforts alone. Assume that in successive years he takes into his employment one additional man, together with equal additional amounts of capital in the form of farming equipment. In the second year, if it is a large piece of land, the increased output may be greater than the amount produced in the first year, and in the third year the increase may possibly be even greater still. After some years, however, the additional output of one year will be smaller than the additional output of the previous year. In other words, the Law of Diminishing Returns will begin to operate. Obviously, this must occur sooner or later, otherwise it would be possible to increase the output from a small piece of land indefinitely simply by putting more men and equipment to work upon it. If this policy of setting more men to work on the same piece of land were continued, eventually the absurd situation would arise where the men would be so crowded together that they would find it physically impossible to move.

Table I shows how the Law of Diminishing Returns operates when a fixed amount of land is cultivated.

Table I

Diminishing Returns to Land

Units of land	Number of men employed (each with equal amount of farming equipment)	Output per year (lb of potatoes)	Addition to output	Average output per man
1	1	100	100	100
1	2	210	110	105
1	3	330	120	110
1	4	460	130	115
1	5	600	140	120
1	6	730	130	121.6
1	7	850	120	121.4
1	8	960	110	120
1	9	1,060	100	118
1	10	1,150	90	115
1	11	1,230	80	112
1	12	1,290	60	107
1	13	1,305	15	100
1	14	1,315	10	94

This table shows that until the employment of five men there is a more than proportionate return—that is, there are *increasing returns*—whereas when the number of men employed is increased beyond five the successive additions to total output decrease—that is, there are diminishing returns. After the employment of eleven men there are steeply diminishing returns.

This can be illustrated by a diagram:

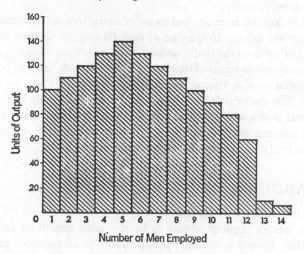

Fig. 2. Diminishing Returns.

Each column represents the addition to total output resulting from the employment of an additional man. The shaded area shows the maximum output (under existing technical conditions) achieved by the employment of fourteen men. An improvement in technique—for example, the use of a new machine—would increase output or achieve a similar output at less cost, that is, by the employment of fewer men.

The operation of the law can also be seen if one considers a self-sufficient country trying to produce more food to satisfy an expanding population. The most fertile land might be used first, and if this did not yield a sufficient output less fertile land would have to be brought into cultivation. If the same number of men and equipment were employed on each square mile of the less fertile land as on the more fertile land the output would be less. If the population increased further, and even less fertile land had to be cultivated, the additional output would be smaller than before. With each increase in population, even less fertile land would have to be cultivated, and so increased output would be achieved only under conditions of decreasing returns. During both World Wars, Great Britain found it necessary to increase its output of food, but this could be done only by ploughing up inferior land, and so production was subject to diminishing returns. The operation of this law of Diminishing Returns in relation to the expansion of population seriously perturbed Thomas Malthus in the late eighteenth century.

The law has also been applied to other extractive occupations, such as mining and fishing. In the case of coal mining, as the area worked recedes farther from the shaft, each addition to output is obtained only at increasing cost in terms of time and labour. With fishing the position is somewhat similar, though replenishment of supply in this case is possible. The essential feature of the Law of Diminishing Returns as considered in this section is that one factor of production is fixed and varying amounts of the other factors are combined with it. By its very character land is more likely to be fixed than other factors.

III. LABOUR

4. The importance of labour

Some writers consider labour to be the most important factor of production. Labour is certainly indispensable to all forms of production, but under modern conditions of production so are the other factors. Labour differs from land and capital in that it is supplied by human beings, and because of that, ethical and moral considerations must be taken into account when dealing with it. In applied economics this human aspect of labour cannot be ignored, but in pure economic theory labour is economically no different from land or capital, being simply one of the resources that are essential to production. Though its economic role may be a passive one, labour can be far from passive if employers act in ways regarded as detrimental to its interests. Labour differs too from the other two productive resources in that it is not only a factor of production but also the end for which all production is undertaken.

5. The supply of labour

There is some ambiguity in the term, supply of labour. The supply may be taken to mean the total number of people—men, women and children—of working age. Even the phrase "working age" is not precise and needs to be defined. Again, supply of labour may be taken to mean the supply of *labour service* available, and since it is the service of a factor, rather than the factor itself, that takes part in production, this is the more useful concept. The supply of labour service can be varied either by a change in the number of working population or by a change in the number of hours worked in a given period of time. The supply of labour available in a country depends, then, on three factors:

(i) the total population of the country; (ii) the proportion of the population available for employment; and (iii) the number of hours worked by each person per year.

Economists have, therefore, always been interested in population changes. The proportion of the population available for employment will depend mainly on the standard of civilisation reached by the country concerned, the extent of its industrialisation, its social organisation and perhaps the attitude of its people to work. In a poor country it may require the maximum efforts of both men and women, young and old, to eke out even a bare existence, whereas in a highly industrialised State the provision of the necessities of life may require the employment of only a fraction of the total population. If the people regard all forms of manual work as menial, as in the Athens of Aristotle, the size of the labour force will depend on the number of slaves the country possesses. In a highly civilised country the size of the labour force will be influenced by (i) keeping children longer at school, though this may be more than counterbalanced by the improvement in the quality of the labour, and (ii) the age at which people retire from work.

In a poor country both men and women may have to continue at work so long as they are physically able to do so; in a richer country fewer women may be compelled to work, and the men may retire from work while still physically strong and mentally alert. The changing social attitude in Great Britain during the twentieth century to the employment of women, both unmarried and married, has had a considerable influence on the supply of labour in this country. At the beginning of the century it was considered to be degrading for young girls in middle-class families to undertake paid work, and married women did so only if their husbands' wages were very low. Two World Wars changed all this. By the 1960s women formed a third of the total labour force in Great Britain.

The social development of the country may result in the adoption of a shorter working week, with a reduction in the number of hours worked per day, and with paid holidays. In Great Britain, in the early years of the industrial system, conditions prevailed similar to those that existed when people either worked on the land or were independent craftsmen, when the hours of work were limited only by the hours of daylight, and holidays were confined to "holy days" such as Sundays and Saints' days, and perhaps an annual local "feast" day. Gradually working hours have been reduced, so that nowadays most workers in Great Britain enjoy a five-day week of eight hours per day, with holidays of up to three weeks each year on full pay. If the hours of work are excessively long a reduction in hours may actually increase the amount of work done, but after a point each reduction in the number of hours worked is equivalent to a reduction in the labour force. In effect, however, the shorter working week has meant the opportunity for more overtime at a higher rate of pay.

6. Efficiency of labour

It has already been pointed out that two factors which reduce the supply of labour—the longer period of education and the shorter working week—might be offset to some extent by a consequent increase in the efficiency of labour. By increased efficiency is meant the ability to achieve a greater output in a shorter time without any falling off in the quality of the work—that is to say, increased productivity per man employed. The efficiency of a country's labour force depends on a number of influences:

(*i*) *Climate.* This can be an important influence on willingness to work, for extremes of temperature or high humidity are not conducive to concentration even on congenial tasks.

(*ii*) *Health of the worker.* The efficiency of the worker is closely related to his state of health which depends on his being adequately fed, clothed and housed. Not only will attention to the physical welfare of employees reduce time lost from sickness, but it will improve their general efficiency. The cost of a health service might be offset to some extent by increased production.

(*iii*) *Peace of mind.* Anxiety is detrimental to efficiency. A social security scheme relieves people from worry about the future by providing for them in times of sickness, unemployment and old age. At one time people may have been tempted to save at the expense of health to provide for these contingencies. Others may be worried about their work or their private problems. Large firms realise that this is detrimental to efficiency and appoint personnel officers to help employees with such problems.

(*iv*) *Working conditions.* The general conditions under which people work can effect their output. Minimum standards have been laid down under a long series of Factory Acts, and, more recently, the *Health and Safety at Work Act* (1974) and factory inspectors pay particular attention to such things as ventilation, overcrowding and the fencing of machinery. In the past the consideration given to the welfare of employees was mainly inspired by humanitarian motives. Research, however, has shown that it is in the employers' own interest to pay attention to the welfare of employees in such matters as heating, lighting, ventilation and noise and by the provision of "rest pauses" and "tea breaks," since anything that reduces fatigue will increase output. The provision of recreation facilities and canteens has the same objective.

(v) *Education and training*. This factor has three aspects: general education, technical education and training within industry. A high standard of general education is essential for developing intelligence and providing a foundation upon which more specialised vocational training can be based. Technical education is available to most people only in their own time, generally by attendance at evening classes, though many firms are now willing to release employees from work for one or more half-days per week. Vocational education consists chiefly of subjects of study related to the profession or trade of the student. The third type of training is known as training within industry, and each firm must undertake this for its own employees. To a greater or less extent each firm has to train its own employees in the way it desires its work to be done, for example, in the proper handling of the particular machines used.

(vi) *Efficiency of the factors*. The productivity of labour will be increased if the quality of the other factors is high. The more fertile the land, the greater will be the output per man, other things being equal. Similarly, the greater the amount and the better the quality of the capital employed, the greater will be the productivity of the labour. Efficiency of organisation is even more important since this determines whether the best use is being made of factors of production. We have already seen that division of labour increases the efficiency of labour. The greater the amount of specialisation, the more capitalistic the method of production, the greater will be the output per man.

7. Productive and non-productive labour

Writers on economics formerly discussed at great length the question whether particular kinds of labour were productive or not. The group of economists known as physiocrats regarded labour employed in agriculture as productive labour, and, though Adam Smith widened the term to include labour engaged in the manufacture of goods, he classed domestic service and other direct services as non-productive. Only 54 per cent of labour in Great Britain is at present engaged in industrial occupations, the rest being employed in commerce, or in supplying direct services. We have already stressed that production is not complete until commodities have reached consumers, so that the distribution of goods becomes the final stage of production; and, further, production is now taken to include the production of all kinds of services. To class some labour as productive and some as non-productive is therefore not only pointless but also inaccurate. The only labour that can be considered to be unproductive is misdirected labour, where effort has been wasted on the production of something that is incapable of fulfilling the purpose for which it was intended.

IV. CLASSIFICATION OF FACTORS OF PRODUCTION

8. Objections to the conventional method of classification

There are two main objections to classifying factors of production into rigidly defined groups of land, labour and capital:

(i) *Substitution between units of the same factor is not always possible.* In the first place, factors are not homogeneous—that is, each group does not consist of a number of identical units, any one of which could be substituted for any other. All land is not alike—in fact, it is impossible for two pieces of land to be exactly alike, for no two pieces of land can have exactly the same situation. Nor can all land serve the same purposes. Land used for grazing cannot necessarily be switched to wheat growing. Differences of climate and soil may prevent the substitution of one crop for another; minerals can be worked only where deposits are found.

Many forms of capital too are not interchangeable since they serve a particular purpose—a railway could serve no other purpose than the one for which it was originally intended, though a motorway and motor vehicles could be substituted for it.

It is exactly the same with labour, many kinds of which are not interchangeable. A shortage of doctors cannot be made good by drafting lawyers, teachers and accountants into the medical profession. There are many kinds of land, many kinds of labour and many different kinds of capital. It would be more logical to recognise hundreds or even thousands of separate factors—each distinctive type of land, labour and capital being considered a factor in its own right—than to limit the number of factors to three or even four.

(ii) *Substitution between factors is often possible.* Although each unit of a factor such as land is not a perfect substitute for either capital or labour, it is frequently possible to substitute some land for either capital or labour, that is, more labour might be employed on a smaller piece of land or more capital in the form of machines or fertiliser. Almost everyone is aware that capital can be substituted for labour as this is a process that has been going on at an ever increasing rate for two hundred years or more. Differences, therefore, between the three factors, land, labour and capital, are only superficial; economically they are similar to one another. Since under conditions of large-scale production the co-operation of all the factors of production is required at all times, it is the business of the producer to decide how much of each he requires. He cannot dispense with any of them, for he must employ a certain amount of each, but above this minimum he has a degree of choice. Though he cannot dispense with all his labour and substitute land or capital for it, he can often, for example, employ a little less labour and more capital, or a little more labour and less land. This is known as the *Principle of Substitution*. How much of each factor to employ will depend on the method of production considered most efficient—that is, more economical. If labour is dear—that is, if wages are high—relative to the cost of new machinery, then there will be a strong inducement to substitute machinery for labour wherever this is possible. Again, if land is cheap relative to labour and capital, as in the United States in the nineteenth century, extensive rather than intensive farming will be practised.

Thus, the classifying of factors of production into three groups is open to objection, first, because substitution between units of the same factor is not always possible, and secondly, because substitution between different factors often is possible.

It is more useful to distinguish between specific and non-specific factors. The great advantage of this method of classification is that it emphasises the similarity of the factors, for within each of the two categories examples of all three factors, land, labour and capital, can be found.

9. Specific factors

A factor is said to be specific if it is of a specialised kind, and therefore cannot easily be used for any purpose other than that for which it was originally intended. There is probably very little land that was not at one time open to alternative uses, for most land can either be built upon or devoted to some branch of farming. Once land has been built upon, however, it becomes more specific, for then the cost of transferring it to an alternative use will be very considerably increased. Much of the sheep-grazing land of the Pennine moorland lying between Lancashire and Yorkshire, however, is fairly specific, since most of it cannot be used for any other purpose, though some may be used for roads.

Labour may be highly specific, especially where a long period of study or training is required, or special aptitude is needed. A dentist has to take a university course lasting several years and pass certain examinations before he is qualified to practice, while no amount of training will make a person without natural talent into an artist. There are degrees of specificity depending on the ease or difficulty of transferring other labour from one to another occupation. The greater the skill required and the longer the period of training, the more specific will be the labour. Sometimes an attempt is made to make labour more specific by artificial means. Craftsmen may insist on unnecessarily long periods of apprenticeship, or professional bodies may make their qualifying examinations to some extent competitive in order to restrict the number of successful candidates.

Many kinds of capital, too, are highly specific. A blast-furnace cannot be used for any other purpose, and some machinery is so intricate in character that likewise its use is limited to a single purpose. A railway system too would fall into this category. In the case of partly finished manufactured goods the nearer they are to the final stage of production, the more specific they are likely to be.

10. Non-specific factors

Any factor of production that can fairly easily be transferred from one use to another can be considered to be non-specific.

It was noticed above that most land could be used either for building or farming. Farmland can be switched from one type of farming to another sort. For example, during the nineteenth century much wheatland in England was turned over to grassland for grazing cattle or sheep. During the past thirty years a great deal of grassland has been brought under the plough again.

The easier it is to learn a job, the less specific will be the labour required to undertake it. There are probably few occupations where nothing at all has to be learned, but whereas it may take years to acquire the knowledge or skill required for some, there are others where probably half an hour's instruction may be sufficient. Unskilled labour is therefore non-specific. In good times and bad there are men who go from one type of job to another and never stay long at any, at one time working as a dustman, at another maybe as a builder's labourer and later perhaps as a cleaner of buses. With regard to labour, it is perhaps worthy of note that, though it may not be easy to increase the supply of a particular type of specific labour from the ranks of the non-specific, the reverse movement is possible: a shortage of unskilled labour could be made good by drawing on the supply of skilled labour, though this would obviously be economically wasteful.

Finally, there is non-specific capital. Most ordinary tools would fall into this category; a hammer could be used by workers in many totally different occupations. Machinery can frequently be adjusted to serve a different—though generally similar—purpose. Buildings also can often be converted to other uses.

Raw materials are generally non-specific capital. For example, raw wool has many alternative uses—cloth, carpets, hosiery—while iron ore may eventually become one of a hundred different articles. With regard to partly finished goods, the nearer they are to the finished state, the more specific they are likely to be. Thus woollen cloth is more specific than raw wool.

V. MOBILITY OF FACTORS

11. The meaning of mobility

The term mobility, as applied to factors of production, means the ease with which a factor can be transferred from one form of employment to another. It is taken to include the concept of specificity considered above. There are, therefore, two aspects to mobility as applied to factors of production: mobility in the sense of specificity—movement from one employment to another, that is, occupational mobility—and mobility in the geographical sense of movement from one place to another, that is, geographical mobility.

Geographical mobility and specificity, however, do not always go together. Some factors are highly specific, and it may be impossible or at least very difficult to transfer them from one form of production to another, and so in this sense of the term they may be considered to be immobile. On the other hand, non-specific factors are generally mobile geographically.

The term mobility can be applied to both land and capital as well as to labour, though land and some forms of capital cannot be moved from one place to another. Capital, however, though durable, wears out in time, and when it is due to be renewed its location could be changed. Businessmen are usually very mobile in both senses of the term. Not only are they prepared to go to any part of the country but they often move from one industry to another of a very different kind on the technical side, as for example from road haulage to oil refining, or from one of the textile industries to motor-car manufacture.

12. Geographical mobility of labour

Labour might be thought to be the most mobile factor in the geographical sense. Human beings are capable of physical movement, and at the present day people travel on average more miles each year than at any previous period of the world's history. In medieval England very few people ever spent even a day away from the places where they were born. At an earlier period, however, whole peoples, impelled by economic forces, moved away from their previous homeland in search of new places in which to live. After the discovery of the New World emigration from Europe—sometimes for economic and sometimes for political or religious reasons—began as a mere trickle, but in the late nineteenth century became a flood.

In Great Britain in the late eighteenth and early nineteenth centuries there was some movement of landless farm workers from the South of England to the new factory towns of the Midlands and the North. During the 1930s this tendency was reversed and many people left Durham, Lancashire and South Wales to seek work in South-eastern England. Apart from emigration to the United States, which received immigrants from nearly every country in Europe, people have often shown great reluctance to move from one country to another, the possibility of higher wages not always being a sufficient inducement. Differences of race, language and style of living, and a dislike of dwelling among foreigners, particularly inhabitants of neighbouring States, between which national rivalry has existed, have made most people prefer not to leave their native lands. Nevertheless, there are many examples of people who regularly cross national frontiers on their way to work, as for example from Italy to Switzerland and from the Netherlands and Yugoslavia to Germany.

Persecution for political, religious or racial reasons has often proved as strong an incentive to movement as economic reasons. French weavers came to England in the seventeenth century to escape the persecution that was being meted out to Protestants in France. During the later 1930s there were considerable movements of people in Europe for these reasons—Jews, liberal democrats, socialists and communists fleeing from Germany in the early part of the period, and refugees from communism later. The Second World War caused a gigantic upheaval of the people of Europe, and large numbers of "displaced persons" came to Great Britain. In recent years many people came to this country from the West Indies, Pakistan and India, the reason in this case being economic. In spite of all these examples of movements of peoples, economists generally are still inclined to agree with Adam Smith that "a man is of all sorts of luggage the most difficult to be transported."

Even during the great depression of 1929–35, when unemployment was less severe in some parts of Great Britain than others, there was often unwillingness, especially among older workers, to leave the districts most severely affected to seek work elsewhere, the unemployed expecting work of the desired kind to be brought to them.

The longer people live in one place, the more attached they become to it and the more reluctant they are to move elsewhere, for ties of friendship become stronger, and many of them become more closely associated with the social activities of the place. To move to another town means going to live among strangers and often losing old friends. After living a long time in one town a certain position of social importance may have been achieved, which may be completely lost by moving elsewhere. A man's work can be made uncomfortable by his immediate superiors, and if he is satisfied with the conditions under which he works he may prefer not to risk the unknown. All these may be considered as non-monetary advantages of staying in one place, and it may take quite considerable monetary inducement to overcome them. Another important thing making for immobility of labour is the housing question. Whether a person rents or owns a house, removal to another town involves considerable financial sacrifice. Houses to rent are not always easy to obtain. If a house is owned it will have to be sold and heavy legal charges incurred in addition to the cost of removal and there are wide differences in the prices of similar houses in different parts of the country.

13. Occupational mobility of labour

Movement of labour from one occupation to another generally takes place indirectly. Though it might not be possible for example, to expand the Civil Service by drafting people from textile mills, a redistribution of labour between these two occupations may be brought about through a number of intermediate stages. The Civil Service may attract people from other kinds of clerical work, these posts then being filled, say, by shop assistants, who in turn may perhaps be replaced by mill workers. Assuming the Civil Service to be offering the most attractive type of work and the mill the least attractive, an increase in the demand for workers in the former occupation will eventually lead to a reduction in the amount of labour available for the other, but this result will be achieved only after considerable changes have also taken place in the distribution of labour between other occupations.

The easiest method, however, of transferring labour from one industry to another is by the entry into industry of school-leavers. A declining industry will attract few new entrants, and so vacancies brought about by retirement and other causes will not be filled, with the result that the total labour force in that industry will be reduced. On the other hand, an expanding industry will attract a larger proportion of new entrants, often by offering a higher rate of pay, and so will increase its labour force. Redistribution of labour among different occupations can be brought about gradually in this way, but it is a method that is very slow in working itself out.

14. The most important factor

As already noted, it has often been asserted that labour is the most important factor of production. The classical economists in the early nineteenth century adopted this view. They wished to show that the value of a commodity depended on the amount of labour involved in its production. For political reasons this idea was again stressed later. Consequently, these economists emphasised the fact that land was a gift of Nature, while capital, they said, owed its origin to labour expended upon its production in the past. In their view, labour was an active factor, whereas land and capital were passive. In fact, economically all factors are similar in being productive resources required in all forms of production, and so labour is no more active economically than land or capital.

It was further pointed out by these early economists that some land was not worth cultivating, and therefore no one would pay anything for its use, while there was no parallel of "wageless" labour. There are, however, a few people—their number fortunately being small—who on account of mental or physical disability are unable to undertake ordinary forms of employment. These "unemployables" are very similar economically to the "useless" kind of land. It was also stated that labour has some choice in the kind and amount of work it is willing to perform. There is probably a greater element of truth in the statement today than at the time when it was first made. Again, labour was declared to be the most important factor, because, if unemployed, it suffers a lower standard of living, whereas if land and capital are unemployed their owners merely suffer a loss of income. This appears to be a somewhat ingenuous argument. The services of all factors of production are owned by men and women, whether the factor be labour, land or capital, and whichever factors are unemployed (if labour is unemployed it is fairly certain that other factors also will be unemployed), the owners of those factors will suffer a decline in their incomes and a lowering of their standard of living.

A case can be made out on behalf of each of the other factors for considering it the most important in production. Take land, for example. It has been said that "the use of a certain area of the earth's surface is a primary condition of anything that man can do."[1] Of capital it can be argued that the greater the amount used in production, the greater the output, and the claim has been made that the increasing rate of recent economic progress has been due mainly to the application of more capital to production, the comparative poverty of those countries with little capital being contrasted with the greater wealth of those with a plentiful supply. None of the factors is of much economic importance unless production is efficiently organised. The fact is that all factors are important to production, for the co-operation of all is required, and no useful purpose is served by singling out any one of them for special commendation.

VI. THE ENTREPRENEUR

15. Are there three factors of production or four?

So far we have assumed there to be only three factors of production, namely, land, labour and capital, and this was the view of early nineteenth century economists as, indeed, of many today. Marshall,[2] however, thought that *organisation* was sometimes worthy of being considered a separate factor, and since then many other economists have recognised the *entrepreneur* (or organiser) as an independent factor.

Those who do not differentiate between labour and the organising function prefer to speak of the *human* factor and argue that some organising is required of all labour, though more in some cases than others. The only distinction they make between the manager and a low-ranking employee, therefore, is that the manager is primarily concerned with organisation and devotes most of his time to it, whereas at the other end of the scale the organisation required of an employee is only a preliminary to his ordinary work, and this occupies only a small fraction of his time. Though human beings perform both labour and entrepreneurial functions these two services are sufficiently distinc-

---

[1] A. Marshall: *Principles of Economics*, IV, II, 2.
[2] A. Marshall: *Principles of Economics* (1890), p. 139.

tive to warrant being regarded as supplied by different factors. The organising undertaken by the entrepreneur is not only on a wider scale but is also different in kind from that of an employee. The entrepreneur is responsible not only for deciding what method of production shall be adopted but also for organising the work of others. He has to make many other important decisions, such as what to produce and how much to produce. Perhaps the primary function of the entrepreneur is to bear the risk and uncertainty of production.

Land, labour and capital are of no economic importance unless they are organised for production, and to the entrepreneur they are just masses of productive resources. How they shall be employed and how much of each shall be used are questions to be decided by the entrepreneur and not by the owners of the other factors. Land, labour and capital are passive factors, whereas the entrepreneur is the active factor and therefore different in function. Some people not unnaturally are reluctant to regard labour merely as a productive resource since labour is supplied by human beings. Whether the entrepreneur is regarded as a separate factor or not, the functions of the entrepreneur are vital to production.

16. Functions of the entrepreneur

There are two distinct functions of the entrepreneur:

(i) *Uncertainty-bearing.* There are many risks which have to be faced in business. Some, such as fire, loss of goods in transit, etc., can be insured against because statistics are available which enable insurance companies to calculate their probability. In addition to insurance, there are a number of other ways by which risk can be reduced. Hedging, for example, is a sort of insurance against price fluctuation. Statistics, based on market research, provide the entrepreneur with more accurate information, and so reduce the risk he has to bear. Whenever risk is reduced in this way, though, the pure entrepreneurial function is also lessened, for the risks that the entrepreneur must bear are those that cannot be insured against because their probability cannot be actuarily calculated. This type of risk is termed uncertainty. In an advanced economic system producers generally do not produce goods only in response to direct orders, production being carried on in anticipation of demand. Modern methods of production have become so complex that the time interval between the taking of the decision to produce and the marketing of the product has been considerably lengthened. The longer this interval, the greater is the possibility for a change of demand to occur, with the result that future demand becomes difficult to predict. This is the kind of uncertainty-bearing that devolves upon entrepreneurs. "The most fundamental fact in connection with organisation, it has been said, is the meeting of uncertainty."[1] The importance of the entrepreneur, therefore, has increased with the increasing complexity and uncertainty of production.

(ii) *Management control.* The managerial function of the entrepreneur involves responsibility for broad decisions of policy and the ability to ensure that these decisions are carried out. In the large modern limited company there are different degrees of management and so some of the entrepreneurial function may be delegated to men primarily engaged in providing labour service. It is, therefore, more important that the entrepreneur should understand men and be able to select the right man for the job than that he should possess expert technical knowledge. This is shown by the way successful entrepreneurs often move around between firms engaged in widely different forms of production—in much the same way as Cabinet ministers frequently exchange one Government department for another. It is said that men of high entrepreneurial ability are few in number. To a certain degree the entrepreneur can choose between employing more of one factor or more of another—more capital, perhaps, and less labour—but if he is to produce most efficiently he will have to combine his factors as nearly as possible in the best or optimum proportion. On the combined decisions of entrepreneurs, therefore, depends the assortment of goods that will be available to consumers.

Where production is on a small scale and undertaken by a sole master-craftsman, the entrepreneurial function is easy to locate, for the factors —labour and organisation—are combined in the same person. The typical modern business unit is, however, the limited company, and in a company it is not easy precisely to locate the entrepreneurial function. In the case of the large limited company risk is borne by the shareholders (though many of them never attend a shareholders' meeting) while the day-to-day control of the business is in the hands of a manager or managing director.

[1] F. H. Knight: *Risk, Uncertainty and Profit*, p. 317.

RECOMMENDATIONS FOR FURTHER READING

J. R. Hicks: *The Social Framework*, Chapters 6 and 7.
A. Marshall: *Principles of Economics*, Book IV, Chapters 1–6.

QUESTIONS

1. State the law of diminishing returns and outline its significance for short-period costs of production. (Bolton)

2. What are the functions of the entrepreneur? How are these functions fulfilled in a large public company? (ULCI)

3. In what manner may the economic well-being of the community be affected by labour efficiency? How may the productivity of labour be increased? (RSA)

4. Explain how insurance protects a businessman against risks. Is there any type of risk that is not insurable? (IT)

5. What factors influence the efficiency of labour? What steps can an employer take to increase the efficiency of the labour he employs? (CIS)

6. "It is the entrepreneur who bears most of the risks of industry." Examine this statement, bringing out the main functions of the entrepreneur in connection with the organisation of industry. (IB)

7. Explain the functions of the entrepreneur and show where he is to be found in modern industry. (CIS)

8. What are the chief "business decisions" which an entrepreneur has to make? (ACCA)

9. What do you understand by the phrase: "*mobility* of factors of production"? To what extent are factors of production "mobile" in the sense in which you have defined the term? (DPA)

10. What do you understand by "the law of diminishing terms"? Do you consider it to be universally applicable? (Exp.)

11. Explain the functions of the *entrepreneur* and describe how they are performed in the various forms of large-scale enterprise in the United Kingdom today. (GCE)

12. Explain what is meant by the law of diminishing returns. (GCE)

13. How can the mobility of labour be increased? Why is it important? (Degree)

CHAPTER 4

CAPITAL

I. THE MEANING OF CAPITAL

1. The capital of a retailer

Different people define capital in different ways. To those unacquainted with economic theory the term presents less difficulty, as they generally take it to mean money. If John Brown says that he would set up in business for himself if it were not for the fact that he possesses insufficient capital his hearers will take it to mean that he has not enough money for the purpose. A businessman, however, does not want money for its own sake. If Brown contemplates opening a retail shop he will use his money–capital to secure suitable premises, fit them out suitably for the particular branch of the retail trade he intends to enter, purchase a certain amount of stock, and, if he is wise, keep some cash in reserve. Having now spent nearly all his money in this way, can it be said that Brown has less capital than he had at first? In fact, what has happened is that the form of Brown's capital has changed and now consists mainly of real things—a shop and its fittings, a quantity of stock together with only a small amount of cash.

The more durable part of his capital, that should require renewal only at fairly long intervals, is known as his *fixed* capital, and that part of his capital that he requires for the everyday running of his business, and which is constantly changing its form, is known as his *circulating* capital. The premises and fixtures comprise Brown's fixed capital, while his stock, cash in hand and any debts owing to him by customers to whom he has granted credit comprise his circulating capital. The form of this capital changes every time a transaction takes place: whenever he sells anything he depletes his stock and increases his cash; whenever he buys stock he increases his stock and reduces his cash. His cash in hand is known as *liquid* capital, because in this form it is capable of being converted into some form of either fixed or circulating capital. In the case of the manufacturing business the fixed capital consists of factory premises and machinery, while raw materials, partly finished goods and money set aside for the payment of wages form the circulating capital.

2. Capital to an accountant

The accountant, too, tends to consider capital as money, for he assigns money values to all the assets of a business as, for example, when he draws up a balance sheet. Suppose that after being in business for a year Brown employs an accountant to draw up a balance sheet for him. It might read as follows:

Table II

John Brown's Balance Sheet at Dec. 31st, 19—

Liabilities		£	Assets		£
Sundry Creditors . . .		380	Premises		5,400
Loan		3,000	Fittings		600
Capital		5,350	Stock		2,100
			Sundry Debtors . .		210
			Cash in hand and at Bank .		420
		£8,730			£8,730

Here capital is taken to mean the excess of assets over liabilities, or the "net worth" of the trader, and so represents the capital *owned* by Brown as distinct from the capital he *employed*. The capital employed by him, however, includes the whole of his assets, excepting debts owing to him—that is, £8,520 (£8,730 − £210). In this case the capital employed is much greater than the capital owned.

3. Capital to an economist

To the economist capital is a factor of production, or, as is sometimes said, wealth used for the production of further wealth. It can be confusing if capital is treated as if it were the same thing as wealth. In Chapter 2 wealth was defined as a stock of goods existing at a given time that yield utility, have a money value, are limited in supply and the ownership of which is transferable from one person to another. If capital is a factor of production it must be restricted to a particular sort of wealth—that used to assist production, for not all wealth is used to assist production. Thus, all capital is wealth, but all wealth is not capital. The stained glass in York Minster is wealth—even though its money value cannot be assessed—but it is not capital. On the other hand, a blast-furnace is obviously an example of that particular type of wealth known as capital. Even if this distinction between wealth and capital is accepted, there is still considerable difference of opinion as to which goods are capital and which are not.

Before discussing this question further, however, it is necessary to define consumers' and producers' goods.

Consumers' goods. The ultimate aim of all production is to provide consumers with those goods which yield them satisfaction. These are goods in the form in which they are wanted by the people who actually wish to make use of them, and comprise such things as bread and other foods, clothing, household furniture, books, etc. All these are consumers' goods or, as they are sometimes called, final products.

Producers' goods. Unlike consumers' goods, these things are not desired for their own sake, but only because of the assistance they render to the production of other goods. They comprise factory buildings and industrial plant, tools and machinery, raw materials (raw cotton, raw wool, iron ore, wood pulp, etc.), all goods that have not reached the final stage of manufacture (undyed cloth, steel, newsprint, etc.) and means of transport (railway systems, roads, lorries, etc.). Producers' goods are sometimes called capital goods or intermediate products.

There is not, however, a hard-and-fast line of demarcation between these two types of goods. Cotton thread used by a tailor would clearly be a producers' good, but if purchased by a housewife it might be considered to be a consumers' good. A motor car might be a producers' good to a sales representative who uses it entirely for business purposes, but to a man who runs his car solely for pleasure it would be a consumers' good. If the sales representative uses his car at the week-end to take his family for a day's outing in the country, does it then become a consumers' good? In this case, it would seem, the same article at one time serves as a producers' good and at another as a consumers' good.

Stocks of consumers' goods held by manufacturers, middlemen or wholesalers, and retailers are sometimes classed as capital. This can be justified on two grounds. It is consistent with accountancy practice, for in a balance sheet the value of unsold stocks are included among the assets of the firm. To the economist, too, the act of production is not finally completed until the goods have actually been handed over to the people who desire to make use of them, and so wholesale and retail distribution are merely the latest stages in the process of production, and by definition goods that have not reached the final stage of production are producers' goods. To avoid ambiguity, however, it is better to restrict capital as an economic term to the more generally accepted forms of producers' goods listed above, and to exclude unsold stocks of consumers' goods.

Even so, this does not quite resolve the difficulty, for some consumers' goods are durable, and strongly resemble capital goods, in that they yield services to their owners over a considerable period of time, though durability is not an essential attribute of capital goods. Houses come within this category, and nearly a quarter of the total wealth of Great Britain is in this form. In the case of a landlord who owns a number of houses, which he lets to tenants in return for payment of rent, there is no doubt that these houses comprise the landlord's capital, but what of a house occupied by the owner himself? One way to resolve the difficulty is to regard houses as personal or social capital, but this is more of a classification according to ownership than according to function.

In the modern world a good deal of production is devoted to the manufacture of armaments. Such things cannot be regarded as either consumers' goods or producers' goods. They resemble capital goods in one respect—their production withdraws factors of production from the manufacture of consumers' goods, but they certainly do not assist the production of other goods!

II. CAPITAL, MONEY AND INCOME

4. Capital yields income

There is another aspect of capital that is sometimes stressed—the fact that capital yields income. In fact, this is a feature of all forms of property. As already noted, income is an addition to an existing stock of wealth. Adam Smith said that a person's capital was "that part of his stock from which he expects to derive an income." Marshall made this definition more precise by expressly excluding land, which also yields income. Capital is a factor of production, and the extent of a country's stock of it is an important influence on that country's volume of production. For the service capital renders to production its owner receives payment; a sort of hire-charge paid by those using it. The owner of shares in a company receives a share of the profits in the form of a dividend. Shares may be said to yield an income, but this income is earned by the real assets, the capital goods, which the shares represent. Capital is a stock of a certain kind of goods existing at a given time; income is an addition to a stock of goods over a period of time.

Capital considered as a stock of producers' goods used to assist in the production of other goods is the economist's approach to capital.

5. Money as capital

When Robinson Crusoe found a quantity of gold coins in the wrecked ship he was at first doubtful whether they were worth the trouble of his taking them ashore. Smiling at the sight of this money, he addressed it in this way: "What art thou good for? Thou art not worth to me, no, not the taking off the ground. One of these knives is worth all this heap." Being a prudent man, however, he took the gold with him.

To a solitary person in Crusoe's situation money was useless, and he could only hoard it. The tools he found on the ship and those he made were capital goods, factors of production capable of being used in the production either of further capital goods or of things to satisfy his immediate wants—that is, consumers' goods. The money was not capital to him, for it could not help in the satisfaction of his smallest want. Money is simply a means of exchange, and becomes capital only when it gives command over producers' goods.

Even in a modern economy the community *as a whole* cannot regard money as either wealth or capital. To increase the quantity of money will not make that community one iota richer than it was before, for unless there is a corresponding increase in the quantity of goods, the value of money will fall—that is, prices will rise—and so the increased quantity of money will purchase no more than could be bought previously.

Money can, however, be exchanged for capital goods or any other kind of goods. An individual can, therefore, reasonably consider his money to be wealth. It has been seen that for this reason the accountant and the businessman look upon money as capital, and when taking stock of the assets of a business, assess their value in terms of money. When a new company is formed the capital it requires is stated as a sum of money. When people save, they save money. When they invest by buying shares in a new company they purchase them for money, but the company desires the money only because it can be converted into real capital goods—factory buildings, machinery, raw materials, etc. In ordinary speech investment is usually regarded as a monetary action, but to the economist investment means the actual production of capital goods. Each share in a company represents the ownership of a certain fraction of capital goods. In the strict economic sense, therefore, the shares themselves cannot be regarded as capital, but merely as titles to the ownership of capital.

Some Government stocks are similar to shares in that they represent real assets as, for example, Transport Stock—railways, canals, docks, etc. The same applies to Gas Stock, Electricity Stock and the other compensation stocks issued to the former owners of nationalised industries. The position, however, is quite different with most Government stocks, for a large proportion of them represent Government borrowing in the past to finance wars, and therefore they represent no tangible assets. Again, if an individual holds, say, £500 of 8½% Treasury Stock he may justifiably look upon it as personal capital, for it yields him an income, but the country as a whole is obviously no richer because its people hold over £30,000 million of Government securities, that is, Government debt. By the same argument the country as a whole is no poorer because of this huge national debt.

III. CAPITAL AND OTHER FACTORS

6. Capital and labour

Capital, therefore, has to be produced, and some factors of production—land, labour and some capital itself, organised by the entrepreneur—have to be employed for this purpose. Early Man made his first step forward when he fashioned for himself his first simple tool from a rough piece of stone, thereby providing himself with a crude item of capital. Thus, labour was combined with land (the raw material) to provide a third factor of production—capital. From this simple beginning ever more efficient and complicated forms of capital have been gradually evolved. According to Karl Marx, author of *Das Kapital*, capital was nothing more than stored-up labour from the past ("crystallised" labour, as he called it), while land was a free gift of Nature, and so its ownership could not entitle anyone to an income from it. Since he did not recognise the entrepreneur as a separate factor, he argued, therefore, that there was really only one factor of production—labour—that was worthy of reward.

The accumulation of modern forms of capital, however, requires some factors of production to be employed on the production of capital goods when otherwise they might have been used for the production of consumers' goods. Thus, the accumulation of capital involves sacrifice—the sacrifice of present satisfaction in order to be able to enjoy a greater satisfaction in the future. By increasing its stock of capital a country can increase its volume of production and so raise the standard of living of its people.

7. Capital and land

Some of the arguments formerly put forward to show that land was different in kind from the other factors have already been considered, and reasons given for their rejection. If capital is defined as wealth used in the production of further wealth, such a definition would logically include land. By land Ricardo meant the "original and inalienable powers of the soil." but these qualities are very difficult, if not impossible, to define or in practice separate from other qualities of land for there is little land (if any) of economic use that does not owe something to having had human effort and capital expended upon it. Land, in ordinary speech, is as much wealth as anything else, and indeed down to comparatively recent times it was the principal form of wealth. It has been said that any distinction made between land and capital is obviously arbitrary, for the conception of land as distinct from capital is "in flagrant and irreconcilable contradiction with the usages of language."[1] An accountant, compiling a balance sheet, would include land owned by a farmer or a railway as part of the capital of each. Similarly, it might be argued that in Aristotle's time slaves were a form of capital.

The difficulty of framing mutually exclusive definitions of land, labour and capital, and the futility of the many subtle distinctions often made between them, only serve to emphasise once again the economic similarity of these factors. It is convenient to use the terms land, labour capital, but it should be remembered that these names only broadly indicate certain groups of economic resources.

IV. CAPITALISTIC PRODUCTION

8. Capital and division of labour

The essential feature, however, of capital as an agent of production is that its employment makes possible a "capitalistic" method of production. Division of labour makes possible the use of capital in the form of machinery. The essential feature of division of labour is specialisation of processes, and the greater the extent to which specialisation is taken, the more "capitalistic" is said to be the method of production. In this sense the word "capitalistic" merely means making use of more capital goods, and it would be applicable equally to production under communism, where capital is collectively owned, as to production under capitalism, where private ownership of capital exists. The term "roundabout" is also frequently used to describe a capitalistic form of production.

Division of labour, by giving each man a smaller task and allowing him to become more proficient in a single operation leads, as already pointed out, to a large increase in output. How much greater, then, will output be if at each stage of production a machine is employed to do the repetitive work. The greater the number of processes into

---

[1] P. Wicksteed: *Common-sense of Political Economy*, Vol. I, p. 366.

which production is divided and the greater the amount of machinery (that is, capital) that can be employed, the greater will be the total output. The more capital that is employed (that is, the more capitalistic or more roundabout the method of production), the larger the output. Capital, then, makes possible even greater specialisation, with the result that output can be still further increased. Thus, not only are the countries with the largest stocks of capital those able to achieve the greatest volumes of production but they are also the ones best able to accumulate more capital. Not only, therefore, do their peoples enjoy the highest standards of living but they are also the ones most likely to continue to raise their standards of living in the future. Conversely, not only are countries with little capital poor but their rate of progress also is slower than that of the richer nations, so that the gap between rich and poor nations tends to widen.

9. "Waiting"

The use of capital therefore makes possible a larger output than could otherwise have been achieved, but before a capitalistic method of production can be adopted the capital itself has to be made. Consider again the case of Robinson Crusoe, alone, as he was at first, on his desert island. Having salvaged from the wrecked ship a certain amount of capital in the form of a chest of carpenter's tools, some nails and spikes, he made himself a raft. His earliest efforts towards providing himself with food, clothing and shelter depended principally on his own exertions. If in such circumstances he wished to speed up production of a commodity necessary to his existence he would first have to make the capital required. To quote from his Journal: "The want of tools (a shovel or spade) made my work go on heavily ... my other work *having stood still* because of my making these tools." This element of "waiting" is an important aspect of capital formation. During this period of waiting Crusoe had to sacrifice some present satisfaction; he may have had to curtail the amount of time he could afford to devote to hunting or fishing, or more probably, in his circumstances, he would have to sacrifice his leisure. His incentive to do so would be the knowledge that with the help of the tools he was making he would be able with less effort on his part to produce things more quickly and in greater quantity in the future.

An example from actual life closely akin to this was provided between the two World Wars by the USSR. In 1928, when the first Five-Year Plan was launched, it was a country with little capital in proportion to its area and the size of its population, though it possessed vast undeveloped mineral resources. For a period of five years, therefore, it was determined that production should be devoted chiefly to making capital goods, such as factory buildings, industrial plant, blast-furnaces, power-stations, machinery, etc. What the Russian people wanted, of course, was more consumers' goods, but they were told that they would have to *wait* until the necessary capital equipment with which to make them had been accumulated. The completion of the first Five-Year Plan in 1933 was succeeded by a second of similar duration. The first plan covered more particularly the production of heavy capital goods, the second being devoted to lighter capital goods. This meant that the people had to continue to wait a further period of five years, but with the hope of a vast flow of consumers' goods coming off the production lines in the future. The Second World war, however, broke out before this hope could be realised, and the consequent destruction of capital equipment made a further period of waiting necessary. Not until the 1960s was the output of consumers' goods appreciably increased.

10. The structure of production

It is clear, therefore, that in order to make production more capitalistic, greater specialisation of processes is first required. The greater the degree of specialisation, the greater will be the number of processes. The larger the desired output, the more intermediate stages there will have to be in the process of production, the number varying according to the size of the required output. The more capitalistic the method of production, the longer will be the time interval between the taking of the decision to begin production and the time when the goods begin to flow on to the market. Professor Hayek[1] speaks of the lengthening or shortening of the period of production as altering the structure of production. To increase specialisation by introducing more intermediate stages, and so making production more capitalistic, is thus considered to be a lengthening of the structure of production. Similarly, to shorten the structure of production would mean making production less capitalistic. If the structure of production is lengthened, the period of "waiting" will be longer, but output will eventually be much greater.

V. CAPITAL FORMATION AND CONSUMPTION

11. Capital accumulation

It was possible for Robinson Crusoe to supply himself with a small

[1] F. A. Hayek *Prices and Production*, Lecture II.

quantity of capital only by giving up to its construction some of the time he would otherwise have devoted to other pursuits. In an economic system where no money was employed the sacrifice involved in accumulating capital would be clear; production of goods desired for their own sake—that is, consumers' goods—would have to be curtailed in order that capital or producers' goods might be produced. Since each country has only limited resources of land, labour, and capital, there will be no resources available for making producers' goods, if they are entirely given over to the production of consumers' goods. A country's stock of capital at any given period of time is, then, the result of sacrifice by its people in the past, and any further increase in its stock of capital can be achieved only by forgoing the satisfaction of some present wants. Putting this in another way, it merely means that the quantity of goods consumed in a period must be less than the total produced if capital formation is to take place. For:

$$\text{Capital formation} = \text{Production} - \text{Consumption}$$

If the quality of a country's resources is so poor that it requires the application of nearly all of them to enable its people to provide themselves only with the bare necessities of existence, it will have little opportunity of increasing its store of capital, and the accumulation of capital will be a slow, painful process. In all countries the early stages in capital accumulation are slow, but once having acquired some stock of capital, this in turn can be used to assist further capital accumulation—that is to say, the rate of accumulation proceeds with cumulative effect. Thus, to provide a developing country with capital will speed up its economic progress.

Capital formation depends on saving. Money often tends to hide the real working of economic forces—the so-called "money veil"—but even in a monetary economy the accumulation of capital proceeds on similar lines to that outlined above. Abstention from consumption enables capital to be produced. Such abstention is called *saving*. Thus Robinson Crusoe was able to save even though his was a non-monetary economy. In a modern economic system where money is in use saving means refraining from spending on consumers' goods. If consumers spent their entire incomes on consumers' goods there could be no accumulation of capital goods, for the entire existing productive resources of land, labour and capital would be required to satisfy this demand. If, on the other hand, consumers decide to save part of their incomes—say, one-sixth—then one-sixth of the country's resources can be devoted to making capital goods:

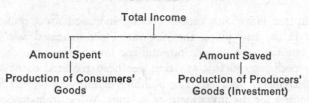

Thus the production of capital goods depends on saving. In economics the term investment is used to mean the actual production of capital goods, and so it can be said that investment depends on saving. A more detailed consideration of saving and investment must be postponed till later, but it may be noted at this stage that saving by itself does not guarantee that investment will take place—it simply makes investment possible. Saving reduces the demand for consumers' goods and frees resources that might otherwise have been used for their production, but if this results in these freed resources merely remaining idle it is quite clear that no capital formation will ensue.

12. Capital accumulation in Great Britain

Capital accumulation is not likely to take place unless people are reasonably sure that their property will be secure, and so saving will be greater in a State where law and order are maintained. Saving, too, is a habit that takes time to develop. Unless opportunities for investment exist, there will be less inducement to save.

Before the eighteenth century there were few outlets for people's savings. The Government borrowed mainly to finance wars, and savings lent by people for this purpose were dissipated without any production of real capital. Lending to the Government, however, developed the habit of saving, and in the eighteenth century enabled the new trading companies to obtain the funds with which to finance their activities. In spite of the losses incurred by many investors at the time of the South Sea Bubble (1720), people continued to put their savings into new ventures. During the second half of the eighteenth century the expansion of the turnpike-road system, with increasing expenditure on road improvements, presented people with new opportunities. The Industrial Revolution of the late eighteenth and early nineteenth centuries provided further outlets for the investment of savings. The early factory businesses were small and generally financed by the savings of the small proprietors, their friends and relations, or, as in the case of the woollen industry, by merchants. Profits were rarely wasted in riotous living, but instead were put back into the business, the owners often leading very frugal lives.

During the nineteenth century saving increased for a number of reasons. In the first place, the National Debt increased at a much slower rate than the population, and for long periods the debt was actually declining, so that taxation per head required to cover the interest payments declined. The building of railways offered further opportunities for the investment of savings. When joint-stock companies were permitted limited liability this reduced the risks of small investors, and so not only encouraged the formation of new companies, thereby increasing investment opportunities, but also increased the incentive to save, at a time when opportunities for this kind of investment were increasing. Not only did opportunities for investment increase but also with the rising standard of living there came increased ability to save.

13. The maintenance of capital

Some capital is by its nature more durable than other forms of capital—a loom, for example, will last longer than the yarn fed into it. Raw materials and partly finished goods are forms of capital that are about to be converted into consumers' goods. In order to maintain stocks of these things, their supply must be constantly renewed. Even more durable forms of capital eventually wear out, though the machines used in some industries have been known to be in continuous use for over fifty years. Railway engines too have often had very long lives, but buses and aircraft are less durable. Each year, however, some capital wears out and has to be replaced. All such capital has to be made good before any addition can be made to a country's total stock of capital. Therefore a certain amount of production each year must be devoted to the replacement of worn-out capital, for, if progress is to be maintained, new capital must be produced in excess of that required to cover depreciation.

Should old capital in good condition be scrapped? People are apt to boast of the durability of some of the capital goods produced in this country. They will point with pride to a machine that has given half a century of service and praise the workmanship that has made this possible. Economically, however, this may not be a good thing. For economic progress to be maintained it is not only necessary for worn-out capital to be renewed but also for out-of-date capital to be replaced. To scrap machinery, however old, that is still in good running order appears at first glance to be wasteful, but it is much more wasteful to continue to use obsolescent machinery when more efficient machinery is available. The main question to be answered in such cases, however, is: will the newer capital be more efficient than the old? If the answer is in the affirmative, then the old capital should certainly be scrapped and replaced by new. The loss resulting from scrapping obsolete capital is easily outweighed by the increased efficiency of the new, up-to-date capital installed to replace it. The extraordinary longevity of some of the machinery in both the cotton and woollen industries was one of the reasons for the long delay in re-equipping these industries with modern capital. Therefore, in order to maintain capital intact a certain amount of production every year has to be given up to the replacement of worn-out and obsolete capital.

14. Capital consumption

If a country ceases to add to its stock of capital it will fail to make economic progress; if it fails to make good depreciation of its capital—that is, if it does not replace worn-out capital—it is said to be consuming capital. Depreciation of capital can take two forms—the wearing out of machinery, etc., and the using up of stocks. Capital consumption may occur if too great a proportion of a country's resources are devoted to the production of consumers' goods, since it means that insufficient resources are employed in making producers' goods. This is only another way of saying that the community as a whole is spending too much of its income on the satisfaction of current wants and that not enough saving is taking place. In such circumstances the stock of capital goods will be gradually reduced—that is, the country will become poorer, for as capital becomes worn out there will be no new capital to replace it. This will have a cumulative effect and after a short time the production of all kinds of goods will begin to decline. The condition will be very similar to that of an individual who is living beyond his means; he will be able to satisfy more of his wants for a time, but in the end he will be poorer.

Living on capital. A person is said to be "living on his capital" if he is having to supplement his current income by drawing on past savings in order to make both ends meet. When he has exhausted his savings he will have to accept a lower standard of living. When a country is consuming capital the consequences will be very much the same. A country that fails to maintain its stock of capital is sometimes said to be "living on capital". Such a condition is now most likely to occur only in war-time. Some capital may be consumed as a direct result of enemy action; factories, machinery, roads, railways, harbours may be destroyed, but even if little or no loss is caused in this way, the nation's energies may be concentrated to such an extent on the effort to win the war that only a bare minimum of consumers' and producers' goods will be made, most productive resources being given up to the manufacture of weapons of war, and as much labour as can be spared being drafted into the armed forces. At such times it may be necessary to run the risk that the war can be won before capital equipment at home deteriorates to such an extent that production begins to fall. Great Britain took this risk during the Second World War (1939–45), when for nearly six years the country was living on capital. When the war ended even the most casual observer could not fail to notice the bad condition of many buses and the frequency of breakdowns. Roads, too, were in need of repair. Maintenance of the railways had been neglected as much as was consistent with safety and because they had been greatly over-worked during the war, they found themselves in 1945 with a shortage of rolling stock, coaches, wagons and engines, and with much equipment in need of repair. In factories also there was a great need of new machinery. A growing population requires an increasing supply of capital goods. The population of Great Britain increased by over $1\frac{1}{2}$ million between 1939 and 1945, but because of the necessity to concentrate on the war effort there was no increased provision of schools, electric generating plant, gasworks or water supplies. Much capital, then, had been consumed and had to be made good before further capital accumulation could take place.

Just as Robinson Crusoe could increase his stock of capital only by reducing production for his immediate needs, so a modern State can increase its stock of capital in a short time only by severe sacrifice of current production and consumption of consumers' goods. Production normally has four objectives—to produce consumers' goods, to provide for depreciation, to accumulate capital and to produce for export:

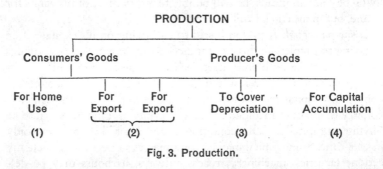

Fig. 3. Production.

With the exception of the normal expansion of production arising from increased productivity, production for one of these four purposes can be increased only if there is curtailment of production for the other three purposes.

RECOMMENDATIONS FOR FURTHER READING

J. R. Hicks: *The Social Framework*, Chapters 8–10.
Irving Fisher: *The Nature of Capital and Income*, Chapters 4–6.

QUESTIONS

1. "Capital is the most important single factor in the development of an economy." Explain and discuss this statement. (SE London)

2. Consider the part played by capital in production and attempt an economic analysis of the sources from which an entrepreneur may obtain capital. (Norwich)

3. "Capital is the most important single factor in the development of an economy." Explain and discuss this statement. (RSA)

4. What do you understand by the term "capital"? (CIS)

5. Discuss the various forms in which the capital of a country exists. (Exp.)

6. One of the major problems today is the replacement, renewal and extension of capital equipment. Discuss how this tends to be achieved in a system of private enterprise. (IHA)

7. "Most economists agree that to secure a steadily expanding level of production in an industrial community 10 to 15 per cent of the national income should be invested in new capital development." Comment on this statement and explain the relation between the production of Capital Goods and that of Consumption Goods. (ACCA)

8. Discuss the different aspects of the statement that a nation may be "living on its capital." (CIS)

9. There are various ways in which an entrepreneur can obtain finance for the purpose of founding or expanding an enterprise. What are the principal sources of such finance? (IB)

10. What is meant by maintaining capital intact? (Degree)

CHAPTER 5

POPULATION PROBLEMS

I. GREAT BRITAIN—THE PAST

1. Economic importance of population problems

Great interest is taken today in population problems both for social and economic reasons. This, however, is not a new interest for economists for nearly two hundred years have been keenly interested in the population problem and, says Marshall, "in a more or less vague form it has occupied the attention of thoughtful men in all ages of the world."[1] The form taken by the problem has varied with the particular conditions of place and time. At one period the aim might be to keep up the number of males, to make good the ravages of war; at another time maybe, there was a fear lest the growth of population should outrun food supplies.

Linked up with the question of food production, the population problem was one of the earliest of Man's economic problems. Early peoples were keenly alive to it, and had their own methods of tackling it. The spread of Christianity, with its cultivation of respect for human life, aggravated the population problem of peoples who had previously kept down numbers by such practices as infanticide. There are three main reasons why population problems are of great economic importance: (*i*) labour is one of the factors of production; (*ii*) people require to be adequately fed if efficient labour service is to be provided; and (*iii*) the aim of all production is to satisfy people's wants.

Population problems are both varied and far-reaching in their effects. For most of his history Man's main concern, like that of other animals, has been with food and shelter. Even though for many people in the twentieth century this problem no longer exists, it is still a serious question for people in many countries. For the world as a whole the most serious problem is the relationship between the rate at which population is increasing and the rate at which the world's output of food can be expanded. Another, perhaps even more serious aspect of this question is the problem of distribution, that is, ensuring that increased supplies of food go to the undernourished

[1] A. Marshall: *Principles of Economics,* IV. iv. 1.

peoples. The efforts of Governments to increase the rate of economic growth of their countries will be nullified if it results in population increasing at an even more rapid rate as, in fact, has already happened in India.

The size of a country's population in relation to its supplies of other factors of production, too, is of great economic importance. Too small a supply of labour may make it impossible for a country to achieve the maximum rate of economic growth, and its people will be poor because they are too few in numbers to enjoy the advantages of large-scale production; if a country is over-populated in proportion to its stock of capital and land, again the people will be poor because output per head will be low. Other problems of a social and economic character include the effects of changes in population on its age distribution, especially when this means a large increase in the number of people retiring from work. These, then, are some of the population problems that have to be considered.

In Great Britain in the late eighteenth and early nineteenth centuries the danger of over-population appeared to men like Malthus to be imminent, though apparently the march of events later in that century showed such fears to have been ill-founded. By the 1920s the whole character of the problem seemed to have changed from a fear of over-population to one of under-population. By the middle of the twentieth century, though the fear of a decline in population in Great Britain had not been entirely removed, some writers, taking a wider view and considering the world as a whole, were becoming alarmed by the prospect of a population too vast for the resources of the world to feed.

2. Growth of population in Great Britain since 1801

It is only since 1801, when the first census was taken in Great Britain, that accurate population statistics have been available. Though particulars of the population of the country before that date must, therefore, of necessity be based only on estimates, it is generally agreed that up to the year 1700, when it has been calculated that the population of Great Britain was 6.5 million, population had been increasing at a very slow rate, as Table III shows.

During the preceding six centuries there had been little difference between the birth-rate and the death-rate, both of which were high, and for considerable periods the population barely replaced itself, and in some years actually declined. Famine, pestilence and war were largely responsible for the high death-rate. Infant mortality was exceptionally high—in the eighteenth century probably not more than half the

Table III

Estimated Population of England 1066–1750

Year	Population (million)
1066	1.5
1345	4.0
1350	2.5
1570	4.2
1630	5.6
1670	5.8
1750	6.5

children born survived to the age of twenty-one—and though it fell throughout the nineteenth century it still stood at 142 per 1,000 live births in 1900. During the twentieth century the infant mortality rate fell to 67 per 1,000 by 1930 and to 17 per 1,000 by 1970.

By the time of the first census in 1801 the population of Great Britain had reached a total of 11.5 million, an estimated increase of 50 per cent in the course of a hundred years. During the following century growth was even more rapid, the population increasing by three and a half times between 1801 and 1901, to give a total of 37 million. After 1901 the rate of growth slackened compared with the previous hundred and fifty years, but the population continued to increase. Table III shows both the irregular and the slow rate of growth of the population of England for upwards of 700 years. Since 1801 the census returns have provided more accurate figures for the growth of population of the United Kingdom:

Table IV

Population of the United Kingdom 1801–1971

Year	Population (million)
1801	11.9
1831	17.8
1861	24.5
1891	34.2
1901	37.0
1921	44.0
1951	50.2
1961	51.6
1971	55.6
1975 (est.)	56.1

Changes within Great Britain and Ireland are of interest. In 1750 Ireland had a population only slightly less than half that of England and Wales and more than two and a half times that of Scotland. By 1901 England and Wales had a population nearly eight times that of Ireland, while Scotland had drawn level with Ireland. During the second half of the nineteenth century the population of Ireland declined by one-third, largely as a result of famine and emigration.

3. Causes of population growth during the nineteenth century

Why, then, did the population of Great Britain, after growing slowly for hundreds of years, increase at so rapid a rate in the late eighteenth and nineteenth centuries? The main cause was the steep fall in the death-rate. In 1740 Great Britain had a death-rate estimated at 31.7 per thousand; by 1820 it had already been reduced to 25.0 per thousand. The death-rate continued to fall during the ensuing one hundred and fifty years, at first slowly but after 1870 more rapidly:

Table V

The Death-rate in the United Kingdom

Year	Rate per 1,000
1870	22.1
1880	19.7
1890	19.6
1900	17.4
1910	14.2
1920	12.7
1930	12.2
1940	13.9
1950	11.8
1960	11.5
1970	11.7
1974	12.0

Until 1870 there was little change in the birth-rate.

In earlier centuries pestilences from time to time swept across Europe, and occurrences such as the Black Death of 1349 and the Great Plague of 1665 were only more serious examples of such visitations. The high death-rate affected all classes, mortality being particularly high among children. Samuel Pepys, the famous diarist was a fifth child but by the time he was seven years of age he had become the eldest, the four older children all having died. The big Victorian families were the consequence of a fall in the death-rate among children rather than an increase in the size of the family. Development of medicine, with science replacing superstition, the opening of hospitals—new ones were opened in Great Britain at an average rate of one per year from 1700 to 1825—and improved sanitation lessened the incidence of epidemics, and many diseases that had previously been prevalent were completely or partially eradicated, as for example, typhus, scurvy and smallpox.

It is no accident, however, that this decline in mortality coincided with the agrarian and industrial revolutions. The cultivation of root-crops made it possible to feed cattle during the winter, instead of having to kill off most of them during that season, as had previously been necessary. This meant that supplies of milk and fresh meat were maintained throughout the whole year. A second factor making for improved nutrition was that improved means of transport made a supply of green vegetables more generally available. Two of the main causes of the slow growth of population during the Middle Ages had been the frequency of epidemics and famine in years of bad harvests. Even as late as 1701 a succession of bad harvests in Scotland caused a famine that wiped out more than half the population in some areas. The improved milk supply and the wider distribution of green vegetables were largely responsible for removing the danger of famine.

Although the fall in the death-rate was the chief factor, there was also a slight increase in the birth-rate. This was the result of young people marrying at an earlier age, especially after it was no longer necessary to serve a lengthy period of apprenticeship, during which it had been forbidden to marry. The establishment of the factory system enormously expanded the demand for the labour of both women and children. After marriage a woman could reasonably be expected to earn her own keep, and it was only a few years before children were old enough to work in the factories, and thereby add to the family income. Fluctuations in the marriage rate in the early nineteenth century were linked to changes in the price of corn; later in that century the trade cycle became the chief influence.

4. Malthus

Although in a vague sort of way his predecessors were aware of the population problem, the Rev. T. R. Malthus (1766–1834) was the first economist to give it serious attention. Though a prolific writer on economic subjects, he is chiefly remembered for his work on what he called "the principle of population." First published in 1798 under the title of an *Essay on the Principle of Population as it affects the Future Im-*

provement of Society, Malthus during the course of his lifetime revised his work five times, each of the later editions embodying additions and alterations both to the title and to the essay itself. Malthus was much abused by his contemporaries for his pessimistic outlook, but his purpose in writing his essay had been to refute the current idea that conditions of life were gradually moving towards an earthly paradise. At the time of the publication of the first edition it had become apparent that the population of Great Britain had begun to increase at a more rapid rate than previously. Such a growth of population was a new phenomenon, and it led Malthus to speculate on the possible consequences of this new trend. At the same time wages were low and prices high, and there was real distress among lower-paid workers. Large families were encouraged by the Speenhamland system (so-called because it was first introduced at the village of that name near Newbury in Berkshire) whereby the Poor Law authorities supplemented the wages of agricultural workers according to the sizes of their families.

Malthus declared that there was a "constant tendency in all animated life to increase beyond the nourishment for it." In the animal world the struggle for existence results in the survival of the fittest, whereas the greater the advance made by civilisation, the less is the effect of this tendency on the human race. No populous country, he said, could obtain the necessaries of life so easily as a thinly peopled country. People, according to Malthus, unless checked in some way, doubled their numbers every quarter of a century. During his own lifetime he noticed that the increased demand for wheat, consequent on the growth of the population, was causing wheat to be grown on inferior land where the yield per acre was low. This led him to state that while population increased in geometrical progression, food production could be increased only in arithmetical progression, a gross exaggeration of the situation, though he did not use these terms with mathematical precision. He sought, therefore, to show that the means of subsistence placed a limit on the growth of population, an increase in the means of subsistence bringing about an increase in the population, unless this was checked by "vice or misery" due to famine, war or pestilence. In the second edition of his work he added "moral restraint," by which he meant abstention from early marriage.

Malthus summed up his argument in three propositions:

(*i*) Population is necessarily limited by the means of subsistence.
(*ii*) Population invariably increases where the means of subsistence increase, unless prevented by some powerful and obvious check.

(*iii*) These checks are all resolvable into moral restraint, vice and misery.

Malthus was impressed by two things: the rapid increase in population in Great Britain and the Law of Diminishing Returns as currently understood, as applied to food production in this country. Each successive increase in population, he thought, required the bringing into cultivation of ever less fertile land. "The best lands are taken up first, then the next best, then the inferior, at last the worst; at each stage the amount of food produced is less than before." If existing cultivated land were farmed more intensively the same inexorable law would operate, and again there would be diminishing returns. Consequently, it would be impossible to maintain an expansion of food production to keep pace with the increasing population. Great Britain could probably have supported a much larger population than it had at the time when he wrote his essay, but not a population increasing as rapidly as it was by the end of the eighteenth century. Unless this excessive growth of population were checked the standard of living of the people in this country would be bound to fall. Thus ran Malthus's argument. To him the only hope lay in checking the growth in population, and the remedy he suggested was moral restraint.

Malthus was not, however, unaware of the great improvements in farming methods that were taking place in his own day. These improvements in both agricultural and pastoral farming made possible a much larger output than had previously seemed possible. He was not, however, fully alive to the effects of this agrarian revolution, but considered it to be of temporary effect only and so merely postponing the day when food production would be insufficient for the population's needs.

5. Did History prove Malthus wrong?

For a long time it was usual to say that the history of the nineteenth century eventually proved Malthus's argument to be wrong. It was pointed out that although the population of Great Britain increased at a faster rate during the nineteenth century than it did in the fifty years preceding the publication of the first edition of his essay, yet the people enjoyed a higher standard of living at the end of the century than at the beginning. The explanation was to be found, (*a*) in the opening up during that period of many new lands—the United States of America, Australia, New Zealand, South Africa, and some of the countries of South America, and (*b*) in the improvement in transport, which made it possible to bring food from the New World to the Old. At this period most of these new countries were primarily producers of foodstuffs and raw materials, and were able to supply food to Great Britain, thus enabling this country to devote more capital and labour to the production of manufactured goods. As a result Great Britain was able to support a much larger population than would have been possible if it had had to feed itself directly from its own resources. Great Britain thus became an industrial country, dependent on the New World for the greater part of its food supply, which it paid for by the export of manufactured goods.

Perhaps Malthus generalised too easily from the circumstances of the time in which he lived, but he could hardly have been expected to foresee the future tremendous economic development of the New World, though he does appear to have been vaguely aware of this possibility. But does this opening up of the New World invalidate his arguments? Just as the effect of the agrarian revolution was, according to Malthus, merely to postpone the evil day, so in like manner might not the effect of the development of the New World be again of a temporary nature, its ultimate result merely being to cause the crisis to occur at a higher level of population? Nor can Malthus's critics altogether be blamed for being impressed by the economic development of the newer countries, which made the potential food production of the world appear almost limitless, and the picture painted by Malthus a pessimistic exaggeration. Around them there seemed to be ample evidence that industrial areas could support dense populations. In forecasting a severe decline in the standard of living in Great Britain by the end of the nineteenth century if population continued to increase, Malthus was undoubtedly wrong, for the population was greater and the standard of living much higher in 1900 than in 1800, but for the world as a whole the ideas of Malthus were revived with increased potency in the twentieth century, when the upsurge of population known as "the population explosion" occurred.

II. GREAT BRITAIN—THE PRESENT AND FUTURE

6. The fall in the birth-rate

The population problem of the twentieth century can be considered from two angles: (a) from the point of view of Great Britain, and (b) from the point of view of the world as a whole. In this country the Malthusian spectre of over-population was replaced for a time in the

1920s by fear of a declining population. In the early Victorian period the average family comprised between five and six children, but after 1875 the birth-rate began to fall, and on the whole continued to do so for the next hundred years. In the forty years 1801–41 the population of Great Britain increased by 76 per cent, whereas in the forty years 1901–41 the increase was just under 26 per cent. The average number of children per family fell from 5.5 in 1850 to 2.2 in 1930, and family size is a more important factor than the birth-rate. In 1870, for example, the expectation of life at birth was only 41 years for boys and 45 for girls, but by 1976 it had risen to over 68 years for boys and over 74 for girls.

It is generally agreed that the reduction in family size was due to deliberate limitation by the parents. Birth control came to be widely practised. The Malthusian picture of the miseries likely to accrue from over-population if the expansion of population went unchecked was the basis of increasing propaganda in favour of family planning in the later years of the nineteenth century. The influence of Malthus is seen in the choice of name for the organisation founded by Annie Besant and Charles Bradlaugh for the propagation of their ideas—the Malthusian League.

The reasons why parents desired smaller families are to be found in the social and economic changes of the period. In the opening years of the industrial revolution children became wage-earners at a very early age, and therefore soon ceased to be a burden on their parents. The Factory and Education Acts gradually raised the age at which children were permitted to work in factories, and by the end of the nineteenth century children were no longer a source of income to their parents, but instead had become an expense. There was a widespread desire about this time among people of all classes to raise their standard of living, and this was more difficult if the family was large. The desire for a higher standard of life may lead to later marriages, and a likely effect of this will be to reduce the average family size. There was, too, greater insecurity of industrial life under the factory system than had previously been the case, and this insecurity became greater with the increasing complexity of industrial production. Before the introduction of social insurance a large family was a great hardship in times of unemployment or sickness. Parents, too, came, to desire to do better for their children—for example, by giving them a better education than they themselves had enjoyed—and this increased the cost of bringing up a family. There is no doubt, too, that the rate of population growth is related to the level of employment. The 1930s saw the longest and most severe slump Great Britain had ever experienced, and it is not surprising, therefore, that these years of high unemployment coincided with a falling birth-rate.

Table VI

The Birth-rate in the United Kingdom

Year	Rate per 1,000	Year	Rate per 1,000
1880	35.2	1945	16.3
1885	32.9	1950	16.2
1890	30.2	1955	15.4
1900	30.3	1960	17.5
1905	27.3	1965	18.4
1910	15.1	1967	17.2
1915	21.9	1969	16.6
1920	25.5	1970	16.3
1925	18.3	1971	16.2
1930	16.3	1972	14.9
1935	15.2	1973	13.9
1940	14.7	1974	13.2
		1975	

Another factor making for small families was the emancipation of women of the better-educated classes, for the rearing of a large family became incompatible with their higher status or the pursuit of a career. Perhaps not least in importance was the fact that the small family became fashionable. These factors making for the smaller family influenced the educated classes to a greater extent than others, so that the larger families tended to be found among the less-cultured sections of the community.

7. Population projections

Periodically since the 1920s population projections have been made for Great Britain. (A population projection is a forecast of the future trend of population.) Such projections have to take into account many variables, as for example, the death-rate, the birth-rate, average family size, emigration, immigration, and any other influences on population changes. Calculations, therefore, are of necessity based on an assumption that present tendencies will continue. The forecasters of the 1920s noted that for half a century the birth-rate had been falling. (*See* Table VI above.) To some extent this had been offset by a falling death-rate. (*See* Table V on page 71.) In 1870, for example, the expectation of life at birth was only 41 years for boys and 45 for girls, but by 1976 it had risen to over 68 years for boys and over 74 for girls. It was pointed out therefore that if these tendencies continued the population of Great Britain would gradually rise to around 48 million by 1944, after which year it could be expected to fall, slowly at first to about 46 million by 1956 and probably to 36 million by 1976. If this forecast had proved to be even approximately correct Great Britain's population problem of the second half of the twentieth century would have been that of a declining population. This view was supported by the *Report of the Royal Commission on Population* (1949) which forecast a fall in the number of births during the next fifteen years, whereas after 1955 the number actually increased. The Commission estimated that to prevent a future decline in the population of Great Britain required an annual total of at least 700,000 births. In fact, the average number of births since 1958 has been over 930,000 and in most years has exceeded one million. In addition to being appointed "to examine the facts relating to the present population trends in Great Britain," the Royal Commission also had to consider "what measures, if any, should be taken in the national interest to influence the future trend of population." Since at that time concern was felt at the possibility of the population declining, it proposed that larger families should be encouraged by increased family allowances, and larger income tax allowances for children.

The Royal Commission further suggested that, as the number of people aged over sixty-five would increase, they should be encouraged to continue at work to a higher age than formerly. Fears of a declining population—at least in the immediate future—proved to be unfounded. Since 1945 the death-rate in Great Britain has remained steady at between 11.1 and 11.8 per 1,000. During the same period the birth-rate continued to rise slowly until it reached 18.7 per 1,000 in 1964. Since then it has shown a tendency to fall. In fact, the birth-rate was exactly the same in the 1970s as in 1950. The higher birth-rate of the 1950s and 1960s as compared with the 1930s can be explained almost entirely by the fact that this period was one with a high level of employment. High earnings at a relatively early age have greatly reduced the average age at which people now marry, with the result that families have tended to be somewhat larger. There has, too, been a swing of opinion against the one-child marriage which was so common in the 1930s.

Population projections made in the 1950s were based on the assumption that the rise in the birth-rate after the Second World War would be only temporary. It was thought, therefore, that the effect of the war would be merely to postpone the date at which the population of the country might be expected to decline—probably towards the end of the century. The population projections of the 1960s, however, indicated the possibility of the population of Great Britain continuing to increase for a considerable time. A population of 72 million was forecast for the year 2000. However, a projection made in 1970 reduced the estimated population for the year 2000 to 67 million.

8. Emigration and immigration

Another factor influencing the growth of population has been the migration of peoples from one country to another. At certain periods in the development of the countries of the New World immigration has been of more importance than the natural rate of increase in expanding population. For example, during the ten years 1880–90, the United States received no fewer than 5 million immigrants. During the past twenty years Australia has had a *net* increase in its population by more than 2 million as a result of immigration. Most of these new arrivals were emigrants from Europe, but Ireland was the only European country that suffered a serious fall in its population in consequence.

Much of the emigration was due to over-population and the conditions of the time in the countries from which the emigrants came— Ireland, Italy, the countries of Central Europe and the Balkans.

During the period of 1871–1931 Great Britain experienced average *net* emigration of over 90,000 persons per year. In the years immediately before the Second World War this country received immigrants from Germany and Austria, including many people with high academic qualifications, and in post-war years many more immigrants came from Europe—the so-called "displaced persons." During 1931–51, therefore, this country for the first time had a *net* gain from migration which averaged 23,000 per year.

In recent years Great Britain's population has been affected by both emigration and immigration. During the years 1951–72 a considerable number of people left this country to make their homes in Australia, Canada and New Zealand. During these years, however, a large number of immigrants came to Great Britain from the West Indies, India and Pakistan, and later from Kenya, and this influx offset the loss from emigration to the extent of 5,600 per year.

In the past countries receiving large numbers of immigrants have often found it necessary to impose restrictions on their entry. The United States, for example, during the 1930s had to restrict the number of immigrants it was prepared to accept. Eventually Great Britain, too, had to adopt a similar course, an Act of 1965 limiting the number of immigrants entering this country. As a result after 1966 Great Britain again began to experience a *net* loss of population from migration (in 1974 a net loss of 85,200). Even Australia, which for so long had been anxious to build up its population, found it necessary to restrict immigration. A new slant was given to population movement in 1974 when over 20,000 people left the United Kingdom for other countries in the European Economic Community (the EEC).

III. THE WORLD

9. The "population explosion"

Since the 1930s the population problem in Western Europe and the United States has been the possibility of a decline of population in the future. At that time the decline seemed imminent and in fact, in France during 1937–45 a temporary decline in its population actually set in. Since 1945 a general rise in the birth-rate in those countries put back the probable date of decline. As already noted, the population of Great Britain is not now expected to decline until well into the twenty-first century. For the world as a whole, however, population continues to expand at an increasing rate and as yet there is no sign of any serious check to its growth.

Until about 1650 the population of the world increased very slowly. It has been estimated that at that date the population of the world was approximately 540 million. Since then expansion has become increasingly rapid. Even Western Europe, in spite of the slackening off in the rate of growth, had 20 million more human beings in 1975 than in 1950. By 1975 the world's population had reached 3,600 million, and it was increasing at the stupendous rate of 70 million a year. For a long time the greatest numerical increase in population per year has occurred in Asia, but in recent years both North and South America have shown greater *rates* of increase. Between 1950 and 1974, for example, the population of the United States increased from 152 to 211 million—an increase of 39 per cent, while that of Latin America increased from 160 to 220 million—40 per cent. Actually, the greatest rate of increase of all occurred in Africa—41 per cent—though by 1950 its population had only reached 300 million. Meanwhile, during the same period the population of Asia increased by only 30 per cent, but this meant an increase in numbers of over 500 million. Of this increase in the total for Asia, India accounted for 172 million as its population increased from 360 to 532 million. Table VII shows the distribution of the world's population in 1970.

Table VII

World Population by Continents

	1970	2000 (est.)
Europe (including USSR)	694	915
Asia	2,008	3,800
Africa	366	510
North America	232	300
Latin America	281	700
Australasia	18	35
	3,600	6,300

The huge increase in the population of Asia has been brought about mainly by a sharp fall in the death rate in that part of the world, expectation of life in India having increased from 33 to 55 years between 1950 and 1970. Improved medical facilities have reduced the impact of many diseases, much of this being due to the efforts of the World Health Organisation (WHO). As a result the death-rate in India has fallen during the past forty years from 40.4 to 16.3 per thousand, although during the same period the birth-rate fell only from 50.8 to 39.4 per thousand, thus doubling the excess of births over deaths.

Table VIII shows how the population of the world has increased during the past 15 years. (Note the huge increase since 1950.)

Table VIII

World Population

Year	Population (million)
1870	1,300
1880	1,380
1890	1,470
1900	1,550
1910	1,670
1920	1,810
1930	2,014
1940	2,245
1950	2,521
1960	2,930
1970	3,600
1975	4,050

It has been estimated that by the year 2000 the population of the world will be in excess of 6,500 million.

To feed the expanding population of the world it is necessary to double the production of food every fifty years. Large numbers of people in many parts of the world today are grossly undernourished by Western standards, and even if population were not increasing so rapidly, it would still be desirable to expand food production.

Not only does an expanding world population increase the demand for food, but the rate of economic growth during the 1950s and 1960s was such that it led to a huge increase in the demand for all kinds of raw materials, thereby raising their prices. Since many of these commodities come from developing countries, where the standard of living tends to be low, this was to their advantage, but for the importing countries it aggravated their difficulties with balances of payments.

10. World population and food production

The problem of increasing the world's food supply has been aggravated in some parts of the world by neglect to maintain the fertility of the topsoil. As a result of soil erosion, there has been considerable loss of fertility, largely due to short-sighted farming methods, adopted by farmers looking for immediate returns and with little thought for the future. Where natural vegetation exists soil formation takes place, but when brought under the plough the soil is easily carried away as a result of erosion. Good stock-rearing districts in the United States have been turned into a great infertile dust-bowl. A very serious view was taken of the problem of food production by Lord Boyd-Orr. "Apart from the prevention of war," he said some years ago, "maintaining the fertility of the top few inches of soil is the biggest problem facing mankind."[1] This view was supported by the late Professor Sir Dudley Stamp, who adds: "Unless soil erosion is checked the whole world is committing suicide."[2]

The fear of Malthus of over-population in relation to food supply and the consequent fall in the standard of living was, therefore, revived, and this time, it was pointed out, there were no new continents to be opened up. It seemed that after all Malthus might turn out to be right.

Between 1939 and 1952 the population of the world increased by 13 per cent while food production increased by 9 per cent. It was this fact that coloured the world population problem in the early 1950s,

[1] Lord Boyd-Orr: University of London Sanderson-Wells Lecture.
[2] L. Dudley Stamp: "Feeding the World's Peoples" (article contributed to the *Westminster Bank Review*).

and led to the belief that over-population of the world was imminent if not already upon us. But these years covered a World War and its aftermath and, in fact, emphasise the extent to which that war had dislocated the world economy.

Without decrying the seriousness of the problem a few voices were raised even at the time to point out that the world was far from having reached its limit of food production:

(*i*) For some time governments had been aware of soil erosion and many of them, including the United States, had already established conservation services.

(*ii*) Under the auspices of the Food and Agricultural Organisation of the United Nations (the FAO) research on an international scale is being carried out on problems of food production in many lands.

(*iii*) There are still considerable areas of land in the world as yet uncultivated on which food crops could be cultivated, especially in Northern Canada and Northern Europe, and much additional land could be made suitable for agriculture by further irrigation schemes. In the New World farming is still mainly carried on extensively, the output of many crops being very much less per acre than in most countries of Western Europe.

(*iv*) More intensive farming in many areas would increase the world's output of food. In the past half-century great progress has been made with the development of chemical fertilisers, and there seems to be no reason to think that progress in this direction cannot be continued. Successful experiments, too, have been made with quicker-ripening crops which makes possible their cultivation in places where there is only a short growing season. There is, too, the further possibility of obtaining more food from the sea.

(*v*) It has been estimated that no less than one-third of all food produced annually is destroyed by insects while in storage. If this difficulty could be only partially overcome the amount of food available for consumption could be very considerably increased.

(*vi*) With increased mechanisation replacing the use of animals or human labour, primitive methods of farming all over the world are giving way to more efficient methods.

Great efforts, therefore, are being made to expand the world's output of food, for there is no doubt that the output of food is capable of being very considerably increased. It has been estimated, for example, that India could produce twice the amount of food it does at present. Between 1955 and 1965 food output increased by 14 per cent and population by 10 per cent. By the 1970s it was estimated that food production was expanding annually by 2.8 per cent, though there was a setback to this favourable trend on account of the poor harvests of 1974.

Without any increase in population it would still be necessary to increase food production for the food produced in the world is not evenly distributed among the world's peoples. In the more advanced economies of Western Europe and North America there is ample food, but in many parts of the world the amount of food per head is less than is regarded as sufficient for the maintenance of health. This makes it particularly necessary to slow down the rate of population growth in the more densely populated regions of the world. Direct help by the richer to the poorer nations has not been an outstanding success. The best way to assist the poorer countries appears to be to show them how to help themselves to increase their output of foodstuffs. By a series of Five-Year plans India has attempted to raise the standard of living of its people, but down to 1970 most of the benefit from the increase in the country's national income has been offset by the increasing population. The Governments of both India and Japan, however, are taking active measures to check population increases. In India, particularly, it is realised by the Government that the present rate of increase must be checked if the standard of living of the people is to be raised, and since 1950 it has sponsored family limitation programmes. Similar efforts are being made in some parts of Africa, for example, Kenya. As yet there appears to be little family planning practised in Latin America where the influence of the Catholic Church is against it. A fall in the birth-rate, however, is likely to be slow to take effect; it is nearly a hundred years since the birth-rate in Great Britain began to decline, and the population of this country is still increasing.

Even though it is now thought that food production is capable of being increased far into the foreseeable future, one cannot believe that it can be expanded indefinitely. Unless the rate at which the population is increasing is checked, it would seem that a time must of necessity arrive—even though every improvement in farming, of course, postpones it—when the food output her head of the population will begin to decline. Thus, the problem propounded by Malthus could return in the future on a world rather than a national basis.

IV. SOME FURTHER ECONOMIC CONSIDERATIONS

11. The optimum population

Numbers alone, however, do not show whether or not a country is under- or over-populated, a fact which Malthus himself seems to have realised. "A careful distinction," he says, "should always be made between a redundant population and a population actually great." In a vague sort of way he seems to have been aware that a particular density of population per square mile might be too large for one country but not for another. For the production of any commodity requires the employment of a number of factors of production, of which labour is only one, and these have to be combined in a certain proportion in order to obtain the maximum output.

The amount of labour which, combined with the other factors of production, yields the maximum output is the *optimum* population for that particular country. What is the optimum population for any country therefore depends on its natural resources and its stock of capital. If the population of a country falls short of the optimum it can then be considered to be under-populated; if its population exceeds the optimum it is clearly over-populated. Thus a country poor in natural resources and lacking capital might be economically over-populated, although in terms of numbers its population is small. Similarly, a country is under-populated if there is insufficient labour relative to other factors of production to make the best use of them. The optimum, however, is not fixed, for over a period of time, conditions are liable to change, and what was formerly the optimum may cease to be so under changed conditions of production. If it were possible to increase the supply of other factors proportionately to the increase in population the optimum might be raised. The supply of land, however, cannot be appreciably increased, but the experience of Great Britain in the nine-teenth century provides an example of how the optimum population can be raised if accompanied by an increase in capital.

Though the economists of the 1930s expressed concern at the possi-bility of the population of Great Britain beginning to decline, other people feel that these small islands are already overcrowded and that a little more elbow room would make for more comfortable living for all. During the Great Depression of 1929–35 the argument was put forward that a decrease in the population would reduce the numbers of the unemployed. In fact, this is far from being the case. With a decline in population there would probably come a falling off in total demand,

and this would add to the difficulties of reducing unemployment. A small population would probably mean a reduction in productive capacity, thereby checking economic growth. It is possible too that any difficulties that might arise with the balance of payments would be aggravated, and not improved by a reduction in population.

Whether or not a decrease in the population of a country is likely to be a good or a bad thing in the long run depends, therefore, on whether the present population is above or below the optimum for that country. Obviously, if the population is above the optimum a reduction in numbers will be an advantage, for this will increase output per head. A reduction, therefore, in the population of India would clearly be economically advantageous to that country, as probably would an increase in the population of Australia. Clearly, if the present population is at or below the optimum any reduction in numbers will result in a fall in output per head.

12. Age distribution of the population

The following table shows the distribution according to age groups of the population of the United Kingdom at 30th June 1974:

Table IX

Age Distribution of the Population (thousands) 30th June, 1974
United Kingdom

Age groups	Total	Males	Females
Under 5	4,124.4	2,119.9	2,004.5
5–9	4,594.8	2,356.9	2,237.9
10–14	4,532.3	2,326.0	2,206.3
15–19	4,048.7	2,079.7	1,969.0
20–24	3,911.5	1,990.0	1,921.5
25–29	4,150.0	2,104.3	2,045.7
30–34	3,409.8	1,733.4	1,676.4
35–39	3,238.0	1,643.8	1,594.2
40–44	3,204.5	1,612.1	1,592.4
45–49	3,330.1	1,655.8	1,674.3
50–54	3,685.1	1,803.9	1,881.2
55–59	2,926.2	1,402.0	1,524.2
60–64	3,185.1	1,491.5	1,693.6
65–69	2,817.4	1,253.0	1,546.4
70 and over	4,898.6	1,735.8	3,162.8
Total	56,056.5	27,305.1	28,751.4

Source: *Annual Abstract of Statistics.*

If the birth-rate and death-rate remained steady, so would the distribution of the population within the various age groups. The largest number would be in the lowest age group and numbers would gradually decline in each succeeding age group. Graphically represented this

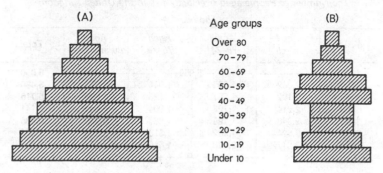

Fig. 4. Population Pyramids.

would give a regular pyramid as shown in Fig. 4(A). A graph of population distribution in Great Britain took this form as recently as 1901. As already noted, the birth-rate was high down to 1911, low from 1914 to 1945 and rather higher since 1945. As a result of these changes and two world wars and the fact that people are living longer, the distribution within the age groups has been distorted. (*See* Fig. 4(B).) During the first half of the twentieth century the proportion of elderly people in this country increased, their numbers doubling between 1901 and 1951 although during that half century the total population increased by only 31 per cent. During 1951–71 the proportion of elderly people increased even more rapidly and can be expected to continue to increase until about 1976. After that date the proportion of people of working age will expand, an increase of 6 million being expected between 1971 and the year 2000. Table X shows how the distribution of the population of Great Britain changed between 1901 and 1974:

Table X

The Changing Age Distribution of the Population

Age	1901	1974
	%	%
0–15	34	24
16–64	60	61
65 and over	6	15

The following table shows how the number of old people has been increasing in recent years:

Table XI

The Number of People aged over Sixty-five in the United Kingdom
(Thousands)

Year	Aged 65–69	Aged 70–74	Aged 75–79	Aged 80 and over	Total
1945	←	5,050		→	5,050
1950	2,062	1,605	1,044	769	5,480
1955	2,102	1,657	1,125	832	5,716
1960	2,214	1,723	1.204	1,000	6,141
1965	2,348	1,798	1,287	1,102	6,535
1970	2,624	1,932	1,318	1,160	7,034
1974	2,817	2,173	1,410	1,316	7,716

Thus there were two million more old people in 1974 than in 1945.

13. Economic consequences of changed age distribution

Serious economic consequences can follow from a redistribution of population within the mean age groups.

(*i*) *Change of demand*. Some change of demand can be expected. To the extent that the demand of the under-twenties differs from that of the over-sixties there will be a decline in employment in industries making goods for the young relative to employment in industries producing things for the old. This will be additional to the normal changes in demand due to changing taste and fashion, and new commodities coming on to the market. Adjustments have regularly to be made to meet changes of demand, and if a country is making economic progress it will be found that at any given time some industries are expanding while others are declining. But labour is not very mobile, and cannot easily be switched from the declining to the expanding industries, and thus structural unemployment is likely to be aggravated.

(*ii*) *The labour supply*. Changes in the size of the working population affect the supply of one of the factors of production—labour. Table X (page 87) shows that the proportion of people of working age increased between 1901 and 1974. Other factors, however, affect labour supply—the extent to which women go out to work, the length of the working week and holidays, the school-leaving age and the age of retirement. Nevertheless, a change in the size of the working population can be of considerable economic importance.

(iii) The dependent population. The greatest change shown by Table X is the fall in the proportion of children and the large increase in the proportion of elderly people. Both these groups are dependent economically on the efforts of the working population. Such a change not only involves a reorientation of the social services but also a further change in demand, in this case in public investment. With an increasing number of elderly people the cost of retirement pensions also increases. To offset this, the Phillips Committee (1954) recommended that the retirement age for men should be raised from sixty-five to sixty-eight and for women from sixty to sixty-three, but there has been little support for this proposal.

RECOMMENDATIONS FOR FURTHER READING

J. R. Hicks: *The Social Framework*, Chapters 4 and 5.
I. Bowen: *Population.*
Report of the Royal Commission on Population (1949).

QUESTIONS

1. Comment on the world's "population explosion." What does this mean and what are the likely economic consequences? (Bournemouth)

2. What is meant by saying that a country is overpopulated? Is Great Britain overpopulated? (UEI)

3. Examine the probable economic consequences of a sharp decline in the size of the working population of the United Kingdom. (RSA)

3. Enunciate Malthus' theory of population and describe the conditions obtaining in England when he wrote which lent support to his theory and the changing views of economists since as to the soundness of his theory of population. (LC Com.)

5. "Cheap labour makes cheap food: cheap food stimulates population: the increase of population makes labour still cheaper." Would you accept any or all of these statements? Give reasons. (CIS)

6. What theories did Malthus produce in regard to population? What truth, if any, do you think they contain? (ACCA)

7. What economic factors would you wish to be taken into account before deciding whether a net increase in population as a result of immigration into Britain is desirable? (IB)

8. Examine the economic effects of the present trend towards an ageing population in the United Kingdom. (GCE)

Part Three

THE ORGANISATION AND STRUCTURE OF PRODUCTION

CHAPTER 6

THE ORGANISATION OF BUSINESS IN A MIXED ECONOMY

In a State-planned economic system production is the sole responsibility of the State. In the case of free or private enterprise, however, production is in the hands of individuals or groups who attempt to anticipate consumers' wants. Thus, nationalised industries are usually extremely large, whereas in the case of free enterprise the size of the business unit varies in type and size from that of the sole proprietor employing only a small amount of capital to the huge public limited company, the largest of which are multinational organisations, which may reckon their capital in hundreds of millions of pounds or dollars. The feature of a mixed economic system, such as that prevailing in Great Britain today, is that some forms of production are operated by the State while others are left to free enterprise. At the present day, therefore, there is in this country great variety of business organisation —the sole proprietor, partnership, private and public limited companies, co-operative societies for the private sector of the economy, and the public corporation for the public sector.

I. THE SOLE PROPRIETOR

1. Features of the "one-man" business

The oldest type of business unit is that of the sole proprietor—the "one-man" business. As recently as the eighteenth and the early nineteenth centuries most manufacturing businesses were of this type, and even today, though large-scale production has made it increasingly difficult for individuals to set up in business for themselves, there are still a few people who succeed in doing so. In the 1920s and 1930s many men found scope for their abilities in the revival of road transport but, at the present time, the retail trade is probably the easiest to enter for the man with a little capital who wishes to set up on his own account, though the opportunities are declining even in this field.

In this type of business a single person undertakes the risks of production. He probably provides all the capital, though to make a start he may have to borrow from friends or relations. He is thus the owner of the business, shouldering the entire responsibility for its management and operation. Success or failure depends primarily on his ability to produce things that other people want and at a price which they are prepared to pay, that is, upon his efficiency as a producer. If he is successful he reaps his reward in the form of profits, which accrue solely to him, though subject to taxation by the State; but if he is unsuccessful he must bear the entire loss himself. Businesses of this type are generally small, at least at first, but many of them have in the course of generations become quite large, though usually when that has occurred the structure of the business has been changed to a form more suitable to large-scale production. A man with only a little capital can build up a business of fairly considerable size by living frugally and devoting most of the profit to the expansion of the business. Many large old businesses in Great Britain today, in a wide variety of industries, originated in this way.

2. Advantages of the sole proprietor

The following are some of the advantages of this type of business:

(*i*) Self-interest is a powerful motive making for the success of the one-man business. He has every incentive to make his business as efficient as possible. He is in full charge and can devote as much of his time and energy to it as he wishes.

(*ii*) There is no need for him to consult anyone else when embarking upon a new line of policy. His decisions can be put into effect immediately without his having to convince others that they are in the best interests of the business. Because of its smallness he can manage the whole business and so attain a high standard of efficiency.

(*iii*) Also, because of the smallness of the business he can maintain a closer and more personal contact with both his employees and his customers. Often he himself has worked for others and understands the employee's point of view. He is known personally to his employees and is aware of their private problems, so that there often exists an intimacy between management and workers which is not easy to foster in large concerns, where management tends to be very impersonal. Further, his personal knowledge of his customers' idiosyncrasies and financial standing makes it easy for him to meet their wishes and to be prudent in the granting of credit.

(*iv*) It is a convenient type of business unit where special lines are produced for a limited market. Where variety is to be preferred to standardisation of the product, the small firm can still hold its own.

3. Disadvantages of the sole proprietor

The following disadvantages of this type of business may be noted:

(*i*) The smallness of the capital may hinder expansion.

(*ii*) His own personal abilities determine the success of the business, and on his death or retirement continued success depends on the ability of the person who inherits the business, but there is no assurance that his successor will possess the necessary ability.

(*iii*) Since he bears all the risks, he is personally liable for all of the debts and obligations of the firm. He cannot, for example, limit his liability to the capital he has invested in the business.

(*iv*) This type of business is unsuitable for any form of production where economies of scale are available.

II. THE PARTNERSHIP

4. The ordinary partnership

One of the ways by which the sole proprietor can expand his business is to turn it into a partnership. There are two advantages to be derived from this method of expansion: it enables "new blood" to be introduced into the business, and it makes possible an increase in capital. There is a special kind of partnership known as a limited partnership (*see* below), but this type of partnership is not popular, since limitation of personal liability is more easily secured in the private company. The *Companies Acts* limit the number of partners in a firm to twenty, except in the case of professional people. A Deed of Partnership should be drawn up by a solicitor to regulate all matters affecting the partners.

A partnership has many of the advantages and disadvantages of the sole proprietor, but a partnership has greater continuity of existence than has the business of a sole proprietor. Partners have equal powers and responsibilities, and each is jointly liable with the other partners for all the debts and obligations of the firm, and in a trading firm a partner can make a contract which is binding on his co-partners. It would obviously be most unwise to enter into partnership with anyone unless convinced of his integrity, judgment and business acumen. The profits are usually distributed among the partners in proportion to the amount of capital each has invested in the business.

5. The limited partnership

This kind of partnership was made possible by the *Limited Partnership Act* (1907). The liability of the limited partner is restricted to the amount of capital he has invested in the firm. His rights are also restricted.

Though he may have access to the books of the firm, and offer advice to the ordinary partners, he may not take any part in the management of the firm nor can he bind the firm, or withdraw any part of his capital. Though there may be more than one limited partner, there must always be at least one ordinary partner. Limited partnerships must be registered with the Registrar of Companies, and as stated above are not very popular. The private limited company of two or more persons has largely made this type of partnership unnecessary.

Where there is more than one general partner this type of business has the advantage over that of the sole proprietor in that it is possible to share the function of management. For example, in a small manufacturing business one partner may assume responsibility for technical matters, and the other for administration and sales. In a partnership it is clear that *all* the managerial functions are shared among the partners —the risks of production, the work of management and the control of the business.

III. THE LIMITED COMPANY

6. The development of the joint-stock company

The partnership owed its existence as a form of business enterprise to the need for a greater amount of capital than the sole proprietor could supply. The joint-stock company developed out of the partnership for precisely the same reason, and in fact the early joint-stock companies were legally no more than large partnerships. In ancient times works necessitating the employment of large amounts of capital could be undertaken only by rich, despotic rulers, with masses of slaves, or conscripted labour at their disposal, or the capital might be provided by exacting tribute from subject peoples. The Hebrews, for example, were heavily taxed to help pay for the temple built by Solomon, and Pericles defrayed the cost of the Parthenon at Athens out of funds contributed by subject allies. Such undertakings might be carried through as works of public necessity, or for the ruler's self-aggrandisement, or in honour of national gods. In this way the magnificent aqueducts, palaces, temples and tombs of the Ancient World came to be built.

Industry was carried on only on a small scale until the time of the Industrial Revolution, and required only limited amounts of capital. Overseas trade, however, required the building of ships, and, with the passage of time, these were of ever larger dimensions and so more expensive to build. The pioneer navigators of the fifteenth and six-teenth centuries had to seek the patronage of monarchs to defray the cost of their voyages. Columbus, though a Genoese, obtained the help of Ferdinand and Isabella of Spain; the Cabots of Bristol had some support from Henry VII.

As a substitute for this method of financing ventures, the joint-stock company was developed. It is not surprising, therefore, to find that the earliest joint-stock enterprises were trading companies, the British East India Company, founded in 1600, being one of the earliest.[1] The distinctive feature of the joint-stock company is that a large number of people provide the capital in varying amounts and receive shares in the profits (if any) in proportion to the amounts they have invested in the company. In this way it becomes possible to raise large sums, providing the sponsors of a proposed new company can persuade the public that its prospects are well founded. This development received strong impetus early in the eighteenth century when a number of these trading companies earned large profits for their shareholders. The early success of the South Sea Company led unscrupulous people to exploit the cupidity of an ignorant public by floating bogus companies. The collapse of the South Sea Company, after a period of frenzied speculation, brought about the bursting of the bubble in 1720 and led to the passing of an Act later in the year to control the establishment of joint-stock companies. In future there were to be two types: (a) chartered companies set up by Royal Charter, and (b) statutory companies, established by specific Acts of Parliament. The Bank of England was established by Royal Charter whereas railways in Great Britain were built by companies established by Acts of Parliament. The increasing scale of production consequent on the Industrial Revolution increased the popularity of the joint-stock company, and in 1825 a third type of company was permitted—the registered company. The control of a joint-stock company depends on the voting rights vested in the shares. The voting at shareholders' meetings is usually proportionate to the number of ordinary shares held, so that a shareholder owning over 50 per cent of shares has the control of the company in his own hands. At the present time over $4\frac{1}{2}$ million people in Great Britain hold shares in limited companies.

7. Limited liability

Probably the most important development in modern industrial organisation has been the evolution of the principle of limited liability. This simply means that the liability of the shareholder is limited to the

[1] Two companies had, however, been incorporated in 1565 for the mining of copper and zinc. (See A. L. Rowse: *The England of Elizabeth*, Chapter IV.)

fully paid up value of the shares he holds, so that if the company should find itself in difficulties and unable to meet the demands of its creditors the shareholder can lose no more than the amount he has invested, the rest of his property being free from any claims by the company's creditors. Where there is no limited liability the unfortunate shareholder may have to sell his private possessions to meet the debts of the company, as occurred in the case of some bank failures in the early nineteenth century. In such circumstances cautious people hesitate to become shareholders in companies, whereas with limited liability the maximum possible loss is known in advance, so that people become more willing to subscribe to an issue of shares.

The Act of 1720 allowed limited liability to both chartered and statutory companies, but the act of 1825, which permitted the registration of new companies, rather surprisingly abolished limited liability. This privilege was not fully restored for thirty-seven years, an Act of 1855 permitting limited liability where the shares were of a nominal value of £10 or over. An Act of 1862, however, allowed any company to have limited liability, whatever the nominal value of its shares. Banks were expressly excluded from the Act of 1855, but limited liability was extended to them in 1858. Companies may be of limited or unlimited liability, but those with unlimited liability are now extremely rare. Indeed, the Acts of 1948 and 1967 refer only to limited companies.

8. Types of companies

Companies are of two main types:

(i) *The private company*. This kind of company has three important features: the number of shareholders may be as few as two, but the maximum must not exceed fifty, not counting past and present employees of the company; a shareholder cannot transfer his shares without the consent of the company nor can any invitation be made to the general public to subscribe for shares. The close company is one under the control of five or fewer persons (or families). Most private companies are of this type. A man and his wife, for example, could form a private (close) company to run a retail business.

(ii) *The public company*. In this type of company there must be at least seven shareholders, but no maximum number is fixed. Seven persons or more wishing to form such a company draw up a *Memorandum of Association* giving particulars of the type of business to be undertaken, the amount of its nominal or authorised capital and the kinds of shares to be issued. A second document, known as the *Articles of Association*, has then to be compiled, giving particulars of the internal working of the proposed company, including such things as voting rights of shareholders, powers and duties of directors, etc. The next step is the *registration* of the company with the Registrar of Companies, after which a *Prospectus* can be issued and an appeal be made to the general public to subscribe for its shares.

The public limited company is thus able to raise very large amounts of capital from small investors, and gigantic undertakings, with capital running into many millions of pounds, become possible. The construction of railways is an outstanding example of the kind of enterprise which the public limited company made possible.

The raising of large amounts of capital is further assisted by the easy transferability of shares on the stock exchanges. Limited companies are also an advantage to the large investor, who is enabled to spread his investments over many companies, and not have all his eggs in one basket. The various *Companies Acts* (1869–1974) were principally designed to protect people from unscrupulous company promoters. For example, the annual balance sheet has to be made public as a safeguard against fraud, the Act of 1948 declaring further that it must be "a fair and true record."

9. Types of shares

The capital of a limited company is divided into shares. These may be in units of 5p, 10p, 20p, 50p, £1, £5, £100, etc., but small denominations are usually preferred. There are a number of different kinds of shares, and a single company may issue two or three different types in order to attract different classes of investors, some of whom may be willing to undertake greater risks than others. Shares are not always fully paid up (for example, only 70p may have been paid for a £1 share) but the company can call up the balance if required.

(i) *Ordinary shares.* Generally these shares carry no fixed rate of dividend (unless deferred ordinary shares are issued), and receive a share of the profit only after all other claims have been met. The dividends paid by firms producing goods for which there is a steady demand may not vary much from one year to another, and even the difference between trade boom and slump may not be very great. Other firms may be greatly influenced by general conditions of trade, and in a boom dividends on ordinary shares may rise to 100 per cent or more, but in a slump may fall to as low as $\frac{1}{2}$ per cent, or even to nothing at all. Clearly, those people who invest in ordinary shares are bearing the principal risk, but in the hope of a commensurate reward.

(ii) *Preference shares*. These shares usually have a fixed rate of dividend, and their holders are paid in full before any payment is made to the ordinary shareholders. To persuade people to invest in preference shares a higher rate of dividend has to be offered than the yield on Government stocks.

There are several varieties of preference shares, and hybrid types which combine features of both the ordinary and the preference shares. Two may be mentioned: (a) Cumulative preference shares, which are entitled to receive arrears of dividend owing from previous years before any allocation of profit is made to the ordinary shares; (b) Participating preference shares, where, in addition to the fixed dividend, a bonus depending on the amount of profit is payable.

(iii) *Debentures*. In addition to the issue of various types of shares, a company may obtain further capital by applying to the public for a loan. This loan capital is obtained by the issue of debentures. Debentures are not shares, and the holders are creditors, and not members of the company, like the shareholders. They are therefore entitled to receive interest whether the company makes a profit or a loss. Debentures carry a fixed rate of interest, usually a little lower than that paid on the preference shares. They are generally redeemable—that is, repayable at par at some future date. Mortgage debentures are those issued on the security of the firm's assets.

An example will illustrate the method of distributing the profits of a company. Assume that the Northern Manufacturing Co. Ltd. has a share capital of £400,000 divided into £300,000 in ordinary shares of 50p each and £100,000 in 7% cumulative preference shares of £1 each, with a loan capital of £50,000 in 6% debentures of £1 each. It will require £3,000 per annum to pay the interest on the debentures and £7,000 to cover the dividend on the preference shares. If one year the company makes a profit of £6,000, after the debenture-holders have been paid, the preference shareholders will have to be satisfied with 6 per cent instead of the 7 per cent to which they are entitled, and there will be no dividend at all for the ordinary shareholders. If next year the profits total £12,500, after the debenture-holders have been paid, the cumulative preference shareholders will receive £8,000 (£7,000 + £1,000 arrears) and the ordinary shareholders £4,500, giving them a dividend of 1½ per cent. If at a later date the company makes a profit of, say, £55,000 the debenture-holders and the cumulative preference shareholders receive in full the payments to which they are entitled, thereby leaving £45,000 for the ordinary shareholders who will thus receive a dividend of 15 per cent.

In a limited company, therefore, it is the shareholders who bear the greater risk. At the shareholders' meeting they elect a management committee, known as the board of directors, who in their turn may elect one of themselves as managing director, or appoint a salaried general manager from outside. If a managing director is appointed he will probably be one of the large shareholders, and so will bear some risk as well as being responsible for the management of the business. The salaried manager may owe his appointment entirely to the Board's confidence in his managerial abilities, though it is said that few managers' salaries are independent of profits, some holding substantial blocks of shares while others may be paid a bonus based on profits. In any case a paid manager's tenure of office is likely to be short-lived if the board regards the profits as unsatisfactory.

IV. THE CO-OPERATIVE MOVEMENT

10. Co-operation in production

Producers' co-operatives have had little success in Great Britain. Under this form of business unit the workers themselves own the business and elect some of their number to manage it, the profit then being divided among them. The chief difficulty, however, has been to secure efficient management, for popular election is not the best method of securing the most able managers, nor is appointment by election conducive to the maintenance of discipline in the factory. A number of co-operative societies of this type have been established at different times in England and elsewhere, but they have generally been small concerns, because the workers have been able to supply only a small amount of capital. At the present time there are twenty-one firms in membership of the Co-operative Production Federation, mostly engaged in the manufacture of boots and shoes or clothing. Over 80 per cent of their output is purchased by co-operative societies. Profits are distributed as dividends on sales, with bonuses to employees.

During the mid-1970s there were several further experiments with producers' co-operatives in the case of firms threatened by closure, the Government giving a measure of financial assistance and the employees usually providing some of the capital. In view of the conditions of the time when these co-operatives were established their lack of success was not unexpected.

Co-operation among farmers, however, has been steadily gaining ground, so that today farmers' co-operatives in Europe cover more than 60 per cent of the farming population. For a long time, the dairy industry has been organised on co-operative lines in Denmark, where farmers combine to purchase and manage the dairies, to which they send the milk from their farms. The proportion of the total quantity of milk supplied by each farmer is recorded, and he is then credited with a proportion of the dairy's output of butter, cheese, etc. The profits of the enterprise are divided among the farmers in the same proportion. The past thirty years has seen a great extension of co-operation in farming in Great Britain. Most farmers in England and Wales are members of purchasing societies and marketing schemes, which lead to more effective buying and selling. There are farmers' co-operative societies for the purchase of fertilisers, seeds and feeding stuffs, for the sale of wool and for the operation of bacon factories. Marketing Boards have been established for a number of farm products, including hops, potatoes, milk, tomatoes and eggs.

11. Consumers' co-operative societies

A much greater measure of success has attended the development of consumers' co-operative societies, though most of the early co-operative ventures of this type failed. The movement really dates from 1844 when twenty-eight weavers opened a shop at Rochdale. Thus, it began as a working-class movement, the aim being to provide factory workers with cheaper food than they could buy in other shops. The success of the Rochdale undertaking led to many more co-operative societies being formed in industrial districts, and though progress was slow at first, membership of the movement reached half a million by 1880 and 3 million by 1901. After 1918 development was more rapid and the total membership reached its peak of 13 million in 1965, since when it has fallen somewhat. Since 1951 the share of the co-operative societies in retail trade has been declining. The *Gaitskell Report* (1958) made recommendations to improve their efficiency, one of which was that societies should be merged to form larger regional units. In 1901 there were 1,438 societies of varying size, the smallest with fewer than 1,000 members and the largest—the London—with a membership of over a million. As a result of amalgamation the number of societies for some years has been falling. The *Gaitskell Report* suggested that the number should be reduced to about 300, and by 1974 the number had fallen to 242. The co-operative societies' share of the retail trade in 1975 was 11 per cent, although for the sale of groceries their share was 20 per cent.

An entrance fee of from 1p to 10p is usually required of members, each of whom may hold as many shares as he wishes. Each member, however, has only one vote at members' meetings, which elect the committee and the society's president. There are some similarities between a co-operative society and a limited company. The members' meeting of the co-operative society corresponds to the shareholders' meeting of the limited company, but whereas each shareholder usually has a vote for every share he possesses, each member of a co-operative society only has one vote irrespective of the number of shares he holds. The shareholders of a limited company elect a board of directors, while the members of a co-operative society similarly elect a committee of management. Each of these bodies is responsible for general policy. and each appoints paid officials to take over the day-to-day management of the business. The members of a co-operative society also elect their president whereas the election of the chairman of a limited company is left to the board of directors. The chief executive of a co-operative society is variously known as the general secretary, the secretary-manager or the chief executive officer, while the limited company has a general manager or managing director. As already noted, the profits of a limited company are distributed among the shareholders according to the type of shares they hold,whereas for a long time the feature of a co-operative society was that its profits were distributed among members in proportion to the value of their purchases.

The Co-operative Wholesale Society and the Scottish Co-operative Wholesale Society, which amalgamated in 1973, were established to supply the retail societies with stock. Their organisation is similar to that of the retail societies except that at their general meetings the voting power of the member societies, like their share of profits, is proportionate to their purchases from the wholesale societies. In their turn the wholesale societies own many factories and tea-plantations.

The CWS is also interested in retailing through Co-operative Retail Services Ltd., which in 1974 had thirty-four branches, each with its own group of shops. The aim of the CRS has been two-fold: (a) to establish retail societies in areas where this could not be accomplished by local effort; and (b) to assist established societies. There is also the Co-operative Bank and the co-operative Nationwide Building Society.

12. Advantages and disadvantages of co-operative societies

An advantage of the co-operative society in the past was the stability of trade that resulted from the loyalty of members, who supported the movement for its own sake. Secondly, it is claimed to be democratically managed. This, however, may be more apparent than real, especially in the larger societies, where many members are as apathetic as the average shareholder of a limited company, so that the management tends to fall into the hands of a small group. It is said, too, that since the customers and the profit receivers are one and the same, there is not the same conflict of interest between them.

Criticism is often levelled against the co-operative societies regarding the lack of business experience of many members of the Committees, and it is often said that the method of promotion is not conducive to efficiency. It is a frequent complaint that the co-operative societies are able to compete unfairly against the other retail traders, because their profits are exempt from corporation tax which falls on the profits of other business undertakings, the dividend on purchase being regarded as a discount rather than a distribution of profit. Another objection frequently made is that some co-operative societies (which include among their members people of all shades of political opinion) use some of their funds for political purposes, the Co-operative Party associating itself with the Labour Party. Co-operation, however, is a social movement, and each society allots a certain sum every year for the propagation of its ideals.

V. PUBLIC ENTERPRISE

Public undertakings can be owned and operated either by Local Authorities or by the State.

13. Operation by Local Authorities

Public utilities were among the first business undertakings of Local Authorities. They appeared to be particularly well suited to run this type of business since competition would generally have required considerable wasteful duplication of capital. Many Local Authorities formerly owned gas and electricity undertakings, and most of the larger authorities, too, used to operate road passenger services in their own areas. Many Local Authorities are still responsible for water supplies while Hull is unique in having a municipal telephone service and Birmingham in having a municipal bank. Many holiday resorts operate commercial activities for the benefit of visitors.

The owners of these various undertakings are the ratepayers but, unlike the shareholders in a limited company or the members of a co-operative society, they are not allowed to decide for themselves whether they are willing to accept the risks of ownership nor, as in these other forms of business management, can they vote directly for the election of a management committee. The management of a local service is vested in a committee of the council, and this committee appoints a salaried manager. Risk is borne by the ratepayers. When profits were earned, and this was generally the case, they provided relief for the rates (and this was often considerable) while losses were borne by the ratepayers (and in more recent times losses were often heavy). Although road passenger transport was nationalised in 1968 the operation of local bus services was transferred to the new metropolitan counties set up in 1974.

14. State undertakings

The public corporation is a type of business unit that was devised during the 1930s to operate those undertakings which, it was thought, should not be left to free enterprise, though Parliament at the time was not favourably disposed to outright nationalisation. Among these were the Port of London Authority, established in 1908, the Central Electricity Board (1926), the British Broadcasting Corporation, set up in 1927 to take over the British Broadcasting Company, the London Passenger Transport Board (1933) and a number of other undertakings. Similar public corporations were set up for British European Airways (1946), British Overseas Airways (1946), the North of Scotland Hydroelectric Board (1943) and the National Film Finance Corporation (1948).

The nationalisation policy of the Government of 1945–51 brought the Bank of England, the coal-mining industry, gas and electricity production and some forms of transport under State control, the public corporation being regarded as the most suitable type of organisation for the nationalised industries. A number of new public corporations, therefore, were established to operate them, now known as the National Coal Board, the Gas Corporation and the Electricity Council. Under the Act of 1947 which nationalised transport, a public corporation known as the Transport Commission was set up, but in 1962 it was replaced by four boards—Railways (British Rail), London Transport, British Transport Docks and British Waterways. Further reorganisation of transport occurred in 1968 when two new public corporations were established—the National Freight Corporation and the National Bus Company (a public corporation in spite of its name). For the nationalised iron and steel industry the British Iron and Steel Corporation was set up in 1967. For nearly three hundred years the only commercial undertaking in Great Britain operated by the State was the Post Office.

Until 1970 it was operated as a Government department and its profits went to the relief of taxation, but in that year it became a public corporation and since then it has been run as a commercial undertaking in the same way as the other nationalised industries.

The form of organisation of these various public corporations differs in detail but each is associated with a Government department headed by a minister of the Crown who is responsible to Parliament, and in all cases Parliament is responsible for general policy. On the establishment of a new public corporation it is granted a Charter. For example, the BBC was granted a Charter that had to be renewed at intervals, the application for renewal providing an opportunity for debate in Parliament on the policy of the Corporation. Once a Charter has been granted, a corporation has freedom of operation for a prescribed period, day-to-day management being free from parliamentary influence, though usually there is some ministerial control. The management of a public corporation is in the hands of a committee, the chairman and members of which are appointed for fixed periods by the appropriate minister, subject to parliamentary approval. The financial side of a public corporation is operated independently of the Treasury. There are no shares and no shareholders. The business risks of the public corporation are borne by taxpayers and, particularly in the case of British Rail, this has required, periodically heavy grants from the Exchequer. The nationalised industries are considered more fully in Chapter 28.

QUESTIONS

1. Distinguish between the following forms of business organisation:
(a) A public corporation (such as the National Coal Board);
(b) A public limited company;
(c) A co-operative form of enterprise. (City)

2. Discuss the principles and the organisation of a co-operative society. In what ways do they differ from a nationalised industry? (RSA)

3. What are the advantages of the limited liability company over other types of business organisation? (CIS)

4. What are the characteristic features of:
(a) Co-operative retail trading societies;
(b) Public limited joint-stock companies; and
(c) Partnerships? (Exp.)

5. Distinguish between a joint-stock company and a co-operative society. (IB.)

6. Consider the main economic effects of the introduction of the system of limited liability. (BS)

7. What is meant by a joint-stock company? What are the advantages of this type of organisation? (GCE)

8. "The public corporation can be controlled neither by the consumer nor by Parliament." Consider, having regard to this criticism, the part that this form of organisation could usefully be made to play in the economic sphere. (Degree.)

CHAPTER 7

THE SCALE OF PRODUCTION

I. THE TENDENCY TO EXPAND

1. The firm and the industry

Production, then, is carried on by a large number of firms of different types and sizes, ranging from the smallest of one-man businesses with very little capital to huge limited companies with hundreds of thousands of shareholders and issued capital of several hundred million pounds sterling. An industry may be large or small, and may consist of both large and small firms. The firm may be defined as an independently administered business unit. An industry consists of a number of firms producing broadly similar commodities, though it is not always easy to differentiate industries completely one from another. It is usual to speak, for example, of the woollen industry, the cotton industry, the motor-car industry, the shipbuilding industry, and these terms give a broad indication of the branch of production concerned.

If the entire output of a whole industry is produced by a single firm, then the firm and the industry are clearly one and the same, as is the case with monopolies. In Great Britain the nationalised industries, such as coal-mining, electricity and gas production, are of this type. In some forms of production the average size of the business unit is small and the number of firms large. This is true of the retail trade, where the business of the sole proprietor is still the most common form of organisation. In some kinds of production the business unit tends to be very large—railways, the iron and steel industry and the chemical industry (ICI, for example, being responsible for a quarter of the total output of this industry in Great Britain), while in other forms of production such as the wool-textile industry the firms are mostly of medium size.

2. The motive for expansion

In the first place, it has to be assumed that it is the aim of every producer to maximise his profits. This being so, he will adopt that form of production where his costs are lowest, and take all measures open to him to effect economies. It is probably not always true that in all circumstances the producer will seek to maximise his profits. To do so may require an increase in his scale of production and involve obtaining additional capital, and he may not wish to do this. He may prefer the more personal relationship between employer and employee that is possible only in a small firm, or he may shrink from the responsibility of controlling a larger firm, perhaps feeling himself not competent to undertake such a task. For any one of these reasons he may prefer not to attempt to maximise his profits. Generally, however, producers will strive to maximise their profits, and without the assumption that this is so in all cases it would be impossible to construct a theory of the firm. In economic theory it must be assumed, therefore, that the producer will expand his firm if economies of scale are open to him.

3. The growth of large-scale production

One of the main features of industrial development during the last century and a half has been the increasing size of the business unit. There were a number of reasons for this development. Specialisation or division of labour went hand in hand with improvements in means of transport. Without adequate transport facilities large-scale production would be impossible, for every increase in output requires an expansion of the market for the commodity and distribution over a wider field. The development of the limited company, too, has been an important factor in making possible large-scale production involving huge amounts of capital. Then there has been a great expansion in the demand for all kinds of things consequent on the rise in the standard of living in recent times. When most people were living near subsistence level they could afford to buy little except the necessaries of life, and in such circumstances there could be no market for mass-produced goods.

These developments made large-scale production possible. The prospect of greater profits was an incentive to the producer to expand his scale of production, for many economies were open only to the large firm, thereby giving it the great advantage of having lower costs than its smaller competitors. In a few cases the hope of securing a measure of monopoly power as a means of keeping up prices may have been a further spur to expansion. Growth was often gradual, expansion often being achieved by producers putting back into the firm a large proportion of their profits. In this way many large businesses were built up. Another way was by the amalgamation of two or more existing firms to form a new larger undertaking. The British railways grew from small local companies to great national systems in this way before nationalisation turned them into one huge concern. Many railways contributed to the making of the London, Midland and Scottish Railway, the largest being the Midland Railway and the London and North-Western Railway, but many of the constituent companies themselves had been brought into being by the amalgamation of a number of still smaller companies. The "Big Four" English banks came into existence in similar fashion, partly by expansion and partly by amalgamation. The British motor-car industry now consists of only four large companies, three of which are subsidiaries of foreign concerns. In 1913 there were 198 independent motor-car manufacturers in Great Britain, and thirty-six as recently as 1939. The larger constituent units of British Leyland themselves expanded partly by natural development and partly as a result of mergers.

II. ECONOMIES OF SCALE

4. Internal and external economies of large-scale production

The economies to be derived from large-scale production are of two kinds: those which any single firm by its own individual policy can achieve and those open only to an industry as a whole. Economies that are possible to a single firm are called internal economies. Economies of this kind are considered in this chapter. Further economies are possible to an industry as a whole when most of the firms in a particular line of production comprising it are concentrated in one area. Economies arising from localisation of industry are known as external economies, and these are considered in Chapter 8.

5. Economies of large-scale production

The following are some of the principal internal economies of scale:

(i) *Economies in the use of factors of production.* To produce a large output at a lower cost per unit of production than a smaller output clearly means that total cost must increase less than proportionately to the increase in output. Consider the case of a small firm that has decided to build a new factory in order to double its output. It will probably not be necessary to double the plant, raw materials and labour to gain this greater volume of production. It would be rare, for example, for the new factory to require twice the area of the old, and therefore the cost of the land per unit of output will fall. Nor is it likely that it will be necessary for it to double its labour force, for greater division of labour will probably be introduced, so that average output per man-hour can be expected to increase. In such a case it will then become possible for the firm to employ fully qualified specialists. If the small firm employs specialists they will have to spend part of their time doing work requiring less skill, for which the large firm can employ lower-paid labour. As a result, the larger firm will attract more efficient labour to itself, if only because it is able to offer its employees better prospects of promotion, since it will have a larger number of better-paid posts to fill. Greater division of labour will also make possible a more capitalistic method of production and the employment of more highly specialised machinery. Some types of capital are of necessity very large, and can be used, therefore, only by the larger firms, for the small firm has not sufficient work to keep such large "indivisible" units of capital fully employed. These large units of capital are, however, often more economical in their use of power and generally require fewer men to tend them. It would, therefore, be uneconomic for the small firm to use such capital, for it would find the cost of such plant or machinery too great for its resources. The large undertaking, too, can make more economical use of its materials, for what might be waste to a small firm can often be used in the manufacture of by-products. Chemical manufacturers particularly are constantly developing new lines of production in this way.

(ii) *Economies in administration*. In the earlier stages of its growth it is unlikely that the costs of administration of the firm will keep pace with increasing output. While the firm is still of medium size, to double the output will not require a doubling of the office staff, for here again the large firm may be able to enjoy the benefits to be derived from division of labour, and specialised office machinery may be introduced. One advantage of greater specialisation will probably be that the manager will be able to devote himself increasingly to administrative and managerial duties. With growth in size, administrative economies, however, generally cease, and in the later stages of expansion the cost of administration may rise quite steeply. As will be seen shortly, the increasing complexity of management is in fact the main factor that sets a limit to the growth in the size of the firm.

(iii) *Marketing economies*. A large firm can generally buy more cheaply than a small one, for it can buy its raw material in bulk, and so obtain it at a lower price. The small firm has to pay merchants for "breaking bulk" and selling in smaller quantities. Similarly, in distribution the large retailer can buy direct from the producer at a lower price than that charged by the wholesaler. The merchant or manufacturer who has a large order to place usually finds himself in a strong bargaining position, for suppliers are anxious to secure his orders, and will generally cut their prices to obtain them. In proportion to output the selling costs of the large undertaking are lower than those of the small. A firm with a nation-wide market can afford to advertise in the national daily papers, and so bring its products to the notice of potential buyers in all parts of the country. The cost of such advertising would be prohibitive to the small firm. Expansion of a firm's output would not necessitate a proportionate increase in the number of its sales representatives. The large firm, therefore, usually enjoys economies in both buying and selling.

(iv) *Other economies of large scale:* (a) *Finance.* The large firm also often has an advantage over the small concern on the financial side. Many firms borrow their working capital from the banks. There is not, however, a standard rate at which banks lend to businessmen, the rate of interest that will be charged depending on the standing of the borrower, the security offered, the amount borrowed, the purpose for which the loan is required and the bank's estimate of the risk involved. Generally large firms are considered to be the safer borrowers, and there is a tendency for the rate of interest charged by banks to vary inversely with the size of the firm. The smaller, less-favoured firms usually pay a higher rate of interest on bank loans than the larger, more favoured firms.

(b) *Research.* At one time it was chiefly the chemical and allied industries that spent money on research, but nowadays most industries are alive to its importance. Again the large firm has advantages over the small, for it can have its own laboratories and employ a large number of trained research workers. Since they are in the full employ of the firm, any discoveries they make become the property of their employers. Imperial Chemical Industries, Ltd., makes research one of its most important activities, and on the Board is a Director with the special function of co-ordinating the research work carried out in the firm's various laboratories. In the wool-textile industry very few of even the larger firms have their own laboratories, and as in other industries where the average size of the firm is not large, there is a Research Association which draws its funds partly from the industry and partly from Government grants and fees. Realising that economic progress and growth depend to a large extent on technical advance, the British Government itself sponsors research in many fields of activity. In such cases research must be for the advantage of the industry as a whole, and though this may be desirable from the point of view of the community, the individual firm assesses its value less highly than research carried out entirely for its own benefit.

(c) *Welfare.* The efficiency of the workers can be increased by improving the conditions under which they work, and by the provision of canteens and other welfare facilities. These can more easily be provided by the larger firms, most of which nowadays make some such provision. Any benefits to be derived from this service are possible only for the larger firms, for the expense is too heavy for the smaller ones.

III. LIMITS TO EXPANSION

6. Limits to the scale of production

If by expanding the scale of production economies can be obtained it might be asked why firms do not go on expanding indefinitely. A number of things, however, set a limit to the expansion of the firm:

(i) *The extent of the market.* The scale of production is, obviously, dependent in the first place on the demand for the commodity. Production on a large scale cannot be undertaken unless there is sufficient demand to warrant it, though it is often possible to stimulate the demand for a commodity. However, the extent of the demand for a commodity is probably more likely to affect the size of the industry than the size of the individual firms comprising it.

(ii) *Individuality* versus *standardisation.* Mass production means the standardisation of the product, or at least restriction of production to a limited number of varieties. The extent to which variety of product is required will have a limiting effect on the scale of production. For example, in order to create as wide a market as possible for their products, motor-car manufacturers in Great Britain at one time produced a much wider range of models than they do today when many differ only slightly from one another. By the standardisation or semi-standardisation of their models the scale of production has been increased and the average cost of production greatly reduced. Standardisation is possible, however, only if buyers are prepared to accept some restriction of their choice. Consumers may be willing to accept a degree of standardisation in the case of motor cars (the different styles of the various manufacturers giving sufficient variety), but it is doubtful whether they would accept greater standardisation in textiles—especially of the material for women's clothes. Indeed, standardisation of pattern and quality might be fatal to the export trade in woollens and worsteds, where variety and high quality have been their main attraction. This fact, therefore, offsets the disadvantage of smallness of size of the average firm in the woollen industry. Standardisation of the product may cheapen production, but it is liable to check progress, on account of the expense of altering the plant for a new design of the product. For example, it has become an extremely expensive business to alter the styling of the mass-produced motor car of today.

(iii) *Increasing cost and complexity of organisation*. Even if there is a sufficiently wide market to make-large scale production practicable, there are other things that check the growth of the firm. First among these is the increasing cost and complexity of organisation as it expands. Imperial Chemical Industries, Ltd., for example, have found it necessary to have fourteen operational divisions, each with a divisional chairman and Board of Directors, and seven functional departments (covering such things as research, personnel, development), each presided over by a director with a seat on the main Board, to co-ordinate and control policy in regard to these matters throughout the firm.[1] When the railways were nationalised the old area divisions were largely retained, and a co-ordinating body had to be created to link them together. Another problem that the very large firm has to face is to find someone with the ability to manage it. It is said that the supply of competent managers is limited, and perhaps the difficulty of securing capable and efficient managers is the chief brake on the expansion of firms. In this connection it is of interest to note that ICI dispensed with the post of managing director because the duties of this office had become too onerous, and replaced him by a number of executive directors, in charge of the operational divisions of the firm.

(iv) *Increasing costs and falling price*. It has been seen that after a certain point substitution between factors of production is possible. How much of each of the factors will be employed depends on how much has to be paid for them. If a particular producer wishes to increase his scale of production he will have to engage more factors. It will be seen later that an increased demand for a factor tends to raise its price. Assuming that when the producer makes his decision to expand production all factors are fully employed, he will be able to increase his supply of them only by drawing some away from other employments, and to do this he will have to offer them higher payments. Consequently, his costs of production will begin to increase. At the same time, unless there is a change in demand, a larger output can be sold only by lowering the price. Under perfect competition each firm produces only a small proportion of total output, and so an increase in the output of one firm will not substantially affect either total supply or price. In actual conditions of imperfect competition, however, this is not so. Suppose, however, that total cost to the producer (including his own reward and "normal profit") is £500 per week for an output of

---

[1] See *Large-Scale Organisation*, edited by G. E. Milward, pp. 144 et seq.

100 units of a commodity, and assuming these are sold for £600 (that is, at £6 each), then the profit will be £100 per week. If by increasing his output to 150 units of the commodity per week his costs increase to £650, but since to sell the greater output he has to reduce his price to £5.40, his total receipts will be £810, thus giving him a profit of £160, that is, £60 more than at the lower output. Obviously in this case there were economies of large-scale production. If, however, beyond an output of 150 per week costs begin to rise more steeply and total receipts increase less than proportionately owing to the falling price of the commodity, a time will arrive when to increase output by one unit more will raise total costs as much as total receipts. Clearly, it will not pay an entrepreneur to expand production beyond this point. In this case an output of 175 units per week might represent the most profitable output of the firm, and so further expansion would not take place.

(*v*) *Increased risk.* As the scale of production increases, so do the risks of production. The greater the output, the greater, therefore, will be the loss from an error of judgment. Unwillingness to bear greater risks may be another limitation on the growth of firms.

7. Disadvantages of large-scale production

The large firm suffers from the following drawbacks:

(*i*) *Bureaucratic control.* The larger the firm, the more bureaucratic its organisation tends to be. In order to ensure the carrying out of the policy that the management has decided upon, rules and regulations are necessary and must be strictly adhered to. The large firm is more impersonal than the small, and contact between management and staff is therefore less easy.

(*ii*) *Sluggish response to changes.* However important the decision a sole proprietor has to take, he alone is responsible for making it. If he is a man who rapidly makes up his mind he can decide at once and quickly put his ideas into effect, for he is under no obligation to consult anyone else. In this case changes in policy or organisation can be introduced without delay. In a large firm, however, only decisions on minor matters can be left to subordinates, and important questions have to be referred to superiors. For example, the manager will have to convince his board of the soundness of a change of policy before he is allowed to carry it out.

(*iii*) *Loss of the motive of self-interest.* It is claimed on behalf of the sole proprietor that his own interests and those of the firm are one, with the result that there is less waste and greater efficiency. Nevertheless, the interests of most managers of large firms are bound up with those of the firms that employ them. Even if they are not shareholders, their own remuneration is probably closely linked with the success of the business, and should a manager fail to make progress, his tenure of office will probably be cut short. However, even if due allowance is made for this, the man who runs his own business is often spurred on by a pride of achievement that is unlikely to influence the salaried manager to quite the same extent.

8. The survival of the small firm

The growth in size of the firm has not prevented the survival of the small firm, in spite of the fact that, though there are some disadvantages of large size, these are more than counterbalanced by the advantages of large-scale production. The size of the business unit tends to be small if the work involves the provision of direct services, such as those of the doctor, the dentist, the solicitor, the accountant, or where the work can be done only by craftsmen, as in bespoke tailoring, or where a personal service is provided, such as that of the domestic plumber or electrician.

Many small retailers have managed to survive—though their number continues to fall—in spite of the competition of supermarkets, multiple shops, co-operative societies and department stores, mainly because they have been able to give personal attention to the particular requirements of their own groups of customers who have shown themselves willing to pay a little more for this service.

It has been pointed out that large-scale production is possible only when there is a wide market for the commodity. The small firm, too, comes into its own when variety of product is preferred to standardisation. Obviously in those cases where there is only a limited demand for a commodity, small firms can produce enough to satisfy it. It may be, too, that in some forms of production costs quickly begin to rise as production expands, and so the most economical unit is the small firm—that is, the optimum size of the firm is small. Similarly, when the technical side of a large firm has grown beyond this optimum it may be more economical for it to put out some processes to small firms rather than undertake them itself.

IV. THE OPTIMUM FIRM

9. What is the optimum firm?

At a certain size the costs of production of a firm per unit of output will be at a minimum. At that size there will be no motive for further expansion, for at any other size, either larger or smaller, it would be less efficient. Such a firm is known as the optimum firm—that is, *the best or most efficient size of firm*.[1] Between one industry and another the optimum size will vary, for, as has already been seen, the small firm is most efficient for some purposes and the large one for others. It is fairly easy in theory to conceive of an optimum size of firm in any particular industry, though in practice it would be difficult—if not impossible—to decide in an actual case whether a firm had reached the optimum or not. It has been further suggested that there may be more than one optimum, a low and a high, expansion from the lower to the higher position being difficult because at any intermediate point between the two optima the firm would be less efficient.

For example, a survey of the Lancashire cotton industry carried out some years ago showed the firms engaged in cotton-spinning to be distributed according to size as follows:

Table XII

Cotton-spinning Firms

Number of spindles	Number of firms
Less than 20,000	23
20,000–40,000	38
40,000–80,000	78
80,000–200,000	110
200,000–1,000,000	26
Over 1,000,000	5

Of 280 firms, 188 (that is, 67 per cent) fell within the third and fourth groups. If it can be taken that most firms will be clustered round the optimum, then in cotton-spinning the optimum at that time might be taken to be the firm with between 80,000 and 200,000 spindles.

In cotton-weaving the position was as follows:

Table XIII

Cotton-weaving Firms

Number of looms	Number of firms
Less than 200	438
200–400	194
400–800	253
800–2,000	153
Over 2,000	25

[1] See E. A. G. Robinson : *The Structure of Competitive Industry*.

The distribution of firms in this section of the industry indicates the possibility of there being a minor optimum (the firm with under 200 looms) and a major optimum (the firm with between 400 and 800 looms). A comparison of the two lists seems to show that the optimum in the spinning section of the industry was larger than the optimum in the weaving section.

Again, the optimum in any industry may itself vary from one period to another. Under perfect competition there would probably be a tendency for all firms to expand towards the optimum. The optimum, too, may change as a result of changing conditions and the development of new techniques. Changes in the relative prices and efficiency of factors will affect the optimum proportion in which factors are combined. For example, a rise in the price of labour may reduce the amount of labour in the optimum proportion. In a society where economic progress is rapid these changes will be constantly taking place, with the result that, though firms are always tending towards the optimum, they never reach it. The actual size, however, may be near to what was previously thought to be the optimum. The idea of the optimum firm is a useful concept; at any given moment there must be a certain size of firm at which production will be most efficient.

10. The reconciliation of differing optima

The chief difficulty confronting any firm striving to reach the optimum is the possibility that the main divisions of the firm may have different optima. For example, the optimum administrative division may not suit the optimum technical division, which may require an administrative department either greater or less than the optimum of the other department. In the heavy industries, where the most economical technical unit is very large, an administrative unit much greater than the optimum may be required. In firms where the technical unit is relatively small (for example, woollen weaving) the required administrative unit may be much smaller than the optimum. From the point of view of finance it has been seen that the large firm can borrow more cheaply than the small, and so the optimum firm from the standpoint of finance is large. The big firm, too, can obtain additional permanent capital more easily than the small firm. Similarly, there may again be a different optimum for the marketing side of the firm. Large-scale buying enables expert buyers to be employed and lower prices to be paid, and large-scale selling also yields economies, for example, in the employment of sales representatives. The producer is thus faced by the problem of reconciling these different optima.

If the technical unit is too great relative to the administration one way out of the difficulty in some cases might be to reduce the size of the technical unit, for example, by limiting production to fewer varieties of the commodity. Or, it may be possible to reduce the size of the technical side by putting out some processes to small firms, as occurs in the motor industry. Or again, it may be possible to split the technical unit into a number of productive departments, each with its own Board of Management. A central board would then be required to formulate general policy and to co-ordinate the activities of the departmental or divisional boards. Thus, although the nationalisation of British railways increased the complexity of management, this may have been counterbalanced by technical economies.

If the technical optimum is small and the administrative optimum is large reconciliation may be achieved by duplicating the technical unit. In a weaving-shed this would merely require the addition of more looms. If there is insufficient demand for the product to make this course feasible the firm might widen its range of products. However great may be the difficulty of achieving this objective, the entrepreneur has the incentive of lower costs to spur him on.

V. THE LAWS OF RETURNS

11. The problems of proportions

Reference has already been made to the Law of Diminishing Returns in connection with the factor of production, land. It was noticed that at one time it was thought that one of the special features of land was that production in which it played an important part was peculiarly subject to this law. The application of the law is no longer restricted to land since it applies in similar circumstances to all factors of production.

The Law of Diminishing Returns states that if the amount of one or more factors used in a particular form of production is fixed, and increasing amounts of other factors are combined with the fixed factor or factors, then both the average output in relation to the variable factor and successive additions to total output will eventually diminish. If this were not so there would be no limit to the yield from one small area of land.

Suppose first, for example, that land and capital are fixed in amount and that varying amounts of labour are used with them, then, as Table XIV shows, there may be increasing returns up to the employment of four men, but after that diminishing returns may set in.

It should be noted that the table shows the output and average product per man for eight different firms, working with a different combination of factors, and not for a single firm recruiting additional men at varying stages of production. The table shows that after a certain point the employment of more men reduces the average output per man, and so illustrates the Law of Diminishing Returns with reference to labour.

Table XIV

Diminishing Returns with Labour the only Variable Factor

Number of men	Fixed amount of land units	Fixed amount of capital units	Output units	Average physical product per man
1	2	8	10	10
2	2	8	30	15
3	2	8	60	20
4	2	8	100	25
5	2	8	120	24
6	2	8	132	22
7	2	8	140	20
8	2	8	146	18

The following production table shows how diminishing returns will eventually set in if the amounts of labour and land are fixed and capital is the variable factor.

Table XV

Diminishing Returns with Capital the only Variable Factor

Units of capital	Area of land fixed	Number of men fixed units	Output units	Average physical product per unit of capital
1	6	2	3	3
2	6	2	14	7
3	6	2	30	10
4	6	2	52	13
5	6	2	75	15
6	6	2	96	16
7	6	2	119	17
8	6	2	132	16.5
9	6	2	144	16
10	6	2	150	15

The table shows that in this case the Law of Diminishing Returns begins to operate when the amount of capital employed reaches seven units, after which the average output per unit of capital declines. Here, then, is an illustration of the Law of Diminishing Returns in relation to capital.

A third table could be constructed to show the operation of the law with land as the variable factor—a very unlikely occurrence. In these examples two factors have been taken as fixed and only one as variable. In actual conditions it is more likely that two of the factors would be variable and only one fixed.

If this law is stated as the Law of Eventually Diminishing Returns it becomes applicable to any kind of production. There may be increasing returns in the early stages as a result of increasing the amount of the variable factor, but sooner or later the Law of Diminishing Returns will begin to operate. In all cases, this law comes into play as a result of varying the proportion between the factors on account of the difficulty of increasing the factors in equal proportions. Indeed it has been suggested that a better name for it would be the *Law of Proportions*.

Within certain limits, the proportions between the factors can be varied. It has previously been noticed that, though a certain amount of each factor is required, choice can be exercised between employing more of one factor or more of another—for example, more capital and less labour, or more labour and less capital. In other words, it is often possible to substitute some of one factor for some of another. This is known as the *Principle of Substitution*. If, therefore, one factor is scarce it becomes possible to use more of the other factors. If one factor is fixed output can be increased only by using proportionately more of the other factors.

12. Returns to scale

If the factors land, labour and capital had to be combined in a fixed proportion in order to carry out any particular kind of production there would be no problem of proportions to be solved, though the scale of production would still have to be decided, for the factors can be combined in the same proportion to make firms of many different sizes, for example:

Table XVI
Change of Scale with Fixed Proportions

Firm	Area of land	Number of men	Units of capital
A	1	20	8
B	5	100	40
C	10	200	80

All three firms, A, B, C, have their factors combined in the same proportion, but B is larger than A, and C much larger than B. It may be that merely to expand the firm from size A to size B will yield increasing returns. If so, there would be said to be *increasing returns to scale*. Perhaps if the firm expands from size B to size C diminishing returns will set in. In some cases the expansion of a firm may be accompanied by constant returns.

It will be seen, therefore, that there are really *two* sets of laws relating to returns, one resulting from varying the proportions in which the factors are combined, and the other arising from increasing the scale of production.

It is not easy, however, to conceive of either increasing or diminishing returns being solely the result of an increase in the size of the firm. Indeed, some economists are inclined to doubt whether *pure* returns to scale are possible at all. A glance back at the economies of large-scale production listed above[1] will show that most of the advantages of large-scale production arise because it is not always necessary or even possible to increase all the factors of the firm proportionately as output expands. It might be of interest to pick out those economies which can be regarded as being "pure" returns to scale. In such cases increasing returns appear to be due to varying the proportions between the factors, though obviously this can be achieved only by increasing the size of the firm.

To produce a small output a small firm is required, and at this size it may not be possible to combine the factors in the best or optimum proportion. In actual conditions the *indivisibility* of some factors prevents the optimum proportion being achieved, for some factors are not divisible into small units. Capital, for example, often consists of large indivisible units such as blast-furnaces; and labour can be employed only in exact units, fractions not being possible. Thus over a wide range of output the same amount of one of the factors may have to be employed. At a small output, therefore, there will be excess capacity, the large, indivisible factor not being fully employed, but if output is increased there will be increasing returns until this factor is working at full capacity. Any further expansion of output will require the duplication of this large indivisible factor, and this may check further expansion.

[1] See pp. 110–13.

13. Application of Laws of Returns to agriculture and manufacture

Ricardo and his followers related the Law of Diminishing Returns solely to land, and it used to be said that this Law operated principally in agriculture, while the Law of Increasing Returns related more particularly to manufacturing industry. It is clear, however, that at different times and in different circumstances each law could apply either to agriculture or to manufacturing. In the early stages of the opening up of a new country the factors may be disproportionately combined—a large amount of land, but comparatively small quantities of labour and capital. The addition of more labour and capital will probably produce for a time a more than proportionate increase in output, so that increasing returns will occur. In most old countries, however, land is scarce relative to other factors, and so if it is desired to produce more food at home this can be accomplished only under conditions of diminishing returns. Any attempt to increase agricultural output in Great Britain today can be carried out only under such conditions, but though it may appear to be uneconomic to do so, it may be justified on other grounds, for example, because of an expanding world population or possibly for strategic reasons.

Similarly, either law can operate in manufacturing, though expansion in manufacturing is more likely to stop short of the point where diminishing returns set in. When factors are not combined in the optimum proportion on account of the indivisibility of large units of some factors, diminishing returns will occur, but expansion of production, resulting in the proportion in which the factors are combined being brought nearer to the optimum, will be accompanied by increasing returns. But eventually diminishing returns will set in both in manufacture and in agriculture, though expansion will generally proceed much farther in manufacture than in agriculture before this occurs. There may also be increasing returns resulting strictly from an increase in the scale of operations—that is, *pure* returns to scale—in either branch of production, mere size of itself producing greater efficiency. Similarly, expansion of both manufacture and agriculture may be accompanied by constant returns or by diminishing returns, in the latter case the unwieldy size of the firm resulting in a loss of efficiency.

14. The Laws of Returns and the optimum firm

By definition the optimum firm in any industry is the most efficient size of firm, that is, one where the average cost of production per unit of output is at the minimum. Upon what does this standard of efficiency depend? The concept of the optimum firm can be linked with the Laws of Returns, and it can therefore be considered from two angles. The optimum firm must first have its factors of production combined in the optimum proportion; secondly, it must have reached the size where it can enjoy to the full economies of scale. In other words, the firm must expand so long as it continues to work under conditions of increasing returns, whether these conditions arise from improved proportions or economies of scale; and expansion will cease at the point immediately before diminishing returns, from either cause, set in. The firm then will have reached the optimum for the industry at that particular time, for it must be remembered that what are the best proportions at one period may not necessarily be the best at another, since new conditions may arise, new methods of production may be developed, or the relative prices of factors of production may change.

The development of the optimum firm may take place in the following manner: assume that y represents the variable factor and x the combination of fixed factors; the first stage in the firms' growth is towards the optimum proportion of factors, increasing amounts of y being combined with fixed amounts of x:

Table XVII

Variation of Proportions

Factors		Total product	Average product per unit of y	
x	y			
5	1	10	10	Increasing returns to proportions
5	2	24	12	
5	3	39	13	
5	4	52	13	
5	5	63	12.6	Decreasing returns to proportions
5	6	74	12.3	
5	7	82	11.7	

Optimum proportion }→

With the combinations $5x+4y$ factors the average output per unit of y employed reaches a maximum. This is therefore the optimum proportion in which to combine the factors.

The second stage in the development of the firm is its growth of scale. In the following table the optimum combination of factors is maintained at different scales of production:

Table XVIII

Returns to Scale

	Factors		Total	Average production per unit of y	
	x	y			
	5	4	52	13	Constant returns to scale
	10	8	104	13	
	15	12	156	13	
Optimum scale } →	30	24	320	13.3	Increasing returns to scale
	60	48	600	12.5	Decreasing returns to scale

At first, doubling or trebling the amount of each factor employed results in a proportionate increase in output, and so there are constant returns to scale. If the scale of production is increased (the same proportions being maintained between the factors) until $30x+24y$ factors are employed there are increasing returns to scale, but the firm will not expand beyond this size, for after this point decreasing returns to scale set in. At this size the firm is at its optimum both as regards the proportion between its factors and also with regard to its scale of production.

Until the optimum is reached the firm will be working under conditions of increasing returns, and if it expands beyond the optimum there will be diminishing returns. Similarly, any reduction from the optimum will produce diminishing returns, just as any reduction from a point beyond the optimum will give increasing returns. Using the

Table XIX

The Optimum Firm and the Laws of Returns

Number of men (land and capital being fixed)	Output units	Average physical product per man	
1	10	10	Increasing Returns
2	30	15	
3	60	20	
4	100	25	→OPTIMUM
5	120	24	Diminishing Returns
6	132	22	
7	140	20	
8	146	18	

production table given above, it can be seen that expansion of output up to 100 units of the commodity is accompanied by increasing returns, as also is any reduction of output from any amount over 100 down to 100. On the other hand, there will be diminishing returns if output is reduced below 100 or increased beyond that amount.

This can be shown graphically:

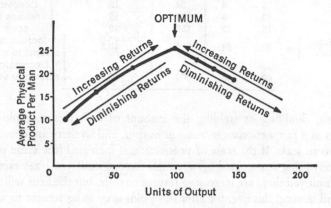

Fig. 5. The Optimum Firm and the Laws of Returns.

The optimum firm can thus be related to the Laws of Returns, with diminishing returns occurring when moving away from optimum, and increasing returns occurring as the optimum is approached. In actual conditions it may be impossible for a firm to reach optimum size, since it may be unable to employ the factors of production in the optimum proportion. This is most likely to occur where large indivisible units of capital are employed.

RECOMMENDATIONS FOR FURTHER READING

F. H. Knight: *Risk, Uncertainty and Profit*, Chapter 7.
E. A. G. Robinson: *The Structure of Competitive Industry*.

For the Laws of Returns:
G. J. Stigler: *The Theory of Price*, Chapter 8.

QUESTIONS

1. What are the advantages and disadvantages of large-scale production? (Bournemouth)

2. Distinguish between internal and external economies and indicate the main economies of large-scale production. (S E London)

3. Examine the economic principles that promote the growth in size of a business and discuss the problems that emanate from such growth. (RS A)

4. Discuss the economic factors which promote the growth in the size of some business undertakings, while others remain small. (RSA)

5. It was at one time thought that the small business would not be able to survive the competition of the large-scale enterprise, but this has proved to be incorrect. To what do you attribute the continuance of the small business and what do you consider to be the most favourable conditions? (LC Com.)

6. Discuss the economies of large-scale production. Explain why some small firms still exist. (IT)

7. Describe some of the economies which can be achieved through large-scale production. In view of these economies, how is it that, in the same industry, small firms can flourish side by side with big firms? (Exp.)

8. What do you understand by the term "optimum firm"? (IB)

9. In what sense is it true to say that the large firm has become the representative business unit in the advanced industrial countries? (CIS)

10. Is it true to say that agriculture is peculiarly subject to a law of diminishing returns? (CIS)

11. The way in which the factors of production may be substituted one for the other is an important element in deciding the economic policy of an employer. Explain why this is so. (IHA)

12. Outline precisely what is meant by the *economies of large-scale production* and show how these may lead to the growth of monopoly in an industry. (GCE)

13. What are *external* economies and diseconomies of scale? What would be the relevance of these to the location of a new factory in the London area? (GCE)

14. Discuss the factors affecting the size of firms and the degree of vertical integration in any *one* industry with which you are familiar. (GCE)

15. "Conditions of increasing returns can be regarded as exceptions to the operation of the law of diminishing returns." Discuss. (Degree)

16. On what factors does the size of an industry and the number of firms comprising it depend? (Degree)

CHAPTER 8

LOCATION OF INDUSTRY

I. INTRODUCTORY

1. Principles of location

Under competitive conditions a producer must select that location for his business where his costs of production will be at least as low as those of his competitors, as otherwise he will be unable to compete against them on equal terms. All the older influences, therefore, on location of industry ultimately depend on their effect on costs of production. Thus, the basic principle underlying location of industry is that the production of a commodity tends to be located where it can be carried on at lowest cost.

For a variety of reasons total costs of production may be lower in one place than another. The following are some of the main influences on location of industry:

(*i*) *Land*. In general the nearer that land is situated to the centres of large towns the more expensive it is likely to be either to buy or to rent, since in such places there are more uses competing for it.

(*ii*) *Power*. Depending on the form it takes, power, too, may be cheaper in one place than another. This was particularly the case when most of industry was dependent on coal for power, for coal becomes increasingly expensive the farther it has to be carried. However, coal has become less important as an influence on location of industry since the development of other forms of power such as gas, electricity and oil.

(*iii*) *Nearness to raw materials*. Especially in cases where they are heavy or bulky and therefore expensive to transport, nearness to raw materials can be a dominant influence on location of industry. Where more than one raw material is required, as in iron-smelting, the industry will be located near the source of the raw material that is wanted in the greatest quantity. Thus, for the iron-smelting methods employed in the nineteenth century three tons of coal were required to smelt one ton of iron ore, and so the industry came to be located on the coalfields, especially those nearest to where iron ore was to be found. When in the twentieth century new methods of production were developed requiring a much smaller amount of coal the iron ore began to be smelted in the East Midlands near to its sources of supply.

(*iv*) *Labour*. Every industry requires a supply of suitable labour to be available. The converse, however, is not true: an area of high unemployment does not necessarily of itself attract new industry, since there are other influences on costs. Another factor in the situation that has arisen in recent years has been the behaviour of labour. Not only may the labour in some areas be unsuited to some methods of production but it may also be more prone to absenteeism and inclined to cease work at the slightest provocation, such dislocations of production reducing output and increasing average costs. This has been the experience of the motor industry, especially in some of its newer centres of production.

(*v*) *Accessibility to markets*. Nearness to markets is particularly important in the case of consumers' goods intended mainly for home consumption, while for industries that export a large proportion of their output easy access to a port is equally important. The farther a producer is from the market for his goods the higher will be his costs of distribution. The more expensive it is to transport a commodity in relation to its price the nearer to the market must be its place of production. Relatively cheap commodities such as bricks are generally manufactured near to where they are to be used.

(*vi*) *External economies of scale*. Some industries in Great Britain became concentrated in particular areas. Clearly, the firms which successfully established themselves in such areas did so because they found costs of production lower there than elsewhere, the region obviously having particular advantages for the industry concerned. Concentration was further encouraged because localisation of itself brings with it other economies. As previously pointed out, economies resulting from greater division of labour consequent on the expansion of a single firm are termed internal economies of scale, while economies arising from regional division of labour made possible by localisation of industry are termed external economies of scale.

Consideration of the various principles of location clearly shows the outstanding part played by costs of transport—for power, for raw materials and for the finished product—in the location of industry.

Sometimes, however, it may appear at first sight that the location of an industry has taken place almost by chance. For example, both Henry Ford and William Morris began making motor cars in their home towns, Detroit and Oxford, without seriously considering the advantages of those place for the industry, but if at that time motor cars could have been made more cheaply elsewhere both men would either have had to move to areas of cheaper production or go out of business. In fact, under modern conditions both locations proved to have many of the advantages enumerated above. In its early years, when assembly was carried out by hand, the British motor industry was widely dispersed, but as the scale of production increased production eventually came to an end in the less advantageous areas.

2. A non-economic influence on location

All the influences on location of industry so far considered have been economic in character, that is, they have had a bearing on costs of production. To these influences on location, however, another in recent times has been added, namely, that of the Government. Since 1945 for social reasons the British Government has been interested in the location of industry. Excessive concentration of an industry in a particular area, even if it does reduce costs of production, has its disadvantages and leads to problems of overcrowding and traffic congestion. The Government too has been anxious to keep down the level of unemployment in regions with unemployment above the national average, and these have generally been areas with highly localised industries. For these reasons the Government has considered it desirable to channel new industry into areas other than those that firms would have selected for themselves. This means that firms have been required to set up in regions where their costs would be higher than elsewhere. To encourage them to do so the Government has had to offer them financial incentives. In the case of some of the lighter industries making consumers' goods, however, costs of production vary less between one region and another.

Since there are many different costs to cover it is extremely unlikely that one area will have advantages over others in all respects. For example, the higher cost of raw materials may be offset by cheaper access to markets, and so for some commodities the advantages of one district over another may be only marginal. In such cases there would be no special hardship to the firm in the Government's selecting its location.

Just as the different influences on location vary in their importance for different industries, so too the relative importance of these influences can change over a period of time. New forms of power may be developed, new methods of production may be discovered, new means of transport invented, or demand may change. This may result in the decline of industries in some localities, though sometimes industries remain in particular areas even though the original advantages that determined their location have been lost, so providing an example of industrial inertia. It is because over the years the influences on location of industry change that it is necessary to consider this problem in the light of experience during three separate historical periods: (*i*) during the nineteenth century—the age of localisation; (*ii*) between the two World Wars (1919–39) when new influences on location of industry arose; and (*iii*) the period of planned location of industry since 1945.

II. THE AGE OF LOCALISATION

3. Localising influences

The basic heavy industries that developed and expanded in Great Britain during the nineteenth century were highly localised. Before that time most manufacturing industries had been widely dispersed, the woollen industry, for example, being carried on wherever sheep could be reared. Even so some centres, such as West Yorkshire, East Anglia and the Cotswolds, because of some local advantages, were more important than others. The application of steam power to manufacturing, however, concentrated industry on the coalfields, but this would not have been possible had there not been at the same time a revolutionary improvement in means of transport. Particular industries became localised on particular coalfields—cotton in South Lancashire, wool textiles in West Yorkshire, pottery in North Staffordshire, and the iron and steel industry in various places where iron ore was found near coal.

The principal factors tending to bring about localisation of industry were as follows:

(*i*) *Nearness to coal.* In the early days of the Industrial Revolution water-power was employed for a time, and the first factories were built near fast-flowing streams. When steam power was introduced nearness to coal became the chief localising influence, for the price of coal increased steeply the farther it had to be carried from the mines. As a result, costs of production were lowest on or near the coalfields. Coal also replaced charcoal in the smelting of iron ore. The result was that all the basic industries—cotton, wool, iron and steel—were established on or near coalfields.

(*ii*) *Nearness to raw materials.* This was particularly important where the cost of the raw materials formed a large proportion of the total costs of production. Nearness to supplies of iron ore, limestone and (for Sheffield) millstone grit influenced the location of iron-smelting. Middlesbrough owed its growth to its nearness both to the coal and to the Cleveland iron-mines, just as in more recent times Scunthorpe and Corby grew rapidly because of their nearness to supplies of iron ore, which became more important since less coal than formerly is now being used in iron-smelting. Boots and shoes came to be manufactured in Northampton and neighbouring towns because of nearness to supplies of leather.

(*iii*) *Nearness to components*. In the case of an industry such as the motor industry where the principal stage of production takes the form of assembling a large number of parts it is very important, if costs are to be kept to a minimum, that the industry be located near to where these components are manufactured.

(*iv*) *Minor influences*. The presence in the Pennines of ample supplies of soft water for cleaning the fibres was an important influence on the location of the Yorkshire and Lancashire textile industries. The use of soft water reduced the cost of this process. Another minor influence on the location of the cotton industry was the humid atmosphere of Lancashire.

A feature, therefore of the late eighteenth and early nineteenth centuries was the drift of population to the coalfields of the North and Midlands.

4. Advantages of localisation of industry

A number of advantages accrue to an industry when it is concentrated in one area:

(*i*) *Regional division of labour*. We have already seen that division of labour within the firm increases output and cheapens production. When an industry is highly concentrated in an area this principle can be extended to a whole industry. When firms are close together it becomes possible for individual firms to specialise in single processes or in particular varieties of a commodity. This has been called territorial division of labour. In the cotton industry and the worsted section of the woollen industry, for example, some firms are engaged solely in spinning, weaving, dyeing or some other process. In the wool textile industry there is specialisation of product, fine worsteds being made in Huddersfield, heavy woollens in Dewsbury and carpets in Halifax.

(*ii*) *A supply of skilled labour*. Localisation of industry brought into being a reservoir of skilled labour for the local industry. A new firm might establish itself in a particular area because a supply of suitable skilled labour was available there.

(*iii*) *Development of subsidiary industries.* When an industry is highly localised subsidiary industries grow up to cater for the needs of the major industry, and so textile machinery for the cotton industry is made in Lancashire, and for the woollen industry in West Yorkshire. The financing of industry, too, can be more easily undertaken where bank managers have specialised knowledge of the local industry. Though small local banks have disappeared, the larger institutions generally appoint as branch managers men with experience of the economic problems of the area.

(*iv*) *Organised markets.* Finally, localisation of industry often leads to the establishment in the area of highly organised markets, such as the Liverpool Cotton Exchange.

The existence of these facilities acts as a magnet to new firms entering the industry.

Where localisation does not occur. (*i*) In some cases heavy costs of transport may outweigh the advantages of localisation, as for example, with building materials. In districts where there are local supplies of stone most buildings will be constructed of stone; in other districts only public buildings and very large houses will be of this material. It has already been pointed out that bricks are usually made near to where they are to be used.

(*ii*) Personal services clearly have to be supplied wherever they are required. Retail services cannot very easily be concentrated as most consumers prefer shops near their homes, though improved transport services compelled many village shops to close, and the development of mail-order business has widened the market for the large city stores. In the case of direct services of a personal kind, concentration is not possible, and doctors, dentists, teachers, etc., are distributed over the country generally according to the density of population.

5. Disadvantages of localisation of industry

There is, however, a serious drawback to a district being dependent on a single basic industry. Even if full employment is successfully maintained, there will still be the risk of structural unemployment resulting from a change in demand. At any given time there are always some industries that are expanding because of an increasing demand for their products, and other industries that are declining owing to decreasing demand. Such changes are a feature of a progressive economy. If the declining industry is highly localised mass unemployment in that area may result, even though the rest of the country is enjoying full employment. This was the experience of Belfast, parts of Scotland, South Wales and North-east England during the 1960s.

Similarly, during a depression some industries will be found to be expanding; even during the Great Depression (1929–35) the motor-car industry, the manufacture of electrical apparatus and of artificial silk were all expanding industries. On the other hand, the cotton industry became a declining industry after 1929, largely due to the contraction of the export trade—the result of increased foreign competition—and even if there had not been a general trade slump at that time, it is possible that there would have been high unemployment in Lancashire. The coincidence of cyclical and structural unemployment during the Great Depression produced the so-called "distressed areas"—those parts of the country where the level of unemployment was well above the national average. Another disadvantage of extreme localisation is the growth of great conurbations, where one town merges into another, with consequent overcrowding, lack of open spaces and traffic congestion.

III. NEW INFLUENCES ON LOCATION OF INDUSTRY

6. The new industries

Between the two World Wars the coalfields ceased to attract new industries. Nearness to coal, however, still remained the principal influence on the location of heavy industries, where the cost of power forms a high proportion of the total cost of the product. Even where the orginal advantages of their situation had passed away, it was difficult for such industries to move because of the large amount of fixed capital involved. It was the new industries which tended to be established away from the coalfields, mainly because they were light in character, that is, the cost of power was not their principal cost. The new industries of this period included the manufacture of electrical equipment and accessories, because of the expanding use of electricity, radio sets and components. There was, too, a great increase in the number and variety of packaged branded goods and patented foodstuffs. In spite of heavy unemployment, the general standard of living was rising, with a consequent expansion of the production of consumers' goods. Heavy industry is primarily occupied with the production of capital goods; light industry is mainly concerned with consumers' goods. Capital goods generally do not require to be as widely distributed as consumers' goods. The products of the light industries, too, were mainly intended for the home market. Thus the new industries were different in character from the older industries, and this had great influence on their location. During this period the main influences on industrial location were:

(*i*) *New means of transport*. The development of railways encouraged localisation of industry and regional specialisation; the development of road transport during the 1920s tended to promote a wider dispersal of both population and industry.

(*ii*) *New forms of power*. During the twentieth century coal ceased to be the sole source of power, alternative forms of power—gas, electricity and oil—having been developed. These were capable of being transmitted to all parts of the country more cheaply than coal, so that industry became no longer restricted to the coalfields.

(*iii*) *Nearness to large centres of population*. Large conurbations came into existence during the nineteenth century as a result of people being attracted to the new industries then developing on the coalfields. During the 1920s and 1930s a large centre of population became of itself an attraction to the new consumer-goods industries, as a market for their products. Where production was undertaken mainly for the home market a firm setting up near London for example, could have a fifth of its potential customers almost on its doorstep. London could also deal with exports. Few new industries were established on the coalfields, where unemployment was heaviest, because of other disadvantages, such as the unsuitability of much of the labour and the high local rates levied in most of these areas. As a result, labour tended to go to the new industries instead of the new industries moving to where there were supplies of unemployed labour.

The drift to the South. The inter-war period, then, showed a reversal of the nineteenth-century tendency of population to increase more rapidly in the North. During this period London, South-East England and, to a lesser extent, the Midlands, attracted the newer industries. Since, too, the heavy industries of the older manufacturing areas felt the impact of the Great Depression more severely than the rest of the country, there was to some extent a drift of population from Northern England and South Wales to the expanding industrial areas of the Midlands and the South-East. The extent of this change in the distribution of population is shown by the fact that there was an increase in the number of insured workers in the London area of over half a million, while considerable losses were experienced by Durham, South Lancashire and South Wales. As a result London began to eat up the countryside on its outer fringes, the further growth of a population already vast accentuating the problem associated with its being a large conurbation. In the West Midlands the effects of the Great Depression on the older industries was counterbalanced by the extraordinary growth of the motor industry during this period, and there was also some drift of population into this region.

7. Government intervention

Areas of localised industries are clearly then more liable to severe unemployment than areas with greater variety of industry. This was apparent in the Great Depression, when 35 per cent of insured workers in the "Distressed Areas" were out of work (in the cases of Jarrow and Merthyr the percentage was 75), while unemployment in Bedford-shire, Hertfordshire and Middlesex never rose above 6 per cent.

Special Areas. There had been an attempt in the 1930s to encourage new industries to be set up in places where there was heavy unemploy-ment, the Acts of 1934 and 1937 giving the Government powers to assist those areas, which had been designated Special Areas. Trading estates were established in Durham, West Cumberland, South Wales and Central Scotland, factories at low rentals being made available to firms willing to go there, the Government itself undertaking to train workers for new occupations. Although some measure of success was achieved, it was difficult at that time to persuade firms to establish themselves in places to which they did not wish to go, and with heavy unemployment in the country it was not possible to refuse to allow firms to set up elsewhere. After the outbreak of war in 1939 the Government itself established over a hundred new factories in the Special Areas.

IV. PLANNED LOCATION OF INDUSTRY

8. The purpose of planned location of industry

As already indicated the Government had made tentative efforts in the mid-1930s to encourage new firms to set up in areas of severe un-employment. In 1937 a Royal Commission had been appointed to inquire into the distribution of industry and population in Great Britain, the *Barlow Report* (1940) being the outcome. The report stressed the social, economic and other drawbacks of highly localised industries with large masses of people living in great conurbations, and recommended (*i*) that the Government should take over responsibility for the location of industry, and (*ii*) that the further expansion of London should be checked by the building of a number of new towns. Controlled location of industry was advocated too by Lord Beveridge as an essential condition for the maintenance of full employment. In 1945 the British Government, therefore, accepted responsibility both for the maintenance of full employment and for planned location of industry.

However, even if demand is successfully maintained at a high enough level to ensure full employment the problem of structural unemployment still has to be faced. Owing to changes in demand there will always be some industries in a progressive economy that are declining while others are expanding. In the case of highly localised industries the problem is more serious. Dispersal of existing heavy industries would be too costly, and so the only way to alleviate the situation was to give greater diversification of industry to such areas so that, if it occurred, structural unemployment would be more widely distributed and those made redundant more easily absorbed into other industries. In general, therefore, the policy adopted has been one of "taking work to the workers" rather than moving workers to where there was work, though this has had to be the policy when uneconomic coal-mines have had to be closed.

9. The Development Areas

In 1945, therefore, Parliament passed the *Distribution of Industries Act*, which made the Board of Trade responsible for the location of industry. This Act designated certain parts of the country as Development Areas, the first four districts to be selected being the pre-1939 Special Areas, generally with enlarged boundaries:

(*i*) the North-East;
(*ii*) West Cumberland;
(*iii*) South Wales and Monmouthshire;
(*iv*) Clydeside and the Lanarkshire coalfield together with the Dundee district.

In 1946 two more Development Areas were designated:
(*v*) South-east Lancashire;
(*vi*) the Wrexham coalfield.

Two years later there were two further additions to the list:
(*vii*) Merseyside;
(*viii*) Inverness and district.

The aim in northern Scotland was to check the drift of population to the South by the development of a new industrial area dependent on hydro-electric power. In 1953 yet another Development Area was created:

(ix) North-east Lancashire.

Development Districts. Although during the years 1950–60 full employment in the country at large was generally maintained, pockets of unemployment arose in certain districts outside the Development Areas. To meet this situation the *Local Employment Act* (1959) was passed. The Act abolished the Development Areas (although this proved to be only a temporary change), replacing them with Development Districts. With the exception of South Lancashire most of the former Development Areas became Development Districts, and to these were added parts of Cornwall, North Wales, the Furness District of Lancashire, West Cumberland, the greater part of Central Northern Scotland and the whole of Northern Ireland. Many of the Development Districts were smaller than the former Development Areas. The Act of 1959 empowered the Government to assist any part of the country where unemployment had been 4 per cent or more for over a year. The Board of Trade was given power to erect factories in any of the Development Districts and to recommend to the Treasury firms to be helped by grants or loans. No firm above a certain size was to be allowed to set up anywhere in the country without first obtaining an Industrial Development Certificate, and these certificates were easier to obtain in the Development Districts than elsewhere. This was a period when the motor industry was desirous of expanding and most of the motor-car manufacturers would have preferred to expand on their existing sites. In fact they were given Industrial Development Certificates only on condition that they opened their new factories in Development Districts on Merseyside and in Scotland, where of course they would be eligible for Government assistance. The Government also assisted the contraction of the cotton industry in 1958–59.

The new Development Areas. In 1966 the boundaries of the areas eligible for Government assistance were again modified by the *Industrial Development Act*, and renamed *Development Areas*. The new areas were fewer in number and wider in extent than previously and included the whole of Scotland, the whole of Northern England north of a line from Morecambe Bay to Flamborough Head, the whole of Wales and Northern Ireland, together with Cornwall and North Devon. Later they were expanded to include the whole of Lancashire and Yorkshire. (*See* the map, Fig. 6, page 141.) It has been emphasised throughout this chapter that, before the days of planned location of industry, firms tended to seek those locations where their costs of production would be at a minimum. If they had been free to please themselves, therefore, few firms would have gone to the Development Areas. For twenty years assistance mainly took the form of providing cheap premises, but this inducement was not sufficient if a firm's costs remained higher than elsewhere. In 1967, therefore, the Government introduced the Regional Employment Premium. Firms in the Development Areas were to receive for at least seven years £1.50 for every man they employed, with smaller premiums payable in the case of women, boys and girls. In addition, firms in these areas received preferential treatment in connection with Selective Employment Tax during the period that this tax was in force. The policy of "taking work to the workers" was continued, but in some cases people were helped by the payment of removal expenses if they could obtain work only in another district. To encourage occupational mobility of labour redundancy payments were made available to those made redundant by economic progress. By these means it was hoped to reduce the imbalance in unemployment rates in different parts of the country.

10. For and against planned location of industry

For a number of reasons a greater measure of success attended Government efforts to influence location of industry after 1945 than during the 1930s. For one thing Government intervention has been on a much more massive scale in recent years. Then, the economic conditions of the two periods were quite different, the earlier one being a time of widespread unemployment, while the later one, at least until 1969, was generally one of full employment. In the earlier period, therefore, new firms were to be welcomed anywhere; in the later period firms were prepared to go to wherever labour was available.

It might be asked whether planned location of industry is sound on economic grounds? Most firms that have been encouraged to set up in the Development Areas, if they had been left to decide for themselves, would probably have gone elsewhere, and in the case of highly localised industries, to the region where their particular industry was concentrated. It must be remembered that when industries became localised it was because production could be carried on more efficiently in those areas, and external economies associated with localisation could be enjoyed. Any scheme of dispersal will rob the firms settling in other areas of these external economies, and in a recession these firms may be the first to be affected, especially since more than half the new firms are only branches of firms with headquarters elsewhere. For example, the new branches of firms in the motor industry opened on Merseyside and in Scotland find themselves at a greater distance than they would wish from the places from which they obtain their components. Most of the newer industries in the Development Areas, however, are of the light type engaged in the production of consumers' goods, and these have less to gain from localisation.

If the scheme for greater local diversification of industry is based on the assumption that full employment will be permanently maintained the effect should be to spread structural unemployment over a wider area and so prevent serious pockets of mass unemployment arising. There is no doubt, for example, that the decline of the cotton industry had less effect on the level of employment in South Lancashire on account of the Government's policy in encouraging new industries to establish themselves in that area. The great variety of industry has made it easier for many workers previously employed in the cotton industry to obtain alternative employment. With the development of road transport and the newer forms of power, the advantages of localisation are perhaps less strong today than they were in the nineteenth century.

11. Regional economic planning

In 1965 the short-lived Department of Economic Affairs published a national plan outlining proposed industrial and economic development over the next five years. As part of the plan Great Britain was divided into ten economic planning regions, and though the national plan had to be abandoned, these regions have been retained as a means of tackling the economic problems peculiar to these particular areas. They comprise: (*i*) Scotland, with Edinburgh as the regional capital; (*ii*) Northern England (capital, Newcastle upon Tyne); (*iii*) Yorkshire and Humberside (capital, Leeds); (*iv*) the North-West (capital, Manchester); (*v*) East Midlands (capital, Nottingham); (*vi*) West Midlands (capital, Birmingham); (*vii*) Wales (capital, Cardiff); (*viii*) South-West (capital, Bristol); (*ix*) East Anglia (capital, Norwich); and (*x*) South-East (capital, London). In effect Northern Ireland forms an eleventh region for economic planning. In each region two bodies were set up—a Regional Economic Council to formulate regional plans, and a Regional Economic Planning Board to co-ordinate the regional work of the various Government Departments concerned. The aim of regional planning is

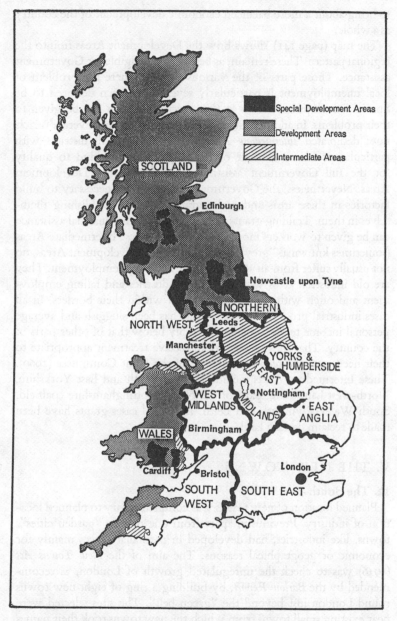

Fig. 6. Economic Planning Regions.
Reproduced by permission of the Controller of H.M. Stationery Office.

to bring about a more balanced economic development of the country as a whole.

The map (page 141) shows how the Development Areas fit into the regional pattern. These remain, as before, areas eligible for Government assistance. Those parts of the various regions where the problem of local unemployment is particularly severe have been declared to be Special Development Areas so that special attention can be given to their problems. In addition, it will be noticed, there are several districts now designated *Intermediate Areas*, these being small districts with particular problems of their own though not of a kind to qualify for the full Government assistance available to the Development Areas. Nevertheless, the Government is prepared if necessary to build factories in these areas and make grants to firms establishing themselves in them. Training grants are also available and financial assistance can be given to workers moving into them.[1] These Intermediate Areas (sometimes known as "grey" areas), unlike the Development Areas, do not usually suffer from an above-average level of unemployment. They are old industrial areas with declining industries and falling employment and often with much derelict land within their borders. In all cases industrial progress in recent years has been sluggish and average personal income tends to be considerably below that of other parts of the country. That these areas should receive treatment appropriate to their needs was the recommendation of the Hunt Committee (1969). These Intermediate Areas include parts of South and East Yorkshire, North-west Lancashire, parts of the North Nottinghamshire coalfield, South Wales, Plymouth and Leith. In several cases grants have been made to reclaim derelict land.

V. THE NEW TOWNS

12. The South-East

Planned location of new towns was complementary to planned location of industry. Previously, apart from one or two "garden cities", towns, like industries, had developed in particular places mainly for economic or geographical reasons. The aim of the *New Towns Act* (1946) was to check the unregulated growth of London, as recommended by the *Barlow Report*, by building a ring of eight new towns round London just beyond the "green belt". The sites selected were near existing small towns from which the new towns took their names —Crawley in Sussex, Bracknell in Berkshire, Hemel Hempstead,

---

[1] These provisions, however, do not apply to Plymouth and Leith.

Welwyn Garden City, Stevenage and Hatfield in Hertfordshire, and Harlow and Basildon in Essex. The Act of 1946 set up a Development Corporation for each town, loans from the Treasury providing the initial finance for these undertakings. The new towns were not intended to serve merely as outer dormitory suburbs for overspill population from London—their distance from the metropolis, it was hoped, would preclude that—but rather as new industrial entities, towns in their own right, providing work for the people living in them. To ensure this development housing accommodation was guaranteed to all employees of firms moving into these places from London. Since mainly young people have been attracted to these towns, the average age of the inhabitants of the new towns tends to be low.

The plan for checking the further expansion of London aimed at eventually rehousing half a million people in the new towns nearest to the congested areas where they were previously living.

Because the amount of office employment in London is regarded as excessive the Greater London Area has been designated a region in which office development can be controlled. The Government itself took the lead by moving some departments to other regions—Glasgow, Newcastle upon Tyne, Cardiff and Newport. Only half the number of civil servants involved (31,000) were expected to move, the remainder being recruited locally. In 1963 a Location of Offices Bureau (LOB) was set up to provide information and advice on alternative locations for business offices for business firms. Quite a number of firms have moved from Central London, about half of them going to the outer suburbs of Greater London, and about half that number to places twenty to forty miles from Charing Cross. In 1976, however, the Greater London Council decided to discontinue its policy of encouraging industry to leave Central London.

The original aim was to build towns with populations of between 50,000 and 80,000 but in most cases the population target was later raised. Progress was slow at first but after the initial difficulties had been overcome their growth became more rapid. By 1973 Basildon had over 84,000 inhabitants, Harlow 81,000 and Crawley 70,000. An Act in 1959 set up a Commission of the New Towns to take over the liabilities of the individual Development Corporations when they reached an advanced stage of development. By 1973 Crawley, Hatfield, Hemel Hempstead and Welwyn Garden City had been dealt with in this way. The new towns have been remarkably successful in attracting industry.

13. Other new towns

New towns have also been planned for other parts of the country. In general the aim is similar to that for the new towns of the South-East, namely to check the further expansion of large conurbations and to build towns offering work to the people living in them. In a few cases the aim was primarily to provide better living conditions in urban surroundings. New towns of the self-sufficient type are being developed at Newton Aycliffe and Washington in County Durham, Corby in Northamptonshire (which was already expanding rapidly for economic reasons—its nearness to the newly developing iron and steel industry of the East Midlands), Skelmersdale in Lancashire and Runcorn in Cheshire, Telford in Shropshire, Redditch in Worcestershire, Cwmbran and Newtown in Wales and Monmouthshire, and at five places in Scotland—Glenrothes in Fifeshire, Cumbernauld in Dunbartonshire and Livingston in West Lothian, East Kilbride and Stonehouse in Lanarkshire and Irvine in Ayrshire. Telford is the only new town to be given a new name. Dawley was established to take overspill population and industry from Birmingham, but its development was slow and in 1968 it was combined with Wellington and Oakengates to form the new town of Telford. Of the other new towns Peterlee in County Durham was planned to provide community living for miners who previously lived in small scattered villages. Killingsworth, planned to take overspill population from Newcastle upon Tyne, is more of a residential outer suburb than a new town. Of the Scottish new towns East Kilbride has made most progress.

New developments. There has recently been a change of ideas as to what the size of the new towns should be. In the early days of new town planning the aim was to build relatively small towns, and this policy was pursued in the case of all the towns listed above. A number of much larger places have been planned, perhaps more appropriately termed "new cities". One of these is to be situated immediately to the south of the River Humber, a second is being developed round Milton Keynes (the home of the Open University) in Buckinghamshire, and a third to the south of Preston in Lancashire. Each of these is intended eventually to have a population of at least a quarter of a million people. An entirely new development is to expand a number of existing towns of moderate size into larger places—Peterborough (where considerable progress has been made), Northampton, Swindon, Aylesbury, Ashford (Kent), Thetford (Norfolk) and possibly Worcester.

For Northern Ireland a new city of 100,000 to 150,000 population has been planned, to be known as Craigavon, and two smaller new towns are to be built to take overspill from Belfast.

RECOMMENDATIONS FOR FURTHER READING

W. H. Beveridge: *Full Employment in a Free Society*, Part IV.
S. R. Dennison: *The Location of Industry*.

QUESTIONS

1. Account for the influence which the Government exercises on the location of industry in Great Britain. Consider its effectiveness in recent years. (Norwich)

2. Why are industries often able to remain and prosper in a certain locality long after all natural advantages that first induced them to settle there have ceased to exist? (Yorks)

3. An industry will tend to become localised in the place where it can be carried on most profitably. What are some of the main causes of localisation? (RSA)

4. What economic arguments would you advance to persuade entrepreneurs to site their new factories in development areas? (RSA)

5. What do you understand by the localisation of industry? What causes it and what economic and social results accrue as a result of it? (AIA)

6. What do you understand by localisation of industry? What problems may be caused by change in location? (Exp.)

7. Discuss the economic factors that are modifying the distribution of industry and population in your own country. (IT)

8. What are the forces that tend to bring particular industries to particular areas? (CIS)

9. What are the main factors determining the location of industry? In the light of your analysis consider the inter-war growth of the industrial population in London and the Home Counties. (IB)

10. Explain with examples why some industries are highly localised while others are carried on in small units scattered throughout the country. (GCE)

11. Explain how changes in the occupational distribution have affected the geographical distribution of population in the United Kingdom during the last fifty years. (GCE)

12. Argue the case for and against a policy of local diversification of industry in Great Britain. (Degree)

Part Four

THE TOOLS OF ECONOMIC ANALYSIS
(i) Supply and Demand

CHAPTER 9

MARKETS

Part Four of this book is devoted to a consideration of two important tools of economic analysis—namely, (i) the supply and demand technique, and (ii) the concept of the margin. By means of these tools many problems in applied economics can be investigated.

First, however, it is necessary to notice the environment in which the forces of supply and demand operate—the market.

I. PERFECT AND IMPERFECT MARKETS

1. What is a market?

It is the function of a market to enable exchange to take place, and in a monetary economy this means the business of buying and selling of goods or services of some kind. In ordinary speech the word *market* appears to have two meanings: it may denote a particular place, possibly a special building, where a market is held, such as Covent Garden Market in London; or it may indicate the extent of the sale for some commodity, as in the phrase: "There is a wide market for this or that commodity." There are many examples still to be found of markets in the narrower sense of the term. Most small country towns have market days, when stalls are erected in the market-place and business is transacted in the open air. In some of the larger towns there are permanent covered retail markets, and there are many wholesale markets of this type too. The right to hold markets was at first granted to lords of the manor, to monasteries or to municipal corporations by Royal Charter, but since 1858 a number of Acts of Parliament have been passed giving local authorities power to establish markets. However, an area, large or small, can be considered as a market if within it buyers and sellers are in easy contact with one another.

The development of communications—transport, postal, telephone, and telegraph services—banking and the grading of commodities have all helped to widen markets. Dealings in some commodities are now world-wide, and for these there may be said to be a world market. The essential feature of a market, however, whatever its extent, is that buyers should be able to deal with sellers, the market being the sum total of such dealings. "The market," says Wicksteed, "is the characteristic phenomenon of economic life," and "the constitution of markets and market prices is the central problem of Economics."[1] The economic importance of the market lies in the fact that it is the place where prices are determined.

2. Perfect markets

One of the most frequent assumptions made in economics is that of the perfect market. For a market to be perfect the following conditions would have to be fulfilled.

(*i*) *Homogeneous commodity*. In the first place, the commodity dealt in must be such that any one unit of it is exactly like any other—that is, that the commodity is homogeneous. This being so it is of no consequence then from which seller a buyer makes his purchase, for there will be nothing to distinguish the supply of one seller from that of another. If the commodity offered for sale is tea all the sellers will be simply selling tea, and not Brown's Tea, or Black's Tea or Green's Tea. Formerly a great many more commodities than at present would have very nearly fulfilled this condition, but the past few decades have seen a vast extension in the "branding" of all kinds of things—jam, tea, tinned goods, even fresh fruit. By dint of extensive advertising the producer tries to convince consumers that his brand is different (that is, better in some way) from those of other producers, and so the commodity ceases to be homogeneous. In fact, different brands are, strictly, different commodities, though clearly close substitutes for one another.

(*ii*) *A large number of buyers and sellers*. This is the second condition for a perfect market. If there are only a few suppliers it may be possible for one of them to increase his profits by curtailing his supply, and so keeping up the price. If, on the other hand, there is a large number of sellers no one of them will be able materially to influence total supply, and so each will try to put as big a supply as possible on the market. Similarly, if there are many buyers one of them can hope to reduce price by curtailing his purchases. Combinations of buyers are difficult to form, and even when they are formed easily tend to break up. For one thing, it is difficult to persuade a sufficient number of them to combine, and for another, there is no strong community of interest among buyers.

(*iii*) *Buyers and sellers must be in close touch with one another*. In early

[1] P. Wicksteed: *Common-sense of Political Economy*, Book I, Chapter VI.

days when communication was difficult the only way by which this condition could be fulfilled was for buyers and sellers to be present together in the same place. By telegraph and telephone buyers and sellers can now be brought into easy contact with one another, even though they may be thousands of miles apart. Thus, improved communications have widened the extent of markets. For a market to be perfect it is essential that all buyers and sellers should be immediately aware of what is happening in any part of the market. In this way an increased supply or a change in demand in one part of the market will affect price throughout the entire market.

(*iv*) *No preferential treatment*. In a perfect market there must be no preferential treatment of favoured customers, or discrimination against a group of either buyers or sellers. By imposing tariffs on foreign imports countries can break up the world market for a commodity into a number of smaller markets. What happens in one part of the world market will not then necessarily affect to the fullest extent all parts of that market. If a market is perfect, similar goods will command the same price in all parts of the market, for if one seller offered to sell at a price higher than the market price his sales would fall to zero for, the commodity being homogeneous, there would be no inducement to buyers to pay one seller a higher price than others were charging.

(*v*) *Portability or transferability of commodity*. Finally, it is necessary that the commodity dealt in on a perfect market should be capable of being easily transported from one part of the market to another.

3. Imperfect markets

It will be clear that the conditions required for a perfect market are of a kind to make the development of such markets under actual conditions very difficult, if not impossible, to achieve. Indeed, an absolutely perfect market exists only as a theoretical concept though some markets approach fairly near to perfection. Examples of these are the markets for foreign exchange (especially in the case of freely fluctuating or floating exchange rates), the securities markets (stock exchanges) and some of the highly organised wholesale produce markets, such as those for cotton, wool and wheat. In the real world markets are to a lesser or greater extent imperfect.

Some retail markets, especially those for low-priced goods, are notoriously imperfect, for many people will not spend time shopping around to find where prices are lowest. In the retail trade it is impossible for all buyers to be in close touch with the sellers. Generally, communication between retail buyers is poor, and many who would buy at the cheapest shops do not do so merely because they do not know where these particular shops are to be found. Then, many people continue to buy at certain shops, even though well aware that they charge higher prices than some others. This may be due simply to a dislike of changing their suppliers, or it may be that the dearer shop is more conveniently situated, or perhaps they find the shopkeeper always pleasant and cheerful or it may be too much trouble to look elsewhere, especially if the saving is likely to be small. The cheaper the article to be purchased the less is the consumer likely to worry about its price, and the more imperfect, therefore, will the market probably be. Preference for one shop rather than another may be due to a belief that the dearer shop sells a better quality of goods, so that the commodity is not, therefore, regarded as homogeneous.

Where there are only relatively few buyers and sellers, as in the market in antiques, the market tends to be imperfect, though in this case imperfection may be caused by buyers and sellers lacking knowledge of what is happening in other parts of the market. Also, where the commodity cannot be transported from one place to another the market is almost certain to be imperfect. Houses probably provide the best example of such a commodity. Houses of similar type may differ widely in price between one town and another, or even between different districts in the same town; but the commodity cannot be moved from the cheaper to the dearer part of the market. If there are great differences in the prices of similar houses in different towns this can have considerable influence on the mobility of labour. A government, too, by import duties, taxes or subsidies, can increase the imperfection of a market.

Only if a market is imperfect can similar commodities be sold at different prices after allowance has been made for costs of transport.

4. Types of market

It has so far been assumed that markets exist only for the buying and selling of commodities. This, however, depends on what we mean by a commodity. It is possible to speak of a labour market, in which case the "commodity" dealt in is labour, the "buyers" being the entrepreneurs, the "sellers" the workers, and the "price" being the wage or salary. Entrepreneurs require some of each of the factors of production —land, labour and capital—before they can undertake any form of production, and the services of each factor are purchased in a market. Such markets are known as factor markets.

It is important also to distinguish between different kinds of com-

modities, and to differentiate between the markets for consumer goods
—sometimes called markets for final products—and the markets for
producer goods or intermediate products. The market for consumer
goods can be further subdivided into wholesale and retail markets.
Then there are the various financial markets—the capital market (the
market for new securities), the stock exchange (mainly the market for
the transfer of existing securities), the money market (the market for
short-term loans), the discount market (the market for bills of exchange), and the foreign exchange market (the market for foreign
currencies). In all these markets the buyers and sellers of a commodity
or service are brought together.

The determination of price in the market becomes, therefore, one of
the most important problems of economics. In fact, it is so fundamental a part of the subject that one economist[1] has defined economics
as "a study in prices".

II. WHOLESALE MARKETING

5. Middlemen

Formerly the normal channel by which commodities passed from
the producer to the consumer was by way of wholesaler and retailer.
Nowadays there is great diversity in methods of distribution,[2] in some
cases the goods being handled by a single wholesaler, in other cases by
several middlemen and in others the goods passing direct from producer to retailer, or even to the consumer. The wholesaler is frequently described, almost as a term of reproach, as a middleman. He
is often looked upon almost as a parasite, his intervention in distribution only serving, it is thought, to make goods dearer to the consumer. The fact that costs of distribution are sometimes greater than
costs of manufacture encourages this view. If, however, the wholesaler
performed no useful function, would not all producers and retailers
by-pass him and divide his reward between them? The fact that this is
not generally done seems to indicate that the wholesaler is of use to producer and retailer. In fact, where the wholesaler is cut out it generally
merely means that someone else—producer or retailer—has to do his
work. Only if wholesalers receive excessive payment for their services,
or if it can be shown that goods are passing through too many hands, do
middlemen as such lay themselves open to criticism.

---

[1] H. J. Davenport: *Economics of Enterprise*, Chapter II.
[2] In this chapter the term *distribution* is used in its ordinary sense of commercial distribution and not in the economic sense used in Chapter 17.

The number of middlemen between producer and retailer varies from one trade to another, according to the particular needs of each trade. Sometimes the employment of a large number of middlemen is due to the existence of greater division of labour in the wholesaling function, especially where an intermediate process requires special knowledge or skill, or where distribution is complicated by irregularity of supply, or the existence of a large number of small producers, or the absence of any method of standardising the commodity. In such cases the intervention of a greater number of middlemen may result in fact in more efficient distribution, just as in industry greater division of labour achieves more efficient production. In foreign trade distribution is more complex, and so clearly more middlemen are required.

6. Functions of the wholesaler

What, then, are the services of the wholesaler to distribution? Some of his main functions may be briefly mentioned:

(i) *The "breaking of bulk"*. The manufacturer generally does not wish to have to undertake the distribution of his product, preferring to dispose of it in large quantities as it is produced. In order to provide themselves with variety of stock, most retailers, on the other hand, buy in small quantities. The wholesaler forms a link between them, and attempts to satisfy the needs of both. It is possible, too, that if the wholesaler were omitted, transport costs would be even higher, for the manufacturer would have to send a larger number of parcels, each a long distance if he supplied retailers direct. Wholesalers are more conveniently situated for particular districts. Each receives a large parcel from the manufacturer, and then splits it up into smaller parcels which then have only short distances to travel. The following diagram will make this clear:

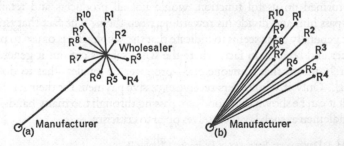

Fig. 7. The Breaking of Bulk. (*a*) Distribution through Wholesaler
(*b*) Omission of Wholesaler. R^1 to R^{10} = Retailers

The wholesaler's more convenient situation also enables the retailer to obtain additional supplies more readily than he could from the manufacturer.

(*ii*) *Warehousing.* Manufacturers produce in large quantities, which they want to dispose of quickly in order to keep their factory space clear for further production. The wholesaler can relieve the manufacturer of the trouble and expense of holding large stocks. By allowing a regular supply to enter the market, especially where production is irregular, the wholesaler helps to prevent wide fluctuations of prices. The holding of stocks by the wholesaler is a valuable service, as it acts as a lubricant to the economic system, enabling distribution to work smoothly and preventing the development of "bottle-necks".

(*iii*) *Expert buying and selling.* Sometimes expert knowledge of the commodities bought and sold is required, and so the employment of specialists is essential, particularly where goods are bought and sold in those organised produce markets where it is necessary for the buyer to examine, test and assess the value of samples, as in the case of wool and tea.

(*iv*) *Marketing the product.* Manufacturers have to produce in anticipation of demand, but the wholesaler can often assist them by passing on to them information regarding consumers' demand which he has obtained from the retailers with whom he deals. This service is of great importance to manufacturers. Wholesalers, too, can assist manufacturers in developing the market for their products.

(*v*) *Financing production and distribution.* In addition to financing the holding of stocks, the wholesaler often helps to finance both the manufacturer and the retailer more directly. Manufacturers expect to be paid for their products as soon as possible, while many retailers have insufficient capital to carry large stocks of unsold goods. By prompt payment to the manufacturers and by allowing credit to the retailer the wholesaler helps to finance the activities of both.

(*vi*) *Preparing the product for sale.* The wholesaler often processes or prepares for sale the goods he receives from the manufacturer before passing them on to the retailer. This may take the form of packing, grading or branding. Sugar refining and the blending of tea are often carried out by the wholesalers of those commodities.

This brief survey of the functions of a wholesaler clearly shows the essential nature of his work. Indeed, all distributors are really engaged upon the final stage in the process of production. Division of labour requires specialisation of production in a limited number of places, but only a small percentage of the goods produced are required where they are made. Most of the goods, therefore, are of little economic value until they have been transferred to places where there is a demand for them. The greater the extent of specialisation, the greater will be the amount of distribution required, and therefore the greater is likely to be its cost. The increasing cost of distribution is thus the result of increasing specialisation and division of labour. Exchange is the logical corollary of specialisation, and similar commodities in different places are in the strict economic sense really different commodities. The middleman who assists distribution and exchange makes possible this greater volume of production. His work can therefore be considered to be productive.

7. Types of middlemen

Only those wholesalers who carry stocks have warehouses, such as dealers in manufactured goods and some dealers in foodstuffs and raw materials. In Canada and the United States wholesalers store wheat in elevators until it is required. In some trades this type of wholesaler is known as a factor, as for example in boots and shoes and tobacco. Some wholesalers, however, only organise the distribution of the commodity from the producer to the retailer, and so do not carry large stocks themselves, as for example, coal merchants and motor-car distributors, while others specialise in financing the holding of stocks.

The main functions of import and export merchants are indicated by their names. The importer may have an entire ships' cargo consigned to him, and he will be responsible for its warehousing after it has been disembarked, after which he will make arrangements for its sale, generally to regional wholesalers, on one of the produce exchanges. This work is carried out by another group of middlemen who are experts in their own particular trades. Unlike the middlemen previously mentioned, they rarely own the commodities in which they deal, but are merely agents who are employed by other wholesalers, usually being paid on a commission basis. These are the brokers and the del credere agents, the latter guaranteeing payment for the goods they sell, and so receiving a higher rate of commission.

A smaller-scale wholesaler is often to be found in provincial towns. Sometimes these people buy from large regional wholesalers, as in the grocery and provision trades, the large number of retailers making it impossible for the large wholesalers to deal directly with them all. The local wholesalers, being in closer contact with the retailers in their area, are able to grant credit with less risk. Small-town wholesalers are also found in the tobacco trade, in which the numbers of retailers is very large, though most of them have only a small turnover. Their needs can best be served by a wholesaler in the same town, for the large tobacco retailers usually buy direct from the manufacturers. Thus the number of middlemen engaged in the distribution of a product depends on the particular character of the trade concerned.

8. The omission of the wholesaler

There are some cases where the wholesaler has been cut out, goods being sent direct from manufacturer to retailer, or even direct from manufacturer to consumer. Since, as already shown, wholesaling is a vital link in distribution, the elimination of the wholesaler merely means that either the manufacturer or the retailer must take over his work. For a manufacturer this will involve the establishment of a warehouse, so that he can undertake the function of storing and the setting up of a selling department, and engaging a staff of sales representatives. Instead of dealing with comparatively few bulk orders to wholesalers, he will now have to deal with a huge number of small orders to suit the requirements of his retail customers, and this will necessitate his having to employ a large additional staff in his administrative, packing and forwarding departments. In other words, such a manufacturer will have to incur the expenses of the wholesaler, and in relation to the extra capital employed it is unlikely that his profit, as a percentage of his capital, will be any greater than it was when he confined himself to manufacturing. If he decides to sell direct to consumers he may have to open his own retail shops or set up a mail-order department, thereby incurring also the expenses of retailing.

Clearly, therefore, advertisements of sale direct from producer to consumer are often misleading and aim at influencing the ignorant and more gullible type of consumer. The manufacturer, however, may wish to ensure that his product is put on the market, and may think that a general wholesaler will not push its sale sufficiently. In such a case he may think the trouble and expense of doing his own wholesaling worth while, and either open his own retail shops, if his turnover justifies it, or appoint a limited number of retailers as his sole agents. Or, if he is a manufacturer of branded goods—that is, goods bearing registered trade names—he may prefer to advertise and market his product himself as far as the retailer.

The marketing of boots and shoes is done mainly through manufacturers' own shops, and consequently the number of wholesalers in this trade has declined. Even where there is insufficient demand for the product to make it economic for the manufacturer to open his own shops, he may prefer to appoint a limited number of agents for his goods in each town—a common practice with manufacturers of radio and television sets—and again act as his own wholesaler. The manufacturers of branded goods often prefer to deal direct with retailers, and this has brought about the disappearance of many small provincial wholesalers. The development of large-scale retail trade, through multiple-shop organisations and department stores, has led these businesses also to set up their own wholesaling departments.

III. HIGHLY ORGANISED MARKETS

9. The development of organised markets

The wholesaling of many commodities is carried on in highly organised markets, buyers and sellers meeting in a particular place in order to transact business. Such markets tend towards a high degree of "perfection", for, since buyers and sellers are in close touch, one price for the same commodity rules throughout the market. There is a tendency for an organised market to develop when the following conditions are fulfilled:

(*i*) The commodity should be fairly durable, in order that stocks can be held.

(*ii*) The annual production of the commodity must be sufficiently large to make it possible to deal in large consignments.

(*iii*) It is an advantage, too, if the commodity can be graded, but if not, its quality can be tested by means of samples.

(*iv*) If the price of the commodity is apt to fluctuate widely, owing to the difficulty in the short period of increasing or curtailing the supply, this will encourage the establishment of an organised market. It will also encourage the emergence of merchants specialising in bearing risk, with the development of some means of reducing risk of loss due to price fluctuations.

Commodities that fulfil these conditions are foodstuffs and raw materials, particularly those imported from abroad. Thus organised markets have been established for wheat, tea, coffee, sugar, cotton, wool, rubber, timber, lead, tin, copper, etc. The main markets for all these commodities are found in London, though there is a cotton exchange and a sugar exchange at Liverpool and a number of provincial corn exchanges.

10. Produce exchanges

Highly organised markets exist, then, for many commodities, buying and selling being concentrated in some specific place or building, Usually business is carried on according to a definite set of rules, though the actual method of conducting business on a produce exchange depends primarily on whether the commodity is capable of being graded. The main advantages to be derived from grading are:

(*i*) the commodity need not be actually on view in the market, and in fact business can be done by telephone;

(*ii*) it makes possible dealings in futures (*see* Para. 11).

Both cotton and wheat can be accurately graded, the grading of the former being carried out by the Liverpool Cotton Association (consisting of merchants, brokers and spinners), and that of the latter by the London and Liverpool Corn Trade Associations. Unfortunately the grades adopted for cotton in Liverpool and the United States are not identical, and this often causes delay on the arrival of the cotton at Liverpool, where the quality has to be decided. Where grading is possible, business is usually conducted by private treaty—that is, by individual bargaining between buyer and seller.

Where grading of the commodity is not possible, as in the case of wool and tea, it becomes necessary for prospective buyers to take samples of the lots to be offered for sale. These commodities are then sold by auction to the highest bidders. Selling brokers acting on behalf of overseas producers are responsible for the warehousing of the wool after its arrival in port until arrangements have been made for its sale at the London auctions, which for fine wool take place six times each year. Buying brokers, acting on behalf of wool merchants, top-makers, spinners and merchants engaged in the entrepôt trade, inspect the wool, take samples and make their estimate of the quality before attending the auction.

At the London Commercial Sales Rooms such commodities as tea, coffee, cocoa, sugar, etc., are sold by auction, dutiable commodities, such as tea being imported on consignment and stored in bonded warehouses until auctioned. As with wool, expert buying brokers are employed to sample the commodities before bidding at the tea auctions.

11. Forward marketing

It is because cotton can easily be graded that a market in "futures" developed. Ten distinct grades of cotton are recognised by the Liverpool Association, and thus it is possible to sell raw cotton before its arrival in Liverpool. The commodities dealt in on a futures market are futures, these originally being contracts to deliver goods at a future date at an agreed price. Dealings in futures take place in both wheat and cotton. Prices for immediate delivery are known as "spot" prices. If a merchant thinks the spot price of cotton is likely to rise in the next few months he will buy futures if they are quoted at a lower price than that which he expects to prevail in the future, as a hedge against a rise in the price of raw cotton. Speculators do not buy or sell the actual commodity, but instead buy or sell futures. The existence of such speculators makes it possible for those owning and holding the actual goods to protect themselves against price fluctuations by themselves buying or selling futures. If the holder of a commodity which cannot be marketed for (say) six months fears a fall in price he can sell futures now, and so assure himself of receiving the present price. In this way he insures himself against a fall in price. Obviously, the buyer of the futures is speculating against such a fall in price, for he hopes to be able to sell at a higher price six months later. The existence of a futures market is particularly advantageous in the case of commodities subject to wide fluctuations of price.

The difficulty of satisfactorily grading wool prevented for a long time the development of a market in futures for that commodity, although such markets were operated with some measure of success at both Antwerp and New York. The wide fluctuations in the price of wool during 1950-2 led to demands for the establishment of a futures market for wool in Great Britain, and in 1953 a wool futures market was opened in London. This now makes it possible for wool merchants also to insure against price fluctuations through the medium of futures. Futures markets have also been established for coffee and cocoa.

The activities of the speculators are often condemned. Speculators on commodity markets, however, must have expert knowledge of the markets in which they deal. Their activities tend to iron out price fluctuations, and so make markets more nearly perfect. If a commodity is in plentiful supply immediately after harvest its price then will be low; but as the supply shrinks the price would tend to rise until the next harvest. If, however, speculators enter such a market immediately after the harvest and buy while the price is low they will tend to force up the price at such times. Then, by holding stocks and releasing them later, they prevent the price from rising later as high as it otherwise would have done. Such speculation steadies prices. Speculation on the financial markets is considered in Chapter 25 below.[1]

[1] See pp. 462-3.

RECOMMENDATIONS FOR FURTHER READING

A. Marshall: *Principles of Economics*, Book V, Chapter 1.
J. G. Smith: *Organised Produce Markets*.

QUESTIONS

1. What are the essential features of centralised and organised commodity markets? (Bournemouth)

2. Describe the stages involved in marketing a product. Illustrate your discussion with examples of the marketing of actual products. (City)

3. Why does the wholesaler play a very important part in the distribution of certain classes of goods, while in other classes he plays a small part or is entirely absent? (RSA)

4. What is meant by "hedging"? How far is hedging possible in the absence of organised markets? (RSA)

5. Discuss the functions of the middleman with particular reference to recent criticisms that he is unnecessary and receives too high a remuneration for his services. (LC Com.)

6. Write a note on economic markets. (CIS)

7. The middleman is sometimes described as an unnecessary feature of the economic organisation. Discuss this view. (Exp.)

8. What are the essential features of a centralised and organised market? Illustrate by reference to any such market with which you are familiar. (Exp.)

9. What functions are performed by middlemen and what determines their regard? What happens when an industry is nationalised? (RSA)

10. Why is it that some commodities have a restricted market and others a very wide one? (AIA)

11. Write a short account of market speculation as an economic function and show its effect upon prices. (IB)

12. Does speculation on the organised commodity markets increase or diminish the range and frequency of price fluctuations? (Degree)

13. What are the advantages of having markets where one can buy and sell what has not yet been produced? (Degree)

CHAPTER 10

DEMAND CURVES AND SUPPLY CURVES

I. PRICE DETERMINATION

1. Haggling

If there are few sellers and few buyers in the market the prices at which the commodities will be sold will probably be determined by haggling. In a sale by private treaty this method obtains, and the prices at which houses are sold are often arrived at in this way. A prospective buyer may approach a prospective seller, and after finding that the seller is asking £8,400 the buyer may offer him £8,000. If the seller prefers to keep the house himself rather than accept £8,000, and if this sum is the maximum the buyer is prepared to pay, there is no basis for further bargaining. However, it is more likely that there is a range of prices that would satisfy the seller, and he may, for example, be willing to accept £8,100, though he may be hopeful of obtaining more than that. Similarly, the buyer may be willing to pay up to £8,250, though he hopes to obtain the house for less. The actual price agreed upon will therefore lie somewhere between £8,100 and £8,250. If the buyer is keener to buy than the seller is to sell the price will be nearer £8,250. If, on the other hand, the seller is keener to sell than the buyer is to buy the price will be nearer £8,100. This range of prices over which bargaining is possible can be represented diagrammatically as follows:

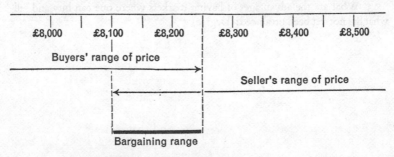

Fig. 8. The Range of Bargaining.

2. Sales by auction

Another method of determining the price at which a commodity shall be sold is to put it up for auction. In such a case there is one seller and a number of prospective buyers. The auctioneer offers an article for sale and asks for bids for it. Anyone desirous of purchasing it is then at liberty to make an offer, and the article will eventually be sold to the highest bidder—that is, to the keenest buyer: the one prepared to pay the highest price. The actual price he will pay depends on how much the second keenest buyer is prepared to pay. If four people—A, B, C and D—are bidding against one another for a house they may be willing to pay £8,400, £8,200, £8,100 and £7,800 respectively. The house may be sold to A for £8,225, because at that price B, C and D have all dropped out of the bidding. Sometimes rivalry between two bidders forces up the price to a level that neither of them would have paid had each not been carried away by a desire to score a victory over his rival. The important thing to notice, however, whether the sale is by auction or private treaty, is that the cost of building the house does not enter into the determination of the price at which it can be sold, since once it has come into the market, its price depends not on its cost, but on the relation between the keenness of buyers to buy and the keenness of sellers to sell.

3. Offers at fixed prices

These two methods of determining price—private treaty or selling by auction—are still in operation at highly organised wholesale markets. It was seen in the preceding chapter that raw wool is sold by auction and raw cotton by private treaty. Either method of sale can be adopted for consumer goods, particularly when the sales are infrequent. Works of art are often sold by auction. For consumer goods in regular demand both methods of sale are too cumbersome and would take up an unnecessary amount of time. For things such as foodstuffs, clothing, household goods, etc., it is customary for the sellers to mark their goods at definite prices. British shopkeepers would be astonished if their customers wanted to haggle over prices, though haggling is still customary in some parts of the world. What has really happened is that the sellers have selected from the range over which they were prepared to sell, some price at which they think they can dispose of their stocks. If their judgment is correct they will be able to sell all their stock at this price; if the price is too high they will find that business is slack, and sooner or later they will have to lower their prices; if they fix the price too low they will quickly sell out all their stock, though they will probably raise their price when they find demand stronger than at first they had anticipated. Evidently then there is some price at which the whole of the stock, neither more nor less, could be sold. What this price will be depends on the strength of the demand for the commodity relative to the supply.

II. DEMAND

4. The meaning of demand

By demand is meant the quantity demanded at a particular price, for it is impossible to conceive of demand not related to price. To want or need a thing is not the same as to demand it. Sometimes the term *effective* demand is used to distinguish demand from need. Most housewives would probably like to have a constant supply of hot water, and they might say that they needed water-heaters for the purpose. The demand for such heaters, however, may be fairly small if their price is high. It is quite certain that if the price were lowered more of them would be sold, whereas if the price were doubled fewer would be demanded. Similarly, most housewives probably buy a smaller quantity of strawberries at the beginning of the season, when the price is high, than they buy later, when the price is lower. Generally at a high price less will be sold than at a low price, assuming, of course, that no change takes place in the intensity of demand.

5. Individual demand schedules

It thus becomes possible to compile an individual's hypothetical demand schedule for a commodity. Demand schedules are difficult to estimate, for statistics cannot be compiled to show demand at prices different from those ruling at a given time. For example, if the price of a certain commodity were 13p per tin Mrs Gamp, a housewife, might buy six tins per month; if the price were 16p per tin she might buy only four tins per month, but at a price of 11p per tin she might buy eight per month. Mrs Gamp's demand schedule might therefore run as shown in Table XX.

It is necessary to emphasise again that this does not indicate any change in demand on the part of Mrs Gamp, but merely expresses what her *present* behaviour with regard to the purchase of this commodity would be at a series of different prices. With no change in the intensity of her demand for the commodity she will buy only three tins per month if the price is 20p, or eight tins per month if the price is 11p. Such a demand schedule is purely hypothetical, but it serves to illustrate the principle that more of a commodity will be bought at a low than at a high price.

Table XX

An Individual Demand Schedule (1)

Price per tin (pence)	Demand per month (number of tins)
20	3
18	$3\frac{1}{2}$
16	4
14	5
13	6
12	7
11	8
10	9

Table XXI

An Individual Demand Schedule (2)

Price per tin (pence)	Demand per month (number of tins)
20	0
18	1
16	$1\frac{1}{2}$
14	2
13	$2\frac{1}{2}$
12	3
11	4
10	6

Table XXII

An Individual Demand Schedule (3)

Price per tin (pence)	Demand per month (number of tins)
20	$3\frac{1}{2}$
18	$3\frac{1}{2}$
16	4
14	4
13	4
12	4
11	$4\frac{1}{2}$
10	$4\frac{1}{2}$

Other housewives will have different demand schedules for the commodity, because the intensity of their demand for this commodity is either stronger or weaker than Mrs Gamp's. For example, at all possible prices Mrs Prig may purchase a smaller quantity than Mrs Gamp, and so Mrs Prig's demand schedule might be as shown in Table XXI (page 165).

On the other hand, the demand of Mrs Bardell may vary little over this range of prices, and her demand schedule might read as shown in Table XXII (page 165).

6. Composite demand schedule

Theoretically, the demand schedules of all consumers of a commodity can be combined to form a composite demand schedule, representing the total demand for that commodity at various prices. This might be called the market demand schedule.

Table XXIII

A Market Demand Schedule

Price per tin (pence)	Quantity demanded per month
20	100,000
18	120,000
16	135,000
14	150,000
13	165,000
12	180,000
11	200,000
10	240,000
9	300,000
8	350,000

These prices are called *demand prices*. Thus, the demand price for 200,000 tins per month is 11p per tin.

7. Demand curves

The above demand schedule can be represented graphically (Fig. 9). The vertical scale *OY* represents the price per tin, and the horizontal scale *OX* represents the number of tins purchased. By convention the vertical axis is marked *OY*, and the horizontal axis *OX*, and it is usual also to show price along the vertical scale and the quantity along the horizontal. From this demand schedule it is possible to plot a demand curve (*see* Fig. 10). The curve *DD* then represents the state of demand

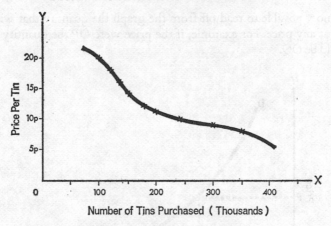

Fig. 9. The Demand Curve (1).

for this commodity at a particular time and under particular conditions. Such a graph is merely a convenient way of showing at a glance the relationship between price and the quantity bought, and so it is not necessary to have the price and quantity scales marked off mathematically. It is sufficient to know that prices and quantity increase evenly from O towards Y and quantity from O towards X respectively. The graph then becomes:

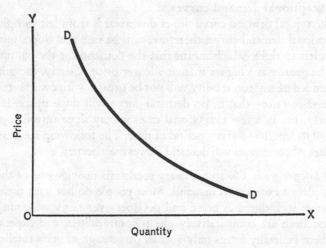

Fig. 10. The Demand Curve (2).

It is now possible to read off from the graph the quantity that will be sold at any price. For example, if the price were *OP* the quantity sold would be *OQ*.

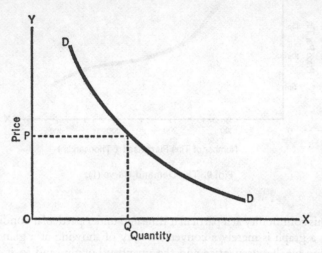

Fig. 11. The Demand Curve (3).

The First Law of Supply and Demand—*the lower the price, the greater the quantity that will be demanded*—can be seen at a glance.

8. Exceptional demand curves

The typical demand curve slopes downwards from left to right. An exceptional demand curve, therefore, will be one that slopes upwards from left to right, which means that the demand for the commodity will be greater at a higher than at a lower price. Clearly, the quantity demanded of any commodity will not be greater with every successive increase in price—that is, no demand curve will slope upwards in its entirety, but in a few exceptional cases it may slope upwards over a part of its length at a given period of time. The following are examples of cases where exceptional demand curves may occur:

(*i*) *Inferior goods.* Cheap necessary foodstuffs provide one of the best examples of exceptional demand. Most people do not vary their purchases of such things as bread and potatoes over fairly wide ranges of prices. Both are comparatively cheap commodities, and expenditure on them generally forms only a small percentage of one's total outlay of food. Even a very considerable fall in price would not encourage most people to buy more, though a steep rise in price, if continued, would eventually lead to less being bought. In the case of the very poor, however, it may be that, at the low price, they are able to buy a certain amount of these cheaper foodstuffs and still be able to afford in addition a small amount of more expensive foods, such as cakes and green vegetables. A rise in the prices of bread and potatoes, however, may mean that less of the more expensive commodities, cake and green vegetables, would be bought, even though their prices remained unchanged, their place being taken by increased amounts of bread and potatoes. The effect therefore of the rise in the price of bread and potatoes might be to increase the quantities of these commodities demanded, although the amount bought of the more expensive foods was reduced. Commodities of this type are sometimes known as *Giffen Goods*.

(ii) *Fear of a future rise in price*. If it is believed that the price of a commodity is likely to be higher in the future than at present, then, even though the price has already risen, more of the commodity may be bought at the higher price. This often happens with stock exchange securities, especially in the case of speculative buying. If the price of a security has been low for a long time a slight rise in its price may be taken to indicate that the price is going to rise still further in the future.

On the outbreak of war in 1939 the prices of many commodities rose slightly, but there was a big increase in the quantity of goods bought, because many people expected a further rise in prices. Demand similarly increased in the United States and some other countries at the outbreak of the Korean War in 1950 and during the Cuban crisis of 1962. Fear of higher prices in the future, therefore, may cause more to be bought at a higher than at a lower price.

(iii) *Articles of ostentation, etc.* There are some commodities that appear desirable only if they are expensive. Some articles of jewellery fall within this category. At a comparatively low price a smaller quantity might be sold than at a higher price, merely because the higher price gives the article greater exclusiveness in the eyes of purchasers. A fashionable dressmaker or milliner might often increase her sales by raising her prices. A luxury car might sell more readily at £7,500 than at £4,000. Since we cannot be expert buyers of everything, we tend to judge the quality of many things largely by the prices at which they are sold.

III. SUPPLY

9. Supply schedules and curves

The second factor that affects prices is supply. By the supply of a commodity is meant the quantity that will come on to the market over a particular period of time at a certain price. Just as demand is not the same as need, and means effective demand or demand at a price, so it is with supply. The supply of a commodity does not comprise the entire stock in existence, but only that amount drawn into the market by the price ruling at the time. The supply of oil is not the estimated resources of all the world's oil-fields, but only that amount which particular prices will bring on to the market. As one would expect, sellers will generally put a greater quantity on to the market the higher the price. As with demand, it is possible to construct a supply schedule showing the amounts that will be offered for sale at different prices by individual firms, these then being combined to form a market supply schedule for the commodity. The supply schedule then might run as shown in Table XXIV.

Table XXIV

A Supply Schedule

Price per tin (pence)	Quantity offered for sale per month
17	400,000
16	370,000
15	350,000
14	320,000
13	285,000
12	240,000
11	200,000
10	160,000
9	120,000
8	80,000

These prices are *supply prices*. For example, at a supply price of 14p 320,000 tins of a commodity per month will be supplied. From this supply schedule a supply curve can be plotted (Fig. 12). Again it will be sufficient to express the curve generally (Fig. 13). Since a greater quantity is usually supplied the higher the price, the typical supply curve slopes upwards from left to right. This illustrates the second Law of Supply and Demand—*the higher the price, the greater the quantity that will be supplied*. From this diagram it can be seen that at the higher price,

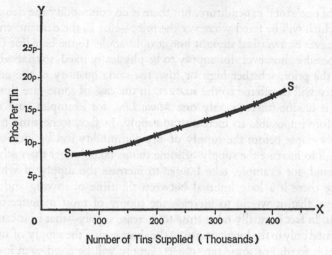

Fig. 12. The Supply Curve (1).

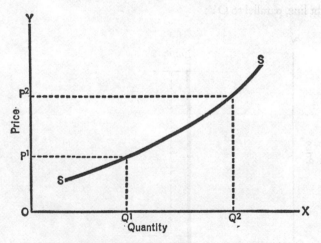

Fig. 13. The Supply Curve (2).

OP^2, a greater quantity, OQ^2, will be put on to the market than at the lower price, OP^1, the amount offered for sale at this price being only OQ^1.

10. Exceptional supply curves

It is possible to conceive of the demand for a commodity being fixed over a narrow range of prices, especially if its cost forms only a small part of one's total expenditure, but there is no commodity the demand for which will be fixed whatever the price—that is, the demand curve will never be a vertical straight line at right angles to the base line OX. It is possible, however, for supply to be physically fixed, so that whatever the price, whether high or low, the same quantity of the commodity will be offered to the market. In the case of some rare things, each is unique (there is only one *Mona Lisa*, for example), and it is therefore impossible to increase the supply. In fact, some time must usually elapse before the supply of any commodity can be increased, though to increase the supply of some things takes longer than others. It would, for example, take longer to increase the supply of wheat, where there is a long interval between the time of sowing and the harvest, than it would to increase the supply of most manufactured goods. In fact it usually takes time to increase supply—that is, it can be increased only in the long run, for in the short period the supply of most things is fixed. For some rare objects supply will be fixed even in the long run. A supply curve, showing a fixed supply, will be a vertical straight line, parallel to OY:

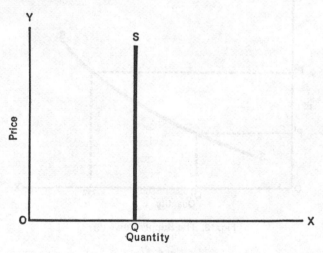

Fig. 14. Fixed Supply.

Just as in exceptional cases a portion of the demand curve can slope backwards, indicating that a larger quantity is demanded at a higher price, so it is possible to find a portion of a supply curve sloping backwards. This would mean that a smaller supply would be offered at a higher than at a lower price. This might occur in the case of labour (supply being taken to mean the number of hours worked), for men may wish to work shorter hours if wages (the price of labour) are high. This regressive supply curve is discussed in connection with wages.

IV. EQUATING DEMAND WITH SUPPLY

11. Equilibrium price

The price at which demand and supply are equal is the equilibrium price. At this price the same quantity will be supplied as is demanded. This can be seen if the market demand schedule (page 166) is set alongside the supply schedule (page 170) for that commodity:

Table XXV

A Combined Supply and Demand Schedule (1)

Price (pence)	Quantity demanded (number of tins)	Quantity supplied (number of tins)
20	100,000	400,000
18	120,000	370,000
16	135,000	350,000
14	150,000	320,000
13	165,000	285,000
12	180,000	240,000
11	200,000	200,000
10	240,000	160,000
9	300,000	120,000
8	350,000	80,000

It will be seen that if the price of the commodity is 11p per tin the quantity demanded will be 200,000 tins, and the quantity supplied will also be 200,000 tins. Under these conditions of demand and supply, then, 11p will be the equilibrium price. This can also be represented graphically by superimposing the demand curve upon the supply curve (Fig. 15). At the point of intersection of the two curves demand and supply are equal. The *equilibrium price*, therefore, *OP*, at which price the quantity *OQ* will be supplied, *equates supply and demand*. This is the third Law of Supply and Demand. Price in a perfect market is thus determined by the interaction of the two forces of supply and demand, the intensity of demand at a particular time in relation to the conditions of supply. At one time it was thought that the price of a commodity was determined solely by its cost of production, but cost of production only influences supply, and as we have just seen, this is only one of the two forces that affect prices. If, however, supply were fixed, price

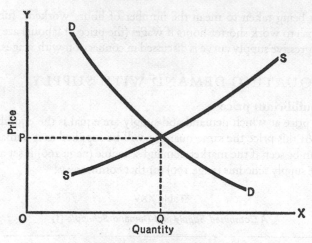

Fig. 15. The Equilibrium Price.

would depend principally on demand. Since supply often tends to be fixed in the short period, the shorter the period, the more important is demand. This is shown in Fig. 16. At all prices the quantity available is OQ; the price OP equates demand with this supply.

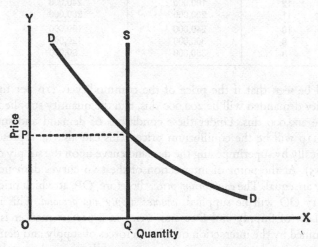

Fig. 16. The Equilibrium Price with Fixed Supply.

12. Market price and normal price

The determination of price by the interaction of the forces of supply and demand occurs through the working of what is known as the *price mechanism*. Both the quantity supplied and the quantity demanded vary with price, and so at the equilibrium price these two forces of supply and demand are brought into balance.

If the equilibrium price is charged in a market there will be just sufficient of the commodity available to meet demand at that price—that is, there will appear to be no shortage, for all buyers can be supplied at the prevailing price. Nor will there be any surplus, since the sellers will just be able to dispose of their entire stocks, for at the equilibrium price the market will be cleared. At any price higher than the equilibrium price the sellers will find some of the commodity left on their hands unsold; at a lower price than the equilibrium price demand will exceed supply and there will be said to be a shortage of the commodity.

The actual price charged in the market may be only the short-term equilibrium price, for in the short period the forces of supply and demand may be subject to temporary influences. The short-period equilibrium price is the *Market Price*. However, when conditions of supply and demand have settled down so that the rate at which the commodity is consumed is equal to the rate at which it is produced, then a long-period equilibrium price will be established. This is known as the *Normal Price*.

RECOMMENDATIONS FOR FURTHER READING

K. E. Boulding: *Economic Analysis*, Chapters 4 and 5.
H. Henderson, *Supply and Demand*, Chapter 2.

QUESTIONS

1. "The amount demanded of a commodity will usually be greater the lower the price, other things remaining the same." Explain this statement with special reference to the significance of "other things remaining the same." (UEI)

2. What exactly do you understand by the laws of demand and supply? Is it always true to say that a fall in price is followed by an increase in demand? (RSA)

3. Explain briefly how the price-system works. (ACCA)

4. How are prices settled in a competitive market? (IT)

5. Within what limits may the prices of goods move in a free market? (AIA)

6. Illustrate in diagrammatic form the equilibrium between demand and supply under conditions of perfect competition and decreasing cost. Explain the various parts and the meaning of the diagram. (CIS)

7. Under what circumstances could demand for a product rise when its price increases? (CIS)

8. Estimate the significance of demand curves in practical business as distinct from theoretical economics. (SIAA)

9. Consider the proposition that increased supply leads to a reduction in price and that a lower price results in decreased supply. Show how this statement can be true, despite the apparent paradox that increased supply leads to decreased supply. (IB)

10. Draw a typical short-run average total cost curve, and explain its characteristic shape. (IB)

11. Explain the distinction between a movement *along* a supply curve and a *shift* of such a curve. (GCE)

12. In what circumstances would a fall in the price of a commodity lead to a reduction in the quantity bought? (Degree)

13. What determines equilibrium in a single market and what forces tend to establish it? (Degree)

CHAPTER II

DEMAND AND SUPPLY RELATIONSHIPS

I. CHANGES IN DEMAND AND SUPPLY

1. Changes in demand

Before the effect of changes in demand can be considered it is important to be quite clear exactly what is meant by a change in demand. As we have already noted the typical demand curve shows that at a higher price a smaller quantity will be demanded than at a lower price. The fact that at a price of 11p 20,000 more tins of a commodity will be demanded than at a price of 12p does *not* indicate a change in demand since this simply involves a movement along the *same* demand curve, which represents the *same* state of demand at a particular time.

Consider the following diagram:

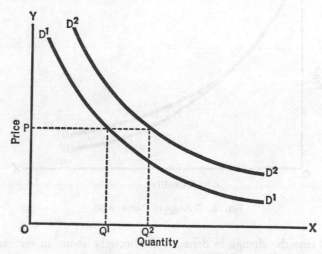

Fig. 17. Change in Demand (1).

The state of demand before the change is represented by the curve D^1D^1. In these conditions at the price OP, the quantity demanded was

OQ^1. Assume now that for some reason a change of demand occurs, the new state of demand being represented by the curve D^2D^2. At the old price, OP, the quantity now demanded is OQ^2, which is obviously greater than the former quantity, OQ^1. In fact, under the new conditions of demand a larger quantity is demanded at each of the old prices. The new curve therefore illustrates an increase in demand. If the new curve had been entirely to the left of the original curve this would have shown a decrease in demand. Confusion frequently arises because sometimes movement along the same demand curve is spoken of as an increase or a decrease in demand. Strictly, an increase or a decrease in demand is the result of a change in demand, and therefore requires a new demand curve. To avoid ambiguity, it is better to speak of an increase or a decrease in the quantity demanded when this is simply the result of a change of price, and therefore refers to the same demand curve.

A change in demand need not, as in the above diagram, affect the whole of the demand curve. The new curve may partly overlap the old:

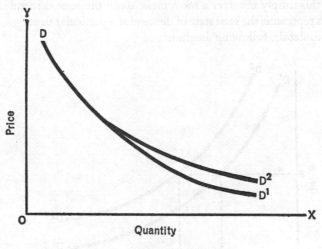

Fig. 18. Change in Demand (2).

In this case the change in demand has brought about an increase in demand only over the lower ranges of prices.

2. Causes of changes in demand

There are a number of reasons why demand may change:

(*i*) *Changes of taste or fashion*. The intensity of demand for something depends on the keenness of people to buy it, but it is often difficult to discover what determines this keenness. Taste may depend on a number of factors, though education and training are often important influences, but taste probably varies as much between different groups of people at the same period as between one period and another, and it changes only slowly. There is undoubtedly a greater appreciation of good music today than there was thirty-five years ago, and so the demand for symphony concerts and opera has increased, but the change from one year to the next would be scarcely perceptible.

Fashion is apt to change more arbitrarily, and often apparently without reason. Few men now wear bowler hats, whereas in 1910 this was the most popular hat for men. In 1920 few men went hatless, whereas fifty years later many men rarely wore a hat. This change of fashion, therefore, has decreased the demand for men's hats, and especially for bowler hats. Some fashions may be related to the weather, and a warm summer will increase the demand for ice-cream. Some children's toys seem to have a brief period of popularity and then are seen no more, demand vanishing almost overnight. Advertisers and propagandists try, and often succeed in changing tastes or fashions. Temperance societies by their propaganda attempt to reduce the demand for alcoholic drink, while the manufacturers of such drinks try to stimulate demand by means of advertising.

(*ii*) *New commodities replace old*. New commodities are constantly being put on the market while others become out of date and their production ceases, the demand for the new things replacing the demand for those that are no longer demanded. Over the past fifty years the demand for electric lamps has greatly increased, while the demand for gas-mantles has declined. Though a piano is now to be found only in a few homes, there are not many homes without a radio, television or radiogram. The attaché case ousted the Gladstone bag, just as later the brief case took the place of the attaché case.

(*iii*) *A change in the quantity of money*. An increase or a decrease in the quantity of money will affect demand, for it is unlikely that the prices of all goods will change proportionately to the change in the quantity of money. The demand for some commodities will increase, while the demand for others will fall.

(*iv*) *A change in real incomes*. A change in real income means a change in the quantity of goods that the money income will buy. Thus, a person's money income may rise, while his real income falls, if prices rise more than wages. On the other hand, his real income may rise, though his money income falls, if his wages fall more slowly than prices. An increase in people's real income may have little effect on the demand for the cheaper foodstuffs, or indeed on food at all after a certain point, but it may have a very considerable effect on the demand for luxuries and semi-luxuries.

(v) *Changes in the distribution of incomes.* Inequality of incomes between different groups of people may be lessened by taxing the well-to-do more heavily than people with low incomes, by subsidising food, and by the State providing free social services which are of greatest benefit to people in the lower income groups. This may result in an increase in demand for many things with a consequent rise in their prices.

(vi) *Changes in population.* Two kinds of change may be noted, (a) an increase or decrease in the total population or (b) a change in the proportion between the different age groups, though if the first of these changes takes place it is almost certain to bring about the second change also. The effect of population changes has already been considered, and it was pointed out that if an increase occurred in the proportion of old people in the population and a reduction in the proportion of children, it would tend to increase the demand for the assortment of goods old people wanted and reduce the demand for goods primarily required for children.

(vii) *Changes in the prices of other goods.* The demand for one commodity may change as a result of a change in the price of some other commodity. To some extent all prices are affected in this way. A general increase in the prices of foodstuffs will reduce the demand for food to a less extent than a rise in the price of other goods, but its effect will be to reduce the demand for other things, if incomes remain unchanged. There are cases, however, where the demand for two or more commodities is more closely related. When things are fairly close substitutes for one another, a fall in the price of one will reduce the demand for the other. A rise in the price of branded cocoa drinks may increase the demand for cocoa; a rise in railway fares may increase the demand for bus travel. Sometimes commodities are used together, and then a change in the price of one will affect the demand for both, even though the price of the second commodity remains unchanged. A rise in the price of motor cars, for example, might reduce the demand for petrol.

(viii) *Expectation of the trend of future trade.* The demand of business men for factors of production depends on their expectation whether business activity is likely to be maintained in the future, since they have to produce in anticipation of demand. This particularly affects the demand for new capital. If a slump is feared the demand for new machinery or plant will fall off.

(ix) *Expectation of future changes in prices.* This generally affects businessmen more than consumers. Expectation of a rise in the price of a raw material will stimulate the demand of merchants and manufacturers for it, whereas fear of a fall in prices will make them more cautious, and so check demand. Exceptional demand (that is, where more is bought at a higher than a lower price), resulting from a fear of a further rise in price, really falls within this category. This was considered in the previous chapter.

(x) *Taxation.* Taxes may be imposed either to lessen inequality of income or deliberately to reduce the demand for a commodity. Spirits, tobacco and, since 1973, petrol are heavily taxed as much to reduce consumption as to raise revenue. Duties have often been imposed on imported goods in order to reduce the demand for them.

3. Changes in supply

In the same way that a change in demand requires a new demand curve, so it is with a change of supply. The fact that more will generally be supplied at a high than at a low price does not indicate a change of supply, but simply shows the effect of a change of price on existing conditions of supply at a particular time. As with demand, this ambiguity can be avoided if one speaks of changes in the quantity supplied when different positions on the same supply curve are under consideration. A change of supply results in a different quantity being supplied at each of the former prices.

Consider the following diagram (Fig. 19) on page 182. In this case the change is an increase in supply, showing that at the old price OP the quantity OQ^2 will now be supplied, instead of the smaller quantity OQ^1. At all prices a larger quantity than before will be supplied.

4. Causes of changes in supply

The following are some of the reasons why conditions of supply may change:

(i) *Where the producer consumes more of his own product.* An improvement in people's standard of living may result in their consuming more of their own output of a commodity. For this reason the exports of meat from Argentina have been less in recent years than formerly. Similarly, Russia exports less wheat today than it did before 1914.

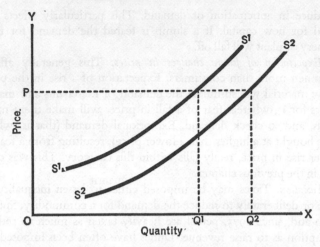

Fig. 19. Change in Supply.

(*ii*) *Changes in the cost of production.* If the businessman has to pay more to secure the services of the factors of production he employs, his costs of production will rise. Since no producer could remain in business for long if he failed to cover his costs of production, a rise in costs will generally tend to reduce the supply of a commodity coming on to the market, other things being equal. A fall in his costs will have the opposite effect.

(*iii*) *Changes in the technique of production.* This is probably the most important factor affecting supply. The development of a new method of production or the invention of a new machine may make possible a big expansion of output at lower cost and so increase supply.

(*iv*) *Effects of the weather.* In the case of agricultural products the actual output cannot be precisely estimated in advance, owing to vagaries of the weather. Over a series of years, the variation in output between one year and another may be very considerable. Because of the long interval between seed-time and harvest, the response of supply to changes in the price of farming products is slow.

(*v*) *Effect of taxation.* Taxation of commodities is likely to raise their prices. The imposition of a tax on a commodity is equivalent to an increase in its cost of production and so will generally result in a decrease in supply. A reduction of taxation will have the opposite effect.

II. EFFECTS OF CHANGES IN DEMAND AND SUPPLY

5. Effects of changes in demand

(i) *An increase of demand.* Consider first the effect of a change in demand, assuming the conditions of supply to remain unchanged. As previously emphasised, this requires the drawing of a new demand curve. SS represents the condition of supply for the commodity, D^1D^1 is the old demand curve and D^2D^2 the new demand curve after the change (in this case, increase) of demand. Before this change the equilibrium price was OP^1, at which the quantity OQ^1 was supplied.

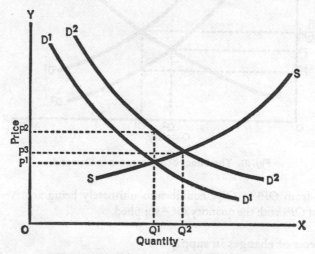

Fig. 20. The Effect of an Increase in Demand.

Supply adjusts itself slowly to changes of price, and in the short period supply may appear to be fixed. The immediate effect, therefore, of the increase in demand is for price to rise from OP^1 to OP^2 because supply remains for a time at OQ^1 as before. Sooner or later the effect of the rise in price will be to evoke the supply of a larger quantity of the commodity. The point of intersection of the supply curve and the new demand curve indicates the new equilibrium position, the quantity supplied being OQ^2 and the price finally settling down at OP^3. The effect of the increase in demand has been both to raise the price and increase the quantity supplied. The fourth Law of Supply and Demand therefore states that *an increase in demand tends both to increase price and to call forth a larger supply.*

(ii) A decrease in demand. A fall in demand will bring about a fall both
in price and in the quantity supplied (Fig. 21).

Again there is an immediate effect, for a reduction in the quantity
supplied does not take place at once. The immediate effect is for price

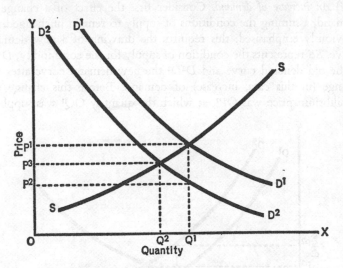

Fig. 21. The Effect of a Decrease in Demand.

to fall from OP^1 to OP^2, equilibrium ultimately being achieved at a
price of OP^3 with the quantity OQ^2 supplied.

6. Effects of changes in supply

(i) An increase in supply. Immediate and long-run effects occur in the
case of changes in supply, but generally demand responds more readily
to changes in price than does supply (Fig. 22). *DD* represents the state
of demand, S^1S^1 the conditions of supply at first, and S^2S^2 the conditions of supply after an increase of supply, perhaps the result of technical improvements which have reduced costs of production. As a
result of the change a larger quantity than before will be supplied at
each price. The old equilibrium price was OP^1, at which the quantity
OQ^1 was supplied. The new equilibrium price is OP^2, at which the
quantity OQ^2 is supplied. The effect of the increase in supply has been
to increase the quantity supplied and also to lower the price. The fifth
Law of Supply and Demand, therefore, states that *an increase in supply
tends to lower price and to increase the quantity demanded.*

(ii) A decrease in supply. A decrease in supply will pull the supply

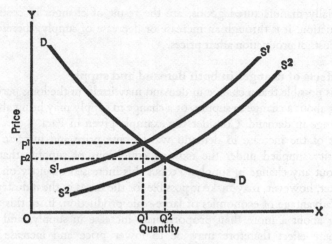

Fig. 22. The Effect of an Increase in Supply.

curve to the left of its original position, and the effect will be to raise price and reduce the quantity demanded.

Consider the following diagram:

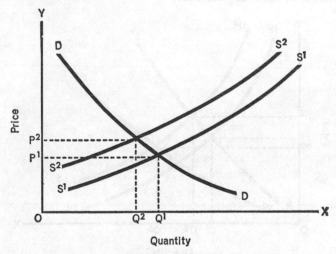

Fig. 23. The Effect of a Decrease in Supply.

The new price, OP^2, is higher than the old, OP^1; the new quantity supplied is OQ^2, and this is smaller than the old, OQ^1. Such a change in the conditions of supply might be brought about by increased costs of production. Thus, changes in the supply of many commodities, especially manufactured goods, are the result of changes in costs of production. It is through an increase or decrease of supply, therefore, that costs of production affect prices.

7. Effects of changes in both demand and supply

It is possible that a change in demand may itself, in the long period, bring about a change in supply, or a change in supply may bring about a change in demand. Consider the example given in Para. 5 (*i*). The effect of the increase in demand was to raise price and increase the quantity supplied under the existing conditions of supply—that is, without any change in supply. To put this increased quantity on the market, however, may make it possible for the firms in the industry to take advantage of economies of large-scale production. If so, this will bring about a more than proportionate increase in supply, and the ultimate effect therefore may be to lower price and increase the quantity supplied. In the reverse case of the falling off in the demand for a commodity the decrease in the quantity demanded may increase the average cost of production and so lead to a rise in price, as is the case with the manufacture of motor cars.

Consider the following diagram:

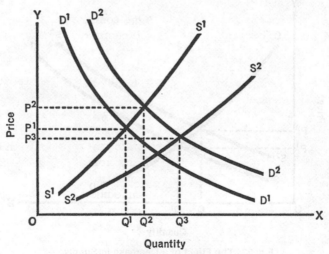

Fig. 24. Change in Both Supply and Demand.

The original equilibrium position indicated by the intersection of the original supply and demand curves $S^I S^I$ and $D^I D^I$ shows that the quantity OQ^I would be supplied at a price of OP^I. Demand then increased from D^1D^1 to D^2D^2. Before any change took place in supply a new equilibrium position was established after price had risen from OP^1 to OP^2, and after the quantity supplied had increased from OQ^1 to OQ^2. Finally, after the change in supply the ultimate effect was to bring about equilibrium at a price of OP^3, at which quantity OQ^3 was supplied. Thus the ultimate effect of this change in demand was to reduce price and increase output. The reader may find it of interest to work out graphically the following further cases:

(*i*) The ultimate effect of an increase in demand where the increase in the quantity supplied can be obtained only at increased costs of production (that is, where expansion of an industry is under conditions of increasing costs).

(*ii*) The ultimate effect of a decrease in demand where the decrease in the quantity supplied raises cost of production.

(*iii*) The ultimate effect of a decrease in demand where the decrease in the quantity supplied lowers costs of production.

III. INTER-RELATIONSHIP OF DEMAND AND SUPPLY

8. Inter-related demands

(*i*) *Joint or complementary demand.* One commodity may be complementary to another, and so the two commodities may be jointly demanded, as for example bread and butter, tea and sugar, strawberries and cream, lamb and mint sauce, pens and ink, motor cars and petrol. In such cases changes in demand are generally in the same proportion for each of the linked commodities; if the demand for bread increases by 10 per cent, then the demand for butter will probably increase by about 10 per cent, though the proportions can often be varied. But it is unlikely that conditions of supply will be the same for both commodities, and so changes in price resulting from a change in demand will not necessarily be in the same proportion for both commodities For example, let us assume that two commodities, A and B, are in joint demand, and an increase in demand occurs (see Fig. 25 on p. 188). OQ^2 represents a similar proportionate increase over OQ^1 in each case, but because the conditions of supply are not the same for each commodity (the supply of A being more responsive than B to changes of price), the price of commodity A will rise by only approximately $33\frac{1}{3}$ per cent, whereas the price of commodity B almost doubles.

If a change should occur in the conditions of supply bringing about an increase in supply of commodity A, the state of demand in this case

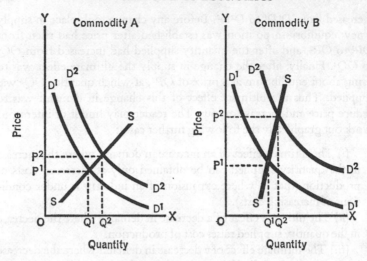

Fig. 25. Joint Demand.

remaining the same, the price of commodity *A* will fall and the quantity demanded will increase. Since *A* and *B* are complementary the increased demand for *A* means an increased demand also for *B*, and the conditions of supply for *B* being unchanged, its price will rise.

(*ii*) *Derived demand*. The term *derived* demand is frequently used where demand for one commodity is the direct result of the demand for another, as, for example, in the case of the demand for factors of production. The demand for land, labour and capital is derived from the demand for the commodities produced by these factors. The producer's demand is for a number of factors jointly—for example, the woollen manufacturer has a joint demand for land, labour, factory buildings, machinery, raw wool, coal or other source of power, and transport. The demand for every one of these things can be said to be derived from the demand for woollen cloth, carpets or other woollen goods.

Joint, complementary or derived demand are similar to one another, in that an increase in the demand for one commodity brings about an increase in the demand for the other.

(*iii*) *Composite demand*. Sometimes a commodity can be used for two or more purposes, and the demand for it may vary as a result of a change in the demand for one of these purposes. Steel may be used for making motor cars, or in shipbuilding; bricks may be used for building either houses or schools; wool may be demanded for making either into cloth or into carpets. This is known as composite demand, and it applies to most raw materials. An increase in the demand for carpets will raise the price of wool, and increase the amount of wool going to carpet manufacturers, but in the short period the supply available to cloth manufacturers will be reduced and they also will have to pay a higher price for wool.

(*iv*) *Competitive demand.* If two commodities are fairly close substitutes for one another an increase in the quantity demanded of one of them will reduce the demand for the other. To some extent all commodities are in competitive demand with one another, because for most people the purchase of more of one thing necessitates the purchase of less of others, so that a change in demand for one thing to some extent affects the demand for all others. Where two things serve more or less the same purpose, to have more of one means that less of the other will be wanted. An increase in the quantity of butter demanded would probably reduce the demand for margarine; an increased demand for mutton might reduce the demand for beef; a change in the demand for fish might conversely affect the demand for meat.

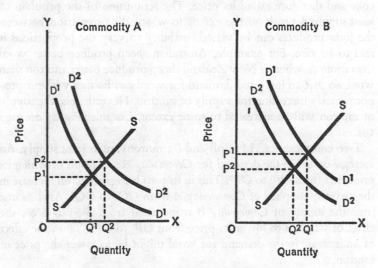

Fig. 26. Competitive Demand.

Consider Fig. 26. The two commodities *A* and *B* are in competitive demand and an increased demand for commodity *A* occurs.

The increased demand for commodity *A* raises the price from OP^1 to OP^2 and increases the quantity supplied from OQ^1 to OQ^2. As a consequence of this increased demand for a commodity A there is a fall in the demand for commodity B from D^1D^1 to D^2D^2, as a result of which its price falls from OP^1 to OP^2 and the quantity supplied falls from OQ^1 to OQ^2.

In the case of competitive demand an increased demand for one commodity will reduce the demand for the other.

The demand for all factors of production is competitive to the extent that factors are capable of being substituted for one another. The employment of more capital, for example, may mean a decreased demand for labour.

9. Inter-related supply

(i) *Joint supply*. Some commodities are produced together, so that change in the supply of one can be brought about only by similarly changing the supply of the other. Wool and mutton, beef and hides, gas and coke and the various types of oil are examples of such joint supply. The use of natural gas in Great Britain has curtailed the production of gas from coal, and so at the same time reduced the supply of coke and therefore raised its price. The seriousness of the problem of joint supply depends on the extent to which the proportion between the joint products can be varied. Inability to vary the proportions is said to be rare. For example, Australian sheep produce better wool than mutton, whereas New Zealand sheep produce better mutton than wool, so that an increased demand for wool can be met without proportionately increasing the supply of mutton. Nevertheless, the supply of mutton will be increased to some extent. Consider Fig. 27 on page 191.

Two commodities, A (wool) and B (mutton) are in joint supply. An increase occurs in the demand for *Commodity A* as a result of which its price rises from OP^1 to OP^2. This in its turn brings about an increase in the quantity supplied of *Commodity A* from OQ^1 to OQ^2. At the same time the supply of *Commodity B* is increased from S^1S^1 to S^2S^2, the effect of which is to lower its price from OP^1 to OP^2. Thus, the effect of an increase in the demand for wool might be to lower the price of mutton.

(ii) *Competitive supply*. To expand the production of one commodity generally requires a reduction in the output of another. This is particularly true of farming products in a country such as Great Britain. To increase the supply of an agricultural product such as wheat means ploughing up more grassland and rearing fewer grazing animals. More meat may be produced, but only at the cost of less milk, or vice

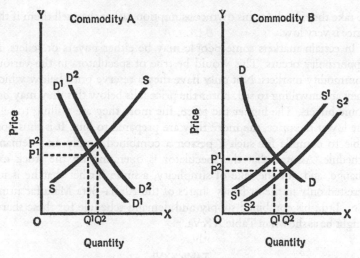

Fig. 27. Joint Supply.

versa. There is a wider application, for every country's supply of factors of production is limited, so that if factors are used for one form of production, obviously they cannot be used for another. It is equally true, therefore, to say that an expansion of manufacturing means less farming. During the nineteenth century Great Britain neglected its farming, but this made possible the vast industrial expansion that occurred during that period. Only by increased mechanisation of farming during the past thirty years has Great Britain been able to increase its output of food, without at the same time curtailing industrial production.

10. Do the supply and demand curves represent independent forces?

It has already been seen that a change in the demand can bring about a change in supply, and that a change in supply may cause a change in demand. Can it be that the supply and demand curves are even more intimately related, and, indeed, are responsive to the same influences? Is the supply curve really only a part of the demand curve? In some cases this may be so. If the seller has a reserve price—that is, a price below which he is not prepared to sell, a price at which the commodity is preferred to money—then in effect the seller himself enters the market at that price, and when he refuses to sell he is in a way buying back his own goods. It is common at auctions for the sellers to have reserve prices. Even the farmer who takes eggs to market may decide to take them back for his own consumption rather than sell them if the price is very low.

In certain markets some people may be either buyers or sellers, as opportunity occurs. This would be true of speculators in the various commodity markets. Not only have they a reserve price below which they are unwilling to sell, but if the price falls below this they may become buyers. The higher the price, the more they are willing to sell; the lower the price, the more they are prepared to buy. It is thus possible to compile for such a person a combined supply and demand schedule. Assume that the speculator is operating on the stock exchange, and, for the sake of simplicity, assume further that he is interested only in the ordinary shares of the Alpha-Beta Manufacturing Co., Ltd., his combined supply and demand schedule for these shares might be as shown in Table XXVI.

Table XXVI

A Combined Supply and Demand Schedule (2)

Price	Quantity bought or sold + = Bought — = Sold
£	
0.80	+1,000
0.85	+ 450
0.90	+ 250
0.95	+ 100
1.00	0
1.05	— 50
1.10	— 200
1.15	— 400
1.20	— 700

This combined supply and demand schedule can be represented graphically in Fig. 28 on p. 193. Thus it becomes possible to represent both supply and demand by a single curve. The supply curve then becomes merely a part of the demand curve reversed.

IV. THE CONCEPT OF ELASTICITY

11. Elasticity of demand

By elasticity of demand or supply is meant the degree of responsiveness of demand or supply respectively to changes of price. If a slight

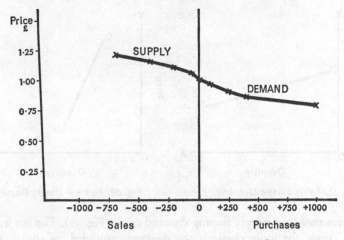

Fig. 28. A Combined Supply and Demand Curve.

change in price causes a big change in the quantity demanded, then demand is said to be elastic. If, however, a fairly considerable change in price makes little difference to the quantity demanded, then demand is said to be inelastic. Demand is perfectly inelastic if the same quantity is demanded whatever the price.

Elasticity determines the shape of the demand curve. If demand is perfectly elastic the demand curve will be a straight line parallel to the base line (Fig. 29). If demand is perfectly inelastic the demand curve

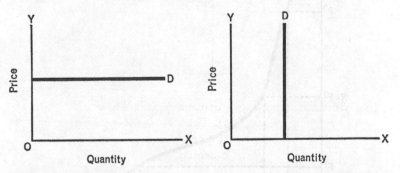

Fig. 29. Perfectly Elastic Demand.   Fig. 30. Perfectly Inelastic Demand.

will be a straight line at right angles to the base and parallel to OY (Fig. 30). Between these two extremes are an infinite number of possibilities. A fairly elastic demand will be represented by a gradually sloping demand curve (Fig. 31). A fairly inelastic demand will be

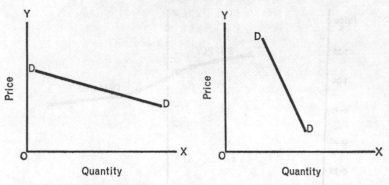

Fig. 31. Fairly Elastic Demand.　　　Fig. 32. Fairly Inelastic Demand.

represented by a steeply sloping demand curve (Fig. 32). The less steep the curve, the more elastic is the demand, provided, of course, the curves to be compared are drawn on graphs with identical price and quantity scales. Probably there is no commodity for which the elasticity of demand is the same at all prices, and most demand curves will show different elasticities over different parts of their lengths (Fig. 33). This demand curve shows that at low prices up to OP^1 demand is inelastic, but between prices OP^1 and OP^2 demand is elastic, becoming inelastic again at high prices over OP^2. Reading from the graph, it can

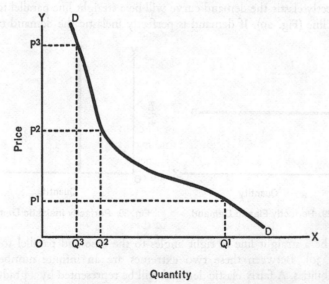

Fig. 33. A Demand Curve with Varying Elasticity.

be seen that when the curve is steep, as between prices OP^2 and OP^3, there is little change (OQ^2 to OQ^3) in the amount demanded, and so demand is inelastic: whereas when the curve has a more gradual slope, as between the prices OP^1 and OP^2, there is a considerable change in the quantity demanded (OQ^1 to OQ^2), and so demand is elastic between these prices.[1]

Elasticity of demand and change of supply. If demand is elastic an increase in supply will result in a large increase in the quantity demanded,

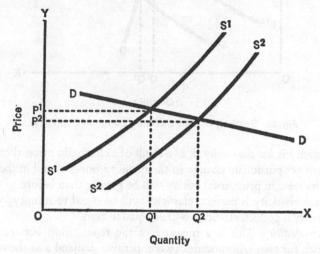

Fig. 34. Elasticity of Demand and Change of Supply (1).

but a small change in price (Fig. 34). If demand is inelastic an increase in supply will result in a small increase in the quantity demanded, but a big fall in price (Fig. 35).

12. Measurement of elasticity of demand

If a change in the price of a commodity brings about a proportionate change in the quantity demanded, then the elasticity of demand is considered to be *equal to unity*. In such cases there is no change in total expenditure on the commodity.

Elasticity is *greater than unity* if, as a result of a change in price, there is a more than proportionate change in the quantity bought. In the case of an increase in price, total outlay on the commodity will be less than before.

[1] The reader must beware of assuming from these illustrations that the *degree of elasticity* is the same for any point on a straight line "curve."

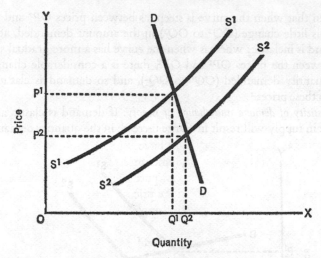

Fig. 35. Elasticity of Demand and Change of Supply (2).

Elasticity is *less than unity* if, as a result of a change in price, there is a less than proportionate change in the quantity bought, and in the case of an increase in price, total outlay will be greater than before.

When elasticity is perfect, elasticity will be equal to infinity; when inelasticity is perfect, elasticity will be equal to zero.

Cross-elasticity. This is a measure of the relationship between the demands for two commodities in competitive demand and shows the effect of a change in the price of one commodity on the demand for the other. An important special case of cross-elasticity is income elasticity of demand, which measures the change in the quantity bought resulting from 1 per cent change in income.

13. Influence of time on elasticity of demand

In the short period a fall in price may have little effect on demand, as it may take time for a change of price to take effect. There are several reasons why this may be so:

(*i*) It may be some time before all consumers become aware of the change in price.

(*ii*) If it is thought that price is likely to fall further, consumers will not increase their purchases at once.

(*iii*) From habit people may have become accustomed to buying a certain assortment of goods and so may be reluctant to change. This may be more important in the case of an increase in price. During a period of inflation those people whose incomes have risen proportionately less than prices may be unwilling to accept a lower standard of living and so, hoping the inflationary condition is only temporary, they may draw upon past savings in order to be able to obtain the same quantity of goods as before the rise in prices took place.

(*iv*) Some goods are durable, and consumers will obviously not replace them until they are worn out, even if their price has fallen.

(*v*) In the case of complementary commodities, jointly demanded, a fall in price of one of them will have little effect if the price of the other rises by a greater amount. Sometimes, in order to take advantage of a fall in price, it is necessary to purchase other commodities. For example, to benefit from a fall in the price of electricity, a householder would have to install more electrical appliances.

14. The basis of elasticity of demand

A number of factors influence the responsiveness of demand to changes of price:

(*i*) *The possibility of substitution.* The most important influence on elasticity of demand is whether there are close substitutes for the commodity. The closer the substitutes, the more elastic is likely to be the demand for the commodity, but the substitute must be within the same price range. From the point of view of use, a Rolls-Royce may be a perfect substitute for a small car, but economically it is no substitute at all, for even a very large change in the price of the small car will have no effect on the demand for large expensive cars. The demand for cocoa is elastic because fairly close substitutes for it exist at approximately the same price. If there are no close substitutes within the same price range the demand for a commodity is likely to be inelastic.

(*ii*) *The degree of necessity.* Whether goods are luxuries or necessaries is not therefore the chief determinant of elasticity of demand. Indeed, the demand for some expensive luxury goods may be very inelastic, not because they are luxuries but rather because they lack close substitutes. Similarly, the demand for bread and potatoes is inelastic because they have no close substitutes within the same price range and not because they are necessaries. If there are close substitutes it matters little whether the commodity is a necessary or a luxury, but if there are no good substitutes the extent to which the commodity is a necessary may then affect the elasticity of demand for it.

(*iii*) *Consumers' incomes.* Generally, the higher a person's income, the more inelastic will be his demand for commodities. The demand of a millionaire for all commodities may be quite unaffected by any changes of price. For most people, however, a choice has to be made, and choice becomes more exacting the lower the person's income. Redistribution of income in favour of people in the lower-income groups will tend, therefore, to make demand for some commodities more inelastic (that is, those things more particularly demanded by such people) and for other things more elastic (that, is those things desired by people in the higher income groups).

(*iv*) *Cheap commodities*. The smaller the proportion of total income expended on a commodity, the more inelastic will be the demand for it. For example, the price of a box of matches or a newspaper might rise considerably before it had much effect on the demand for it.

(*v*) *Habit*. It has already been noted that once certain habits of expenditure have been formed, they may be sufficiently strong for a time to offset the effect of changes in price over a certain range. This has been particularly noticeable in the case of tobacco, for though the price has been enormously increased by taxation, the demand for it has remained almost unchanged. The demand for tobacco, obviously a luxury, has proved to be fairly inelastic, partly because the smoking habit is strong, and partly also because there is no close substitute for tobacco.

15. Elasticity of demand and total income

If a small quantity of a commodity is supplied its price will be higher than if a larger quantity were supplied. How much the price of a commodity rises as its quantity is reduced depends, as already seen, on the elasticity of demand for it. It is of interest to notice how the total income of suppliers will be affected by changes in the quantity supplied. This income will be shown by the area of the rectangle formed by the length representing quantity and the breadth representing price, since total income = price × quantity (Fig. 36).

For example, if DAD represents the demand curve for a commodity and A the point at which the supply curve cuts the demand curve, then OQ is the quantity supplied, and OP will be the price at which this quantity can be sold. Total income of suppliers will then be OQ (quantity) × OP (price)—that is, the rectangle $QOPA$.

Consider now the effect of a change in the quantity supplied. Suppose that the supply is increased from the quantity OQ^1 to the quantity OQ^2, and that demand is elastic (Fig. 37). It is clear that the expansion of output more than balances the fall in price for the rectangle Q^2OP^2B is greater in area than the rectangle Q^1OP^1A. When

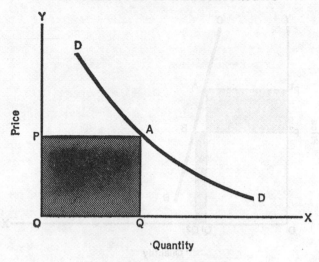

Fig. 36. Total Income.

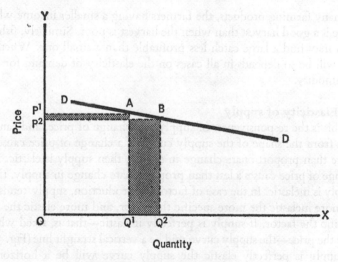

Fig. 37. Total Income with Elastic Demand.

demand is elastic an increase in the quantity supplied will increase the total income of suppliers. If, however, demand is inelastic the greater quantity can be sold only after a large fall in price, and so the total income of suppliers is less than before, as a comparison of the two rectangles Q^1OP^1A and Q^2OP^2B shows (Fig. 38). This is probably true

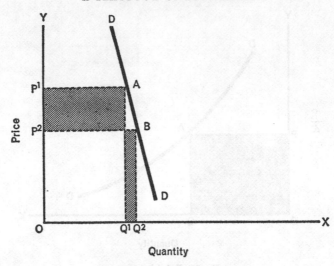

Fig. 38. Total Income with Inelastic Demand.

of many farming products, the farmers having a smaller income when there is a good harvest than when the harvest is poor. Similarly, fishermen may find a large catch less profitable than a small one. Whether this will be so depends in all cases on the elasticity of demand for the commodity.

16. Elasticity of supply

This is the responsiveness of supply to a change of price, and can be seen from the shape of the supply curve. If a change of price causes a more than proportionate change in supply, then supply is elastic. If a change of price causes a less than proportionate change in supply, then supply is inelastic. In the case of factors of production, supply tends to be more inelastic the more specific the factor, and more elastic the less specific the factor. If supply is perfectly inelastic—that is, fixed whatever the price—the supply curve will be a vertical straight line (Fig. 39). If supply is perfectly elastic the supply curve will be a horizontal straight line (Fig. 40).

These, however, are extreme cases. The greater the degree of inelasticity, the steeper will be the slope of the curve. Elasticity may vary over different parts of the same supply curve (Fig. 41). Differences in the steepness of the slope of the curve, however, do not necessarily indicate differences in elasticity. For example, the elasticity of any straight line passing through O, whatever may be its slope, is the same—unity.

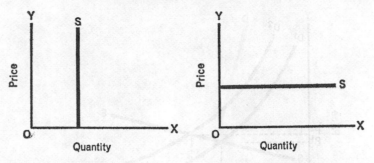

Fig. 39. Perfectly Inelastic Supply.   Fig. 40. Perfectly Elastic Supply.

Fig. 41. A Supply Curve with Varying Elasticity.

Elasticity of supply determines the effect of change of demand on prices. If supply is fairly elastic an increase of demand will bring about a big increase in the quantity supplied, but only a small increase in price (Fig. 42).

If supply is fairly inelastic an increase in demand will bring about only a small increase in the quantity supplied, but will cause a big rise in price (Fig. 43).

The more elastic the supply, the less variable will be the price.

Time has a greater influence on elasticity of supply than on elasticity of demand. In the short period, supply may be fixed, and it may take some time for an industry to adjust itself to a change of output. Elas-

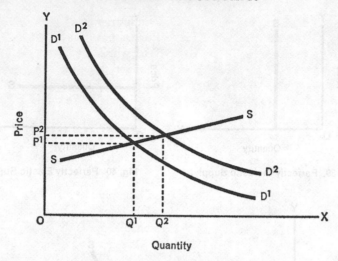

Fig. 42. Elasticity of Supply and Change of Demand (1).

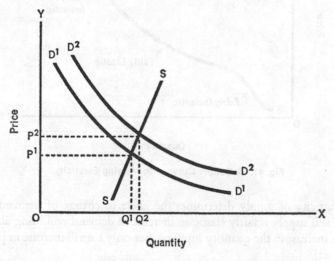

Fig. 43. Elasticity of Supply and Change of Demand (2).

ticity of supply will therefore depend on the time it takes an industry to make this adjustment. Supply will be increased by existing firms expanding their output, and by new firms being drawn into the industry. Supply will be reduced by existing firms contracting their output, and by some firms leaving the industry. The expansion or contraction of output is easier in some industries than others. In some kinds of fruit-growing, for example, at least two years must elapse before there is any yield from new plants; whisky requires seven years to mature, and vintage wines much longer than that. Elasticity of supply depends on the ease with which changes in output can be accomplished.

V. PRICE CONTROL

17. The price mechanism

Demand, supply and price, then, depend on one another, and the equilibrium price equates demand with supply. It has already been seen that all goods are scarce relative to the demand for them, and the price mechanism is one method which enables goods to be distributed among the people who want them. Changes in either supply or demand will be reflected by changes in price, an increase in supply or a falling off in demand bringing about a fall in price, and a decrease in supply or an increase in demand causing price to rise. An increase in demand tends to make entrepreneurs increase supply, just as a fall in demand will make them reduce supply. The price mechanism not only distributes "scarce" goods among consumers but also distributes "scarce" factors of production among entrepreneurs.

The demand of consumers encourages entrepreneurs to expand supply, and this stimulates the demand for factors of production. The demand of consumers, therefore, through the price mechanism, determines what assortment of goods shall be produced, how much of this and how much of that. Under perfect competition the sovereignty of consumers is complete, and goods and resources go where they are most in demand. Furthermore, no elaborate administrative machinery is required to operate the price mechanism, and yet by means of it a vast assortment of goods and services can be produced and distributed in a way which people as a whole prefer. Adjustments to changes in conditions of supply or in intensity of demand can also be made without administrative action. These are its main advantages. On the other hand, it is pointed out that in actual conditions the market is imperfect, and in any case the demand of consumers is not the best way of determining what shall be produced, for it may result in the production of large quantities of, say, tobacco and only small quantities of, say, butter. The alternative is for a State planning committee to decide what shall be produced, but this requires a system of controls to ensure that industries obtain the share of resources apportioned to them.

18. Price control and rationing

In conclusion, it will be useful briefly to consider some aspects of price control. The State may fix prices for any one of a number of reasons. It may be considered desirable to protect buyers in general or the poorer section of the community, and in this case maximum prices will be fixed. It may be that the aim is to protect agricultural producers against a fall in income due to bumper harvests (*see* Para. 15), and so minimum prices will be fixed. Other weapons of price control are taxation (to raise prices) and subsidies (to reduce prices). The purpose of raising prices by taxation may be to check the consumption of certain commodities considered to be harmful, or in order to check imports in the case of balance-of-payments difficulties. Subsidies may be imposed on certain foodstuffs in an attempt to keep down the cost of living or to encourage output.

Consider now the effect of the State's fixing of maximum prices for consumer goods. Such action will be necessary only if the equilibrium price, as determined by supply and demand, is considered to be too high. Let *DD* and *SS* be the appropriate supply and demand curves for

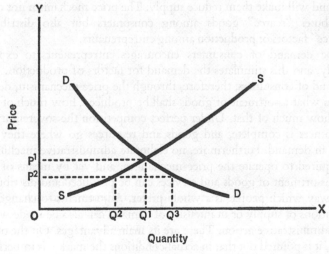

Fig. 44. Price Control and Rationing.

the commodity (Fig. 44). The equilibrium price will be OP^1, and the quantity supplied will be OQ^1. Assume that the State now fixes OP^2 as the maximum price. At this price the quantity demanded will be OQ^3, but suppliers will now be willing to put on the market only the quantity OQ^2. The quantity demanded at this controlled price will be OQ^3, and this will exceed the quantity supplied by Q^2Q^3. Even if the State subsidised suppliers in order to call forth as large a supply as was forthcoming under equilibrium conditions, the quantity demanded will still exceed, by Q^1Q^3, the quantity supplied. If no further action is taken by the State retailers will now find that they have insufficient supplies to meet the demand of their customers. There will be a shortage of the commodity, with the result that customers will be dependent on the favour of retailers, goods not being offered for sale to everyone who wishes to buy. If prices are controlled below the equilibrium, either the State or the retailers will have to introduce some form of rationing.

RECOMMENDATIONS FOR FURTHER READING

K. E. Boulding: *Economic Analysis*, Chapter 7.
A. Marshall: *Principles of Economics*, Book V, Chapters 5, 6.
H. Henderson: *Supply and Demand*.
G. J. Stigler: *Theory of Price*, Chapters 5–8.

QUESTIONS

1. What is meant by elasticity of demand? Why is the demand for the exports of the United Kingdom, in general, more elastic than its demand for imports? (NC)

2. Consider the likely effects of the following on the supply of, demand for and price of houses: (a) a fall in building society interest rates; (b) a rise in bricklayers' wages; (c) a rise in house rents; (d) an increase in the real national income; and (e) a reduction in the price of building plots. (Southampton)

3. What kind of price changes would you expect to see in the market for (a) wool and mutton, (b) butter and margarine, if the demand for both wool and butter increased sharply? (RSA)

4. Consider the different factors which may influence the effective demand for a commodity. When is the elasticity of demand greater than unity? (RSA)

5. Show with examples, the practical importance of a large and of a small elasticity of demand. (CIS)

6. Explain how the income elasticity of demand for a product can lead to an increase in demand even though the price of that product rises. (CIS)

7. (a) State briefly what is meant by "joint" and "composite" demand.

(b) What is elasticity of demand?

(c) What does an economist mean when he says that over short periods demand may be more elastic than supply, while over long periods supply may be more elastic than demand? (ACCA)

8. Define and explain the following economic terms: (a) elasticity of demand; (b) joint supply. (IMTA)

9. It has been said that the keynote of economic analysis is attention to the nature and working of the price mechanism. Explain this point of view, indicating carefully what is meant by the term "price-mechanism" in this context. (IHA)

10. The following table shows the demand schedule for commodity X:

Price per unit	Quantity demanded
12p	600
10p	700
8p	800

(a) define elasticity of demand;

(b) calculate the elasticity of demand for each price reduction;

(c) explain whether the demand for X is elastic or inelastic;

(d) explain whether and, if so, how (c) could be answered by some method other than calculating elasticities? (IB)

11. Define "elasticity of supply." Why might one expect the elasticity of supply of a commodity to be greater in the long run than in the short run? (GCE)

12. What determines the elasticity of supply of wheat: (a) in the short run, and (b) in the long run? (GCE)

13. Discuss the merits and demerits of a price system as a means of allocating resources. (GCE)

14. Explain the concept "elasticity of supply with respect to price." Why might supply elasticities be lower in the short run than in the long run? (GCE)

15. What determines the extent of the price change that follows any given change in supply? (DPA)

16. Illustrate some of the defects in the price system which in your view should be remedied by State action. (Degree)

17. "The so-called supply curve is simply a part of the total demand curve." (Wicksteed.) Explain and examine this contention. (Degree)

18. Describe and discuss critically the problems involved in attempting to measure the elasticity of demand for a product. (Degree)

CHAPTER 12

THE BASIS OF DEMAND

I. MARGINAL UTILITY

An understanding of the technique of supply and demand provides the key to the solution of many problems in economics, but it is not a master key, and it requires to be supplemented by a second tool—the marginal analysis. By means of this it becomes possible to understand the basis upon which demand and supply curves are constructed. It is the purpose of this chapter to investigate the basis of demand: the following chapters will then deal with the basis of supply.

1. The margin

What, then, is meant in economics by the margin? The marginal unit of anything is the last to be added to a supply or the first to be taken away from it. If a student already possesses three books on economics and is contemplating buying a fourth, this fourth book might be considered to be his "marginal" volume. Whether he buys it or not will depend on whether he thinks that the additional benefit to be derived from this fourth book is worth the price he will have to pay for it—that is, he considers its *marginal* worth to him. If a farmer has fifty acres of land under wheat a rise in the price of wheat may tempt him to devote another acre to wheat. This additional acre is the *marginal* unit. Alternatively, if he had decided to withdraw one acre from wheat cultivation the acre that ceased to grow wheat would be the *marginal* unit.

Marginal considerations concern the smallest possible increase or decrease in the stock or supply of anything. For this reason this branch of economics is sometimes called *microeconomics*. It is always marginal considerations that determine whether a person will add to his existing stock of a commodity. The marginal significance of any commodity, therefore, depends on how much of it is already possessed. If a student already possesses a number of books on economics the marginal significance to him of books on economics is likely to be low; if he has only one book on economics the marginal significance of such books may be high—unless he is a student of chemistry and has no interest whatever in economics! The margin is obviously not fixed, for an increase in one's supply will simply push the margin farther away, just as a decrease in one's supply will bring the margin nearer. A change in price will have a similar effect, a fall in price pushing the margin farther away and a rise in price bringing it nearer. It is therefore possible to speak of the marginal unit of a supply. Similarly, the term margin, can be used in connection with cost, income or production, so that we can speak of marginal cost, marginal income and the marginal product.

The marginal unit is thus not a particular unit or any particular type or quality of unit. Some ambiguity arises from the use of the word in such phrases as "the margin of cultivation." Official use of the term "marginal land" tended to make some people apply it to land of a particular grade of fertility, farmers being urged to expand production by cultivating marginal land. But what is marginal at one time is not necessarily marginal at another, and if present marginal land is cultivated this does not get rid of the margin but merely pushes it farther away. The development of the United States in the nineteenth century gradually pushed the frontier farther to the west, but the frontier still remained, although its geographical position kept changing.

2. Utility

As used in economics, the term utility may be defined as the amount of satisfaction to be derived from a commodity or service *at a particular time*. The utility of bread is the satisfaction to be obtained from consuming bread at a particular moment of time. There are two points to note. In the first place, the utility of a commodity has nothing to do with its usefulness; it may or may not be useful, though it must yield satisfaction. Nor has utility any ethical connotation. If we want something whether it is good or bad for us, it possesses utility for us. The ordinary meaning of the word must therefore be put aside. It would perhaps have been better if Wicksteed's term, "significance," had been adopted instead of "utility."

The second point to be emphasised is its applicability to something *at a particular time*. A commodity does not possess a specific amount of utility. To a starving man bread will have great utility, whereas for a man who has just dined well, bread, for the moment, may possess no utility at all. If the starving man is given a good meal bread will also cease for a time to have utility for him. Utility therefore depends on the individual's own *subjective* estimate of the amount of satisfaction to be obtained from something. Thus there is *no such thing as intrinsic value*, for the same commodity has at the same time different utilities for different people, and even for the same person the utility of a thing is not constant but differs at different times and in different circumstances.

3. Diminishing marginal utility

The marginal utility of a good will thus be the amount of satisfaction to be obtained from the possession of a little bit more of it, or, alternatively, the loss of satisfaction due to giving up the smallest possible amount of it. The demands of two different people for a commodity may differ for two reasons: (i) they may differ in their estimate of its desirability; (ii) they may already possess different quantities of it. Assuming that no change takes place in the strength of an individual's desire for it, its marginal utility to him will vary with the quantity possessed. The student with only one book on his subject has a high marginal utility for such books. When he acquires a second book marginal utility falls, and after acquiring a third, marginal utility falls again. With each additional book he obtains, the marginal utility of such books for him successively declines. Eventually a time will arrive when their marginal utility will be so low that an additional volume will have no utility at all for him. The marginal utility of a commodity therefore declines as one's supply of it increases until satiety is reached. It would be exactly the same with a homogeneous commodity such as tea, each unit being identical, for marginal utility depends on the amount possessed. As a hungry man consumes more and more food, the marginal utility of food gradually declines for him. It is therefore the *marginal* utility of a thing, and not its *total* utility, that is important economically, for a person's demand for anything depends on the marginal utility of the commodity to him. Marginal utility can be applied to money, its marginal utility being the satisfaction to be obtained from the expenditure of one more unit of it. The law of Diminishing Marginal Utility is a general law of life, as in fact it applies to everything.

Since utility is the strength of the satisfaction to be derived from a thing, it cannot be measured. Assume, however, for the moment that the utility of tea for Mrs Gamp can be measured in units of utility.

Table XXVII shows that for Mrs Gamp the marginal utility of a first packet of tea stands at "60 units of utility." After purchasing one packet of tea its marginal utility falls to 42 and with each successive packet purchased the marginal utility of the commodity falls, until for her eighth packet of tea its marginal utility has declined to seven units of utility. Each additional packet of tea has less utility than the preceding one, showing that as one's stock increases marginal utility declines. Another method of illustrating the Law of Diminishing Marginal Utility is to consider how much Mrs Gamp would be willing to pay for each successive packet of tea. For example, for the first packet she might be willing to pay 30p, for the second 20p, for the third 15p, for the fourth 12p, for the fifth 10p, for the sixth 8p, for the seventh 6p, for the eighth 4p and for the ninth 2p.

Table XXVII

Marginal Utility

Packets of tea	Total utility (units of utility)	Marginal utility (units of utility)
1	60	60
2	102	42
3	132	30
4	156	24
5	176	20
6	191	15
7	201	10
8	208	7

The concept of diminishing marginal utility was developed about the same time (1871) by William Stanley Jevons in England and by Karl Menger in Austria, each working independently of the other. It is usual to couple with these two names that of Leon Walras, the Swiss economist, although his work was not published until 1874.[1] Jevons, however, used the rather misleading term "final utility" for marginal utility.

4. The origin

In the above example concerning tea the minimum unit taken was one packet. Smaller units might have been taken, but a very small amount may be of little use. Clearly, if the quantity possessed is too small to be of effective use it cannot have much utility, and an additional amount may then have greater utility than the first unit. In fact, the Law of Diminishing Marginal Utility begins to operate only after a certain point, called the *Origin*. Until the origin is reached—that is, until the minimum amount of the commodity that can be used

[1] See Sir A. Gray: *The Development of Economic Doctrine*, p. 341 n. The author also shows that Gossen, in a work published in 1854, was the first to propound a marginal theory.

effectively has been obtained—successive increments will show increasing utility.

5. Diminishing marginal utility is the basis of demand schedules

In Para. 3 the diminishing marginal utility of tea to a housewife, Mrs Gamp, was considered. She was willing, it will be remembered, to pay 30p for her first packet, but for a ninth she would only pay 2p. It can be assumed that if she is willing to pay 30p for one packet and 20p for a second, then if the price is 20p she will purchase two packets. Similarly, if she is prepared to pay 15p for a third packet she will buy three if the price is 15p. The following table illustrates this situation:

Table XXVIII

Diminishing Marginal Utility

Price	Amount purchased (*packets of tea*)
(*pence*)	
30	1
20	2
15	3
12	4
10	5
8	6
6	7
4	8
2	9

It is clear that this table is, in fact, Mrs Gamp's demand schedule for tea. If she estimates the marginal utility of tea at 30p, that is the price she is prepared to pay for it; if she considers the marginal utility of tea to be worth only 2p she will pay no more than that amount. For example, if the price is 12p, and assuming she has no tea in stock, she will purchase one packet (for 12p), because she assesses its marginal utility at 30p; she will purchase a second packet because she now assesses its marginal utility at 15p, and a fourth because the price she pays (12p) is still equal to what she considers its marginal utility to be worth. If the price is 12p she will not, however, increase her purchase of tea beyond four packets, because the marginal utility of a fifth packet is less than the price of the tea. No rational person will pay a price higher than his estimate of the money value of the marginal utility of the commodity.

6. Consumer's surplus

Consider once more Mrs Gamp's purchase of four packets of tea at 12p per packet. She was willing to pay 30p for the first packet, whereas in fact she paid only 12p for it. Similarly, she was willing to pay 20p for the second packet, but actually paid only 12p. Again she obtained the third packet for 12p, and would have been willing to pay 15p. Her actual expenditure on tea was 48p, but she obtained four packets of tea which she considered to be worth 30p, 20p, 15p and 12p respectively—a total of 77p. Therefore she obtained 77p worth of satisfaction for 48p—a surplus of 29p. This is known as Consumer's Surplus.

Let us assume that a new book is published at £4.50. Those people who consider that the amount of satisfaction they will derive from it not to be worth this price will obviously not buy it. Of those who buy a copy some would have been willing to pay more than £4.50. Thus a person who would have been prepared to pay £5.50 for the book can be considered to have obtained a consumer's surplus of £1.00 worth of satisfaction.

7. Equilibrium distribution of expenditure

It was seen that all things are relatively scarce, and that more of one thing can be enjoyed only by having less of another. A choice has therefore to be made, and this implies that each individual has a scale of preferences, a sort of list of his wants arranged in the order in which they press upon him. Though utility is not measurable, wants, however, can be arranged in order of preference. We can say that we prefer one thing to another, though we cannot calculate exactly the extent of this preference. It is clear now that the order in which commodities and services are arranged on such a scale is determined by their *marginal* utilities, and not by their *total* utilities. Bread and water being necessaries of life, have a high total utility, and yet may occupy low positions on a person's scale of preferences because their marginal utility is low. For a consumer has to decide not between, say, bread and water, on the one hand, and, say, cake and milk, on the other, but between a little more bread and a little less cake, or a little less bread and a little more cake.

Assume that a housewife goes to the market to purchase three commodities, *A*, *B* and *C*, and obtains the following quantities of each:

A	B	C
10 units	7 units	4 units

To maximise her total satisfaction she must buy so much of each commodity that its price in each case is exactly equal to her estimate of the money-value of its marginal utility. This must be so, because she has decided that the tenth unit of A stands higher on her scale of preferences than an eighth unit of B or a fifth unit of C; that a seventh unit of B is to be preferred to an eleventh unit of A or a fifth unit of C; that a fourth unit of C is preferable to an eleventh unit of A or an eighth unit of B. If the marginal utilities of these three commodities were not equal she could increase her total satisfaction by buying more of one and less of another. When deciding how much of each to buy it was their respective marginal utilities in relation to their prices that she considered—whether she should buy a little more of A and a little less of B or C, or a little more of B and a little less of A or C, etc. If she has no motive for changing the quantities of these three commodities that she has bought she will have achieved an equilibrium distribution of her expenditure. Perfect equilibrium can, however, be obtained only if all three commodities are capable of being divided into the smallest possible units.

Where there are many competing demands for a commodity, the more urgent will be fulfilled first. An increase in supply and a lower price not only allow more of the commodity to be used for existing purposes but also enable new uses for it to be developed. If electricity is dear its use may be restricted to lighting; if it becomes cheaper its use may be extended to cooking; if it becomes cheaper still it may come to be used for all kinds of other appliances—radiators, vacuum cleaners, washing machines, etc.

8. Some criticisms of the Law of Diminishing Marginal Utility

The following are some of the main criticisms that have been levelled against the concept of diminishing marginal utility:

(i) *"The more one has the more one wants."* There are some things the marginal utility of which increases as one's supply increases. (This is, of course, quite apart from the fact that marginal utility in all cases increases until the origin is reached.) Supporters of the theory of diminishing marginal utility say that such cases are rare, but their opponents believe that they are common enough to make diminishing marginal utility far from being a general law. Instead of becoming satiated as more of something is enjoyed, the desire for more grows, so that the more one has of some things the more of them one wants. This may often be true of money, its accumulation merely increasing the desire to accumulate more. It is also true of anything for which a taste has to be cultivated, whether it be for fine wines or fine art, travel or sport. If acquisition stimulates the collecting instinct marginal utility increases even more strongly, whether the objects collected be postage stamps, gramophone records or pictures. Strictly, however, as a taste for something is being developed, a change of taste is taking place, and this creates a new condition of demand. In other words, the person who at one time did not care for Beethoven is not really the same person (economically, at least) as the one who has later developed a taste for Beethoven's music.

(ii) *Habit and impulse.* Much expenditure tends to become habitual, for people do not trouble to weigh carefully the marginal utilities of all the things that they buy, especially where the purchase of cheap, trivial articles is concerned. Few people, too, at some time or another have failed to resist an impulse to buy something which at a more rational moment they would have refused. Economists, however, assume that customers always behave rationally.

(iii) *Large indivisible commodities.* The Law of Diminishing Marginal Utility assumes that all goods can be divided into small units, so that one's supply can be increased or reduced by the tiniest amount, whereas many durable goods are large and indivisible, as for example houses, furniture, motor cars. There are, however, many people who buy such things on hire purchase and so pay by instalments. In a sense, therefore, if payment for a television set is spread over one hundred weeks each weekly instalment represents the purchase of one-hundredth of it.

II. VALUE

9. The problem of value

At one time writers on economics devoted a great deal of attention to the question of value. Why, they asked, should the price of one thing be £2 and that of another only £1? We have already seen that price depends on the interaction of the forces of supply and demand. The early economists, however, generally ignored the influence of demand and related price solely to cost of production. In the short period, once an article is offered for sale in the market its cost of production has no direct bearing on its price. Whatever it may have cost to produce, no consumer will be willing to buy it unless its marginal utility to him coincides with its price. If a speculative builder has erected a house at a cost of £10,000 he will not be able to sell it for that sum unless he can find someone whose marginal utility for such houses is £10,000. How much he sells the house for will, of course, determine his future building activity. If he finds he can sell it for £10,400 he may immediately set about building another similar house, but if he can sell it for no more than £9,600 he will cease building such houses. Costs of production, therefore, affect price indirectly through supply—high cost curtailing supply, and low cost tending to expand supply. In the short period, however, value depends entirely on marginal utility, which is the basis of demand.

10. Early theories of value

It will be useful to glance briefly at some of the early theories of value. They are essentially similar, usually being different forms of the Labour Theory of Value. To Adam Smith there were two kinds of value, which he named "value in use" (this depending on the utility of the commodity), and "value in exchange" (this determining the price at which it could be sold). He found it necessary to make this distinction in order to explain the so-called "paradox of value," which greatly troubled early writers on economics. Water had great value in use, but generally a low exchange value, whereas diamonds had much less value in use, but had a high exchange value. It is clear, after considering marginal utility, that this paradox arose because the writers did not distinguish between *total* and *marginal* utility. In countries such as Great Britain, where water is plentiful and can be used for purposes low on the scale of preferences, the total utility of water is great, though its marginal utility is often low. In the case of diamonds the supply is relatively small, and so marginal utility tends to be high, though the total utility of diamonds is small. After noting this paradox, Adam Smith explained value in terms of "value in use." Therefore, the value of a thing depended on the amount of labour expended upon its production, for he said that it was "natural" that an article the making of which required two days' labour should have double the value of another article that was the result of only one day's labour. "Labour is the real measure of the exchange value of all commodities," he said.

Ricardo also recognised two forms of value, and agreed with his predecessor that the value of most things depended on the amount of labour required to produce them, but that there was another group of things, such as works of art and other rare articles, the exchange value of which depended on their scarcity. The supply of goods in the first category, he thought, could be increased "almost without any assignable limit," whereas the supply of goods in the second category could not be increased. It is not surprising that the Labour Theory of Value was eagerly seized upon by writers seeking support for political views. Karl Marx and his followers reiterated the view that the value of a commodity depended on the amount of labour required for its production, in order to be able to assert that the worker was entitled to the entire fruit of his labour. According to Marx, a thing can have value only if it is a product of human labour.

The Cost of Production Theory of Value as enunciated by J. S. Mill is really a refinement of the Labour Theory of Value. According to this theory, the value of any commodity is determined by its cost of production, including, of course, labour costs, but also including the profit of the entrepreneur.

11. Some criticisms of the early theories of value

The following are some of the main criticisms of the early theories of value:

(i) *The difficulty of measuring labour or cost of production.* How is the amount of labour required in the production of a commodity to be measured? Adam Smith used time as his measuring rod, but workmen are not all of equal efficiency, and the less skilled may take longer than the skilled over a particular piece of work, and so put more labour into it. Labour, too, may be misdirected, and an article incapable of fulfilling the purpose for which it was intended can have no value however much labour has gone to its manufacture, for even Marx admits that "nothing can have value without being an object of utility." Marx was aware of both these objections to the labour theory and so he defined the amount of labour required as "socially necessary labour," for, he said, "misdirected labour does not count as labour."

The term "cost of production" is no more precise than "quantity of labour." The cost of producing a commodity depends on a number of factors, differing between one firm and another, and in any case can be considered only in relation to output. The greater the output of a commodity the lower usually is its cost of production.

(ii) *The early theories are not of universal application.* Apart from the special category of scarce goods mentioned by Ricardo, these early theories all fail to explain the value of rare things, such as works of art or antiques. It is a serious weakness of any theory of value if it does not explain the value of all things. The Law of Diminishing Marginal Utility, however, can be applied equally well to rare things as to articles in common use, for all goods are scarce relative to the demand for them, whether they are rare or not.

(*iii*) *The influence of demand is neglected.* The principal reason for the weakness of the early theories of value is that they ignore the influence of demand, while at the same time they explain very inadequately the influence of supply, scarcity being insufficiently stressed. Labour itself is limited in supply, and that explains to some extent why goods are scarce.

III. INDIFFERENCE CURVES

12. The marginal rate of substitution

The problem of what determines value is still far from solved, and unlike J. S. Mill, who thought nothing further was to be said on the subject, there are some economists who doubt whether the problem ever will be settled. At one time the adherents of the Marginal Utility Theory believed that they had found the solution, but diminishing marginal utility is no longer generally accepted as an explanation of demand. More recently it has given way to the concept of the *marginal rate of substitution* and analysis by means of indifference curves.

Because all goods are relatively scarce, everyone has to make a choice between alternatives; therefore it can be assumed that everyone has a scale of preferences. This, it has been seen, it really a scale of marginal utilities. A little more of one thing is preferred to a little more of another. As Marshall said more than half a century ago: "The term, value, is relative and expresses the relation between two things at a particular place and time." Thus, the value of a thing can be regarded as the relation between preferences, for the value of one thing can be measured only in terms of another.

The valuation of one commodity in terms of another (one of which may be money) is known as the Marginal Rate of Substitution. Just so much of a commodity will be purchased in the market as will equate the Marginal Rate of Substitution of that commodity with the price that has to be paid for it.

Changes in price produce two effects:

(*i*) *A substitution effect.* If there are two commodities that are fairly close substitutes for one another, and there is a fall in the price of one of them, the one that has fallen in price will tend to be substituted for the other.

(*ii*) *An income effect.* A fall in the price of a commodity means that it is possible to buy the same quantity as before for a smaller outlay, and this may lead either to the purchase of more of that particular commodity or a quantity of some other commodity. This is similar, therefore, in its effect to an increase in the consumer's income.

13. The construction of indifference curves

Suppose that there are only two commodities available to the consumer—say x and y. If two commodities are considered these can be represented on a two-dimensional diagram. The Scales of Preference of individuals will differ. However, a consumer, Quilp, having the combination $9x+14y$, may be willing to give up without any loss of satisfaction one x for two more of y, and other combinations assumed to yield him equal satisfaction are as follows:

$23x+\ 7y$	$9x+14y$
$20x+\ 8y$	$8x+16y$
$17x+\ 9y$	$7x+18y$
$15x+10y$	$6x+21y$
$13x+11y$	$5x+24y$
$11x+12y$	$4x+27y$
$10x+13y$	$3x+31y$

It will be noticed that as Quilp's supply of either commodity declines its marginal utility increases, and so he is prepared to give up further units of it only in exchange for more of the other commodity. Thus, when he possesses $20x+8y$ he will give up a unit of y only for $3x$, but when he has $6x+21y$ he is prepared to exchange $3y$ for an extra unit of x. Quilp is indifferent between any of these combinations. If plotted on a graph they will form an indifference curve, AA, any point on which shows a combination of x and y equally agreeable to him (Fig. 45).

Clearly, Quilp will prefer the combination $10x+15y$ to any of those given in the above table, because this is obviously better than $9x+14y$. Thus a second table of indifference can now be compiled showing all combinations of x and y that Quilp considers to yield him equal satisfaction to $10x+15y$. This might run as follows:

$24x+\ 8y$	$10x+15y$
$21x+\ 9y$	$9x+17y$
$18x+10y$	$8x+19y$
$16x+11y$	$7x+22y$
$14x+12y$	$6x+25y$
$12x+13y$	$5x+28y$
$11x+14y$	$4x+32y$

A second indifference curve, BB, can now be constructed, and since

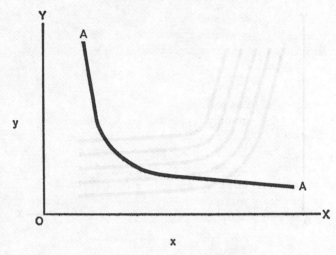

Fig. 45. An Indifference Curve.

any point in the curve *BB* is superior to any point on the curve *AA*, the second curve will fall slightly to the right of the first (Fig. 46).

In similar fashion further indifference curves can be added until a whole series of indifference curves has been drawn (Fig. 47).

Quilp will always prefer a position on a curve farther from *O* than a curve nearer to *O*, because the farther a curve is from *O*, the greater will

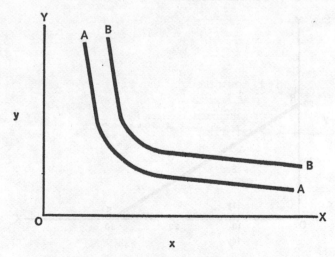

Fig. 46. Indifference Curves.

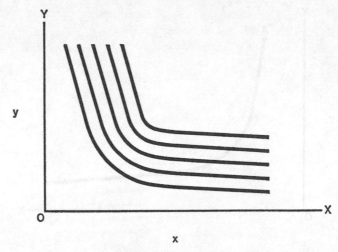

Fig. 47. A Series of Indifference Curves.

be the satisfaction he will obtain. Since, however, he has only a limited amount of money to spend, this will limit his choice and prevent his selecting a curve very far to the right of O. Assume that if he spent the whole of his money on *x* this would give him 30*x*, or if he spent it entirely on *y* it would give him 20*y*, then because of his limited resources his actual choice must lie somewhere along the line *RS* that connects these two extreme choices:

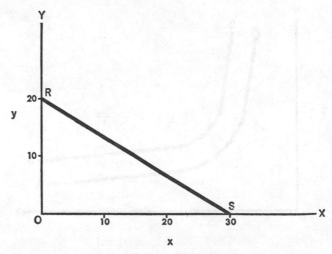

Fig. 48. Limits of Choice.

If Quilp's indifference curves are now superimposed on this diagram the following will be the result:

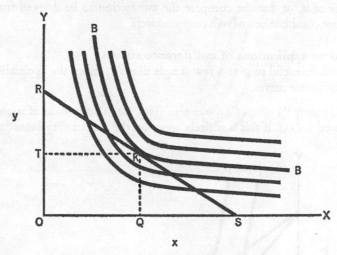

Fig. 49. Choice and Maximum Satisfaction.

Quilp's choice must be at some point on the line *RS*, and to obtain the maximum satisfaction, his choice must also be on the indifference curve farthest from *O*, and this must be the curve *BB*, which just touches *RS* at *K*—that is, the curve to which *RS* is a tangent. Quilp's actual combination of *x* and *y* will therefore be the quantity *OT* of *y*, together with the quantity *OQ* of *x*. If Quilp's demand changes as a result of his receiving an increase in income, or for some other reason, this will move the line *RS* farther away from *O*, and so enable him to move to a higher indifference curve. If the price of *y* rose, this would bring *R* nearer to *O*, reduce the slope of *RS* and bring *K* down to a lower indifference curve.

Indifference curves are therefore useful to illustrate choice between two alternatives. If choice lies between more than two, then *x* can be taken to represent one, and *y* the combined amount of the others. In favour of indifference curves it is claimed that they merely imply that the consumer is capable of balancing against one another different possible combinations of two commodities, so that it is no longer necessary to make the unreal assumption that he can measure in terms of money the utility of each additional increment of a commodity. Whether demand is analysed with the aid of the marginal utility concept or by means of indifference curves, some assumption of human behaviour is required. The main point is: is it more realistic to assume that the individual values a commodity in terms of a little bit more or a little bit less of it, or does he compare the satisfaction to be derived from different combinations of two commodities?

14. Some applications of indifference curves

It will be useful to give a few simple illustrations of the application of indifference curves.

(i) *To show the effect of a rise in price* (Fig. 50). The amount of money possessed is OM. If this is entirely spent on the commodity before the

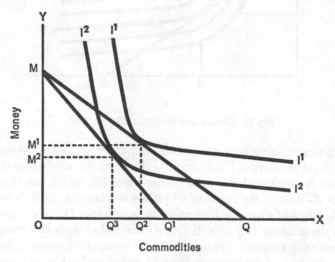

Fig. 50. Effect of a Rise in Price.

rise in price takes place the quantity OQ can be bought. After the rise in price only the quantity OQ^1 can be bought.

Before the rise in price, the maximum satisfaction was obtained by purchasing OQ^2 of the commodity and retaining OM^1 of money, because this was the combination of the commodity and money indicated by the point on MQ at which the indifference curve I^1 was a tangent.

After the rise in price, maximum satisfaction is obtained by purchasing the quantity OQ^3 and retaining OM^2 of money. This combination is on indifference curve I^2, which is nearer the origin, O, than the indifference curve I^1, showing that total satisfaction has been reduced.

(ii) *To show the effect of a fall in income* (Fig. 51). The income at first is OM, and if this is completely spent, the quantity OQ of commodities could be bought. Maximum satisfaction is obtained when OM^2 of income is retained after purchasing OQ^2 of commodities, for this combination is on the consumer's highest indifference curve.

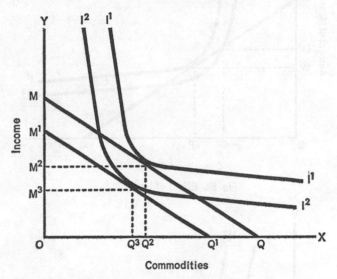

Fig. 51. Effect of a Fall in Income.

Income falls to OM^1, and total purchases cannot now exceed OQ^1. As a result, the highest indifference curve available to this consumer is now I^2. The curve is lower than the curve I^1, and so the consumer has suffered, as one would expect, a loss of satisfaction.

(iii) *To show the effect of rationing on consumer's satisfaction.* Before rationing was introduced, this consumer purchased OQ^1 of the commodity and retained OM^1 of his money. (If he had spent the whole of his money he would have been able to purchase the quantity OQ.)

As a result of rationing he can buy only the quantity OQ^2, but this leaves him with a larger amount of money unspent—namely, OM^2. This combination of money and the commodity is on a lower indifference curve (I^2 instead of I^1) and so, although he has more money to spend on other things, his total satisfaction is less than before. The closer the rational quantity OQ^2 is to the previous quantity bought, OQ^1, the nearer the new indifference curve to the old, and the less the loss of satisfaction.

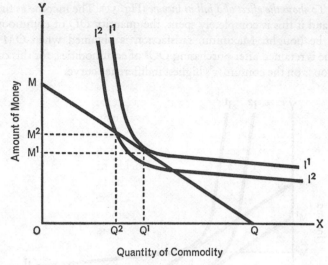

Fig. 52. Effect of Rationing.

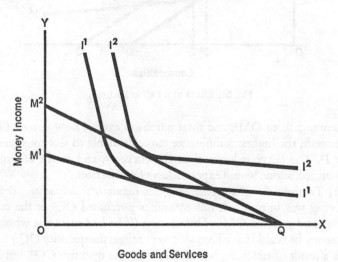

Fig. 53. The Effect of Inflation.

(iv) *To show the effect of inflation.* Assume that the prices of goods and services increase proportionately to income, so that if the entire income is spent, the same quantity of goods and services as before can be bought. Will, then, the satisfaction of the consumer also remain unchanged? The consumer's income increases from OM^1 to OM^2, but this will still buy only the same quantity, OQ, of goods as before. If he purchases the same quantity of goods as before he will have more money left unspent than he had previously, although its value in terms of what it will buy is the same. Nevertheless, this consumer is now on a higher indifference curve, and therefore appears to derive more satisfaction from the disposal of his income. If he had spent his entire income his satisfaction would have remained unchanged, for the quantity of goods he purchased would also have remained exactly the same. However, he has more money left unspent, though this is of only the same real value as the smaller amount left unspent before, but evidently, according to the diagram, it yields him more satisfaction. Experience during the past thirty years of the falling value of money seems to indicate that it is probably true that many—perhaps most—people prefer to have a large money income rather than a smaller money income, even if real income in terms of the goods it will buy is the same in both cases.

It is necessary, however, to warn the reader that some economists object to money being employed as one of the two choices which indifference curves may be used to illustrate on the ground that, unlike other things, money is not wanted for its own sake but only as a medium of exchange. Nevertheless, people have to make a choice between spending and saving.

RECOMMENDATIONS FOR FURTHER READING

A. Marshall: *Principles of Economics*, Book III, Chapter 6.
P. Wicksteed: *Common-sense of Political Economy*, Book I, Chapters 1–3.

For Indifference Curves:
K. E. Boulding: *Economic Analysis*, Chapters 33, 34.

QUESTIONS

1. Define and indicate clearly the relationship between *total utility, marginal utility* and *value*. (RSA)
2. What relation has the amount of labour expended in the production of a commodity to the selling price of that commodity? (AIA.)
3. What is meant by consumer's surplus? (ACCA)
4. Explain and discuss the statement that the price actually paid for a commodity is a money measure of the marginal utility of that commodity. (IB.)
5. "Where we talked of 'marginal utility,' we now talk of 'marginal pre-

ference'; and where we drew curves of 'marginal utility,' we now draw 'indifference curves.'" Explain with diagrams. (CIS)

6. Explain what is meant by consumer's surplus. What are the effects of (a) indirect taxes, and (b) rationing, on consumer's surplus? (IMTA)

7. Explain why water, which is an essential, normally has a low price, while diamonds, which are much less necessary, are expensive. (IB)

8. The table below sets out the total utility (measured in utils) that a consumer expects to derive from varying amounts of two goods A and B. The price per unit of A is 10p and of B (per unit) 5p.

| | Good A | | Good B |
Units	Total utility	Units	Total utility
10	912	30	502
11	1,020	31	560
12	1,080	32	585
13	1,110	33	600
14	1,120	34	610

a) Draw up marginal utility schedules for both goods.

b) How much of good A and good B would the consumer wish to buy?

(c) Explain the reasoning by which you reached your answer to (b), above. (IB)

9. Normally, more of a good will be demanded at a lower than at a higher price. Outline and comment on any theory which helps to explain why this is so. (GCE)

10. What factors determine the demand for washing machines? (GCE)

11. How does rationing of consumer goods affect the satisfaction that the consumer can obtain in the expenditure of his income? (Degree)

12. In what ways has the use of indifference curves aided economic analysis? (Degree)

13. What does the indifference technique contribute to the analysis of demand? (Degree)

CHAPTER 13

THE BASIS OF SUPPLY:
UNDER PERFECT COMPETITION

I. MEANING OF PERFECT COMPETITION

1. The application of the margin to supply

In the previous chapter the concept of the margin was used to explain the basis of demand curves; the marginal analysis will next be used to explain the derivation of supply curves. It was shown that the demand for a good depends on the *marginal* utility—not on the *total* utility of the commodity. It is similar with the supply curve, which shows how much of a commodity will be put on the market over a range of prices. The amount of any commodity that will be produced at a given price will depend on its cost of production, but just as demand did not depend on total utility, it is marginal cost, and not total cost, that is the main determinant of how much will be supplied.

2. Perfect competition

Demand for most commodities comes from a large number of potential buyers, who act quite independently of one another, rarely making any concentrated effort to influence price by withholding their demand. Even when attempts have been made to persuade consumers to act together they have rarely had much success, for it is difficult to persuade buyers to combine even for a limited period. In studying demand there is therefore no need to assume that there are many buyers, for such conditions are the normal experience of real life.

In the case of supply, however, for some commodities there are many producers, for others only a few. Thus the derivation of supply curves has to be considered under the influence of different environments, of which three may be recognised—perfect competition, imperfect competition and monopoly. The first and third of these— perfect competition and monopoly—are simply theoretical concepts, but it is necessary to consider supply under these unreal conditions before attempting a more realistic interpretation. The basis of supply will be explained first in an environment of perfect competition.

The assumptions of the perfect market were considered in Chapter 9. Though the existence of a perfect market does not necessarily ensure perfect competition, the two terms are very similar in meaning. Perfect competition relates more especially to the environment in which the production of a particular commodity is carried on. For a perfect market there must be a large number of buyers and sellers, and the commodity in which dealings take place must be homogeneous. Similarly, the primary assumptions of perfect competition are that there should be a large number of firms, each producing only a small fraction of the total output, so that no firm can influence the price of the commodity in the market by increasing or decreasing its output. Such firms must take the price of the commodity as fixed. At this price an individual firm can sell any quantity it pleases; to increase its sales it has no need to cut its price, for however great its own output, it still remains only a tiny fraction of the total output for the industry, and therefore it makes no material difference to the total supply of that commodity. In other words, the demand for the product of a *single* firm is perfectly elastic. Since, further, the commodity is homogeneous, there is no reason to prefer the product of one firm to that of another, and so, though a firm can sell any amount at the market price, its sales would be zero at any price above this. Under perfect competition, too, there is no restriction on the entry of new firms into an industry.

A certain ambiguity exists regarding the meaning of the term perfect competition. In addition to the assumption just given, should one also assume perfect mobility of factors, their complete divisibility and an absence of all kinds of economic friction? If this were so, a change in demand from one commodity to another would immediately cause resources to be transferred from one form of production to the other, price moving to the new equilibrium without there being any intermediate effects. This difficulty would have been resolved if the suggestion made by an economist[1] many years ago had been followed. He suggested that the term be restricted to complete perfection in all respects, and the name "pure competition" be given to the less perfect conditions. Since this suggestion has not been generally followed, we are compelled to use the term perfect competition for a competitive state that is less than completely perfect, and thus it is all the more necessary to make quite clear the assumptions on which it is based.

[1] E. H. Chamberlin: *The Theory of Monopolistic Competition* (1933).

II. COSTS

3. Costs of production

The term "cost of production" also is ambiguous, for cost of production has meaning only when it is related to output. No answer can be given to the question: what is the cost of production of a fountain pen? for there is no such thing as *the* cost of production of any commodity. If only one pen is to be produced its cost of production will be very high: if 100 pens per week are to be produced it is fairly certain that the cost of production per pen will be much lower. If output is raised to 1,000 pens per week the cost of production per pen may be higher, lower or the same, depending on whether, between these two outputs, cost is increasing, decreasing or constant.

The word "cost" is ambiguous also because it has a variety of meanings; there are fixed and variable costs, prime and supplementary costs, average cost and marginal cost. It is best, therefore, to avoid the use of either the word "cost" or the phrase "cost of production," unless the output is clearly stated.

4. Fixed and variable costs

Some costs vary with output, whereas others are said to be fixed because—at least over a fairly considerable range of output—they do not vary. For example, once a firm has provided itself with a factory and installed the necessary machinery, these costs remain the same whether the firm is working at full or at only half capacity. The same amount of rent and rates will have to be paid in either case. The number of clerks employed in the office does not vary with every change of output, and so the cost of administration is looked upon as a fixed cost in the short period. If, however, the firm is engaged in spinning wool the amount of raw material required will be directly related to output. If the machinery is driven by electricity less power will be required if the firm is working below capacity. Whether the employees are on piece rates or paid by the hour, the wage bill will increase the larger the output. Rents, rates, interest on loans and any allowance for depreciation of machinery (machinery may depreciate even faster if idle) and administrative expenses are *fixed* costs; wages of labour, cost of power and raw materials are *variable* costs.

If, however, a firm is compelled by a falling off in the demand for its product to work short time for a lengthy period it is probable that administrative expenses also will have to be reduced. So another classification of cost groups the cost of administration with the variable costs, and calls these *prime* costs. The other fixed costs are then termed *supplementary* costs. The following diagram will help to make this clear.

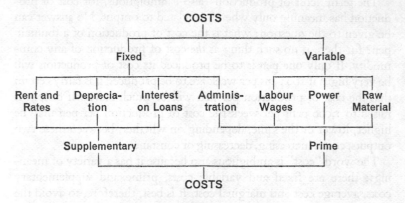

Fig. 54. Classification of Costs.

The importance of making a distinction between prime and supplementary costs is that in the short period a firm will generally continue in production if it covers only its prime costs. If it closes down temporarily it will still have to meet its supplementary costs, so it will suffer no great loss by continuing in production if its revenue from the sale of its products covers only its prime costs. The loss of goodwill, and the difficulty of restarting production, consequent on the loss of its labour force and the depreciation of idle assets, all weigh against ceasing production if it is thought that a recession of trade is likely to be of short duration. In the long period, obviously, a firm must cover all its costs, supplementary as well as prime. Indeed, the distinction between fixed and variable costs is largely a short-period distinction. The so-called variable costs are merely those that are variable in the short period; administrative costs become variable in the medium period; and even the supplementary costs become variable in the long period; for when machinery wears out it need not necessarily be replaced and premises can be converted to other uses.

5. Average and marginal cost

Marginal cost is the addition to total cost that results from increasing total output by one more unit. Average cost is the average cost of producing each unit of output. Consider the following example:

Table XXIX

The Cost Schedule of a Firm (1)

Output	Fixed cost	Variable cost	Total cost	Average cost	Marginal cost
Units	£	£	£	£	£
100	100	700	800	8.00	—
101	100	706	806	7.98	6
102	100	709	809	7.93	3
103	100	710	810	7.86	1

To increase output from 100 to 101 units adds £6 to total cost. Marginal cost, therefore, is £6. To increase output from 101 to 102 units increases total cost by a further £3, and so marginal cost is now £3. It is clear from this table how important it is to relate cost of production to output. If only 100 units are manufactured their total cost is £800. At an output of 103 units, however, the average cost per unit is only £7.86. The greater the proportion that fixed costs bear to total costs, the greater is the difference in average costs at different levels of output.

Consider now the following cost schedule of a firm:

Table XXX

The Cost Schedule of a Firm (2)

Output	Total cost	Average cost	Marginal cost
Units	£	£	£
20	270	13.5	—
30	330	11.0	6
40	400	10.0	7
50	500	10.0	10
60	630	10.5	13
70	840	12.0	21

The table shows that if average cost is falling, marginal cost will be less than average cost; if, however, average cost is rising, then marginal cost will be greater than average cost. It also shows average cost and marginal cost are equal when average cost is at a minimum. When, therefore, average cost and marginal cost are represented graphically the marginal cost curve should cut the average cost curve at the lowest point on the average cost curve (*see* Fig. 55).

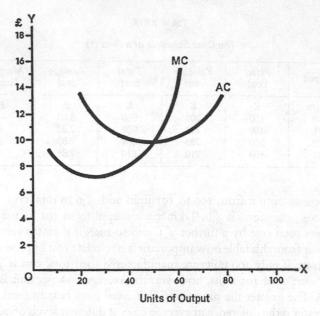

Fig. 55. Average Cost (AC) and Marginal Cost (MC).

III. OUTPUT

6. Normal profit and the size of an industry

In economics cost is taken to include *normal profit*. By normal profit is meant the payment necessary to keep an entrepreneur in a particular line of production. Normal profit will vary between one industry and another, being greater where uncertainty is greater. If a firm persistently earns less than what is considered to be normal profit for the industry the entrepreneur will leave that industry and seek more profitable employment elsewhere. The *marginal firm* will thus be the one just capable of earning normal profit. If profits in the industry fall, the marginal firms will be the first to leave, and a new margin, again comprising firms just earning normal profit, will be created. If profits rise, all firms will earn more than normal profit, and so new firms, whose costs previously were too high, will be drawn into the industry. Thus, an industry expands or contracts according to whether the firms comprising it earn more or less than normal profit. Profit above normal is sometimes called *surplus profit* or *net revenue*. If normal profit is reckoned as part of cost the marginal firm's profit—that is, surplus profit or net revenue—will be zero.

7. The most profitable output

It is an assumption of economics that all people, both consumers and producers, at all times behave rationally. Thus it is assumed that the aim of each entrepreneur is to try to maximise his profits, although in actual conditions this is not always true, for it may necessitate an expansion of his business that, for any one of several reasons, he may be unwilling to undertake. It is, however, essential to make this assumption if a satisfactory theory of the firm is to be built up.

Profit will be at a maximum at an output where marginal cost is equal to marginal revenue. By marginal revenue is meant the additional revenue accruing to a firm as a result of selling one more unit of its output. Since to a firm working under conditions of perfect competition the price of its products is fixed, marginal revenue must be equal to the price of one unit of the commodity, since the increase in revenue from the sale of an extra unit is the price of that unit. Profit must therefore be at a maximum when marginal cost equals marginal revenue. So long as marginal revenue is greater than marginal cost, it will be to a firm's advantage to go on increasing its output, for in such circumstances each addition to its output will add to its profit. But if output is pushed beyond this point the addition to cost will be greater than the addition to revenue, and so total profit will be less. Marginal cost must therefore equal marginal revenue, and this is true of all forms of competition—perfect or imperfect.

It has already been shown that in perfect competition marginal revenue is equal to price; thus marginal cost also must be equal to price. It has been seen above that for the marginal firm average revenue is equal to average cost (since there is no profit other than normal profit), and since average revenue is the same thing as price, then in the case of the marginal firm operating under conditions of perfect competition the following conditions are fulfilled:

Marginal revenue = Marginal cost;
Marginal cost = Price;
Price = Average revenue = Average cost.

Therefore:

Price = Marginal cost = Marginal revenue = Average revenue = Average cost.

The main point to emphasise is that in perfect competition price is equal to marginal cost. This can be seen from Table XXXI:

Table XXXI

The Marginal Firm under Perfect Competition

Output	Average cost	Total cost	Marginal cost	Average revenue (price)	Total revenue	Marginal revenue	Surplus profit
Units	£	£	£	£	£	£	£
50	12	600	—	10	500	10	—100
60	11	660	6	10	600	10	— 60
70	10.4	730	7	10	700	10	— 30
80	10.1	810	8	10	800	10	— 10
90	10	900	9	10	900	10	—
100	10	1,000	10	10	1,000	10	—
110	10.1	1,110	11	10	1,100	10	— 10
120	10.2	1,230	12	10	1,200	10	— 30

At an output of 100 units of the commodity marginal cost is £10, marginal revenue is £10, average revenue (price) is £10, and average cost is £10. Output will not be pushed beyond this point because surplus profit will be negative at any higher output—that is, there will be less than normal profit.

Under perfect competition firms always operate at an output where marginal cost is rising (as in Tables XXIX and XXX), since under perfect competition no firm will restrict its output, and diminishing returns will set in sooner or later. Tables similar to the above can easily be constructed to show that if price is £6 the most profitable output will be 60 units; if price is £8 the most profitable output will be 80 units; and if price is raised to £12, then output will be increased to 120 units.

8. High-cost and low-cost firms

In any industry some firms are more efficient than others, and therefore make higher profits. This is not necessarily due to some firms being more efficiently managed than others; it may be due to the advantages of situation or some other influence outside the control of the entrepreneur. Whether a firm is a high-cost or a low-cost firm depends on the quality of the factors of production it employs, and the entrepreneur is only one of these factors. Nevertheless, the standard of efficiency of the management is of paramount importance, and the efficiency of the other factors may in no small measure be dependent on it, as for example the quality of its capital—whether it is up-to-date or obsolescent. The firm's location may have been deliberately selected on account of its suitability for its particular line of production. In an area where an industry has been long established the local labour may be superior to that in other districts.

Consider now the cost schedule of a low-cost firm working under perfect competition:

Table XXXII

Perfect Competition: a Low-cost Firm

Output	Average cost	Total cost	Marginal cost	Average revenue (price)	Total revenue	Marginal revenue	Surplus profit
Units	£	£	£	£	£	£	£
80	7.3	590	—	10	800	—	210
90	7.5	675	8.5	10	900	10	225
100	7.6	765	9.0	10	1,000	10	235
110	7.8	860	9.5	10	1,100	10	240
120	8.0	960	10.0	10	1,200	10	240
130	8.2	1,065	10.5	10	1,300	10	235
140	8.4	1,175	11.0	10	1,400	10	225

Again, it will not pay the firm to expand its output beyond 120 units, because that is the point where marginal cost is equal to marginal revenue, and this is clearly its most profitable output. The low-cost firm differs from the marginal firm in that total revenue exceeds total cost, so that surplus profit, additional to normal profit, is earned over a range of output.

It is sufficient for a firm to earn normal profit for it to continue in production, since surplus profit is really a form of economic rent, being a payment to factors over and above what is necessary to keep them in their present employment.

9. The firm and industry in equilibrium

(*i*) *Equilibrium of the firm.* Under perfect competition a firm will be in equilibrium when it is of no advantage to it to increase or decrease its output, or to change its method of production by altering the proportion in which its factors of production are combined. Its average cost will be at a minimum, for marginal cost is equal to average cost at a minimum average cost (*see* Para. 5). In such circumstances any change in output or in the method of production will result in a smaller total profit.

(*ii*) *Equilibrium of an industry.* Under perfect competition an industry will be in equilibrium when there is no tendency for the size of the industry to change—that is, when no firms wish to leave it and no new firms are being attracted to it. This means that the highest-cost or marginal firm will be making normal profit, neither more nor less, for if its profit were above normal new firms would wish to enter the industry, and if it had been making less than normal profit some firms would wish to leave. If every firm in the industry is making normal profit, and no more, the industry can be said to be in *perfect equilibrium*. Under perfect competition economic forces will generally exert their influence on industry in the direction of this goal. Lack of complete divisibility of factors and differences in their quality may, however, result in the industry having a permanent cost structure of high- and low-cost firms. When its marginal firm is making more than normal profit an industry is said to be in *imperfect equilibrium*.

10. The response of supply to changes in price

A rise in the price of the commodity calls forth a bigger supply, and this is brought about partly by existing firms expanding their output and partly by new firms being attracted into the industry. The entire additional output is not provided by existing firms, because under perfect competition no firm will expand beyond the optimum size. A fall in price produces the reverse effect. It has been seen that some firms have high and others low costs, and that a fall in price drives out the high-cost (that is, marginal) firms, just as a high price makes it possible for new high-cost firms to come in. These high-cost firms found production unprofitable before the rise in price. The ease with which this adjustment of output to price takes place determines the elasticity of supply of a commodity. If expansion or contraction of an industry is easy supply will be elastic; if expansion or contraction is difficult supply will tend to be inelastic.

If marginal cost is rising very sharply—that is, if the marginal-cost curve is steep—it will require a considerable rise in price to call forth an increase in supply. The shape of the supply curve therefore depends on the shape of the marginal-cost curve. If one is steep, so also is the other, and hence a steep marginal curve indicates that supply is inclined to be inelastic.

If there are many firms enjoying more than normal profit it shows that the industry is too small. This may arise because special difficulties stand in the way of firms wishing to enter that particular industry, and these hold back newcomers, with the result that the price of the product is high. If there are many firms with less than normal profit it shows that the industry is too large, but that for some reason firms are unable or unwilling to leave it. In this case the price of the product will be low, and the industry may agitate for the fixing of a higher price. To accede to the industry's request, however, will provide no remedy, for it will merely perpetuate its excessive size. The ease or difficulty of contraction of an industry depends largely on its cost structure. If there is considerable difference between the costs of individual firms, with only a few firms at each level—that is, if the "cost ladder" of the industry is steep—contraction of the industry is easy, the few high-cost firms dropping out if there is a fall in price. If, however, there is little difference between the costs of one firm and those of another, contraction is difficult and the industry will tend to remain over-large.

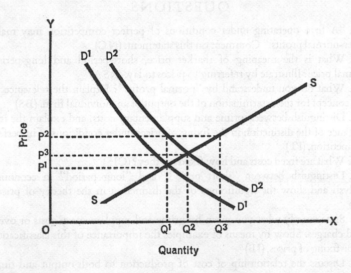

Fig. 56. Excess Capacity.

Where the response of supply to a fall in price is slow, producers may plan to produce more than the new equilibrium position justifies. For example, the impact effect of an increase in the demand for a commodity may be to raise its price to OP^2 (Fig. 56). At this price producers have an incentive to produce the quantity OQ^3, and so additional factors may be drawn into the industry to enable this quantity to be supplied (Fig. 56).

Equilibrium will eventually be established at the price OP^3, where the quantity supplied will be only OQ^2. Thus, all the additional capacity provided to meet the increase in demand will not be required, with the result that the industry—at least for a time—will suffer from excess capacity.

RECOMMENDATIONS FOR FURTHER READING

K. E. Boulding: *Economic Analysis*, Chapters 22–24.
J. E. Meade: *An Introduction to Economic Analysis and Policy*, Part II.
E. H. Chamberlin: *Theory of Monopolistic Competition*, Chapter 2.
Joan Robinson: *Economics of Imperfect Competition*, Chapters 7 and 9.
G. J. Stigler: *Theory of Price*, Chapters 9 and 10.

QUESTIONS

1. "A firm operating under conditions of perfect competition may make super-normal profits." Comment on this statement. (NC)
2. What is the meaning of market price, short-period and long-period normal price? Illustrate by referring to prices today. (RSA)
3. What do you understand by "normal profits"? Explain the relevance of this concept for the determination of the output of an individual firm. (BS)
4. Distinguish between prime and supplementary costs, and explain the importance of the distinction in the fixing of prices under conditions of imperfect competition. (IT)
5. What are fixed costs and how fixed are they? (CIS)
6. Distinguish between "short period" and "long period" in economic analysis and show the significance of the distinction in the theory of prices. (IB)
7. State exactly what you mean by prime and supplementary costs or overhead charges. Show by means of examples the importance of this classification in the fixing of prices. (IB)
8. Discuss the relationship of cost of production to both output and time. (CIS)
9. Bring out clearly the connection between Cost of Production and Price. (CCS)
10. Explain the problems raised in agriculture by the intervals which elapse between the producer's decisions and the consequent effects upon supplies reaching the market. (Degree)
11. Examine critically the view that perfect competition leads to an optimal allocation of resources. (Degree)

CHAPTER 14

THE BASIS OF SUPPLY: UNDER MONOPOLY

I. OUTPUT UNDER MONOPOLY

1. Absolute monopoly

For a monopoly to be absolute two conditions must be fulfilled. Firstly, the production of the commodity or service must be in the hands of a single producer. (The monopolist could, of course, be a combine comprising all the producers of the commodity.) Secondly, there must be no substitute for the commodity.

The second condition would be even more difficult to fulfil than the first, since there are few things for which there is not some sort of substitute. There may be no very close substitute for coffee, but if its price rose considerably the demand for it would be influenced by the existence of other beverages such as tea, cocoa, beer, wine, etc. A person's demand for any commodity is affected by his demand for all other commodities, the assumption that everyone has a scale of preferences implying that every purchase involves a choice between alternatives. A monopolist producer of motor cars is free from competition from other producers of motor cars, but he still is subject to competition from producers of other things, not merely other forms of transport but also quite different things such as, for example, houses. Thus, absolute monopoly does not occur in real life.

Just as monopoly occurs when there is a single producer of a commodity, so monopsony means that there is only one buyer of a commodity or service. For example, there is only one "buyer" of the services of railway engine drivers, the industry now being nationalised.

2. The monopolist and demand

Even though a monopolist may have complete control over the supply of a commodity, he cannot control demand, though he may sometimes attempt to influence it by means of advertising. He has therefore to take account of the fact that more can be sold at a low than at a high price—that is, his power is limited by consumers' demand. He can increase his sales only by lowering the price not only of his additional but of his entire output. Thus the monopolist can, if he wishes, fix his price, and then allow consumer-demand to decide what quantity he shall sell; or he himself can decide what output to produce, but in that case the price at which this output can be sold will depend on consumer-demand. This is what is meant by saying that even a monopolist is subject to the "sovereignty" of the consumer. For example, if DD represents the demand for a commodity the monopolist, if he wishes, can charge the price OP^a, but if he does he will sell only the quantity OQ^a. If he decides on an output of OQ^b, then he can sell

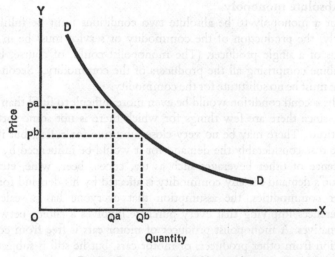

Fig. 57. Demand and the Monopolist.

this quantity only if he charges the price, OP^b. By reducing his output, therefore, from OQ^b to OQ^a the monopolist would be able to raise the price of the commodity from OP^b to OP^a. He can decide either his output or the price at which he will sell, but not both.

Elasticity of demand and monopoly. Whether a monopolist can increase his revenue by restricting his output depends on the shape of the demand curve—that is, on the elasticity of demand for the commodity. The monopolist will increase his revenue only if a reduction in output brings about a more than proportionate increase in price. Thus the more inelastic the demand for the commodity, the greater is the opportunity to obtain monopoly profit. Consider the following cases, where A, B and C are commodities with different elasticities of demand

—the demand for *A* being fairly inelastic, the elasticity of demand for *B* being equal to unity and *C* being in fairly elastic demand. In all cases it is assumed that production is in the hands of monopolists, and that at first the output was 100 units and the price £3 per unit, so that the total revenue of each was £300. Suppose now that each producer reduces his output to 75 units. The new price will then depend on the elasticity of demand for each commodity. The price of *A*, for which there is a fairly inelastic demand, will rise to £9; the price of *B*, for which the elasticity of demand is equal to unity, will rise to £4; and

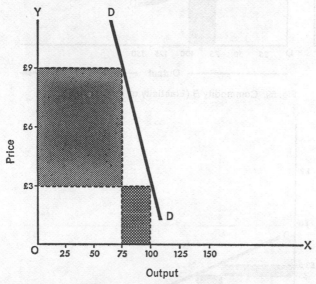

Fig. 58. Commodity *A* (Inelastic Demand).

the price of *C*, for which demand is fairly elastic, will rise only to £3.5. Figures 58, 59 and 60 show the effect of curtailment of output in these three cases.

It is clear therefore that the effect on total revenue of a reduction of output depends on the elasticity of demand for the commodity. In the case of *A*, where demand is inelastic, total revenue increases from £300 to £675; for *B*, with unit elasticity of demand, total revenue remains the same; for *C*, where demand is elastic, total revenue falls from £300 to £262.50. Where demand is elastic the monopolist cannot increase his income by curtailing output, but he may try to increase demand through advertising. Demand, however, is not the

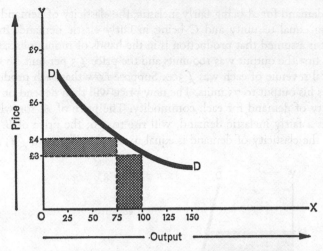

Fig. 59. Commodity *B* (Elasticity of Demand = Unity).

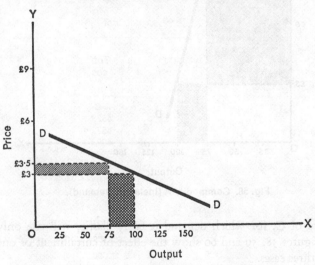

Fig. 60. Commodity *C* (Elastic Demand).

sole determinant of monopoly output: the problem of cost also has to be considered.

3. Monopoly output

The essential feature of monopoly is that the monopolist can influence the price of the commodity by expanding or contracting supply. The monopolist's aim will be to produce that output which will yield him maximum profit. The monopolist's output is shown in the following tables, giving the cost and revenue schedules of three monopolists, the first working in conditions of increasing marginal cost, the second in conditions of decreasing marginal cost and the third in conditions of constant marginal cost. In perfect competition, it will be remembered, firms always expand their output to a point where marginal cost is increasing (*see* pages 232–3).

(i) *Increasing marginal cost.* From Table XXXIII it can be seen that if the monopolist has an output of 70 units (per week) he can sell them at £8.75 each, his total revenue being 70 × £8.75 (£612.50), and his total cost (including normal profit) £432.50. If the total cost is subtracted from the total revenue this leaves the monopolist a surplus (or monopoly) profit of £180.

Table XXXIII

The Cost and Revenue Schedule of a Monopolist:
Increasing Marginal Cost

Units of output	Average revenue (price per unit)	Total revenue	Marginal revenue	Average cost	Total cost	Marginal cost	Surplus profit
	£	£	£	£	£	£	£
70	8.75	612.50	—	6.17	432.50	—	180.00
80	8.50	680.00	6.75	5.72	457.50	2.50	222.50
90	8.25	742.50	6.25	5.42	492.50	3.50	250.00
100	8.00	800.00	5.75	5.50	550.00	5.75	250.00
110	7.75	852.50	5.25	5.67	620.00	7.00	232.50
120	7.50	900.00	4.75	5.92	710.00	9.00	190.00

If he increases his output to 80 units he has to reduce the price to £8.50 in order to sell his entire output. This increases his total revenue by £67.50 to £680 but since his total costs increase by only £25 he achieves a higher surplus profit than before—namely £222.50. His marginal revenue is £6.75 (£67.50 ÷ 10) and his marginal cost is £2.50 (£25 ÷ 10). (It is necessary to divide the difference in total revenue and total cost shown in the table by 10, because the table shows outputs only at intervals of 10 units.) The monopolist will continue to expand his output so long as marginal cost does not exceed marginal revenue. In this case he will not exceed an output of 100 units, because at this point his surplus profit is at a maximum. This occurs where marginal revenue equals marginal cost. Under perfect competition marginal cost is equal to price, but under monopoly average revenue (price) is greater than marginal cost. In the above examples the monopolist's output is 100 units, the price is £8 and his marginal cost only £5.75. The graph (Fig. 61) shows the monopolist's output to occur when marginal revenue equals marginal cost, but also where average revenue (price) exceeds marginal cost by AB.

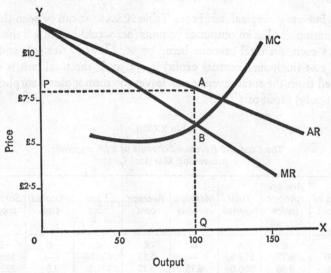

Fig. 61. Monopoly Output with Increasing Marginal Cost. (MC = marginal cost. AR = average revenue (demand curve). MR = marginal revenue).

(ii) *Marginal cost decreasing.*

Table XXXIV

The Cost and Revenue Schedule of a Monopolist:
Decreasing Marginal Cost

Output	Price	Total revenue	Marginal revenue	Average cost	Total cost	Marginal cost	Surplus profit
	£	£	£	£	£	£	£
20	12.50	230	—	6.20	135	—	95
30	9.00	270	4.00	5.70	170	3.50	100
40	7.50	300	3.00	5.00	200	3.00	100
50	6.50	325	2.50	4.50	228	2.80	97
60	5.50	330	0.50	4.20	250	2.50	80

As before, the monopolist will not increase his output beyond the point where marginal cost equals marginal revenue, for at this point his surplus profit is at a maximum.

(iii) Marginal cost constant.

Table XXXV

The Cost and Revenue Schedule of a Monopolist:
Constant Marginal Cost

Output	Price	Total revenue	Marginal revenue	Average cost	Total cost	Marginal cost	Surplus profit
	£	£	£	£	£	£	£
50	15	750	—	9.00	450	—	300
60	14	840	9	8.30	500	2	340
70	13	910	7	7.80	550	5	360
80	12	960	5	7.50	600	5	360
90	11	990	3	7.20	650	5	340
100	10	1000	1	7.00	700	5	300

Again surplus profits is at a maximum when marginal revenue is equal to marginal cost. Cases (*ii*) and (*iii*) also can be shown graphically (Figs 62 and 63).

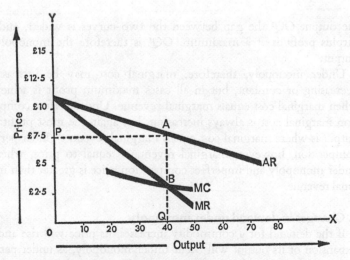

Fig. 62. Monopoly Output (Decreasing Marginal Cost).

All three tables show that in the case of monopoly, average revenue (price) is greater than average cost or marginal cost or marginal revenue.

Figure 64 on page 249 shows that a monopolist's output therefore will be that at which there is the greatest difference between his total revenue and his total costs, since this yields him his maximum profit. Total cost is, as usual, assumed to include normal profit. At

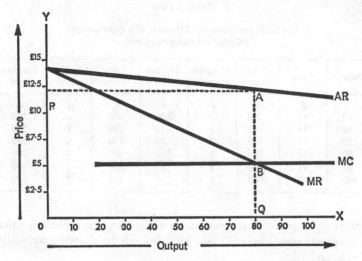

Fig. 63. Monopoly Output (Constant Marginal Cost).

the output OQ^I the gap between the two curves is widest, and so surplus profit is at a maximum. OQ^I is therefore the monopolist's output.

Under monopoly, therefore, marginal cost may be increasing, decreasing or constant, but in all cases maximum profit is achieved when marginal cost equals marginal revenue. Under perfect competition marginal cost is always increasing, but again the most profitable output is where marginal cost equals marginal revenue. Under perfect competition, however, marginal revenue is equal to price, whereas under monopoly and imperfect competition price is greater than marginal revenue.

4. Changes in demand under monopoly

If the demand for a commodity increases, its price will rise and an expansion of its output will occur under monopoly, as under perfect competition (Fig. 65). D^ID^I represents demand and MR^I marginal

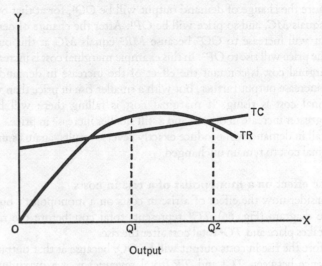

Fig. 64. Monopoly Output. (TC = Total Cost. TR = Total Revenue.)

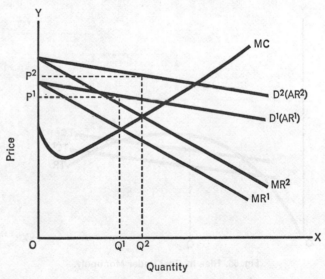

Fig. 65. Change of Demand under Monopoly.

revenue before a change in demand. D^2D^2 represents demand and MR^2 marginal revenue after the change in demand. MC is the marginal cost curve. If the expansion of output makes possible economies of scale the marginal cost curve will move farther to the right.

T.E.—15

Before the change of demand output will be OQ^1, for at that output MR equals MC, and so price will be OP^1. After the change of demand output will increase to OQ^2 because MR^2 equals MC at this output, and the price will rise to OP^2. In this example marginal cost is increasing. If marginal cost is constant the effect of the increase in demand will be to increase output further, but with a smaller rise in price than when marginal cost is rising. If marginal cost is falling there will be an even greater increase in output and a still smaller increase in price.

A fall in demand will produce exactly reverse results, again assuming marginal cost to remain unchanged.

5. The effect on a monopolist of a rise in costs

Consider now the effect of a rise in costs on a monopolist's output. In the diagram (Fig. 66) TC^1 represents total cost before the rise in costs takes place and TC^2 total cost after the rise.

Before the rise in costs output will be OQ, because at that output the difference between TC^1 and TR (total revenue) is at a maximum. It

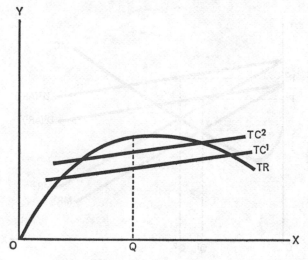

Fig. 66. Rise in Cost under Monopoly.

will be seen that if the increase in costs is the same whatever the output, as with TC^2, the monopolist will have no incentive to alter his output, since his profit is at a maximum at the same output as before, though of course reduced in amount.

The effect of a fixed lump-sum tax on a monopolist would be similar to an increase in his costs. Even if the tax was equal to his entire surplus profit, the monopolist would still have no motive for changing his output, (*OQ*).

A lump-sum tax equal to surplus profit at the monopoly output and at all lower outputs, but decreasing with each output beyond monopoly output, would encourage the monopolist to increase his output. The heavily dotted line (Fig. 67) represents total cost after the imposition of such a tax. The monopolist will expand his output from OQ^1 to OQ^2 because his surplus profit is now greatest at his larger output. It

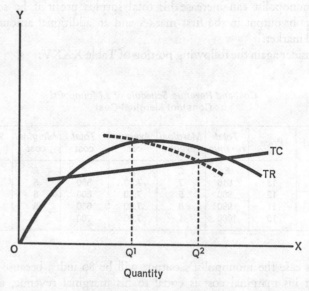

Fig. 67. Taxation of a Monopolist.

has been suggested that the imposition of a tax of this kind would encourage a monopolist to expand his output, to sell which he would have to reduce his price, but such a tax would be impossible to calculate.

II. DISCRIMINATING MONOPOLY

6. Price discrimination

By price discrimination is meant the charging of different prices to different groups of consumers for a similar commodity or service. This is possible only under conditions when:

(*i*) the production of the commodity is undertaken by a monopolist;

(*ii*) consumers are members of separate markets, so that the commodity or service cannot be transferred from one market to another;

(*iii*) elasticity of demand for the commodity is not the same in each market; and

(*iv*) the cost of keeping the market separate is not too great.

The monopolist can increase his total surplus profit if he sells his monopoly output in the first market and an additional amount in a second market.

Consider again the following portion of Table XXXV:

Cost and Revenue Schedule of a Monopolist
Constant Marginal Cost

Output	Price	Total revenue	Marginal revenue	Average cost	Total cost	Marginal cost	Surplus profit
	£	£	£	£	£	£	£
70	13	910	7	7.80	550	5	360
80	12	960	5	7.50	600	5	360
90	11	990	3	7.20	650	5	340
100	10	1000	1	7.00	700	5	300

In this case the monopolist's output will be 80 units, because at this output his marginal cost is equal to his marginal revenue, and his surplus profit is at a maximum of £360. If he were to put 100 units of the commodity on this market instead of 80 he would have to reduce the price from £12 to £10 per unit; his total revenue would increase by £40, but his total cost would rise by £100, so that his surplus profit would fall to £300. If instead he increases his output to 100 units but sells 80 units only in the first market, he can increase his total surplus profit by disposing of the additional 20 units for any sum above their marginal cost of £100. Assuming that his price in the second market is £5.50, then:

Total cost of producing 100 = £700
Sale of 80 at £12 each   = £960 ⎫
Sale of 20 at £5.50 each   = £110 ⎬ £1070
⎭

Surplus profit = £370—an increase of £10.

The reason why he is able to increase his total surplus profit in this way is that in order to increase sales in the first market he had to reduce the price of his *entire* output, whereas if the markets can be kept separate he can sell the additional output at a low price in the second market without having to reduce his price in the first market.

How much he will sell in each market will depend on the elasticity of demand for the commodity in each market. His total profit for the two markets will be at a maximum when he produces that output at which marginal cost is equal to marginal revenue in each market, for if this condition is not fulfilled it would be more profitable to transfer some of the output from one market to the other. In the above example (Table XXXV) this condition was fulfilled in the first market at an output of 80 with selling price at £12, marginal revenue and marginal cost both being £5. To maximise his profit from the two markets together he will charge such a price in the second market that in that market also marginal cost equals marginal revenue at that output. If elasticity of demand is the same in each market there will be no incentive for the monopolist to charge different prices, for he cannot increase his profit by so doing. When a monopolist divides his own output between two markets the price will be higher and the quantity sold less in the market where demand is more inelastic.

To make price discrimination possible markets may be kept separate by tariffs. In the above example the first market may be the home market, and the monopoly might be maintained by a high tariff on foreign imports. The extra output is then exported and sold much more cheaply abroad, the high tariff also serving the purpose of preventing a foreign purchaser making a profit by re-exporting the commodity back to the home market. This practice is generally known as dumping. Producers have often complained of foreign manufacturers dumping their goods at prices, which they said, were below *cost of production*. This complaint shows again the ambiguity of the term *cost of production*. Consider once more the above example. Assume the commodity to be produced under conditions of perfect competition in the second market at an average cost of £6. If the price of the imported article is only £5.50 this is obviously below the *average* cost of production of producers in either market, but is above the *marginal* cost of a monopolist selling in separate markets. A protective tariff is almost certain to be demanded by home producers as a protection against such dumping.

Sometimes markets are not so clearly separated. For example, a new novel may sell for £3.10; later a cheaper edition at £1.25 may be published; later still there may be a paperback edition at 40p. These markets may be completely separated from one another by time, but there is nothing to prevent a prospective purchaser waiting until the cheapest edition is brought out. If, however, most of the consumers who buy the £1.25 edition are people who would not in any case have been willing to pay more, then the prospect of a cheaper edition will not seriously affect the sales of the more expensive first edition. Similarly, the 40p edition may serve a third market. In such a case, in order to assist price discrimination and make it less obvious, there may be some attempt at differentiation of the commodity by means of different bindings.

Price discrimination and consumer's surplus. A bookseller may be able to sell ten copies of a particular book if its price were 60p, six copies if the price were £2.50, but only two if the price were £4.50. If actually the book is published at £2.25 two people can obtain for £1.25 a book for which they would have been willing to pay £4.50, with the result that each of them enjoys £2.25 worth of surplus satisfaction; three others who were willing to pay £2.50 each have £0.25 worth of surplus satisfaction. When discriminatory prices can be charged consumer's surplus can be reduced to a minimum and the producer's surplus profit thereby increased. If everyone had to pay the maximum price he was willing to pay for everything he bought, consumer's surplus would completely disappear.

7. Further examples of price discrimination

Railway freight rates used to provide one of the most frequently quoted examples of discriminatory charges. Goods were arranged in twenty-one categories, the more expensive the commodity, the higher the charge for carrying it. The railway classification of goods was based on the principle of "charging what the traffic will bear," since if all goods had been charged at the same rate, some of the cheaper goods would never have been carried at all. This method of charging came into existence when the railways were monopolist carriers. Discriminatory charges were possible because the markets were quite separate—a high category commodity could not be transferred to a lower class in order to obtain the advantage of the cheaper rate (woollen cloth, for example, could not be passed off as coal!). In the case of discriminatory passenger fares the markets are not quite so easily kept separate. It will not pay to issue cheap return tickets, available for travel by ordinary trains if this ruins the market for tickets at the full rate. To prevent this, restrictions are imposed on the use of cheap tickets—for example, the tickets may not be available until too late an hour for most ordinary travellers. If the issue of cheap tickets brings people to the railways who would not otherwise have travelled, then it is clear that the two markets are separate. Where special excursion trains are run the separation of markets becomes easier. The railways, too, have heavy fixed costs, and marginal cost is relatively low, for the additional cost of running an extra train is comparatively small, though the cost of maintaining the additional rolling stock is very high relative to its use.

Airlines similarly charge discriminatory fares, with lower rates for mid-week or night travel or at certain seasons. A lower fare is often charged to those travelling for pleasure than to those on business by linking fares to "packaged" holidays. Cheaper fares are often available to students or people travelling in groups. Lower excursion fares may depend on the length of time that must elapse before the return journey is undertaken. The aim of all these restrictions on cheap fares is to restrict their issue as far as possible to people who would have been unwilling to pay the full fare.

Before the introduction of the National Health Service in 1948 doctors were said to have different scales of charges for different groups of patients, the poor being charged at a lower rate than the rich. This was possible because the service was personal and could not be transferred from one person to another.

Gas and electricity undertakings, like railways, have very heavy fixed costs and relatively low variable costs. The two-part tariff—a fixed minimum charge and a further charge proportional to the amount consumed—is an attempt to apportion the charge over fixed and variable costs. Marginal cost, therefore, is low and so sometimes lower charges are made where large quantities of the commodity are consumed. Again the markets are distinct for the lower price can be obtained only after a stated amount of gas or electricity has been consumed. Sometimes price discrimination in the case of electricity can be applied also to the purpose for which it is used, a lower charge being made for its use as power than for lighting. Or discrimination may be in favour of a certain type of consumer, industrial concerns being charged at a different rate from householders. Since there must be sufficient plant to meet the heavy demand at peak periods, lower charges may be imposed at other times to encourage consumption at off-peak periods, as with storage heaters, which consume electricity only during off-peak periods but supply heat at other times, separate meters being required to keep the markets separate. For this reason long-distance telephone calls are cheaper in the evening than earlier in the day. In all cases the aim is to tap new markets, success depending on the elasticity of demand for the commodity or service and the ease and extent to which the markets can be kept separate.

RECOMMENDATIONS FOR FURTHER READING

K. E. Boulding: *Economic Analysis*, Chapter 25.

E. A. G. Robinson: *Monopoly*.

Joan Robinson: *Economics of Imperfect Competition*, Chapters 3 and 10–15.

E. H. Phelps Browne: *A Course in Applied Economics*, Part II.

QUESTIONS

1. Consider the limitations on a monopolist's power. (Bolton)
2. Are monopolies always contrary to the public interest? (Yorks)
3. Explain the system of price discrimination and show how it is practised. (RSA)
4. What do you understand by the phrase: "charging what the traffic will bear"? (LC Com.)
5. "The monopolist can sell his product at whatever price he likes." Comment on this statement and show how the monopolist reaches an equilibrium position. (BS)
6. Can it ever be profitable to charge different consumers different prices for the same product? Illustrate your answer by reference to costs. (CIS)
7. How, exactly, does a monopolist decide the price he will charge for his product in order to maximise his profits? (IT)
8. Is it inevitable that the monopoly price of a commodity must be higher than its competition price? In your answer, outline the major differences in the determination of these two types of price. (IHA)
9. What is the relevance of elasticity of demand to the fixing of prices under monopolistic conditions? In what circumstances could a monopolist charge differential prices? (Exp)
10. "Given a certain elasticity of demand, the supply which the monopolist will produce (and therefore the monopoly price) will depend upon the condition of production." Discuss this statement. (IB)
11. Explain the term Monopoly in your own words; and discuss the effects of monopoly (a) under private, (b) under public ownership. (ACCA)
12. "A monopolist will always charge a higher price and produce a lower output than a competitive industry." Critically examine this statement. (GCE)
13. What do you understand by price discrimination? In what circumstances is it (a) practicable, (b) profitable? (GCE)

14. Discuss the view that charges for electricity should vary with the time of day during which electricity is used. (Degree)

15. "Monopoly is objectionable because it leads to a misallocation of the factors of production." Discuss. (Degree)

CHAPTER 15

THE BASIS OF SUPPLY: UNDER IMPERFECT COMPETITION

I. IMPERFECT COMPETITION

1. Competition is imperfect

Though it was realised that in actual conditions neither perfect competition nor perfect markets existed, it was thought at one time that economic forces nevertheless exerted a pull towards an equilibrium where competion and the market were perfect. Such hindrances to perfect competition as existed were considered to be exceptional.

At the opposite extreme from perfect competition was monopoly. Under perfect competition there is a large number of firms producing a homogeneous commodity, so that buyers have no preference for the product of any particular seller; whereas under monopoly there is a single producer for whose product there is no close substitute. Under perfect competition sellers accept price as something beyond their control and have no incentive to restrict supply; the monopolist, on the other hand, can influence price by restricting his output.

Actual conditions lie between the two extremes of perfect competition and monopoly. Unfortunately in ordinary speech—and in Acts of Parliament too—forms of very imperfect competition are described as monopoly. In fact the *Fair Trading Act* (1973) defined a monopolist as a producer of 25% of the total output of a commodity. In a number of ways competition is far from perfect. Sellers often combine together; entry to an industry may be difficult if a large amount of capital is involved, or if there are considerable economies of scale, and new competitors may be kept out by devices such as patent rights; or similar products may be artificially differentiated by branding. In these and other ways competition has been rendered imperfect, and far from being exceptional, these conditions are now the rule. Under perfect competition there is a single price at which the entire supply can be sold.

A feature of imperfect competition, however, is that there is no single selling price for a commodity.

Production in conditions of imperfect competition is more difficult to study than either perfect competition or monopoly, for whereas these are both well-defined cases because they happen to be extremes, imperfect competition has many varieties ranging from near perfection to near monopoly, so that generalisation becomes difficult.

2. Types of imperfect competition

Imperfect competition takes too many forms for all of them to be discussed here, and consideration must be restricted, therefore, to a few well-defined types. In some forms of imperfect competition we find a large number of producers, but imperfection results from differentiation of the commodity or in the service provided. This is generally known as *monopolistic competition*. Another type of imperfect competition occurs where there are only a few producers, this being known as *oligopoly* (Greek *oligoi* = few). Duopoly (two producers or sellers) is thus a special case of oligopoly. If the commodity is homogeneous we have perfect oligopoly; if there is differentiation between the products of different sellers we have imperfect oligopoly. The following table shows the distinguishing features of the different environments in which production can take place:

Table XXXVI

Features of Competition and Monopoly

Type	Producers	Commodity
Perfect competition . . .	Many	Homogeneous
Imperfect competition:		
(i) Monopolistic competition	Many	Differentiated
(ii) Perfect oligopoly (or duopoly) .	Few (or Two)	Homogeneous
(iii) Imperfect oligopoly (or duopoly)	Few (or Two)	Differentiated
Monopoly	Single	Single

II. MONOPOLISTIC COMPETITION AND OLIGOPOLY

3. Monopolistic competition in the retail trade

A feature of monopolistic competition, as of perfect competition, is that there are many producers or sellers, but unlike perfect competition, the commodity or service is not homogeneous. The retail trade provides an interesting example of monopolistic competition.

Differentiation takes many forms. Two shops may be selling similar goods, and yet there may be differentiation in the form of better service at one shop, or greater convenience of situation. In the case of shops in the suburbs of a town, it is unusual to find two shops in the same branch of trade very close together (though this is common enough in the town centre). Suppose A and B to be two grocers' shops. Each has a sort of hinterland in which its customers live, and within its own hinterland each shop has some measure of monopoly, owing to the greater convenience of its situation to people living in that area. Competition between A and B is therefore restricted to the small area between the two shops where the two hinterlands overlap. To people living well within the hinterland of A, Shop B is not a perfect substi-

Fig. 68. Shopping Hinterlands.

tute. If the two shops are close together some people may still prefer one to the other because they consider that it offers a better service. The differentiation between them may be nothing more than the contrast between the pleasant smile of one shopkeeper and the surly nature of the other. As a result, if one retailer cuts his prices he will not attract all the customers away from the other retailer.

On the other hand, shops in one branch of trade are often found in the same locality of a town because they wish to reduce to a minimum differences between them. So, in London, tailors are concentrated in or near Savile Row, jewellers in Bond Street and doctors in Harley Street.

The typical retailing unit is the small shop. The retail trade is easy to enter because no special training is needed and the amount of initial capital required is relatively small. It now offers almost the sole remaining opportunity to the small man to set up in business for himself. Consequently, the effect of retailing being carried on under conditions of monopolistic competition is to produce *excess capacity* rather than surplus profit, for the high-cost firms are not driven out, as they would be if competition were perfect. Other factors making for excess capacity in the retail trade are: (*i*) many small shops are family businesses, and other members of the proprietor's family assist him at peak periods for little or no wages; (ii) a very small retail business may consist merely of a room of a dwelling house converted into a shop, retailing being only a sideline to the proprietor's main occupation. It has been suggested that retailers should be licensed in order to reduce excess capacity. In fact some local authorities already restrict the number of certain kinds of shops—for example, those selling fish and chips. In some trades, for example the sale of newspapers, wholesalers will supply only a limited number of retailers in a district. Control over the entry of new firms by licensing may provide a more efficient system of retailing, but if this results in fewer retail shops it will mean a loss of convenience for some consumers, and at the same time a strengthening of the monopolistic position of those retailers who are able to secure licences. The cost to the consumer of greater efficiency in retailing is a curtailment of his choice of supplier. Some people, of course, may prefer greater freedom of choice to efficiency, but others, as the success of the supermarkets shows, prefer lower prices to freedom of choice and better service.

4. Oligopoly

A common form of imperfect competition is oligopoly, which occurs where there are only a few producers. Two forms of oligopoly can be distinguished—perfect and imperfect:

(i) *Perfect oligopoly*. In the case of perfect oligopoly the commodity is homogeneous. This is true also of perfect competition, but in perfect competition there are many producers. Because the commodity is homogeneous there can be only one price under either perfect competition or perfect oligopoly. Under perfect competition, however, each firm must take price as being something outside its control, whereas under perfect oligopoly this is not so. Under either form of oligopoly a firm contemplating a cut in price must consider the possible effect of such action on the price policy of the other firms in the industry. Where the commodity is homogeneous, consumers have no preference for one producer as against another, and so if oligopoly is perfect a cut in price by one producer must lead to similar cuts by other producers. Generally, but not always, price leadership will be with the largest firm. In Great Britain suger refining and the manufacture of cement provide examples of perfect oligopoly.

(ii) *Imperfect oligopoly*. When production is in the hands of only a few firms and the commodity is not homogeneous—that is, where there is some differentiation between the product of one firm and that of another—imperfect oligopoly exists. If firm A cuts its price, there is no certainty that firms B, C, D and E will all follow suit immediately. Meanwhile firm A may find that its sales have expanded sufficiently to increase its surplus profit. Any advantage in price-cutting goes to the first firm to indulge in it, but this can yield only a temporary advantage, for what A has done can also be done by B, C or D, and a price-cutting war may follow. The smaller the number of firms, the more severe will be the competition. so that duopoly tends to produce the most extreme example of cut-throat competition. In the end, the duopolists, in order to avoid their ruining each other, may decide to divide the market, each agreeing to allow the other a monopoly in its own area. Sixty years ago a tobacco war resulted in such an agreement. Cut-throat competition can take the form of price-cutting or it may take the form of a keenly competitive advertising campaign. Price-cutting may be by an actual reduction in prices or through the offer of gifts or trading stamps exchangeable for gifts or cash. Advertising may be supplemented by free samples or the offer of coupons entitling the customer to a temporary reduction in price.

5. Imperfect oligopoly in branded goods

In imperfect oligopoly there are only a few producers, each one of whom tries to differentiate his product or service in some way from those of others. The extent of this differentiation may not always be very great, for all are producers of similar products, but because of some slight difference the product of one is not regarded as a perfect substitute for the product of another. For example, they may all be makers of strawberry jam, but Cheeryble's strawberry jam is not regarded as a perfect substitute for Boffin's strawberry jam, because some consumers believe Boffin's to be superior in quality to Cheeryble's, while others believe Cheeryble's to be the better. Excelsior chocolates may differ only slightly from Superb chocolates, but some people may prefer Excelsior because they are more attractively packed, or merely because they prefer the name. As a result Superb chocolates are not regarded as a perfect substitute for Excelsior chocolates, even though the differentiation may be trivial and in no way adding to the quality of the commodity. Differentiation tends to make the demand for a commodity more elastic. Most branded goods are produced and sold under conditions of imperfect oligopoly.

As a result of this differentiation, Boffin may be able to charge a penny more for his jam. If competition were perfect this would result in all consumers buying Cheeryble's jam, and Boffin's sales would fall to zero. Under monopolistic competition some people will still prefer Boffin's jam, because they do not look upon Cheeryble's as a perfect substitute for it. Again, if the makers of Superb chocolates cut their price they will not gain all those customers who previously preferred Excelsior chocolates, for many consumers do not consider Superb chocolates to be a perfect substitute for Excelsior.

Under conditions of imperfect competition, therefore, there is always an opportunity for surplus profit to be made by any firm that is first in the field with something new. The possibility of surplus profits will attract a train of imitations (except so far as the idea is protected by patent rights) and profits will again fall. The innovation will have to be no more than an "improvement" of an existing commodity, for it is essential that its differentiation from the products of other firms should be slight; otherwise, if it is an entirely new article, a new market will have to be created. For example, if Dorrit, a competitor of Boffin's and Cheeryble's in the market for strawberry jam, invents an improved method of preserving the commodity, Boffin and Cheeryble will not be driven out of the market, for some of their customers will remain loyal to them. Dorrit, however, may for a time capture a much larger share of the market, and increase his surplus profit until other firms imitate his product.

This possibility of surplus profit, even for a temporary period, is the great stimulus to the invention of the many new gadgets that come on to the market, for many customers like to try something new. With the same aim manufacturers of branded goods often add new brands to their range of products. It has been known for a manufacturer deliberately to market two brands, sold under different names, but otherwise identical, in order to obtain a larger share of the market.

Reference has already been made to the practice of differentiating similar varieties of products by branding. This may take the form of an invented name (often a misspelling of the name of a commodity, for example, the name "Sope" for a brand of soap), or the name of the firm may be used in a distinctive way. The invented name is the more popular, and some of these words have almost been accepted into the language. The *Trade Marks Acts* give protection to the manufacturer against the improper use of his trade name by unscrupulous rivals, provided the name has been legally registered. An important result of the branding of goods is that the manufacturer himself often prefers to market the commodity direct to the retailers, and such goods are extensively advertised.

To the retailer the branding of goods has both advantages and disadvantages. Since the goods are made up in packets or containers of uniform weight and quality, they are more conveniently handled, and there is no necessity for the retailers to inspect them before placing his order. On the other hand, retailers have to carry stocks of a large number of different varieties of similar goods in order to pander to the whims and fancies of their customers.

6. Resale price maintenance

For a long time manufacturers of branded goods insisted on a fixed price, and this safeguarded the smaller retailers against price cuts by their larger competitors. The fixed price, however, was to the disadvantage of the more efficient retailers who as a result were debarred from trying to increase their turnover by reducing their prices, and so in conditions of imperfect oligopoly the maxim "small profits, quick returns" ceased to operate. Resale price maintenance was thus a consequence of the sale of branded goods.

Resale price maintenance was first introduced in the 1890s after agitation by the smaller, independent retailers against price-cutting by multiple shops and department stores, which at that time were seeking to increase their turnover by this method. More recently, however, pressure for the retention of price maintenance came chiefly from manufacturers. Insistence on resale at a fixed price was due chiefly to the manufacturer's desire to place his product with as many retailers as possible, in order to secure for himself the maximum number of selling points. To do this he had to ensure that the more efficient retailers did not under-cut the others, since price-cutting might drive the less efficient out of business. Thus, the sale of fixed-price branded goods still further encouraged excess capacity in retailing. Another effect of price maintenance was to substitute competition in service for price competition between retailers. Both the Lloyd Jacob Committee (1949) and the *Restrictive Trade Practices Act* (1956), however, condemned as a restrictive practice concerted action by manufacturers against retailers who had cut the prices of their products. The *Resale Prices Act* (1964) made resale price maintenance illegal, except where manufactureers could satisfy the Restrictive Practices Courts, set up under the Act of 1956, that it was in the public interest for a fixed price to be retained. The effect of this legislation has been to increase competition in retailing to the advantage of the multiple shops and supermarkets, and a large number of the smaller independent traders have been driven out of business. In 1961 there were 542,000 retail shops in Great Britain, but by 1966 the number had fallen to 504,000, and by 1972 to 473,000. The number of shops is expected to fall still further in the future.[1] Customers, however, have gained from lower prices but the larger shops are often less conveniently situated and customers generally have to provide their own transport for their purchases.

7. Selling costs

Selling costs are costs incurred in order to stimulate sales, and thus advertising is the principal selling cost. Advertising can be undertaken for either of two purposes. Sometimes it is simply a way of making an announcement more widely known, this type being known as informative advertising, and to this there are no economic objections. Most advertising, however, is of the persuasive or competitive kind, and its purpose is to persuade consumers that a certain manufacturer's brand of a particular commodity is different from, and superior to, all other brands. Under perfect competition, therefore, there could be no advertising of this second type, on account of the homogeneity of the commodity, although sometimes an industry as a whole might advertise in some form such as *Eat more bread* or *Eat more fruit*. Selling costs are therefore a consequence of imperfect competition, being particularly associated with imperfect oligopoly and, to a lesser degree, with monopolistic competition. In the case of branded goods a fall in price is likely to increase sales only slightly, for people often prefer one brand to others. Regular advertising is essential, too, if the names of the various brands are to be kept constantly before consumers. To some extent, therefore, all advertising is informative. In the production of some commodities selling costs form a very high proportion of total costs, being as high as 45 per cent, for example, in the case of patent medicines. Selling costs are regarded as one of the greatest wastes of imperfect competition. Consequently, economists condemn competitive advertising, partly because of the wasteful employment of factors of production on advertising when they might have been used in some other form of production, and partly because this kind of advertising only increases costs of production. An advertising campaign may, of course, be advantageous to an individual producer, but not to the community as a whole.

III. THE PROBLEM OF MONOPOLY POWER

8. Bases of monopoly power

Although absolute monopoly does not exist in the real world, nevertheless a large measure of monopoly power can sometimes be obtained, as in the following circumstances:

[1] *The Future Pattern of Shopping* (HMSO).

(i) *Where one firm (or group of firms working together) controls a large proportion of the total supply* of a commodity. These are sometimes called natural monopolies. For example most of the world's supply of rubber comes from Malaya; and Canada has almost a monopoly of the world's output of nickel. The few producers of tin have often combined to make price agreements. Brazil is the principal producer of coffee and it is distributed through a central agency, the Coffee Institute of Brazil.

(ii) *Where large, specific plant is required*, as in some branches of the iron and steel industry. In such cases it is difficult for new firms to enter the industry, because of the considerable amount of capital required to do so. Even if capital is available, however, it will not be drawn into such industries immediately profits rise above normal, for where an industry consists of a small number of large firms the addition of one more firm may make the industry over-large and unprofitable. As a result, existing firms enjoy a certain degree of monopoly, but if profits rise much above the normal for a lengthy period rival firms will, of course, be tempted to enter the industry, and so in the long period surplus profit may disappear.

(iii) *Where duplication of a service would be wasteful.* Wherever fixed costs are very heavy proportionately to variable costs, as in the case of many public utilities, such as electricity, gas and water undertakings, an inferior service would result if rival suppliers each laid pipes or cables down every street. To the extent that gas and electricity undertakings compete against one another, wasteful duplication to some extent already exists in many places, and these services would be more efficient if it could be avoided. When the British railway network was under construction Parliament actually encouraged the wasteful duplication of lines in the mistaken view that greater competition would be beneficial to travellers. The result was that eventually Great Britain found itself with a less efficient railway system. Keen as was the desire of Parliament to maintain competition between railways, it had to allow them—until the coming of the motor vehicle—a monopoly over large portions of their systems. It may be that at the present time in spite of the closing of many railway branch lines there is still some wasteful competition between road and rail services. Similarly, the early motor-bus operators were small firms, and often competed against one another over the same routes until 1931 when, in the interest of the safety of the passengers rather than economic efficiency, road traffic was regulated, and competition in road passenger operation abolished. Competitive postal services would obviously be wasteful.

(*iv*) *Branded goods.* By the use of trade marks and trade names, manufacturers try to differentiate their products from those of other producers. Though the element of monopoly is restricted, this practice gives rise to imperfect competition in the form of imperfect oligopoly.

(*v*) *Patent rights.* A patent is a grant by the Crown to the inventor of a new machine or process, giving him a monopoly of its use, in the first instance, for a period of sixteen years, with the possibility of renewal for a further five years or in some cases ten years. Copyright is somewhat similar, and grants the owner the sole right to reproduce a literary or musical work for a period of time, in the case of an author of fifty years after his death, and for gramophone records of fifty years after the making of the matrix. Both patent right and copyright, therefore, give rise to forms of imperfect competition.

(*vi*) *Local monopolies.* These may arise in a number of ways. In the first place, where transport costs are very heavy and only one firm is near the market for the commodity, this firm may be able to raise its charges by an amount equal to the costs of transport of its nearest

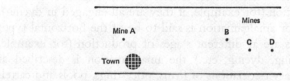

Fig. 69. Local Monopoly.

rival, and as a result obtain surplus profit. Suppose, for example, there is a coal-mine, A, near a certain town, and no other mines nearer than B, C, D. Suppose, further, that the cost of raising a ton of coal is the same in all cases, but that it costs 45p per ton to carry coal from mines B, C and D to the town. The mine A will be able to charge nearly 45p per ton more than the others and yet sell its coal a fraction more cheaply in the town, thereby obtaining a monopoly profit. In the same way local brickworks and stone quarries enjoy an element of local monopoly, as also did village shops before the development of road passenger transport.

Another way in which a somewhat similar type of monopoly may arise occurs when an old-established firm has acquired a very high reputation for the quality of its work, with the result that it may be able to charge higher prices for its products, and be able to continue to do so even though after a time the quality of its product is no better than that of its rivals.

(*vii*) *Tariffs.* A producer's monopoly in the home market may be protected from foreign competition by means of a tariff on imports.

(*viii*) *Restrictions on entry to occupation.* In order to keep up rates of pay a professional organisation may make entry more difficult by insisting upon a longer period of training than is really necessary, or depend on the passing of certain examinations. In many cases the character of the occupation may require a high standard of knowledge and training, as in the medical and legal professions, but in some cases it has merely become a device for restricting the number of people permitted to practice a particular calling. Similarly, trade unions may insist on an unnecessarily long period of apprenticeship.

9. Types of monopolistic association

In order to obtain the advantage of monopoly, firms may form themselves into voluntary associations, or they may combine together permanently.

Horizontal and vertical combines. Where the firms are all at the same stage of production (for example, if they are all engaged in dyeing), the association or amalgamation is said to be of the horizontal type; where the firms are at different stages of production (for example, spinning, weaving, dyeing, etc.) the amalgamation is described as vertical. Voluntary associations of firms, price rings, pools and cartels are of the horizontal type, whereas trusts are generally of vertical structure.

(*i*) *Voluntary associations.* These agree either to fix a minimum price or to restrict output. Price agreements are easier to enforce among the members than agreements to limit output, and so quite loose associations such as the price ring, were to be formed for this purpose. The *Restrictive Trade Practices Act* (1956), however, made it illegal for a group of firms to agree not to sell below an agreed price, and the *Resale Prices Act* (1964) abolished resale price maintenance.

(*ii*) *Cartels.* More complex organisation is required for the cartel, especially if the aim is to restrict output. The first cartels were set up in Germany, the member firms establishing a central selling agency. The members retained their individuality and independence as producers, except that they agreed not to exceed a stated output. There is a tendency, however, for such voluntary agreements to break up. Changing conditions make the more progressive firms increasingly desirous of securing a larger share of the market. Unless a cartel includes all producers, those outside it will take advantage of the higher prices to expand their output. If sponsored by the Government the setting up of a cartel or central selling agency can be made compulsory, and the British Marketing Boards for milk, hops, potatoes, and eggs are cartels of this type. Restriction of output is not the aim, except in the case of hops, but in all cases production for the market is restricted to producers holding the necessary licences. Examples of international cartels are Shipping Conferences at which the shipping lines agree to charge the same passenger fares and make the same freight charges, and the International Air Transport Association which acts in a similar capacity for the international airlines. The Organisation of Petroleum Exporting Countries (OPEC) was, as the name indicates, a cartel of oil exporters. It was established in 1960, but it was not until 1974–5 that it was strong enough to take concerted action to bring about a steep rise in the price of oil.

(iii) *Trusts.* One of the chief weaknesses of the cartel is that the members retain independence of management and, in many cases, the right to withdraw from the association after an agreed period. A complete amalgamation of firms, overcomes this difficulty, for the old firms—at least, the weaker of them—completely lose their identity. The Trust, which is of American origin, is a large-scale amalgamation of firms, frequently of the vertical type, the shareholders in the constituent firms receiving Trust certificates in exchange for their shares.

(iv) *The holding company.* This is a modern development for bringing a number of firms under a single control. It is a purely financial institution which uses its capital to acquire controlling interests in other firms—often in different industries to give greater diversification of product—generally by taking up 51 per cent or more of their shares to form what is known as a group of companies. The holding company has become the typical form of business organisation in both Great Britain and the United States. Although it has control over its subsidiaries, it can, however, retain their original names and the goodwill attached to them. A serious drawback to the holding company is that it makes possible what is known as "pyramiding"—that is, the control of a huge amount of capital by a person who may possess only a relatively small proportion of it. Suppose, for example, Z is a holding company with a capital of £100,003, in which Snodgrass holds shares to the value of £50,002. The holding company, Z, acquires controlling interest in companies A, B and C. Company A has two subsidiaries, D and E, while company C has one subsidiary, F. The following diagram shows the structure of the organisation:

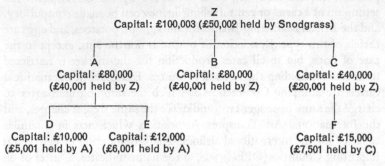

Fig. 70. A Holding Company.

There are six manufacturing companies—A, B, C, D, E and F—with a combined total of £237,000, entirely under the control of Snodgrass, whose total investment is only £50,002—that is, only a little over 21 per cent of the total capital involved. Sometimes only a limited number of the ordinary shares issued by a limited company carry the right to vote at shareholders' meetings, most of the ordinary capital being in the form of non-voting shares. Since the issue of non-voting shares makes pyramiding easier, it has been suggested that no more issues of such shares should be permitted.

(*v*) *State monopolies.* The oldest State monopolies in Great Britain are the Royal Mint and the Post Office. In several European countries the State for a long time has had a monopoly of the manufacture of matches and tobacco, and from an early date in many countries railways have been State-owned. Broadcasting became a State monopoly in Great Britain in 1926. The nationalisation of a number of industries after 1945 created a batch of State monopolies in this country, in some cases where previously there had been a large number of competing firms, as in coal-mining and road haulage.

10. Advantages and disadvantages of monopoly and imperfect competition

(*i*) *Advantages.* In some cases production or distribution can be carried out more efficiently if it is in the hands of a monopolist. It has already been seen that competition in the supply of gas, electricity and water would be wasteful and result in higher prices to consumers. Rationalisation of an industry—that, is reorganisation to secure greater efficiency—makes possible the elimination of excess capacity by closing down production centres where costs are high, and concentrating production in places where costs are lower; instead of all factories working below capacity, a smaller number will then work at full capacity. The Government recently assisted the Lancashire cotton industry to re-organise itself in this way. Similarly, at an earlier period Wool-combers Ltd, had purchased many wool-combing businesses in order to close them, and so reduce the total capacity of the industry.

Under monopoly it becomes possible to reduce the number of varieties of products, whereas under competitive conditions each firm strives to offer as many designs as possible. A reduction, for example, in the number of models of motor cars would to some extent reduce consumers' choice, but the production of an excessive number of designs increases their average cost. Fewer models would mean "longer runs" in the factories and workshops. The same applies to cloth and many other things. Standardisation is the basis of cheaper production. Restriction in the number of designs, however, may not always be a desirable policy. It would not, for example, be in the interests of British worsted manufacturers to put cheapness before variety of pattern, for it is chiefly in the market for high-quality goods that they can compete successfully against foreign manufacturers.

(ii) *Disadvantages*. Though the chief aim may often be to obtain economies of large-scale production, the creation of monopoly brings with it the danger of the misue of monopoly power by exploitation of the consumer. For, under monopoly, prices are almost certain to be higher, and output lower, than would be the case under perfect competition.

The principal disadvantage, however, of monopoly is that consumers lose some of their freedom of choice, and the assortment of goods produced is not that desired by them. Under perfect competition it is the demand of consumers that determines what goods and how much of each shall be produced. By restricting output the monopolist prevents as large an amount of resources going into the production of his commodity as consumers would wish, and so resources are forced into other forms of production which consumers consider to be less desirable. Under monopoly, prices are likely to be more stable than under perfect competition, but output is more liable to fluctuate, and so, therefore, is the level of employment.

So long as a number of firms are competing against each other to supply the market with a particular commodity, each firm has a strong incentive to make itself as efficient as possible. Each firm will readily adopt improved methods of production in order to try to push ahead of its rivals. Under monopoly this incentive is weakened, and if new inventions are costly to introduce there may be reluctance to abandon the older methods. Perhaps one of the chief drawbacks to nationalisation is the loss of this spur to efficiency.

11. Control of monopoly power

One of the chief problems confronting a State aiming to maintain a free economy is how to prevent the exploitation of consumers by producers who possess an element of monopoly power. Labour has been protected by factory legislation and by trade unions (themselves monopolists) and nowadays there is probably a greater danger of the trade unions exploiting the rest of the community than of labour itself being exploited. Company law has been tightened up to regulate more effectually the activities of limited companies. Consumers, however, have never succeeded for long in organising themselves to protect their particular interests. In general, however, monopolists have been disinclined to exercise their power to the full for fear of attracting State action against them.

Attempts have been made in a number of ways to control monopoly:

(i) *Legal restriction*. When it has been recognised that some degree of monopoly is unavoidable, if wasteful competition is to be obviated, charges and profits have often been legally restricted. Canal and railway rates in Great Britain at an early date were subject to Parliament's control. In the case of some monopolies—gas, electricity and local transport undertakings, for example, where these were operated by limited companies—no increase in dividend was permitted unless at the same time they reduced their charges. When road passenger traffic was regulated in 1931, no changes in either service or fares were allowed without the sanction of the Traffic Commissioners for the area.

(ii) *State or municipal operation*. Monopolies of the public-utility type have for long been considered to be best administered by local authorities or the State, the presumption being that neither of these authorities would exploit consumers. Most municipalities in Great Britain formerly operated passenger transport services, and many of them also owned their own electricity and gas undertakings until these services were nationalised. The postal service from the seventeenth century was looked upon as an appropriate activity of the State, and the Post Office took over telegraph and telephone business in 1897. When it was decided in 1933 to co-ordinate the various types of passenger transport serving London—buses, tramways, underground railways—a public corporation, the London Passenger Transport Board was set up. In this country it was considered desirable, too, that broadcasting should be a monopoly, and though at first it was under the control of the British Broadcasting Company, it was eventually taken over by the British Broadcasting Corporation.

(*iii*) *Legal action against monopolies.* In the United States action was taken against monopolies by the State as long ago as 1890 when the Sherman *Anti-Trust Act* was passed declaring trusts to be an illegal form of business organisation. The American policy of making monopolies illegal was not particularly successful during the quarter-century following the passing of the Sherman Act, although under the anti-trust laws a number of extra-large companies were broken up. Often, however, this only resulted in the companies being reorganised to comply with—or more likely to evade—the law. More recently, however, the courts of the United States have vigorously attacked many undesirable monopolistic practices, including some of those employed by oligopolists, and the firms concerned have been compelled to cease these activities.

In Great Britain action against monopoly was not taken until 1948 when under the *Monopolies and Restrictive Practices Act* a Commission was set up to inquire into the conditions of manufacture of a number of commodities. Altogether the Monopolies Commission reported on a great many commodities, including matches, electric lamps, motor-car tyres, linoleum, cigarettes and tobacco, wallpaper, household detergents, colour films. The Commission, however, found it extremely difficult in many cases to decide whether prices and profits were reasonable. It is of interest to note that the Act setting up the Monopolies Commission defined a monopolist as a producer of at least one-third of the total output of a commodity. The power of the Commission was limited to reporting its findings to Parliament. Under the *Restrictive Trade Practices Act* (1956), however, five Restrictive Practices Courts were established to decide whether existing agreements among producers or distributors, all of which had to be reported to a Registrar, were in the public interest, and these courts have power to enforce their decisions. Any agreement found to be undesirable must be immediately dissolved. Since the passing of the Act the members of some trade associations, however, have made "open price" arrangements, the price-leader informs its rivals of the price that it intends to charge, and these other firms can then of their own volition decide to charge the same price if they so wish. This practice is as yet outside the jurisdiction of the courts.

The *Resale Prices Act* (1964) encouraged competition by abolishing resale price maintenance except in cases specifically exempted by the Restrictive Practices Courts. The *Monopolies and Mergers Act* (1965) empowered the Board of Trade to inquire into any proposed merger and to refer it to the Monopolies Commission if it was thought to constitute a monopoly. Since then the Commission has refused to sanction more than one proposed merger. By the *Fair Trading Act* (1973) the Monopolies Commission became the Monopolies and Mergers Commission. This Act gave greater protection to consumers and set up an Office of Fair Trading to consider complaints reported to it.

Thus in both Great Britain and the United States more effective action is now being taken against monopolists and oligopolists.

RECOMMENDATIONS FOR FURTHER READING

K. B. Boulding: *Economic Analysis*, Chapters 27 and 28.
E. H. Chamberlin: *The Theory of Monopolistic Competition*, Chapters 3–6.
Joan Robinson: *Economics of Imperfect Competition*, Chapters 25 and 26.
M. Hall: *Distributive Trading*.

QUESTIONS

1. Why and how does the State attempt to control monopoly practices? (SE London)

2. Define imperfect competition and account for its prevalence. (Wales)

3. "Combination does not necessarily imply monopoly, nor does monopoly involve combination." Illustrate this statement by examining the several types of combinations of business units with which you are familiar. (RSA)

4. Write a short essay on the main features of cartels, combines and trusts in industry and their advantages and disadvantages to the consumer. (LC Com.)

5. Distinguish with examples, between horizontal and vertical combination. (AIA)

6. How does a trust differ from a cartel in structure and policy? (IT)

7. It has been suggested that combines operate at the expense of the consumer. What do you understand by this statement, and do you consider it necessary to modify it in any way? (LC Com.)

8. Discuss the use and limitations of advertisement as an aid to trade. (Exp.)

9. What is meant by imperfect competition? Distinguish any types of imperfect competition which are known to you. (CIS)

10. Explain briefly the major points of difference between "perfect" and "imperfect" competition. (CIS)

11. To what extent is advertising undersirable from the viewpoint of the community? (IB)

12. Why do monopolies arise? Discuss the possible causes of the emergence to monopolistic organisations, with special reference to the conditions in the United Kingdom. (GCE)

13. Explain carefully the machinery existing in the United Kingdom for controlling either (a) monopolies or (b) restrictive practices. (GCE)

14. What are the advantages and disadvantages in the practice of putting branded consumable goods upon the market? (Degree)

15. "Monopolistic competition involves a less economical use of resources than perfect competition." Do you agree? (Degree)

Why are monopolies considered to be harmful? Can they ever be beneficial? (Degree)

Part Five

THE NATIONAL INCOME AND ITS DISTRIBUTION

CHAPTER 16

THE NATIONAL INCOME

I. PERSONAL INCOME AND NATIONAL INCOME

1. Types of income

As a result of the employment of its factors of production during a year a country achieves a certain output of goods and services—its total volume of production for that year. For their services to production, factors are generally paid in money, these payments being variously known as rent, wages, interest and profit. It is tempting to regard these four payments as the rewards accruing to the four factors of production for their share in the work of production—rent to land, wages to labour, interest to capital and profits to the entrepreneur. Unfortunately, this is too simple a concept. Wages are easily recognised as the particular reward of labour, but it is not nearly so easy to assign the other payments to appropriate factors. Rent is paid for the use of land, but there are often elements of rent both in wages and in profit, and it is not always easy to distinguish between interest and profit. All these four types of payment are, however, income, and all income is received by someone. The total income of a community depends, then, on the total volume of production—in fact, as will be shown shortly, it *is* the total volume of production. The purpose of this chapter is to consider the national income and its importance, and then in the following chapters to discuss how this income is distributed among different sections of the community. In other words, these later chapters will be devoted to that branch of economics known as distribution.

From the point of view of the entrepreneur payments made to factors are costs of production—the cost of producing the goods and services that comprise the total volume of production. To the factors of production, however, these payments are income. Some of the factors of production are persons; others are inanimate things, such as most forms of capital. Payments, however, can be made only to persons, and not to inanimate objects. Payment is made for the services of a factor, and these may be personal services, such as those of labour or the entrepreneur, or impersonal services, such as those of land and capital, and in the case of impersonal services payment is made to the owners of the factors.

Income, therefore, is derived from two sources:

(*i*) the performing of personal services;
(*ii*) the ownership of factors providing impersonal services.

Figure 71 shows the different sources of income, the term *property* being used for any impersonal thing that yields an income.

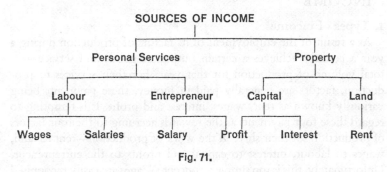

Fig. 71.

2. Inequality of income

Inequality of income can be attributed, then, to one of two causes: (*i*) differences in payments made for personal services; or (*ii*) differences in the amount of property possessed. A discussion of the causes of differences in wages in different occupations must be reserved for Chapter 18. Many people have only income of this kind; others derive considerable income from the ownership of different kinds of property. Incomes derived from the possession of property vary enormously, because property is very unequally distributed. Property of all kinds—land, buildings, shares in companies, Government securities, etc.—can be acquired either by inheritance, or by saving, or in both these ways. It should be noted that it is not merely the possession of property that yields income; the owner receives payment because he allows someone else the use of his property, that is, he is paid for a service he renders to someone else. Large accumulations of property have been built up partly by inheritance and partly through saving, successive generations of owners having added to their possessions during their lifetime. For this reason taxes in some countries are levied on both income and wealth, especially where the aim is to reduce the inequality of income.

Before the growth of large-scale industry during the past hundred and fifty years or so, the rate of accumulation was slow, for most property consisted of land and buildings, and openings for profitable investment were few. In England the system of inheritance, whereby all the landed property and most of the personalty were left to the eldest son, tended to increase inequality. The younger sons generally entered the professions or trade, and some of them—especially those who took up law or trade—saved enough in their lifetimes to purchase estates for themselves and found new landowning families. In countries where on the death of the father the property was shared among all the children in the family there is a more widespread ownership of property and less inequality, though less efficient operation of the estate usually following each subdivision of it. Industrial development has increased the possibility of building up a large accumulation of property in one's lifetime, and big fortunes have been made in many different types of production. In Great Britain some income from property is usual among even the lower-salaried grades of the middle classes and the better-paid artisans. Thrift, for long preached as a great virtue, is still practised by people within a wide range of income derived from work. National Savings Certificates, Premium Bonds and balances in the National (formerly Post Office) and Trustee Savings Banks are widely held, and in the largest companies shareholders often number many thousands. The custom of home ownership has increased enormously in Great Britain in the last quarter of a century, and though much of such property is mortgaged with Building Societies for long periods, the houses eventually become the property of the occupiers, and as such yield income—in this case notional—on the rent that otherwise would have to be paid. The thrifty are not limited to any particular income group—just as spendthrifts are to be found among rich and poor alike—though obviously the thrifty rich are capable of saving more than the thrifty poor. Inequality of income has, however, been reduced by steeply progressive income taxes, which make it difficult to accumulate large amounts of property by saving, and by heavy death duties which reduce the amount of property that can be acquired by inheritance.

3. The national income = the volume of production

The terms *national income* and *volume of production* are really alternative names for the same thing, for the amount paid for a commodity in effect comprises a number of payments for the various services undertaken in its production, and all payments become income to those who receive them. Consequently, the national income can be regarded either as the money value of all goods and services produced during a particular period—usually a year—or the sum of all personal incomes derived from economic activity during that time. A Census of Production records the quantity of ships, motor cars, sewing-machines, wireless sets, bedroom suites, carpets, worsted cloth, cotton goods, boots and shoes, wheat, oats, potatoes, jam, etc., produced in the country during a certain year; but it does not show how much medical and dental service, how much teaching, how many hours of entertainment and music have been provided. Even if it did show the total of services, as well as of goods, produced in the year, the total would still be a heterogeneous mass that could not easily be compared with that of other years.

A common denominator must therefore be found, and the money, value of all these things provides an obvious unit of measurement, though by no means a perfect one, for money itself may change in value. Marshall defined national income as "the aggregate net product of, and the sole source of payment for, all the agents of production."[1] Sir John Hicks has given the following definition: "The national income consists of a collection of goods and services reduced to a common basis by being measured in terms of money."[2]

The total volume of production, then, is expressed as a sum of money. For example, it was calculated that in 1974 the total volume of production of the United Kingdom was worth £73,977 million, that is to say, the total value of all the goods and services produced in this country in that year came to that amount. Since every cost of production is a payment for a service, the total income of the producers of those goods and services, therefore, must also have been £73,977 million. Entrepreneurs received payment for the goods they produced, and paid out rent, wages and salaries and interest on loans for the use of the factors they employed, keeping the balance (profit) as their own reward. Those people who provided services were paid either in fees or salaries, and the value of their services was assessed at the amounts they received. For clarity, some complications have for the moment been omitted, but some of these will be considered shortly. It is evident, therefore, that the total volume of production and the total of all incomes are, in fact, one and the same. In other words, the price paid for a commodity is equal to the sum of the payments to the factors of production that have assisted in its manufacture.

The calculation of the national income can consequently be approached either from the side of the output of goods or from the side

---

[1] A. Marshall: *Principles of Economics*, VI. I. 10.
[2] J. R. Hicks: *The Social Framework*, Part IV.

of income. If full information were available, either method of calculation should yield exactly the same result. A third approach is possible—from the side of consumption. Since income is either spent or saved, the total amount spent on consumers' goods, added to savings, should also be equal to the national income.

4. Increased interest in the national income

Though economists from the time of Alfred Marshall onwards have given some consideration to the national income, it is only in comparatively recent times that the study of its measurement and distribution has assumed a prominent place in economics. This has been rendered possible because Governments have now begun to take more interest in the subject, for serious analysis and study were impossible until current statistics were available, the compilation of which was too vast a task for the resources of private institutions devoted to economic study. The British Government has established a permanent body known as the Central Statistical Office, which since 1941 has provided the material for the Government's annual White Paper and Blue Book on the National Income and Expenditure and for many other matters of economic importance. In the United States the National Bureau of Economic Research of the Department of Commerce fulfils a similar function. Most countries now are interested in the subject, as also is the United Nations Organisation, because the income is the best guide to economic welfare.

II. THE CALCULATION OF THE NATIONAL INCOME

5. The Gross National Product

Preliminary details of the national income for the previous year are given in a *White Paper* published annually in March, this being followed in September of each year by a more detailed *Blue Book on National Income and Expenditure*. Table XXXVII on page 284 shows the *Gross National Product at factor cost*. The total value of all the goods and services produced in this country in a particular year is known as the *Gross Domestic Product*. This is calculated at what is known as *factor cost*, that is, excluding subsidies and taxes imposed on any goods or services. It is, in fact, the cost of total output to producers. After account has been taken of net income from abroad (the value of exports of all kinds less the value of imports) we have the *Gross National Product at factor cost*.

Having calculated the Gross National Product it now becomes possible to calculate the national income. All that is required is to make an estimate of the capital consumption that has taken place during the year and deduct this from the Gross National Product.

Thus, it will be seen that the national income is in effect the net national product, that is the total volume of production after allowance has been made for that part of production that has been devoted to making good the depreciation of existing capital equipment.

Table XXXVII

Gross National Product at Factor Cost

Product or service				1974	197–[1]
				£ million	£ million
Goods and services produced by					
Agriculture, forestry and fishing	.	.		2,116	
Mining and quarrying	.	.	.	1,021	
Manufacturing	.	.	.	20,645	
Building and construction	.	.	.	5,645	
Gas, electricity, water	.	.	.	2,255	
Transport and communication	.	.		6,648	
Distribution	.	.	.	7,003	
Insurance, banking and finance	.	.		6,750	
Public administration and defence	.	.		5,312	
Ownership of dwellings	.	.	.	4,310	
Public health and education	.	.		4,854	
Other services (net)	.	.	.	6,066	
Gross domestic product	.	.	.	72,625	
Net income from abroad	.	.	.	1,352	
Gross National Product	.	.	.	73,977	

[1] The reader is recommended to complete this column with the latest figures available.

Table XXXVIII

National Income (1)

	1974	197–[1]
	£ million	£ million
Gross national product	73,977	
Less capital consumption	8,431	
National Income	65,546	

[1] For the latest figures.

6. National income and expenditure

A second method of calculating the national income is to take the total of all incomes derived from economic activity (Table XXXIX). Whether the national income is calculated as the total volume of production or the total of all incomes derived from economic activity the two totals must be the same. Indeed, the volume of production and the national income are the same thing. It is clear that this must be so, since what is paid by a consumer for a commodity becomes income to all those who have had a share in its production. Every commodity, it is said, represents merely a collection of the services of those who have obtained the raw material, changed its form in some way, transported and marketed it at the wholesale and retail stages.

Table XXXIX

National Income (2)

Type of income	1974	197–[1]
	£ million	£ million
Wages and salaries	45,490	
Pay in cash and kind of the Forces . .	1,078	
Employers' insurance and other contributions	5,433	
Professional earnings	1,214	
Income from farming	1,599	
Profits of other sole traders and partnerships	5,122	
Profits of companies	9,706	
Profits of public enterprises	2,426	
Net income from abroad	1,352	
Other income	597	
Total income	73,977	
Less capital consumption	8,431	
National Income	65,546	

[1] For the latest figures.

Employers' insurance contributions appear in the table because it is now general practice to regard them as part of employees' incomes deducted at source. Since some of the incomes shown in Table XXXIX were earned in producing new capital to make good capital consumption an allowance must be made for this as was done in Table XXXVIII.

A third method of calculating the national income is to take the total of all expenditure incurred during the year, personal and public. This is shown in the Table XL on page 286.

Table XL

Total Expenditure

	1974	197–[1]
	£ million	£ million
Personal consumption		
Food	9,837	
Clothing	4,477	
Rent and rates	5,848	
Fuel and light	2,268	
Alcoholic drink	3,972	
Tobacco	2,237	
Household goods	5,736	
Books, newspapers, etc. . . .	797	
Cars and motor-cycles and running costs	4,872	
Travel	1,598	
Insurance	864	
Catering (meals and accommodation) .	2,431	
Entertainment	948	
Other goods and services . . .	7,630	
Total personal consumption . . .	51,760	
Expenditure of public authorities . .	16,641	
Gross domestic capital formation . .	9,908	
Subsidies	2,766	
Net income from abroad . . .	1,352	
	82,337	
Less indirect taxes on goods and services .	8,360	
Gross national expenditure at factor cost .	73,977	
Less capital consumption	8,431	
Net national expenditure	65,546	

[1] For the latest figures.

III. THE MEASUREMENT OF THE NATIONAL INCOME

7. The importance of the national income

Why, then, is so much interest taken in the national income? In Chapter 2 we say that the aim of production is to increase economic welfare. In the first place, economic welfare depends on the volume of production, for an increase in the volume of production will increase economic welfare, provided (*i*) that it does not increase inequality of income, and (*ii*) that it is not achieved at the cost of health. A reduction in inequality of income will generally increase economic welfare, unless it results in a fall in production. As an indication of economic progress, Alfred Marshall considered national income a more suitable measure than national wealth. "The money income, or inflow of wealth," he says, "gives a measure of a nation's prosperity, which, untrustworthy as it is, is yet in some respects better than that afforded by the money value of its stock of wealth."[1] An increase in the national income in real terms is an essential prerequisite to a rise in the general standard of living of a people.

The fact that in this country the State began to measure the national income in 1941—at perhaps the greatest crisis in the nation's history—is an indication of the practical importance by that time attached to knowing the volume of production. Since then it has become an important adjunct to economic planning. Directly and indirectly the public sector of the economy has been expanding, the State playing an ever more important role in the national economy. The acceptance by the State of responsibility for full employment has made it more than ever necessary for it to know the trend of business activity, and particularly the proportion of the national income devoted to investment. Nowadays one of the principal aims of economic policy of Governments throughout the world is to improve the standard of living of their people. In the first place, the standard of living of a people depends on the size of the national income, for clearly the greater the volume of production, the greater the quantity of goods and services available for distribution. An increase, therefore, in the national income makes possible a rise in a people's standard of living. A second influence on the standard of living is the way in which the national income is distributed, for in general, the less the inequality of individual incomes, the higher will be the general standard of living.

8. Economic growth

The rate of increase of its national income provides a measure of a country's rate of economic growth and, therefore, of the standard of living of its people. Tables XLI and XLII show how the national income of the United Kingdom has increased in recent years.

It would be erroneous, however, to assume from a reading of this table that on average the people of this country were enjoying a standard of living in 1974 nearly double that of 1960. The past thirty years have been a period of almost continuously rising prices and this fact accounts for a good deal of the increase in the national income. This

[1] Alfred Marshall: *Principles of Economics*, p. 80.

has been particularly true of the years since 1970 during which prices rose more steeply in Great Britain than ever before. The only way to compare one year with another, therefore, is to recalculate all the prices in terms of those ruling in a particular year. For purposes of comparison the *Blue Book on National Income and Expenditure* takes the year 1970 as its base. When this is done the expansion of the national income becomes much less impressive.

Table XLI

The Growth of the National Income (1) *Actual Prices*
No allowance for changes of prices

Year	£ million	Year	£ million
1870	929	1964	29,163
1910	2,062	1966	33,042
1938	5,175	1967	34,854
1946	8,783	1968	37,333
1950	10,786	1969	39,180
1952	12,771	1970	43,012
1954	14,590	1971	44,228
1956	16,846	1972	49,468
1958	19,621	1973	57,451
1960	21,883	1974	65,546
1962	24,872	1975	

Table XLII

The Growth of the National Income (2) *Constant Prices*
Calculated in terms of 1970 prices

Year	£ million
1950	26,305
1960	34,228
1962	35,900
1964	38,080
1966	39,753
1968	41,687
1969	42,240
1970	43,012
1971	43,818
1972	44,764
1973	47,113
1974	47,171
1975	

According to Table XLI, where no allowance is made for rising prices, the national income increased in money terms by no less than 98 per cent, but if Table XLII is used, prices being assumed to be constant, the increase was only 18.5 per cent, giving an average rate of growth of only about 2.3 per cent per year. Governments nowadays are particularly concerned to promote economic growth, the rate at which the volume of production expands being taken as a measure of a country's economic progress. During the 1960s the rate of economic growth of West Germany and Japan was most impressive, and it was generally felt that Great Britain was lagging behind as its rate of growth was much less. In fact, for the world as a whole the rate of economic growth accelerated during the nineteenth century, but the outstanding period of economic growth was the thirty years, 1945–75, when it is estimated that total world production increased by no less than four times, the increase in real terms being as great as in the previous two thousand years. If national income figures are used as a basis for comparing standards of living of people in different countries —or even of the same country at different periods of time—allowance must be made for (*i*) price changes; (*ii*) differences in the size of the population; (*iii*) the rate of exchange between different currencies (*iv*) the amount of production given up to the manufacture of such things as armaments; (*v*) the amount of work the people do for themselves and for which they receive no payment; (*vi*) how the national income is distributed among the people, that is, whether there is great inequality of income or not. Different peoples, too, demand different assortments of goods, and in some countries with less well developed economic systems with less division of labour people perform more services for themselves. In 1974 the national income, expressed as an average per head of the population, was £1,700 for the United Kingdom, £3,200 for West Germany, £2,500 for France, over £3,400 for the United States and about £650 for Russia. The only possible basis on which such comparisons can be made is to average the national income per head of the population. But before that can be done the total income for one country has to be recalculated in terms of the currency of the other at the rate of exchange prevailing at the time, and this may not give a very accurate indication of the relative internal value of the two currencies as other influences affect exchange rates.

9. Factors determining the national income

There are a number of influences on the size of a country's national income. It is for the following reasons that one country may have a larger national income than another.

(i) *The stock of factors of production.* The quantity and quality of a country's stock of factors of production will be one of the most important influences on the size of its national income. Land may be fertile or infertile, for reasons outside the control of the community. Climate and quality of the soil are the prime factors that determine the type of agriculture that can be undertaken, for handicaps of climate can be overcome only to a limited extent. Irrigation can offset lack of rainfall; glasshouse production can mitigate a lack of heat; but the Sahara Desert is too vast to be treated in the one way, just as the Canadian tundra is too vast for the other. Agricultural production, too, may vary quite considerably from one year to another, because of vagaries of the weather.

The quality of the labour will depend partly on the inborn intelligence of the people, though perhaps mainly on the quality of its education and training. The supply of labour must be large enough to make the best use of other factors, but too great a supply will mean smaller shares for all. In other words, the population should be as near as possible to the optimum.

Capital can vary from very simple, primitive tools to the most modern types of automated industrial plant. The extent of a country's stock of modern forms of capital is the most important influence on its total volume of production. The supply of factors in any country is limited, and whether or not the best use is made of them will depend on the entrepreneurial ability available, for only if the factors are combined in the optimum proportions will the maximum output be achieved. Since the countries that have the largest amounts of capital find it easiest to increase their stock, the difference between rich and poor nations tends to widen in spite of the assistance to the less developed countries by those more economically advanced.

The quantity and quality of factors of production (especially capital) vary enormously between one country and another, and this is perhaps the main cause of differences in their standards of living.

(ii) *The state of technical knowledge.* A second influence on the national income is the state of technical knowledge in a country. Until the middle of the eighteenth century methods of production had remained substantially unchanged for many centuries, but since then technical progress has become ever more rapid, especially in the more economically advanced countries. The most recent development has been the introduction of automation, an important feature of which is the linking together of machines by automatic control. There is a wide difference between the state of technical knowledge of the most advanced industrial countries as compared with the developing ones.

(*iii*) *Political stability*. If production is to be maintained at the highest level, political stability is essential. The development of many countries—for example, some of the South American Republics—has been hindered in the past by political instability. At some period of their history all countries have suffered setbacks to their economic progress on account of political instability resulting from wars or revolutions.

10. Some difficulties in measuring the national income

Measurement of the national income is beset with difficulties:

(*i*) *Information is incomplete*. Although the Inland Revenue returns provide particulars of sources of income that are subject to Income Tax, and the Department of Employment collects information on wages, there still remain some items that have to be estimated. Then, some income is not recorded, as for example when a joiner, electrician or plumber does a job in his spare time for a friend or neighbour.

(*ii*) *The danger of double counting*. The cost of raw materials and of finished goods must not both be counted, for that would mean that the cost of raw materials would be included twice. In reckoning the output of a firm the cost of materials purchased from other firms must be deducted. All services performed by one firm for another, including transport, insurance and banking, must therefore be excluded, as their cost is included in the price of the product.

(*iii*) *Unpaid services*. Only those goods and services for which payment is made are taken into account. Any services that people do for themselves, or do gratuitously for others—a woman making her own clothes, or doing embroidery; a man painting his house or growing a few vegetables—have to be excluded. It is very difficult to know exactly where to draw the line between what to count and what to omit but the only practicable method seems to be to exclude all unpaid employment. This method of surmounting the difficulty, however, produces some anomalies. The fewer services people do for themselves—that is, the greater the division of labour—the larger will be the national income, even if no increase in actual output results. If Jingle, a house-painter, attends to his own garden, and Trotter, a gardener, paints his own house, neither of these tasks will add anything to the national income. If, on the other hand, Jingle paints Trotter's house, and Trotter does some gardening for Jingle, the national income is increased by the charge each makes for the work he has done.

Therefore, the greater the extent to which division of labour is carried
—that is, the less people do for themselves—the greater will be the
national income, even though the actual volume of production is the
same in both cases. For this reason the national income of India—only
about £52 per head in 1974—appears to be lower than it actually is.
If the Mersey Tunnel or the Forth Bridge were freed from toll, or if
a charge was made for using the Woolwich ferry, the national income
would be affected, but clearly in neither case would there be any
change in the volume of services provided.

(*iv*) *Depreciation*. If the *net* national income is to be calculated, then
the amount set aside for replacing worn-out or out-of-date fixed
capital assets must be deducted from the total. If the national income is
considered in terms of volume of production of the reasonableness of
this is at once clear. For example, the production of lorries to replace
vehicles that are no longer fit for service obviously does not increase
the total stock of such vehicles. Similarly, the replacement of an old
machine by a more efficient one does not increase the stock of capital
of this sort though it clearly improves its quality. It has already been
seen that the British practice in calculating the national income is to
allow for depreciation.

(*v*) *Housing*. If Cratchit lives in a house for which he pays his landlord a rent of £52 per annum this rent is clearly income to the landlord; it will not, of course, be net income, for out of it the cost of
repairs to the property will have to be met. If Cratchit buys this
house he will no longer pay rent—at least, not to some other person.
This rent payable to himself is known as notional income. For purposes of calculating the national income it is justifiable, therefore, to
credit Cratchit with an addition to his income equal to the rent of the
house in which he lives as owner-occupier. In the *Blue Book on National
Income and Expenditure* this item is included under the heading *Ownership
of dwellings*, while newly built houses come under the heading, *Building
and construction*.

(*vi*) *Public income and expenditure*. Government expenditure falls into
three main categories: (*a*) the maintenance of internal law and order
and external defence; (*b*) the provision of social services including
education, medical and dental services and social security payments;
and (*c*) the payment of interest on the national debt. Part of the expenditure in category (*b*) falls on local authorities, as also does some of the
expenditure of an entirely local character, as, for example, street lighting and the upkeep of parks. Government income is principally derived
from taxes, while Local Authorities raise revenue by levying rates.

State activity in Great Britain also includes the operation of nationalised industries. Much of Government expenditure presents no difficulty if it is considered as a collective payment by the Government on behalf of taxpayers for the various services provided, but from the taxpayers' point of view it becomes compulsory consumption. The national debt payment, however, is interest on a debt created in the past, which taxpayers pay to holders of Government stocks. Since it is merely a transfer of income from one group of people to another, income from this source must not be included in addition to the full incomes of those who paid it, otherwise there will be double counting. Similarly, social security payments for sickness, etc., also are transfers of income from one group of people to another. Such transfer income must not be counted twice.

As already noted, indirect taxes, such as purchase tax and duties on beer and tobacco, are deducted from the market price of the commodities on which they are levied, in order to show output at factor cost, that is, the cost in terms of the payments to the factors of production used in their manufacture.

(*vii*) *Foreign payments*. There are people in this country who receive income from abroad in the form of dividends from shares in foreign enterprises, or interest payments on foreign Government Stocks; and there are foreigners also who receive dividends and interest from their investments in this country or who send gifts to relatives abroad or make use of this country's shipping, banking and insurance facilities, and therefore have to pay for them; or again, the Government may receive interest payments for loans made in the past to foreign countries, or foreign tourists may come to Great Britain and spend money on hotel accommodation and transport. From all these sources income may come from abroad, or for any one or all of these reasons payments may have to be made to foreign countries, but to some extent payments and receipts will offset one another. These items must therefore be added to (or subtracted from) internal income. In calculating the national income of a country, only its net income from abroad (total receipts less payments) will be included. This can be either a credit or a debit item.

(*viii*) *Inventory revaluation*. The term *inventory* denotes the value of stocks and work in progress at the end of the year, as shown in a firm's balance sheet. In the trading account compiled the opening and closing stocks are the inventories of the current and the preceding years. In periods of rising prices gross profit will be increased on account of the appreciation in value of stocks held, though the replacement cost of such stocks will also increase. Business profits include such gains, but in the calculation of the gross national product a deduction is made for straighten appreciation whenever this occurs.

(ix) *Changes in the value of money.* Money is a poor measuring rod, since its own value is liable to change, but it is, nevertheless, the only common denominator we possess for adding together the heterogeneous mass of goods and services that comprise the national income. Nevertheless, the total national income in terms of money has little meaning. Comparison between one year and another is impossible unless the relative value of money at the two dates is known. As already indicated, the *Blue Book on National Income and Expenditure* now includes tables showing total expenditure of consumers (i) at current prices, and (ii) in terms of prices ruling in a selected base year (at present 1970), so that comparison between different years becomes possible. (*See* Tables XLI and XLII.)

11. Social and private net product

A. C. Pigou[1] drew a distinction between what he called social and private net product. The national income shows the value of the goods and services produced during a certain year, but it takes no account of any harmful effects of production. There are some things the production of which adds to the national income, but which at the same time create a disservice. The net social product might therefore be defined as the private net product *less* the value of any disservices entailed in its production.

All people who live in industrial towns have to suffer to a greater or lesser degree from the effects of an atmosphere heavily laden with smoke, petrol fumes and other impurities. Laundry bills are heavier and the sickness rate is higher in such places than in more salubrious districts. If the atmosphere is also polluted with impurities, if it is near large airports or chemical or tin-plate works, curtains and other household fabrics may deteriorate more rapidly than elsewhere. So far economic progress has been achieved only at the expense of much dirt and grime, noxious fumes in the streets, and river and coastal pollution, although the establishment of "clean air" zones has reduced it somewhat. From the private net product a deduction to cover these disservices must be made in order to obtain the social net product.

In this category too might be placed the manufacture of intoxicants, for if it can be shown that the consumption of intoxicants leads to an increase in crime, thereby creating additional expense to the State for

[1] A. C. Pigou: *Economics of Welfare.*

the maintenance of prisons and larger police forces. Social welfare would be increased if the production and sale of such commodities was curtailed.

Profits from organised gambling such as the running of football pools and bookmakers' businesses, add to the private but not to the social net product.

All the so-called "wastes" of imperfect or monopolistic competition increase the private net product by amounts greater than the social net product. This is especially true of competitive advertising, for its effect is merely to persuade people to buy one thing instead of another, nothing being added to the total volume of goods and services produced.

The expansion of the national income owes a great deal to scientific research, but the application of research to new means of destruction adds nothing to the social net product.

Some people believe that the employment of married women in industry reduces the social net product, since it may lead to neglect of children, though this loss may be reduced by setting up day nurseries.

Similarly, the social net product will exceed the private net product wherever the production of a commodity or the provision of a service is conducive to healthier conditions. Examples of such things are the provision of parks and other open spaces in large towns, the substitution of electric power for coal, or the extension of "clean air" zones in the larger towns.

RECOMMENDATIONS FOR FURTHER READING

J. R. Hicks: *The Social Framework,* Part IV.
A. C. Pigou: *The Economics of Welfare,* Part II, Chapter 8.
W. Beckerman: *An Introduction to National Income Analysis.*
Blue Book on National Income (HMSO) (annually in September).

QUESTIONS

1. Define the national income. Upon what factors does the growth of the national income depend? (Bolton)

2. Describe the methods of calculating the national income. What difficulties are encountered in its measurement? (Huddersfield)

3. National income figures are used to measure the standard of living in a country. What are the limitations of this when comparing either two different years or two different countries? (Yorks)

4. What is meant by the real national income? What are the main difficulties involved in a comparison of the real national income today with that of twenty-five years ago? (B S)

5. How would you compare the national income of different countries to discover in which country the average worker had the higher standard of living? (CIS)

6. Is it either possible or sensible to compare the national income of Britain with that of an under-developed economy? (CIS)

7. What do you understand by the income of (a) an individual and (b) a nation? (CIS)

8. What main economic factors affect the standard of living? (IB)

9. What factors determine the level of national income per head within a country? (IB)

10. Describe the methods of calculating the national income. How far can the national income be used as a measure of economic growth? (IB)

11. "The national income consists of a collection of goods and services reduced to a common basis by being measured in terms of money." Comment upon this statement and discuss the view that the national income provides the best single measure of a nation's economic progress. (IB)

12. Account for the rise in National Income since 1939. (GCE)

13. Why is the National Income per head higher in the United Kingdom than it is in Italy or Greece? (GCE)

14. Explain what is meant by: (a) money national income; (b) real national income. (GCE)

15. How has real national income per head changed in the United Kingdom in the past thirty years? What do you consider to be the chief causes of this change? (GCE)

16. Define *real national income*. What difficulties arise in measuring it? (GCE)

17. What determines the extent of the differences between the standards of living in two countries? (GCE)

18. "The standard of living in country A is twice as high as in country B." Discuss the conceptual and practical difficulties involved in this statement. (Degree)

19. What factors will influence the possibility of doubling the standard of living in the United Kingdom during the next twenty-five years? (Degree)

CHAPTER 17

THE THEORY OF DISTRIBUTION

I. THE MARGINAL PRODUCTIVITY THEORY

1. The factor market

In Chapter 9 we considered commercial distribution, that is the various methods employed to distribute goods from their place of manufacture to the people who want to use them. We have now to consider distribution in its economic sense, namely what determines the share of the national income received by labour and the owners of the other factors of production. This forms one of the main branches into which economics was traditionally divided.

In the markets for consumers' goods prices are determined by the interaction of the forces of supply and demand. This problem of pricing has already been considered. The marginal analysis was used to explain the bases upon which supply and demand are founded, marginal utility underlying demand, and the concepts of marginal revenue and marginal cost being employed to determine supply. These same tools of economic analysis can be applied also to the pricing of the factors of production. The entrepreneur's costs consist of payments made for the services of various factors, the quantity of each factor employed depending largely on its price. Instead of the term price, for the payments made to factors of production, the terms rent, wages, interest and profit are used. Demand in the market for consumers' goods comes from consumers; demand in the factor market comes from entrepreneurs for the services of factors of production. The basis of demand in the market for consumers' goods is the marginal utility of the commodity to consumers; the basis of demand in the factor market is the marginal productivity of the various factors to the entrepreneurs. The demand for factors, however, is a *derived* demand, since it depends on the demand for the commodities in the production of which they are employed.

2. The marginal productivity of a factor

Marginal productivity is similar to the other marginal concepts previously considered. The marginal product of any factor is the addition to output and income[1] of the entrepreneur arising from the employ-ment of an additional unit of that factor. If perfect competition is assumed a large output can be sold at the same price as a small output, and so if the employment of one more man in an enterprise results in the production in a week of say, forty-four units of a commodity that can be sold for £1 each, then the marginal productivity of the factor, labour, in this enterprise is £44 per week. The employment of more men will reduce the marginal productivity of labour in exactly the same way that an increase in a consumer's supply of a commodity reduces its marginal utility to him. The more labour (or any other factor) the entrepreneur employs, the lower will be the marginal productivity of that factor. The following table shows the marginal productivity of labour when different numbers of men are employed:

Table XLIII

The Marginal Productivity of Labour
Price = £1 per unit

Number of men	Units of output	Total revenue	Marginal productivity (units of output)	Marginal productivity (income to firm)
40	589	£589	—	—
41	633	£633	44	£44
42	671	£671	38	£38
43	704	£704	33	£33
44	733	£733	29	£29
45	759	£759	26	£26
46	783	£783	24	£24

When forty-one men are employed, the marginal physical pro-ductivity of labour is forty-four units of the commodity and the marginal revenue productivity is £44. If forty-two men are em-ployed, marginal productivity falls to thirty-eight units, or £38. How much a consumer will buy of a commodity depends on its price, more being bought the lower the price, so that the demand curve for the commodity slopes downwards. Similarly, how much labour the entrepreneur in the above example will employ will de-pend on the price—that is, wages—of labour. If he has to pay labour a wage of £29 per week he will employ forty-four men, but if the wage is £44 per week he will employ only forty-one men, since

[1] The increase in income is sometimes called marginal *revenue* productivity to dis-tinguish it from an increase in output (marginal *physical* productivity).

he will never pay more for a factor—whether it be land, labour or capital—than the value of its marginal product. It is obvious that this must be so. If he paid more than this his net revenue would be less. For example, if he already employs forty-four men, and is considering the employment of an additional man, he will not pay him more than £26, that being the value of the marginal product. If he were to pay more his total profit would be less than before.

Under perfect competition then, according to this theory, no factor will receive more than the value of its marginal product, and in fact the price paid by the entrepreneur will be equal to its marginal productivity. A similar demonstration to the above can be made to show that the price paid for land or capital will be equal to the value of its marginal product. A fall in the price of any factor will increase entrepreneurs' demand for it, just as a rise in the price of a factor will decrease entrepreneurs' demand for it. This line of reasoning formerly led economists to believe that employment varied inversely with wages, unemployment being the result of wages being too high, but Lord Keynes disagreed with this view. In any case, the theory applies only to perfect competition, and at most marginal productivity influences only the demand for a factor; the influence of supply must also be taken into account when the determination of a factor's price is being considered.

The marginal productivity theory has been subjected to much criticism. The concept is certainly highly theoretical, since the employment of one more unit of a factor may be impossible, so that in practice the value of its marginal unit cannot be calculated.

II. THE SUPPLY AND THE DEMAND FOR FACTORS OF PRODUCTION

3. The demand for factors

The demand for factors is a derived demand. Factors of production are not wanted for their own sake; they are required only for the production of other goods and services, and it is the demand for these other goods which determines the strength of the demand for the factors used to produce them. Land is not wanted for itself, but merely as a site where some form of production can be carried on—for a factory, shop or house, road or railway, or on which to grow crops or rear animals. The demand for labour is derived from the demand for things made in factories or grown on the land and from the demand for commercial and direct services. The various forms that capital takes—

factory buildings, machinery, raw materials, etc.—are obviously not wanted for their own sake, but only because of the demand for things they help to produce. Since production takes place in anticipation of demand, the demand for factors of production in the present will depend on the anticipated future demand for the commodities in the production of which they are to be employed.

4. Influences on the elasticity of demand for factors

Three important influences on the elasticity of demand for factors of production can be distinguished:

(i) *The elasticity of demand for the final product.* By elasticity of demand for factors is meant the response of demand for their services to changes in their prices. The demand for a factor will be elastic if a slight fall in its price results in a large increase in its employment. Since the demand for factors is a derived demand, the elasticity of demand for the commodity, for the production of which the factors are required, will determine the elasticity of demand for the factors. If the demand for the commodity is elastic, then the demand for the factors required in its manufacture will be elastic; if the demand for the commodity is inelastic the demand for the factors also will be inelastic. For example, fluctuations in employment will be greatest in those occupations where the labour is engaged in the production of commodities for which there is an elastic demand.

(ii) *The amount of the factor required.* A second influence on the elasticity of demand for factors is the extent to which a factor is required in a particular form of production. If a factor plays only a small part—that is, if its payment forms only a small percentage of the total cost of producing a commodity—the demand for that factor will be fairly inelastic. For example, the cost of building an ocean liner will not be appreciably affected by the price of chronometers, and so the demand for chronometers and the factors required to make them will be fairly inelastic.

(iii) *Substitutability between factors.* The greater the ease with which factors can be substituted for one another, the more elastic is likely to be the demand for them, for a slight rise in the price of one factor will result in more of the alternative factor being employed. High wages may result in less labour and more machinery (capital) being employed if the work is of a kind that can be done by machinery. On the other hand, if machinery becomes relatively dear more labour may be employed. The more specific the factor, however, the more inelastic will be the demand for it.

5. The supply of factors

Consider now some of the influences on the supply of factors of production:

(i) *Land.* The supply of commodities depends on their cost of production, and so the higher the price, the larger the quantity that will be put on to the market. On the supply side it is more difficult to carry the analogy of the commodities market into the factor market. Land, for instance, has been described as a "gift of Nature", and as such it has no cost of production. Though the total supply of land is more or less fixed, the supply for a particular purpose is rarely fixed. The total available supply of land in England amounts to 50,874 square miles, and this is distributed among a variety of uses (Table XLIV). Although

Table XLIV

Land Utilisation in England

Use	Per cent of total
Woods and plantations	5
Rough grazing	11
Permanent pasture	43
Arable land	26
Other (including urban) land	15

the total area has varied little over the past hundred and fifty years, that given up to permanent pasture has greatly increased during the period, at the expense of land devoted to arable farming. The expansion of large cities, their suburbs encroaching more and more upon the countryside, the building of new towns, the construction of motorways with their huge intersections and junctions, other wide main roads with dual carriageways, and the building of large airports have all taken land from other uses, a not inconsiderable amount having previously been good farmland. In the past much woodland has been cleared, and the Forestry Commission has had to undertake the planting of trees. Variations in the distribution of crops on the arable land are also possible. For example, less grain may be grown and more root crops produced, or vice versa. Thus there are often many competing uses for land, and though a high price cannot call more land into existence, the offer of a high price for land for a particular use will increase the supply coming into the market for that purpose. Nevertheless, the supply of some kinds of land is strictly limited, as for example the number of sites facing on to the main street in a city centre; in this case a high price cannot call forth an increased supply.

(*ii*) *Labour*. With regard to the supply of labour, it is doubtful whether high wages will increase the total supply, though the early economists thought that any rise in wages above subsistence level would inevitably lead to an increase in population by reducing deaths from malnutrition. High wages may, however, lead to earlier marriages, and even if the average size of family remains unchanged, the shortening of the period between generations will increase total supply. As with land, there are many competing demands for labour, and high wages in one occupation will cause more labour to seek employment there. It requires no real extension of the meaning of words to apply the term *cost of production* to labour. Even if no special training is required, children have to be kept at school at least until the statutory leaving age, and though family allowances, cheap milk and school meals, free education and maintenance grants have reduced the cost somewhat, the bringing up of a family still involves considerable expense. Where special training is required, especially if this entails a university education, membership of an Inn of Court or a long period as an articled clerk, with little or no remuneration, the cost of production of such labour may be very heavy. The supply of a particular type of labour can be increased in either of two ways: more workers may be drawn away from other occupations, or people not previously working—for example, married women and men who had retired—drawn into employment; or the number of hours worked by each person may be increased.

(*iii*) *Capital*. The supply of capital presents little difficulty because, like consumer goods, capital goods have to be made by the ordinary processes of production and so generally the higher the price, the greater the supply that will be forthcoming. A change in costs of production will affect the quantity supplied at each price. The basis of supply in this case is saving, for without saving in some form there can be no production of capital goods at all.

6. Elasticity of supply of factors

The elasticity of supply of a factor of production means the responsiveness of its supply to changes in price. The more specific the factor, the more inelastic will be its supply, for in the short period the supply of most specific factors cannot be increased, though the supply of some factors may be fixed in both short and long periods. Let us consider each factor of production in turn:

(*i*) *Land*. An increase in the demand for milk will raise the price of milk, and the higher price will call forth a bigger supply. To increase, the supply of milk more dairy cattle and grazing land will be required, and to bring this about will take time. The supply of grazing land may be fairly elastic in the long period, for other farmland can be turned over to grass. On more than one occasion in recent years British farmers have increased beef production at the expense of milk or vice versa. It would be easy, however, to increase the supply of some kinds of fruit or rubber, for several years must elapse (five in the case of rubber) before new trees begin to yield any return. No price, however high, can increase the total frontage for shop sites in London's Bond Street or Regent Street.

(*ii*) *Labour*. Two things influence the elasticity of labour: the extent to which it is occupationally specific and its geographical mobility. The longer the period of training, the more specific the labour becomes, and this not only causes a period to elapse before supply can adjust itself to a higher price, but the possibility that price may fall again during the period of training will tend to check the number of new entrants. It may be, too, that the number of new entrants is limited. In some professions this occurs when members are restricted in the number of articled clerks they may employ. In some cases numbers may be limited by the accommodation available in the training establishments. During the 1960s the supply of university graduates increased very slowly in spite of an increased demand for them, since to do so required the establishment of many new universities. Where special aptitude is required, an increase in supply is even more difficult to bring about. Similarly, where labour is specific, a fall in wages does not quickly lead to a reduction of supply.

Even if the work is not highly specific, men become less occupationally mobile as they become older. This is a serious problem in the case of declining industries; men who have spent their lives in one occupation may be too old to re-train for another. The older coachmen clung to the roads in the early nineteenth century, though it was plain to everyone else that the railways had sounded the death-knell of the coach. A hundred years later, when buses replaced trams, some of the older tram-drivers were too old to learn to drive buses, and often only reluctantly accepted other jobs.

Though wages may be higher in one area than another, labour is often unwilling to move. Further, it is not always true that the higher the wage, the more hours the worker is prepared to work. The marginal utility of leisure increases steeply as the working day lengthens, and if the work is unpleasant, the higher the wage per hour, the fewer the number of hours the worker may be willing to work. Absenteeism increases in many occupations as the wage rate increases. This provides an example of what is sometimes called "the regressive supply curve". It shows that after a certain point the higher wage calls forth a smaller supply in terms of the number of hours worked (Fig. 72).

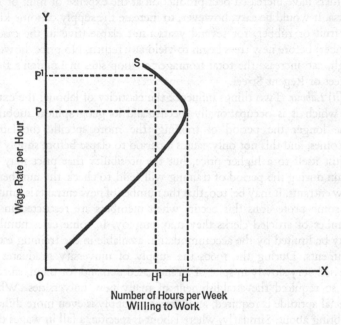

Fig. 72. A Regressive Supply Curve.

The vertical scale represents the wage rate per hour increasing from O towards Y; the horizontal scale represents the number of hours the worker is willing to work, increasing from O to X. At a wage OP he is willing to work OH hours; at any lower wage he is willing to work only for a shorter period; if, however, his wages rise above OP his willingness to work again declines, and at the wage OP¹ he would work only OH¹ hours.

(iii) Capital. With capital too, its elasticity of supply depends to a certain extent on its specificity, though in most cases a rise in the price of capital will increase the amount produced. In the case of a simple machine, an increase in supply may be brought about very quickly— that is, its supply will be elastic. For a raw material such as flax a longer period will be required to increase its supply; for a raw material such as wool it may take even longer. In the case of a very large and costly unit of capital, such as a blast-furnace or an ocean liner, a rise in price will not immediately result in an increase in supply. Indeed, it may require a very steep rise in price, maintained over a considerable period, to bring about an increase in supply in such cases.

7. Supply and demand curves for factors

It thus becomes possible to construct supply and demand curves for factors of production. The intersection of the supply and demand curves for any factor, as in the case of a commodity, gives the equilibrium position at which supply equals demand, and shows the amount of the factor supplied at the equilibrium price. For example, if the supply and demand curves for a particular type of labour are as shown in Fig. 73 it means at the wage OW the number of men willing to

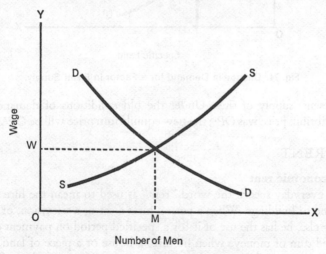

Fig. 73. The Equilibrium Wage.

undertake this kind of work will be OM. The steeper the supply curve—that is, the more inelastic the supply—the smaller the difference in the number of men employed at different levels of wages.

The effect of changes in supply or demand can be shown by inserting a second supply or demand curve. An increase in the demand for this kind of labour would therefore result in more men being employed, and at a higher wage than before.

Similar diagrams could be used to show the effect of changes in the supply or the demand for land or capital. If supply is fixed, as in the case of some urban sites, the price will depend on demand, a change in demand producing a very considerable rise in price (Fig. 74). OL

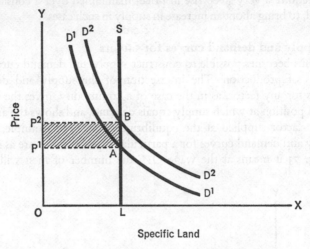

Fig. 74. Change in Demand for a Factor in Fixed Supply.

represents supply of sites. Under the old conditions of demand the equilibrium price was OP^1; the new equilibrium price will be OP^2.

III. RENT

8. Economic rent

In everyday speech the word "rent" is used to mean the hire price of land or buildings. When a person hires a car or a television, or anything else, he has the use of it for a specified period on payment of an agreed sum of money; when he hires a house or a piece of land he is said to rent it, and the periodic payment is termed rent. In the ordinary sense, then, rent is simply a price for the use of the services of a factor of production, land, or land together with capital (buildings), paid by the tenant to the owner. Rent, as the hire price of land, however also includes interest on capital.

At one time economists followed everyday practice and restricted the term rent to land, but it is now used in relation to any factor. It has, too, been given a more precise meaning. Rent can be defined in slightly different ways, but its main characteristic is that it is a surplus, that is additional income, accruing to a factor which was not foreseen when that factor entered a particular line of production. The Italian economist Pareto considered economic rent to be the surplus received by any factor of production above its opportunity cost—that is, any surplus over and above what was necessary to keep that factor in its present employment. Rents can therefore be received by labour, capital or the entrepreneur, as well as by land.

Consider the demand schedule for a certain type of labour given in Table XLV. The higher the wage, the more labour will offer itself for

Table XLV

A Demand Schedule for Labour

Wage offered per hour (pence)	Number of men offering their services
30	50
35	70
40	100
45	160
50	250
55	380
60	540

employment. If the wage offered is 30p per hour only fifty men offer themselves for employment; at 35p seventy men offer themselves; at 40p a hundred men are willing to do this kind of work, and so on. Suppose now that the actual wage agreed upon is 55p per hour. At this wage three hundred and eighty men are available for employment, and although two hundred and fifty men would have accepted a lower wage, 55p per hour must be paid to all. Some men, therefore, will receive more than is necessary to keep them in that particular kind of employment, and so part of the wages can be considered to be economic rent. Fifty of these men will be paid at the rate of 55p although willing to work for 30p, and so their renumeration really consists of 30p wage, plus 25p rent. In this sense most labour receives wages and rent as payment for its services. The payment of this labour force will be made up as follows:

Transfer earnings. The more difficult it is for a factor to secure alternative emplonment—that is, the more specific it is—the less it will be necessary to pay it in order to retain its services, once it has been put to a particular use. For example, a blast-furnace cannot be used for any purpose other than that for which it was originally intended, and so

Table XLVI

Rent in Wages

| Number of men | Pence per hour | | Payment received (pence) |
	Wages	Rent	
50	30	25	55
20	35	20	55
30	40	15	55
60	45	10	55
90	50	5	55
130	55	—	55
380			

in one sense its entire earnings can be considered to be rent. The amount that a factor could earn in its best-paid alternative employment is sometimes known as its *transfer earnings*. Any payment in excess of this amount is a surplus above what is necessary to retain the factor in its best-paid employment, and so is a rent. In the above example, to obtain the services of three hundred and eighty men it was necessary to offer 55p per hour. If this type of employment were not available some of them might be able to obtain alternative employment at 50p per hour, others at 45p per hour, etc., and so another table might be constructed to show how much of their remuneration is rent, as shown by their transfer earnings:

Table XLVII

Transfer Earnings and Rent

Number of men	Transfer earnings (pence)	Rent (pence)	Payment received (pence)
80	50	5	55
180	45	10	55
90	40	15	55
30	35	20	55
380			

The more specific the factor, the greater the proportion of its earnings that consist of rent.

9. How rents rise

Alternatively, however, rent can be defined in terms of its origin. Rent can be said to be the surplus accruing to any factor of production, the supply of which cannot easily be increased, and arises from an increase in the demand for the services of that factor. Rent is, then, the result of dynamic or changing conditions; and under perfect competition it would not persist for long. It can be seen, therefore, why rent was formerly restricted to land, for land is a factor most kinds of which are fixed in supply. The number of corner sites at the intersection of two principal shopping streets in a town is definitely limited to four. With the development of the town the demand for these sites will increase and the price to be paid for their use will rise. Any increase in the earnings of such land is due to its scarcity and the impossibility of increasing its supply in response to an increase in demand.

Consider again the diagram (Fig. 74) on page 306. This shows the effect of a change in demand on the price of a factor, the supply of which is fixed. Before the increase in demand took place the factor's income was represented by the rectangle OP^1AL; as a result of the increased demand for it the factor's income became OP^2BL, the shaded portion P^1P^2BA representing the rent now accruing to this factor.

10. Quasi-rent

This term is really no longer required. Following Alfred Marshall, it was used of all rents received by factors other than land, but it is unusual now to differentiate between land and other factors in this way. If the factor is highly specific it will receive rent so long as its supply falls short of the demand for its services. Since in the long period the supply of most specific factors can be increased, rent is often of temporary duration. The higher incomes of such factors will attract factors wherever possible from other employments, and so with the increase in the supply of the factor the rent will eventually disappear. If the supply of a factor is perfectly elastic supply will immediately adjust itself to changes in demand, and so no rent will arise; if the supply of a factor is less than perfectly elastic an increase in demand will enable it to earn a rent, at least for a time. Thus, a second feature of quasi-rents is that they tend to be temporary, received by the factors concerned in the short period only until supply catches up with demand.

Rent in wages. Many kinds of labour are highly specific because of the long period of training or the special ability required. As with land, the supply of some kinds of labour may be almost perfectly inelastic. Just as perfect substitutes cannot be found for particular sites in a city centre, so there may be no perfect substitutes for a prima donna, a great violinist, a film star, a comedian or a heavyweight boxer. The incomes of such people consist mostly of rents, which will persist so long as the demand for their services remains, for supply cannot be increased. The supplies of most kinds of specific labour are not generally as inelastic as this, for usually in the long period the supply can be increased, though the period of training may be of many years' duration. An increased demand for the services of barristers would enable them to raise their fees (and so receive rent), but the possibility of high earnings would eventually attract more people into this profession, so that perhaps in four or five year's time the supply would again equal demand, with the result that rent would disappear and the level of barristers' fees would fall. The special ability required of a successful barrister may be rare and not capable of being deliberately trained, and such a person would then be in a similar position to the prima donna who, because close substitutes could not be found, would continue to command high remuneration—that is, would still receive rent. This is sometimes known as a "rent of ability".

Rent in interests and profits. The supply of some forms of capital is inelastic in the short period, and so an increase in demand will give rise to additional income or rent. The supply of large, expensive plant will not immediately expand in response to an increase in demand for the commodities for the production of which it is required. The heavy cost of erecting additional plant will tend to restrain the entry of new firms into the industry until there is a clear indication that the increased demand for the commodity is likely to be maintained. If high profits persist, new firms will eventually enter the industry, but meanwhile such capital will receive rent. High profits earned by a railway serving two large cities will not immediately lead to the construction of a second railway to connect them, but if the first railway cannot cope with the expansion of traffic, and if the increase seems likely to be permanent, sooner or later a second railway will probably be built. An increase in the demand for houses—due perhaps to people getting married earlier—cannot easily be met, for the building of a large number of new houses takes time, and so houses will become scarce and the high prices paid for them will include a substantial amount of economic rent.

11. Rent, price and cost of production

A test to discover whether the earnings of a factor contain rent or not is to answer the question: does this extra payment arise *because* higher prices are being offered, or does it *cause* prices to be higher? In fact rent income *results from* the high price of the product or service, and does not *cause* the high price. The rent of a piece of land depends on the price of the product of the land; if the rent of agricultural land is high it is because the price of the crop grown on the land is high, and the price of the crop will be high if the demand for it is strong. If the price of the product is high, then the price of the land will be high. Similarly, the rent of city sites is high because the demand for them is high. If there was a vacant site near the centre of a large city there might be competition to acquire it for the erection of a department store, an hotel or an office block. If three firms made bids for it the size of the bids would depend on each firm's estimate of what its customers or clients would be willing to pay. If eventually an hotel is erected on the site the charges for hotel accommodation will be high, not because of the higher rents, but because of the high demand for hotel accommodation in that locality. Therefore, it is the fact that people are prepared to pay high charges for hotel accommodation on that site that makes the rent high, and not the other way round.

An entrepreneur who requires the services of a specific factor of production, the supply of which cannot easily be increased, will have to pay a scarcity price or rent if he wishes to employ it. To the entrepreneur, of course, such rent payments form part of his costs of production. But if he were relieved of the payment of rent the price of the product would not fall because, owing to the scarcity of the factor, supply could not easily be increased, and price in the short period is determined principally by demand.

12. Monopoly profit and rent

Rent arises as a result of an increase in demand, where the supply of a factor cannot readily be increased. The monopolist makes a profit above normal (that is, a surplus profit) because he deliberately restricts output in order to keep up price. In the one case scarcity is due to an increase in demand; in the other scarcity is artificially created. The monopolist's profit is a surplus; so is rent. Neither monopoly profit nor rent is necessary in order to retain factors of production in their present employment. There is, then, a strong similarity between rent and monopoly profit. There is, however, an important difference: rent is the *result* and not the cause of high prices, whereas the monopolist's restrictionist policy is the *cause* of the high price of his product. Many professional bodies and some trade unions (particularly unions of skilled workers) deliberately restrict entry to their professions or trades by examinations (which tend to become competitive), restriction of numbers or insistence on a lengthy period of apprenticeship, so that their additional incomes resulting from these practices are more akin to monopoly profit than to rent.

13. The Ricardian theory of rent

The English economist best known for his theory of rent is Ricardo, whose book *The Principles of Political Economy and Taxation* was published in 1817. Like the other classical economists, he thought that the value of a commodity depended on the amount of labour put into its production. The cost of production of farming products, however, presented difficulties, for it appeared to vary according to the fertility of the soil—wheat, for example, being grown at much lower cost on fertile land than on land of inferior quality. It was this problem that led him to formulate his theory of rent—that part of his work for which he came to be best known. Ricardo defined rent in what he called the strict sense (to distinguish it from the ordinary sense in which Adam Smith and others used the term) as "that portion of the produce of the earth which is paid to the landlord for the use of the original and indestructible powers of the soil."

Rent, according to Ricardo, then arises in the following way. If a country has an "abundance of rich and fertile land," there will be no rent, for no one will be willing to pay for the use of land if there is a greater supply of it than is required for all purposes. There would thus be no rent if all land was of best quality and unlimited in quantity. Rich and fertile land, however, is not unlimited in quantity in any country, nor is land uniform in quality. According to Ricardo it is for this reason that rent arises. As he says, "when land of the second degree is taken into cultivation, rent immediately commences on that of the first quality, and the amount of that rent will depend on the difference in the quality of these two portions of land." Land at the margin of cultivation—that is, land that it is only just worth cultivating—Ricardo considered yielded no rent. More fertile land will yield a greater return, and the value of this excess yield over that of land at the margin of cultivation ("no-rent" land) is its rent. The greater the difference between a country's poorest and the best-cultivated land the higher then the rent of the best land.

Suppose the value of the crops from four pieces of land of equal area, and equal distance from the market but of different fertilities, to be £60, £48, £40 and £35. Assuming that the £35 yield comes from the land that is only just worth cultivating, that is "no-rent" land, and the rent on the other three pieces of land will be the excess yield over £35, that is, £25, £13 and £5 respectively:

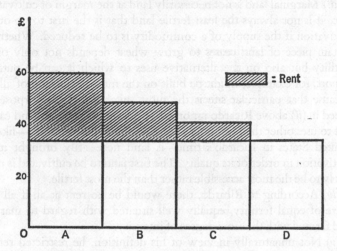

Fig. 75. The Ricardian Theory of Rent. (A, B, C, D represent equal areas of land.)

As population increases, ever less fertile land will be drawn into cultivation, and the rent of previously cultivated land will rise, and with the operation of the law of diminishing returns, profit from the cultivation of land will tend to fall.

Rent, Ricardo thought, could also arise if land is cultivated more intensively. Two pieces of land may be of equal quality, but if more capital and labour are applied to one, this will earn rent equal to its excess return. As land is cultivated more intensively, each additional amount of labour and capital applied to it will yield a less return—and therefore less rent—than the previous application, again giving diminishing returns.

14. Some criticisms of the Ricardian theory

The following are some of the criticisms levelled against Ricardo's theory:

(*i*) His theory is based simply on natural variations in productivity of different pieces of land as a result of differences in their fertility.

(*ii*) He ignored the fact that there might be competing uses for a particular piece of land—that a piece of land might be farmed or built upon—though he did admit the possibility of advantageous situation with regard to the market.

(*iii*) Marginal land is not necessarily land at the margin of cultivation, since it is not always the least fertile land that is the first to go out of cultivation if the supply of a commodity is to be reduced. Whether a certain piece of land ceases to grow wheat depends not only on its fertility but also on the alternative uses to which it can be put. An airport, for example, might be built on the most fertile land of all just because that particular site is the most suitable for this purpose. As noted in (*ii*) above Ricardo ignored the important fact that land can be put to uses other than farming. Nor, in a developing country—like the United States in Ricardo's time—is land necessarily brought under cultivation in order of its quality. The first land to be cultivated is more likely to be the most accessible rather than the most fertile.

(*iv*) According to Ricardo, there would be no rent at all if all land were of equal fertility, equally well situated with regard to markets, and farmed with the same degree of intensity.

(*v*) Not unnaturally in view of his definition, he restricted rent to land. As defined by modern economists, rent has become a much more useful concept, since it can apply to any of the factors of production.

(*vi*) Ricardo, however, asserted that rent was not a cost of production, since the cost of producing a commodity on the poorest land determined its cost of production.

15. Rent as an object of taxation

Since rent is a payment over and above what is necessary to keep a factor in its present employment, it has been argued that economic rent is an unearned increment, and therefore a suitable object of taxation, for, provided that the tax does not exceed the rent, it will have no adverse effect on production. Henry George and others have, for example, advocated the taxation of any increased value in land sites, on the ground that such increased value owes nothing to effort on the part of the owner. This is quite true, but in equity, if rent accruing to land is taxed, rents accruing to other factors should also be taxed. The main difficulty, however, is to distinguish between that part of a factor's income that is unearned economic rent and that part of its income that is earned. It would be difficult, if not impossible, to devise a satisfactory scheme for the taxation of all forms of economic rent. However, such attempts were made by the British Government both in 1948 and 1966, but without success.

RECOMMENDATIONS FOR FURTHER READING

K. Boulding: *Economic Analysis*, Chapters 9–12.
P. Wicksteed: *Common-sense of Political Economy*, Vol. I, Chapters 8 and 9.
A. Marshall: *Principles of Economics*, Book VI, Chapters 1–2, 9, 11.

QUESTIONS

Theory of Distribution.

1. Examine the causes of inequalities in the real income of individuals. What are the present-day tendencies? (RSA)

2. (*a*) How were the factors of production allocated among industries in the days of *laissez-faire*?

(*b*) On what principle are they allocated when the central authority has the determining voice? (ACCA)

3. "It has now become certain that the problem of distribution is much more difficult than it was thought to be by earlier economists, and that no solution of it which claims to be simple can be true." (Marshall) Discuss. (ACCA)

Rent

4. Explain the statement "Rent is a surplus". Why are rents in the city higher than in the country? (RSA)

5. Is rent a cost of production? (CIS)

6. "The prices at which I sell are high because my rent is high," says a shop-keeper. Is this correctly stated? (IHA)

7. Distinguish between agricultural rent, site rent and house rent. How do developments in transport affect site values? (IT)

8. Discuss the theory of rent with special reference to (*a*) a tobacconist shop, (*b*) a ladies' dress shop, both in a fasionable centre of a large city. (IB)

9. What warrant is there for extending the concept of rent to the factors of production other than land? (IHA)

10. "The profits of monopoly are most properly regarded as rents." Discuss this statement. (CIS)

11. What economic forces help to determine the annual rent of a plot of land in the centre of a city? (GCE)

12. "Shops in city centres charge higher prices because land in city centres is more expensive." Comment. (GCE)

CHAPTER 18

WAGES

I. THEORIES OF WAGES

1. Real and nominal wages

Wages and salaries. In ordinary speech a distinction is frequently made between wages and salaries. Both, however, are payments for labour service and so economically there is no difference between them. Some people might attempt to differentiate between them by saying that wages are payments for manual work, salaries for non-manual work; others might say that wages are paid weekly and salaries at longer intervals; yet others might say that wages are paid for a definite amount of work, as measured by time or piece, so that if less than a full week is worked a proportionate deduction from the weekly wage will be made, whereas salaried workers suffer no such deductions. Only the last distinction is of any economic importance. Wages are a variable cost, varying with output, whereas salaries in the short period are a fixed cost since they do not vary with output. This distinction is made in book-keeping, wages being included in the Trading Account, drawn up to enable gross profit to be calculated, while salaries are included in the Profit and Loss Account, as one of the expenses to be deducted from gross profit in order to arrive at net profit. Except, therefore, in discussions of variable and fixed costs, the economist regards wages and salaries, that is, income received from work, as alternative terms for the share of labour in the national income.

It is important, however, to distinguish between real and nominal wages. Nominal wages are wages in terms of money, and the term *money wages* is perhaps to be preferred. In comparing wages at different periods of time it is not sufficient to know that in 1913 few men received more than £1 per week; that their average earnings were £3.50 per week in 1938, £12 in 1955 and £50 in 1974. Such statements are frequently made, the inference being the economic position of these men had improved by fourteen times between 1913 and 1974. Wages are wanted only for what they will buy, real wages being wages in terms of the goods and services that can be bought with them. "The labourer," says Adam Smith, "is rich or poor, is well or ill rewarded, in proportion to the real, not to the nominal price of his labour."

In comparing the nominal wages of people in different occupations account must be taken of payments in kind, such as free uniform for policemen, railway workers and many others, free travel to and from work for those engaged in passenger transport undertakings, the use of a car by some business executives, free board and lodging for some hotel workers and hospital nurses.

It is further necessary to distinguish between wage rates and earnings. During the period 1964–74 wage rates in Great Britain rose by 148 per cent but earnings rose by over 170 per cent, for in most industrial occupations a considerable amount of overtime was being worked. In many industries the introduction of the five-day working week has often simply meant that work on Saturday mornings has ranked for overtime.

2. The marginal productivity theory of wages

According to the marginal theory of distribution, as we have seen, the producer will pay no more for any factor of production than the value of its marginal product, since to do so will raise his costs by a greater amount than his revenue. As applied to labour this provides us with the marginal productivity theory of wages. This theory has been criticised for the following reasons:

(i) It is too theoretical a concept, since it does not appear to agree with what actually takes place.

(ii) In practice it is impossible to calculate the amount or the value of the marginal product of any factor of production.

(iii) The employment of one man more or one man fewer may completely upset the method of production in use at the time. To employ an extra man may simply mean that there will be more labour than is necessary; to take away a man may remove a vital link in the chain of production. For this reason a small rise or fall in wages is not likely to bring about an immediate change in the amount of labour employed.

(iv) The productivity of labour does not depend entirely on its own effort and efficiency, but very largely on the quality of the other factors of production employed, especially capital.

(v) According to this theory, the higher the wage, the smaller the amount of labour the entrepreneur will employ. Surveys that have been taken appear to indicate that not all employers take account of the wage rate when considering how many men to employ, being influenced more by business prospects.

(*vi*) Lord Keynes said the theory was valid only in static conditions, and therefore, to lower the wage rate in a trade depression would not necessarily increase the demand for labour.

(*vii*) In any case the marginal productivity theory is applicable only under perfect competition, a condition which does not exist.

3. The market theory of wages

Another approach to the problem of wage determination is to regard wages as a price—the price of labour—and, therefore, like all other prices determined by the interaction of the market forces of supply and demand. We have already seen that it is possible to conceive of factor markets as well as commodity markets, the price of a factor of production then depending on the demand for it in relation to its supply. Therefore, in the case of wages, it is necessary to consider the labour market.

(*i*) *The supply of labour.* We have already noted that there is some ambiguity in the concept of a supply of labour, since supply can mean either the total number of people available for employment or the total number of hours worked. In the case of a commodity its supply depends on its cost of production. Though it may be difficult to conceive of cost of production being applied to labour in general, the term can, however, be related to those forms of specific labour which require earnings to be sacrificed during a period of training.

(*ii*) *The demand for labour.* In the factor markets demand is a derived demand. It is, too, an anticipated demand, since commodities are generally produced in anticipation of future demand for them. Thus the demand for labour is derived from the anticipated demand for the goods and services it is required to produce. Expectation of favourable conditions of business activity, therefore, will stimulate a demand for labour. Another influence on the demand for labour is the possibility of substitution. For example, at a particular time the producer may be able to substitute capital for some labour, but whether he does so will depend on the relative prices of these two factors of production. Conditions for substitution, however, may change—a new machine or a new development may reduce the demand for labour. On the other hand, an increase in real capital investment, public or private, will increase the demand for labour.

(*iii*) *The price mechanism and the labour market.* Through the price mechanism supply is brought into equality with demand. An increase in demand in relation to supply, therefore, should raise the price of labour, that is, wages, while a fall in demand in relation to supply should cause wages to fall. Though it is generally true that a rise in its price can be expected to increase the supply of a factor coming on to the market, it is not certain that the supply of labour can always be increased by an offer of higher wages, since after wages have reached a certain level leisure may be preferred to further income, therefore providing an example of a regressive supply curve (*see* Fig. 72 on page 304).

The Market Theory of Wages, however, does not run counter to the Marginal Productivity Theory. In the same way that marginal utility forms the basis of individual demand, so marginal productivity forms the basis of demand for labour and other factors of production.

4. The bargaining theory of wages

Earlier theories of wages, some writers believe, have been rendered invalid, or at least inadequate, as a result of collective bargaining by trade unions. The Marginal Productivity Theory rests on the assumption of perfect competition, whereas collective bargaining makes competition imperfect. It becomes necessary, therefore, to study the determination of wages, like production, in conditions of both perfect and imperfect competition. The forces that determine wages under perfect competition continue to influence wages even though competition is imperfect. Collective bargaining provides an example of what is sometimes called bi-lateral monopoly, the trade union being the monopolist supplier and the employers' association the monopolist (or more correctly, monopsonist) buyer of a particular kind of labour.

Those who support the Bargaining Theory of Wages assert that the level of wages in an industry depends on the bargaining strength of the trade union concerned, so that, they say, differences in wages in different occupations are the result of differences in the strength of the respective trade unions. The power of a trade union depends on a number of things—the size of its membership, the amount of its "fighting" fund (of less importance since Social Security payments were made to strikers' families) and the extent of the dislocation to the national economy or the inconvenience it can cause to consumers by a strike. Clearly, a strike of milliners is going to inconvenience the community less than a strike of transport workers at a popular holiday period or a strike of electricity workers or coal miners during the winter months. Nevertheless, however great the bargaining skill of some trade-union leaders, this is less important than the prevailing economic conditions. In times of full employment the trade unions will be in a strong position; in a depression they will be weaker. The success, however, of the more powerful industrial unions has led to demands for stronger action from employees in occupations unused to strikes.

It might, therefore, be asked: to what extent, then, can a trade union raise the wages of its members? In this connection it is necessary to distinguish between real and nominal (money) wages. Adherents of the Marginal Productivity Theory of Wages argue that real wages can be increased only if they are below the value of the marginal product of labour, since real wages can never for long exceed this. They also point out that real wages can be increased only by employing less labour in relation to other factors of production or by increasing the efficiency of labour. In inflationary conditions it is easy to increase nominal wages but not so easy to raise real wages. Thus, if a trade union obtains an increase in wages the benefit to its members tends to be short-lived, since other wage increases follow and prices rise. A permanent increase in real wages can be achieved only by an increase in the volume of production, that is, as a result of economic growth, and in recent times Great Britain has found it difficult to maintain the average annual growth rate of 3–4 per cent achieved over the past fifty years.

Efforts have been made in recent years to increase real wages and not merely nominal (money) wages by increasing the productivity of labour while checking excessive rises in wages. Although in most cases a measure of success was achieved in the short term, a sharp rise in wages occurred immediately the policy was relaxed. This was particularly so in 1969–71 when after the ending of the incomes policy in 1969, wages rose steeply.

5. Wages in service occupations

Associations representing workers providing services—clerical, postal, teaching, etc.—have generally been less successful in securing increases in wages for their members than the large, powerful trade unions. This fact seemed to add point to the Bargaining Theory of Wages. These associations have generally attempted to apply the "principle of comparability" with wages of those in similar occupations, though it is often very difficult to compare work in different occupations, since no two jobs are alike. The laws of the market, however, have an important influence. When labour is plentiful in relation to the demand for it their wages tend to be low. Only when there is a strong demand for labour in relation to the supply are people in service occupations able to secure increases in wages. At such times alternative openings for employment are often available to them.

The Priestley Commission which inquired into pay in the Civil Service favoured "a fair comparison with comparable work"; the Guillebaud Committee accepted the same principle for railway workers; the Pilkington Committee, which undertook a similar task for doctors and dentists, stressed that their earnings should be compared with the incomes of people in other professions with equivalent qualifications, and in the case of the police the Willinck Committee favoured higher wages than in similar occupations in order to attract more recruits to the service. Similarly, the Wilberforce inquiries in 1971 and 1972 into pay increases, respectively for electricity workers and coal miners, based its recommendations on the need to treat them as "special cases". To offer more than is paid in other occupations in inflationary conditions can however, only lead to demands from others for parity of treatment.

Bargaining strength is clearly an important influence on wage determination, but at the present day, though the market has been rendered imperfect, the influence of the market forces of supply and demand continue to be of great importance.

6. The effects of inventions

Ever since the Luddites took to smashing machinery during 1811–16, workers have been suspicious of the introduction of new machines, which it was thought inevitably reduced the demand for labour, and so caused unemployment. It has often been impossible to adopt new inventions until the trade union concerned has satisfied itself that the interests of its members would not be adversely affected. There have been many instances of new machines that would have increased production not being used for several years, for fear of the workers going on strike. On occasions the use of new machinery had been permitted only on condition that as many men as previously were employed on this work!

There is no doubt that in the long run new inventions are to the advantage of labour, though it has to be admitted that the immediate effect of the installation of a new machine has often been to increase frictional unemployment. In the long run, however, additional employment will be created, for the machines themselves have to be made, while the effect of using them has generally been to increase output and to lower prices, with the result that the real wages of other workers have risen and in consequence their demand for all kinds of goods. As a result, employment in other industries, and perhaps also in the industry in which the new machinery has been introduced, will be stimulated. During the Great Depression of 1929–35 this view was challenged, and it was seriously suggested that a halt should be called to scientific progress. The ultimate benefit of new techniques was admitted, but it was feared that if technical progress was too rapid further unemployment would arise before those previously thrown out of work could be found other jobs.

The effect of a new invention or innovation on employment and wages depends on whether it is a *labour-saving* or a *capital-saving* invention. Possibly there may be a third group where the effect is neutral. An invention may be labour-saving if it reduces the demand for labour, whereas a capital-saving invention will reduce the demand for capital. If the wages of labour are higher, as in times when the demand for labour tends to exceed the supply, this will act as a stimulus to the invention of labour-saving machinery. Only by the adoption of the most up-to-date techniques, however, can productivity be increased; and this is a prerequisite of higher real wages. The ultimate effect of most inventions has therefore been a rise in real wages and, therefore, in the standard of living.

II. DIFFERENCES IN WAGES

7. No single labour market

It has already been seen that an equilibrium distribution of expenditure in the market was achieved by a housewife when the marginal utilities of all the commodities she had purchased were equal, for only then had she no incentive to dispose of a little of one commodity in order to obtain a little more of another. An equilibrium distribution of labour among different occupations might then be expected to occur when the wages of labour in all occupations are equal.

Why, then, do wages vary between one occupation and another' The reason is that there is no such thing as a single labour market, for there are as many markets for labour as there are types of labour, for labour is not a homegeneous commodity. If there is a shortage of doctors the services of plumbers cannot be enlisted, nor can butchers make good a deficiency of accountants. One kind of labour may differ from another because of its ability to undertake certain work, or because of the special training required. Where special aptitude is needed, little can be done to meet a shortage of supply, though sometimes, even in such a case, training may improve the aptitude of a lower-grade worker. The special training required for some occupations makes it difficult to increase the supply of labour in the short period. The better-paid occupations might be expected, however, to attract more entrants than those that are poorly paid. This would increase the supply of labour and reduce wages in these better-paid occupations, and at the same time, because of the reduced supply of labour wages in the poorer-paid occupations would rise. Equilibrium would eventually be achieved only when wages in all occupations were equal.

There are several reasons why this does not happen. The period of special training may be long and expensive. Attendance at a university for three, four or five years may be required, and the necessity to pass an examination at the end of the course adds a measure of uncertainty. Though the earnings of those who successfully complete such periods of training generally amply compensate for the expense incurred, many parents, even when they can afford it, are unwilling to allow their children the opportunity of qualifying for these better-paid occupations because they may feel that at, say, sixteen years of age, when a decision has to be made, it is time for their children to begin to earn their own living. Many blind-alley jobs are well paid for beginners, just as most well-paid posts can be obtained only by those who have been willing to accept a low rate of pay in the early years of their careers. Some differential payment for skilled work is necessary, therefore, in order to encourage people to undertake the period of training required. Many people too would be unwilling to accept posts carry responsibility if they did not receive greater remuneration.

The main influence on the separation of labour markets, therefore, is lack of occupational mobility. The fact too that labour is not completely mobile in a geographical sense helps still further to keep labour markets separate. However, in times when the demand for labour greatly exceeds the supply, as in inflationary conditions, many people frequently change their jobs.

8. Non-monetary considerations

Another influence on wages is that some occupations possess advantages of a non-monetary nature. Some kinds of work are more congenial than others and are carried on under pleasanter conditions; in some employments the worker has a greater degree of independence than in others; in some occupations there is a high degree of security from dismissal except for serious misconduct as, for example, in the

Civil Service and Local Government. In some cases an occupation may carry a degree of prestige that gives satisfaction to the worker—or to his wife—as in most professions, and to some extent even in the more lowly white-collar occupations, though in recent times the rate of pay has tended to become a more important factor. Other occupations are subject to disadvantages of some kind. Some work is dangerous— for example, that of steeplejacks—some occupations are more subject to unemployment than others, especially seasonal unemployment— for example, bricklayers; sometimes the hours of work are inconvenient, requiring very early or very late attendance, or shifts may have to be split, as with those employed in public transport; in some occupations it may be necessary to work on Saturdays or public holidays—as for example in a public utility service; for some kinds of work it may be necessary to spend long periods away from home—for example, fishermen and sales representatives.

Wage differences can arise from all these causes. Generally, the greater the advantages of the occupation, the lower the wages, and the greater the disadvantages of the occupation, the higher the wages. The reason for this is that non-monetary considerations affect the supply, which tends to be greater when there are non-monetary advantages and less when there are disadvantages. However, it is not always necessary to offer higher wages in order to persuade people to do disagreeable work. If the work requires some measure of skill, it will probably be better paid than more congenial work requiring an equivalent amount of skill, but disagreeable work often requires little skill, and generally the supply of labour available for this kind of work is greater than the demand for it, so that it is often poorly paid. Nevertheless, in inflationary times when the general demand for labour tends to exceed the supply, many of the more disagreeable jobs become difficult to fill unless higher wages are offered, especially when the demand for higher wages is backed by a strike with disagreeable consequences for the community.

9. Women's wages

Until recently it was normal practice for women to be paid less than men, even for similar work. The fact that many of them were married and so not entirely dependent on their own earnings in the past often made them willing to work for much lower wages than they could otherwise have accepted. In the textile industries, in the earliest days of the factory system, it was customary for all adult members of the family to go out to work, and the family income was often of greater importance than the incomes of the individual members. The effect of this was to depress men's wages in these industries. Apart from the textile industries and domestic work, there were formerly few openings for women, and so there was a tendency for the supply to exceed the demand, with the result that payment was low. The demand for women in many industries was low because their productivity was thought to be low. Many kinds of work done by the men were considered to be unsuitable for women, and in occupations requiring considerable physical strength this was largely true, but the experience of two World Wars showed that women were capable of many kinds of work formerly considered to be suitable only for men, such as transport and engineering.

In most of the professions, especially those that until fairly recently were closed to women, there is no differentiation between men and women with regard to payment, but in these occupations there is often a wide difference in the earnings even of different men. Women barristers can earn as much as male members of the profession if they can obtain a sufficient number of briefs. Similarly in the medical profession women's incomes can equal those of their male colleagues if they can attract a sufficient number of patients. In the Civil Service, local Government and the teaching profession (except at university level) there used to be lower scales of salary for women, but for some time now there has been equal pay in these occupations. In most kinds of factory work, however, two rates of pay persisted until 1975. If men and women are doing equal work with equal efficiency there is no economic reason why they should not receive equal pay. An increasing number of women now take up clerical posts in commerce, which were once looked upon as men's occupations, one reason for the change being that employers formerly found it cheaper to employ young women.

Most girls still look upon the period of employment after leaving school as a temporary interval until they marry, and so do not remain long enough at a particular kind of work to consider making a career of it. The average age of female clerks, therefore, is low, as also are their average wages. For this reason employers often do not consider it to be worth their while to train women for the more responsible positions, as so frequently this training would be wasted. Most men—and some women, too—dislike working under a woman. Some employers think that men are more reliable than women, and if men and women receive the same pay, prefer to appoint men. It frequently appears that many highly efficient women are less tolerant of human short-comings in others than equally efficient men, and so make less capable managers.

Another reason why in the past women were generally paid less than men was that trade-union organisation among women was weaker.

Even now that the principle of equal pay for equal work has been accepted, it is often very difficult to decide precisely what is equal work. Superficially two posts may seem to be alike, and filled equally well in the one case by a man and in the other by a woman, and yet one of them may be far more efficient in that particular type of work than the other.

Some men's organisations for a long time opposed equal pay for men and women, even when it was clear that they would be doing equal work, on the ground that most men have family responsibilities, and equal pay would result in many unmarried women being able to enjoy a higher standard of living than was possible to married men. It was pointed out that the Armed Forces recognise the married man's position by granting him a marriage allowance. This, however, is a social rather than an economic question, and not unrelated to the population problem. The payment of different rates to the married and the unmarried employee would be impracticable in industry, for if this were so, in a trade depression married men would be the first to lose their jobs. The payment of a marriage allowance under the National Insurance scheme would require a huge increase in the weekly contribution. An extension of the present system of Income Tax allowances might be more feasible. However, the difference in the standard of living between married couples and single women has been lessened since more women continue to work after marriage.

The Royal Commission on Equal Pay (1946) published Majority and Minority Reports. The Majority Report favoured differentiation between the earnings of men and women on the ground that men possess greater physical strength and are generally more efficient than women, that the sickness rate was higher among women, that they were more likely than men to absent themselves from work for trivial reasons, and were generally less ambitious than men and in crises showed less initiative. The Minority Report admitted that where physical strength was concerned, men were more capable than women, but it was claimed that with this exception women were equally as efficient as men, the fact that in the past women had been promoted to few posts of responsibility being ascribed to the prejudice of employers and the jealousy of male employees.

The increasing acceptance of the principle of equal pay in many occupations has been less a triumph of principle than of expediency— shortage of labour during much of the time since 1945. There is general agreement among the more economically advanced nations that there should be equal pay for men and women. The Treaty of Rome (1957), which established the European Economic Community (*see* Chapter 26) supported this principle. The ILO (International Labour Office) convention on equal pay, to which Great Britain subscribed in 1971, also supported the principle of equal pay. In Great Britain, by 1970, women in most professions and the civil service had achieved equality of pay with men. To remove discrimination against women, both as regards pay and other conditions of work, two Acts were passed in 1975—the *Equal Pay Act* and the *Sex Discrimination Act*. However, the difficulty of deciding what is equal pay has already been pointed out. The Act of 1975 proposed that pay for "broadly similar" work should be the same, while the ILO had suggested the term "work of equal value" as the basis for job evaluation. The fact remains that many kinds of work done by women are quite different from any work done by men, so that there is no basis of comparison. The Act of 1975 made discrimination against *either* sex unlawful, not only in employment but in other lines of activity too.

III. EARLY THEORIES OF WAGES

10. The subsistence theory of wages

According to this theory, wages tend to keep to a level that will provide the workers only with a bare subsistence. If wages for a time rise above this level it inevitably leads, it is said, to an increase in the population, and increased competition among workers for employment causes wages to fall again. If wages fall below subsistence level fewer children are born and malnutrition raises the death-rate, so that competition for employment is reduced and wages tend to rise. This "iron law" of wages was looked upon as a natural law by the French School of economists, known as the Physiocrats, who based it upon their observations of conditions of life among the French peasants of the eighteenth century. "Wages are fixed and reduced to the lowest level by the extreme competition of the workers," said Quesnay (1694–1774), who first put forward this theory. The theory of population, expounded by Malthus later, was based on this "iron law".

The main objections to this theory of wages are:

(*i*) Even if true in eighteenth-century France, and in some densely populated countries today, it was certainly not true of England in the nineteenth century. During that century real wages almost doubled, while the population increased by over two and a half times. Nor did rising real wages after 1850 lead to a rise in the birth-rate, for in fact the exact opposite occurred, the birthrate falling from 35 to 28.7 per thousand between 1850 and 1900.

(*ii*) The Subsistence Theory of Wages approaches the problem entirely from the side of supply, the demand for labour being completely ignored. If a rise in wages led to an increase in population the larger supply of labour might be more then balanced by an increase in the demand for labour.

(*iii*) The most serious objection to this theory, however, lies in the ambiguity of the term "subsistence level". What is considered to be the bare minimum for human existence varies between one period and another, and things at one time looked upon as luxuries of the rich often eventually come to be regarded as necessaries. Tea is a good example of this tendency. At the present day very few households are without radio and television sets. What is considered to be bare subsistence in the 1970s would have been thought a very substantial standard of comfort in the 1840s.

11. The wages-fund theory of wages

If the Subsistence Theory were valid all efforts to raise wages would be doomed to failure, since according to that theory wages were bound to remain at subsistence level. The Wages-fund Theory was an attempt to show, without discarding the Malthusian theory of population, that in certain circumstances wages could rise. This theory approached the question more from the side of demand, the demand for labour depending on the amount of capital available for the payment of wages. Since production takes time, producers have to pay wages in advance of the marketing of their products. At the time when the Wages-fund Theory was developed it was thought that a fund of capital had to be accumulated in advance before wages could be paid. Thus the size of the fund at any given moment, it was thought, limited the total amount available for wages. The size of this fund was determined by past accumulation of capital. According to this theory, wages then were not fixed but depended on the relation between the wages fund and the size of the population. An increase in population would lower wages unless this was accompanied by a corresponding increase in capital accumulation. Wages could be improved (*i*) by restricting the growth of population, or (*ii*) by an expansion of the wages fund. Taxation of employers, by reducing their ability to accumulate capital, would thus result in lower wages. Though the wages fund was capable of expansion or contraction over a period, yet at any given time its size was fixed, and so, therefore, was the total sum available for the payment of wages. Though the Wages Fund Theory did not specifically say so, it appeared to imply that if one group of workers obtained a rise in wages it could be only at the expense of other workers, whose share of the fund was thereby reduced. If this were so wages could rise in one industry only at the expense of another, since it was impossible for the general level of wages to rise unless capital increased more rapidly than the population.

Though somewhat crudely expressed, there are elements of truth in this theory. The proportion between the factors of production is an important influence on production, and by increasing the productivity of labour the accumulation of capital tends to raise wages. There is, however, no such thing as a fixed fund set apart for the payment of wages that has to be accumulated in advance, for at the present day production can be financed on credit. In conditions of full employment, however, with production at a maximum, one aspect of the theory appears to come into its own, since in these conditions (assuming no increase in productivity takes place) one group of workers can obtain a rise in their *real* wages only at the expense of all other workers, since if in consequence a rise in prices results, the *real* wages of all other workers will fall.

IV. SYSTEMS OF WAGE PAYMENT

12. Wages rates

Standard rates. The payment of a standard rate to all workers engaged on similar work is an advantage to both employer and employee. Without standard rates an employer would have to make an individual wage bargain with each employee before engaging him. The calculation of the cost of labour becomes easier to the employer when he knows the exact cost of each additional hour of labour. Standard rates, whether per hour or per piece, are essential to collective bargaining, for otherwise it would be impossible for a trade union to make an agreement with the employers regarding wage rates.

Time-rates and standard rates. Various methods of calculating wages are in operation, but the best known are the time-rate and the piece-rate systems. Where time-rates are in operation all employees engaged on similar work are paid an agreed sum per hour. Good, bad and indifferent workers receive equal payment if they work the same number of hours. Under this system it becomes necessary to keep records of the number of hours worked by each employee, a time-clock being installed, and workers having to "clock in" and "clock out", their times of arrival and departure being recorded on cards. It is a further necessity of this system that workers have to be kept under constant supervision in order to prevent slacking. The quicker and more efficient workers may receive the same pay as those who are slower and less efficient, but the better workers may have greater security of employment, for if it becomes necessary to curtail production the first to be dismissed will be the less-efficient workers—those who, because of their poor physique, carelessness, unreliability, or temperament have a low net productivity.

Piece-rates. In order to give the workers an incentive to work harder, a number of different systems have been tried, all of which aim at making the wages received by the worker dependent on the amount of work done. Of these, the simplest, and therefore the most favoured system, is the straight-forward piece-rate method, where the employee receives a fixed payment for a definite, measurable amount of work. If he receives 50p for each unit of work and in a week completes sixty units his wages for that week will be £30; if the following week he accomplishes sixty-four units of work his pay will be £32. Such a system is easy for the worker to understand, since he himself can easily check his earnings. Piece-rates can, however, be operated only where each individual's work can easily be measured, though where groups of employees work together the principle can be extended to the group. If the work is of a continuous nature, and cannot easily be standardised and measured, such as the work of shopkeepers, teachers and bus drivers, payment by piece-rates is not possible, though attempts have sometimes been made to pay shop assistants a bonus based on the value of their sales, and in the nineteenth century teachers in inspected schools were paid according to the number of "passes" in examinations conducted annually in the schools by HM Inspectors. If the quality of the work is more important than the quantity piece-rates are an unsuitable method of payment.

Advantages of piece-rates

(i) The quicker workers can earn more than those who are slow or inclined to waste time.

(ii) Output will probably be increased and the cost per unit reduced. The employer's variable costs (including expenditure on wages) will increase as output increases, but his fixed costs (rent, rates, etc.) will remain as before. His total costs, therefore, will not increase pro-portionately with output.

(*iii*) The cost of supervising employees while they are working will be reduced, because any slacking will affect the employees themselves by reducing their earnings.

(*iv*) The work of costing becomes easier, for the employer knows the exact cost of the labour required for a given unit of output.

Disadvantages of piece-rates

(*i*) The attempt to increase earnings may result in work being rushed. Thus it will be necessary to employ "passers" or inspectors to check the quality of the work done and to reject unsatisfactory work.

(*ii*) The more careful and conscientious workers, who take a longer time over their work, will earn less than those whose work is just satisfactory. The highest earnings will generally go to those whose work is only just good enough to be accepted.

(*iii*) Workers may be induced by the possibility of higher earnings to speed up their work to such an extent that overstrain may injure their health. Employees new to the system often tend to overwork in the early part of the day or week, and then fatigue may slow down their output so much that their eventual earnings are lower than those of a steady worker. Working at excessive speed also increases the liability to accident, and in their own interest men may have to be warned to work more slowly and more carefully.

(*iv*) A complaint made by workers in the past against the piece-rate system was that the wage rate per piece was reduced when it was found that workers were earning considerably more than they previously earned on time-rates. Piece-rates, however, are difficult to fix, and a "fair" rate can be determined only by experiment. A change too in the market conditions for a commodity may necessitate some adjustment of the rate. Considerable attention has been given in recent years to the question of fixing the rates of pay for particular work, especially where the work varies greatly in difficulty. The time taken by workers has been scientifically evaluated by time-and-motion studies.

(*v*) In the past, piece-rates often led to dissatisfaction on the part of the employees because they had no proof that they were being paid for all the work they had done. This led in 1872 to the coal-miners ob-taining the right to appoint a check-weighman at each colliery to see that each miner was credited with his correct output. In 1891 the textile trades adopted the "ticket" system, which entitled each worker to a "ticket" showing the work to be done and the payment for it.

There was a tendency until recently to introduce piece-rates wherever this was possible, but some firms nowadays, for example in the motor-car industry, have reverted to time-rates.

13. Bonus systems

From time to time various modifications of the simple piece-rate system have been adopted, all aiming at reducing the additional amount to be paid in wages for increased output on the part of the workers. A serious drawback to many of the bonus systems that have been tried is that they are more complicated than the straight-forward piece-rate system, and therefore more difficult for the employee to understand. There are three main types of bonus systems: the premium-bonus, the task-bonus systems and the Bedaux system:

(i) *Premium-bonus systems.* In the *Rowan* system (so called because David Rowan of Glasgow first introduced it) each unit of work has a standard time assigned to it. Time-rate wages, say, £1.20 per hour, are in operation, and if the worker completes the work in the "stand-ard" time (say, eight hours) he will be paid 8 × £1.20, that is, £9.60. On a straight piece-rate system this would be the payment received whether the time taken was less or greater than eight hours. If, however, he works very hard and finishes this particular job in six hours, he will be paid at £1.20 per hour for six hours (£7.20), with in addition a bonus equal to the percentage of time saved. In this case the time saved is two hours out of eight hours, and so the bonus will be 25 per cent of £7.20. He will thus receive £9.00 for six hours' work.

Under the *Weir* or *Halsey* system the bonus is half the hourly rate of the time saved. In the above example if the bonus is calculated on the Weir system payment would be for six hours at £1.20 per hour—that is £7.20 + two hours at 60p per hour = £8.40. Table XLVIII com-pares earnings under these two systems, where the standard time is eight hours and the rate 60p per hour.

(ii) *Task-bonus systems.* In these systems piece-rates are paid, but in addition a bonus is payable only if the task is completed within a certain standard time. The severity of the task varies, sometimes, as in the *Gantt* system, being double that of the average worker, and no bonus is paid if the worker just fails in his task. In other systems such as the *Emerson* a more reasonable task is set, and the bonus payments vary according to how near the worker approaches it.

(iii) *The Bedaux system.* Invented in New York in 1911 by Charles Bedaux, and introduced into England in 1926, this system attempts to

Table XLVIII

Rowan and Weir Bonus Systems

Time taken hours	Rowan System			Weir System			Ordinary piece-rate
	Time payment	Bonus	Full payment	Time payment	Bonus	Full payment	
	£	£	£	£	£	£	£
7	8.40 +	1.00 =	9.40	8.40 +	0.60 =	9.00	9.60
6	7.20 +	1.80 =	9.00	7.20 +	1.20 =	8.40	9.60
5	6.00 +	2.24 =	8.24	6.00 +	1.80 =	7.80	9.60
4	4.80 +	2.40 =	7.20	4.80 +	2.40 =	7.20	9.60
3	3.60 +	1.50 =	5.10	3.60 +	3.00 =	6.60	9.60

apply a uniform system of bonus payment to work of varying degrees of difficulty and strain in the same factory. Each type of work is analysed, and according to the strain involved a proportion of time is allowed as "rest". For all kinds of work there is a standard unit of time, known as a B-unit (B for Bedaux), but in an easy job this may consist of fifty-five seconds of work and five seconds of rest, whereas in a more difficult job it may comprise forty-five seconds of work and fifteen seconds of rest. Standard times, calculated by experts supplied by the Bedaux Company, are worked out for all types of work carried on in the factory. The bonus is calculated as in the Weir system, as a percentage (usually 75) of the hourly rate for the time saved.

14. Profit-sharing

Profit-sharing is another method by which some firms have tried to give their employees a more direct interest in the prosperity of the firm. Workers are permitted to hold a certain number of shares, so long as they remain in the employment of the firm, and so they receive a share in the profits. Profit-sharing schemes have been inspired by two motives: (*i*) an incentive to increase output, and (*ii*) in order to stimulate good relations between management and employees. Though there are still a large number of profit-sharing schemes in existence, the number of such schemes has steadily declined during the past forty years or so. Trade unions have always been suspicious of them, since in the early schemes it was often made a condition that the employees should not be members of trade unions. The addition to wages is really a collective bonus depending on the profits earned by the firm. Some of these schemes have been carried on successfully for long periods, and many of the firms operating them proudly boast that they have never been concerned in either a strike or a lock-out. It is claimed, too, that where profit-sharing is in operation less supervision is necessary, and that workers are more careful in their handling of the firm's equipment. A serious objection to profit-sharing is that the bonus is paid only at long intervals: there is too long a time lag between putting forward an extra effort and being paid for it.

15. Wages and the cost of living

Some trade unions have secured agreements whereby the wages of their members vary with the cost of living. The Index of Retail Prices will be considered later. Its main feature, however, is that a certain date is selected as a base year and given an Index Number of 100, a rise in the cost of living of 5 per cent over the base year giving a new Index Number of 105. When wages are linked to the Index of Retail Prices it is agreed that if the index rises a certain number of points wages are to be increased by a certain amount, and similarly if the index falls, wages are to be reduced. This gives wage rates a certain degree of flexibility, but there are two main objections to linking wages to the Index of Retail Prices:

(i) The original Index (known then as the Cost-of-living Index) was based on the expenditure of a working-class family, and had July 1914 as its base. At the present time, however, the index is based on the expenditure of people with a much higher standard of living. People in different income groups distribute their expenditure differently, and changes in the Index Number may affect one income group only to a slight extent, whereas other terms of expenditure, not allowed for in the Index, may affect them to a much greater extent.

(ii) If wages rise or fall proportionately to the rise or fall in the cost of living, and assuming the Index Number to be representative of the standard of living of the workers concerned, real wages become stabilised. For this reason many trade unions are opposed to having wages linked to an index, as their aim is to raise the standard of living of their members. Consequently when the price index is rising they demand wage increases in excess of the rise shown by the index, but if the index falls cuts in wages would be resisted.

V. INDUSTRIAL RELATIONS

16. The development of trade unions

The Industrial Revolution made possible the development of organisations of employers and of employees whose interests seemed to diverge the larger industry grew. In the Middle Ages the guilds included within their membership not only masters but also journeymen and apprentices both of whom had good hopes of themselves eventually becoming masters, so that in those days there was no real divergence of interest between masters and men. The decline of the guilds left both employers and employees unorganised, but the State intervened to regulate wages and working conditions, the Justices of the Peace being empowered to fix wages in their own localities. By the time of the Industrial Revolution this system had lapsed, and each employer decided for himself what wages he would pay. Employees, therefore, began to combine together in order to try to improve the conditions under which they worked. The *Combination Acts* of 1799 and 1801, however, prohibited combinations formed for the purpose of raising wages, on the grounds that such associations were in restraint of trade. These Acts remained in force until 1824, when, largely as a result of the efforts of Francis Place, they were repealed, only to be restored in a modified form the following year. Employees, however, obtained the right to hold meetings and to strike.

A great increase in the number and membership of trade unions followed upon the Acts of 1824 and 1825 and many strikes occurred, but after 1845 disturbances became less frequent, though a recurrence of violence on the part of the trade unions in 1867 led to the setting up of a Royal Commission to inquire into their organisation. The immediate result was the passing of the *Trade Union Act* of 1871, which, with the Acts of 1875 and 1876, clarified the position of trade unions and defined their legal position more precisely, giving them protection for their property, the right to "peaceful picketing" and the freeing of their members from possible charges of conspiracy. The last decade of the nineteenth century saw the development of what was called the New Unionism, which brought unskilled workers within the orbit of the trade-union movement. As a result of the admission of unskilled workers the membership of the unions greatly increased.

In 1900, however, the position of the trade unions was again challenged when the Taff Vale Railway successfully sued a trade union because some of its members had induced other employees to break their contracts, but the *Trade Disputes Act* of 1906 freed the unions from a repetition of such charges. If proper notice was given a strike was not to be regarded as a breach of contract, but in the case of *Rookes v. Barnard*, the House of Lords in 1965 found that in certain circumstances a threat to strike might be unlawful.

Then in 1909 the right of a trade union to use its funds for political purposes was put to the test in the Osborne case, when a member objected to part of his subscription being applied to that purpose. The decision of the courts was that it was illegal for trade unions to engage in political activity. This led to the passing of the *Trade Union Act* of 1913 which permitted unions to contribute to the support of a political party, though members who wished were allowed "to contract out".

The Trades Union Congress in 1926 called a general strike of all the unions in support of the coal-miners, who had been on strike for some time. The general strike failed, and this type of strike was made illegal by the *Trades Disputes and Trade Unions Act* of 1927, but this Act was repealed in 1947.

17. Organisation of trade unions

Trade unions are combinations of employees formed for the purpose of collectively bargaining with employers. The oldest trade unions were the craft unions, which restricted membership to skilled workers engaged in a particular craft. These tend to be the smaller unions, and are especially concerned about the enforcement of apprenticeship regulations in order to restrict entry. The large unions are generally industrial unions, which admit both skilled and unskilled workers, and include all types of workers in the various branches of a particular industry. For example, in the wool textile industry there are small craft unions of warp dressers, twisters, loom tuners, etc., but nearly three-quarters of the employees in the industry are members of the National Union of Dyers, Bleachers and Textile Workers, an industrial union. Many unions are grouped together in federations (for example, the National Association of Unions in the Textile Trades), and most unions are affiliated to the Trades Union Congress. Unions vary greatly in size, some having barely a hundred members and two others each having over a million members.

Each union has local branches which send representatives to district and national committees. Before the development of national insurance many unions offered their members sickness benefit, and some of them (generally the craft unions) also provided unemployment benefit. Although in consequence of mergers the number of trade unions in Great Britain has fallen by about a third, their total membership increased from $1\frac{1}{2}$ million in 1900 to over $11\frac{1}{2}$ million in 1974, of whom 3 million were women.

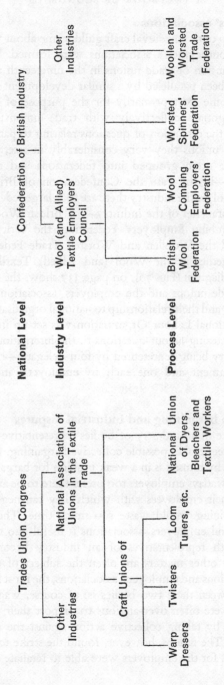

Fig. 76. Associations of Employers and Employees in the Wool Textile Industry.

18. Employers' associations

The break-up of the medieval craft guilds came about when separate masters' and journeymen's associations were formed. The development and expansion of trade unions in the nineteenth and twentieth centuries have been paralleled by a similar development of employers' associations. Some exist primarily for the purpose of enabling employers to negotiate collectively with trade unions; others exist principally for the discussion of questions relating to particular trades. Like the trade unions they vary considerably in size, though small associations are often grouped into federations and affiliated to a national body—in this case the Confederation of British Industry. Thus in the wool textile industry there are four large federations covering the main branches of the industry—the British Wool Federation, the Wool Combing Employers' Federation, the Worsted Spinners' Federation and the Woollen and Worsted Trade Federation. These are linked together in the Wool (and Allied) Textile Employers' Council. The diagram (Fig. 76), on page 337 shows the general structure of the trade unions and the employers' associations in the wool textile industry and their relationship to national organisations.

The International Labour Organisation was set up in 1919 for the purpose of discussing labour questions to the international level, each member country being represented by four delegates—two appointed by the Government and one each by employers' and employees' organisations.

19. Collective bargaining and industrial disputes

The existence in an industry of bodies representative of employers and of employees makes possible collective bargaining, for the individual employee by himself is in a weak position for bargaining with his employer. Nowadays employers too prefer there to be an organisation representing their employees with which they can negotiate, for individual bargaining would waste too much time. The existence of trade unions and employers' associations is useful also to the State if discussions with representatives of an industry become necessary. Though many other matters are often the subject of discussion between trade unions and employers' associations, the most frequent cause of dispute between these two bodies is, of course, wages. The early trade unions were often over-anxious to support their claims for increased wages by taking collective action against the employers by calling strikes. The unions, however, found the strike to be a double-edged weapon, for the employers were able to retaliate by a lock-out if the union refused to accept a reduction in wages. The strike, however, became mainly a weapon of last resort, to be used only when negotiations had failed and deadlock had been reached.

Collective bargaining depends, however, for its success on the willingness of each side to accept any agreement made on their behalf by their representatives. In recent years, however, there have been many "unofficial" strikes called by discontented groups of members with their own particular local grievances, and frowned upon by the officials of the union concerned. Some of these unofficial strikes have occurred when the local branch of a union has insisted on a "closed shop" policy—that is, that all employees should be members of a union—or when some of the members have been unwilling to accept an agreement negotiated by the unions. As an alternative to the strike the unions have developed a new weapon—"working to rule", that is, deliberately working at a slow pace whether working rules exist or not.

During the 1960s there was a shift of power in many trade unions from their national leaders to the shop stewards in individual factories and workshops. The national body might negotiate a wage agreement covering an entire industry, but the shop stewards regarded this only as a basis for further negotiations with their particular employers. This development greatly increased the influence of the local representatives of the unions, who often used their newly acquired powers to call local strikes at individual factories whenever they felt they had a grievance with the management, often over quite trivial matters. These "unofficial" strikes had a serious disruptive effect on production, reduced the prestige of the unions and their leaders, and led to demands in many quarters for a reform of trade union law to make unofficial strikes illegal.

Conciliation and arbitration. For over half a century the State has shown itself anxious to provide machinery for settling industrial disputes to avoid recourse being made to the strike. In 1896 a *Conciliation Act* gave powers to the Labour Department of the Board of Trade (later transferred to the Ministry of Labour—now the Department of Employment) to enquire into disputes, to bring the two sides together, and upon the application of one of them, to appoint a conciliator, or, if both sides were agreeable, an arbitrator. In industries where no machinery previously existed for negotiation between employers and employees Joint Industrial Councils have been sey up. They are generally known as Whitley Councils, because the Rt Hon. J. H. Whitley was chairman of the committee which in 1916 recommended their establishment. Both trade unions and employers' associations are represented on these committees, which meet at regular intervals. There are also Whitley Councils for those in the Civil Service, and in the employment of Local Authorities. Since 1919 there has been in existence a permanent Industrial Court with independent members, as well as representatives of employers and employees, to which reference can be made in the case of specific problems, but its decisions are not enforceable.

20. Reform of the trade unions

Unofficial strikes, restrictive labour practices and inter-union disputes discredited the trade union movement. Since too in service industries, such as transport, and energy, it is consumers rather than employers who feel the brunt of strikes, a widespread demand developed for reform of trade union. The prestige of the unions had been high down to 1955, but after that date it began to decline.

(i) *The Donavon Report*. A Royal Commission under the chairmanship of Lord Donavon was set up in 1965 to inquire into both trade unions and employers' associations, its report being published in 1968. It recommended that strikes should be permitted only in the case of registered trade unions. The Report favoured local agreements which should be registered and supervised by a Commission of Industrial Relations. It also recommended that the smaller unions should be merged to form larger units. To people who wanted a reform of the unions the Report was very disappointing.

(ii) *"In Place of Strife"*. The Government proposed to go further than the recommendations of the *Donavon Report* and in a White Paper, entitled *In Place of Strife*, outlined its proposals. Reforms were to be introduced to put an end to unofficial strikes and a Commission of Industrial Relations was to be set up. The Department of Employment was to have power to delay by twenty-eight days the calling of a strike and to impose fines for breaches of its orders. Strong opposition from the trade unions, however, compelled the Government to withdraw the bill to implement these proposals.

(iii) *The Industrial Relations Act* (1971). With a change of government came the passing of the *Industrial Relations Act*, the aim of which was to improve industrial relations. Under the Act a code of industrial relations practice was drawn up, including a list of unfair practices, to give guidance to both employers and trade unions. Collective agreements between trade unions and employers were to be legally binding. Provision was made for trade unions and employers' associations to be registered. This gave both organisations certain privileges, trade unions for example being permitted to call official strikes, whereas a strike called by an unregistered trade union was to be regarded as unlawful. In certain cases where the economy or public safety and health were likely to be affected the Department of Employment could restrain industrial action for a period of up to sixty days, the so-called "cooling-off period," in order that efforts could be made to settle the dispute. Alternatively, the Department of Employment could order a secret ballot to be taken on the issue. Unless specifically agreed upon, the "closed shop" (that is, employment by a firm only of members of the appropriate trade unions) was not to be permitted. There were clauses in the Act, too, for the protection of the worker as, for example, entitling him to a longer period of notice according to the length of time he had worked for his firm. National Industrial Relations Courts (to be known as Industrial Courts) were established to uphold the code of industrial practices and to hear any complaints of unfair practices.

The passing of the *Industrial Relations Act,* met with open defiance from the trade unions, the TUC encouraging them not to register in spite of the loss of privileges this entailed. Since all the large unions refused to register, the Act became unworkable and as a result the attempt to bring a degree of order into industrial relations failed, and eventually caused the downfall of the Government. The new Government which came to power in 1974 immediately repealed the *Industrial Relations Act* and replaced it by the *Trade Unions and Labour Relations Act,* amended 1975, which legalised the closed shop. The unions were persuaded to accept a measure of control of wages by the acceptance of a "Social Contract" between them and the Government.

RECOMMENDATIONS FOR FURTHER READING

M. Dobb: *Wages.*
J. R. Hicks: *Theories of Wages.*
Report of the Royal Commission on Equal Pay. (1946.) (HMSO)
Department of Employment: *Industrial Relations Handbook.* (HMSO)
E. H. Phelps Brown: *A Course in Applied Economics,* Chapter VIII.

QUESTIONS

1. What are the main causes of inequality of personal incomes in a country? (SE London)

2. "The labourer is rich or poor, is well or ill rewarded in proportion to the real, not to the nominal, price of his labour." (Adam Smith.) Elucidate this statement in the light of conditions at the present ttime. (RSA)

3. Why do wages vary between different occupations? (CIS)

4. Does the fixing of wages by collective bargaining, as is common in Great Britain, supersede the market mechanism? (CIS)

5. What are the economic consequences of automation? Would you advocate that automation should be accelerated in this country? (CIS)

6. What do you understand by the "net advantages of an occupation"? To what extent is there a tendency for all occupations to offer equal net advantages? (IB)

7. What are the main causes of the inequality of personal incomes in a country? (GCE)

8. Why do solicitors earn more than their clerks? (GCE)

9. Salary claims by trade unions are often made on the grounds of higher salaries in "comparable occupations". What analytical arguments might be used in support of such a case? (GCE)

10. "Marginal productivity theory cannot explain the salaries of civil servants." Explain. (Degree)

11. Discuss the contention that rates of wages should be adjusted to take account of alterations in the cost of living. (Degree)

Trade Unions.

12. Explain what you understand by "collective bargaining" and outline the main objectives pursued by trades unions on behalf of their members through this process. (ULCI)

13. What are the economic arguments for and against making collective agreements legally enforceable? (CIS)

14. "The main case for an incomes policy rests on post-war experience suggesting that full employment, price stability and free collective bargaining are inconsistent policies." Discuss. (IB)

15. What is a trade union? In what manner and to what extent does it differ from other types of economic associations? (IB)

16. Discuss the relative merits of trade union organisation based on (*a*) the craft, or (*b*) the industry, from the point of view of the efficiency of a country's economic life. (CIS)

17. In what circumstances might a trade union bring about a permanent increase in the wage rate of the workers in a particular occupation? (GCE)

18. Explain what you understand by collective bargaining. How does it affect the wage structure in the United Kingdom? (GCE)

CHAPTER 19
INTEREST AND PROFIT

I. THE NATURE OF INTEREST

1. The payment of interest

Income, as was seen in Chapter 16, comprises payment for services rendered to production, and is derived from either direct personal service or the ownership of property providing impersonal services. Wages are the payment for labour, and are generally easily distinguished. Rent, interest and profits are not so easily assigned to particular factors of production. This difficulty has already been considered in the case of rent, elements of rent being found in each of the other forms of incomes. Interest and profit are often difficult to distinguish from one another in practice. Interest may be looked upon as a payment for the use of capital, and profit as the reward of the entrepreneur for his services; or interest may be regarded as income from *money* capital, and profit as income from *real* capital, though interest and profit are often inextricably mixed. Interest then becomes a payment for the use of a certain sum of money for an agreed period of time. If a person borrows £100 at a rate of interest of 5 per cent per annum he will in one year's time have to repay £105—that is, the £100 that he borrowed together with £5 interest.

The medieval Church, following the Mosaic Law[1] and the Greek philosophers, condemned usury. For the lender to receive back from the borrower more money than he had lent was considered unjust. This attitude to the payment of interest is, however, more readily appreciated if the difference between borrowers today and borrowers in ancient or medieval times is taken into consideration. At the present time the most important lenders are the various banks. The people who find it easiest to borrow are those whose financial position is basically sound. The businessman borrows only because he thinks he can use the money in a way that will yield him more in profit than he has to pay in interest. In less industrialised societies those who sought loans were usually poor people who found themselves in difficulties as a result of some misfortune—perhaps a fire or a bad harvest—so that

[1] Exodus xxii. 25.

by accepting interest the lender appeared to be taking advantage of another man's misfortune. The moneylender of today who does business with the poor is no more respected a member of society than was Shylock, but even so he provides a service for clients who would be unable to borrow elsewhere. From the time of Henry VIII onwards many statutes were passed regulating the rate of interest. The Usury Laws, however, were not repealed until 1854, though they had not been enforced for some time. The rates charged by pawnbrokers continue to be regulated, and moneylenders' charges are subject to review by the courts.

Some opposition to the payment of interest was based on the view that it cost the lender nothing to make a loan and Karl Marx and his followers maintained this opinion. The purchaser of a motor car has to pay for it, and a person who hires a car has to pay for the use of it for a period. It appears to be reasonable, therefore, for a borrower to have to pay for the use of a sum of money for a period, since both the owner of the motor car and the owner of the money are providing services, and both forgo something in return for the payments. Interest is paid because a loan provides a service, and because loanable funds are scarce relative to the demand for them.

2. Present-day borrowers and lenders

Borrowing and lending are indispensable activities in an advanced economic system. At the present day the chief lenders are:

(i) Banks, which lend to businessmen and private individuals (on loan account or overdraft) and to the Government (by the purchase of Government securities).

(ii) Building societies, which assist private individuals and business to purchase house or business property.

(iii) Finance companies whose main business is to finance hire-purchase transactions.

(iv) Moneylenders, who lend to private individuals.

The above make lending their main function. Other lenders include:

(v) Insurance companies, which lend to the Government (by the purchase of Government securities) and to business (by the purchase of debentures and shares).

(vi) Individuals, who lend to the Government and to business (in a similar manner as do insurance companies) and to banks, building societies and finance companies (by making deposits).

(*vii*) Businessmen, who may lend part of their reserves to the Government (by the purchase of Government securities), to local authorities or to banks (on deposit account).

All these lenders, except individuals, obtain funds for lending by borrowing in their turn, so that the extent of their borrowing determines the amount they are able to lend.

The chief borrowers, therefore, are the Government, businessmen and private persons; banks and building societies borrow by accepting deposits. The following diagram shows the intricate pattern of present-day borrowing and lending:

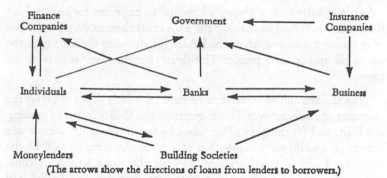

(The arrows show the directions of loans from lenders to borrowers.)

Fig. 77. Borrowing and Lending.

3. Elements of interest

There are three elements in gross interest:

(*i*) *Payment for risk*. In one case £6 may have to be paid for the use of £100 for a year: in another case £9 may have to be paid for a similar loan. Why should there be any difference in the "hire-price" of two equal sums of money for the same period of time? Why do insurance companies charge higher premiums to some people than to others for insuring motor cars? The reason is exactly the same in both instances: more risk is involved in one case than in the other. Part of the interest charged on a loan is therefore a payment for risk—the risk that the loan may not be repaid. Generally, some sort of security has to be given for a loan—something that the lender can turn into cash if the loan is not repaid. In such cases the risk to the lender is reduced, and so the risk payment will be smaller. The person who offers to lend without security will charge a higher rate of interest because his risk of loss is greater.

(ii) Payment for the trouble involved. When goods are sold on the hire-purchase system the price to be paid will be higher than that charged to a person who pays cash. Again part of the higher price is a risk payment, but a charge is also made for the inconvenience which this type of sale causes the seller. The reason why a pawnbroker charges a high rate of interest on loans is partly because there is a great risk that the loan will not be repaid, and partly because of the work entailed in granting such loans. Lending money, then, causes the lender a certain amount of work; he has to keep a record of the transaction and he may have to collect the interest. Thus part of the interest payment is a charge for the lender's trouble.

(iii) Pure interest. Any charge additional to payment for risk and for the trouble involved in making the loan must therefore be for the use of the money, to compensate the lender for allowing the borrower the use of his money for a period. This third element, then, is pure or net interest.

Thus the amount of interest to be paid on a loan depends on (*a*) the character of the borrower, (*b*) the expenses the lender incurs in making the loan, and (*c*) the prevailing rate of pure interest. Of these three factors (*a*) and (*b*) are variable, but at a particular time (*c*) will be the same for loans of equal amount and for the same length of time, though the rate of pure interest may vary between one period and another. Consider the following three borrowers, A, B and C, each of whom borrows £100 for a year. A at 8 per cent, B at 10 per cent and C at 15 per cent.

Table XLIX
Elements of Interest

	Amount of loan	Rate of Interest	Payment for use of money (Pure Interest)	Expenses of lender	Payment for risk	Total payment
	£	%	£	£	£	£
A	100	8	7	0.50	0.50	8
B	100	10	7	1.00	2.00	10
C	100	15	7	1.00	7.00	15

Although different rates of interest are paid by the three borrowers, the amount of pure interest is the same in all three cases. If the rate of pure interest rises it will increase the cost to all borrowers.

4. The rate of interest and the rate of yield

In order to raise a new loan, the Government may have to offer 8 per cent interest to persuade a sufficient number of people to subscribe to it. New stock or bonds to the required amount will be issued, and these may bear some such name as Eight per cent National Bonds 1994–8. The name is required to distinguish the bonds from other issues, and the dates signify that the bonds are not redeemable—that is, repayable—before 1994 or later than 1998, the Government having the option of repaying at any time convenient to itself between these two dates. If the bonds are issued at par this means that £100 of bonds can be bought for that amount, and 8 per cent is the rate of interest to be paid on them. A person purchasing £100 of bonds will therefore acquire an income of £8 per annum. Some time later the Government, again wishing to borrow, may find that now it can only obtain the sum required by paying 10 per cent, and a new issue of, say, ten per cent State Bonds 2002–8 may be offered to the public The stock exchange—the market for securities—will then experience a decreased demand for Eight per cent National Bonds because they carry a lower rate of interest. This decreased demand will push down the price, so that less than £100 will have to be paid for £100 of these bonds. In this case the price will probably fall to about £80, for at that price the rate of yield (£8 on £80) will be 10 per cent, the same rate of interest as on the new issue. On the stock exchange the prices of bonds and other securities fluctuate daily, and the rate of yield varies with each change of price. If the price of £100 of National Bonds rose to £110 the rate of yield would rise to just under 7¼ per cent (£8 on £110). The important feature of all such securities is not the fixed rate of interest they bear, but the rate of yield at any given time, for it is this that reflects the prevailing rate of interest.

II. SAVING

5. Borrowing and saving

People borrow money not because they want it for its own sake but only because it gives them command over goods and services. Nobody will seek a loan unless he considers that the value of the satisfaction to be derived from the goods or services on which the money is to be spent is at least equal to the interest that he has to pay. Most loans are wanted by businessmen to finance production. The essential feature of a loan, therefore, is that the lender for an agreed period forgoes in favour of the borrower his claim to a quantity of goods and services. The supply of loanable funds depends on the amount of saving that has previously taken place, the saver forgoing the consumption of a certain quantity of goods and services, which then become available to the borrowers. It is important, therefore, to consider the different types of saving and the reasons for saving before considering the factors that determine the rate of interest.

Types of saving. The importance of saving lies in the fact that it makes possible real investment—that is, the accumulation of capital goods. Saving reduces the demand for consumers' goods, and so enables more of a country's resources to be devoted to the production of producers' goods or capital goods. Any course of action, therefore, that brings about a reduction of consumer spending can be considered to be saving. Thus, there are a number of kinds of saving:

(*i*) *Individual saving.* This is what most people understand by saving. They are prepared to abstain from current consumption in order to build up a fund of purchasing power for use at a later date, or in order to provide themselves with a future source of income.

(*ii*) *Corporate saving.* Only about half the total amount of saving comes from private individuals, most of the remainder being provided by the undistributed profits of limited companies. By the decision of the directors, the shareholders have to forgo this amount of profit, which otherwise might have been distributed among them.

These two types of saving are both voluntary.

(*iii*) *Compulsory saving.* In ordinary speech, saving and taxation are regarded as two quite distinct things, but the economic effect of each can be similar, since each results in a curtailment of consumption, and so makes possible capital investment. If individuals are unwilling to save it may be necessary for the State to compel them to curtail their consumption, and to do this it would impose additional taxation to bring in the amount to be "saved."

(*iv*) *Forced saving.* The demand for consumers' goods may be checked by a moderate inflation if this results in a rise in prices without a corresponding rise in incomes. By curtailing consumption, resources are released for the production of capital goods, and this has the same economic effect as other kinds of saving. It is sometimes called "forced saving."

6. Reasons for saving

In general it is probably true that the higher the rate of interest, the greater the amount that will be saved, for it is generally agreed that a low rate of interest discourages saving and encourages spending. Though, by and large, this may be true, there are many exceptions, for in some cases the rate of interest has little effect on saving, and sometimes a lowering of the rate may actually result in more being saved. It is necessary, therefore, to consider why people save, for the extent to which the rate of interest affects saving will depend on their motives for saving. The following, then, are some of the reasons for saving:

(i) *For unforeseen contingencies.* Most people prefer to have some reserve of cash which they can fall back upon in time of need. In the past the most likely purpose for such a reserve was the possibility of sickness. The extension of national insurance to the whole community reduced the need of saving for this purpose. Saving of this kind will be unaffected by the rate of interest.

(ii) *For a future need.* In the past one of the most urgent reasons for saving was the desire to put something by for old age. In Great Britain Old Age Pensions were first introduced by Lloyd George in 1908. Since 1948 retirement pensions have been provided under the National Insurance scheme, and these are periodically increased to keep in line with the rising cost of living. More recently, schemes for earnings-related pensions have been introduced. Even when these pensions are supplemented by other contributory schemes, as in the Civil Service, Local Government and many large firms, saving for old age does not appear to have declined. People save in the hope, on retirement, of being able to continue to enjoy the standard of living to which they have been accustomed. Some people, too, may desire for their children a form of education different from that provided by the State, and often begin saving to cover its cost from the time of their children's birth. If a definite sum is required by a certain date more will have to be saved if the rate of interest is low, so that a fall in the rate may actually increase the amount of saving for this purpose.

(iii) *For the purchase of expensive goods.* In some ways this purpose is similar to the previous type, as it is simply deferred spending. Things such as motor cars, houses (even if building societies lend a high percentage of the purchase price) and furniture are expensive, and so to a lesser entent are holidays and many durable household goods. For those who find it difficult to save, because to them present satisfaction far outweighs future satisfaction, there are clothing clubs, the Christmas clubs and the holiday clubs. The effect of hire-purchase is to discourage saving (apart from the initial deposit) and to encourage spending. There are still some people, however, who prefer to save in advance for things they wish to buy. The rate of interest clearly has no direct bearing on such saving, which often merely brings forward or puts back a little the date when the particular satisfaction can be enjoyed.

(*iv*) *To raise social status*. Power, influence and social prestige depend to some extent on personal wealth and income. By saving it is possible for a man to build up a source of future income either for himself or his descendants. It is doubtful how far the rate of interest will affect this kind of saving. A low rate may discourage some, but for others it may merely lead to a redoubling of effort.

(*v*) *As a matter of principle*. At one time people looked upon thrift as a virtue, and considered self-denial a desirable thing in itself. In such cases saving was obviously independent of the rate of interest, but there is probably little of this kind of saving today.

(*vi*) *For speculative purposes*. Saving for this purpose is directly related to the rate of interest. If the rate is high there is a strong inducement to save, whereas if the rate is low saving less becomes worth while.

(*vii*) *Some saving is not planned*. The very rich may save the surplus that remains from their incomes after they have spent all they wish, though heavy taxation of high incomes has reduced the amount saved in this way. The rate of interest clearly has not much effect on this saving. All saving is, however, to a greater or less extent dependent on the saver's wealth and income, for the rate at which wealth increases is cumulative. The more that is saved, the larger the income, and so the easier it becomes to save still more.

In times of persistent inflation the falling value of money generally tends to discourage saving. Money spent in the present has greater value than money saved to be spent in the future. Nevertheless, during 1971–6 when prices were rising more rapidly than ever before in time of peace, saving was actually increasing.

III. THE DETERMINATION OF THE RATE OF INTEREST

7. Some theories of interest

Interest is one of the most controversial subjects in economics. A number of theories have been put forward to explain it:

(*i*) *Supply and demand*. According to one school of thought, the rate of interest, being the price of loans, is determined by the demand for loans, on the one hand, and the supply of loanable funds, on the other, so that the equilibrium rate (or natural rate, as Wicksell called it) is the rate that equates demand with supply.

(ii) *Time-preference.* The supply of loanable funds comes from saving. As with other things, more will generally be supplied the higher the price, so that a high rate of interest will increase the supply of loanable funds. This is probably largely true, though it has been seen above that much saving is independent of the rate of interest. Time preference theories stress the idea that the supply of loans depends on the fact that most people prefer to have a certain sum of money now than at some future time. Interest, therefore, arises because one person prefers £100 now, to (say) £105 a year hence, while another prefers £105 a year hence to £100 now, lending and borrowing being possible only because the satisfaction of immediate wants occupies a higher place on the borrower's than on the lender's scale of preferences.

(iii) *Capital is productive.* There is a demand for loans because capital is productive. As already noted, a greater output is achieved if a more capitalistic method of production is adopted, but this increases the time interval between the taking of the decision to produce and the beginning of the outflow of goods. The more capitalistic the method of production, the longer this time interval will be. In order, then, to be able to undertake a more capitalistic method of production the entrepreneur has to sacrifice a smaller immediate gain for a greater future gain. He is willing, therefore, to pay interest on his borrowed capital because he hopes that his gain from *waiting*, that is, extending the time interval of production, will more than compensate him for what he has paid. Thus interest can be regarded either as the reward of waiting or as a payment for not waiting.

The holding of stocks—generally financed by borrowing—makes possible a more even flow of goods to the market, particularly in the case of agricultural products, merchants buying large stocks of wheat, for example, when supplies are plentiful, storing the commodity and releasing it to the market gradually. In a somewhat similar way the wholesaler eases the distributive process by holding stocks of goods turned out in large quantities by manufacturers and wanted by retailers in small quantities only when their stocks are in need of replenishment.

Marginal productivity of capital.[1] Capital can never receive more than

---

[1] Lord Keynes used the term "marginal efficiency of capital," which he defined as "the relation between the prospective yield of one more unit of that type of capital and the cost of producing that unit." (*General Theory of Employment, Interest and Money*, p. 135.)

the value of its marginal product, because the entrepreneur will employ a little more capital only if the additional income arising from its employment exceeds what he has to pay for it. If the producer can borrow £100 at 12 per cent and use it productively so as to yield him a return of £20 he will gain £8 by borrowing. The incidence of the Law of Diminishing Returns may mean that a further £100 (assuming that he can continue to borrow at the same rate) yields a return of £18, a third £100 a return of £15, a fourth £100 a return of £13, and a fifth only £11. He can increase his profit, therefore, by borrowing up to £400, because at that point the interest he has to pay is equal to the value of the marginal product of the capital. The demand for business loans depends then on the marginal productivity of capital in relation to the rate of interest, and the greater the amount of capital employed, the lower generally will be its marginal productivity. There is a tendency, however, for the marginal productivity of capital to be the same in all forms of production, for capital will be attracted to these lines of production where it will yield the higher return, being drawn away from those employments where the return is lower, so that equilibrium will be achieved only when marginal productivity is in all cases equal. Some capital, of course, cannot easily be transferred to alternative use, but it need not be replaced when it becomes worn out.

The importance of interest to production. The rate of interest is important because it influences capital accumulation. If a new machine costing £500 will add £50 a year to the income of the firm installing it, it will be to the advantage of the entrepreneur to borrow the necessary £500, provided that the rate of interest is less than 10 per cent. As the rate of interest falls, some forms of production previously unprofitable can be undertaken. Since production is undertaken in anticipation of demand, it is the prospective yield of capital, and not its current yield, that influences entrepreneurs. Capital is scarce relative to the demand for it, and so it is the purpose of interest (as with other prices) to distribute it among all the various uses competing for it; and such a rationing of capital by means of the rate of interest is necessary even under a communist regime.

8. The monetary theory of interest

Liquidity-preference. The view that the rate of interest equates the demand for loans with the supply of savings is too simple, for the question is complicated by the fact that banks can create credit and by the public's demand for holding money balances. People require to hold money for everyday purposes—bus fares, for example—with a little in reserve to meet any unforeseen calls upon them. If more is held than is necessary for these purposes it must be because they prefer to keep their resources "liquid"—that is, in the form of money rather than in the form of other assets, such as stocks and shares. To keep one's resources liquid, however, involves a loss of interest. But if the prices of securities are expected to fall in the future it will be advantageous to postpone purchasing them, since a fall in their prices will increase their yield. In such circumstances, then, more money will be held—that is, liquidity-preference will be strong. If the prices of securities are expected to rise, it will be advantageous to purchase them without delay, and so less money will be held—that is liquidity-preference will be weak. Liquidity-preference and the rate of interest affect one another. The monetary authorities decide what the total quantity of money shall be, but the general public's liquidity-preference decides how much money will be held— that is, people themselves determine the demand for money. According to this theory, the rate of interest is not determined by people's willingness to save, but by their attitude towards liquidity. The rate of interest can therefore be considered as the reward for parting with liquidity. This question will be discussed further in Chapter 21 in connection with the demand to hold money.

It is likely that each one of these explanations of the determination of the rate of interest contains some truth, for it may be partly determined by real forces such as the productivity of capital and partly by monetary forces such as liquid-preference. Controversy is largely the result of difference of emphasis.

9. Long-term and short-term rates of interest

Differences in the liquidity of securities affect their rates of yield. $2\frac{1}{2}\%$ Consols are an example of a non-liquid security, for there is no date when they are due to be redeemed. Many Government stocks are dated, two dates usually being given, the Government having the option to redeem them at any time between these two dates. Generally the longer the period of redemption, the higher is the rate of yield, though there have been exceptions to this when the short-term rate of interest has been very high, as, for example, on the occasions when the Bank rate has been high. The stock exchange quotations for some Government stocks on the 7th January 1976 are given in Table L.

In all cases the quotations refer to stock of £100 nominal value. Their yields vary inversely with their prices. On the 3% Gas Stock the gross redemption yield was approximately 11.9 per cent, whereas on the $2\frac{1}{2}\%$ Consols it was 14.3 per cent.

Table L

Stock Exchange Prices

3½% Treasury Stock 1979–81	.	83¼
3% British Transport Stock 1978–88	.	47⅞
3% Gas Stock 1990–95	.	33¼
3½% Funding Loan 1999–2004	.	28⅞
2½% Consols	.	17¾

There are, however, securities that fall due within a very short period of time, such as bills of exchange (trade bills and Treasury bills), which generally mature in three months. Since these bills are fairly liquid, they generally bear only a low rate of interest. This is the short-term rate of interest. The two rates—long-term and short-term—generally follow one another up and down, though the short-term is more liable to fluctuations. On account of the greater risk of a change of yield over a long period of time, the long-term rate is usually higher than the short-term, except when the short-term rate is very high. That the two rates tend to rise or fall together is largely the result of the action of speculators, who sell their long-term securities if their price is high and buy short-term securities with the proceeds, reversing this process later if the price of short-term securities rise. The yield on bills is likely to be small (except when interest rates are high) because they are a fairly liquid form of asset. The cost of keeping one's assets liquid, therefore, is the short-term rate of interest, and so this, depending largely on liquidity-preference, is generally regarded as the fundamental rate, the long-term rate being determined by it.

IV. PROFIT

10. Gross profit and net profit

Suppose that Pecksniff is the sole proprietor of a retail business. In order to show his gross profit he periodically draws up a trading account as shown in Table LI. This shows that his gross profit for this period of six months is £6,100. Pecksniff will then proceed to draw up a Profit and Loss Account in order to find his net profit as shown in Table LII. Pecksniff's net profit for this period of six months is therefore £1,700, and this has been calculated by deducting his expenses from his gross profit. Even this simple illustration shows one important characteristic of profit, namely that, unlike wages, it is not a fixed sum, but a residual amount received after all payments have been made.

Table LI

Trading Account

For the period 1st January to 30th June

			£				£
Jan. 1.	To opening stock .		1,850	June 30.	By sales . .		15,610
June 30.	„ purchases .		9,300	„ 30.	„ closing stock		1,640
„ 30.	„ gross profit .		6,100				
			£17,250				£17,250

Table LII

Profit and Loss Account

				£				£
June 30.	To wages .	.		3,200	June 30.	By gross profit .		6,100
„ 30.	„ rent .	.	.	460				
„ 30.	„ rates .	.		300				
„ 30.	„ lighting .			130				
„ 30.	„ heating .	.		110				
„ 30.	„ depreciation	.		200				
„ 30.	„ net profit .	.		1,700				
				£6,100				£6,100

A sole trader, he will probably regard as profit the whole of the
amount that the business yields him—£1,700 in the above example.

11. Elements of profit

Before setting up in business on his own account, Pecksniff may
have been employed as branch manager of a multiple-shop, saving a
portion of his income each year for the purpose of accumulating the
capital necessary for a business of his own at some future date. Suppose
that as manager of the Northampton branch of Multiple Drapers Ltd.
his salary was £2,000 per annum, and that his savings finally amounted
to £7,000 which he had invested in Government Stock at 9 per cent.
At that time his income for six months would be:

	£
Salary as manager of the shop	1,000
Interest on his savings	315
Total income for six months	£1,315

In business on his own account his income for six months is his net profit of £1,700. As a sole trader he has been acting as manager of his own shop, and also using his own capital, which otherwise would have yielded him interest. His net profit can therefore be split up as follows:

Table LIII

Elements of Profit

	£
Salary as manager of his own shop (assuming his services to himself to be worth as much as Multiple Drapers Ltd. previously paid him)	1,000
Interest on his capital	315
Pure profit	385
	£1,700

Thus, as Table LIII clearly shows, it is possible to distinguish three elements in profit: (*i*) wages of management; (*ii*) interest on capital; and (iii) pure profit.

If Pecksniff's business had been a private limited company with capital of £10,000, his salary then would have been reckoned as working expenses, and the company's profit for six months would have been £385. Assuming the profit for the next six months to be the same, and that the whole amount was distributed among the shareholders (a most unlikely event), the company would have been able to declare a dividend of 26 per cent for the year. The distributed profit of a company, therefore, contains two elements: interest on capital and pure profit.

Pure profit. This is a payment for taking risk. People would be unwilling to provide capital for business enterprises if there was no possibility of a greater return than could be obtained from "safe" investments such as Government stock. Earlier in this chapter it was said that interest can be considered as income from money capital, and profit as income from real capital, but it is clear now that income from real capital also includes an element of interest.

Some writers look upon pure profit as the peculiar reward of the entrepreneur for his share in the work of production; others, who refuse to recognise the entrepreneur as a factor of production, stress the concept of profit as the surplus remaining after all the expenses of production, including wages of management, have been met. These two concepts are, however, not nearly so divergent as might at first appear. Profit goes to the owners of the business, who risk holding assets in that form. In both cases, however, profit is a payment for bearing risk. In Chapter 3 it was seen that uncertainty-bearing was the principal function of the entrepreneur, uncertainty covering all risks that could not be insured against, whereas contractual payments are made for the services of labour. The income of the entrepreneur is residual and also, unlike wages, it can be negative—that is, a firm can make either a profit or a loss.

Under perfect competition a certain level of profit is necessary if capital is to be retained in a particular line of production, and this has been called *normal profit*. Apart from this, pure profit would tend to disappear under static conditions. Profit arises, then, under dynamic conditions. In the more extreme forms of imperfect competition— those forms that approach most nearly to monopoly—profit above normal arises as a result of restriction of output, so that monopoly profit is more in the naure of a rent than a true profit, since it has its origin in the scarcity of the product, even though in this case scarcity is created by the monopolist himself.

12. Causes of uncertainty

Pure profit occurs in dynamic conditions because there will always be uncertainty in conditions that are liable to change. The entrepreneur may be fully conversant with the state of the markets for his factors, and for his final product, at the time when he embarks upon production, but since production usually takes place in anticipation of demand, and a time interval must elapse between the taking of his decision to produce and the beginning of the outflow of his goods to the market, no entrepreneur can be sure what will be the eventual demand for his product. In other words, uncertainty is present. In static conditions there would be no pure profit, for uncertainty is the result of dynamic change.

The following are some of the influences liable to produce uncertainty:

(*i*) changes in population, either in numbers or in its distribution among different age-groups, with consequent changes in demand;

(*ii*) changes of fashion which can cause sudden changes of demand;

(*iii*) a rise or fall in total money income or a change in the distribution of income among consumers;

(*iv*) the introduction of new forms of capital, with consequent changes in the technique of production;

(*v*) ignorance of the price and output policy of rival firms.

If any of these changes takes place uncertainty will arise, and entrepreneurs may earn pure profit. If for any reason uncertainty declines, then pure profit will also decline.

13. Differences in profit

So long as uncertainty exists there can be no general rate of profit, for profit will vary between different industries according to the extent of uncertainty in each line of production. Therefore, as one might expect, in well-established industries, where conditions are less subject to change, uncertainty is at a minimum, and so pure profit tends to be low. In such industries there will also be only slight differences in the amount of pure profit earned by different enterprises.

Wherever differences in the amount of pure profit earned by entrepreneurs occur in the same industry these differences can be explained only in terms of variations in entrepreneurial skill. The greater the uncertainty, the greater will be the possibility of profit, but also the greater the risk of loss. People are willing to put their capital into risky undertakings only because of the possibility of high profit. Uncertainty is always high in the case of new products and so the expectation of high profit is the inducement to capital to enter new fields of activity. If an industry yields high profit this will encourage new firms to enter, and so in time tend to reduce profit in that industry. The entrepreneur aims at maximising his profit, and this induces him to adopt new techniques. Profit, therefore, encourages enterprise.

Differences in profit in different industries are, therefore, the result of differences in uncertainty. On the other hand, differences in profit between firms in the same industry are due to differences in the skill of entrepreneurs in bearing uncertainty.

14. Profit and cost of production

The residual character of profit has already been stressed. This being so, two questions may be asked. Is profit a cost of production? Does profit enter into price? Wages of management are clearly a cost of production, as was shown in the case of a limited company. If capital is provided in the form of debentures they become a charge on the firm, and so interest on this form of capital also becomes a cost of production. In the case of the dividend on ordinary shares it is difficult to distinguish between interest and pure profit, but the interest element is clearly a cost. Unless entrepreneurs receive what is regarded as the "normal profit" for an industry, capital will move elsewhere, and so normal profit, the minimum reward the entrepreneur is prepared to accept should also be regarded as a cost of production. Any further profit, however, is due to the entrepreneur's own skill and judgment in overcoming uncertainty, and is a surplus earned only by the more successful entrepreneurs. This element of profit is not a cost, and therefore it does not influence the price of the commodity. High profits, therefore, are not the cause but the consequence of high prices, which in turn are the result of a high level of demand.

Both profit and rent, then, are surpluses, but rent is a surplus accruing to any factor of production as a result of a condition generally outside the factor's control—the difficulty in the short period of increasing the supply of a specific factor to meet an increase in the demand for its services. Rent is therefore unearned, for no factor can as a result of its own exertions obtain rent. Profit, however, differs from rent in being earned, for it is the entrepreneur's reward for the successful bearing of uncertainty.

RECOMMENDATIONS FOR FURTHER READING

F. H. Knight: *Risk, Uncertainty and Profit*, Chapters 1, 2, 7–10.
A Marshall: *Principles of Economics*, Bk. VI, Chapters 6–8.
P. Wicksteed: *Common-sense of Political Economy*, Vol. I, Chapter 7.

QUESTIONS

Interest

1. What reasons may be advanced for and against the payment of interest? (RSA)
2. "The rate of interest is the reward for parting with liquidity for a specified period." Assess the adequacy for this definition of the rate of interest. (CIS)
3. What are the factors that tend to link together the movements in long-term and short-term rates of interest? How far are these factors operative in present conditions? (IB)
4. "The rate of interest is not the 'price' which brings into equilibrium the demand for resources to invest with the readiness to abstain from present consumption." (Keynes.) What do *you* think determines the rate of interest? (ACCA)
5. What factors influence the level of savings in an economy? (GCE)
6. What place does the Keynesian theory of interest leave for thrift and the productivity of capital? (Degree)

Profit

7. Distinguish between profit, rent and interest. (IMTA)
8. How would you distinguish between interest and profits? (CIS)

9. What is meant by the "profit-motive"? In your answer bring out carefully the nature and genesis of profits. (IHA)

10. Examine the contention that if profits were reduced wages could be increased in any given industry. (IT)

11. "Profits are the reward for risk-taking." Discuss this statement with reference to the present-day financial structure of industry. (Exp.)

12. "Profits tend to equality." Point out the ambiguities in this statement and submit a clear statement about the relations between profits in different industries. (IB)

13. On what factors does the profitability of an enterprise depend? (Degree)

14. "Super-normal profits are a rent and may be taxed away without affecting business enterprise." Discuss. (Degree)

Part Six

BANKING AND FINANCE

CHAPTER 20

THE ORIGINS AND FUNCTIONS
OF MONEY

I. THE ORIGIN OF MONEY

1. Disadvantages of barter

The use of money facilitates exchange. Under the most primitive conditions of human existence each family provided for its entire needs, though even then there would probably be some division of labour among the members. In so small a group, held together by family ties, each member might make a contribution to the common tasks and be content to receive a share from the common pool according to his needs. As soon as peaceful intercourse took place between different groups of people the possibility of exchange would arise if one group were able, by reason of differences of climate or geology, to produce something another group lacked. Division of labour, by making it possible for people to specialise in those occupations for which they are best fitted, raises the standard of life, but makes exchange necessary. The man who devotes his whole time to working in iron is compelled to exchange some of the things that he has made for food and clothing. Before money came to be used goods had to be exchanged for goods; the smith, for example, might exchange a spade perhaps for a quantity of meat or wheat, just as today a schoolboy might exchange a penknife for a handful of marbles.

The exchanging of goods for goods is known as *barter*. It has three serious drawbacks. In the first place, it makes exchange dependent on what is called a "double coincidence of wants." Thus it is not sufficient for the smith to find someone requiring a spade; if he wants wheat in exchange for the spade he must find a farmer who not only wishes to dispose of wheat but who at the same time requires a spade. Since farmers are likely to want spades, this might be less difficult than the task of a goldsmith in search of a butcher who is in want of a gold trinket of some kind. Even after two men who are able to satisfy each other's wants have been brought together, there is the further difficulty of deciding how much wheat has to be given for a spade or how much meat for a gold ornament. Different rates of exchange have to be determined to cover every transaction before it can take place. A third problem arises if one party to a transaction has only a large commodity, such as a table, to offer, but requires only a small quantity of something—perhaps a stone of potatoes—in exchange. Barter, therefore, involves a waste of human effort and is a clumsy method of exchange, but even under a system of barter there is need of a unit of account in which to assess the values of different commodities, even though no medium of exchange is in use.

2. Early forms of money

The difficulty of bringing two people together, each of whom was able to supply something the other desired in exchange for what the other could offer him, led to the development of an intermediate stage. There would be some things that were in general demand, and so instead of seeking out a farmer in need of a spade, the smith might, for example, exchange his spade for a quantity of salt, and then exchange the salt for wheat. Anything in common use and generally acceptable could serve in this way as a medium of exchange. Thus goods first employed as money were those that were most marketable—that is, those considered to be valuable for their own sake.

To be generally acceptable, goods have to be either useful or ornamental, and so cattle, hides and leather, furs, tea, salt, cowrie shells and many other things at different times and in different places served as money. Adam Smith declared that in his own day salt was still being used as money in Abyssinia, shells in some parts of India, dried cod in Newfoundland, tobacco in Virginia and sugar in the West Indies. Immediately after the Second World War cigarettes for a time served as a medium of exchange in West Germany. All these things, however, have their own individual drawbacks. Cattle are not all of equal quality; they are bulky and not easily taken around by a shopper; the units are too large, and so can be used only for large purchases; and their owners would suffer loss if the cattle were to die. Tea and salt are more easily divisible, but both are liable to deterioration when stored. Cowrie shells, though used as money in China, are fairly abundant in the Indian Ocean, and there are places where one could easily replenish one's stock.

Qualities of good monetary media. A good medium of exchange must not only be (*i*) generally acceptable, but must also be (*ii*) fairly durable, (*iii*) capable of being divided into reasonably small units, and (*iv*) easy to carry about. A fifth necessary quality is that it should be relatively scarce, though not too scarce. The precious metals, at first silver and later gold, fulfilled clearly these conditions, and they quickly superseded other things as money, silver being in use for this purpose in the earliest days of recorded history. Though there has been considerable variation at different times in the output of gold and silver from the mines, the amount mined in any one year has never formed more than a small percentage of the total amount in existence. Commodities more valuable than gold, such as diamonds and platinum, have never been used as money because the amounts required for the purchase of cheap things would be too small to handle. In early times a sixth quality was required before a commodity could be used as money—namely, that it should be valuable for its own sake. However once a commodity had been selected for use as money its value tended to increase. When, during the nineteenth century, many countries replaced silver by gold as their monetary standard the value of silver fell considerably, while the value of gold rose.

II. TYPES OF MONEY

3. Coins

One of the main advantages of using the precious metals as money was their divisibility, and at first merchants paid for what they purchased by weighing out an agreed amount of the metal. Though the use of the precious metals in this way was a great improvement on previous media of exchange, the disadvantages of this method of making payments must soon have become apparent. It was not long, therefore, before coins came into use. A coin is nothing more than a definite amount of metal, its weight and fineness being guaranteed by the official stamp of the issuing authority. At first, for example, the Jewish shekel was a certain weight of metal, but later it came to mean a coin, and similarly, the pound sterling was originally a pound by weight of silver. Coins were the most convenient form of money yet used, but there was always the danger that the issuing authority might make them of less weight than they were reputed to be. The responsibility for the issue of coins soon came to be regarded as the sole prerogative of the State. Monarchs in financial straits, however, were often tempted to debase the coinage by reducing their content of the precious metals. Henry VIII had recourse to debasement of the coinage on an extensive scale, the coins issued between 1543 and 1551 containing each year less silver than the year before, until eventually the amount of silver in the coins was only one-seventh of the amount they had originally contained.

Merchants in those days looked upon coins simply as a convenient means of handling quantities of the precious metals, and they were not to be deceived by such unscrupulous behaviour, for whenever the issuing authority resorted to debasement the value of the coins fell. In such cases the merchants would again have recourse to weighing the coins themselves. Thus more coins would be required in payment if the precious metal content of the coins had been reduced. If the debasement was the result of mixing base metal with the precious metal the value of the coins would be proportionately reduced, and this again would result in a rise in prices. During the reign of Henry VIII prices, therefore, rose steeply, but since the debased coins were still legal tender, the king and other debtors were able to pay their debts more easily, that is, so long as creditors would accept such coins in payment. About this time prices also rose for another reason—new discoveries of silver in Central and South America led to a new source of supply of the precious metal and increased the amount available in Europe for coinage.

Gresham's Law. Whenever debasement of the coinage occurred the better coins passed out of circulation, thus providing an example of Gresham's Law, which states that "bad money drives out good." This so-called law takes its name from Sir Thomas Gresham, Elizabeth I's finance minister, to whom fell the task of putting the currency on a sound basis again.

It is not, however, universally true that bad money drives out good. The base coins may not circulate at all if people refuse to accept them, for the fact that coins have been declared to be legal tender will not make them serve as money unless they are generally acceptable. If there are insufficient of the inferior coins in circulation to meet the needs of trade some of the good coins will circulate along with the bad. As people come to regard money merely as a medium of exchange, and not as something desirable in itself, they may continue to accept a form of money of less value than it purports to be, either from habit or a realisation that any commodity can cerve as money if it is generally acceptable and relatively scarce.

4. Legal tender

Any means of payment that a debtor can legally compel his creditor to accept is legal tender. In Great Britain at the present time Bank of England notes—£20, £10, £5 and £1—are full legal tender up to any amount. Coins, however, are only limited legal tender. The reason for this limitation is now largely historical. Before 1914 the gold sovereign and half sovereign were worth their full face value, and so were full legal tender. The silver and copper coins were even then worth less than their face value—that is, they were merely token coins. The coins in use in Great Britain today are worth as metal only a small fraction of their face value. Inconvertible paper money temporarily in circulation in this country during the Napoleonic War and the First World War and permanently since 1931 has no value apart from its use as money, so that all the money now in use in Great Britain is token money, and it has been said that our coins are really "bank-notes printed on metal."[1] The most commonly used means of payment—the cheque—is not legal tender, nor are bills of exchange, postal orders or money orders. For a short time in 1914 and again in 1939, in each case during the early months of war, postal orders became legal tender.

Bi-metallism. If both gold and silver coins of full face value were minted supporters of bi-metallism believed that money would be more stable in value, though difficulties would clearly arise if a change took place in the relative values of the two metals. For example, if the price of silver rose, while that of gold remained unchanged, the silver coins would become worth more than their face value, and would tend to be driven out of circulation in accordance with Gresham's Law. Fluctuations in market prices occur daily, and so it is impracticable to have both gold and silver coins of their full face value in circulation at the same time.

5. Paper money

Paper money had its origin in the receipts given by goldsmiths to clients who deposited money and other valuables with them for safe custody. The nature of the goldsmith's business made it necessary for him to have a strong room in which to store his valuable stock, and in times when acts of violence were of common occurrence it was natural for people to make use of the goldsmith's facilities for storing things of great value. For this service a charge was made. If a client, Tigg, deposited £50 in silver coins with Tapley, a goldsmith, he would receive a receipt for that amount. When some time later Tigg, in the course of business, made a purchase from Pinch for £50 he could either take his receipt to Tapley, obtain his £50 in cash and then hand it over to Pinch, or instead he might endorse the receipt with instructions to Tapley to pay the £50 to Pinch, who in turn might pass on his

[1] G. Crowther: *An Outline of Money*, p. 16 n.

claim on yet another merchant. It would be unusual at first for receipts to cover such convenient amounts as the £50 of this example. More often they might be awkward amounts, such as £98 or £43.

When the usefulness of these goldsmiths' receipts for making payments was realised it became the practice to issue receipts in smaller denominations. Instead of a receipt for £50, Tigg, perhaps, might accept ten separate receipts each for £5. In this way the bank-note came into existence. In London the goldsmiths became the first bankers, and they soon found the issue of bank-notes to be a profitable business. Thus the bank-note was a receipt for a debt, an I O U, showing that the banker owed the bearer of the note a stated sum of money, the banker being expected to redeem the promise printed on his note and exchange it on demand for actual cash. Confidence in the early bankers grew only slowly, but as people became more accustomed to bank-notes the banker eventually found it unnecessary to keep a stock of cash equal to the total value of all the bank-notes that he had issued, and so he could employ some of his cash profitably. At the present time the only bank in England that possesses the power to issue bank-notes is the Bank of England, though several banks in Scotland, Northern Ireland and the Isle of Man are permitted to issue a strictly limited amount in notes.

6. Convertible and inconvertible money

If a bank-note can be exchanged on demand for gold or silver coins it is said to be convertible. The earliest bank-notes had to be convertible, because people were willing to use a medium of exchange only if it was of value for its own sake, and it was a long time before people were willing to accept as money something of no value in itself. The convertible bank-note was not, in the strictest sense, itself money but merely a substitute for money, that is, a claim to the sum of money named upon it. On the other hand, there is no compulsion on the issuing authority to exchange inconvertible paper money for gold or any other form of money of full face value.

Inconvertible paper is the final stage in the development of the bank-note. So long as it can be used to purchase what people want to buy, it is not necessary for the medium of exchange to be valuable in itself. So long as people have confidence in the medium, so long will it be generally acceptable, but once this confidence is lost it can no longer serve as money—a fact of which people living in a country that has suffered a major inflation are only too painfully aware. Confidence in a currency will be lost if an excessive amount of it is put into circulation.

If paper money has to be convertible on demand this limits the amount that can be issued; but if notes are inconvertible States may be tempted to choose the easy way of covering expenditure by merely printing more notes. That is the great danger associated with the use of inconvertible paper money.

The issue by private institutions of paper money—whether convertible or not—has always been regulated in some way by the State. Regulation may take the form of limiting the issue to a definite fraction of one or more of the issuing authority's assets. For example, in the United States of America the Federal Reserve Banks were at one time legally compelled to hold gold certificates up to a minimum of 40 per cent of their note issue.

In England the *Bank Charter Act* of 1844 limited the power of the Bank of England to issue notes. Except for £14 million, the Bank's notes were to be backed in full by gold, additional notes being issued only if the bank acquired an equivalent additional amount of gold. That part of the note issue not backed by gold is known as the *fiduciary issue*. Before 1914 Bank of England notes in denominations of £5 and multiples of £5 were convertible and circulated along with gold sovereigns and half-sovereigns. During 1914–25 Bank of England notes ceased to be convertible, but in 1925 they, as well as the £1 and ten-shilling Treasury Notes issued by the Government during 1914–28, again became convertible, but only in large amounts—in exchange for gold bars each weighing 400 oz. and worth approximately £1,560 each. Since 1931 bank-notes in England have been inconvertible, and the promise of the Bank of England printed on them now has little meaning.

7. Bank deposits subject to withdrawal by cheque

The final stage in the development of money is the use of bank deposits as money. The cheque as a means of payment is most widely used in Great Britain and the United States. The greater political stability of these two countries and the greater confidence of businessmen in banks—in spite of some banking crises—have been responsible for this development. The use of cheques is, however, rapidly expanding now in most countries.

In Great Britain the Act of 1844 restricted the note issue to an amount insufficient for the needs of a rapidly expanding economy, and so bank deposits were used to make good this deficiency. In order to obtain the right to draw a cheque it is necessary to open a current account at a bank. A cheque-book is then obtained, and if a payment has to be made a cheque can be drawn for the required amount. The person receiving the cheque deposits it with his own banker, who collects the amount for him from the bank on which the cheque has been drawn.

It is to be noted that it is the bank deposit that is considered to be money, and not the cheque, for the cheque itself is merely an order from the owner of a bank deposit to his banker to transfer a certain sum to the payee named on the cheque. The validity of a cheque therefore depends on whether the drawer of the cheque has a sufficient amount in his current account to meet the cheque. If he draws a cheque for £80 when his bank account shows that he has only £5 to his credit the bank will dishonour the cheque and the payee will find that he has been given a worthless piece of paper. Cheques therefore are not legal tender and so a creditor has the right to refuse to accept this method of payment. Cheques, however, are widely acceptable, especially when payment is made through the post, and by permitting bank deposits to be transferred from one person to another, enable bank deposits to serve as money.

In one way cheques resemble bank-notes: they both have to do with bank debts. The bank-note is an acknowledgement by a bank that it owes the bearer a certain sum, and as the bank-note passes from hand to hand, the bank's debt is transferred from one person to another; similarly, a bank deposit is an acknowledgment of the bank's debt to a particular depositor, who by means of the cheque can transfer the bank's debt to some other person. The bank-note is likely to be more generally acceptable because the bank is more widely known and enjoys the public's confidence to a greater degree than do most drawers of cheques. At the present time it is estimated that approximately 90 per cent of all business payments made in Great Britain are made by cheque. When calculating the total bank balances that can be drawn upon by cheque, and so used as money, it is usual to include sums on deposit account as well as sums on current account, the assumption being that transfers can easily be made from one account to the other. The total of bank deposits in Great Britain at the present time is more than six times as great as the total cash in the country. It is clear, therefore, that bank deposits now form the chief type of money in this country.

The principal stages in the development of money therefore can be seen from the various media of exchange that have been employed at different periods:

    (*i*)   commodities in general demand, such as cattle;
    (*ii*) precious metals by weight;

(*iii*) definite weights of metal in the form of coins;
(*iv*) goldsmiths' receipts for deposits of cash;
(*v*) bank-notes convertible into cash on demand;
(*vi*) inconvertible paper money; and lastly
(*vii*) bank deposits, transferable from one person to another by cheque.

III. FUNCTIONS OF MONEY

8. Advantages of using money

The following advantages can be claimed on behalf of money:

(*i*) It enables a person who receives payment for his services in money to obtain in exchange for it the assortment of goods from that particular amount of expenditure *which will give him maximum satisfaction*. No two persons have exactly the same wants, and so any other system of distribution would yield less satisfaction to most people. For example, a system of rationing will give some people more and others less than they want of some commodities. When commodities are rationed a person cannot forgo one thing in order to enjoy more of another. If money were not in use wages would have to be paid in kind, and most people would regard this as even worse than rationing.

(*ii*) Without the use of money, *division of labour* would be difficult, if not impossible, to sustain. Exchange is essential if there is to be division of labour, and exchange is simplified if money is employed rather than a system of barter. It is only when money is used that it becomes possible, therefore, for people to specialise efficiently and effectively.

(*iii*) When money is employed it becomes *easier to make loans*. A borrower never wants money for its own sake, but only for the command it gives him over real resources. Lending can, of course, take place without the intervention of money, as when a man borrows his neighbour's lawn-mower, or when a farmer or a manufacturer hires a machine. The use of money, however, makes it possible for a firm to borrow for the payment of wages or for the purchase of raw material or to generalise its borrowing.

(*iv*) Deferred spending, too, would be impossible without money. By refraining from spending a portion of one's current income for a period it becomes possible to save up a larger sum of money to spend later.

9. Functions of money
Money performs four main functions:

(i) *A medium of exchange.* Money comes into use because of the inconvenience of barter. A system of exchange which requires the bringing together of two people who have "a double coincidence of wants" will reduce the exchange of goods to a minimum. It has been seen that the use of a medium of exchange occurred at quite an early stage in the development of trade. By acting as a medium of exchange, money facilitates the exchange of goods, and historically, this was probably its earliest function.

(ii) *A measure of value and a unit of account.* A second drawback to barter is the difficulty of determining a rate of exchange between different kinds of goods, especially in the case of large, indivisible articles. It is possible, therefore, that even while a barter system was still in operation this difficulty may have led to the use of some commodity as a means of assessing the relative values of a heterogeneous group of things. It is probable that some commodity was serving as a unit of account even before a medium of exchange was in use, and so in point of time money may have fulfilled this function even before it became a medium of exchange, for it is not necessary for a commodity to be generally acceptable—the first characteristic of money—for it to be used for making calculations. The unit of account, however, could have been used merely to assign prices to commodities, and not as a means of payment. For example the Anglo-Saxon shilling served only as a unit of account, since no such coin was minted, the silver penny being the principal coin in use at that time. Almost anything can serve as a unit of account, since goods will still be exchanged for goods, and it will not be necessary to handle the unit of account.

Commodities that would be inconvenient as money because they lack divisibility or portability can quite well serve as units of account. For purposes of calculation it is possible, for instance, to speak of hundredths of a cow or fractions of a sea-shell; or even such intangible things as hours of labour could be used. Some unit of account would be required even if the State, on the grounds that "money is the root of all evil," determined to do without money. It would still be necessary to find some means of deciding which of two methods of producing a commodity was the more economical; it would be necesary to decide between the production of a little more of one commodity and a little more of another. For purposes of calculation a unit of account would be needed. Where a medium of exchange is in use, this is obviously the most convenient unit of account, and so money generally fulfils this second function. If, however, people for any reason lose confidence in their money, as occurred in Germany in 1923 or Hungary or China in 1946, the national currency may cease to serve as the unit of account and be replaced perhaps by a foreign currency or some acceptable commodity.

Some writers point out that the value of a good cannot be measured, since value is subjective and determined by each person for himself. Commodities therefore can be arranged only in order of preference. Therefore, they say, money cannot be regarded as a measure of value. They have to admit, however, that it is a great convenience to be able to assign money-prices to goods, and money-prices are partly determined by market demand, which is made up of a large number of individual subjective demands.

(*iii*) *A store of value*. Without the use of money it would be impossible to build up stores of many things for future use. Money, therefore, makes it possible for a person to provide for old age. By forgoing current consumption he can accumulate a reserve of purchasing power for use in the future, though there is no certainty that the things he wants will be available when he wants them. While a person keeps his assets in the form of money—a liquid asset—he is free to turn them into whatever fixed assets he pleases. In a period of falling prices, however, the money-value of real assets falls; at such times money gains in value. But if prices are rising, the value of money will fall. In a period of inflation money therefore becomes a very poor store of value, as many people in Europe found in the years following each of the World Wars. In Great Britain £1 would buy nine times as much an 1913 as in 1976.

(*iv*) *A standard for deferred payments*. The use of money makes it possible for payments to be deferred from the present to some future date; it also enables contracts to be made in the present for the future delivery of goods. Credit transactions cannot easily be carried out unless money is used. The vast credit structure of the modern world is based on the use of money, and much of production today depends on credit facilities being available. Just as money, however, ceases to be a store of value in times of severe inflation, so it will cease to be a standard for deferred payments once people's confidence in it has been lost, and future contracts will cease, or will be made in some other currency or commodity.

RECOMMENDATIONS FOR FURTHER READING

G. Crowther: *An Outline of Money*, Chapter 1.
D. H. Robertson: *Money*, Chapter 1.

QUESTIONS

1. Indicate the main functions of money and state the extent to which, in your view, these functions are being satisfactorily fulfilled at the present time. (City)

2. Why has the use of money and credit become necessary in modern economic life? (RSA)

3. What is money? (ACCA)

4. Describe the functions of money, and examine critically the extent to which the various forms of money in use today fulfil these functions. (Exp.)

5. It has been stated that anything generally acceptable will serve as money. Examine this statement. (IMTA)

6. What are the functions of money? Show that they can be efficiently discharged only when its general purchasing power is secured against violent changes. (LGB)

7. What do you understand by the quantity of money? How does the quantity of money influence prices? (CIS)

8. Indicate the main functions of money, and state the extent to which, in your view, it is satisfactory in fulfilling these functions at the present time. (CIS)

9. Describe Gresham's Law and indicate the restrictions to which it is subject. (IB)

10. What functions are performed by money? What things perform these functions in the United Kingdom? (GCE)

11. In what way does money differ from all other economic goods (DPA)

12. "The most important invention ever made for the development of civilisation was that of money." Discuss this dictum. (Degree)

CHAPTER 21

THE VALUE OF MONEY

I. THE PRICE LEVEL

1. The value of money and the price level

Price is the relation between a quantity of money and a quantity of goods. Even if it is agreed that value is subjective and therefore cannot be measured, so that price and value are not the same thing, it is convenient to regard market prices as indicators of the relative value of commodities in terms of money at a particular time. Since money itself is used as the measure of value, its own value can be seen only indirectly through the prices of other things. If the prices of goods rise, this is equivalent to saying that the value of money has fallen, for fewer goods than before can then be obtained in exchange for a given sum of money. If a basketful of commodities costs £3 in 1939, whereas a similar assortment of goods in 1945 costs £6, this shows that between 1939 and 1945 the value of money fell by a half.

Between 1938 and 1976 the value of money in Great Britain fell to a seventh of its former value—that is, prices on average increased by seven times during these thirty years. On the other hand, between 1925 and 1931 prices in Great Britain were falling, and so during that period the value of money was rising. By 1976 the value of money in France had fallen to $\frac{1}{360}$ of its value in 1914, prices in France having risen by 360 times during that period. The value of money is thus shown by the level of prices, a general rise in prices indicating a fall, and a general fall in prices indicating a rise, in the value of money. The price of a commodity is the amount of money that has to be given for it; the value of money is the quantity of goods it will buy.

2. Changes in the value of money

A study of changes in the value of money thus becomes a study of prices. Indeed, it is easier to understand this problem if it is considered from the angle of price rather than from that of the value of money, so long as one remembers that prices vary inversely with the value of money.

Three distinct trends in price movements can be noticed—long, medium and short-period movements:

(i) *A long-period movement of prices.* Over the centuries there has been a general tendency for prices to rise, that is, for the value of money to fall. In the eleventh to fourteenth centuries money was scarce and most people handled very little money, most payments being in kind or by so many days' labour per week on the lord's demesne. At that time a sheep cost only a few pence. The level of prices, however, was higher at the end than at the beginning of almost every century from 1100 to 1900, and there is little doubt that the twentieth century will see the largest increase in prices of any century. The exceptions to this were 1400–1500, when prices were fairly steady, and 1600–1700 when slight falls in prices occurred.

The following diagram illustrates the long-term trend of prices to rise in Great Britain:

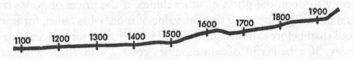

Fig. 78. The Long-period Rise in Prices.

(ii) *A medium-period movement of prices.* A second feature of price fluctuation was noticeable during the nineteenth century. Periods of from twenty-two to twenty-nine years during which there was a tendency for prices to fall alternated with periods of similar length during which there was a tendency for prices to rise. The relation between the rate of increase in the quantity of money and the rate of increase in the production of goods available for the money to buy seems to have been the basis of these price movements. During the nineteenth century the monetary importance of gold increased, and the quantity of money was therefore closely related to the amount of gold available. Generally the amount of gold mined each year forms only a small percentage of the total supply, and so it not likely seriously to affect prices, but on occasions when new gold-mining areas were being developed the influence of the new supplies on prices was much greater. A large increase in the supply of the monetary metal may be expected, other things being equal, to cause a rise in prices. As more countries substituted gold for silver as their monetary standard, there was relatively less gold available for each, and so there was a tendency for prices to fall. The nineteenth century, too, saw a vast expansion of industrial production, but, like the output of gold, the rate of expansion was more rapid at some periods than at others. If the supply of gold was increasing more rapidly than the supply of other goods prices tended to rise; if the output of other goods increased more rapidly than gold prices tended to fall.

Four periods of medium-term fluctuation of prices, therefore, can be distinguished:

(*a*) *1820–49*. This was a period during which prices were generally falling as the output of goods was increasing more rapidly than the output of gold.

(*b*) *1849–74*. This was a period of generally rising prices. In 1847, gold was discovered in California and in 1849–51 in Australia. After 1844 there was also a gradual extension of the use of cheques, and in spite of the Bank Charter Act of that year restricting the issue of banknotes, the output of goods failed to keep pace with this increase.

(*c*) *1874–96*. This was a period of falling prices. The demand for gold increased as Germany adopted a gold coinage in 1873, and France in 1878. Production of commodities had again been expanded relatively to the output of gold.

(*d*) *1896–1945*. This was another period of rising prices. Gold was discovered in South Africa in 1884–5, and eventually this area produced half the world's annual output. Again the output of gold exceeded the output of other goods.

The following diagram illustrates the medium-term movement of prices:

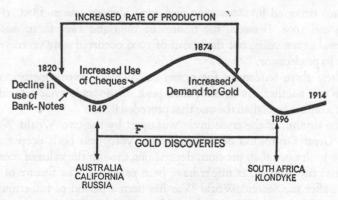

Fig. 79. The Medium-period Movement of Prices.

(iii) A short-period movement of prices. The short-period variation in prices is associated with the trade cycle, but discussion of this phenomenon must be reserved for Chapter 29. Meanwhile, it will be sufficient to note that during the nineteenth and early twentieth centuries the ups and downs of business activity showed certain regular recurring features. Booms and depressions succeeded one another at regular intervals; on average a period of eight years separated one depression from the next, the interval never being less than five years and never greater than eleven. Once a depression had set in, recovery at first was slow, but after a few years boom conditions would develop. During this upswing of the cycle prices at first would remain steady, but at the height of the boom they would rise rapidly. The downswing of the cycle was characterised by a fall in prices and trade activity, often after an economic crisis of some kind. The value of money, therefore, increases in a depression and falls in a boom, although graphs of fluctuations in production and prices do not entirely coincide. The following graph shows the trade cycle during the latter part of the nineteenth century:

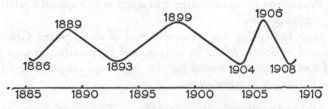

Fig. 80. The Short-period Movement of Prices.

Booms occurred in 1889, 1899 and 1906, depressions in 1886, 1893, 1904 and 1908. Between the booms of 1889 and 1899 there was an interval of ten years, but the boom of 1906 occurred only seven years after its predecessor.

These three tendencies for prices to fluctuate were superimposed upon one another. As a result, each peak of the trade cycle tended to be at a higher level than the one that preceded it.

The rhythm of the trade cycle was upset by the two World Wars. The Great Depression of the inter-War years was both deeper and more prolonged than previous depressions, though the value of money did not rise as much as might have been expected. The feature of the years after the Second World War has been a period of full employment and inflation of unprecedented length with only minor recessions alternating with periods of over-full employment until the more serious world recession in 1974-6 with unemployment at a higher level than at any time since the 1930s. During the whole period inflation persisted and, contrary to experience in the nineteenth century and the Great Depression of the 1930s, actually reached its most serious level while unemployment was increasing. Throughout this period, therefore, the value of money was falling, and after 1971 at a very rapid rate, especially during 1974-6.

II. THE DETERMINATION OF THE VALUE OF MONEY

3. The Quantity Theory of money

In the seventeenth century it was noticed that there was a connection between the quantity of money and the general level of prices, and this led to the formulation of the Quantity Theory of money. In its crudest form it stated that an increase in the quantity of money would bring about a proportionate rise in prices. After being long discarded, the theory was revived in the 1920s by Professor Irving Fisher, who introduced into it the concept of the velocity of circulation. Money circulates from hand to hand. Micawber, the greengrocer, spends 50p at Bumble's, the tobacconist; Bumble uses the 50p to make a purchase from Swiveller, the grocer, who in his turn spends it at Cuttle's, the confectioners; Cuttle then buys 50p worth of greengrocery from Micawber. Thus, the 50p has returned to where it was before the first transaction took place. In this case the same coins were used for four separate transactions; 50p did the work of £2. In the course of a year each unit of money is used many times. If one unit of money is made to serve four transactions this is equivalent to four units of money each being used in only one transaction.

As modified by Irving Fisher, the Quantity Theory came to be expressed by the equation of exchange:

$$MV = PT$$

The symbol M represents the total amount of money in existence—bank-notes, etc., and bank deposits.

The symbol V represents the velocity of circulation. This is difficult to calculate, though the combined totals of the bankers' clearing houses in relation to the quantity of money gives some indication of it.

MV therefore represents the amount of money used in a period.

On the other side of the equation, P stands for the general price level, a sort of average of the prices of all kinds of commodities—producers' goods as well as consumers' goods—and services.

The symbol T is the total of all the transactions that have taken place for money during the period.

The equation of exchange shows us that the price level, and therefore the value of money, can be influenced not only by the quantity of money but also by (i) the rate at which money circulates, and (ii) the output of goods and services. Thus prices might rise without any change taking place in the quantity of money if a rise occurred in the velocity of circulation. On the other hand, prices might remain stable in spite of an increase in the quantity of money if there was a corresponding increase in the output of goods and services.

4. Some criticisms of the Quantity Theory

Even in its revised form, however, the Quantity Theory has been subjected to the following criticisms:

(i) It is not a theory at all, but simply a convenient method of showing that there is a certain relationship between four variable quantities—M, V, P and T. It shows only that the total quantity of money, as determined by the actual amount of money in existence and the velocity of circulation, is equal to the value of total trade transactions multiplied by their average price. As such it is obviously a truism, since the amount of money spent on purchases is obviously equal to the amount received from sales. Not only must MV be equal to PT, but MV is PT, since they are only two different ways of looking at the same thing.

Even if the equation of exchange is only a truism, it would not be quite correct to say that it demonstrates nothing. For example, it shows that it is possible for there to be an increase in the quantity of money without a general rise in prices. It informs us, too, that if there is to be a change in one or more of the variables of the equation, there must also be a change in one or more of the other variables. Clearly it would be wrong to read into it more than this.

(ii) The four variables, M, V, P and T, are not independent of one another as the equation of exchange implies. For example, a change in M is likely of itself to bring about a change in V or T or both. It is probable that a rise in prices will follow an increase in the quantity of money, but this will most likely be brought about because the increase in the quantity of money stimulates demand and production.

(iii) A serious defect is to allow the symbol P to represent the *general* price level. Price changes do not all keep in step with one another. In its original form the equation was criticised because it implied that an increase in the quantity of money would automatically bring about a proportionate increase in all prices. A study of price changes between 1939 and 1976 shows that some prices increased during these years by as much as six times while others rose by only 50 per cent. Clearly, then, there is no *general* price level, but instead, as the Index of Retail Prices shows, a number of sectional price levels, one for food, another for clothing, another for fuel and light, and so on.

(*iv*) The Quantity Theory only attempts to explain *changes* in the value of money, and does not show how the value of money is in the first place determined.

(*v*) The Quantity Theory approaches the question of the value of money entirely from the supply side, completely ignoring the influence of demand. Though true of the original theory, it was not true of Fisher's modification of it. Since the demand for money is the demand to hold money, the greater the strength of the demand to hold money, the lower will be the velocity of circulation. Thus, the desire to hold money varies inversely with the velocity of circulation, and so the introduction into the equation of V to some extent disposes of this criticism.

(*vi*) The most serious criticism of the Quantity Theory is its inadequacy as a theory of money, since it takes no account of the influence of the rate of interest.

Large falls in the value of money during periods of severe inflation, however, can probably be explained by the quantity equation, since it does contain at least one fundamental truth—namely, that there is a connection between the quantity of money and its value. Though few modern writers would more than grudgingly admit this, Professor K. Boulding, however, thinks the quantity equation is more useful than most present-day writers are prepared to recognise.[1]

5. The money supply and the demand for money

As we have already seen, the value of a commodity depends on the relative strength of the forces of supply and demand. Since this provides a satisfactory general theory of value, should it not be employed to explain the value of money also?

Caution, however, is required in applying this technique to the determination of the value of money since, unlike commodities, money

[1] K. E. Boulding: *Economic Analysis*, Chapter 15.

is not wanted for its own sake, and the term *demand for money* means demand to *hold* money, as distinct from investing it. The concept of the supply of money presents less difficulty, though again, unlike other commodities, its supply is not related to its cost of production.

(*i*) *The money supply.* At the present day two kinds of money are in use in Great Britain: (*a*) cash, in the form of inconvertible Bank of England notes and coins; and (*b*) bank deposits held on current account and transferable by cheque. Today bank deposits form about four-fifths of the total money supply. The total amount of money of these two kinds is sometimes represented by the symbol M^1. The size of M^1 is dependent on the credit policy of the Bank of England and the monetary authorities, as we shall see in the next chapter. The size of the Bank of England's note issue nowadays depends primarily on the volume of bank deposits.

A wider concept of the money supply is indicated by the term M^3 (the symbol M^2 is no longer in use). This comprises M^1 together with deposits on deposit account held by both banks and discount houses. Table LIV shows the composition of the money supply.

Table LIV

The Money Supply

	1939	1945	1972	1976
	£ million	£ million	£ million	£ million
Bank of England notes	526	1,300	3,750	5,900
Bank deposits (all banks in UK)	2,248	4,692	24,501	43,963
Total	2,774	5,992	28,251	49,863

In 1976 the total for M^1 was £49,863 million and for M^3 it was £53,076 million.

(*ii*) *The demand for money.* The demand for money is a more difficult concept than the demand for goods and services. As stated above, the demand for money means the demand to hold money, that is, to keep one's resources in liquid form instead of in some form of investment. It is necessary, therefore, to inquire why people hold money, since, clearly, this involves a loss of the interest it might otherwise have earned. According to Lord Keynes, there are three motives for holding money:

(*a*) *The transactions motive.* A certain amount of money is needed for everyday requirements, the purchase of food and clothing and other ordinary expenses. How much is it necessary to hold for these purposes will depend on two factors: a person's income and the interval between one pay-day and the next. Generally, the higher the income, the more money will be held, though millionaires are notorious for declaring that they are short of cash. The weekly wage-earner will need to hold less than a person who receives his salary monthly, for in the one case sufficient has to be held to cover expenses for only one week, whereas the other man has to make provision for four weeks. Similarly, in business, cash has to be held to cover expenses, such as wages, during the period of production.

(b) *The precautionary motive*. Most people like to keep something in reserve, in case an unexpected payment has to be made. One of the commonest of unforeseen contingencies is sickness, and formerly this was probably the main reason for people keeping a little money in reserve. The introduction of the National Insurance scheme, however, made it less necessary to hold money for this purpose. Certain household expenses—for example, those due to breakages—are also of this nature, though again, so far as these contingencies can be covered by insurance, there will be less need to hold money for renewals.

(c) *The speculative motive*. Holding money involves the sacrifice of the interest it would have yielded if it had been invested. In considering the function of money, however, it was noticed that it can serve as a liquid asset. To have an asset in the form of money means that whenever one so wishes, it can be exchanged for some other asset. Because there are advantages in keeping one's assets liquid, some inducement in the form of interest is necessary to make people forgo liquidity. We have already seen that the strength of the desire for liquidity is called *liquidity-preference*, and it is this that decides what proportion of their assets people will hold in the form of money.

How much is held for the transactions motive and the precautionary motive depends on daily needs and habit, and, in the short period, the amount is unlikely to vary very much. The demand for money for the first motive is fairly inelastic, somewhat less inelastic for the second and most elastic for the third. If more is held than is required for the first two purposes it must be held for speculative reasons—that is, it will depend on expectations regarding the future trend of the rate of interest. If people think the rate is likely to rise—that is, if they think the price of stocks will fall in the future—they will hold money, since any loss of interest which this involves will be counter-balanced by the lower prices to be paid later. On the other hand, if they think the rate of interest is likely to fall they will invest their money at once, while the prices of stocks are low. Expected future prices of other assets will determine how much money is held. Many consumers will postpone some of their purchases—particularly of durable consumers' goods—if they think there is a possibility of a fall in prices in the near future. In a boom, then, when prices are rising, less money will be held; in a depression, when prices are falling, more money will be held.

The advantage of this theory of the value of money is that it employs the general theory of value. Secondly, unlike the Quantity Theory, it gives a prominent place to the influence of the rate of interest.

A second equation of exchange. It is possible to construct a second equation of exchange allowing for the demand to hold money:

$$p = \frac{M}{kR}$$

The symbol k is used to represent the proportion of a community's total income held in money; R stands for the country's output of goods and services—that is, *real* income; M, as in the previous equation, represents the country's stock of money (cash and bank deposits) at a given time; p is the general price level of consumers' goods. (P in the former equation, it will be remembered, represented the general price level of all kinds of goods, including producers' as well as consumers' goods.) This equation takes account of the total volume of production (R) and the demand to hold money (k). An increase in either of these will reduce the general price level of consumers' goods. If other things remain the same an increase in the demand for money will bring about a fall in prices. The greater the proportion of money that is held, the lower will be the velocity of circulation; the less money that is held, the greater will be the velocity of circulation. The symbol V of the first equation thus varies inversely with k of the second equation.

III. INDEX NUMBERS

6. Measurement of changes in the value of money

The usual method adopted to measure changes in the value of money is by means of index numbers of prices. A number of these indices have been compiled, but the main principle in all cases is the same: a group of commodities is selected, their prices noted in some particular year which becomes the base year for the index number and to which the number 100 is given. If the prices of these commodities rise by 1 per cent during the ensuing twelve months the index number next year will be 101. A fall in price of 1 per cent would be shown by an index number of 99. Indices of wholesale prices have been complied by the Board of Trade, *The Economist* and the *Statist*. The index of the Department of Trade and Industry now takes 1963 as its base year for wholesale prices, the index number for manufactured goods being 110 in 1966 and 136 in 1971.

The best-known index number is the former Cost-of-Living Index, complied then by the Ministry of Labour (now the Department of Employment). This took July 1914 as its base. In 1921 it stood at 240, falling to 100 in 1929 and to 85 in 1933, after which date it began to rise again, reading 96 in 1939 and 132 in 1945. It was superseded by a new Interim Index of Retail Prices, for which 1947 was selected as base year. It was revised again in 1952 and 1956 and, following a new survey, the index was completely revised with January 1962 as the base. It was revised once more in 1974.

7. The problem of weighting

The greatest difficulty facing the compiler of an index number is to decide how much of each commodity to select. This is the problem of weighting. Different "weights" will yield different results, as the following example illustrates. Assume that there are only three commodities, A, B, C, the prices of which are 50p, 20p and 10p, respectively. By taking one unit of each—that is, without any weighting—the index number for the base year is constructed as follows:

	Base Year		
Commodity	Price	Weight	Index
A	50p	1	100
B	20p	1	100
C	10p	1	100
		—	
		3	300

Index for all items = 100

Assume that one year later the price of A is 45p, B 25p and C 15p:

Commodity	Price	Weight	Index
A	45p	1	90
B	25p	1	125
C	15p	1	150
		—	
		3	365

Index for all items = 121.6

The index number in the second year is 121.6, showing an increase in price of 21.6 per cent over the base year.

If the commodities A, B, C are differently weighted a different result will be obtained. For example, suppose that one unit of A, four of B and twenty of C are taken. The index number will then be compiled as follows:

	Base Year				Second Year		
Commodity	Price	Weight	Index	Commodity	Price	Weight	Index
A	50p	1	100	A	45p	1	90
B	20p	4	400	B	25p	4	500
C	10p	20	2,000	C	15p	20	3,000
		25	2,500			25	3,590
	Index for all items = 100				Index for all items = 143.6		

By weighting C heavily this index shows a rise in prices of 43.6 per cent, *although individual prices show only the same change as before.* By weighting commodity A heavily an index number can actually be compiled from the same data to show a *fall* in prices!

	Base Year				Second Year		
Commodity	Price	Weight	Index	Commodity	Price	Weight	Index
A	50p	10	1,000	A	45p	10	900
B	20p	1	100	B	25p	1	125
C	10p	1	100	C	15p	1	150
		12	1,200			12	1,175
	Index for all items = 100				Index for all items = 97.9		

The importance of correct weighting will now be clear. The choice of weights is, however, no easy matter. The method employed in the case of the old Cost-of-Living Index Number was to make a survey of the distribution of expenditure of working-class families, the 1914 index being based on a survey taken in 1904. For the 1947 index number the survey took place in 1937–8, and the weighting was based upon the assortment of goods purchased by families with annual incomes of less than £250. In 1952 the weighting of the index was again revised. A new inquiry was undertaken, and following this the weighting, introduced in 1956, was based on the expenditure of people with incomes up to £1,000 a year. A revised index was introduced in January 1963 with January 1962 as 100. In 1974 the index was again revised with

January 1974 as the base. Since 1962 the weighting has been modified each year.

The collection of data presents difficulties, for many people resent inquiries into the ways in which they spend their money, and even when they are prepared to give this information they are often unwilling to admit the full amount they spend on things such as drink, tobacco and entertainments.

It is instructive to compare the weights used in the index at different periods, as shown in Table LV.

Table LV

Weighting of the Index of Retail Prices

Commodity groups	1914	1947	1952	1956	1962	1975
	%	%	%	%	%	%
I. Food . . .	60	34.8	39.9	35.0	31.9	23.2
II. Alcoholic drink .	—	} 21.7	16.8 {	7.1	6.4	8.2
III. Tobacco . .	—			8.0	7.9	4.6
IV. Housing . .	16	8.8	7.2	8.7	10.2	10.8
V. Fuel and light .	8	6.5	6.6	5.5	6.2	5.3
VI. Durable household goods .	—	7.1	6.2	6.6	6.4	7.0
VII. Clothing and footwear . .	12	9.7	9.8	10.6	9.8	8.9
VIII. Transport and vehicles . .	—	—	—	6.8	9.2	14.9
IX. Miscellaneous .	4	3.5	4.4	5.9	6.4	7.1
X. Services . .	—	7.9	9.1	5.8	5.6	5.2
XI. Meals taken outside home .	—	—	—	—	—	4.9
	100	100	100	100	100	100

The changes in the weights of the various groups of goods and services is of particular interest in showing how people's distribution of expenditure changes as their standard of living rises. For example, Groups I, IV, V and VII, covering the basic wants of foods, clothing and shelter, formed 96 per cent of the total expenditure of a family in 1914, but less than 60 per cent in 1947 and only 52 per cent in 1970. The most striking change is the fall in the proportion of expenditure on food—from 60 per cent in 1914 to 35 per cent in 1962 and 23.2 per cent in 1975. The changes in weighting show clearly how as the standard of living rises, expenditure on things other than basic necessaries increases. The expansion of private motoring is shown by the increased expenditure in Group VIII (Transport and Vehicles) from 6.8

per cent of the total in 1956 to 14.9 per cent in 1975. The heavy allowance for Groups II and III in the 1947 index is of interest in showing how people in the lower-income groups actually spend their incomes, but if it is used as a basis for claims for higher wages increases in the prices of semi-luxuries and less necessary things have an undue influence on the index. Similarly, a fall in the prices of less-necessary things will bring about a fall in the index number, perhaps to the disadvantage of people in the lowest income groups. Group XI (Meals taken outside the home) was added in 1968.

8. Other problems of index numbers

The weights to be given to different commodities and services having been determined, the next problem is to decide what grades and quantities to take into account. By including more than one grade an attempt is made to make a representative selection. An even greater difficulty occurs when the price of a commodity remains unchanged, although the quality has declined. In recent revisions of the index, however, adjustments have been made for changes in quality, account being taken, for example, of changes in the strength of beer! On account of seasonal variation in their prices, green vegetables and fresh fruit were excluded from the 1914 Index, but since 1947 they have been included during the months when they are in season.

Other difficulties associated with the construction of index numbers are:

(i) The choice of a base year. This should preferably be a year when prices are reasonably steady, and so years during periods either of severe inflation or deflation are to be avoided. The first half of 1914 was quite a good date to select, as would have been 1938 or the early part of 1939. The outbreak of war in 1939 caused the postponement of a new index number, at first because of the abnormal conditions of the war period and later because of the difficulties of the immediate post-war years.

(ii) Index numbers are of limited value for comparisons over long periods of time because (a) new commodities come on to the market; (b) changes in taste or fashion reduce the demand for some commodities and increase the demand for others; (c) the composition of the community is liable to change; (d) changes may occur in the distribution of the population among the various age-groups; and (e) the rise in the standard of living. The 1914 price index was probably representative of upwards of 60 per cent of the population, but by 1938 it was applicable to less than 30 per cent. It is for this reason that periodic revision of the Index of Retail Prices is essential if it is to retain any degree of accuracy.

(*iii*) Even people in the same income groups do not distribute their expenditure over the same range of commodities or buy similar proportions of them. The higher the general standard of living, the greater these differences are likely to be. Thus an Index of Retail Prices can be used to show variations in the cost of living only for the particular income groups on whose expenditure it is based. For example, the higher the income, the smaller the proportion of it that will be spent on food. The 1914 index was appropriate to a more homogeneous group than the latest index with its relatively high upper-income limit.

On account of the many difficulties associated with their compilation, and their many drawbacks, and in spite of the great care now taken in compiling them, index numbers are not a very reliable means of comparing changes in the value of money over long periods of time. Nevertheless, they do give an approximate indication of changes over short periods—month-to-month fluctuations, for example —or for comparing one year with the preceding one.

9. The index of retail prices[1]

The data for this index is collected in three ways:

(*i*) The prices of some foodstuffs, clothing and household goods are ascertained by inquiry of shops in each of 200 places, selected as representative of different population groups—for example, twenty-five are in Greater London, twenty-five are towns with populations over 200,000, fifty are towns with populations between 50,000 and 200,000 and so on.

(*ii*) The prices of branded goods, tobacco and beer are obtained by inquiry of the manufacturers of these commodities.

(*iii*) Information regarding rent and rates is obtained from Local Authorities and Property-owners' Associations.

Commodities and services are divided into ten groups, each of which is further subdivided into a number of sections. Group I (food), for example, includes nineteen sections covering such items as bread, beef, fish, etc. Separate indices are calculated for each group and even for individual items within each group, as well as an overall index for all

[1] See "Interim Index of Retail Prices: Method of Construction and Calculation," published by Her Majesty's Stationery Office, for an excellent account of the method of compiling the 1947 index-number.

Table LVI

Index of Retail Prices
(15th January 1974 = 100)

	1974 Weights	Base: Jan. 1974	Sept 1974	Feb. 1975
All items	1,000	100	110.0	121.9
I. Food	232	100	111.5	122.5
Bread, etc. . .	33	100	107.5	121.3
Meat and bacon .	62	100	116	128
Tea, coffee, cocoa .	11	100	116	129
II. Alcoholic drink . .	82	100	111.6	119.5
III. Tobacco	46	100	121.6	124
IV. Housing	108	100	105.8	111.1
V. Fuel and light . .	53	100	115.8	127.8
Coal and coke .	11	100	105	126
Electricity . .	25	100	126	135
VI, Durable household goods	70	100	110.5	119.8
Furniture . . .	34	100	113	121
VII. Clothing and footwear .	89	100	112.9	121
Men's outer clothing .	16	100	111	120
Women's outer clothing	23	100	112	119
VIII. Transport and vehicles .	149	100	113.5	132.6
IX. Miscellaneous goods .	71	100	115.4	127.9
Books, newspapers, etc.	17	100	121	141
X. Services	52	100	110.3	116.7
Postage and telephone .	11	100	113	116
Entertainment . .	22	100	104	107
XI. Meals outside home .	48	100	111.7	120.5

Source: *Monthly Digest of Statistics* (HMSO)

items. Table LVI shows the Index of Retail Prices for All Items, the ten main Groups and also for a few typical items within some of the groups. This table shows how necessary it is to think in terms of sectional price levels.

The following table shows the rise in the index number of retail prices since 1962 and inversely, therefore, the fall in value of money:

Table LVII

Index of Retail Prices since 1962

1962	100	1972	164.3
1964	107.0	1973	179.4
1966	116.5	1974	100
1968	125.0	1975	121.9
1970	140.2	1976	
1971	153.4		

IV. INFLATION

10. Effects of changes in the value of money

(*i*) *On the level of production.* If prices are rising, business activity will be stimulated. Since production is carried on in anticipation of demand and as all costs do not increase immediately prices begin to rise, profit margins will be greater than anticipated. There is therefore less risk to the producer. In order to take advantage of rising prices he will increase his output as much as he can, for so long as rising costs lag behind rising prices his profits will be greater than before.

If, however, prices are falling, profit margins will be smaller than was anticipated when production was undertaken. A severe fall in prices may result in a loss, for costs of production will not fall proportionately with commodity prices, wages being particularly difficult to adjust. To producers the outlook will appear black, and therefore they will tend to become more cautious and restrict their output.

If it is desired to maintain a high level of production gently rising prices are then to be preferred to falling prices.

(*ii*) *On the distribution of incomes.* The incomes of different groups of people are not equally affected by price changes. Any advantage accruing to one group of people as a result of a change in the value of money must be at the expense of other groups. Those who suffer most from rising prices are people with fixed money incomes. Those who suffer when prices are falling are the profit-receivers.

Consider first those people whose incomes are derived from profits. It has been noticed above that when prices are rising profits are generally higher than was anticipated. In the past a rise in prices, therefore, immediately resulted in higher profits, so that profit-receivers generally tended to be at least as well off as they were before. A fall in prices also immediately affects their incomes, which fall as profits fall, and if the fall is severe losses may be incurred. During the severe inflation of 1974–5, however, rising prices were accompanied by falling production and rising unemployment with the result that profit receivers suffered a fall in their incomes.

Wages in the past did not generally rise immediately as prices rose, but production was stimulated and as a result producers became willing to pay higher wages in order to expand production. Thus, though wages eventually rose, wage increases usually tended to lag behind prices. In times of rising prices, therefore, wage-earners found that their real wages had fallen, but since the demand for labour was high there was less unemployment, so that the total amount of real income distributed as wages was greater than before. When prices were falling there was a similar time-lag with decreases in wages, so that those who succeeded in keeping their jobs gained in real income, but unemployment was greater and so the total amount distributed in wages was less. However, in the prolonged period of rising prices that has occurred since 1945, though wage rises lagged behind price increases, eventually they caught up with prices, and in recent years wages have increased more rapidly than prices. During the severe inflation of 1972–5 *real* incomes of wage earners for a time actually increased until control of incomes was adopted in 1975.

The third section of the community comprises those who receive fixed incomes. Among these will be retired people. If they are living on annuities bought with past savings their money incomes will remain unchanged. If they have invested their savings in gilt-edged securities their position will be similar. Thus, in a period of rising prices all people on fixed incomes find that their real incomes decline, but when prices are falling—a rare event, though it did happen during 1925–31— their real incomes increase. However there are fewer people on rigidly fixed incomes today than was formerly the case. More people nowadays invest their savings in shares in limited companies or in unit trusts, and so they too have joined the profit-receivers. At one time most pensions were fixed and so the money income remained the same whether prices were rising or falling. The real incomes of these people improved during the 1930s but fell severely during the years after 1939. The prolonged period of rising prices since 1945 led to some pensions being increased slightly, but only after their value in real terms had considerably declined. From time to time small increases were made in National Insurance retirement pensions and in the pensions of retired teachers, civil servants, local government officers and retired members of the armed forces. Banks, insurance companies and some other firms periodically increased the pensions of their former employees. It was not, however, until 1971 that the principle was accepted that pensions paid by the State should be kept in line with the cost of living. Since then National Insurance pensions and the pensions of people formerly in public employment have been reviewed annually and adjusted to compensate for any rise in the cost of living.

In some occupations incomes used to be fixed for long periods, adjustments being made only after great changes had occurred in the value of money. During the short periods of rising and falling prices in the past, salaried workers could be regarded as fixed-income receivers.

After 1960 most salaries at least kept pace with the rise in prices and by 1974, as with wage earners, the real incomes of salary earners were increasing. In Great Britain the salaries of judges varied little during the hundred years before 1953; the highest grades in the Civil Service obtained their first adjustments of salary in 1950, after eleven years of rising prices. In most of these cases salary increases generally failed to keep pace with the fall in the value of money. Something, therefore, has been done to mitigate the effects of inflation, at least so far as wages, salaries and incomes are concerned. In many cases, however, savings have been reduced by inflation. Small savers who put their savings in trustee savings banks or invested in National Savings Certificates and other Government securities or building societies have found that the real value of these investments has consistently declined. This led more people to turn to stock exchange securities, mainly through the medium of unit trusts, though the sharp fall in stock exchange prices during 1969–70 showed that these investments in the short run do not provide a sure hedge against inflation. A new development occurred in 1975 when the Government introduced two index-linked investments: (i) Retirement Certificates for people of pensionable age only, the interest being related to the index of retail prices; and (ii) a Save-as-you-earn scheme, similarly related to the price index, open to all. Although, therefore, something has been done to reduce the impact of inflation, such action does nothing to get rid of the inflation itself.

Those who gain when prices are rising are the ones who lose when prices are falling and vice versa. There is, however, a long-period tendency of prices to rise, and present-day economic policy is likely to encourage this. On balance, therefore, the advantage seems to lie with those who gain from rising prices. All debtors gain and all creditors lose when the value of money is falling, the reverse being true when the value of money is rising. Thus changes in the value of money tend to bring about an arbitrary redistribution of income.

11. Meanings of inflation

The term *inflation* appears to have at least three meanings:

(i) Any increase in the money supply, however small, can be regarded as inflationary, just as any decrease in the quantity of money is deflationary. The terms *inflation* and *deflation* are used in this sense to describe the credit policy of the Central Bank. Inflation occurs when the central bank expands the money supply and deflation when it reduces it. Expansion of the money supply will raise the general level of prices. If, however, the money supply is accompanied by a proportionate increase in the output of goods and services (assuming no change occurs in the velocity of circulation) the general price level will remain unchanged.

(*ii*) Inflation, as understood in the post-1945 period, connotes something more than an increase in the quantity of money. It describes an unstable situation. Inflation occurs when the volume of purchasing power is *persistently* running ahead of the output of goods and services, so that there is a *continuous* tendency for prices—both of commodities and factors of production—to rise because they fail to keep pace with demand for them. This type of inflation can therefore be described as *persistent inflation*. In ordinary speech inflation is often taken to mean high prices, but high prices do not necessarily indicate the existence of inflation, for equilibrium of Supply and Demand can be established at any level of prices, and once equilibrium has been achieved inflation disappears.

(*iii*) The term *inflation* is often taken to mean a runaway inflation. At such periods the excessive creations of money result in huge increases in prices. This type of inflation has been variously described as *runaway*, *galloping* or as *hyperinflation*.

12. The inflationary gap

Inflation may be the consequence of banking policy, but a hyper-inflation is most likely to occur during a war or as a result of a war. Modern wars are enormously expensive, and at such times it is impossible to cover Government expenditure from current taxation. Recourse must then be made to borrowing, but so long as loans come from the general public there will be no inflation, for taxation and borrowing both decrease the amount of purchasing power in the hands of the community, and therefore reduce the demand for consumer goods, so that there will be no tendency for prices to rise. If the Government fails to cover its expenditure by these two methods it will be compelled either to create the additional money itself or to borrow from the banks—that is, permit the banks to create the additional money required. This is known as the inflationary gap. Both World Wars saw huge increases in the quantity of money and in prices. Inflation can occur in times of peace if Government expenditure is greatly in excess of its income from taxation, with a consequent increase in the money supply.

The continuous increase in the money supply after 1945, and especially during 1971–5, was, however, a new experience for Great Britain in time of peace.

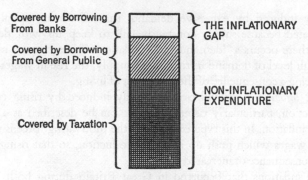

Fig. 81. Government Expenditure.

During neither of the two war periods did the increase in the money supply affect prices to the extent that might have been expected, the increase being to some extent offset by a fall in the velocity of circulation. While a war is actually in progress people respond more readily to patriotic appeals urging them to save, and in any case hours of work are so long that opportunities for spending are in consequence reduced, as well as by the curtailment of the production of consumers' goods. While a war is in progress therefore, inflation tends to be to some extent kept under control, but after the war people's accumulation of savings form a vast volume of potential purchasing power. The result is that inflation arising out of war-time tends to be more serious immediately after the war than during the war itself.

13. Persistent inflation

The inflationary spiral. It is necessary, therefore, to consider what factors induce persistent inflation. The pressure of demand, resulting from the existence of huge amounts of purchasing power, will force up the prices of all goods and services. High prices will lead to demands for wage increases, which employers will generally be willing to concede, since rising prices offer the possibility of increased profits. When demand is pressing it is possible to pass increased costs to the consumer in the form of still higher prices. Most costs of production—wages, raw material, power—rise, and as a result prices are pushed still higher, this bringing in its train a renewal of demands for wage increases. Wages force up prices; prices force up wages. This is the inflationary spiral, which if unchecked can end only with money ceasing to have any value at all.

Demand inflation. This term is used to describe an inflation which is mainly induced by excessive demand, the inflationary spiral being stimulated because supply constantly fails to keep up with demand. Thus there occurs a "demand-pull" inflation. Prices rise as a result of the high level of demand in relation to supply, the rise in wages in this case being a consequence of the rising cost of living.

Cost inflation. If an inflation is mainly induced by rising costs of production, particularly rising wages, it can be described as a "cost-push" inflation. In this type of inflation the motivating force is mainly rising wages which push up costs of production, so that rising prices are a consequence of increased costs.

The inflations that occurred in Great Britain during both World Wars and the two post-war periods were therefore mainly demand inflations. By the early 1950s, however, supply had caught up with demand, and since then inflation has been mainly a cost inflation.

An important cause of the persistence of inflation in Great Britain, the United States and some other countries since 1945 has been the acceptance of responsibility for full employment by the Governments of those countries. As a result, for most of this period the demand for labour has been greater than the supply, and in these conditions demands for higher wages by the trade unions tend to be frequent and competitive. Indeed, one of the consequences of inflation is shortage of labour, with wages rising steeply in those occupations where the shortage is greatest. In such conditions there is also a tendency for employers, who are short of labour, to bid against one another by offering higher wages than the agreed rates—a practice that has come to be known as "wage drift". It seems that with full employment persistent inflation will be difficult to avoid, though it may be temporarily checked by brief periods of stable prices, as in 1953–54 and 1958–60, although so far efforts to keep increases in wages in line with increases in production by means of an "incomes policy" have met with little success.

Another factor that has helped to stimulate inflation in Great Britain throughout the whole period since 1945 has been the failure of successive Governments to cover their expenditure from taxation. This has been particularly the case since 1970. The level of public expenditure has been high throughout the whole period, the aim being to provide the country with a more modern road system, new towns, redevelopment of old town centres, better housing, new schools and universities, a comprehensive health service and better social conditions generally. In addition many nationalised industries have incurred deficits that the State has had to cover, while assistance has been given to ailing firms in the private sector. Then during 1970–3 a great effort was made to achieve a faster rate of economic growth in spite of increasing inflationary pressure. Between 1971 and 1974 the money supply doubled and the Government had to resort to heavy borrowing to cover its expenditure, but the greatest deficits ever incurred in peacetime occurred in 1974 and 1975 and this in spite of a steep increase in taxation.

During the 1970s inflation both in Western Europe and in the United States increased considerably, but in Great Britain the inflation rate accelerated alarmingly. In relation to the currencies of the other leading industrial countries sterling depreciated by over 45 per cent. One cause of accelerating inflation in Great Britain was the attempt during 1970–3 to increase the rate of economic growth, this country having lagged behind other leading nations in this respect. The policy, although achieving little, was pursued regardless of the heavy budget deficits and serious adverse balances of payments that it caused. The trade unions showed their strength by securing wage increases in excess of the rise in prices and with little increase in productivity. The budgets of 1973–6 showed expenditure greatly in excess of revenue. In the five years to 1975 there was, too, a huge increase in the money supply. Surprisingly, however, unemployment rose during these years to the highest level in Great Britain since the 1930s.

14. Hyperinflation

The danger in persistent inflation is that it may become a hyperinflation. Since 1914 a number of hyperinflations have taken place, as for example, in Germany, Austria and Russia in the 1920s and in Hungary, Romania, China and Germany again in the 1940s. Exceptionally severe inflation occurred in some countries of South America during the 1960s and 1970s, Argentina having an annual price rise of 20 per cent per year over the ten years 1962–72. Severe inflations have occurred in some other countries, both during the 1920s and since 1945. All countries of the world have suffered some degree of inflation during the past thirty years.

As inflation proceeds, the velocity of circulation increases to an even greater extent because holding money entails considerable loss. Saving ceases, and there is an increasing anxiety to turn all cash into real tangible things, whether these are really wanted or not. The result is a steeper rise in prices than the increase in the quantity of money warrants. Wages have to be adjusted daily and may have to be reckoned in terms of a foreign currency or a commodity.

During 1922 prices in Germany were five hundred times as high as they had been four years previously; during the final stages of the inflation in 1923 the price even of a postage stamp reached astronomical figures. In Hungary in 1945 prices rose to even greater heights, the purchase of the cheapest things requiring a payment in pengö of a number running into no less than thirty digits! Debtors found that quite considerable debts dwindled away to almost nothing. The gains of debtors were, of course, the losses of creditors. People with savings in bank deposits or Government Stocks had them wiped out; those who had invested in real assets—factory buildings, industrial plant, machinery, houses, land—were more fortunate, as the value of these in terms of money appreciated as the value of money fell.

There can be only one end to runaway inflation. Sooner or later the currency ceases to be acceptable and in the end a new currency has to be introduced and the old one withdrawn. In Hungary the forint replaced the pengö, in Austria the schilling took the place of the crown; in Germany the Reichsmark replaced the mark, the Reichsmark itself being superseded later by the Deutsche Mark.

RECOMMENDATIONS FOR FURTHER READING

G. Crowther: *An Outline of Money*, Chapters 3 and 4 (Section 1).
D. H. Robertson: *Money*, Chapters 2 and 3.
J. L. Hanson: *Monetary Theory and Practice*, Chapters 10 and 11.

QUESTIONS

1. Give a critical account of the Quantity Theory of Money. (S E London)
2. Distinguish between "inflationary" and "deflationary" gaps. Explain why they may be considered undesirable and outline briefly the kind of policies that the Government should employ to remove them. (Southampton)
3. How are changes in the general level of prices measured? Give examples. (RSA)
4. What are chief causes of changes in value of money? What effects are they likely to have on distribution of wealth? (IT)
5. How may changes in the cost of living be measured? (AIA)
6. What are the defects of the Quantity Theory of Money? (IMTA)
7. Explain the difficulties involved in trying to measure the general level of prices. (BS)
8. Describe the practical use of index numbers. How are they constructed? (IB)
9. What is "liquidity preference"? What are the main factors in a community which determine the degree of it? (IHA)

10. Why do people hold money balances if money is only useful when it can be exchanged for goods and services? (GCE)

11. "While the accuracy of the quantity equation in the theory of money is beyond dispute its usefulness is not so certain." Discuss. (GCE)

12. How would you measure the average level of retail prices? What difficulties are likely to arise in doing so? (GCE)

13. What do you understand by the distinction between "cost inflation" and "demand inflation", and what is the relevance to anti-inflationary policies? (Degree)

14. What are the main factors influencing the demand for and the supply of money? (Degree)

CHAPTER 22

THE ENGLISH BANKING SYSTEM: THE COMMERCIAL BANKS

I. THE EVOLUTION OF BRITISH BANKING

1. The origin of banking in England

In England banking had its origin with the London goldsmiths, who because of the nature of their business, had facilities for storing valuables. The first banking function, therefore, was accepting deposits of cash from merchants who lacked a safe place in which to keep their money. The goldsmiths at first made a charge for looking after their customers' money. The second stage came when the receipts for these deposits began to be used as means of payment by merchants, and this led the early bankers to issue bank-notes of fixed denominations which were more generally acceptable. Thus the second function of banks became the issuing of bank-notes. The third stage in the development of banking came when bankers began to lend money. The increasing use of bank-notes meant that fewer people withdrew their deposits in coin from the bankers, who thus found it safe to lend out at interest some of the money deposited with them. This proved to be a profitable business, and so bankers began to offer interest as an inducement to merchants and others to increase their deposits. Next, bankers began to lend their own notes, experience teaching them how much to keep in hand to meet their customers' demand for cash. Later the use of cheques made it possible for banks to lend by allowing customers to have overdrafts—that is, permitting them to draw cheques for agreed sums above the amount standing to their credit at the bank.

2. Private banks

The Bank of England was founded in 1694, primarily for the purpose of lending money to the Government, and though it undertook some ordinary commercial banking, and at an early date became the sole bank in London issuing notes, from the first it left most ordinary business to other banks. Until 1826, however, it had a monopoly of joint-stock banking in England, and in London until 1833. By the end of the eighteenth century the private bankers in London had developed the use of cheques and had established a clearing house. Outside London, private banking was often at first only a sideline to a manufacturer's or a merchant's main business—for example, Samuel Lloyd, who was in the iron and steel business in Birmingham, was the founder of Lloyds Bank. Many private banks sprang from "corn-merchants' offices, chandlers', tea dealers' or mercers' shops."[1] By 1821 there were 843 private banks in England, of which sixty-two were located in London.

The large increase in the number of private banks outside London was the result of the Industrial Revolution: in 1750 there were only twelve such banks, whereas in 1821 there were 781 "country" banks. Most of them were small, unit banks—that is, they had no branches—and in times of crisis many failures occurred. During the fifteen years 1815–30 there were no fewer than 206 bank failures.

3. Joint-stock banks

Banking in Scotland had developed on somewhat different lines, the Bank of Scotland (founded 1695) having no monopoly of joint-stock banking in that country. A number of joint-stock banks had therefore been established in Scotland, and it was noticed that bank failures there were rarer than in England. In the banking crisis of 1825–6, for example, not one of the joint-stock banks failed, though a large number of private banks had to close—only a few in Scotland but over eighty in England. Supporters of joint-stock banking, such as Joplin, pointed to the Scottish banks as proof of the greater strength of joint-stock bankers as compared with private banks.

An Act of 1826 permitted the establishment in England of joint-stock banks with unlimited liability. These banks had power to issue bank-notes, provided that they were situated at least sixty-five miles from London. Joint-stock banks were opened in Bradford and Huddersfield and a number of other towns the following year, and within seven years their number had increased to thirty-two.

An Act of 1833 permitted the establishment of joint-stock banks in London, though in their case without the right to issue notes. The first joint-stock bank to open in London was the London and Westminster, founded in 1834, and this bank had to face opposition from the Bank of England, from the London private banks and from the general public, who for some reason at first looked with suspicion on the new joint-stock banks. By 1836, however, there were ninety-nine joint-

[1] Clapham: *Economic History of Great Britain*, I, p. 264.

stock banks in England, of which twenty-one were in Yorkshire and two in London.

4. The expansion of banks: (i) by opening branches

Small banks, whether private or joint-stock, were unable to withstand crises. Large-scale banking developed in two ways: individual banks extended their activities either by opening branches or by amalgamation with other banks. Private banks, by their very nature, tended to be local institutions, though lack of capital often hindered their expansion, and so branch banking was undertaken chiefly by joint-stock banks. Considerable progress in this direction was made during the fifty years ending in 1890. The number of private banks fell from 321 to 155 between 1840 and 1890, but there were still over 100 joint-stock banks at the end of this period—only five fewer than at the beginning. Branch banking, however, developed only slowly. In 1865 there were only three banks with over thirty branches, the largest being the London and Country, with 127 branches. By 1890 there were nine banks with over fifty branches, the largest at that date being the London and Country (165 branches), the National Provincial (158) and the Capital and Counties (99), but the other 250 banks averaged only ten branches each. By 1890 branch banking had developed to such an extent that ten banks had a total of 949 branches, and by then all important Scottish banks had opened London offices, though in their case this did not deprive them of the privilege of issuing bank-notes.

Advantages of branch banking. The chief advantage of branch banking lies in the greater stability of such banks, for the risk of failure is reduced. When a bank has a number of branches, smaller reserves of cash can be maintained at each branch, as in case of need one branch can obtain assistance from others. Where, as in Great Britain, industries are highly localised, a decline in the basic industry would probably result in many bank failures in that district if banks were single localised units. Though the Great Depression of 1929–35 was most severely felt in the "distressed areas", there was not a single bank failure in Great Britain, because by that time commercial banking in this country was carried on by a small number of banks, each with a network of branches, losses in one part of the country being offset by gains elsewhere. The history of banking during this trade depression was, however, vastly different in the United States, where unit banking is the general practice; 7,000 banks in that country closed their doors during 1930–3, no fewer than 3,000 of them in the two months February–March 1933. In favour of unit banks it is said that, because of their better acquaintance with local conditions, they are able to provide services suitable to the local industry, but this is poor compensation for their weakness in times of crisis, and in any case branch banks generally appoint as managers men who have had previous experience in the same industrial area.

Limited liability. It was not until 1858 that the privilege of limited liability was extended to banks, though many years after that date sixty-nine English banks and all the Scottish banks still had unlimited liability. The failure of the City of Glasgow Bank in 1878, when the demands made upon the shareholders ruined many of them, caused share-holders in other banks with unlimited liability to press for protection, and within a few years all the large banks enjoyed limited liability.

5. The expansion of banks: (ii) by amalgamation

Before 1913. There were two main periods of bank amalgamation. The period down to 1913 saw the development of upwards of forty large joint-stock banks. In this period amalgamations took place (*i*) between small country banks, (*ii*) between London and country banks and (*iii*) between joint-stock and private banks. Joint-stock banks, which had previously had agents in London, were particularly anxious to join up with private banks that were members of the London Bankers' Clearing House, even though to have a branch in London in the case of an English bank meant the sacrifice of the right to issue notes. For their part, the London banks, more affected than the provincial banks by the cheap-money policy of 1892-6, began to seek a country connection. Large-scale industry required large scale banking, and this provided another motive for amalgamation. Finally, the earlier antipathy of the public towards joint-stock banks and its preference for private banks was reversed, many of the private banks gradually losing public confidence.

As a number of the larger banks developed they began to expand further by absorbing other smaller banks. The National Provincial came to London in 1864, the Birmingham and Midland in 1890 and Parr's in 1891. As a result of these amalgamations the total number of banks declined still further, so that by 1913 there were only thirty-seven joint-stock banks (with an average of 165 branches each) and sixty private banks (with an average of fewer than seven branches each). Many private banks—for example, Lloyds and Barclays—became joint-stock banks, though Barclays did not make this change until 1896.

After 1913. In the second period of bank amalgamation large banks of equal importance began to join together, and this movement culminated in the creation of the "Big Five"—the Midland, Barclays,

Lloyds, the National Provincial and the Westminster—each of these banks having between 1,000 and 2,000 branches. Few large provincial joint-stock banks then remained, Martins with over 500 branches being the largest. This development, however, caused some alarm that the movement would end with the creation of a single, large bank. In 1918, therefore, the Treasury set up a Committee of Inquiry, which recommended that no further bank amalgamations should take place without the sanction of the Treasury. The merger of the London and Westminster Bank and Parr's in 1919 was permitted because it was regarded as being based on sound banking principles, most of the branches of the London and Westminster being in the Home Counties, where deposit banking predominated, while most of the branches of Parr's were in the industrial areas of the North and the Midlands, where there was a heavy demand for loans. As a result of these amalgamations the number of joint-stock banks in England and Wales declined between 1913 and 1939 from thirty-seven to thirteen, though the total number of their branches increased to over 10,000.

The most recent series of mergers occurred during 1967–70. After the Treasury had refused to sanction a merger of Barclays, Lloyds and Martins, permission was given to Barclays to take over Martins. The amalgamation of the National Provincial and the Westminster (to form the National Westminster) reduced the "Big Five" to the "Big Four", the only other large English commercial bank being Williams & Glyn's (itself a recent amalgamation of two banks). During this period mergers also occurred between Scottish banks, their number being reduced to three, all of which are now associated with English banks.

In recent years the English and Scottish commercial banks have widened the scope of their activities by acquiring interests in finance companies, mainly engaged in hire-purchase finance, and in some cases by establishing unit investment trusts or by the issue of credit cards. At the present day over 85 per cent of all the banking business in England and Wales is undertaken by the "Big Four". In 1958 the English commercial banks extended their activities by acquiring interests in Finance Companies, mainly engaged in financing hire-purchase.

II. THE PRACTICE OF BANKING

6. Functions of banks

(i) *Accepting deposits*. This is the oldest banking function, and in the earliest days of banking a charge was made for taking care of the money. Nowadays banks pay interest on deposit accounts, the rate usually being 2 per cent below Bank rate. This is the main type of business carried on by Savings Banks, such as the National Savings Bank and the Trustee Savings Banks, which are to be found in most large towns. The Savings Banks also pay interest on deposits, and are popular with small savers. It is usual for the commercial banks to require a few days' notice of withdrawal of money from deposit accounts, though for small sums this requirement is generally waived.

(ii) *Acting as agents for payment.* Commercial banks also permit their customers to have current accounts, on which they can draw without notice by cheque. The accounts standing to the credit of customers in deposit and current accounts form over 99 per cent of the liabilities of a commercial bank, as a glance at the balance sheet on pp. 414–15 will show. In the United States the distinction between deposits on deposit account and deposits on current account is made clearer by the terms used in that country—time deposits (deposit accounts) and demand deposits (current accounts). The cheque has become the principal method of payment in business, and each year sees an expansion of its use by the general public. Its convenience as a means of payment, economising the carrying of cash and providing a safe means for the transmission of money through the post, explains its increasing popularity in Great Britain and the United States. Banks pay no interest on current accounts, and sometimes make a charge for their work in transferring sums of money from one person's account to another's.

When calculating the total volume of purchasing power that exists in the form of bank deposits it is usual to add together the amounts on deposit and current account at commercial banks, though only sums on current account are subject to withdrawal by cheque, since in practice transfers can easily be made from one type of account to the other.

(iii) *Issuing bank-notes.* It has already been seen that the issue of bank notes was the second banking function to develop, the receipts given by the early bankers in exchange for customers' deposits coming to be used as means of payment. For convenience, the receipts were replaced by bank-notes of fixed denominations, each note having printed on its face the banker's promise to pay the bearer on demand the sum stated. A bank-note is thus an acknowledgement of a bank's debt, a sort of promissory note. The issue of bank-notes was an important function of early banks, though about the middle of the eighteenth century the London banks, other than the Bank of England, ceased to issue them. In London cheques came into common use at an earlier date than in the rest of the country, and in the first half of the nineteenth century the country banks were the chief issuers of notes. Once a banker had established himself in the public's confidence, his bank-notes were accepted and circulated as money, and few people desired to exchange them for gold. This made it possible for the banker to lend his own notes, and so the issue of notes became a coveted privilege of a banker and the most profitable side of his business. Many banks, however, at times found themselves in difficulties as a result of over-issuing notes. In most countries legal restrictions have been imposed on the issue of notes by banks. Often the issue of notes is subject to tax as in England in 1804, or Canada (the Chartered Banks), Australia (1910) and New Zealand (to 1933). In England the effect of the *Bank Charter Act* of 1844 was gradually to confine the right to issue notes in this country to the Bank of England, which since 1921 has been the sole bank of issue.

(*iv*) *Lending to customers.* The most profitable business of a banker is lending, and this can be considered to be one of the primary functions of a commercial bank. The early bankers were at first engaged in deposit banking, simply storing cash that had been deposited with them for safe keeping. The use of bank-notes made it possible for a banker to lend his own "promises to pay" so long as he retained the confidence of the business community.

Banks nowadays make advances to customers in the following ways;

(*a*) *By means of a loan account.* In this case the borrower's current account will be credited by the amount of the loan, and at the same time a loan account for this sum will be opened. Thus the borrower pays interest on the full amount he has borrowed. Some banks also grant personal loans.

(*b*) *By means of overdraft.* When a customer obtains an overdraft from his banker this means that he is permitted to draw cheques for a sum greater by the amount of the overdraft than the balance standing to his credit. In this case, if he does not avail himself of the full amount of the overdraft, he pays interest only on the amount by which his current account is actually overdrawn. The overdraft provides an easy and convenient method of borrowing to businessmen.

(*c*) *By discounting bills of exchange.* When a bank discounts a bill of exchange for a customer it is making a payment to a creditor, whose debtor has promised to pay at some future date. Thus, by discounting bills the bank enables the creditor to be paid at once, and at the same time allows the debtor a period of credit. This therefore is really another form of bank lending, the bank collecting the debt when it is due for repayment.

(*v*) *Other services to customers.* Banks act as agents for their customers in the purchase or sale of stock exchange securities, they are prepared to act as trustees or executors, they transact foreign exchange business, obtaining foreign currency for customers or exchanging foreign currency for sterling, and issue bank drafts, travellers' cheques, etc. The commercial banks also undertake acceptance business in connection with bills of exchange. Since 1965 they have provided certain customers with cheque cards guaranteeing their cheques up to £30.

7. Bank loans create bank deposits

Whether a bank lends by overdraft or by means of a loan account, the result is the same—it increases the total volume of purchasing power, that is, the quantity of money. For example, if Dombey's account shows that he has a credit balance of £50 and he obtains an overdraft for £100 he can draw a cheque for £150, and the bank will honour it. This cheque may be paid into, say, Gradgrind's account, which will increase by £150. Dombey's account, however, cannot fall by more than £50 (although, of course, his account will show a debit of £100), so the total combined deposits at the banks of which Dombey and Gradgrind are customers will increase by £100. The loan of £100 to Dombey has increased total deposits by £100. Thus loans make deposits. Banks can also create deposits by purchasing Government stock, which is simply a method by which banks lend to the Government. The bank pays for such purchases by cheques drawn on itself, and the payees of these cheques pay them into their own banking accounts, and so again the banks create deposits. Thus bank deposits are mainly created by the banks themselves. This power of the banks to expand credit is of enormous economic significance, for bank deposits are a form of purchasing power which can be used for the purchase of goods and services, irrespective of the way in which they have been created. The total quantity of money therefore depends largely on the credit policy of the banks.

Superficially it may appear that a bank can lend only what has been deposited with it. From the example just given, however, it is clear that cheques paid by customers are often drawn against overdrafts, though only the drawer's banker is aware of this. The banking system as a whole is responsible for the creation of a very large proportion of the deposits of the various banks.

8. Bank credit and trade credit

It has been seen that when a bank grants credit it creates what it lends, and so total purchasing power is increased. If therefore a manufacturer obtains from the bank a loan of £1,000 the bank does not forgo the use of this sum in order to make the loan. In fact, as has already been seen, bank deposits will rise by £1,000, and so total purchasing power will increase. If it restricted its loans to the amount of cash deposited with it a bank would merely be acting as an intermediary for the transfer of a sum of money from depositors to borrowers. Banks, however, are prepared to expand their lending within the limits imposed by their liquidity rules.

It is rather different when a wholesaler grants credit to a retailer for, unlike the banker, the wholesaler has to forgo for a period the use of the sum the retailer owes him. What the retailer gains the wholesaler forgoes so that there is no increase in total purchasing power. A merchant who grants credit to his customers will require more capital than one who does not, as many owners of small businesses have found to their cost, for if their customers are slow to pay they may find that they have not the means for replenishing their stock. The granting of credit by wholesalers makes it possible for people with little capital to engage in retail trade, for it enables them to sell part of their stock before paying for it. Similarly, a consumer can spend most of his wages before he receives them if retailers supply him with goods on credit.

In the case of trade credit, therefore, the extra purchasing power enjoyed by one person is generally balanced by an equal loss of purchasing power by another, unless, of course, the credit trading itself is financed by banks directly by loan or overdraft, or indirectly by discounting bills of exchange. Nevertheless, trade credit has often been used to finance an expansion of production at times when bank credit has been restricted by the monetary authorities. In some respects, therefore, trade credit is similar to bank credit in its effect on total purchasing power.

9. The clearing of cheques

We have already seen that at the present day the most used means of payment in business is the cheque. When a cheque is received in payment it is paid into the payee's bank which then has to collect the sum required from the drawer's bank. This makes it necessary for there to be some means of clearing the cheques. The London private banks were the first to allow their customers to use cheques, and by 1770 they had established a clearing house. Previous to that, bank clerks had met in the street to exchange cheques.

In recent years the clearing of cheques has been greatly simplified, for there are in effect only two types of clearing now:

(i) *Branch and head office clearings.* Where only one bank is involved, that is, where the drawer and the payee both have their accounts at the same branch of the same bank, it is an easy matter to credit one account and debit the other by the amount of the cheque.

Thus if Pickwick, a customer with the Southern Bank, Canterbury, sends a cheque for £8 to Weller, whose account is with the Dorking branch of the same bank, this cheque will be cleared through the Head Office of the Southern Bank, Pickwick's account being debited and Weller's credited with £8.

(ii) *The London Bankers' Clearing House.* When the two parties to a cheque have accounts with different banks, whether the banks are in the same town or not (with one exception) the cheque will be cleared through the London Bankers' Clearing House. There used to be local clearings for cheques involving two banks in the same town, but in 1968 all provincial clearings were transferred to the London General Clearing except the afternoon clearing at Liverpool. Thus, if Spenlow has an account with the Eastern Bank, Northampton, and draws a cheque for £25 in favour of Drood, who pays it into his account at the Western bank, Exeter, this cheque will be cleared through the London Bankers' Clearing House.

Table LVIII

The Clearing of Cheques

Cheques paid into:							
Northern Bank		Southern Bank		Eastern Bank		Western Bank	
Cheques drawn on:	£	Cheques drawn on:	£	Cheques drawn on:	£	Cheques drawn on:	£
Southern	2,000	Northern	1,900	Northern	1,500	Northern	1,800
Eastern	1,700	Eastern	1,200	Southern	1,100	Southern	1,500
Western	2,100	Western	1,600	Western	1,200	Eastern	1,300

The total amounts to be credited and debited to the four banks can now be calculated:

	Northern	Southern	Eastern	Western
	£	£	£	£
Credit	5,800	4,700	3,800	4,600
Debit	5,200	4,600	4,200	4,900

The differences will be:

	£	£	£	£
Credit+, Debit— . .	+600	+100	−400	−300

It will be sufficient now for the Eastern Bank to give the Northern Bank a cheque for £400 and for the Western Bank to give cheques for £200 and £100, respectively, to the Northern and Southern Banks.

All cheques originating from banks in towns other than those where they have been paid in are sent each day to the head office of the payee's bank, after which they go to the London Clearing House. The procedure there is similar to that at the provincial clearing houses, though the number of cheques and sums involved will, of course, be very much greater. The only difference is in the final settlement. At the clearing house representatives of the banks exchange cheques and so far as possible offset their indebtedness to one another as the following examples show: since each of the English commercial banks keeps a balance at the Bank of England, and differences of indebtedness can be settled by cheques drawn on the Bank of England, a series of book entries will suffice to complete the transfer of hundreds of millions of pounds between people and firms in all parts of the country, without any movement of actual cash. All that remains is for the drawers' accounts to be debited.

There are two separate clearings at the London Bankers' Clearing House. There is the General Country Clearing and, in addition to this, the Town Clearing (twice per day) for the banks in the vicinity of the City. At the present day the daily average for the London clearing is over £6,000 million, involving cheques covering 1,500 million transactions in Great Britain (22,000 million in the United States; 6,000 million in West Germany).

10. Restrictions on the creation of credit by banks

It has been seen that the banks themselves can create deposits. Banks, however, do not have unlimited power to create deposits, their ability to do so being restricted in a number of ways:

(i) *The Clearing House imposes a restriction on an individual bank.* A single bank cannot adopt an expansionist credit policy unless the other banks are willing to do the same. In other words, the banks in their credit policy must keep in line with one another, expanding or contracting credit together. For if one bank expands credit more than others only a fraction of the additional bank deposits thereby created will remain with it, or be paid into it by its own customers, the rest being transferred by cheque to people with accounts at other banks. If it persists in pursuing an expansionist policy it will have persistent debit balances at the Bankers' Clearing House, and in consequence a continuous depletion of its reserves at the Bank of England will occur. The banks look upon these reserves as cash, and if a serious reduction of its cash reserves takes place a bank will soon be compelled to change its policy. Similarly, if a bank adopts an over-cautious credit policy its cash reserves will increase, but its profit-earning assets will be proportionately less than those of the other banks, with the result that its competitors will show higher profits.

(ii) *The liquidity ratio.* Money consists of bank deposits and cash, the former comprising about 78 per cent of the total. Bank deposits are largely the result of bank loans, but the banks have been able to create deposits to this extent only because most people prefer money in that form to cash. Banks lend on the assumption that their customers will wish to exchange only a small proportion of their deposits for cash. So long as a bank retains the confidence of its depositors there will be no abnormal demand for cash, and in order to retain this confidence the bank must always be able to pay cash on demand. A bank must therefore keep a sufficient reserve of cash to meet the demand of its customers for cash. Increasing confidence in banking and the greater use of cheques have reduced the demand for cash in countries which, like Great Britain, have a well-established, mature banking system.

For a long time British banks maintained a ratio of 10 per cent between cash and deposits, as experience had taught them that this was sufficient to enable them to meet all normal calls upon them, for no bank, however efficient its management, could withstand a continuous and abnormal demand for cash. Thus the creation of credit by the banks depends on (*a*) the amount of cash in existence; (*b*) the amount of cash people prefer to hold; and (*c*) limitations on the creation of bank credit, and therefore the size of the cash reserves which the banks deem necessary. As cheques are increasingly used the demand of customers for cash falls and even before 1939 British banks found that to maintain a cash ratio of 10 per cent gave them a greater margin of safety than they regarded as necessary. In 1946 the Bank of England recommended that a cash ratio of 8 per cent should be maintained, and since then the banks have kept to this lower cash ratio.

For a long time the English commercial banks maintained two liquidity rules:

(a) a ratio of 8 per cent between their cash reserves and deposits; and

(b) a ratio of 28 per cent between their more liquid assets (Items 1 to 3 in the Balance Sheet on pp. 414–15) and their total assets.

At one time the cash ratio was regarded as the main limitation on the power of the banks to create credit, but as the *Radcliffe Report* (1959) showed, if the cash ratio fell below 8 per cent the banks could easily restore it by reducing their holding of Treasury bills, whereas such action would have no effect on the 28 per cent liquidity ratio. It was therefore this second liquidity rule of 28 per cent and not the 8 per cent cash ratio that acted as a check on the commercial banks. Though there was no legal compulsion on British banks to maintain their liquidity rules, there is no doubt that the Bank of England would have put pressure on them to do so if it had considered such a course to be necessary.

In 1971 a further change in the calculation of the liquidity ratio to be maintained by the commercial banks was proposed by the Bank of England. It was suggested that the commercial banks should regard as their liquid assets cash in hand and balances at the Bank of England, money at call and short notice, Treasury bills (the three traditional liquid assets of the banks), together with Government stocks within one year of maturity and a proportion of their commercial bills. It was proposed that a ratio of $12\frac{1}{2}$ per cent should be maintained between these assets and a bank's total deposits.

If its liquidity ratio rises it becomes possible for a bank either to accept this increase in its liquidity or expand its loans; if its liquidity falls, it must reduce either investments or loans. If the banks consider changes in the ratio to be due to temporary causes no action will be taken. Shortly before Christmas and in the summer there are heavy seasonal demands for cash, but in January and early autumn the cash generally flows back to the banks. In June and early December, therefore, the ratio falls, but usually returns to normal again in early January and late August. Knowing this, the banks take no action to influence it.

(iii) *The collateral security available.* Before a bank grants a loan it will want to know the purpose and length of time for which it is required and how it is to be repaid. In addition, the borrower will probably be asked to give the bank some kind of collateral security which the bank can turn into cash if the loan is not repaid. It is, however, an important banking principle that the first consideration in such cases is the character of the borrower, for the banker prefers a loan to be repaid and for the collateral security to be at his disposal only in an emergency. The more liquid the security—that is, the greater the ease with which it can be turned into cash without loss—the more acceptable it is to the bank. Life assurance policies form good security because they usually have a "surrender value"—that is, a present cash value. Stock exchange securities and deed of property are frequently given as collateral security, but the prices of stock exchange securities vary from day to day, and in times of trade depression the value of industrial property may fall catastrophically, as both British and American banks found to their cost in the 1930s. Documents of title, such as bills of exchange, bills of lading, warehouse warrants, etc., can be used as collateral security. Sometimes a borrower may be able to persuade someone, whose credit is approved by the bank, to act as guarantor for the loan. The amount of collateral security is obviously not fixed in quantity, for the banks can raise or lower their standards, but at any given time, and taking the banks' standard as given, the amount of security available may tend to limit bank lending.

(iv) *The central bank and the State.* The final restriction on the creation of credit by the commercial banks comes from the monetary authorities, that is, in this country the Chancellor of the Exchequer, the Bank of England and the Treasury, but a consideration of monetary policy must be reserved for Chapter 24.

III. THE BALANCE SHEET OF A COMMERCIAL BANK

11. The theory of banking

A bank is an institution that is prepared to accept deposits of money or claims to money and repay cash on demand. The essential feature of commercial banking is the lending of more cash than the amount held by the bank. Loans to customers form a bank's most profitable activity, but the urge to expand this side of its business in order to increase its profits is tempered by its obligation to pay cash on demand. However, most borrowers do not require actual cash, although a proportion of loans will be wanted in the form of cash as, for example, for the payment of wages. To expand loans will, therefore, to some extent increase the demand for cash. This is a fact that a banker must always bear in mind when he is considering whether to increase his lending. It has been seen that a banker knows from past experience what proportion of his assets to keep in liquid form, but he must be able to convert his other assets into cash if circumstances require it without undue delay and if possible without loss. Thus a banker's main concern is with the liquidity of his assets. This limits the extent both of his willingness to lend and the amount of investment he is prepared to undertake, for, as we have just seen, the banker must maintain certain liquidity rules.

The structure of bank assets can be seen from Table LX.

Table LIX

Bank Deposits (London Clearing Banks)

Year	£ million monthly averages
1945	4,692
1950	5,952
1955	6,400
1960	7,236
1965	8,415
1970	10,271
1972	14,580
1973	18,823
1974	24,715
1975	27,620
1976	

12. The liabilities of a commercial bank

The chief liabilities in the balance sheet of a commercial bank are capital, reserves and deposits on current and deposit account. A hundred years ago capital and reserves formed $12\frac{1}{2}$ per cent of a bank's total liabilities but in 1976 they formed less than $2\frac{1}{2}$ per cent. Thus, at the present day deposits are by far the most important liability of a commercial bank. Bank deposits are of great economic importance since they provide the pricipal form of purchasing power in use today. Table LIX shows how bank deposits have increased in recent times.

Bank deposits increase rapidly in times of easy credit and more slowly during periods of credit restriction. At the present time about 55 per cent of total deposits are on current account, the remaining 45 per cent being on deposit account. This has little economic significance since transfers from one type of account to the other can easily be made. Since 1964 the Trustee Savings Banks allowed their customers to make withdrawals from their account by cheque, thereby adding to the volume of purchasing power. In recent years many American and other foreign banks have opened branches in London, and if their sterling deposits were added to the total given above, total bank deposits would be very considerably increased. In recent years accepting houses located in London have also increased their deposit banking, thereby adding a further £1,000 million to total deposits in 1976.

13. The assets of a commercial bank

The assets of a commercial bank are in effect claims against other people, other institutions or the Government. The distribution of bank assets is the result of a compromise between (*a*) the necessity always to be able to pay cash on demand, and (*b*) the desire for profit. The more liquid the asset, the less profit it will generally yield to the bank. Cash— the most liquid asset—earns no profit at all, whether it be in the tills of

Table LX

Bank Assets (London Clearing Banks)

	1951		1971		1975	
	£ million	%	£ million	%	£ million	%
1. Coin, notes and balances with Bank of England . .	521	8.6	912	8.1	978	4.0
2. Money at call and short notice . .	605	9.8	1,446	13.1	2,842	11.6
3. Bills discounted .	965	15.9	1,228	11.0	1,322	5.4
4. Special deposits .	—	—	393	3.4	615	2.5
5. Investments . .	1,954	32.9	1,234	11.0	1,280	5.2
6. Advances to customers . .	1,912	32.8	5,989	53.4	17,433	71.3

Source: *Bank of England Quarterly Bulletin.*

the bank's various branches or in the bank's balance at the Bank of England. The least liquid of a bank's assets—apart from its premises—is advances to customers, because it is the most difficult to turn into cash at short notice.

Table LX shows the combined assets of the London Clearing Banks in recent years. The percentages show the relation between each type of asset and total deposits.

14. The more liquid assets of a bank

When calculating their total cash the English Commercial banks include their balances at the Bank of England, which forms about 40 per cent of the total. This they are entitled to regard as cash since in an emergency the Bank of England would always allow a bank to make withdrawals in cash from its balance. The more liquid assets comprise items 1 to 3 above—cash, money at call and short notice, and bills discounted.

Money at call and short notice. This item in a commercial bank's balance sheet consists chiefly of short-term loans to the members of the money market; bill brokers, discount and acceptance houses. As the term implies, such loans can be called in by the banks either without notice or at very short notice—one to seven days. This is a very liquid asset, and its existence makes it possible for British banks to keep a smaller cash ratio than would otherwise be prudent. In countries without a well-developed money market banks find it necessary to keep a large proportion of their total assets in the form of cash. Because this asset is useful to them on account of its liquidity, banks make only a small charge to the money market for loans at call or short notice.

Bills discounted. The discounting of bills is an important function of a bank. Bankers look upon bills as a most desirable asset, since they are fairly liquid and yet yield a profit. They are preferred to loans because they provide the bank with a negotiable instrument, which can be rediscounted if necessary, although it is not the practice of banks to rediscount bills which they have once acquired. Bills are sometimes said to be self-liquidating, for they arise as a result of actual trade transactions and fall due for payment at a fixed date. The use of bills of exchange to finance inland trade transactions has declined with the increasing use of cheques. They are also less used than formerly in connection with foreign trade. Most bills discounted nowadays are Treasury bills, which yield a very small profit.

Special deposits. In 1960 the Bank of England for the first time made use of a new instrument for controlling the commercial banks, namely demanding from them sums as Special Deposits as a means of reducing their liquidity, repaying them at times when it was considered desirable to increase their liquidity. Since then this device has been employed on a number of occasions. In 1975 the Bank of England was holding £615 million in Special Deposits. Special Deposits can be regarded as a liquid asset but how quickly they can be turned into cash would depend on the Bank of England.

15. The less liquid assets of a bank

Investments and advances to customers comprise the less liquid, but the more profitable of bank assets. On account of their concern for liquidity, banks do not care for long-term investments. In this country they limit their investments to "gilt-edged" securities—mainly British Government stocks. Advances are generally loans to provide industry with circulating capital, as it is rare for British banks to provide fixed capital. In recent years there has been an increase in personal loans. The following table shows the distribution of bank advances in 1971.

Table LXI
Bank Advances (London Clearing Banks)

1975	£ million
Agriculture and fishing	460
Industry	6,005
Retail trade	474
Wholesale trade	636
Personal and professional . . .	1,015
Financial services	3,210
Local Government authorities . .	210
House purchase	720
Hire purchase financial companies . .	244
Public utilities	672
Others	2,704
	16,353

Source: *Bank of England Quarterly Bulletin.*

It is usual for bank advances and investments to vary inversely, for when bank advances are not in demand the banks increase their investments. In periods of trade depression banks increase their investments at the expense of advances, businessmen in general being unwilling to borrow in such conditions however low might be the rate of interest, but in any case fewer satisfactory borrowers coming forward. With the revival of business activity banks tend to sell investments in order to increase their advances, since advances are a more profitable asset than investments.

RECOMMENDATIONS FOR FURTHER READING

J. H. Clapham: *Economic History of Great Britain*, Vol. I, Chapters 7 and 13.
R. S. Sayers: *Modern Banking*, Chapters 1, 2, 8.
G. Crowther: *An Outline of Money*, Chapter 2.

QUESTIONS

1. In the banking system, loans create deposits. Explain this statement with the aid of simple balance sheets and point out the limitations to the creation of credit. (Bolton)

2. Explain the traditional asset structure of the commercial banks and indicate how the changes in banking regulations introduced in 1971 affect this structure and the operation of the banks. (Chesterfield)

3. What are the main functions of modern banks? (Exp.)

4. Outline the advantages and the possible dangers of bank and trade credit. (IB)

5. Explain the working of the Banker's Clearing Houses. (IMTA)

6. To what extent are the joint-stock banks able to influence the total supply of money in circulation? (BS)

7. "Banks do not create money; they only lend money which has been deposited with them." Discuss. (CIS)

8. Can banks create credit? If so, how? (CIS)

9. What are the principal investments of a British joint-stock bank and what are the general principles which tend to determine the allocation of resources amongst these investments? (IHA)

10. "The secret of successful banking is to distribute resources in such a way as to get a sound balance between liquidity and profitability." Discuss. (AIA)

11. By what means can banks increase the total volume of bank deposits, and how will such action affect the price level? (DPA)

12. Show how the assets of a commercial bank are distributed in accordance with the twin aims of liquidity and profitability. (GCE)

13. Examine the limitations on the power of the commercial banks to change the quantity of money. (GCE)

14. Describe a typical commercial bank's balance sheet. What are the chief factors determining the composition of its assets? (GCE)

15. What are the liquidity principles of sound commercial banking? Why are these principles an inadequate bulwark against monetary instability? (Degree)

CHAPTER 23

THE ENGLISH BANKING SYSTEM: THE MONEY MARKET

I. INTRODUCTORY

1. The financial markets

There are four important financial markets, the scope and functions of which are frequently confused. These are the money market, the discount market, the securities market (the stock exchange) and the capital market. Of these, the securities market is the only one that has a particular building in which its business is carried on. The business of the money market and the discount market is transacted in the neighbourhood of Lombard Street and the Bank of England, where the head offices of the commercial banks and other financial institutions are situated within easy reach of one another.

These four financial markets conveniently group themselves into two pairs. The terms *money market* and *discount market* are often used as if they were synonyms, for the connection between them is very close. The money market is essentially a market for short-term loans, just as the capital market is primarily a market for long-term loans. The second item in a commercial bank's balance sheet in order of liquidity is Money at Call and Short Notice, and this shows how much at a particular time the banks are lending to the discount houses and bill brokers. These firms form the link between the money market, where the commodity dealt in is the short-term loan, and the discount market, where the commodity dealt in is the bill (trade bills and Treasury bills). Since bills are self-liquidating, and can be turned into money at a specified date, they have been called "near money". The bill brokers and discount houses borrow on short-term from the banks in order to provide themselves with funds with which to purchase (that is, discount) bills. Banks do not lend on long-term, and so firms in need of fixed capital must generally have recourse to the capital market. The securities market, or stock exchange, is the market in which existing issues of stocks and shares are bought and sold. The capital and securities markets are considered in Chapter 25.

II. TYPES OF BILLS

2. The promissory note

The promissory note is the simplest type of bill, being a written promise on the part of one person to pay another a certain sum of money at an agreed future date. It usually takes the following form:

West Hill Road,
Manchester, 7.

£187   10 March, 197–.

Three months after date I promise to pay Ralph Nickleby or order the sum of One hundred and eighty-seven pounds, value received.

Harold Skimpole.

Payable at Northern Bank, Ltd.
Mosley St., Manchester.

Fig. 82. Promissory Note.

In this case Ralph Nickleby has supplied Harold Skimpole with goods to the value of £187, but Skimpole desires three months in which to pay, and with Nickleby's consent payment has been made by means of a promissory note. This falls due for payment three months and three days (these extra days being known as "days of grace") after 10th March—that is, on 13th June. On its being presented on that date at the Mosley Street branch, Manchester, of the Northern Bank, payment will be made. This particular bank has been chosen by Skimpole because he keeps his account there. Promissory notes are rarely used in business in Great Britain, though they are still fairly popular in the United States.

3. The bill of exchange

The inland bill of exchange is similar in some ways to the promissory note. Both are means by which a debtor makes acknowledgment of a debt incurred in the course of business and which he proposes to pay on demand, or, generally, at some agreed future date. Most bills are drawn for three months, but both bills of exchange and promissory notes can be drawn for payment at sight or for periods longer or shorter than three months. For both types of bill the debtor is allowed three additional days of grace in which to pay unless they are payable within three days. Stamp Duty is no longer payable on bills of exchange or cheques. The bill of exchange differs from the promissory note in two ways: it is drawn by the creditor, and before it is of any value it has to be accepted by the debtor. They are similar in that they allow debtors to postpone payment.

An inland bill of exchange takes the following form:

---

85 Lower Canal Road,
Bradford.
7th January, 197–.

£544

    Three months after date, pay to me or my order
    Five hundred and forty-four Pounds, value received,
                        H. Veneering.

To S. Wegg
    Foss Way,
      Leicester.

Fig. 83. Bill of Exchange.

After a bill has been accepted it is known as an Acceptance. Inland Bills of Exchange were quite common in 1840, though by 1870 they had been largely displaced by the cheque. They are only rarely used in Great Britain nowadays.

The foreign bill of exchange differs from the inland bill in a number of ways. It used to be made out in triplicate in case the first copy was lost in transit, but this is no longer usual. Before 1914 the import of cotton and wheat was financed by this means, but fewer bills of exchange than was formerly the case are now used in foreign trade transactions. The simplest form of the foreign bill is as follows:

Old Wharf
London.
15th May, 197–.

$700

    Sixty days after sight of this FIRST of Exchange (second and
    third of the same tenor and date being unpaid) pay to my order
    the sum of Seven hundred dollars, value received.
                        J. Podsnap.

To Z. Scadder,
    Eighty-fifth Street,
      New York.

Fig. 84. Foreign Bill of Exchange.

In this example J. Podsnap of London has sold goods to Z. Scadder of New York, and has drawn a bill of exchange in payment which

Z. Scadder will in due course accept and on the due date pay. In the case of a foreign bill the period before it becomes due for payment is calculated from the date of acceptance.

4. The Treasury bill

Treasury bills were created by an Act of 1877, largely at the suggestion of Walter Bagehot. Unlike trade bills, they are purely financial instruments, and do not arise as a result of trade transactions. In fact, they are a special type of accommodation bill. They enable the Government to borrow on easy terms by taking advantage of the facilities offered by the London money market. They are issued by the Treasury in units of £5,000, £10,000, £25,000, £50,000 and £100,000 for periods of three months, the amount offered each week being announced the previous Friday and tenders invited. Each tender must be for a minimum of £50,000. Bills are then allotted to the highest bidders, who can have their bills dated for any day during the following week. Some Treasury bills are issued "on tap" to Government departments with funds available. Treasury bills had their origin in the Government's need to borrow in anticipation of revenue, but the cheapness of this method of borrowing led to a huge increase in their use, so that the value of outstanding Treasury bills at the present day greatly exceeds the outstanding revenue. The Treasury bill takes the following form:

Due 14 June 197–.

TREASURY BILL
Per Acts 40 Vict. c. 2 and 52 Vict. c 6.

£10,000   A

London.   12,438

   This Treasury Bill entitles   or order to payment of Ten Thousand Pounds at the Bank of England out of the Consolidated Fund of the United Kingdom on the 14th day of June 197–.

          (Signed)..........................
          Secretary to the Treasury.

Fig. 85. A Treasury Bill.

Generally, no payee's name is inserted, the bill then being payable to bearer; for safety in transit a name will be inserted if the bill is taken up by a foreign purchaser. Treasury bills are paid when they fall due on presentation at the Bank of England.

III. THE WORK OF THE DISCOUNT MARKET

5. Discounting bills

The members of the money and discount markets are the discount houses, the merchant bankers (or acceptance houses), the English commercial banks, a large number of foreign and overseas banks, and as lender of last resort, the Bank of England.

When Veneering, the creditor named in the bill shown in Fig. 83, agreed to Wegg's request that settlement of his debt be made by a three-month bill of exchange, it was equivalent to Veneering giving Wegg three months' credit. The advantage of this type of settlement is that it gives rise to a negotiable instrument. Three courses are then open to Veneering: (*i*) he can hold the bill until it matures—that is, until it is due for payment; or (*ii*) by endorsing it he may be able to use it in settlement of one of his own debts, if some other merchant is willing to take payment in this form; or (*iii*) he may be able to discount it, that is, sell it to a broker. Whether the bill can be discounted will depend on Wegg's standing in the business world, for the eventual payment of the bill depends on Wegg's ability to meet it. On discounting the bill, Veneering will not receive the full amount for which it was drawn, for interest on £544 for three months will be deducted, the rate depending on the prevailing rate of interest and the risk in holding this particular bill. If Veneering discounts the bill Wegg will really be obtaining a loan, the transaction between Wegg and Veneering in effect being financed by the bill broker who discounts the bill.

Operating in the London discount market there are now nine public limited companies, of which Alexanders, the National Discount Company and the Union Discount Company of London are the largest. These nine firms are responsible for the greater part of the business of the market. In addition, there are three private firms. There are also four firms of "running brokers," but they are only agents who act on behalf of others and do not discount bills on their own account.

The discount houses enjoy the unique privilege of being able to borrow from the Bank of England when it acts in its capacity as "lender of last resort" (*see* pp. 439–40).

6. Accepting bills

A bill of exchange has no value until it has been accepted; and unless the name of the acceptor is well known, no one will be willing to discount, it. Foreign bills may be drawn on firms in all parts of the world, but few bills would qualify for discounting were it not for the existence of specialist accepting institutions. The accepting houses are sometimes known as merchant bankers because their financial business generally developed out of their ordinary trading activities. The oldest of these firms moved into London from Europe in the late eighteenth or early nineteenth centuries during the Napoleonic War, and the most recent was founded in 1921. The names of many merchant bankers indicate their foreign origin—Schroder, Kleinwort, Lazard, Baring, Rothschild. Other merchant banks include Hambros, Hill Samuel and S. Montagu. In their dealings merchant banks specialise to some extent in particular parts of the world, and they have, in the chief commercial centres, their own agents who are thus able to acquire expert knowledge of the credit-worthiness of merchants in the areas in which they operate. For a fee, therefore, they are prepared to accept bills which would otherwise not be negotiable because the first acceptor's name was not known to the discount market. Foreign merchants can open acceptance credits with the acceptance houses, and other merchants can draw bills upon them, and such bills can be discounted in the London discount market. Thus, by guaranteeing payment, they make bills negotiable, and bill brokers and discount houses are then prepared to deal in them.

Acceptance business has never been the sole activity of merchant banks, nor in the case of Rothschilds the most important function. They have frequently undertaken the placing of long-term loans in London on behalf of foreign firms or governments. For example, Rothschilds assisted the purchase of a controlling interest in the Suez Canal by Disraeli's Government in 1875.

When a bill has been accepted either by a commercial bank or by a merchant banker it is known as a "bank bill"; when accepted by a merchant of good standing it is known as a "fine trade bill."

7. Functions of the money market

Although the US dollar has now outdistanced sterling as an international means of payment a much greater amount of business is still transacted on the London market than by any foreign discount market. The bill brokers and discount houses borrow from the commercial banks at a very low rate of interest because the loans can be recalled at short notice. This is an advantage to the banks, as it provides them with a particularly liquid asset, and so enables English banks to keep a lower cash reserve than is possible for most foreign banks. The practice developed whereby bill brokers use these funds to discount bills which they hold for a period, usually a month, after which they rediscount them with the banks. They were able to make a profit by charging a slightly higher rate for discounting bills than that at which they borrowed from the banks. The banks themselves discounted bills, but preferred bills not more than two months from maturity when they acquired them. They also liked bills to have approximately equal amounts falling due each week. Thus they were prepared to rediscount bills for the bill brokers at lower rates than the interest they charged on their short-term loans. This loss the banks regarded as a sort of fee to the bill brokers for holding bills for a period and arranging them in "parcels." Once a commercial bank has acquired a bill it usually holds it until maturity.

The existence of a well-developed money market enables the English commercial banks to avoid borrowing from the central bank. If they should find themselves short of cash they can call in some of their loans to the money market, and so compel members of the money market to borrow from the Bank of England. Borrowing then becomes more expensive to the members of the money market, for the Bank of England charges a higher rate than do the commercial bank both on short-term loans and for rediscounting bills. In addition the Bank of England's eligibility rule restricts its discounting of bills to bank bills or fine trade bills. The intervention of the money market between the commercial banks and the central bank is a distinctive feature of the English banking system.

8. Developments in the money market

During the past fifty years a number of important developments have occurred affecting the London money market. The use of the bill of exchange as a means of international payments has considerably declined. The main reason for this is that the foreign bill of exchange has been largely superseded by the bank draft and the telegraphic transfer of bank deposits from one country to another. If a bank draft is employed the importer obtains a draft for the required amount in the currency of his creditor and pays for it with his own cheque. A telegraphic transfer of a bank deposit from one bank to a bank in another country can be effected by a cable to a foreign bank instructing it to pay a specified sum of money to a particular merchant. Another method of payment now used in foreign trade is the documentary credit, and though this still requires the employment of a bill of exchange, it is drawn on a foreign bank and not on a merchant. The use of the documentary bill has weakened somewhat the position of the accepting houses, the services of which are no longer required in connection with such transactions, since the foreign bank is responsible for payment being made. In consequence, there is no need for the special information regarding foreign firms which only the accepting house, with its foreign connections, could supply. Direct dealing with a foreign merchant was a risky undertaking, but commercial banks can deal safely with well-known foreign banks.

Things were made more difficult for the merchant banks, when the commercial banks entered this field in spite of the contraction of the amount of acceptance business, and reduced still further the amount available to them. The decline in the use of trade bills coincided, however, with a large increase in the volume of Treasury bills. During the 1950s nine-tenths of the bills discounted by the English commercial banks were Treasury bills. During the 1960s, however, things began to change. As recently as 1968 half the bills discounted by the banks were Treasury bills, but by 1975 Treasury bills formed less than one quarter of the bills coming into the hands of the banks. From the point of view of both discount houses and accepting houses the Treasury bill is not so desirable as the trade bill, since such bills do not require to be accepted. Nor do Treasury bills have to be arranged in "parcels", since they are always issued in convenient amounts, and not in irregular amounts like trade bills, and a bank, too, can arrange to have them fall due daily as required. In practice, however, the commercial banks refrain from tendering directly for Treasury bills, preferring to rediscount bills offered to them by the discount houses.

Some bills are taken up by overseas banks and a few by large industrial concerns. Until 1972 the discount houses did not compete against one another when tendering for Treasury bills; they used to meet each Friday to decide the amount of their syndicated bid. Bills were allotted in full to those making the highest tenders, the remainder being taken up by the discount houses.

The decline of their specialist business in the London money market led the accepting houses to widen their activities. In addition to dealing in bills they began to deal in short-dated Government stocks, the supply of which is greater than it used to be. They have also greatly expanded their ordinary banking business—their reply to their loss of acceptance business to the commercial banks—accepting deposits, on which they pay a higher rate of interest than the commercial banks, and making advances. In 1975 their total deposits were £8,310 million as compared with £27,620 million of the commercial banks. They also lend to local authorities. Other functions they have developed include acting as issuing houses in the flotation of new public limited companies (*see* p. 454). Another activity of theirs which has expanded greatly is in connection with mergers, for they have acquired great expertise in negotiations undertaken for this purpose. It is usual for the parties to a proposed merger to appoint merchant banks to act on their behalf, the negotiations then taking place between the two merchant banks. There has been a large amount of this kind of business in recent years. They often, too, act as advisers and trustees of pension funds. Some merchant banks also have their own unit trusts. The decline in bills has been off-set by the development of other negotiable instruments, such as bills drawn on local authorities, certificates of deposit (CD's), which in effect are claims to specified sums of money deposited with the bank named on them. Other negotiable deposits are Finance House deposits and Inter-company deposits, both of recent origin. The best known of these new negotiable instruments are those associated with Eurocur-rency deposits. These are funds that have been deposited with banks in other countries but which are denominated in the currency of the country of origin. The most used Eurocurrency is the Eurodollar which has been employed since 1957. There was a huge increase in the volume of Eurodollars during the 1960s. Eurocurrency deposits are par-ticularly useful to multinational companies.

As the amount of acceptance business declined it began to be said that the continuance of the discount market depended very largely on the willingness of the commercial banks and the Treasury to permit it to exist. However, the existence of a well-developed money market has for a long time been one of the distinctive features of the English bank-ing system. In this country, as already pointed out, the commercial banks when short of cash never themselves borrow from the Bank of England, but instead call in some of their loans to the money market ("money at call and short notice"), and in consequence compel the dis-count houses and bill brokers to borrow from the central bank. In other countries commercial banks borrow directly from their central banks. In England, therefore, the money market acts as a sort of buffer between the commercial banks and the Bank of England. The discount houses, too, regard themselves as providing an important service to the Government, since they are always prepared "to cover the tender," that is, they are willing to take up whatever amount of Treasury bills the Government offers them. Thus, for a number of reasons the English commercial banks prefer the London money market to remain in being. It is doubtful, however, whether the money market could have survived if it had not adapted itself to the changing conditions by developing new activities.

The expansion of ordinary banking business undertaken by the accepting houses and discount houses made it necessary for the Bank of England to bring them within the scope of its control by making them conform to the liquidity rules that apply to the commercial banks in order to make them more responsive to its monetary policy. The discount houses must now hold 50 per cent of their assets in Government securities.

RECOMMENDATIONS FOR FURTHER READING

R. S. Sayers: *Modern Banking*, Chapter 3.
R. J. Truptil: *British Banks and the London Money Market*, Pt. 1, Chapters 3, 4; Pt. II, Chapters 1–3, 6.

QUESTIONS

1. "The discount market is an unnecessary institution, especially in view of recent developments in competitive banking." Explain and comment on this statement. (Bournemouth)

2. What institutions, apart from the Bank of England and the commercial banks, make up the London Money Market? Briefly indicate their functions. (City)

3. Explain the function of the London Money Market and comment on its economic significance for the economy. (RSA)

4. Outline the function of the English banking system and show how Acceptance Houses operate therein. (RSA)

5. Give a brief description of the organisation of the London Money Market. How has the relative importance of its several components altered in recent years? (RSA)

6. Explain clearly the nature of a Bill of exchange. In what ways does its "monetary character" differ from that of a Bank of England note? (Exp.)

7. Who are the chief Lenders and Borrowers in the London Money Market? (LC Com.)

8. What are the discount houses? Explain their role in the London Money Market. (GCE)

9. What are the functions of the contemporary discount market? What do you think of its future prospects? (Degree)

10. What are the present main functions of the London Money Market? (Degree)

11. The London discount market is sometimes described as a buffer between the Treasury and the Bank of England, on the one hand, and the clearing banks, on the other. Explain how the discount market does work in this way. (Degree)

CHAPTER 24

THE ENGLISH BANKING SYSTEM: THE BANK OF ENGLAND

I. INTRODUCTORY

1. Central banking

It has become an accepted principle that a banking system requires a central bank. This is, however, a comparatively recent development, although some of the functions of a central bank were being performed by the Bank of England before the middle of the nineteenth century. The Federal Reserve System, which undertakes central banking in the United States, was set up in 1913. Both France and Germany had central banks in the nineteenth century, but there were still many countries without this type of bank as recently as 1920, central banks not being established in Canada and Argentina until 1935. It was only slowly and by the adaptation of policy to particular circumstances that the practice of central banking developed in England. Not until Bagehot published his *Lombard Street* in 1877 was any attempt made to formulate the principles on which central banking should be based.

The outstanding function of a central bank is to carry out a country's monetary policy. In order to be able to do so it must work closely with the State or be subject to its control, and it must have some means of influencing the credit policy of the commercial banks. In Great Britain at the present time monetary policy is the joint responsibility of the Treasury, the Chancellor of the Exchequer and the Bank of England. The aim of the central bank is not, therefore, to make maximum profit for itself. Nor should it compete against the commercial banks for ordinary banking business. The eight branches of the Bank of England are situated in the principal commercial centres—Leeds, Manchester, Birmingham, etc.—their main function being to supply cash as required to local banks.

The necessity for a close connection between the State and the central bank led some countries to consider it desirable that the central bank should be State-owned. Both the Bank of England and the Bank of France are now nationalised institutions, but before 1946 the Bank of

England was a limited company, its capital being in the hands of its stockholders. It makes little difference nowadays whether a country's central bank is nationalised or not, for its activities are always closely controlled by the State, and in either case it is usual for the State to take at least a share of the bank's profits. The nationalisation of the Bank of England has had little effect on its relations with the Treasury, which since 1931 has had the last word in determining monetary policy. The *Nationalisation Act*, however, gave the Treasury the legal right, after consulting with the Governor, to give directions to the Bank, and also gave the Bank the power to make recommendations to the commercial banks. It is generally agreed that complete independence of the central bank is undesirable because of the widespread economic effects its policy may have upon the community at large, although it might be undesirable for a central bank to be completely subservient to the State, compelled without question to carry out whatever instructions the Government of the day might issue.

The Bank of England also acts as banker both to the British Government and to the other banks. It is, too, the only bank in England with the right to issue bank-notes. When occasion demands it also acts as lender of last resort. All these can be considered to be proper functions for a central bank to undertake, but it should not concern itself with ordinary banking business.

II. FUNCTIONS OF THE BANK OF ENGLAND

2. The Weekly Return

Before considering the functions of the Bank of England it will be useful to examine the Bank's Weekly Return. The *Bank Charter Act* of 1844 divided the work of the Bank of England into two departments known as (i) the Issue Department and (ii) the Banking Department, and required it to issue a weekly balance sheet for each department. This is the Bank Return which is published each Wednesday.

Consider first the Issue Department (Table LXII). The liabilities of this Department consist of the notes issued by the Bank. Most of the notes (a) are in the hands of the banks, the general public and shopkeepers. The notes (b) in the Banking Department are those that have not yet been drawn into active circulation. This is the item to watch if an increase in the note issue is anticipated.

The following are specimen returns for the Issue Department:

Table LXII

Bank of England Weekly Return (1) Issue Department
(2) Wednesday, 15th October 1975

	£ million			£ million
Notes issued:				
(a) In circulation . . .	5,839	(c) Government debt . .		11
(b) In banking dept. . .	36	(d) Government securities .		5,261
		(e) Other securities . .		603
		(f) Coin		1
	5,875	Fiduciary Issue . .		5,875

¹ (3) Wednesday

	£ million		£ million
Notes issued:			
(a) In circulation . . .		(c) Government debt . .	
(b) In banking dept. . .		(d) Government securities .	
		(e) Other securities . .	
		(f) Coin (other than gold) .	
		Fiduciary Issue . .	

¹ This space is provided for the insertion of the latest figures.

The assets of the Issue Department are five in number. Government debt (*c*) consists of loans made to the Government by the Bank of England during the first hundred and fifty years of its existence, generally in return for a renewal of its charter. Government securities (*d*) consist of Government Bonds and Treasury Bills. Other securities (*e*) comprise other first-class securities, including bank bills and eligible trade bills. Coin (*f*) consists of silver. Items (*c*), (*d*), (*e*) and (*f*) together form the backing for the fiduciary issue. Until 1939, when most of the Bank of England's gold was transferred to the Exchange Equalisation Account, 60 per cent of the note issue was backed by gold. Only since 1971 has the note issue been entirely fiduciary.

Consider now the liabilities of the Banking Department (Table LXIII). The item (*h*) is the capital subscribed by the stockholders when the Bank of England was a joint-stock company. On its nationalisation the stockholders received compensation in Government stock yielding an income equal to the dividend previously paid them by the Bank. The Rest (*i*) is the Bank's reserve, accumulated out of undistributed profits.

Public Deposits (*j*) comprise the balance to the credit of the Government account. As taxes are paid in, this item will increase; when the Government makes payments it will decrease.

Table LXIII

Bank of England Weekly Return (2) Banking Department
(1) Wednesday, 15th October 1975

	£ million		£ million
(h) Capital	14½	(m) Government securities .	1,268
(i) Rest	3½	(n) Other securities . .	85
(j) Public deposits . .	21	(o) Discounts and advances	249
(k) Other deposits . .		(p) Notes	36
(ka) Bankers' deposits .	245	(q) Coin	1
(kb) Other accounts .	381		
(l) Special deposits. .	974		
	1,639		1,639

[1] (2) Wednesday,

	£ million		£ million
(h) Capital		(m) Government securities .	
(i) Rest		(n) Other securities . .	
(j) Public deposits . .		(o) Discounts and advances	
(k) Other deposits . .		(p) Notes	
(ka) Bankers' deposits .		(q) Coin	
(kb) Other accounts .			
(l) Special deposits .			

[1] For the latest figures.

Banker's deposts (*ka*) are the balances of the commercial banks, forming part of their cash reserves, since they regard these balances as cash. Increased demand for cash on the part of the commercial banks will cause them to withdraw sums in cash from these balances. Payments by customers of the Commercial banks to the Government (for example, taxes) will cause public deposits to rise and bankers' deposits to fall; a payment by the Government to a customer of a commercial bank will have the reverse effect. Other accounts (*kb*) include the balances of Commonwealth and foreign banks as well as of ordinary customers of the Bank of England, and the size of this item gives an indication of the extent of ordinary business undertaken by the Bank. Special deposits (*l*) are compulsory deposits made by the commercial banks at the request of the Bank of England in pursuance of monetary policy—a new instrument of policy first employed in 1960.

The largest of the assets of the Banking Department is Government securities (*m*), and this comprises Government Stock, Treasury bills acquired directly and "Ways and Means" advances. This is the item affected when the Bank of England buys or sells securities in the open market (open-market operations). Other securities (*n*) are Dominion and foreign securities, and securities obtained by the Bank of England in the open market.

Discounts and advances (*o*) show the extent of the Bank's lending to the money market. When the commercial banks call in money at short notice the discount houses and bill brokers are compelled to borrow from the central bank, the market is then said to be "in the Bank." Lending by the Bank may take the form of rediscounting bills, or making loans with bills as collateral security. If the market is "in the Bank" this item will, therefore, increase. Notes (*p*) form the unused portion of the note issue, the reserve of notes held by the Bank of England to meet demands for cash by the commercial banks. It is the same as item (*b*) in the Return for the Issue Department. Gold and silver coin (*q*) is mostly silver, held like notes (*p*) for issuing when required to the commercial banks.

3. The Government's bank

The financing of war had always severely taxed the resources and ingenuity of kings, and by the late seventeenth century the cost to William III of waging his war on the Continent had become too great to be met by expedients previously employed. It was the Government's need for money for this purpose that led to the founding of the Bank of England in 1694. In return for a charter (often renewed only in exchange for a further loan) granting the privilege of incorporation, the Bank lent the Government £1,200,000 at 8 per cent. Thus was established the first joint-stock bank in England. An Act of 1708, by forbidding firms with more than six partners to act as bankers, ensured for the Bank of England a monopoly of joint-stock banking in England until 1826, and in London till 1833.

From its foundation, therefore, the Bank of England was the Government's bank, although it was not State-owned until 1946. As such, it receives the proceeds of taxes which are paid into the Government's account and shown in the Weekly Return under the heading of public deposits or public accounts. As agent for the Government it makes payments from this account, including the half-yearly payments, of interest on Government bonds. Thus, the national debt came into existence at the same time as the Bank of England, and ever since management of the national debt has been in the hands of the Bank. Direct lending to the Government by the Bank of England is comparatively rare nowadays, although the Bank still does a little by means of "Ways and Means" advances. As the Government's bank, therefore, the Bank of England keeps the Government's account, manages the national debt and lends to the Government.

On account of the huge size of the national debt its management has assumed great importance in the field of monetary policy.

4. The note issue

By the terms of its first charter, the Bank of England was given the right to issue bank-notes at least up to the value of its capital, but it was not always the sole bank of issue in England or even in London. As already noticed, the private London banks ceased to issue notes only when they developed the use of the cheque during the eighteenth century. For a long time other banks outside London continued to issue notes, and it is only since 1921 that the Bank of England has been the only bank in England with the right to issue notes. Bank of England notes were acceptable to the commercial world, and so when provincial banks were established they kept their reserves in Bank of England notes instead of in gold. With the exception of a short period during the first two years of its existence, the Bank of England successfully maintained the convertibility of its notes into gold for a hundred years. The heavy drain on the Bank's resources during the War with Napoleon, however, compelled it to cease payment in gold. To relieve the situation, notes in denominations of £2 and £1 were issued, the £5 note previously having been the lowest denomination. The *Bank Restriction Act* of 1797, which made Bank of England notes legal tender, had been intended as a temporary measure, but it was regularly renewed until 1821, when cash payments were resumed, Bank of England notes again becoming convertible.

The Act of 1826, which permitted the establishment of joint-stock banks outside a radius of sixty-five miles from London, also gave these new joint-stock banks the right to issue notes. This Act prohibited the Bank of England from issuing notes of denominations under £5. In the eighteenth and early nineteenth centuries the only Government control was over the denomination of the Bank's notes. In 1775 the Bank was forbidden to issue notes of less than £1, this minimum being raised two years later to £5, though later the issue of £1 notes was resumed. As already noted, £2 and £1 notes were issued during 1797–1821 and £1 notes temporarily in 1825.

The Bank Charter Act (1844). The over-issue of bank-notes had been responsible for the failure of many banks between 1833 and 1843. The *Bank Charter Act* was therefore an attempt to regulate the note issue. Its chief provisions were:

(*i*) It separated the note-issuing function of the Bank of England from its banking business by dividing the work of the Bank of England into two departments. (*a*) the Issue Department, and (*b*) the Banking Department.

(*ii*) In order to prevent an over-issue of notes it was decreed that, apart from a fiduciary issue of £14 million, all Bank of England notes were to be fully backed by an equivalent amount of gold and silver, though the amount of silver was not to exceed 20 per ent of the value of the gold. A fiduciary issue is an issue backed by securities and not by gold. Had it not been for the fact that the Bank of England had already issued notes in excess of its holding of gold, it is probable that the Act of 1844 would have insisted on all notes being fully backed by gold. In France and some other countries a gold reserve proportional to the note issue had to be maintained, usually 35–40 per cent of the note issue.

(*iii*) No new bank was to be allowed to issue notes. Existing banks having a note issue were not to increase their issues beyond the average circulation for the twelve weeks preceding 27th April 1844.

(*iv*) No bank in London, other than the Bank of England, was to have the right to issue notes, and a provincial bank on opening a London office or amalgamating with a bank with a London Office was to lose this right. Whenever a bank lost its privilege of issuing notes, the Bank of England could increase its fiduciary issue by two-thirds of the amount of the lapsed issue. As a result of this clause in the Act, the fiduciary issue had increased to £19¾ million by 1914. At the time of the passing of the *Bank Charter Act* there were seventy-two banks of issue in England, but by 1914 the number had fallen to thirteen. The amalgamation of Fox, Fowler and Company with Lloyds in 1921 left the Bank of England as the sole bank of issue. Except for £4.3 million, the note issues of the banks of Scotland and Northern Ireland have to be fully backed by Bank of England notes.

(*v*) The Bank of England had to issue notes on demand in exchange for gold bullion at £3 17s. 9d. (£3.88) per standard ounce—that is, gold eleven-twelfths fine.

(*vi*) The Bank of England had to publish a weekly balance sheet—the Weekly Return—for both its issue and its banking departments. This publicity, it was thought, would be a safeguard against any tendency to over-issue notes.

5. The fiduciary issue

The *Bank Charter Act* of 1844 represented a triumph, it is said, for the Currency School, whose members were anxious to prevent an over-expansion of the volume of money by an excessive issue of bank-notes. Indeed, they would probably have preferred all notes to be fully backed by gold with no fiduciary issue, for the Currency School did not yet realise that the development of the cheque as an instrument for the transfer of bank deposits from one banking account to another had resulted in bank deposits becoming money. As the Macmillan Committee (1931) pointed out, bank deposits are more important than bank-notes, for pressure to increase the note issue is generally the result of an expansive credit policy by banks.

In times of crisis the *Bank Charter Act* of 1844 has had to be suspended, as in 1847, 1857 and 1866, but the crisis of 1857 was the only occasion until 1914 when it was necessary to increase the note issue above the legal limit, the suspension of the Act being sufficient to restore calm in the other cases. The clumsiness of this arrangement has evoked frequent criticism. The legal limit for the fiduciary issue was exceeded in 1914, but the decision of the Treasury to put out its own notes for £1 and ten shillings (£0.50) relieved the situation. Until 1928 Bank of England notes and Treasury Notes circulated side by side.

The Cunliffe Committee (1918). Although this committee favoured a more elastic currency than was possible under the *Bank Charter Act* (1844), it considered that Act to have fulfilled its main object by preventing over-issues of notes. It recommended, therefore, that the principle laid down in this Act should be maintained, but that, with the Treasury's sanction, changes in the fiduciary issue should be made whenever this course was thought necessary. It further recommended that the Bank of England should take over the Treasury issue.

The Currency and Bank-notes Act (1928). This act implemented the recommendation of the Cunliffe Committee. From 22nd November 1928 all Treasury Notes were to be replaced by Bank of England notes. The fiduciary issue was raised to £260 million, backed by securities, except for £5½ million backed by silver. Changes in the fiduciary issue were to be made only with the consent of the Treasury, and notes in excess of this amount were to be fully backed by gold. Restrictions on the issue by the Bank of England of notes for amounts less than £5 were withdrawn. Pound and ten-shilling notes became legal tender in the United Kingdom for any amount, and £5 notes were legal tender for any amount in England and Wales. The profits of the Issue Department were to go to the Treasury.

The fiduciary issue since 1928. Between 1928 and 1939 the fiduciary issue varied between £200 and £275 million. An Act of 1939 gave the monetary authorities power to revalue the gold in the Issue Department of the Bank of England each week. Thus a rise in the price of gold would have made it possible to increase the note issue, while a fall in the price would have necessitated its contraction. War broke out, however, shortly afterwards, and most of the gold in the Issue Department was transferred to the Exchange Equalisation Account. From 1939 to 1971, therefore, most of the Bank of England's note issue was fiduciary in character. In 1931 only a third of the note issue was backed by gold, but by 1939 over 60 per cent of notes had a gold backing, whereas during 1939–71 less than 1 per cent was backed by gold. Since 1971 the issue has been entirely fiduciary. In 1939 the fiduciary issue stood at £580 million. Since then it has increased year by year reaching a total of £6,700 million by 1976.

Seasonal variations in the note issue. At certain times of the year larger demands for cash occur. The few weeks immediately before Christmas and the month of July are such occasions, and at these times there are heavy withdrawals of cash from the banks. At Christmas the cash is required for making purchases in the shops, and the shopkeepers later pay it back into the banks, and in the summer the money is spent on travel, hotels, etc., and again after a short interval much of it returns to the banks. In December 1937 the fiduciary issue was increased temporarily to meet this seasonal demand for cash. Since 1948 the fiduciary issue has been temporarily increased each year in July and December and usually reduced again shortly afterwards.

At the present time, therefore, this country has a fairly elastic note issue, as the frequent changes in its volume since 1939 show.

Convertibility of bank-notes. From 1821 to 1914 Bank of England notes were convertible on demand into gold sovereigns. Other note-issuing banks could exchange their own notes for Bank of England notes. During this period gold sovereigns and half-sovereigns were in general circulation. Great Britain left the gold standard on the outbreak of war in 1914 and, as already noted, Treasury notes were issued to replace the gold coinage. On the return to the gold standard in 1925 the gold coinage was not restored, as the maintenance of a gold coinage is expensive. Bank-notes, however, were made convertible for gold, but only in exchange for bars of gold, each weighing 400 ounces. In 1931 Great Britain again left the gold standard, and since then has had an inconvertible paper currency. Pound notes, however, still have printed upon them the phrase: "I promise to pay the Bearer on Demand the sum of One Pound," and although this is supported by a facsimile of the signature of the Chief Cashier of the Bank of England, the promise now has little meaning.

Putting cash into circulation. (*i*) *Coin.* The production of coins is the responsibility of the Royal Mint, a Government Department since 1968 located at Llantrisant near Cardiff. The Mint buys the metal, mints the coins and then sells them to the Bank of England on demand, the Bank in its turn allowing the commercial banks to make withdrawals in coin on demand from their balances at the Bank—that is, from bankers' deposits. The expenses of coinage are met by the Government from its account at the Bank of England, and when coins are sold to the Bank of England the Government's account is credited by the proceeds of the sale. As coins are sold to the Bank of England at approximately three times their cost, the Mint makes a considerable profit.

(*ii*) *Notes.* When the commercial banks make withdrawals from their accounts with the Bank of England bankers' deposits and the notes held by the Banking Department, each fall by the amount of the withdrawal. If the reserve of notes in the Banking Department appears likely to be insufficient to meet the demand of the commercial banks, it will then be necessary to increase the fiduciary issue. This, of course, requires the sanction of the Treasury, but nowadays that is a mere formality.

6. The bankers' bank

A central bank acts as banker to the commercial banks. From the first country banks kept only a limited amount of gold, their resources being chiefly in Bank of England notes, and so the Bank of England came to be the only bank with a large stock of gold. When cheques replaced notes as the principal means of payment, the provincial banks opened accounts with the Bank of England in order to facilitate the clearing of cheques. Some alarm was felt by the country banks when the Bank of England, taking advantage of its powers under the Act of 1826, began to open branches in the leading commercial centres. These fears, however, proved to be groundless, for it was not the aim of the Bank of England to compete against the commercial banks but only to provide facilities for provincial bank clearings similar to those already provided in London. Thus the Bank of England became the bankers' bank for both London and country banks.

The development of a system of branch bankings—a few large banks each with a network of branches—has simplified the clearing system. The "Big Four" and the other members of the clearing house keep part of their cash reserves in the form of deposits (known as bankers' deposits) at the Bank of England. Settlements between banks at the clearing can therefore be made by transfers between the accounts of the commercial banks at the Bank of England. The final adjustment of transactions involving millions of pounds simply requires book entries at the Bank, a credit to one bank, and a debit to another.

The Bank of England, as the bankers' bank, affords the commercial banks similar banking facilities to those that the commercial banks themselves render to their own customers. A person who has a current account with a bank can draw cheques on it and make payments to his creditors, and if he is short of cash he can withdraw sums in cash from his account. In exactly the same way a bank pays its debts to other banks by means of cheques drawn on its account at the Bank of England, and if it requires cash it can withdraw amounts in cash from this account. The commercial banks are therefore fully justified in regarding their balances at the Bank of England as cash. In the same way that a commercial bank must always be prepared to pay cash on demand to any of its customers, so must the Bank of England be prepared to pay cash on demand to the commercial banks.

The Bank of England also acts as banker to the discount houses.

7. The lender of last resort

An essential function of a central bank is that when circumstances require it, it should act as lender of last resort. No commercial bank, however efficiently run and soundly managed, could withstand an abnormal demand for cash. In a banking crisis it becomes the duty of the central bank to allay any tendency towards panic on the part of the general public by assisting the banks to withstand the strain of excessive demands made upon them for cash. In some countries the commercial banks in times of difficulty borrow directly from the central bank. In this country the commercial banks call in their loans to the money markets, and so compel the discount houses and bill brokers to seek assistance from the Bank of England. When the other banks are unwilling to lend, the central bank should be prepared to assist eligible borrowers, thereby acting as "lender of last resort". The Bank of

England does this either (i) by rediscounting bills or purchasing Government stocks, or (ii) by lending against bills or short-dated stock as security for the loan. The central bank can, of course, insist upon its own eligibility rules, and also in order to reduce such borrowing to a minimum, it can demand its own price—that is, charge as high a rate of interest as it deems the situation requires.

As with its other functions, the development of the Bank of England as lender of last resort was gradual. It was already acting in this capacity to some extent before the end of the eighteenth century, but until the Usury Laws—which prohibited more than 5 per cent interest being charged—were modified, the Bank did not willingly assume this role. The Government came to the Bank's assistance in 1847 and 1857 by suspending the Bank Charter Act of 1844, thus enabling the crises of those years to be overcome. It was not, however, until the crisis of 1866 that the Bank of England fully accepted its responsibilities as lender of last resort. For over a hundred years the Bank of England continued to act in this capacity without question. In 1971, however, it qualified its position by declaring that it was no longer prepared in all circumstances to buy stock outright unless it was within one year of maturity.

8. Responsibility for monetary policy

Money has become much more than a medium of exchange. Changes in the money supply and in the value of money influence the level of production and the distribution of the national income. Monetary policy is mainly concerned with varying the money supply. Formerly the Bank of England was responsible for monetary policy, and when Great Britain was on the gold standard its primary aim was to protect the country's gold reserves. Since 1944, when the Government for the first time accepted responsibility for the maintenance of full employment, it has had a more direct interest in monetary policy, which though now regarded as primarily the responsibility of the Chancellor of the Exchequer, requires the co-operation of the Treasury and the Bank of England for carrying it out.

Monetary policy, too, may be dictated by the external situation—the relation between a country's imports and its exports. If imports are considered to be excessive it may be necessary to damp down demand at home by a contraction of credit in order to reduce the demand for imported goods.

Since, however, both rising and falling prices bring about an arbitrary redistribution of income, it would seem to be more equitable to aim at stable prices, but this policy would probably make it more difficult to attain full employment. Perhaps the fairest method would be to keep all incomes stable and allow greater efficiency and higher output to bring down prices so that the whole community could share in the increasing prosperity of a country. Unfortunately, falling prices tend to check production and increase unemployment.

Two possible policies are open to the monetary authorities:

(i) *An expansionist policy.* In considering the effects of changes in the value of money we saw that one of the effects of rising prices (that is, of a fall in the value of money) was to stimulate production. If the volume of purchasing power is deemed insufficient to keep up demand to a level that will yield full employment an expansionist policy will be required. The appropriate monetary policy will then be pursued to expand credit and stimulate demand. A rise in prices will probably follow. Consequently, whenever in recent years there has been a falling away from full employment the monetary authorities have adopted an expansionist or inflationary policy.

(ii) *A restrictionist policy.* Since 1945, however, the problem has been mainly one of trying to check persistent inflation. During most of this time, at least until 1975, therefore, there was over-full employment with the demand for labour greater than the supply. Periodically, then, it was necessary to adopt a restrictionist policy, contracting credit to reduce demand with, in consequence, a temporary loss of full employment, a policy popularly known as a "credit squeeze." Such a disinflationary policy had on several occasions been forced on the British monetary authorities by the external situation, excessive demand having so stimulated imports as to create a large deficit in the balances of payments and, before exchange rates were allowed "to float," a consequent depletion of the country's reserves of gold and convertible currencies.

The main objectives of monetary policy in Great Britain in recent years therefore have been:

(i) to maintain full employment;

(ii) to maintain a reasonably stable internal price level, that is, to keep inflation in check.

(iii) to stimulate economic growth and thereby increase the national income in order to raise the standard of living of the people;

(iv) to maintain stability in the external value of the currency;

(v) to keep the balance of payments in balance.

Whether all these policies can be successfully pursued at one and the same time is extremely doubtful, since some of these aims conflict one with another. For example, is stability of prices compatible with the maintenance of full employment? Can economic growth be achieved without inflation? Do not full employment, economic growth and a rising standard of living all tend to stimulate imports, thereby making a balance of payments more difficult to achieve, and so endangering the external value of the currency? However, the consideration of questions affecting foreign exchange and international trade must be left for later chapters.

9. Other functions of the Bank of England

The Bank of England also performs a number of other functions:

(i) *Ordinary banking business.* From its foundation the Bank of England has always had some ordinary customers, now mostly old-established businesses in the City of London, for whom it has provided the banking facilities that might be expected of a commercial bank. Since it is generally recognised that ordinary banking business is not a proper function of a central bank, new business of this kind is only rarely accepted now by the Bank of England. The position is very different in France, where the Bank of France undertakes most kinds of ordinary banking business. Whereas the Bank of England has only eight branches, the Bank of France has over five hundred.

(ii) *Assistance to industry.* As already pointed out, it is not customary for British banks to provide industry with fixed capital. During the Great Depression of 1929–35, however, the commercial banks found themselves in the paradoxical situation where their only hope of eventually securing repayment from many of their borrowers was to continue lending to them, since at that time a cessation of bank lending would have compelled many large firms to close down. It was not in the national interest to allow this to happen. Encouraged by the Government, and supported by the commercial banks, the Bank of England began to give some assistance to industry, though only in selected cases.

Two subsidiaries, the Bankers' Industrial Development Company and the Securities Management Trust, were established by the Bank of England. Aid was given by taking up debentures in the firms to be helped, such assistance generally being dependent on the reconstruction of a company's capital where this was considered desirable. Among firms that received assistance were the Lancashire Cotton Corporation and Shipbuilders' Security Ltd, both of which organisations undertook the rationalisation of their particular industries. The Macmillan Committee on Finance and Industry in 1931 had recommended that there should be a closer connection between the banks and industry. After 1945 the Bank of England indirectly assisted industry through two finance corporations in which it was an important shareholder—the Industrial and Commercial Finance Corporation Ltd, and the Finance Corporation for Industry Ltd. In 1974 these two corporations were merged to form Finance for Industry (FFI).

(iii) *External business*. The Bank of England acts as agent of the Treasury in many matters affecting Great Britain's monetary relations with the rest of the world, as for example, in the management of the Exchange Equalisation Account, exchange control, relations with other central banks and with international monetary institutions, such as the International Monetary Fund, the International Bank and the Bank for International Settlements.

III. THE TECHNIQUES OF MONETARY CONTROL

10. The traditional instruments of monetary policy

A central bank must have power to expand or contract the volume of purchasing power in a country by its control over the commercial banks. In Great Britain this control became possible because the commercial banks (i) thought it prudent to maintain a known liquidity ratio, and (ii) kept a balance which they were able to regard as cash at the central bank. The maintenance of a known liquidity ratio was, however, only customary in the case of English banks and not legally imposed as in some countries. For a long time the English commercial banks maintained a cash ratio of 10 per cent, but in 1946 it was reduced to 8 per cent at the request of the Bank of England. Until 1972, as has been seen, the banks adhered to a liquidity ratio of 28 per cent between their more liquid assets and their total deposits. So long as a known liquidity ratio is maintained, expansion or contraction of credit by the commercial banks depends mainly on the amount of their liquid assets. The English commercial banks have always regarded their balances at the Bank of England as cash since they can withdraw in cash from these balances at any time. Their cash reserves, therefore, consist partly of cash—Bank of England notes and coin—in the tills of their many branches and partly of deposits—bankers' deposits at the Bank of England. Thus, in the days when a bank's main concern was for its cash ratio, a fall in its balance at the Bank of England was regarded as a reduction in its cash reserves. To restore its cash ratio to the required amount it had then to reduce its deposits through a curtailment of its lending.

In 1972 the Bank of England decided that the former liquidity ratios of the commercial banks should be replaced by a new one of $12\frac{1}{2}$ per cent of their sterling deposit liabilities, that is, their more liquid assets—cash, notes and balances at the Bank of England, money at call and short notice, Treasury bills, Government stocks within one year of maturity and a proportion of eligible commercial bills. It is expected that the effect will be to give the Bank of England greater control over the credit policy of the commercial banks.

The ultimate control over the volume of deposits of the commercial banks rests with the Bank of England. The traditional instruments of monetary policy by which the Bank of England exercises this control were Bank rate and open-market operations. Nowadays monetary policy is the joint responsibility of the Chancellor of the Exchequer, the Treasury and the Bank of England. Consider now each of the instruments of policy available to the British monetary authorities today:

(i) *Bank rate*. Known since 1972 as the Bank of England's minimum lending rate, this is the minimum rate at which the Bank of England will discount—or more correctly, rediscount—first class bills. The rate used to be fixed weekly, usually on Thursdays, though in an emergency it could be varied at any specially convened meeting of the Court of the Bank. The importance of Bank rate lay in the fact that other rates of interest used to depend on it—the rate charged to discount houses, the rates charged on advances to customers and the rate offered on their deposit accounts. These rates all used to move up or down with Bank rate. Thus changes in Bank rate aimed at influencing other rates of interest. If it was desired to check credit expansion Bank rate would be raised in order to make borrowing more expensive and so, it was hoped, reduce the demand for loans. When Bank rate was high some forms of business activity that were previously profitable would cease to be so. A high Bank rate could therefore be expected to check business activity. Curtailment of bank lending would then reduce bank deposits and therefore purchasing power in the hands of the community, thereby bringing about a fall in prices, which in turn would be likely to check business activity still further. By lowering Bank rate the cost of borrowing was reduced, credit expansion encouraged and the reverse train of events set in motion. Such at least, was the theory of Bank-rate changes. Bank rate could also be raised for the purpose of checking an outflow of foreign funds from London and so, before floating exchange rates were introduced in 1972, protecting the country's gold reserve. Probably Bank rate fulfilled its external function more effectively than its internal function. When bank rate was low money was said to be cheap. Since 1971 the lending rate for advances of the commercial banks has not been so closely geared to Bank rate as formerly. Their basic lending rate is now known as *base rate*, and this can be varied, should the commercial banks so wish, without any change occurring in the Bank of England's minimum lending rate.

(ii) *Open-market operations.* Even before 1914, when the Bank of England considered Bank rate to be its chief means of influencing the credit policy of the commercial banks, it was usual for the Bank to supplement it by open-market operations. It took this action, it said, in order to make Bank rate "effective." By intervening in the open market to buy or sell securities, the Bank of England could directly influence the size of bankers' deposits. If it sold securities it received payment by cheques drawn on the commercial banks, for most of the buyers of these securities would have accounts with these banks. At the clearing of these cheques transfers had to be made from the commercial banks to the Bank of England. The balances of the commercial banks at the Bank therefore decreased by the amount the Bank had received for the securities sold. Since the commercial banks considered their balances at the Bank as cash, they had to reduce their deposits by calling in some of their loans if they were to maintain their liquidity ratio. By selling securities the Bank of England could thus bring about a reduction in the commercial banks' deposits and, in consequence, in the volume of purchasing power in the country. By buying securities the Bank could increase the reserves of the commercial banks, and so make possible an expansion of credit and the volume of purchasing power. Though the Bank of England used to regard its open-market operations as only complementary to Bank rate, it is probable that its operation in the open market was the really effective instrument and not Bank rate as was commonly supposed.

At the present day open-market operations are undertaken mainly for the purpose of influencing the rate of interest. The Bank of England intervenes in the discount market and the securities market (that is, the stock exchange). In the discount market it employs a Special Buyer, while in the securities market its operations are in the hands of the Government broker.

11. The efficacy of Bank rate as an instrument of monetary policy

There is considerable difference of opinion as to the effectiveness of Bank rate as an instrument of monetary policy. Critics point out that to raise Bank rate had little effect in checking inflation in a trade boom. In such conditions prices and profits are rising, so that even a very high rate of interest is more than covered by the profit earned. Similarly, at the bottom of a depression a very low rate of interest will not encourage businessmen to borrow if they have little expectation of making a profit. It was conceded, however, that Bank rate was more likely to be effective in checking an expansion of credit than in stimulating recovery from a slump. Thus, it was widely felt that Bank rate had proved its ineffectiveness by its failure to end the Great Depression of the 1930s. As a result, from the year 1932 when a cheap money policy was initiated Bank rate remained at 2 per cent until November 1951, apart from a short period in September–October 1939. Thus, for nearly twenty years Bank rate was in abeyance as an instrument of monetary policy. Nevertheless the cheap-money policy was adopted in the first place in order to stimulate a revival of trade, and though slow to do so, eventually it had the desired effect.

The cheap-money policy was continued after 1939 to enable the Government to finance the war cheaply, and in this it was again successful, but it was pursued after 1945, again to keep down the cost of borrowing, even though conditions had completely changed and when inflation had been the main problem.

Before the adoption of a cheap-money policy in 1932 Bank rate used to fluctuate frequently, often being changed more than a dozen times in the course of a single year—in 1875 it was altered no fewer than twenty-four times. During the twenty years 1862–81 it was changed on average over nine times each year; during the twenty years 1894–1913 it was changed on average four and a half times each year. The decline in the use of Bank rate was clear even before 1914. During 1919–32 the average number of changes per year was two and a half, but since 1951 there has been on average little more than one change in the Bank of England's minimum lending rate per year. Since 1972 the highest level reached by this rate has been 15 per cent (October 1976).

Though the *Radcliffe Report* (1959) emphasised that the liquidity position of financial institutions was of greater importance than the supply of money, it regarded variations in the structure of interest rates as an important influence on liquidity. The supply of money is of some importance, but the structure of interest rates is regarded as the vital factor in the situation.

12. Modern instruments of policy

During the period when Bank rate was discredited, especially the years 1945–51, new instruments of policy were employed—physical controls and then fiscal policy. In 1951 the use of Bank rate was revived, and it was employed first in conjunction with physical controls (until these were withdrawn) and later along with fiscal policy.

Other instruments of monetary policy were introduced and developed to supplement the traditional ones, as a means of influencing the money supply.

Consider now some of these adjuncts to monetary policy:

(i) *Physical controls*. As a legacy from the war there were physical controls—rationing of consumers' goods, control of prices, licensing of building, control of investment and exchange control. These were retained until the early 1950s as a means of fighting inflation, but they succeeded only in suppressing inflation without getting rid of it.

(ii) *Fiscal policy*. The use of the budget as an alternative to monetary policy had been suggested as long ago as the 1930s. Then it was suggested that taxation should be eased at the expense of a budget deficit in order to expand demand and stimulate recovery from the slump which then prevailed. It was a simple matter, therefore, to suggest that in inflationary conditions taxation should be increased to provide a large budget surplus in order to reduce purchasing power and the pressure of demand. In fact, the budget has now become an important instrument of policy. Demand can be checked by increasing taxes, especially those imposed on commodities, or it can be stimulated by a reduction of taxation. The budget as an instrument of policy is considered more fully in Chapter 30. In 1961 the Chancellor of the Exchequer began to make use of the *Regulator* to vary taxes and excise duties between budgets by up to 10 per cent. Since 1974 he has been empowered to vary these taxes by up to 25 per cent.

(iii) *Hire purchase*. The volume of hire-purchase business has increased enormously in recent years. In 1975 a sum of over £2,303 million was outstanding in hire-purchase debt, nearly two-thirds of which was owing to Finance Houses. During 1951–70 regulations governing hire purchase were frequently varied to suit economic conditions, the initial deposit being increased or reduced, and the period of repayment shortened or lengthened. To check a recession the regulations were eased to encourage demand, and in times of inflation this policy was reversed to check an excess of demand. Hire purchase had assumed such large proportions that to expand or contract it had an important influence on demand and production. A serious drawback, however, was that only a limited range of goods was affected. In 1971, therefore, following the recommendations of the *Crowther Report*, the use of hire-purchase controls as an adjunct of monetary policy were abolished.

(*iv*) *The Treasury directive.* As at first employed, this was a direct instruction from the Treasury to the commercial banks to restrict their lending. In 1951 and 1952 they were given a *qualitative* directive, that is, they were requested to restrict advances to purposes regarded as being in the national interest. In 1955 and 1957 they were told to reduce their lending by a required amount whatever the purposes for which loans were required—*quantitative* directives. In 1964, 1966 and 1968 banks were instructed not to increase their advances by more than 5 per cent. Since credit restriction by banks can be offset if borrowers can obtain assistance from other financial institutions, the Bank of England more recently has also made its wishes known to the merchant banks, finance companies and other financial concerns.

(*v*) *Special Deposits.* In order to reduce the cash basis for their credit policy the Bank of England can ask the commercial banks for Special Deposits, usually a percentage of the banks' own deposits. This instrument of monetary policy was employed for the first time in 1960. It is really an alternative to open-market operation and supplementary to the Treasury directive. When the Bank of England in 1960 requested Special Deposits from the commercial banks it asked for an amount equal to 2 per cent of their deposits from the English banks and 1 per cent from the Scottish banks. Since then the Bank of England has called for Special Deposits on a number of occasions, then releasing them as conditions have improved. Since 1971 the discount houses also have been subject to calls for Special Deposits in order to bring them into line with the commercial banks. The Bank Return (p. 432) shows the extent to which banks have had to provide Special Deposits.

It may be said, therefore, that for the purpose of fighting inflation or the onset of a recession the British monetary authorities—the Chancellor of the Exchequer, the Treasury and the Bank of England—have now available to them a variety of instruments with which to implement their policy, namely variations in interest rates, open-market operations, Special Deposits and, if they wished to revive them, the Treasury directive, control of hire purchase and physical controls. The employment, at the same time, of a number of instruments of monetary policy came to be known as a "package deal." It might be argued that though by itself variation of interest rates is not always a very effective instrument of policy—or at least slow to take effect—it may nevertheless have an important part to play when used in conjunction with other instruments of monetary policy.

RECOMMENDATIONS FOR FURTHER READING

R. S. Sayers: *Modern Banking*, Chapters 4, 5 and 9.
G. Crowther: *An Outline of Money*, Chapter 6.
The Radcliffe Report on the Working of the Monetary System (HMSO).
R. G. Hawtry: *The Art of Central Banking*, Chapter 4.
J. L. Hanson: *Monetary Theory and Practice*, Chapter 14.

QUESTIONS

1. How, and how effectively, can the Bank of England implement the Government's monetary policy? What are the Bank's other main functions? (SE London)

2. Explain the role of the Bank of England with reference to the Government's monetary policy. (Yorks)

3. Explain the system by which the volume of purchasing power is regulated in the United Kingdom economy and comment on its effectiveness. (RSA)

4. Examine the relationship of the Bank of England to the London Money Market and show how this relationship affects the credit structure of the economy. (RSA)

5. Using the Bank of England as illustration, say what are the major functions of a central bank. (IHA.)

6. Does an increase in the fiduciary issue of a central bank mean that the currency is being inflated? (IT)

7. Can the central bank really control the quantity of money? If it can, why should it? (CIS)

8. Describe the functions of a central bank: what powers should it possess and by what principles should their exercise be regulated? (CIS)

9. What is meant by the "backing of the Note issue"? Is it a necessary condition of a sound monetary system? (GCE)

10. How are the activities of joint-stock banks influenced by the Bank of England? (GCE)

11 How does the Central Bank control the credit policy of the commercial banks? (GCE)

12. What are the most fundamental powers of a central bank? Give reasons for your selection, and show the relations of other conventional central banking powers to these fundamental ones. (Degree)

13. "The Central Bank cannot simultaneously fulfil the role of lender of last resort *and* successfully control the money supply." Discuss. (Degree)

CHAPTER 25

THE CAPITAL MARKET

I. THE DEMAND FOR CAPITAL

1. What is the capital market?

The various financial markets can be distinguished from one another by the length of the term of the loan. Thus, broadly, the money market can be defined as the market for short-term loans, and the capital market as the market for long-terms loans. It would probably be more accurate, however, to describe the money market as the market for call money or very short-term loans, or even more precisely, as the market for loans to the discount market. The capital market then becomes the market for short-term, medium-term, long-term and permanent loans to the Government, industry and commerce. An important function of the capital market is the raising of capital by new issues to the general public and other investors of stocks and shares. The capital market is essentially the market for new issues.

2. The financing of industry

Industry requires both fixed and circulating capital:

(i) *Circulating capital.* In Great Britain firms generally obtain their circulating capital from the commercial banks. The item *advances to customers* in the banks' balance sheets indicates the extent to which banks supply industry with its circulating capital. For the London Clearing Banks in 1975 this item came to over £16,000 million.

Another source of circulating capital is trade credit. In addition to their other functions, wholesalers act as financiers. By allowing them credit wholesalers enable retailers to sell some of the stock they have purchased before paying for it, thereby helping them to finance the holding of stock. The wholesalers themselves borrow from the banks, so that indirectly the banks provide circulating capital for the retail trade. Of recent years there has been a considerable increase in direct lending by the banks to retailers—especially those operating on a large scale—the amount advanced to retailers reaching a total of £474 million by 1975. The bill of exchange provides another means by which a trader can obtain circulating capital, since it enables payment for goods to be postponed until they have been sold. If, as quite likely may be the case, the bill is discounted by a bank, then the transaction is financed directly by the bank.

Thus, in most cases, directly or indirectly, the commercial banks provide industry and commerce with their working capital. Some very large firms, however, finance themselves by providing their working capital from their reserves which have been accumulated from undistributed profits.

(ii) *Fixed capital.* On account of their concern for the liquidity of their assets British banks in the past have been disinclined to provide fixed capital for industry. They do not care to have their assets in the form of shares in companies, and prefer shorter-term loans, even though in practice these are renewable. Many continental banks, however, used to undertake this type of business, but owing to heavy losses in trade depressions they have tended to abandon investment banking. On the other hand, the British banking system has moved to some extent in the opposite direction, though in general assistance to industry is provided through their subsidiary, the finance corporation now known as Finance for Industry (FFI).

Generally, then, British industry has to look to the capital market to provide it with its permanent capital. A man setting up in business for himself as a sole proprietor usually provides most of his capital from his own past savings, supplemented perhaps by a loan from friends or relatives. One of the principal reasons for the sole trader turning his business into a partnership is generally the need for additional capital for expansion, which the new partners provide. The development of the joint-stock company made it possible for projects requiring huge amounts of capital to be undertaken, the capital being subscribed in large or small amounts by a very large number of investors.

The granting of limited liability to joint-stock enterprises by the Acts of 1855 and 1862 made it possible for the man of small means to invest some of his savings in industry without risking the loss of the rest of his savings or his personal possessions. Industry, therefore, obtains most of its permanent capital from the general public, either directly by subscription or indirectly through other institutions, such as insurance companies and investment trusts. The British insurance companies have enormous funds available for investment, and they hold large blocks of shares in the larger limited companies. The knowledge that shares in public companies can be disposed of on the stock exchange at their market prices makes people readier to respond to a company's appeal for subscriptions to its shares. A company may also raise fixed capital by the issue of debentures, which are loans to the company, debenture holders therefore being its creditors. Since interest on debentures is a cost to a company, the amount to be paid is deducted before net profit is calculated, thereby reducing liability to Corporation Tax. Since the imposition of this tax debentures have become a more attractive method of raising capital.

We have seen that many businesses provide themselves with circulating capital from their own resources; some also finance expansion from their profits. Instead of the whole of the profit being distributed as dividend among the shareholders, a sum is retained to provide additional fixed capital. The sole proprietor would look upon such a fund as his savings, and indeed, similarly, the undistributed profits of a limited company are the company's savings. Many small businesses have grown into large firms in this way. At times tax concessions have to be made in order to encourage firms to plough back some of their profits into the business. Clearly, if a company increases its capital by using some of its profits for this purpose, its previously issued share capital does not give a true picture of the amount of capital employed by the firm. In order to correct this, firms sometimes issue bonus shares to their shareholders, the number received by each shareholder being proportionate to their existing holdings. The dividend paid to its shareholders by such a company often tends to remain at a steady level in spite of its progress, but the price of the shares will rise because the growth potential of the company is considered to be good.

3. The control of investment

Whenever the demand for factors of production is greater than the supply, some method of apportioning them among different uses has to be employed. Under perfect competition they would be distributed among different employments according to the demand for them, equilibrium being achieved when the marginal productivity of each was the same in all occupations. As long ago as 1931 the Macmillan Committee on Finance and Industry recommended control of investment. To support his policy of full employment, Lord Beveridge suggested that since investment was easier to control than saving, the two should be brought into line by imposing control over investment.

Control of investment is necessary in time of war to ensure that investment is adequate in the industries essential to the war effort. Control of investment, however, is not generally viewed favourably in peacetime. Nevertheless, in inflationary times there will be a greater demand for factors of production than the available supply, and the demand too for capital will be excessive. Control of investment can then be used to ration capital among the many uses competing for it. An Act of 1946 therefore continued for some years the regulations for the control of investment that had been introduced during the war. The purpose in continuing this control was, in the first place, to ensure that those capital projects considered to be most important in the national interest should be able to obtain the necessary real resources; in the second place, to make possible the planning of both public and private investment. Control was effected through a Capital Issues Committee, to which application had to be made by those desiring to raise capital by the issue of shares or other securities. In general, control of investment has not found much favour in normal circumstances.

In February 1959, therefore, it was decided that only Local Authorities should have to apply to the Capital Issues Committee if they wished to raise money on the capital market. The Government can restrict its own investment by curtailing capital projects in times when there is a heavy demand for labour and other resources. On a number of occasions in recent years Governments have found it necessary to cut down their investment programmes and have often requested Local Authorities to do the same.

4. The new-issue market

An outline of the procedure for floating a public limited company was given in Chapter 6. When the various formalities have been completed the sponsors can then issue a prospectus and appeal to the public to subscribe for the shares. Accepting houses act as issuing houses. The floatation can therefore be placed in the hands of an issuing house. These institutions act like wholesalers, purchasing the entire share issue from the new company at a price slightly below that at which the shares are to be issued to the public. Underwriting of an issue of shares in this way ensures that the full amount asked for will be immediately forthcoming, less, of course, the payment that has to be made to the issuing house for its services. For the sake of their own reputation in the capital market, the best issuing houses handle new issues only after careful investigation of the new companies which seek their services. Merchant banks often act as issuing houses. A recent development is to introduce a new issue of shares through the stock exchange. Application is made to the stock exchange for a quotation for the shares, this introduction being accompanied by an arrangement with a number of insurance companies and investment trusts to take up the entire issue. By intervening in the capital market in this way the stock exchange has widened the scope of its activities. It has always been closely related to the capital market but it is essentially a market for existing securities rather than an instrument for making new issues.

II. THE SUPPLY OF CAPITAL

5. Savings

The supply of capital to the capital market comes partly from individuals and partly from institutions—that is, from the savings of private individuals or firms. A private individual wishing to invest in a company's shares can instruct his banker or stockbroker to purchase them in his name. When a limited company ploughs back some of its profits in effect it obtains additional capital from its shareholders (who in consequence have to accept lower dividends) instead of having to go into the capital market to obtain it. The supply of capital to the market comes from private savings, either directly, as when a man decides to buy shares, or indirectly when an institution, such as an insurance company, collects people's savings and then itself invests them. British insurance companies in 1974 held over £5,600 million in equities (see Table LXIV), that is, in ordinary shares in public limited companies. Other institutions that invest in equities include investment trusts and unit trusts.

As has already been emphasised, British commercial banks as a matter of policy normally invest only in gilt-edged securities (Government stocks), while trustee savings banks are prohibited by law from taking up any other form of investment than Government securities or similar stocks.

6. Investment trusts and unit trusts

(i) *Investment trusts.* The large investor is usually careful to avoid putting all his eggs in one basket. He safeguards himself against heavy losses by spreading his investments over as wide and varied a field as his resources will allow. If he holds shares in a dozen different companies a loss in one may be offset by a gain in another. A small investor who foolishly puts all his savings into one company runs a grave risk of losing all he has invested should misfortune overtake that particular company, and on occasion this happened to what had appeared up to then to be a soundly based company. The investment trust, however, makes it possible for the small investor to spread quite a moderate investment over a large number of companies, thus lessening his risk of loss. Investment trusts are purely financial institutions which use their capital to purchase shares in a number of other companies, the aim being to spread the risk of investment over a wider field. A single share, therefore, in an investment trust may represent a small fraction of a share in each of several hundred different companies. The management of the trust may be free to vary its investments if it thinks such a course desirable by disposing of shares in some companies and reinvesting in others. An investment trust derives its income from the dividends it receives on the shares it holds, and after deducting expenses of management, what remains is available for distribution among its own shareholders. Some investment trusts specialise in particular fields of activity, such as bank, insurance, mining or commodity shares. There are in existence a number of old-established investment companies, the shares of which are bought and sold in the ordinary way on the stock exchange. To invest in these companies, therefore, it is necessary to buy shares.

(ii) *Unit trusts*. At the present day the most popular form of investment trust, however, is the unit trust, which came into existence during the 1930s, although they attracted little attention from investors until the 1950s. During the 1960s a great many new unit trusts were established and the older ones expanded very considerably. In principle they are similar to the investment trust companies, in that they use their funds to buy shares in a large number of companies—perhaps a hundred or more. They obtain their funds, however, by the issue of units, often in quite small denominations—maybe of 25p or even less—and units can be bought direct from the managers of the trust. In the case of a flexible trust the managers have power to vary the investments of the trust at their discretion. Most unit trusts are formed for limited periods of time, though generally the period can be extended. In 1975 the total assets of investment trusts exceeded £7,200 million. In the same year the combined assets of the unit trusts stood at over £2,800 million. The success of both investment trusts and unit trusts depends on the expertise of their investment advisers.

7. Insurance companies

The probability of many risks can be mathematically calculated, and it is against these that insurance can be effected. Insurance is based upon the principle of the *pooling of risks*. Those who insure contribute to a common fund, out of which payments can be made to those who suffer loss. It is possible to insure against such risks as fire, theft, accident, goods in transit, employers' liability, sickness and a great many other contingencies.

Nearly 40 per cent of the total of insurance business is life assurance, so-called because the risk covered is certain to happen at some time. Most of this is not pure assurance, as the endowment policy is now the most popular. In this case the person whose life is assured undertakes to pay premiums for a limited period of time—ten to forty years or until he reaches a certain age. If he dies before the expiry of this term the assurance company pays an agreed sum to his dependants; if he survives he receives the agreed sum, generally with the addition of a bonus, depending on the company's profits. Thus this type of assurance is partly a method of saving. Life assurance probably dates from the seventeenth century, but other forms of insurance are much older, there being evidence of the existence of marine insurance as early as 916 B.C.! Acts of 1870 and 1909 contain provisions for the protection of policy-holders, one of these being the separation of the "life" fund from the funds of any other kind of insurance business the company may transact.

Insurance companies, therefore, have huge funds at their disposal and available for investment, and during the past thirty years these funds have increased enormously. The total income of all British insurance companies has increased from £60 million in 1900 to over £5,000 million in 1974, of which, in the latter year, over £2,500 million was for life assurance. In 1920 the total funds of all these companies came to about £400 million; in 1974 the total was over £23,000 million. It is interesting to note the chief forms of investment

Table LXIV

Investments of British Insurance Companies 1974

Type of Investment	£ million
British Government Stocks	2,841
Commonwealth and Foreign Government Stocks	1,511
Debentures and Preference Shares . .	3,655
Ordinary Shares	5,610
Mortgages (on property)	3,445
Other investments	6,503
Total	23,565

into which the funds of the forty British insurance companies have gone.

During recent years British Insurance companies have invested heavily in British industry and in property.

8. Finance houses

Hire purchase is a method by which medium-term credit is made available to consumers, and is sometimes known as consumer-credit or instalment credit. Generally, the consumer pays a small deposit and the balance, including interest, in equal instalments spread over a period. The credit may be provided by the retailer from his own resources or more probably nowadays by a finance house. Of the total of over £2,330 million of hire-purchase debt in 1974 £1,037 million was owing to finance houses. It is possible too for a manufacturing business to buy new machinery on this system.

The Radcliffe Committee in 1959 reported that there were in existence at that time seventeen large finance houses, and eighteen smaller companies calling themselves industrial bankers, these together being responsible for the financing of more than 70 per cent of all hire-purchase business in Great Britain. The remaining business was in the hands of over a thousand smaller firms. Ten of the large finance houses are controlled by the English commercial banks.

The finance houses raise funds partly by borrowing from the commercial banks, especially when credit is easy, and partly by accepting deposits from the general public, the interest on deposits tending to be high, especially when credit is tight. Some of the larger finance houses and industrial bankers also undertake a certain amount of ordinary banking business, and since 1971 many of them have been recognised as banks.

9. Building societies

These institutions are registered under the *Building Societies Acts*, their main functions being to assist people to purchase houses by instalments. This they do by allowing suitable people to borrow the purchase price against a mortgage on the property. Houses are too expensive for most people to buy outright, but if payment is spread over a period of twenty years house purchase is very little more onerous than the payment of rent. Building societies accumulate funds in order to be able to lend money to their members for the purchase of houses, repayment of the loan being spread over a long period, during which the society holds a mortgage on the property.

By accepting deposits, issuing subscription shares, and paid-up shares, building societies, like insurance companies, collect small savings. In most cases the societies themselves pay the income tax due to the interest paid. The actual interest received by a depositor depends therefore on the rate of tax he pays: the higher his rate of tax, the greater the gross interest he receives. The rate of interest to be paid by the borrower depends on the ease with which the Society itself can raise funds and therefore the rate of interest it has to pay to attract depositors. Building society rates of interest, however, do not change with every change in bank interest rates. Nevertheless, when these rates are high building society rates also tend to be high, and vice versa. Only the reserves of building societies are available to the capital market, and these go into trustee securities. The rest of their funds are used to provide loans to borrowers.

Most building societies are still small, expansion generally having being achieved by natural growth. The Halifax Building Society and the Abbey National are exceptional in having branches in most parts of the country. Although there has been no amalgamation movement among building societies in general comparable with that that occurred with the commercial banks, there have been nevertheless a number of mergers. During the past thirty years there has been a vast increase in the business of British building societies, their total assets expanding by over fifteen times, and the number of members by nearly ten times during this period, though on account of amalgamations, the total number of societies has tended to fall.

10. The provision of medium-term capital

At one extreme there are banks which prefer to lend for short periods, while at the other there is the capital market enabling industry to obtain long-term or permanent capital. The need for the provision of capital for a term intermediate between these two extremes led to the establishment in 1945 of two institutions to supply medium-term loans. These were the Industrial and Commercial Finance Corporation Ltd., the capital of which came from the Bank of England, and the English and Scottish commercial banks (their contributions being proportional to their deposits), and the Finance Corporation for Industry, the capital of which was provided by the Bank of England, investment trusts and insurance companies. The former has power to grant loans of from £5,000 to £200,000, the function of the latter being to provide loans in excess of £200,000. As long ago as 1931 the Macmillan Committee had pointed out the need for institutions to give such assistance, especially to lesser-known firms that would find a public issue unduly expensive. The Industrial and Commercial Finance Corporation commenced its activities in 1945. Most of its customers were private companies seeking additional capital either for expansion or to finance current production or to provide against the incidence of death duties. Before assistance was given, full details were required of a firm's history, activities and financial position. Help may be given by way of loans for ten to twenty years, secured by collateral security, as with bank loans, or by taking up debentures or preference shares in the firm, or in some cases even by acquiring ordinary shares. In 1974 these two finance companies were reorganised and the Finance for Industry (FFI) was formed, the scope of the new corporation being considerably widened to enable it to assist the Government to help ailing firms in the private sector.

III. THE MARKET FOR SECURITIES

11. The stock exchange

A stock exchange is a place where dealings in stocks and shares take place, a market where those desiring to buy stocks and shares are brought into contact with those who want to sell. It is, therefore, primarily mainly a market for existing securities. There are stock exchanges in the chief financial centres of the world, such as London and New York, and in the more important provincial cities in Great Britain. A number of northern stock exchanges combined in 1965 to form the Northern Stock Exchange. In 1972 it was decided to merge all the stock exchanges in the country to form a united stock exchange. The existence of stock exchanges makes it possible for an owner of stocks or shares to dispose of them if he so desires. Stock exchanges serve the capital market by giving liquidity to permanent capital, that is, to securities that have no redemption date. Some Government stocks such as $2\frac{1}{2}\%$ Consols which have no date of maturity and ordinary shares of public companies are also of this type. If there were no stock exchanges it would be difficult for owners of stocks such as Consols or ordinary shares to dispose of them, and people would therefore be less willing to invest in them. Thus stock exchanges assist the capital market by making securities more liquid, thereby encouraging people to invest in them.

The price at which a security can be bought or sold on the stock exchange will depend, as in other markets, on the relative strength of the demand for and the supply of that particular security at a particular time. All sorts of influences affect the prices of shares, through supply or demand. If business prospects are good the prices of shares will generally be high; if prospects are poor prices will be low. The publication of a company's balance sheet will affect the price of its shares, favourably or adversely, as the case might be. Other factors which influence stock-exchange prices are such things as the general economic situation, changes in interest rates, changes in Government policy, the publication of foreign trade figures or even rumours of impending political changes. At the present day there are a number of large institutional buyers in the market such as insurance companies, pension fund managers, investment trusts or unit trusts and, in the gilt-edged market, the commercial banks. Their influence on prices is considerable. The Government broker intervenes in the gilt-edged market for the special purpose of influencing the rate of yield on Government stocks, making use for this purpose of the funds of those Government departments which have money to invest. If the aim is to keep up the rate of yield on Government stocks the broker will enter the market to sell in order to reduce the prices of the stocks; if the aim is to keep down the rate of yield he will go into the market as a buyer in order to raise the prices of stocks. Thus, the rate of yield on Government stocks is largely determined by the Government itself.

Method of doing business. Only members are allowed access to the London Stock Exchange, and these consist of jobbers, of whom there are about 750, brokers, to the number of over 2,500 and their authorised clerks. The brokers act as agents for prospective investors or people with securities to sell. The actual dealers in securities are the jobbers, who tend to specialise in particular types of stocks or shares. Thus one jobber will specialise in gilt-edged securities, another in mining shares, another in the shares of commercial undertakings and so on. A broker wishing to obtain stock or shares for a client will approach a jobber who deals in the required security and ask him to state a price, but without informing him whether he wishes to buy or sell. The jobber will quote two prices, the higher being that at which he is prepared to sell, and the lower that at which he is prepared to buy. Thus, through the brokers and the jobbers buyers and sellers are brought into contact with one another. The London Stock Exchange is a highly organised market, and business is carried on according to a strict set of rules. Since there is easy telephonic communication between the London and provincial stock exchanges and those abroad, the markets in stocks and shares is nearly perfect, prices tending to be the same in all parts of the

A TEXTBOOK OF ECONOMICS

market, even though, as in the case of some shares, the market may be world-wide.

12. Speculation and its control

There are two reasons why people buy stock exchange securities. Most people buy for the sake of investment, that is, with the intention of holding the securities in order to secure a regular income from their capital. Once having obtained these securities they generally retain them, unless a change in their financial affairs makes it necessary for them to obtain cash. So long as they derive what they consider to be a reasonable income from their investments, they may care little about fluctuations in their market prices. This is particularly the case with Government securities that bear fixed rates of interest. A man with an annual income of £50 a year from Consols may be quite unconcerned whether they stand at 65 or 25 in the market, since this has no effect on his income. He would be interested in the market price only if for some reason he had to sell his stock. Then, just as the stock exchange assisted him to buy stocks or shares, so it will help him to sell whenever he wishes to dispose of them.

There are other people, however, who pay little attention to the income to be obtained from securities, but who are keenly interested in fluctuations in their market prices. When they buy they do so because they consider the price to be low and likely to rise. Then when they believe prices are near the peak they sell, because they judge prices will fall. If the market is keen to buy it is said to be "bullish"; if it is keen to sell it is "bearish." Those who buy hoping that prices will rise are known as "bulls"; those who sell expecting prices to fall are known as "bears." These people are speculators, and their aim is to take advantage of fluctuations in the prices of stocks and shares in order to make a quick profit for themselves. Such profits are known as capital gains. Speculators are also to be found on the highly organised markets dealing in securities, foreign exchange, wheat or wool, etc.

It would be wrong to condemn all types of speculation outright. The existence of speculators in a market means that at all times it is possible to buy or sell. The small holder of securities, suddenly finding himself in need of cash, knows that he can sell his securities at the market prices at any time. If there were no speculators in the market there might be times when it would be impossible to find buyers. Speculation, therefore, helps to make securities more liquid. The activities of some speculators tend to steady prices, for they enter the market as buyers when most other people desire to sell, and so they prevent prices falling as much as they otherwise might; when others are wanting to buy they enter the market as sellers, and so prevent an undue rise in prices.

Speculation, however, is to be deprecated when those engaging in it attempt to influence prices by their own actions, trying to push prices down immediately before they buy, or to raise prices immediately before they sell. The prices of shares are important to the economic system because these prices reflect the relative profitability of different lines of production, and a high return on investment in a particular field attracts new capital into that line of production. Speculation of an undesirable kind may therefore result in capital not being employed to the best advantage, and so lead to the misuse of real resources. The greater the risk, the greater the possible profit, and so in times of trade boom the more risky enterprises often find it easier to obtain capital than the less risky but sounder and more socially desirable under-takings. Excessive speculation can lead to disasters such as the historic crash which occurred in Wall Street, New York, in 1929, and which precipitated the Great Depression.

Control of speculation. Various suggestions have been put forward for restricting the activities of speculators on the securities market:

(*i*) It has been suggested that once securities have been transferred to a new owner he should not be permitted to dispose of them until a certain minimum period has elapsed.

(*ii*) Control of investment, that is, new issues, can prevent any serious diversion of real resources to wasteful uses. It ensures priority for those forms of production considered to be in the national interest.

(*iii*) Bank lending for speculative purposes might be restricted. In Great Britain only a relatively small proportion of bank advances is made to stockbrokers, in contrast to the United States, where it is common practice to borrow to finance stock-exchange speculation. It was this, as much as declining confidence, that caused the crash of 1929 to have such far-reaching effects.

(*iv*) A capital-gains tax can be made to fall more heavily on short-term capital gains.

The main thing that stands in the way of controlling undesirable speculation is often the difficulty of distinguishing between speculative dealings and genuine investment. Care must be taken lest any restric-tion of speculation should hamper the raising of capital on the capital market for legitimate purposes.

RECOMMENDATIONS FOR FURTHER READING

B. Ellinger: *The City*.
E. Lavington: *The English Capital Market*.

QUESTIONS

1. How does the stock exchange assist industrial firms in obtaining funds for expansion? (ULCI)

2. "The stock exchange is a market for second-hand securities." "Without the stock exchange, there would be little capital available for new commercial and industrial ventures." Show how these two statements can be reconciled and indicate the main functions of the market. (Wales)

3. The London Stock Exchange is often described as a "perfect market." Give a sufficient description of its work to justify this attribute; and point out how the division of its members into brokers and jobbers may be considered to help towards the attaining of this perfection. (RSA)

4. It is stated that a stock exchange is essential to the proper function of the capitalist system. Examine the economic arguments for a stock exchange in such a system. (RSA)

5. What is a Bonus Issue?

Discuss the desirability or otherwise of such an issue from the point of view of (a) the company; (b) the shareholder; (c) the National Economy. (LC Com.)

6. What do you understand by share capital and loan capital? What factors might cause a firm to decide to finance expansion by one form rather than the other? (CIS)

7. What do you understand by the market for new capital? (GCE)

8. What part does the stock exchange play in the Capital Market in the United Kingdom? (GCE)

9. What factors determine the market value of a joint-stock company's shares on the stock exchange? (GCE)

10. What is the capital market? Discuss ways in which it might be improved. (GCE)

11. Outline briefly the history and present position of British building societies. (Degree.)

12. Discuss the position of life assurance offices as providers of capital. (Degree.)

Part Seven

INTERNATIONAL ECONOMICS

CHAPTER 26

INTERNATIONAL TRADE

I. THE THEORY OF COMPARATIVE COST

1. The origin of international trade

Trade between different countries developed first where one country could produce something desirable which others could not. The Phoenicians became famous in the ancient world for their purple-dyed cloths, which they bartered for other goods with the people of the countries bordering on the Mediterranean Sea. International trade therefore owes its origin to the varying resources of different regions:

(*i*) Mineral resources can obviously be worked only where they are found. Coal nowadays is mined chiefly in the United States, Great Britain, Germany and Russia; iron chiefly in the United States, France, Sweden and Russia; copper in the United States and Chile. Most nickel comes from Canada; most gold from South Africa, and most silver from Mexico.

(*ii*) Many commodities can be grown only under particular climatic conditions or in certain soils. As a result, most rubber is produced in Malaya and the East Indies; almost the entire world supply of jute comes from the Ganges delta; most of the world's coffee comes from Brazil, and most cocoa from West Africa and Brazil; and Italy comes first for the production of lemons.

(*iii*) The inhabitants of a region may develop a special skill for the production of a commodity, which in time may acquire a special reputation for quality. Wines such as champagne, sherry, port, chianti owe their distinctive qualities partly to the special flavour of locally grown grapes and partly to the local method of manufacture. Scotch and Irish whisky have similarly acquired distinction.

By exchanging some of its own products for those of other regions, a country can enjoy a much wider range of commodities than otherwise would be open to it.

2. International division of labour

If international trade took place only in cases where countries could produce what others could not, the total volume of world trade would not have reached its present-day proportions. A glance through the list of commodities entering into any country's trade will show that it imports many things that it could, if it wished, produce for itself—for example, Great Britain imports wheat, dairy produce, meat and wool, all of which it is itself capable of producing. Similarly, the United States imports motor cars, motor cycles, china ware, wool, cotton and linen goods. The reason for this is simply that a country by its own efforts cannot completely satisfy its demands for these commodities. Early in this book it was seen that division of labour within a country enables it to increase the output of everything it produces, even though specialisation entails an increase in the work of distribution. Just as division of labour within the firm can be extended to division of labour within the industry, so division of labour within a country can be extended to the international field, each country specialising in the production of only a few of the things that it is capable of producing, and leaving to others the production of some of the things that it could have produced itself had it so desired. International division of labour or specialisation results in a vast increase in the total world output of all kinds of goods.

A country's choice of the forms of production in which to specialise will be determined according to its advantages over others in the production of these things. If one country has the greatest advantage over others in the production of woollen goods, then it will tend to specialise in the production of that commodity. Another country may specialise in the production of raw wool. Such advantages will accrue to a country if it can produce particular goods of a certain quality more cheaply than other countries. This is known as the *Principle of Comparative Cost*, which is really an extension of the *Principle of Comparative Advantage* previously considered. This theory of international trade was first developed by Ricardo. Comparative cost is considered in terms of what can be produced by a given quantity of productive resources (factors of production)—that is, it is real or opportunity-cost that is involved. For example, in one country it may take 100 units of productive resources to produce 150 units of milk, or 80 units of wheat. In a second country 100 units of productive resources may produce 100 units of milk, or 60 units of wheat. The first country clearly has the greater comparative advantage over the second in the production of both milk and wheat.

Consider again the Principle of Comparative Advantage as applied to individuals. A successful barrister would find it to his advantage to pay a man to attend to his garden rather than do this work himself, for during the time he would have to spend working in his garden he could earn more in his professional capacity than the amount necessary to pay the wages of a hired gardener. The barrister may be both a better lawyer and a better gardener than the man whom he employs, but it will still be to his advantage to specialise in that pursuit for which he has the greater comparative advantage over the other. By undertaking legal work and using part of his earnings to pay his gardener's wages, the barrister is indirectly cultivating his garden. Similarly, it is to the advantage of a nation to specialise in the production of those things for which it has the greatest comparative advantage over others. By specialising in the production of a few things and engaging in inter-national trade, a country produces its imports indirectly.

Just as division of labour within a country increases the work of dis-tribution, so international division of labour makes necessary a vast increase in the exchange of commodities between countries. The greater the amount of international specialisation, the greater, there-fore, will be the volume of international trade, and the greater will be the output of all kinds of goods by the world as a whole.

3. Advantages of international trade

In order to simplify discussion of the advantages of international trade, it is usual to assume that there are only two countries in the world and that only two commodities enter into trade. Let the two countries be Atlantis and Erewhon, and let the two commodities be cloth (typifying manufactured goods) and wheat (typifying agricul-tural products). There are then three separate cases to consider.

Case I. Where each country can produce one commodity, but not the other. Assume that Atlantis can produce cloth but not wheat, and that Erewhon can produce wheat but not cloth. The earliest trade between regions took place on this basis. Without exchange each country will obviously be poorer. If Atlantis can make a bargain for the exchange of some of its cloth for some of Erewhon's wheat the people of both Atlantis and Erewhon will be better off as a result of this trade, for each will then have both cloth and wheat.

Case II. Where each country can produce one commodity more cheaply than the other. Assume next that the employment, say, for a year of 100 units of resources (factors of production) in Atlantis will produce either 100 units (yards) of cloth or 50 units (bushels) of wheat, and that 100 units of resources in Erewohn will produce either 50 units of cloth or 100 units of wheat. Assume further that Atlantis possesses 2,000 units of resources of factors and Erewhon 3,000 units. If each country employs half its resources for the production of cloth and half for the production of wheat, and no exchange takes place, the total output and consumption for these countries will be as follows:

Table LXV(A)

Country	Units of resources	Units of output		
		Cloth		Wheat
Atlantis	2,000	1,000	+	500
Erewhon	3,000	750	+	1,500
World Total . .	5,000	1,750	+	2,000

If now Atlantis and Erewhon specialise in the production of the commodity for which each has acomparative advantage over the other, Atlantis devoting its production entirely to cloth, and Erewhon producing only wheat, their total output will be as follows:

Table LXV(B)

Country	Units of resources	Units of output		
		Cloth		Wheat
Atlantis	2,000	2,000	+	0
Erewhon	3,000	0	+	3,000
World Total . .	5,000	2,000	+	3,000

As a result of this specialisation the total output of cloth has increased from 1,750 to 2,000 units, and the total output of wheat from 2,000 to 3,000 units. If the rate of exchange is taken to be 900 units of wheat for 900 of cloth, then the consumption of each commodity by the two countries will be as follows:

Table LXV(C)

Country	Units of resources	Units consumed		
		Cloth	+	Wheat
Atlantis	2,000	1,100	+	900
Erewhon	3,000	900	+	2,100
World Total . .	5,000	2,000	+	3,000

As a result of specialisation and exchange, Atlantis has increased its consumption of cloth from 1,000 to 1,100 units and its consumption of wheat from 500 to 900. At the same time Erewhon has increased its consumption of cloth from 750 to 900, and of wheat from 1,500 to 2,100. The gain of the two countries is clear:

Table LXV(D)

Country	Units of resources	Units consumed		
		Cloth		Wheat
Atlantis	2,000	100	+	400
Erewhon	3,000	150	+	600
World Total . .	5,000	250	+	1,000

Both countries, therefore, benefit from international trade.

Case III. Where one country can produce both commodities more cheaply than the other. Assume now that the employment for, say, a year of 100 units of resources in Atlantis will produce either 100 units of cloth or 100 units of wheat, and that the employment of 100 units of resources in Erewhon will produce either 40 units of cloth or 80 units of wheat. As before, assume also that Atlantis possesses 2,000 units of productive resources and Erewhon 3,000 units. If each country devotes half its resources to the production of each commodity, and if no specialisation and exchange took place, the respective outputs (and consumption) in the two countries will be as follows:

Table LXVI(A)

Country	Units of resources	Units of output		
		Cloth		Wheat
Atlantis	2,000	1,000	+	1,000
Erewhon	3,000	600	+	1,200
World Total . .	5,000	1,600	+	2,200

In this case Atlantis can produce both commodities more cheaply than Erewhon, but it has a greater comparative advantage in the production of cloth than of wheat. Specialisation and exchange will still be of advantage to both countries. Atlantis will specialise in the production of cloth, because it has a greater comparative advantage in the production of that commodity; Erewhon will specialise in the production of wheat. In this case it is unlikely that Atlantis will give up entirely the production of wheat, for Erewhon can produce only 2,400 units of wheat, even if it devotes all its resources to the production of this commodity. Assume that Atlantis continues to use 10 per cent of its resources for wheat production. Then as a result of this specialisation, but before exchange takes place, output will be as follows:

Table LXVI(B)

Country	Units of resources	Units of output		
		Cloth	+	Wheat
Atlantis	2,000	1,800	+	200
Erewhon	3,000	0	+	2,400
World Total . .	5,000	1,800	+	2,600

The total world output of each commodity is greater than it was before, the production of cloth having been increased from 1,600 to 1,800 units and wheat from 2,200 to 2,600 units. If an exchange is effected of (say) 700 units of cloth for 1,000 units of wheat each country will be able to consume more of each commodity than was possible without specialisation. As a result of international trade each country, therefore, is richer:

Table LXVI(C)

Country	Units of resources	Units consumed					
		Cloth			Wheat		
		Output	Import or export	Total	Output	Import or export	Total
Atlantis . .	2,000	1,800−	700 = 1,100		200+1,000 = 1,200		
Erewhon . .	3,000	0+	700 = 700		2,400−1,000 = 1,400		
World Total .	5,000			1,800			2,600

Thus, it is *comparative* and not *absolute* differences in cost that are important. This case also provides an illustration of a country (Atlantis is this example) importing a further quantity of a commodity (wheat) which it produces itself. Some people in Atlantis might urge that more wheat should be grown and less imported. It can, however, be clearly seen from this example that there would be no *economic* justification for this. Atlantis, like any other country, has only a limited supply of productive resources, and more wheat can be grown there only if resources are withdrawn from the production of cloth or some other commodity. If Atlantis diverts 100 units of resources from the production of cloth to the production of wheat the country will be poorer, for 100 units of resources will produce in that country either 100 units of cloth or 100 units of wheat but in the above example 70 units of cloth can be exchanged for 100 units of wheat.

4. The terms of trade

By terms of trade we mean the rate at which one country's products exchange for those of another. How much wheat Erewhon will have to give Atlantis for a quantity of cloth will depend, as J. S. Mill pointed out, on the strength of the demand of Erewhon for cloth relative to the demand of Atlantis for wheat.

In Case III above it was assumed that these relative demands were such that 100 units of wheat were exchanged for 70 units of cloth. However great is the demand of Atlantis for wheat, not more than 100 units of cloth will be given for 100 units of wheat. If the price were higher it would be more profitable for Atlantis to increase its own production of wheat by curtailing its production of cloth, for the opportunity cost of 100 units of wheat in Atlantis is 100 units of cloth. Similarly, however great is Erewhon's demand for cloth, the highest price that it will pay for 100 units of it will be 200 units of wheat, for the opportunity cost of producing 100 units of cloth in Erewhon is 200 units of wheat. The price of 100 units of cloth, therefore, will be at some point between 100 and 200 units of wheat.

The terms of trade depend, therefore, on the prices of commodities entering into international trade. The terms of trade are said to be favourable to a country when the prices of its exports are high relatively to the prices of its imports. During the 1930s the terms of trade became more favourable to Great Britain because the world prices of primary products—raw materials and foodstuffs—fell more than the world prices of manufactured goods. On the other hand, for a time after 1945 the demand for primary products was so great that the terms of trade turned sharply against Great Britain and continued to do so until 1953. During 1956–62 the terms of trade again became more favourable to Great Britain, as also during 1965–70, as Table LXVII shows.

Table LXVII

The Terms of Trade

1955	.	.	. 86	1966	.	.	. 103
1956	.	.	. 87	1967	.	.	. 105
1957	.	.	. 89	1968	.	.	. 102
1958	.	.	. 96	1969	.	.	. 101
1959	.	.	. 96	1970	.	.	. 104
1960	.	.	. 97	1971	.	.	. 101
1961	.	.	. 100	1972	.	.	. 101
1962	.	.	. 102	1973	.	.	. 90
1963	.	.	. 101	1974	.	.	. 75
1964	.	.	. 99	1975	.	.	. 80
1965	.	.	. 102	1976	.	.	.

N.B. The larger the number, the more "favourable" the terms of trade.

5. Assumptions of the theory of international trade

The Theory of Comparative Costs shows quite clearly that international trade is to the advantage of all countries taking part in it. It is, however, based on a number of assumptions:

(*i*) the existence of perfect competition;

(*ii*) that there is full employment in all countries;

(*iii*) the absence of currency restrictions; and

(*iv*) that trade is free from artificial restrictions, such as tariffs or quotas.

The effects of interference with the freedom of international trade are considered below.

In addition to these important assumptions a number of others are made in order to simplify demonstration of the theory:

(*v*) that there are only two countries in the world, and only two commodities entering into international trade;

(*vi*) that there are no costs of transport, since to take account of such costs will only reduce the range within which the world price of a commodity will fluctuate by the cost of transport;

(*vii*) that expansion or contraction of production in the two countries Atlantis and Erewhon is possible without either diminishing or increasing returns coming into operation. To allow for the possible effects of the Laws of Returns, however, would unnecessarily complicate the exposition.

In view of these limitations it is hardly surprising that practice often differs from theory.

II. RESTRICTIONS ON FREEDOM OF TRADE

6. Free trade

Effects of restrictions on trade. Import duties aim at checking imports by making them dearer; import quotas more directly limit imports to certain pre-determined amounts; both therefore reduce the total volume of international trade. Preferential duties (that is, the imposition of lower rates of duty to certain privileged countries) and exchange control (limiting the amounts of foreign currency people can acquire) both divert trade from its normal channels. Whatever forms the interference with free trade takes, the results are the same—the production of goods in regions that do not possess the greatest comparative advantages for their production, and in consequence a reduction of the total world supply, thereby making the world as a whole so much the poorer economically.

Decline of free trade. Never, however, since the nation-state came into being has any country completely carried out a policy of free trade. The nearest approach to free trade in Europe occurred during the decade 1860–70, when, largely as a result of the influence of Napoleon III, there was an all-round lowering of import duties. In the late nineteenth century there was a reaction against free trade, and both Germany and the United States built up their industries behind tariff barriers. British prosperity under free trade made this country cling to the doctrine longer than other countries, but the Great Depression (1929–35) caused all countries to seek the protection of high tariffs, and in 1932 Great Britain forsook free trade. Efforts to secure a general reduction of tariffs had only a limited success, the World Economic Conference of 1933 being a complete failure.

Towards freer trade. After 1945 there was a widespread desire to reduce tariffs due to a desire to avoid a return to the conditions of the 1930s when international trade shrank to small proportions. The General Agreement on Tariffs and Trade was signed and this in effect set up a permanent organisation that came to be known as GATT, its members including the leading trading nations of the world except Russia. The aim was to secure a general reduction of tariffs as a means of expanding world trade. A number of international conferences were held and each achieved a measure of success so far as manufactured goods were concerned. Under the influence of President Kennedy the United States began to take a more liberal attitude to free trade, and at the GATT conference at Geneva in 1964–7 the United States took the lead in bringing about an even greater reduction of tariffs which came to be known as the Kennedy Round. The reductions were introduced gradually during 1967–72. This was a most remarkable achievement, for previously the United States had been outstanding in favouring protection. There were two reasons for this change of outlook: (i) economic growth requires a wide market for mass-produced goods and therefore an expansion of international trade; and (ii) a desire to reduce the common external tariff of the European Economic Community (EEC). Unfortunately the difficulties both of Great Britain and the United States with their balances of payments led to a revival in both countries of demands for greater protection of home-based industry, especially against competition from Japan. The American "dollar crisis" of 1971 strengthened the protectionist group in that country. To meet the crisis the United States imposed a temporary surcharge on imports as Great Britain had done for a brief period after 1964. In the recession of 1974–7 there was increasing demand in Great Britain for import controls.

7. The case for protection

(i) *Some non-economic arguments.* If the advantages of international division of labour and trade are as strong and irrefutable as economists assert, the student of international trade may well be puzzled by the extent to which Governments impose restrictions on their foreign trade. The actions of Governments, however, are not swayed entirely by economic considerations. When a country aims at economic self-sufficiency the reasons are generally political. For example, a country may wish to protect its farming industry in order to be able to feed itself in time of war, or it may try to build up an iron and steel industry as part of an armaments programme.

If a conference is called to consider a reduction of tariffs a country that had imposed no restrictions on imports would find itself at a disadvantage, since it would have no concessions to offer. It has been suggested, therefore, that a country believing in free trade should nevertheless impose import duties solely to give it bargaining power when negotiating with others for a reduction of tariffs.

(ii) *To assist new industries.* One of the few economically sound arguments in favour of protection is in the case of "infant" industries— that is, newly established industries. If heavy initial fixed costs have to be incurred by a new industry the cost of producing a small output will be very heavy, but expansion of output may be accompanied by decreasing costs. In the early stages of its development the industry may be unable to stand up to its foreign competitors. Unless protected while "young," the industry will never be able to establish itself. A protective tariff for infant industries, however, can be justified only if it is removed once the industry has become firmly established. The difficulty is to decide when protection is no longer needed, for once tariffs have been imposed it is not easy to secure their removal. There is the danger, too, that protection will be given to industries that have no chance of survival without it, so that resources are diverted from more to less advantageous use.

(*iii*) *To protect a country's standard of living.* In countries where the people enjoy high real wages, it is often felt that their standard of living will be undermined if cheap goods are imported from countries where wages are low. The development of manufacturing industry in the Far East has given special point to this argument. A people's standard of living, however, depends on the quantity and quality of their country's factors of production, and high wages are therefore the *result*, and not the *cause*, of favourable conditions of production. To boycott goods produced in a country where wages are low will therefore depress wages still further there, whereas an increased demand for labour, arising from increased demand for that country's products, will raise wages there. Indeed, the basic principle underlying international trade is that costs of production are not the same everywhere. A serious difficulty arises, however, when areas with the greatest comparative advantages develop after a vast amount of highly specific fixed capital has been laid down elsewhere. Great Britain obtained a long start over other countries in most branches of manufacture as a result of its being the first country to experience an industrial revolution. Cotton goods could be made more cheaply in Lancashire then anywhere else in the world at the time of the industry developed there. Great Britain, however, can take advantage of the changed circumstances to import cheap cotton goods, but this meant that factors of production in Great Britain, previously employed on the manufacture of cotton goods, had then to be used in other forms of production. This meant scrapping a large amount of capital, much of it, however, out-of-date, and developing new industries in Lancashire to avoid structural unemployment there.

(*iv*) *Other arguments for protection.* When the production of a commodity abroad is carried on by a foreign monopolist a high tariff may be demanded in order to protect home producers against dumping of foreign goods on the home market at a much lower price than that at which the monopolist is selling them in his own country. This form of price discrimination was considered in Chapter 14.

Sometimes a tariff is advocated in order to correct an adverse balance of payments. If imports exceed exports, duties on imports will make them dearer, and so reduce their volume. If this policy also checks exports, as it may well do if other countries retaliate for their loss of exports by themselves restricting imports, the eventual result will be to reduce the total volume of trade. An excessive demand for imports is symptomatic of an inflationary condition in a country's economy, a situation that can be remedied only by internal monetary policy and not by the restriction of imports. In a trade depression, however, a tariff may be imposed as an emergency measure, for the Theory of International Trade is based on the assumption that there is full employment. If, however, there is heavy unemployment a Government will be inclined to pursue any policy it thinks will alleviate it, regardless of any ill effects it may have for other countries. As already noted, as short-term measures Great Britain imposed a surcharge on imports in 1964.

8. Import quotas

As an alternative to the tariff, restriction of imports can be brought about by means of quotas. These fix the minimum amount of a commodity that can be imported during a particular period. The amount having been determined, licences are then issued to supply countries, stating the maximum amount each is permitted to supply.

A tariff or an import surcharge restricts imports by increasing their prices; import quotas enable a Government to restrict imports to definite quantities. Unless the prices of these goods are also controlled, restriction of imports by quota will tend to raise their prices. When the amount of a quota is determined by a trade agreement with a foreign Government this may be for a period of years. In such cases a fall in world prices is of no benefit to home consumers. In th case of tariffs it is the Government which gains from the higher prices resulting from the import duties, but when imports are restricted by quotas (unless the Government undertakes the buying) the higher price benefits the importers of the commodity.

9. Multilateral v. bilateral trade

By multilateral trade is meant freedom of countries to trade with whatever other countries they please. Bilateral trade occurs when two countries try to balance their trade with one another, and this may be brought about by a trade agreement between them. A diagrammatic illustration of the advantages of multilateral over bilateral trade is given in Figs. 86 and 87.

(*i*) *Multilateral trade.* Assume that there are three countries—Atlantis, Erewhon and Utopia—taking part in world trade, and that there are no restrictions of any kind on freedom of trade, and that all three currencies are freely convertible. In the following table the arrows indicate the direction of a country's exports, the arrow pointing to the importing country. The sign — denotes exports and the sign + imports. The figures denote units of imports or exports. Transport costs are ignored.

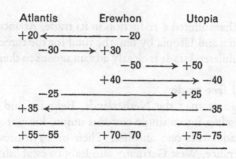

Fig. 86. Advantages of Multilateral Trade.

When multilateral trade is in operation it is not necessary for each country to balance its exports and imports individually with each other country. For example, Atlantis imports 35 from Utopia, although itself exporting only 25 to that country, but this is balanced by an export of 30 to Erewhon, with an import from that country of only 20. The trade of Erewhon and Utopia shows the same features, so that each country exactly balances its trade.

(*ii*) *Bilateral trade.* Assume now that for some reason multilateral trade breaks down and that each pair of countries enters into a trade agreement. Atlantis desires only 20 from Erewhon, and so Erewhon can have only 20 from Atlantis; Erewhon can make an exchange with Utopia of only 40; and Utopia and Atlantis will exchange only 25. In the case of bilateral trade each pair of countries must balance their trade with one another, with the result that the volume of trade between them is determined by the lesser of the two demands for imports. The total trade of the three countries, therefore, will now be as follows:

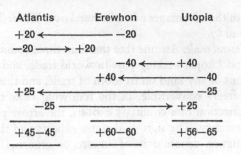

Fig. 87. Bilateral Trade.

Each country has suffered a reduction in its trade, Atlantis by ten units, Erewhon by ten and Utopia by ten, the total for the three having fallen by thirty. Multilateral trade is clearly advantageous to them all.

10. Regional free trade

As long ago as 1947 the Netherlands, Belgium and Luxembourg formed themselves into a single customs union, known as Benelux, to encourage trade with one another. Then in 1952 these three states joined with France, West Germany and Italy to establish the European Coal and Steel Community. It was the success of these two efforts that led these six countries in 1957 by the Treaty of Rome to establish the European Economic Community (EEC), better known in the United Kingdom as the European Common Market. The aim was not entirely economic as it was hoped that economic co-operation would lead in time to political union. They agreed to reduce their tariffs against one another year by year, beginning with a reduction of 10 per cent in January 1959. By 1969 the EEC had established a common market with free trade between members but with a common tariff against the rest of the world.

The UK's attitude to the Common Market was affected by its relationship to the members of the Commonwealth, which all enjoy preferential tariffs in one another's markets. It was on this account that the UK did not become a founder-member of the European Economic Community. Since, however, the UK's trade with countries of the EEC was increasing, this country became anxious not to suffer from being outside this organisation, but in spite of protracted negotiations during 1962–3 and 1967 between the UK and the EEC, agreement could not be reached. Meanwhile the UK had helped to form a second region in which tariffs between members were gradually reduced, known as the European Free Trade Association (EFTA), comprising the United Kingdom, Norway, Sweden, Denmark, Portugal, Austria and Switzerland, with Finland as an associate member. This was a purely economic association without political implications. EFTA kept in line with the EEC in its tariff reductions.

A third area of regional fre trade with seven members was established in 1960, known as the Latin American Free Trade association (LAFTA).

The Theory of International Trade supports the view that a lowering of tariffs between countries will have the effect of increasing their trade with one another. This appears to have been proved in the case of both the EEC and EFTA. After 1958 not only did trade within each group increase but so also trade between the two groups, demonstrating that an increase in international trade is to the advantage of all countries taking part in it.

11. The United Kingdom and the EEC

The Treaty of Rome made provision for the admission of other countries as members of the EEC. In 1961 Greece and in 1963 Turkey were admitted as associate members. In 1963 eighteen African states—most of them former French colonies—became associated with the EEC. In 1965 Nigeria became an associate member. Several other countries have applied for membership.

In spite of its failure to secure admission to the EEC in 1963 and 1967 the UK made a further application in 1970, and after terms of entry had been agreed, this country was admitted to membership in January 1972. Applications from the Republic of Ireland and Denmark were accepted at the same time, and so the EEC increased its membership from six to nine. Entry had to be negotiated as the UK had to protect the interests of New Zealand and developing Commonwealth countries such as Jamaica. The poorer members of the Commonwealth in Africa and the Caribbean became associates of the EEC on the same terms as the former French colonies. The United Kingdom was allowed five years in which to adjust to the new conditions—free trade with the other members of the EEC and a common external tariff with the rest of the world. Thus, EFTA lost two of its members, while the EEC gained three. After some minor modifications of the terms the UK's membership of the EEC was confirmed in 1975 by a referendum.

The main advantages that can be expected to accrue to Great Britain from membership of the EEC is a wider market for its products free of customs duties—four times as large in terms of population, and slightly larger than the home market for US firms. In modern manufacturing industry a wide market is essential if full advantage is to be taken of economies of scale. Competition, however, will be keener, though this could be a spur to greater efficiency. Many industries will gain from increased opportunities for expansion and increased regional specialisation, but some will suffer, and in the early years economic frictions will have to be overcome. One of the inducements impelling the UK to seek membership of the EEC was to increase its rate of economic growth which since 1957 had been slower than that of the Community.

The main disadvantage to membership of the EEC is the necessity to accept the Community's agricultural policy. This means higher prices for farm products and consequently a rise in the cost of living for the people of this country. How much this rise will eventually be is still uncertain. Higher prices, however, should benefit the more efficient British farmers, especially those working large farms. Duties on agricultural products imported from outside the EEC are not received by the importing country, as is generally the case, but paid into a common fund. The United Kingdom, too, will have to make a contribution to the Community's budget of £100 million in 1973, rising to £200 million by 1977.

Some people regret what appears to be this country's movement towards Europe and away from the Commonwealth. In fact, Canada has for a long time been closely linked economically with the United States; Australia has been rapidly increasing its trade across the Pacific in recent years; and since 1960 Great Britain's trade with the Commonwealth has been sharply declining, and equally sharply increasing with Europe.

III. THE BALANCE OF PAYMENTS

12. The visible balance of trade

International trade gives rise to indebtedness between countries. The balance of payments shows the relation between a country's payments to other countries and its receipts from them, and is thus a statement of income and expenditure on international account. Payments and receipts on international account fall into three groups: (i) the visible balance of trade; (ii) invisible items; and (iii) capital movements.

The chief payments and receipts are, of course, for goods—imports and exports respectively. Great Britain's imports are mainly foodstuffs and raw materials, its exports being mostly manufactured goods, though in recent times imports of manufactured goods have tended to increase. Great Britain, therefore, has to pay those countries which supply it with food and raw materials and receives payment from those countries which buy its manufactured goods. Items in the balance of payments which relate to goods are known as *visible* items, and the relation between imports and exports is known as the balance of trade. With one or two exceptions (all since 1956), Great Britain has consistently had an adverse (or passive) trade balance—that is, an excess of imports over exports—every year since 1890. In the nineteenth century, when Great Britain was the workshop of the world, this country generally had a favourable balance of trade.

13. Invisible items in the balance of payments

There are, however, many other payments and receipts which enter into a country's balance of payments, and these are known as *invisible* items, often being called invisible exports in the case of receipts. They arise chiefly as a result of services provided by one country for another and include the following:

(i) *Shipping and civil aviation.* Payment has to be made to shipping and aircraft companies for the carriage of goods and passengers from one port to another.

Table LXVIII
Sea Transport and Civil Aviation

	Sea Transport			Civil Aviation			Overall Balance
	Receipts	Payments	Net	Receipts	Payments	Net	
	£ million	£ million	£ million	£ million	£ million	£ million	£ million
1938	100	80	+ 20				
1952	401	296	+105				
1958	637	615	+ 22	68	60	+ 8	+ 30
1960	644	669	− 25	96	78	+ 18	− 7
1962	647	659	− 12	115	94	+ 21	+ 9
1964	703	728	− 25	135	108	+ 27	+ 2
1966	765	760	+ 5	219	150	+ 69	+ 74
1968	1,053	1,018	+ 35	235	206	+ 76	+ 64
1970	1,361	1,437	− 76	316	279	+155	− 39
1972	1,656	1,687	− 81	410	346	+ 64	− 17
1974	2,621	2,791	−170	619	561	+ 58	−112
1975							

At one time Great Britain enjoyed almost a monopoly of the world's carrying trade, and as recently as 1913 was responsible for carrying 70 per cent of the goods entering into world trade. In spite of the appearance of competitors after the First World War Great Britain still retained over 50 per cent of the carrying trade. The Second World War was a further setback for this country, but by 1970 Great Britain's merchant tonnage, though at that date forming only 12 per cent of the world's total, exceeded that of 1939. An increasing amount of freight is now carried by air and net receipts from this source have more than offset the decline in net receipts from shipping.

(*ii*) *Financial services.* During the greater part of the nineteenth century London was the financial centre of the world, providing banking and insurance services for many countries. As with shipping the two World Wars seriously affected Great Britain's position, but income from this source is still an important credit item to the British balance of payments.

(*iii*) *Investments abroad.* At one time the capital for a considerable amount of industrial development in foreign countries came from British investors. This was supplied in a number of ways. Sometimes British companies with British capital established themselves abroad to build railways (as in South America) or to develop oil-mining (as in Mexico, Iraq and Iran); sometimes British investors put their money into foreign companies; sometimes foreign governments raised loans in Great Britain; sometimes the British Government itself lent to foreign governments. In all cases the effect was the same: dividends or interest had to be paid from other countries to Great Britain, and this income became another invisible receipt. The following table shows how income accruing to Great Britain from foreign investment has increased:

Table LXIX

Income from Foreign Investment

	Receipts	Payments	Net
	£ million	£ million	£ million
1891	—	—	+ 100
1907	—	—	+ 140
1913	—	—	+ 200
1938	205	30	+ 175
1950	271	117	+ 154
1960	634	455	+ 179
1964	888	495	+ 393
1968	1,107	772	+ 335
1970	1,446	899	+ 557
1972	1,762	1,182	+ 580
1974	3,171	1,819	+1,352
1975			

There has been a great increase in foreign investment in this country in recent years. Heavy borrowing on a number of occasions since 1945 has resulted in interest payments increasing.

(iv) *Other invisible items.* Expenditure by British tourists abroad is a payment; expenditure by foreign tourists in Great Britain is a receipt. For a long time this item was a debit but during 1968–70 it became a net credit item. Expenditure of the British Government abroad is now a serious debit item, having risen from only £16 million in 1938 to over £480 million in 1970.

The following table shows the chief items in the British balance of payments:

Table LXX
British Balance of Payments : Current Account

Payments	£ million			
	1938	1970	1974	19–[1]
I. Imports (visible items) . .	835	7,882	21,120	
II. Invisible Items:				
(i) Government expenditure abroad	16	480	880	
(ii) Sea transport and civil aviation	80	1,365	3,352	
(iii) Interest, profits and dividends .	30 } 173	842 } 3,981	1,819 } 8,409	
(iv) Travel (tourism)	40	388	682	
(v) Other items .	7	906	2,416	
Total payments .	1,008	11,863	29,529	
Receipts				
I. Exports and re-exports (visible) .	533	7,885	15,886	
II. Invisible Items				
(i) Sea transport and civil aviation	100	1,506	3,240	
(ii) Interest, profits and dividends .	205 } 405	1,374 } 4,609	3,171 } 9,975	
(iii) Travel (tourism)	28	433	833	
(iv) Other items (net)	72	1,296	2,731	
Total receipts .	938	12,949	25,861	
Balance . .	−70	+631	−3,668	

Source: Annual Abstract of Statistics.
[1] This column can be completed with the latest figures.

14. Effects of capital movements

All the above items in the balance of payments, visible and invisible, affect the current income and expenditure of a country with the rest of the world. The balance of payments is also affected by capital movements. The income from foreign investments is a receipt, but when the investment was originally made, it is a payment. For a long time sterling served as an international currency, but after 1945 it shared this function with the US dollar. Other countries hold balances in these currencies to cover their international transactions. Fear for the safety of these balances, however, may cause holders to convert them into gold, thereby causing an outflow of capital from this country. Capital movements have a disturbing effect on the balance of payments of the countries concerned, as Great Britain has found to its cost on a number of occasions. This danger has been rendered more serious by the increase in the size of these balances. A favourable balance on current account can be turned into an adverse balance by capital movements, as indeed occurred in 1954, 1959 and 1963. In 1955, 1960, 1964, 1968 and 1974, when Great Britain had large deficits in its balance of payments on current account, the situation was aggravated by large deficits also on capital account (see Table LXXI).

15. The British balance of payments

A debit balance on visible trade can be offset by a credit balance on invisible items, or vice versa, so that an overall balance can be achieved. During the early nineteenth century Great Britain generally had a credit balance in its balance of trade, which was mainly devoted to investment abroad, thereby increasing still further its income from foreign investment. As a result, by the second half of the nineteenth century Great Britain was able to import considerably more goods than it exported, the adverse balance in the balance of trade being easily covered by the favourable balance in invisible items.

Table LXXI shows the British balance of payments in recent years. As this table shows, Great Britain has had difficult years, but has achieved a credit balance on current account in most years since 1952, though huge deficits have occurred in recent years. Difficulties have often arisen on capital account, due partly to excessive investment abroad and partly to a temporary loss of confidence in sterling as an international currency, resulting in withdrawals of sterling by foreign holders. Sterling crises, however, tended to occur in those years when Great Britain had an adverse balance of payments on current account, for its reserves of gold and convertible currencies were inadequate to meet

Table LXXI

British Balance of Payments 1938–74

Date	Balance of Trade (Visible Items)	Invisible Items	Current Balance of Payments	Long-term Capital Movements
	£ million	£ million	£ million	£ million
1938	− 302	+ 232	− 70	
1952	− 120	+ 258	+ 138	
1954	− 204	+ 325	+ 121	−191
1956	+ 53	+ 156	+ 209	−187
1958	+ 32	+ 298	+ 330	−193
1959	− 116	+ 248	+ 132	−251
1960	− 404	+ 131	− 273	−185
1961	− 149	+ 135	− 14	+ 77
1962	− 98	+ 191	+ 93	− 93
1963	− 80	+ 204	+ 124	−105
1964	− 519	+ 137	− 382	−116
1965	− 237	+ 188	− 89	− 85
1966	− 73	+ 157	+ 84	− 81
1967	− 557	+ 244	− 313	− 59
1968	− 659	+ 379	− 280	+ 16
1969	− 143	+ 592	+ 449	− 99
1970	− 9	+ 716	+ 707	−204
1971	+ 285	+ 808	+1,093	−273
1972	− 677	+ 791	+ 114	−255
1973	−2,375	+1,165	−1,210	−252
1974	−5,234	+1,556	−3,668	−275
1975				

+ = credit.   − = debit balance.

severe strains. Heavy borrowing from abroad during 1970–5, due largely to the huge increase in the price of oil, caused further difficulty with the balance of payments.

16. The problem of balance

When a country has an adverse or debit balance in its balance of payments it regards it with serious concern; when it has a favourable or credit balance there is satisfaction. Yet for all countries of the world total payments must be exactly equal to total receipts, since every payment is at the same time a receipt. Since, then, all countries cannot achieve favourable balances in the same year, the aim should be a balance, neither more nor less, over a period of time.

In one sense each individual country's balance of payments must balance each year. When all items, both visible and invisible, have been taken into account a balance is achieved by showing how the deficit (if there is an adverse balance) or the amount of the credit (if the balance was favourable) has been covered.

If there has been a deficit it must have been covered in one of the following ways: (*i*) by borrowing from another country; (*ii*) by obtaining assistance from the IMF (the International Monetary Fund) or from the Group of Ten—the world's leading central banks; (*iii*) by imports on credit; (*iv*) by receiving gifts from another country; (*v*) by selling foreign investments; (*vi*) by exporting gold. Most of these methods of covering a deficit in the balance of payments make things more difficult for the country concerned afterwards—loans have to be repaid, goods bought on credit have to be paid for later, the sale of foreign investments reduces future income. Such measures are therefore to be taken only in exceptional circumstances. When the deficit is small it can be covered by an export of gold.

When a country earns a credit balance it can use it to increase its foreign investment or to add to its gold reserves.

RECOMMENDATIONS FOR FURTHER READING

G. Crowther: *An Outline of Money*, Chapter 10.
P. B. Whale: *International Trade*.
R. F. Harrod: *International Economists*.

QUESTIONS

1. Examine the case for and against import duties. (Southampton)

2. Explain what is meant by an adverse balance of payments and examine the methods of correcting it. (UEI)

3. Comment on the view that an extension of international trade will raise the living standards of all those countries which engage in it. (RSA)

4. Explain clearly what is meant by an adverse balance of payments. Discuss the measures which a government can introduce to try to bring about an overall surplus. (RSA)

5. Explain what is meant by the "infant industry" argument in support of protective tariffs. (LC Com)

6. What do you understand by the "Theory of Comparative Costs"? Can it be applied to home trade? (AIA)

7. How does inflation affect our export and import trade? (Exp.)

8. Distinguish between the Balance of Trade and the Balance of Payments and explain the meaning of (*a*) unrequited exports, and (*b*) invisible exports. (IMTA)

9. Why do countries trade with each other? Is it ever desirable for a country to restrict the amount of international trade it permits its inhabitants to participate in? (CIS)

10. "It is comparative advantage, not absolute advantage, which determines the pattern of trade between countries." Elucidate and discuss. (CIS)

11. How is a country affected by a change in its favour of the terms of trade? (CIS)

12. Import controls are a way or correcting an unsatisfactory balance of payments. Discuss the objections to their use. (IB)

13. What part do capital movements play in the United Kingdom Balance of Payments? (GCE)

14. In Malanesia a unit of resources will produce either 100 yards of cloth or 20 units of steel. In Indolaysia a unit of resources will produce 90 yards of cloth or 15 units of steel. Explain the effects of international trade on production of each of the commodities in each country. (GCE)

15. What are invisible exports and invisible imports? Give examples of both and discuss their relative importance for the United Kingdom. (GCE)

16. "The main justification of tariffs is to protect the industries of advanced nations from the unfair competition of backward ones." Discuss. (GCE)

17. Make out a *reasoned* case for imposing an import tariff or quota on a specific good of your choice. (GCE)

18. What is meant by "deterioration in the terms or trade," and for what reasons may this occur? Can such a deterioration ever be to the advantage of the country suffering it? (DPA)

19. "Living beyond their means." Does this well describe citizens in any country with a balance of payments deficit? (Degree)

CHAPTER 27

FOREIGN EXCHANGE

I. THE GOLD STANDARD (TO 1914)

1. International payments

All the early forms of money, as already noted, were commodities that were wanted for their own sake, and many of these things were generally acceptable to people of different nationalities. With money of this kind, therefore, international payments presented no special difficulties, being almost as easy to make as payments between merchants of the same country. When the precious metals, silver and gold, came to be used as money they were even more widely accepted. Then, when coins began to circulate they were readily accepted for their silver or gold content (their value often, for one reason or another, being less than their face value), even though they might not always be wanted as coins. It was only because coins were convenient that they were preferred to metals that had to be weighed out, and merchants were assisted by money-changers in the exchange of coins of different sizes and weights issued under the aegis of different authorities. In all these cases payments arising out of international trade were relatively easy to make, especially in days when the volume of trade was small.

At the present day the most important kind of money in most countries is bank deposits with inconvertible paper money as the principal sort of cash. No one, however, wants inconvertible paper money for its own sake. It is of value to foreigners only if they wish to spend it in its country of origin, though they may be willing to accept it if they know that they can easily exchange it for their own currency. The main means of payment in use today for the settlement of international transactions are: (*i*) the foreign bill of exchange; (*ii*) the bank draft; (*iii*) the documentary credit, for which it is necessary to open a credit at a bank in the exporter's country; and (*iv*) the telegraphic transfer which enables a bank deposit to be transferred expeditiously from the importer's bank to that of the exporter. For all these means of payment between people in different countries the banks act as intermediaries. To facilitate international payments British banks maintain balances in the local currency at their overseas branches in commercial centres abroad or at local banks which act as their agents. Similarly, a large and increasing number of foreign banks have branches in London for the purpose of holding sterling balances. Since London is still the leading financial centre of the world, with the most highly developed money market, more international payments are made in sterling than in any other currency. Consequently the sterling balances held by foreign banks in London are much larger than the balances held abroad by British banks. However, the use of the US dollar for international payments has enormously increased in recent times, one effect of this being the opening in London of many more branches of American banks.

International dealings are complicated by the fact that each country has its own currency, and a balance of payments can be compiled only after prices expressed in many different currencies have been converted to a common denominator, namely, that of the currency of the country concerned. The method by which a balance of payments is brought into balance varies according to the system of foreign exchange in operation at the time. It is necessary, therefore, to understand the working of the various systems of foreign exchange that over the years have been tried if the present day problems of foreign exchange are to be appreciated.

2. Features of the gold standard

On the full gold standard, as it operated down to 1914, the monetary unit consisted of a fixed weight of gold of a definite fineness; the price of gold was fixed by law; and there was complete freedom to buy or sell gold, to import it or to export it. When Great Britain was on the gold standard the Bank of England was legally obliged to buy gold at £3 17s. 9d. and to sell it at £3 17s. 10½d. per standard ounce, eleven-twelfths fine. Changes in the supply of gold or in the demand for it could have no effect therefore on its price in terms of money. A change in the price of gold could be seen only indirectly through changes in the prices of other things: a fall in the price of gold meant that fewer other things could be obtained in exchange for a given amount of it; a rise in its price meant that more of other things could be obtained for the same amount of gold. There was thus a close relation between the supply of gold and the prices of other things.

The mint par of exchange. The rate of exchange between two currencies on the gold standard depended therefore on the quantity of gold in a unit of each. When the gold sovereign (pound sterling) contained the same amount of gold as a French 25-franc piece the rate of exchange between the two currencies was 25 francs to the pound. This was known as the mint par of exchange.

Gold points. A heavy demand for French francs in Great Britain would raise their price there. So long as France was on the gold standard and its paper francs were convertible for gold, the price of francs in Great Britain could not rise above the cost of transporting gold between the two countries. Similarly, the price could not fall by more than this amount, for if it did, paper money could be purchased and exchanged at a profit for imported gold. Thus, when countries are on the gold standard the rate of exchange between their currencies can fluctuate only within these narrow limits—that is, between the specie or gold import and export points. The extent of fluctuations would depend in each case on the cost of transport and insurance, so that on the full gold standard the rate of exchange between sterling and American dollars would be liable to slightly wider fluctuations than the rate of exchange between sterling and French francs.

3. The dual functions of the gold standard

The gold standard really performs two functions, to a certain extent separate and distinct:

(i) *The internal gold standard.* On the full gold standard, gold coins were in circulation and on demand bank-notes could be exchanged for gold. This meant that an adequate reserve of gold had to be kept to meet this demand. In some countries the law insisted upon the maintenance of a gold reserve proportionate to the note issue. In Great Britain the *Bank Charter Act* of 1844 permitted a small fiduciary issue, but the rest of the issue required a full gold backing. The amount of cash in the country then depended on its stock of gold. If this stock increased the quantity of cash could be expanded; if it declined the amount of cash had to be reduced. On the gold standard the volume of cash was then directly and rigidly controlled; the volume of bank deposits being dependent on the amount of cash held by the commercial banks, this kind of money also was indirectly controlled.

(ii) *The external gold standard.* In the international field the gold standard provides stability of exchange rates between different currencies, for the rate could not fluctuate beyond the limits of the gold points. Fluctuating exchange rates, however, handicap international trade, merchants being reluctant to make forward contracts if a change in the rate of exchange is feared. On the gold standard, a country with an adverse or debit balance of payment would have to make up its excess of payments over receipts by the export of gold; while a country having a favourable or credit balance would import gold.

The interaction of the functions of the gold standard. Since a single gold reserve had to serve both internal and external needs, the export or import of gold to meet the needs of the balance of payments would also affect the internal situation. An export of gold reduces the gold basis for the internal currency, the volume of which would therefore have to be reduced. To accomplish this the banking system would have to adopt a policy of *deflation*. Bank rate would be raised, and by open-market operations the central bank would reduce the cash reserves of the commercial banks which, in their turn, in order to maintain their cash ratio, would reduce deposits by restricting loans. As a result, internal prices—including wages—would fall. This would make foreign goods relatively dearer, and the effect would be to check imports, while the export of home-produced goods would be stimulated by their lower prices on the world market. Thus, by increasing exports and reducing imports an adverse balance of payments would be rectified.

If, on the other hand, a country on the gold standard had a favourable balance of payments it would receive an inflow of gold from abroad. This would increase the cash basis for the internal currency, and the banking system would then adopt a policy of credit expansion —*inflation*—in order to increase the quantity of money. This would raise prices and wages, and increase the demand for imports, but exports would be discouraged by their higher prices. In this way, a favourable balance would tend to disappear. Thus, it was said, the gold standard was self-regulating in character, a deficit or surplus being "automatically" corrected.

The diagram on page 494 illustrates the working of the gold standard.

Thus, the "rules" of the gold standard compelled a country to deflate when it was losing gold, and to inflate when gold was flowing in. Provided that these two rules were obeyed the balance of payments was "automatically" brought into balance. The report of the Cunliffe Committee (1918) described the working of the gold standard on these lines. It is extremely doubtful, however, whether the gold standard ever worked quite so smoothly as the Cunliffe Committee believed.

4. Advantages and disadvantages of the gold standard

Advantages. The gold standard had great advantages: (*i*) Except for the fiduciary issue the size of a country's money supply depended on

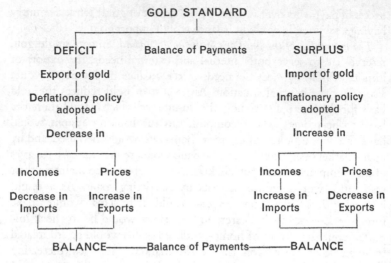

Fig. 88. The Gold Standard.

its stock of gold, and so it became impossible for an over-expansion of credit to occur. Therefore, there could be no hyperinflation on the gold standard. (*ii*) In the international sphere the gold standard provided traders with the benefit of fixed rates of exchange. (*iii*) if a country kept to the "rules" of the gold standard (to inflate when it was gaining gold, and to deflate when it was losing gold) its balance of payments could generally be left to take care of itself.

Disadvantages. It was not until the 1920s and 1930s that it came to be seen that the gold standard had serious defects. (*i*) Internal purchasing power could be increased only if more gold was acquired. Critics of the gold standard pointed out that an expanding economy required the volume of purchasing power to be more elastic than this, for industrial development should not be dependent on a country's stock of gold. (*ii*) The principal drawback to the gold standard, however, was that it linked internal monetary policy too closely to the requirements of the balance of payments, thereby making it impossible for a country to pursue an independent monetary policy. If gold was flowing out, an internal policy of deflation had to be followed irrespective of whether, because of a high level of unemployment, the internal economic situation required a policy of credit expansion. If gold was flowing in, an inflationary internal policy was required even though credit expansion at the time was considered to have proceeded far enough. However, it is only very rarely that this sort of situation was likely to arise. On most occasions the policy required by external difficulties was also equally appropriate to the internal situation. For example, an inflationary internal situation tends to upset the balance of payments by stimulating imports to an excessive degree; and in such circumstances a policy of deflation would bring the internal inflation to an end and at the same time correct an adverse balance of payments. In fact, it is rare that difficulty with the balance of payments on current account is independent of the internal monetary situation. (*iii*) A further disadvantage of the gold standard was the necessity of maintaining an additional gold reserve to support the internal note issue.

II. FLEXIBLE EXCHANGE RATES (1919–25)

5. Determination of the rate of exchange

On the outbreak of war in 1914 the gold standard was suspended, though fixed rates of exchange remained. For some years after the war, however, the rates of exchange between many currencies were permitted to fluctuate freely or, to use a modern term, to float. Thus, the value of the pound sterling in terms of US dollars immediately fell from 4.76½, the rate at which it had been fixed for the duration of the war, to 3.40. On this system the price of one currency in terms of another depended on the relation its supply and the demand for it in the foreign-exchange market. The supply of pounds sterling increased in France if Great Britain imported goods from that country, while the demand for sterling in France depended on the French demand for British exports. A series of different exchange rates would thus emerge between each pair of countries engaging in trade, depending on the relative strength of their demands for each other's products. If, however, sterling could be bought in France and sold at a profit in, say, the Netherlands speculators would immediately intervene in the market and continue to operate until the same rate of exchange eventually prevailed in all centres. Speculation in foreign exchange is known as *arbitrage*.

The Purchasing Power Parity Theory, as refined by Cassel, attempted to show that under a system of flexible exchange rates the rate of exchange between two currencies depended on the relative price levels in the two countries. If, for example, the rate of exchange between sterling and French francs moved from 150 to 200 francs to the pound it was thought to be due to a rise in prices of 33⅓ per cent in France. Though this theory contains an element of truth it is nevertheless open to serious criticism.

(*i*) It is difficult to compare purchasing power in different countries because different groups of people do not all buy the same assortment of goods.

(*ii*) A change of demand can affect the exchange rate. For example, if the British demand for French perfume increased it would increase the British demand for French francs on the foreign-exchange market, and so raise the price of francs in terms of sterling. As a result all French goods, not only perfume, would be dearer to the people of Great Britain and, without any change in the French demand for them all, British goods would be cheaper to French buyers. Apart from imports, however, the relative cost of living in the two countries would remain unchanged. When exchange rates are free to fluctuate they are responsive also to speculative, political and psychological influences. Freely fluctuating exchange rates were revived (under the name of "floating" rates) by many countries in the 1970s including Great Britain.

6. Flexible exchange rates and the balance of payments

On a system of flexible exchange rates, just as on the gold standard, the balance of payments could be left to take care of itself. An adverse balance resulting from an excess of imports, would cause the supply of the country's currency on the foreign-exchange market to increase relatively to the demand for it. Therefore, its price in terms of other currencies would fall. Thus imports, being dearer, would be discouraged, and exports being cheaper, would be stimulated, so that a balance would eventually be achieved. If the rate of exchange between sterling and French francs were 120 francs to the pound, an increase of French imports from Great Britain would increase the supply of French francs in the market, and so cause the franc to depreciate, perhaps to 180 francs to the pound. As a result British people would then be able to buy French goods previously costing one pound for two-thirds of the price, and so French exports to Great Britain would increase. To the French people, however, goods formerly costing 120 francs would cost 50 per cent more, and so they would tend to import less than before from Great Britain. Thus, on a system where exchange rates are free to fluctuate the currency will *depreciate* in terms of others in the case of a debit balance of payments, and to *appreciate* when there was a credit balance.

7. Advantages and disadvantages of flexible exchange rates

Advantages. When its exchange rate is free to fluctuate a country can pursue at any time whatever monetary policy suits the needs of its own internal situation. If it considers that mild inflation to be desirable to stimulate business activity this policy can be adopted. In fact, when flexible exchange rates are in operation a country need never adopt a policy of deflation. On the gold standard the needs of the balance of payments dictate the internal monetary policy, but with freely fluctuating exchange rates the balance of payments is brought into equilibrium by the rate of exchange. On or off the gold standard, however, the internal and external situations affect one another. Inflation at home will increase imports and discourage exports, and so lead to a loss of gold in the one case and depreciation of the currency in the other. No government can ignore for long a situation in which its currency is rapidly depreciating on the foreign-exchange market.

Disadvantages. The chief drawback to freely fluctuating exchange rates is the harmful effects of fluctuating exchange rates on international trade. There is, too, a greater danger of a runaway inflation, for though the gold standard does not prevent inflation (all countries on the gold standard to inflate together), it does put an effective brake on inflation in a single country. Shirking unpopular policies—increased taxation or credit restriction—a weak government may be tempted to take the easy way out of its difficulties by financing its activities through inflation. It is perhaps significant that during 1919–25 when exchange rates were free to fluctuate there were many severe inflations. Again in 1974–6 when Great Britain suffered its most severe bout of inflation this occurred during a period when sterling was free to float on the foreign exchange market.

III. THE RESTORED GOLD STANDARD (1925–31)

8. New forms of the gold standard

(i) *The gold bullion standard.* It was the chaos of the monetary systems in the years following the First World War that made the authorities in many countries believe that recovery could be achieved only by a return to the gold standard. The Cunliffe Committee (1918) recommended that Great Britain should follow this course. In 1922 the gold standard was restored in Austria, in 1924 in Germany, in 1925 in Great Britain and in 1928 in France. Great Britain did not, however, return to the full gold standard, for under the restored standard there was no gold coinage. Paper money was convertible, but only in exchange for gold bars, each weighing 400 ounces and worth at the time about £1,560. The gold bullion standard had two advantages over the full gold standard: (*a*) it was not necessary to incur the expense of replacing worn coins, nor (*b*) was there any need to maintain a gold reserve against the internal note issue, although of course, a gold reserve was still required for international settlements.

(*ii*) *The gold exchange standard.* Some countries sought to obtain the advantages of the gold standard without having a gold reserve at all. Instead they kept their gold exchange standard reserves in a currency based on the gold standard. This was known as the gold exchange standard. The Scandinavian countries adopted this form of gold standard and chose to keep their reserves in sterling—mainly in Treasury bills. The advantage of this system was that a country's reserves could earn interest, whereas the guarding of a stock of gold involves considerable expense. The disadvantage, however, was that countries on the gold exchange standard became dependent on the "parent" country, for if the "parent" country left the gold standard the value of the reserves of all countries linked to it on the gold exchange standard would depreciate. The drawback of this system to the "parent" country was equally great. The slightest sign of strain in that country's balance of payments would lead to heavy withdrawals of capital. Great Britain's difficulties in 1931 were aggravated in this way.

9. The breakdown of the gold standard

Various causes led to the breakdown of the gold standard:

(*i*) *Not obeying the "rules."* The gold standard was successfully operated before 1914 because generally those countries adhering to it obeyed the rules. The first rule, it will be remembered, was that if there was an outflow of gold a policy of deflation must be adopted, and the second rule was that in case of an inflow of gold an inflationary policy was required. During the period of the restored gold standard, however, countries were less willing to keep to the rules. Deflation was both unpopular and difficult to carry out, for a contraction of credit requires a reduction in prices and wages, and trade unions were stronger in 1925 than in 1910 in resisting cuts in wages. It was not possible to deflate to the required extent because wages were difficult to adjust. Deflation was unpopular because it checks business activity, since falling prices reduce profit margins. Similarly, a country receiving gold was often unwilling to inflate for fear that a rise in prices might check its export trade. The United States imported a huge amount of gold, but it was "sterilised," that is, it was not allowed to influence the cash basis for credit expansion. After 1928, France acted in a similar fashion. It should be emphasised, however, that the rules were easier to carry out before 1914 than after 1925, as in the period of the restored gold standard the necessary adjustments—that is, the extent of inflation or deflation—were much greater than had been previously required. To obey the rules during 1929–30 would have required Great Britain to deflate in a time of depression and the United States to inflate while still experiencing a trade boom and inflation.

(*ii*) *Capital movements.* In the pre-1914 period, most big movements of capital were for long-term investments. During the years following the First World War a mass of short-term funds came into existence, and this "refugee capital" or "hot money" moved from one centre to another. Safety rather than the rate of interest was the prime consideration, so that a high Bank rate, instead of attracting foreign investment, came to be looked upon as a sign of weakness and actually caused a withdrawal of funds. The repayment of war debts and reparations payments also added to post-war difficulties.

(*iii*) *The over-valuation of sterling.* When Great Britain returned to the gold standard in 1925 the pound sterling was given the same value in terms of US dollars as it had in 1914. Sterling was an international means of payment and the reasons for selecting this rate was mainly to maintain the prestige of London as the leading financial centre of the world. It was, however, widely acknowledged at the time that this rate greatly overvalued sterling, thereby making this country's imports relatively cheap and its exports dear. The amount of deflation required was too great, and prices and wages could not be reduced to the necessary extent. The consequence was that a trade recession beset Great Britain fully two years ahead of the world trade depression.

In contrast, the French franc at one-fifth of its pre-1914 parity was under-valued and for a time France enjoyed a favourable balance of payments and an inflow of gold.

Devaluation. In exceptional circumstances, when it is clear that a currency is over-valued by the rate of exchange, a country may decide to devalue its currency in order to remain on the gold standard.

When there is a fundamental disequilibrium in a country's balance of payments due to over-valuation of the currency, and the amount of deflation required to correct it is very great, devaluation is justified. Like deflation, it will cheapen exports and make imports dearer (in terms of other currencies), but unlike deflation, there will be no need to reduce *money* wages. It is, however, a remedy to be applied only in case of dire necessity, for stability of exchange rates is the principal advantage of the gold standard, and fear of further devaluation may destroy confidence in a currency. Great Britain, for example, would have been perfectly justified in devaluing at any time during 1925–31. On the other hand, there was really no justification whatever in 1933 for the devaluation by the United States of the dollar to 60 per cent of its previous value in gold, thereby giving a rate of over $5 to £1 sterling. France devalued the franc on several occasions.

Immediate cause of Great Britain's leaving the gold standard. After the collapse of the mark in the great German inflation of 1923 Germany would have been unable to buy from abroad at all had it not been for loans from the United States and Great Britain. The trade depression hit the United States in 1930 and American financial assistance to Germany abruptly came to an end. Fear of the consequences of this led those of Germany's creditors who could do so to withdraw funds from that country. This, and the general collapse of world prices, brought on a financial crisis in Germany in 1931. It was well known too that Great Britain was heavily involved in Germany, and so both its creditors and countries on the gold exchange standard, as well as others with sterling balances, began to withdraw their short-term loans from London. Confidence in Great Britain's ability to remain on the gold standard was further shaken by this country's large budget deficit in 1931. Although both the United States and France came to Great Britain's assistance with loans, it proved to be impossible to withstand the heavy drain of gold, and therefore, in September 1931, Great Britain had to leave the gold standard. During the years 1931–6 one country after another left the gold standard.

IV. EXCHANGE CONTROL

10. Aims of exchange control

When countries left the gold standard in the 1930s there was no desire to return to freely fluctuating exchange rates, for too many people, especially in Central Europe, remembered the severe inflations suffered in the previous decade. In most cases, therefore, some form of exchange control was introduced. The aim might simply be to keep exchange rates stable, as was British policy during 1932–9, and this could be achieved by official intervention in the foreign-exchange market. On the other hand, the aim might be to maintain a rate of exchange either higher or lower than the equilibrium rate of a free market. A country "pegging" the rate at a low level—that is, under-valuing its currency—did so to stimulate its export trade. New Zealand followed such a policy after 1933. A policy of over-valuation might be pursued in order to bolster up confidence in the currency at home, or to cheapen imports during time of war or preparation for war. Thus the German mark was over-valued in 1931. Consequently, strict measures of exchange control were necessary to maintain the exchange rate, for over-valuation encourages imports, and checks exports.

11. Exchange intervention

After Great Britain left the gold standard sterling was at first free to fluctuate, and by 1932 it had steadied itself at about 70 per cent of the value on the gold standard. The aim of British policy at that time was to stabilise the exchange rate for sterling. The British Treasury there-fore established an *Exchange Equalisation Account*, for which the Bank of England acted as agent. The sterling resources of the Account were in Treasury bills, and these funds were used for intervention in the foreign-exchange market. At the time when the British Exchange Equalisation Account was set up, confidence in sterling was returning, and as a result, the Account was able to acquire a considerable amount of foreign currency. The aim was to counteract those fluctuations in the value of sterling on the foreign-exchange market which were due to causes other than changes in the demand for imports and exports—for instance, to cut out, if possible, the effect of movements of refugee capital. If sterling was being sold on the foreign exchange markets, the Account bought sterling; if, on the other hand, there was a demand on the market to buy sterling, the Account sold sterling for other cur-rencies. Thus the system was adopted by Great Britain before 1939 was a very mild form of exchange control, since no restrictions were im-posed on the acquisition of foreign currency by British people.

In 1936 both the United States and France established Exchange Equalisation Accounts. In the same year an agreement was made between these two countries and Great Britain whereby each country undertook to buy back its currency from either of the others in ex-change for gold. These three countries also agreed not to alter the parity of their currencies without consulting one another. Thus, in a modified form, the gold standard was revived in the international field. Rates of exchange, however, were not rigidly fixed as on the gold standard, but reasonable stability over a period was assured. It would have been possible for Great Britain to return to the gold bullion standard in 1933, but the new system was considered to be preferable to it.

On the outbreak of war in 1939, Great Britain, too, imposed a rigid system of exchange control, and, with some modifications, this was continued for some time after 1945. To maintain the over-valued pound Great Britain therefore had to adopt a policy of restriction on exchange transactions. As in the pre-1939 German system, foreign currency could be obtained only through the Central Bank, although in Great Britain each person was allowed a small amount of foreign currency for private purposes. Since 1959 (except during 1966–70) there has been in effect little restriction on the amount of foreign currency available to British residents for foreign travel, but the Bank of England has restricted private investment abroad.

12. Exchange restriction

Germany over-valued its currency by pegging the mark above the equilibrium rate. This encouraged imports and checked exports, so that it became necessary to restrict the amounts of foreign currency available to the German people. If this had not been done, the Germans, remembering the great inflation of 1923, would probably have rushed to change marks for other currencies, and the mark would have become worthless for the second time in eight years.

The German Government then proceeded to build up the most rigid and comprehensive system of exchange control ever known in peace-time. Germans who wanted foreign currency had to apply to the Reichs-bank for it. Foreign currency was available only for purposes approved by the Government. The foreign trade of Germany came under the control of the Reichsbank and soon imports came to be restricted to things useful to a rearmament programme. At the same time Germans who acquired foreign currency were compelled to sell it to the Reichs-bank. Even foreigners who had acquired German marks in Germany were forbidden to exchange them for their own or any other currency, and had to accept credits in *blocked accounts*, on which they could draw only for expenditure in Germany itself. A system of multiple exchange rates eventually developed, the rates varying according to the purpose for which the foreign currency was required. In the end trade with Germany was reduced almost to barter.

V. INTERNATIONAL INSTITUTIONS

13. The sterling area

The division of the world into different currency areas, and parti-cularly the strength of the dollar and the weakness of the pound for some years after 1945, gave new life to the sterling area. The members of the sterling area are those countries which have found it to their advantage to keep their currencies linked to sterling. Its membership has changed from time to time, but it has usually included most of the countries within the British Commonwealth, although Canada has never been a member. An important feature of the sterling area has always been its flexibility and adaptability. It will be useful to trace its development.

(i) *Before 1914*. The sterling area had its origin in the period before 1914 when Great Britain, a mature, industrially developed country, was at the head of an empire of large, diverse, economically un-developed territories. Great Britain's powerful economic position enabled it to devote its balance of payments surplus to loans to these and other countries, for Great Britain possessed the financial institutions necessary for this type of business. The trade of the British self-governing dominions and colonies was chiefly with and largely financed by the home country. Even after the Dominions had de-veloped their own banking systems, the Bank of England continued to act as their central bank and the place, therefore, where they kept their reserves.

(ii) *Between the two World Wars*. The development of a gold-exchange standard, whereby some countries held their reserves in sterling instead of in gold, gave the sterling area a new importance. When Great Britain left the gold standard in 1931, so did all the other countries which kept their reserves in sterling. These countries formed the nucleus of a block that desired to keep their currencies relatively stable. The stability of prices in Great Britain after 1931 was in striking contrast, both to prices in the countries which remained on the gold standard, and to prices in Great Britain itself before 1931. This en-couraged other countries, which preferred to keep their currencies linked to sterling rather than to gold, to join the sterling area. It was, however, an entirely voluntary association, without any central means of control, simply comprising countries desirous of linking their currencies to sterling and keeping their external reserves in London. Generally, fixed exchange rates prevailed between the members, though some of them found it necessary to change the parities of their currencies from time to time. Besides Great Britain, the members of the British Commonwealth and the Scandinavian countries, the sterling bloc at one time also included Argentina, Japan and France.

(iii) *1939-45*. On the outbreak of war in 1939 most of the neutral countries left the sterling area. For the first time it received legal recognition, and Great Britain became the official guardian of the gold and dollar reserves of the entire bloc. In 1939 strict exchange control was imposed between the area and the rest of the world, though its operation was left to individual members, thus even in war-time maintaining the voluntary character of the association. Shipping diffi-culties would, however, have made it difficult for any member to abuse its freedom to import goods from outside the sterling area.

(iv) *After 1945.* The post-1945 currency difficulties and the need of Great Britain and many other countries to curtail their purchases from the dollar area increased the importance of the sterling area. The drain on the area's gold and dollar reserves led to an agreement among members to restrict their use of dollars to the utmost, for after 1945 the main concern of the sterling area was protection of its gold and dollar reserves which, as a banker to the sterling area, Great Britain held. When a member of the sterling area acquired US dollars they were passed over to the British Treasury in exchange for sterling. After 1945 the sterling area, though still an organisation without rules, was given greater cohesion by periodic meetings of members and the establish-ment of permanent committees in London. The sterling area owed its continued existence to the fact that its members evidently considered membership to be advantageous to them. It was no mean achievement for Great Britain to retain its leadership of the sterling area during the changing conditions of the twentieth century. During recent years, however, the proportion of Great Britain's trade with the sterling area has been declining. Long before joining the European Economic Com-munity (EEC) Great Britain's trade with Europe was increasing. Sterling's reduced role as an international currency has also tended to weaken many member countries' link with Great Britain, as also did this country's joining the EEC. Another factor weakening the sterling area was the adoption in 1972 by Great Britain of a "floating" (that is, flexible) rate of exchange. In 1973 the sterling area was reduced to the United Kingdom, the Republic of Ireland, the Isle of Man, the Channel Islands and Gibraltar.

14. The need for a new system

The policies adopted during the inter-war years had reduced inter-national trade to meagre proportions. While the Second World War was still being fought, consideration was already being given, par-ticularly in Great Britain and North America, to the problem of post-war international exchange. The aim was to establish a system of international exchange that would maximise world trade. Trade would have to be multilateral, and so bilateral agreements would have to cease;

exchange rates would have to be reasonably stable, and changes in rates be agreed upon. Devices such as multiple exchange rates and blocked accounts, invented by the exponents of exchange control, would have to be abandoned. All restrictions on the acquisition of foreign currencies would have to be abolished, and all currencies made freely convertible—that is, freely exchangeable at the official rate of exchange for any other currency. The gold standard would have satisfied most of these conditions, but it was felt to be too rigid, since it required the immediate export of gold whenever a country had an adverse balance of payments, however temporary it might be. Against the gold standard there was, too, the loss of independence over internal monetary policy. Flexible exchange rates offered the other extreme, giving freedom over domestic policy, but fluctuating exchange rates. What was desired, if possible, was the advantages of both systems without their disadvantages—a difficult, if not impossible thing to achieve.

Simultaneously, currency plans were worked out in both Great Britain and the United States, the British plan being associated with the name of Lord Keynes. Both aimed at fostering multilateral trade through stable exchange rates and unrestricted convertibility of currencies; both favoured the establishment of an international institution to be responsible for the working of the new scheme, and the introduction of an international currency; both also favoured the retention of gold in international settlements. The main differences between the two plans were due chiefly to the different interests of Great Britain and the United States. The Keynes Plan proposed the establishment of an international institution with power like a bank to grant overdrafts in order to make possible an increase when required in the volume of international currency. It was more expansionist than the American plan, and less dependent on gold. The two plans were discussed at an international conference at Bretton Woods in 1944, the final scheme leaning rather more to the American than to the British plan. Though proposed by both countries the idea of an international currency was not adopted.

15. The International Monetary Fund

Under the Bretton Woods Agreement the International Monetary Fund (IMF) was established to work the scheme, and operations began in March 1947. The principal features of the scheme were:

(i) *Rates of exchange*. By an agreed date member countries had to declare the par values of their currencies. After the great upheaval caused by the war, it was exceptionally difficult to determine with any degree of accuracy what this should be. It was decided that the pound should be worth 4.03 US dollars.

(*ii*) *Convertibility*. All currencies were eventually to be freely convertible, but a transition period of five years was envisaged, during which some measure of exchange control would be permissible.

(*iii*) *Changes of parity*. Once selected, parities were generally to be regarded as fixed, and member countries agreed to consult the Fund before making any change. The consent of the Fund, however, was not required for changes up to 10 per cent, provided that the change was due to a fundamental disequilibrium in the member's balance of payments, that is, disequilibrium resulting from over- or under-valuation of its currency. If the balance of payments was adverse, depreciation was permitted; if the balance was favourable, appreciation of the currency was allowed. If a change of parity greater than 10 per cent was desired, the permission of the Fund had to be obtained first, the Fund to give its decision within seventy-two hours, if the total change was no greater than 20 per cent. For greater changes no time limit was set.

(*iv*) *The pool*. The International Monetary Fund was to be provided with a pool consisting of gold and members' currencies. Member countries had to make contributions to this pool according to the quotas assigned to each. Of this quota, 75 per cent could be contributed in the member's own currency, the remainder being either entirely in gold or in gold and US dollars. Table LXXII shows the quotas of come of the members. Quotas were increased in 1959, 1965, 1970 and 1976. Since 1976 the amounts have been reckoned in terms of Special Drawing Rights (SDRs). Previous to that the unit had been the US dollar. (In 1976 the £ sterling was equal to 1.73 SDRs).

A member country could obtain from the Fund in any one year foreign currency in exchange for its own up to 25 per cent of its quota. Thus Great Britain could, immediately the Fund started its operations, obtain up to $325 million from the pool in exchange for sterling; France could obtain $112.5 million; Australia $50 million. At no time, however, had there to be in the Fund currency of any member of a greater value than double its quota.

The main purpose of the pool was to allow a country to have an adverse balance of payments to a limited extent and for a limited period. Beyond these limits an adverse balance required an outflow of gold, and steps had then to be taken to restore equilibrium. To this extent the new system allowed more latitude than the gold standard. It was not the

Table LXXII

International Monetary Fund Quotas

Country	1945	1965	1976 (Proposed)	
	$ million	*$ million*	SDRs *million*	%
United States . . .	2,750	5,160	8,405	21.5
United Kingdom . .	1,300	2,144	2,925	7.5
West Germany . .	—	1,200	2,156	5.5
France	450	985	1,919	4.9
Japan	—	725	1,659	4.2
Canada	300	740	1,357	3.5
Italy	—	625	1,240	3.2
India	400	750	1,145	2.9
Netherlands . . .	275	520	948	2.4
Belgium	225	422	890	2.3
Australia . . .	200	500	790	2.0
Brazil	150	350	665	1.7
Iran	—	192	660	1.7
Spain	—	150	557	1.4
China	—	—	550	1.4
Mexico	90	270	535	1.4
Sweden	145	325	450	1.2
South Africa . . .	100	200	424	1.1
Nigeria	—	—	360	0.9
Denmark	120	260	310	0.8
Norway	120	240	295	0.8
Pakistan	—	—	285	0.7
Malaysia	—	—	253	0.4
New Zealand . . .	75	150	155	0.6
Bangladesh . . .	—	—	152	0.4
Ireland	50	100	155	0.4

purpose of the Fund, however, to make it possible for a country to have persistent adverse balance.

(*v*) *Scarce currencies.* A widespread demand for a currency would reduce the Fund's stock of it. If this stock fell below 75 per cent of a member's quota the Fund could declare that currency to be *scarce*, and it is then the duty of the Fund to ration the scarce currency among the countries demanding it. Two courses were then open to the Fund: (*a*) it could increase its stocks of the scarce currency by buying some of it for gold; (*b*) it could borrow from the member concerned.[1]

16. Two international banks

(*i*) *The International Bank for Reconstruction and Development.* A new International or World Bank also was established, although the Bank

[1] For the reform of the Bretton Woods system see pp. 512–13.

for International Settlement (BIS) set up after the First World War was still in existence. The International Bank (IBRD) is a separate institution from the International Monetary Fund, and obtains its funds partly from the contribution of its members and partly from the issue of dollar bonds. The purpose of the Bank is to assist countries with more serious difficulties than those for which they might seek assistance from the IMF. Loans, which are usually only made available to Governments, can be obtained from the Bank to assist reconstruction or to further economic development. A number of countries have received financial assistance from the International Bank. Other international financial institutions include the International Finance Corporation (IFC) to assist private capital investment, and the International Development Association (IDA) to promote the economic development of the less-developed areas of the world and thus to supplement the activities of the World Bank.

(ii) *The Bank for International Settlements (BIS)*. This bank was established in 1930 to enable the principal central banks to co-operate in dealing with international financial problems of the day. Though primarily a European institution, its headquarters being in Basle, Switzerland, it might have been expected that the setting up of the World Bank would have made it redundant. It has survived because of the remarkable way in which it has adapted itself to changing conditions. Its transactions are with central banks. It became banker too to a number of international institutions including the Organisation for European Economic Co-operation (OEEC) and the European Coal and Steel Community (ECSC). During the 1960s it made central bank co-operation its main concern. Meetings are held regularly each month to enable the respresentatives of the member central banks to exchange views on current international monetary problems and decide what course of action the bank should take. In addition to its dealings in gold and foreign exchange with its member banks it intervenes in the foreign-exchange market on its own account whenever it considers this course to be necessary. The Group of Ten, comprising the seven leading members of the BIS together with the central banks of the United States, Canada and Japan, on occasions has made loans to the IMF in order to increase the resources of that institution.

VI. RECENT INTERNATIONAL MONETARY DEVELOPMENTS

17. The devaluation of sterling (1949)

In 1945 Great Britain received a loan from the United States sufficient, it was thought, to cover anticipated deficits in the British balance of payments over the next five years. A condition of the Washington Agreement was that sterling be made freely convertible in 1947 so that the Bretton Woods scheme could be put into operation as soon as possible. But 1947 was much too soon, a transitional period of five years having been expected. The drain on Great Britain's resources was so severe that convertibility of sterling was maintained for only five weeks.

The failure of Great Britain to maintain convertibility of sterling, however, made the United States realise the serious effect of the war on the British economy. Marshall Aid to Great Britain and other countries of Western Europe was the result. American assistance speeded up European recovery. Great Britain's difficulties with its balance of payments were largely due to the war, but it was felt in many quarters that the disequilibrium in Great Britain's balance of payments was of a "fundamental" kind, and therefore to be overcome only by a devaluation of the pound. The choice of a rate of £1 = $4.03 had been more or less arbitrary, and it soon became clear that this rate greatly over-valued the pound. In spite of official denials that sterling was to be devalued, fear of it made merchants in dollar areas postpone purchases from Great Britain. In September 1949, therefore, the pound was devalued from $4.03 to $2.80—that is, by about 30 per cent. At the same time a number of other countries devalued their currencies. Devaluation can succeed in correcting an adverse balance of payments only if imports, by becoming dearer, are checked, but this will not occur if the demand for imports is inelastic. Nor will exports be stimulated by the fall in their prices unless foreign demand for them is elastic. Again, if rising prices, resulting from devaluation, lead to wage increases the inflationary spiral will be set in motion and the problem will recur.

Failure to maintain convertibility of sterling in 1947 made the British monetary authorities reluctant to risk a second failure, which could have had a disastrous effect on the commercial and financial prestige of this country. The full development of multilateral trade, however, is impossible unless currencies are freely convertible, and so the achievement of convertibility remained the aim. The crux of the problem was that Great Britain's reserves were inadequate. One by one, however, restrictions on sterling were relaxed. Most important was the reopening of the foreign-exchange market, and although the British monetary authorities through the Exchange Equalisation Account intervened only to keep sterling fluctuations with the US dollar within the range of 2.82 and 2.78, this provided an indicator of the strength of sterling. If the rate was near the upper limit it meant that sterling was strong and in great demand in exchange for other currencies with a tendency for the reserves to increase, but if the rate was near the lower limit it indicated a demand to sell sterling with a consequent fall in the reserves. It was not, in fact, until 1959 that at last sterling was given convertibility.

18. The devaluation of sterling (1967)

The period 1951–67 was punctuated by a series of sterling crises during which lack of confidence in sterling as an international currency led to heavy withdrawals from London. Crises of this nature occurred in 1951, 1955, 1961, 1964 and 1967. On each of these occasions Great Britain was in difficulties with its balance of payments on current account, generally the result of an internal upsurge of inflation, except in 1961 when the revaluation of the West German and Dutch currencies adversely affected sterling. In times of crisis the inadequacy of Great Britain's reserves brought a fear of a further devaluation of sterling.

Since both sterling and the US dollar served as international currencies they have been subjected at various times to severe strain, both countries on occasion having difficulties with their balances of payments. In the case of the United States this was entirely due to the enormous assistance given by that country to developing nations, its balance on current account invariably being favourable. Great Britain's difficulties with its balance of payments were mainly the result of the inadequacy of its gold and dollar reserves during the period when fixed exchange rates were in operation. The United States too experienced a severe drain on its gold reserves which, during the 1950s, had been so large.

In spite of assistance from the IMF, the BIS and the Group of Ten and a high Bank rate, Great Britain in 1967 could not stop the drain on its reserves. The reason for this was the growing feeling abroad that sterling was overvalued at $2.80 to the pound. In fact, in 1967 sterling had to be devalued to $2.40 to the pound. In 1949 most other countries in the Sterling Area and Western Europe devalued their currencies in line with sterling, but in 1967 only a few other devaluations took place. Some British writers would have preferred sterling to have been devalued two or three years earlier in order to end the huge deficits in the British balance of payments.

Though rather slow to take effect devaluation eventually made it possible for Great Britain from 1968 to achieve substantial surpluses in its balance of payments. The severe inflation of 1969–71, however, whittled away the advantages derived from the devaluation of 1967. The succession of sterling crises and two devaluations in twenty years has led to suggestions that more flexible or floating rates should be adopted to give a wider range of fluctuations than was permitted under the Bretton Woods scheme.

19. International liquidity

At the present day most international payments are made either in sterling or US dollars, supplemented by gold. During the past twenty-five years the world economy and world trade have been expanding at a more rapid rate than ever before. The output of gold from the mines could not keep pace with this rate of expansion. Sterling and the US dollar, therefore, played a useful role in making good this deficiency in international means of payment. The falling value of money throughout the world aggravated the situation by widening the gap when countries had difficulties with their balances of payments. To meet this situation the IMF has increased members' quotas several times. As already noted, the Group of Ten agreed to make additional funds available to the IMF if required.

In spite of these efforts it was still felt that the existing means of international payment were inadequate for the needs of the modern world. Eventually it was decided that the IMF should be empowered to issue new reserve units known as Special Drawing Rights (SDRs), the amount available to each member being based on its IMF quota. Thus, at the first allocation in 1970, out of a total of $3,414 million, the United States received $867 million, Great Britain $410 million, West Germany $410 million and France $202 million. The SDR is a composite unit of sixteen leading currencies. SDRs are regarded as a permanent addition to each country's reserves but transferable only between central banks. It is expected that distributions will take place annually.

20. The breakdown of the Bretton Woods scheme

From 1945 to 1971 the US dollar was regarded throughout the world as equivalent to gold, its convertibility for gold being taken for granted. Under the Bretton Woods scheme only the United States was obliged to buy or sell gold at a fixed price. Other currencies were given fixed rates of exchange in terms of gold or US dollars. In fact, parities were related to the US dollar and so only indirectly to gold. During the early years of the operation of the scheme dollars were "scarce," but gradually they became more plentiful and many countries began to hold their reserves in US dollars instead of gold or sterling. At one time it was said of the Bretton Woods scheme that it was a modified form of gold standard: in fact, it eventually became a dollar standard.

In the 1940s and 1950s the position of the dollar as the world's leading currency was unchallenged. As a result it became widely acceptable as a means of international payment. The vast amount of aid given by the United States to many countries, the increasing use of Eurodollars and the cost of the war in Vietnam eventually undermined the US balance of payments. For years the United States had run a deficit though maintaining a credit balance on current account, and these deficits had been a useful addition to international liquidity, but gradually the country's huge gold reserves were depleted, and then in 1971 for the first time in over fifty years the United States found itself with a deficit on current account. In terms of other currencies, especially the Japanese yen, the US dollar was over-valued. Drastic measures were taken. In August 1971 the monetary authorities of the United States declared that the dollar was no longer convertible for gold.

The move towards flexible exchange rates. The action of the US monetary authorities in 1971 threatened the entire IMF system with its fixed rates of exchange and dollar standard. After a bried period of uncertainty floating rates of exchange were widely adopted and other currencies at first appreciated in varying degrees in relation to the US dollar. For some years Canada had had a floating rate, and in 1971 West Germany went over to this system. Great Britain adopted a floating rate in 1972, and other countries followed. The drawbacks to flexible exchange rates were discussed earlier in this chapter. In favour of flexible rates it can be said that there will no longer be crises over devaluation or revaluation, for action will no longer be required to protect a country's gold reserves since the internal monetary system did not now depend on gold. No longer would any country be able to obtain trading advantages by deliberately undervaluing its currency. Nevertheless at Bretton Woods the founders of the IMF deliberately chose fixed exchange rates from a realisation of their advantage to international trade. Not unnaturally, therefore, the IMF is opposed to floating rates and only regarded them as a temporary device until new rates could be negotiated.

The Smithsonian Agreement (December 1971). This was the final attempt of the International Monetary Fund to retain fixed exchange rates, the core of the Bretton Woods system. At a meeting of the Group of Ten in December 1971 the United States agreed to devalue the dollar by 8 per cent and new rates of exchange were fixed in terms of the US dollar. It was also decided that the margin of variability from the new rates should be widened from 1 to $2\frac{1}{4}$ per cent, this giving sterling a rate of \$2.55–\$2.66 to the £. As when sterling was devalued in 1967 all currencies did not keep in line in relation to the US dollar. Some European currencies appreciated in terms of sterling (*e.g.* those of West Germany and Switzerland), some kept in line with sterling (*e.g.* France) and some depreciated slightly (*e.g.* Italy and Sweden). Only the Japanese yen (previously grossly undervalued) appreciated by the full extent of the devaluation of the US dollar.

The exchange rates adopted under the Smithsonian Agreement lasted only six months. Since then flexible rates have been in operation, and gold has ceased to be the international standard. Whether this system of foreign exchange will be more successful in the 1970s than it was in the 1920s remains to be seen. Those who favour floating exchange rates believe that conditions today are quite different from those in the 1920s when flexible rates were last in operation. There is no doubt that under the Bretton Woods scheme during the 1960s many countries became too pre-occupied with balance of payments difficulties. World economic conditions, however, rarely run smoothly for long, and the most serious problem the nations have had to face since the adoption of flexible exchange rates has been the huge increase in the price of oil. Nevertheless, since Britain went over to a floating rate for sterling its value in relation to other leading currencies fell by 40 per cent during the five years to October 1976. In relation to the US dollar sterling has almost continuously declined, falling in late 1975 to \$2.02 to the £.

Reform of the Bretton Woods system. Throughout 1972–4 committees set up by the IMF struggled without success to agree to the lines on which the Bretton Woods system should be reformed. At a meeting of the IMF in Jamaica in January 1976 it was agreed that gold should no longer have any special status in the world's monetary system. Over a period of four years the IMF was to sell 25 per cent of its gold, the profits on this sale to provide a trust fund to assist member countries in difficulties with their balances of payments. A further 25 per cent of the IMF's gold was to be returned to the contributing countries. The

IMF had to accept floating exchange rates (it could not have done otherwise) but envisaged an eventual return to fixed parities. Quotas were revised to take account of the relative changes that had taken place since the last revision in the relative economic importance of members, and this was somewhat to the disadvantage of the United Kingdom.[1] The amount each member country was permitted to borrow was increased from 100 per cent to 111.25 per cent of its quota.

RECOMMENDATIONS FOR FURTHER READING

G. Crowther: *An Outline of Money*, Chapters 7–10.
J. L. Hanson: *Monetary Theory and Practice*, Chapters 7–9, 18, 19.
R. S. Sayers: *Modern Banking*, Chapter 6.
White Papers on *Balance of Payments*.

QUESTIONS

1. Does a floating exchange rate help to remedy an adverse balance of payments? Discuss. (S E London)

2. To what extent can the devaluation of the currency be expected to rectify a deficit in the balance of payments? (Yorks)

3. Give an account of the operations of the International Monetary Fund and suggest how its services might be improved. (R S A)

4. Describe the events leading to the formation of the Exchange Equalisation Account and how it has been operated. Is the Account still operating? (LC Com.)

5. In your estimate would it be possible to create an international currency, and if such a currency system were introduced would it have any practical advantages? (LC Com.)

6. Write a short essay on the transition from the international gold standard system as it worked before 1914 to the managed currency systems of the present time. (SIAA)

7. Consider the advantages and disadvantages of flexible exchange rates. What might be done to reduce the disadvantages? (CIS)

8. What do you mean by the gold standard? What was the difference between the gold standard of 1913 and that of 1925–31? (IB)

9. Describe briefly the functions of the International Bank established under the Bretton Woods Agreement. Having regard to these functions, do you consider it correct to describe the institution as a bank? (IB)

10. What determines the external value of a country's currency in a freely operating foreign-exchange market? (GCE)

[1] The 1976 quotas are shown in Table LXXII (p. 507).

11. In what circumstances will a country benefit from currency devaluation? (GCE)

12. Would a floating exchange rate help to remedy an adverse Balance of Payments? (GCE)

13. It has been contended that the Bretton Woods Agreement was tantamount to a return to the gold standard. Give your reasons for agreeing or disagreeing with this contention. (DPA)

14. What case was or could be made for the return to the gold standard in 1925? How far did subsequent events expose weaknesses in the case? (Degree)

15. Give a brief account of the underlying and immediate causes of this country's abandonment of the gold standard in 1931. (Degree)

16. Do you consider the purchasing-power parity theory to be an adequate explanation of the equilibrium rate of exchange between national currencies? (Degree)

17. In what circumstances would you recommend a country to raise the foreign-exchange value of its currency? (Degree)

18. Compare the role of gold under (a) the gold standard, and (b) the International Monetary Fund. (Degree)

Part Eight

ECONOMICS AND THE STATE

CHAPTER 28

THE EXPANSION OF THE ECONOMIC ACTIVITY OF THE STATE

I. FROM LAISSEZ-FAIRE TO NATIONALISATION

1. *Laissez-faire* and its decline

The emergence of the nation-state in the fifteenth and sixteenth centuries led governments to seek to regulate trade, and particularly to restrict imports. By the eighteenth century the mercantilist system was well-established. This system aimed at increasing the wealth, measured in terms of gold and silver, of a country regardless of the effects on others. Imports were subjected to heavy duties or prohibited outright, and exports were encouraged by subsidies. Then in 1776 came the publication of *The Wealth of Nations*, in which Adam Smith strongly criticised the mercantilist views. Economic intervention by the State he condemned as "folly and presumption." The adoption by Great Britain of a policy of *laissez-faire* in the nineteenth century was largely due to the influence of Adam Smith. For the greater part of the nineteenth century the *laissez-faire* view was held. The State, it was believed, should not intervene in the economic life of the country unless it could be shown to be essential to the welfare of the people. As the century progressed the State found it necessary to intervene to an ever greater extent. Gradually the way was prepared for the abandonment of *laissez-faire* in the twentieth century.

It was only with great reluctance, therefore, that the State at first intervened to regulate the employment of women and children in the mines and factories. It was only slowly, too, that it took upon itself the task of providing free education for all. By 1914, however, a comprehensive body of factory legislation had been built up, elementary education was compulsory and free, secondary education inexpensive, many regulations existed for safeguarding the health of the people, and a limited scheme of national insurance covering old age pensions, sickness and unemployment had been introduced. Throughout the nineteenth century Parliament kept a watchful eye on the activities of the railways, to prevent the development of monopoly, and railway rates were controlled. Amalgamations of railways were frowned upon, just as were bank amalgamations later. The issue of bank-notes was restricted by the *Bank Charter Act* (1844). The development of the limited company eventually led to the growth of a body of company law for the protection of the public. In the sphere of foreign trade, however, the doctrine of free trade, at least in Great Britain, remained triumphant for a few years longer. In these various ways the State began to take an active interest in the social and economic life of the nation. The only commercial undertaking operated by the State, however, during the nineteenth century was the Post Office, a service provided by the State since 1657. It expanded its activities by taking over the telegraph and telephone services in 1897.

2. New forms of State activity (1919–39)

During the First World War the Treasury undertook the issue of £1 and ten-shilling notes, but the Bank of England took over the issue in 1928. During the twenty years, 1919–39, the link between the Treasury and the Bank of England became closer, the policy pursued by the Bank being influenced by the Treasury to a greater extent than ever before. Shortly after Great Britain left the gold standard the Exchange Equalisation Account was established to enable the Treasury to buy or sell foreign currencies or sterling in order to influence the exchange rates of sterling on the foreign-exchange market.

Between the two World Wars State intervention in economic affairs was further increased. Faced by the impact of the Great Depression Great Britain in 1932 had to abandon free trade, a policy to which this country had clung tenaciously for so long, a tariff on a wide range of imports being imposed. The Great Depression was responsible, too, for the Government establishing marketing boards for milk, potatoes, etc., and regulating the import of bacon and some other commodities by import quotas. In cases where monopolies had to be permitted the Government set up public corporations to operate them as, for example, in 1927 when the British Broadcasting Corporation was established. Then in 1933 the London Transport Board was brought into being to take over public transport in the London area.

Social insurance was extended in 1929 to include widows' pensions, and in 1937 the scope of the scheme was widened still further to bring in salaried workers.

In all these ways the State extended its activities in the social and economic fields, By 1939 state activity thus covered a wide range of services:. (*i*) protection of workers by factory legislation; (*ii*) the provision of a national system of education; (*iii*) the provision of welfare services; (*iv*) housing; (*v*) control of monopoly either by regulation of charges (as with railway rates) or by setting up public corporations to operate monopolistic enterprises.

3. State planning

Features of the period since 1945 have been (*i*) the extension and improvement of the social services; (*ii*) increased State intervention in economic affairs; and (*iii*) the nationalisation of a number of industries.

By 1945 all parties in Parliament were agreed that a more comprehensive scheme of social insurance should be provided. Family allowances were introduced in 1946, and the full scheme came into operation two years later. All people, irrespective of income, and whether employed or self-employed, were brought within its scope. Benefits include payments during sickness and unemployment, retirement pensions, widows' pensions, maternity and funeral grants. It is more correctly a scheme of social security rather than of social insurance, for its financing has required an increasing contribution from the national exchequer, in addition to large weekly contributions by employers and employees. With the inflation of the 1960s and the accelerating inflation of the 1970s both benefits and contributions had to be periodically increased. A more ambitious earnings-related graduated pensions scheme was introduced in 1961, only to be superseded by an even more ambitious scheme in 1975.

The greatest advance in the acceptance by the State of responsibility for economic affairs, however, occurred in 1944 when the Government for the first time assumed responsibility for the maintenance of full employment, a policy on which all three political parties in Great Britain were agreed.

During both World Wars the economic life of this country was brought to a great extent under State control. By means of exchange control and control of imports, foreign trade was regulated by the Government. Industries not essential to the war effort were curtailed, and by direction the distribution of labour among different industries was controlled. Many prices were controlled and commodities rationed. Investment, too, was controlled, so that the diversion of real resources to less essential forms of production could be prevented.

Though a wide range of State planning was accepted as a necessity of war few people in Great Britain wished it to continue in peace-time. Nowadays, however, all the major political parties in this country agree that some State planning is necessary, though they differ as to its extent.

Different countries vary in the amount of state planning they undertake. At one extreme is the Communist State, where there is a maximum amount of State planning; at the other extreme there is the State that allows the maximum amount of free enterprise, the price mechanism being subject only to those restrictions necessary for the protection of the community. Between these two systems is the "middle way," taken by Great Britain and most non-Communist countries, an economic system with both a public and private sector, that is a "mixed" system. By 1971 the public sector in Great Britain employed 26 per cent of the total labour force, and owned 42 per cent of the total capital assets of the country.

An important step towards greater State planning in Great Britain took place in 1962, when the National Economic Development Council (usually known as "Neddy") was established. The main functions of this body were (i) to advise the Treasury; and (ii) to consider obstacles to Great Britain's economic growth. The NEDC delegates work appertaining to particular industries to a number of Economic Development Committees ("Little Neddies"), as, for example, for the machine-tool industry, building, wool textiles, chemicals, mechanical engineering, etc. The most comprehensive scheme of State planning was the National Plan published by the Government in 1965, but the economic difficulties of Great Britain in the ensuing years led to its being abandoned.

The extent of State intervention in economic and social affairs in Great Britain is indicated by the number of Government departments now concerned with these matters—the Exchequer, Employment, Industry, Agriculture, Fisheries and Food, Housing, the Environment (including Transport), Posts and Telecommunications, Technology, Education and Science, Social Services. In earlier chapters of this book we have seen how the British Government has widened its interest in economic affairs in recent years. In Chapter 8 we saw how it has attempted to influence the location of industry, at first by the creation of Development Areas and more recently through its proposals for regional planning. Its interest in the National Income (Chapter 16), too, has increased, as it is greatly concerned to stimulate economic growth. Throughout the period since 1945 it has attempted to keep inflation in check (Chapter 21), and to that end it has taken a more active part in promoting monetary policy (Chapter 24) than ever before. Matters affecting the balance of payments (Chapter 26) are also now a prime Government concern.

II. STATE OWNERSHIP IN INDUSTRY

4. Nationalisation in Great Britain

The third feature of the period since 1945 has been the nationalisation of a number of basic industries. Before that date, with one or two minor exceptions, the State had not invaded the industrial field. Towards the end of the nineteenth century nationalisation of "the means of production" became one of the chief items of socialist policy.

Public ownership can be supported on a number of grounds:

(*i*) as a means of protecting the consumer against monopoly;

(*ii*) where competition was wasteful it may be better to create a state-owned monopoly;

(*iii*) it was in the national interest that basic industries such as coal, iron and steel, and transport be brought under public control;

(*iv*) where it was clear, as with airlines, that the industry for many years might have to be subsidised by the State;

(*v*) where an industry was clearly technologically inefficient, as in coal-mining;

(*vi*) where labour relations were particularly bad, as also in the case of the coal-mining industry;

(*vii*) where, because of economies of scale, a service could be provided more efficiently nationally than locally, as with electricity;

(*viii*) where it was necessary for carrying out Government policy, as in the case of the Bank of England;

(*ix*) where it might be to the public danger to allow an industry to be privately controlled, as with atomic energy.

After 1945 an extensive programme of nationalisation was embarked upon in Great Britain, partly for political reasons and partly because, for one or other of the reasons listed above, it was considered that certain basic industries could be better operated by the State.

From the economic point of view the question that has to be decided is whether an industry will be more efficiently run if it is nationalised than it would be under free enterprise. First came the nationalisation of the Bank of England (1946), closely followed by the coal industry and public transport (1947), electricity (1948), gas (1949) and iron and steel (1951). Road transport (partially) and the iron and steel industry, however, were both denationalised in 1953. The iron and steel industry was renationalised in 1967, and road transport in 1968. A public corporation was set up to manage each nationalised industry. The two principal British airlines—British European Airways and British Overseas Airways Corporation—were already operated by public corporations. In 1954 two more public corporations were established—the Independent Television Authority, to break the monopoly of the BBC, and the Atomic Energy Authority, to promote the development of atomic power. In the case of atomic energy all three of the British political parties favoured State control. By 1975 the public sector had an income equal to 60 per cent of the national income.

After the nationalisation of the iron and steel industry further nationalisation was suspended for some years. In 1976 the shipbuilding and aircraft industries were nationalised and the nationalisation of banking and insurance was proposed. In the meantime the State acquired an interest in a number of companies in the private sector of the economy which found themselves in financial difficulties on account of the increasing rate of inflation and the drift into a serious world recession. The greatest State incursion into the private sector occurred in April 1975 when the State invested £1,500 million in British Leyland, the largest car manufacturing firm in Great Britain. This followed closely on the Ryder report which had recommended a drastic re-organisation of this firm. The National Enterprise Board, set up under the *Industry Act* (1975), overlooks the State's interest in private firms receiving State assistance, such as Rolls-Royce, Ferranti and British Leyland. The Government also proposed to set up the Co-operative Development Agency to widen the scale of public ownership and offer greater competition to large-scale retailers.

5. Financial aspects of nationalisation

The previous owners of nationalised firms were paid compensation unless they were local authorities. The stock holders of the Bank of England, for example, received sufficient 3% Government stock to yield an income equal to that which they had been previously receiving. In the case of the coal industry, compensation was fixed at £114,160,000 in Treasury Stock, this sum being distributed among the firms in each region. Transport Stock to the value of £1,024 million was allotted to the shareholders in the railways and canals. Individual agreements were made with road-haulage firms. Some gas and electricity undertakings were owned by municipal authorities, but compensation was given only to the shareholders in the company-owned concerns in the form of British Gas Stock and British Electricity Stock.

Compensation in the form of Government stock has vastly increased the country's internal debt. The nationalised industries were burdened with heavy fixed charges which had to be covered in bad times as well as good, whereas previously dividends paid to shareholders varied directly with profits. The railways at first had the additional burden of having to make payments to a stock redemption fund. From the start The National Coal Board was financed directly by the Exchequer, but the other nationalised industries, particularly the electricity, gas and transport undertakings, at first obtained additional capital by the issue of long-term guaranteed stocks. Since 1956, however, all nationalised industries have been financed by the Exchequer.

6. Price and profit policy of nationalised industries

All the British nationalised industries are monopolies or near-monopolies, though some of them, such as coal, gas and electricity, compete against one another and against oil, while British Rail also competes against the National Bus Company, airlines and the private motor car.

The price and profit policies of the nationalised industries are matters of great economic importance. The constitutions of the public cor-porations operating the nationalised industries do not state that they should be run for profit, although they are expected to pay their way over a number of years. Public ownership of an industry implies that it should provide a service and so be operated in the public interest rather than that the aim should be to make a profit. The phrase "in the public interest," however, has no precise meaning, and if the question of profit or loss is completely ignored no satisfactory economic test of the efficiency of an industry can be applied. It has been suggested, therefore, that since to earn a profit is not the primary aim of a national-ised industry, some kind of audit of efficiency by an audit commission should replace profit as a test of its efficiency.

If problems of output, price and profits are to be decided solely on economic grounds, it is important that a nationalised industry should attract to itself that quantity of factors of production—neither more nor less—that is economically desirable. Thus, prices should be related to costs, particularly where nationalised industries are in competition with one another. Many economists think that the aim should be to break even, thus avoiding either a large profit or a heavy loss. If prices are too high, this will check the development of the industry; if too low, there will be over-expansion at the expense of other forms of production. Under perfect competition it has been seen that price is equal to marginal cost, and if economic considerations are to prevail this might appear on theoretical grounds to be the price a nationalised industry should charge to its consumers. Most of the nationalised industries, however, have heavy fixed costs in proportion to their variable costs, with average costs falling as output increases, so that marginal cost tends to be below average cost. In these circumstances, therefore, a loss will be incurred if a price equal to marginal cost is charged.

If the price to be charged is based on average cost it means that the more profitable activities of a nationalised industry have to subsidise the less profitable. This principle is observed by the Post Office, for the postal charge is the same for a letter from London to an isolated farm in the Western Highlands of Scotland as from Westminster to Chelsea. Average cost, and therefore price, can be reduced by ceasing to operate unremunerative activities—the policy for the railways recommended by the *Beeching Report*.

Since most nationalised industries produce goods or services in fairly inelastic demand it is easy to pass on increased cost to the consumer, and this can have serious effects, for most of these industries produce services or capital goods on which other industries depend. Increased charges for power, transport, and iron and steel, therefore, will increase the costs of all other producers.

It is sometimes argued that, for reasons other than economic, some nationalised industries should be run deliberately at a loss because it is socially desirable that they should do so or because they are of strategic importance or essential to a country's defence. The railways might be considered to fall within this category. Any decision to run at a loss, however, must be the responsibility of Parliament, but if such a course is decided upon it then becomes almost impossible to test the efficiency of the industry. In practice, the State may impose its own price policy. A Standing Committee reporting on the pricing policy of nationalised industries recommended that British Airways should continue to operate certain routes at a loss,[1] and yet the airline was expected to make a profit. The argument has also been been employed in connection with the railways. On a number of occasions the National Coal Board has complained that for some grades of coal it had to charge prices that were too low.

7. Some nationalised industries: (i) Coal

The nationalisation of the coal-mining industry was recommended by the Sankey Commission as long ago as 1919. The *Coal Mines Nationalisation Act* (1946) declared the policy of the National Coal Board to be the efficient development of the industry and the provision of coal in such quantities and at such prices as to "further the public

[1] For example, to the Western Isles.

interest." This Act brought 1,500 mines under the control of the National Coal Board on 1st January 1947. Some 400 mines, each employing fewer than thirty underground workers, retained their independence, although they had to be licensed by the Coal Board. The industry is administered by nine regional Coal Boards, and under them are forty-eight area managements.

Throughout the nineteenth century and down to 1913 the output of coal from British mines continued to increase. From 10 million tons in 1800, production expanded to 80 million tons in 1860, and reached its maximum of 287 million tons in 1913. During the last two decades of this period an export trade in coal was developed. The Great Depression severely affected the industry, for when the home demand for coal fell off it was difficult to revive the export trade, particularly since the depression was world-wide. Germany and Poland, too, had become serious rivals to Great Britain in foreign markets, and the development of hydro-electric power in the Alps and Scandinavia, the increasing use of oil for the generation of electricity, together with the adoption of more economical methods of using coal in industry, reduced the demand for it. Consequently between the wars, coal-mining in Great Britain was a declining industry, and there was a contraction of its labour force. During the 1970s some coal had to be imported from the United States and Australia.

Table LXXIII shows how the output of coal has declined in recent years.

Table LXXIII

Coal Production in Great Britain

Year	Million tons
1913	287
1938	217
1948	200
1954	222
1960	194
1966	174
1968	163
1970	140
1972	117
1974	107

The introduction of mechanisation into the mines raised the average output per man shift from 1.14 tons in 1938 to 1.33 in 1958, to 1.8 in 1966 and to 2.25 in 1974. However, the problem for many years has been labour difficulty, the labour force in the industry falling steadily since 1945 to 602,000 in 1960, to 498,000 in 1964 and to 305,000 in 1971. Successive increases in miners' wages have not attracted sufficient labour. In fact, the supply curve for labour in this industry is probably regressive, so that high wages, coupled with a high level of employment, tended to increase absenteeism.

Coal is no longer the sole source of power, though it is still important for both industrial and domestic purposes. It can be used directly or for the production of electricity, though both oil and atomic energy have become rivals to coal for the generation of electricity. In recent years gas, too, has become a greater competitor to coal than was formerly the case on account of the ease of piping natural gas from the North Sea. Little coal is now used for the production of gas. In consequence the price policy of the National Coal Board has acquired increased significance, and to reduce the average cost of mining coal a number of uneconomic mines have been closed.

8. Some nationalised industries: (ii) Gas and electricity

At the time of nationalisation two-thirds of all electricity undertakings in Great Britain were operated by local authorities, the remainder being in the hands of public companies (mostly in country areas). Before nationalisation some measure of co-ordination by the linking up of one area with another had been achieved under the Central Electricity Board. An act of 1948 nationalised the generation of electricity and established the Central Electricity Authority (later known as the Central Electricity Generating Board), but the setting up of fourteen area boards provides considerable decentralisation. Each area board keeps its own separate accounts, and has at its disposal—subject to the approval of the national authority—any surplus it may earn. Before nationalisation there were almost as many different scales of charges as there were undertakings. Greater uniformity has meant increased charges in the towns and lower charges in the country. A serious drawback to uniformity of charges is that it is liable to lead to uneconomic location of industry. Shareholders in the former electricity companies received compensation in the form of Electricity Stock, but undertakings owned by municipal authorities were taken over without compensation.

Some local authorities formerly owned gas-works, but a great many were operated by companies, a large number being controlled by a single combine, the Gas, Light & Coke Co. Ltd. The nationalisation of the industry in 1949 instituted a form of organisation similar to that for electricity, a Gas Council with twelve area boards being established. In 1972 the Gas Council was replaced by the British Gas Corporation and the area boards were abolished.

Most local authorities made a profit from supplying gas and electricity, and this was partly used for the relief of rates. One effect, therefore, of the nationalisation of gas and electricity was to increase the rates of many local authorities.

9. Some nationalised industries: (iii) Iron and steel

The iron and steel industry, like coal, is one of the basic industries, and it was for this reason that its nationalisation was proposed. It is, too, one of the first industries to be affected by the onset of either a boom or a slump. The older centres of the industry are located on the coalfields, because in earlier days a large amount of coal was used in the smelting of iron ore. The newer centres of the industry, at Scunthorpe in North Lincolnshire and at Corby in Northamptonshire, are near supplies of iron ore.

Down to 1913 the iron and steel industry enjoyed almost continuous expansion, and to meet the needs of the First World War the industry was enlarged to such an extent that excess capacity was the result. By 1924 the output of the industry was only half of what it was capable of producing, and there followed a period of "rationalisation" when the industry was deliberately reduced by the closing down of many plants. The rise in the demand for basic steel and the fall in the demand for wrought iron reduced considerably Great Britain's advantages over its rivals, and the output of both the United States and Germany went ahead of that of Great Britain. The iron and steel industry is one in which economies of scale are available and in all three countries it has been a large-scale industry for a long time. The largest concern in the United States is the United States Steel Corporation, in Germany there are large cartels and in Great Britain, too, there were combines of the cartel type.

The British iron and steel industry was nationalised in 1951. The firms involved numbered ninety-six, and comprised companies producing 50,000 tons of iron ore or 20,000 tons of pig-iron or steel in one year. All the completely owned subsidiaries of the ninety-six companies named in the Act, of which there were about 150, were also taken over. In order to preserve the goodwill of the old firms, they were allowed to retain their original names, and their entire capital was vested in a holding company. Thus the companies became publicly owned, each with a single shareholder—the State. Medium-sized firms outside the scheme were not permitted to expand beyond double their size at the time of the passing of the Act, except under licence. The iron and steel industry, therefore, remained what it had been before nationalisation—a cartel—and with the same drawback that the more efficient firms would have to subsidise the less efficient.

The iron and steel industry was denationalised in 1953 but re-nationalised by the *Iron and Steel Act* of 1967. The industry is now run by the British Steel Corporation, under which are four operational groups.

III. INLAND TRANSPORT

10. The development of competition between the railways and road transport

Industrial development has gone hand in hand with the development of means of communication, for exchange is the corollary of territorial division of labour. The Industrial Revolution was both a cause and a result of improvements in transport. In many countries, in contrast to Great Britain, where even the building of roads had been left to private enterprise, the State assisted this development, mainly because means of transport are of strategic as well as economic importance. In most countries railways are now State-owned, the main exceptions being the United States and the Netherlands.

The British railways were mostly built in the first place to satisfy local needs, but the amalgamations of local lines resulted in the development of the first railway systems in this country. Parliament through fear of monopoly, encouraged competition by sanctioning the building of competitive lines, with the result that a measure of excess capacity was created. In spite of amalgamations, Great Britain, as late as 1914 was still served by twenty-five railway companies of medium size, in addition to over seventy-five small concerns. An Act of 1921 made compulsory their amalgamation into four groups,[1] the grouping being so arranged that some measure of competition remained.[2] During both World Wars the State took over the operation of the railways.

The return to the roads. The development of the railways during 1844–70 had driven nearly all inter-town traffic off the roads. The first competitors of the railway were street tramways, which became their

[1] The Great Western Railway, the London Midland and Scottish Railway, the London and North Eastern Railway and the Southern Railway.

[2] For example, the LMSR and LNER were competitors for traffic between London and Scotland, the GWR and LMSR between London and Birmingham, the GWR and SR between London and Plymouth.

rivals for suburban traffic. It was not, however, until the perfection of the petrol engine that road transport became a serious competitor of the railways. A few buses were in service before 1914, but after 1922 a rapid expansion of this form of transport began. Many of these road-passenger transport firms were run by small operators, each with only two or three vehicles. It is important to emphasise that many of these operators, like most of the tramways before them, wer‾ at first developing new traffic, and not taking traffic from the railways. By expansion and amalgamation many large companies developed, such as the West Yorkshire and Ribble and United companies in the north, and the Southern and Western National companies in the south. All over the country small operators of goods services also sprang into existence about the same time, the small amount of capital initially required making it easy for them to establish themselves. Just as large bus companies came to be established, so large haulage firms soon came into being. Both long-distance passenger and goods services were developed. Alarmed by this development, the railways in 1928 obtained powers to operate road-transport services, and soon afterwards they acquired substantial holdings in the larger road-passenger transport companies. The railways then began to close a number of their small country stations and short branch lines.

The increasing amount of traffic on the roads made it necessary to restrict competition between road operators of both passenger and goods services. The *Traffic Acts* of 1930 and 1933 regulated road transport by introducing a system of licensing for road services. Under the Act of 1930 Traffic Commissioners were appointed, their first business being to restrict the number of bus operators over each route, and to consider applications from operators wishing to establish new routes. Thus, though existing operators were given a monopoly their time-tables and charges were subject to sanction by the Traffic Commissioners. The Act of 1933 restricted the number of hauliers except those carrying their own goods. As a result, freedom of entry to the main branches of road transport was removed. During the ensuing thirty years keen competition between road and rail operators developed.

11. Road v. Rail

Advantages of road transport. (i) For distances up to at least 200 miles, road haulage of goods is speedier than the railway. (ii) The road transport unit is relatively small, and so small loads can be expeditiously dealt with, whereas the railway has to deal with whole train-loads which involves a complicated system of marshalling. (iii) Road transport can

offer a door-to-door service, whereas transport by rail involves collection and delivery. For many goods road hauliers charge lower rates
than the railway. Many manufacturers—especially those making
branded goods—prefer to deliver their products in their own vans. For
passengers, the bus often has the advantage over the railway of a more
frequent service at regular time intervals. The railways often suffered
from the disadvantage of having inconveniently situated stations,
especially in country districts.

The operation of railway and road transport. The construction of railways involved heavy capital investment, whereas the initial outlay of
the small road operator was often little more than the cost of a single
vehicle. Operational costs of a railway are heavy, for it is solely responsible for the upkeep of its track and the maintenance of signalling,
stations, etc. Motorways, and other trunk roads for the use of road
vehicles are constructed at the cost of taxpayers. The road operator had
only to pay for a road fund licence and insure his vehicle, and then
(until 1930 or 1933) he could run wherever he pleased.[1] The marginal
cost of railway transport, however, is low, for the cost of running an
additional train is small; on the other hand, marginal costs of the road
operator are relatively heavy, and nearly proportional to any increase
in his traffic. As has already been noticed, railway rates until 1963 were
based on the principle of charging what the traffic would bear, goods
being arranged in twenty-one classes. Another important feature of
railway charges was their publicity and their subjection to public
scrutiny in order to curb their possible misuse of monopoly power.
In road haulage keen competition prevailed, and so for a long time it
was free from control. Railway charges were based on average costs
for the whole railway; road charges were based on the costs of particular journeys, exceptionally low rates sometimes being charged
for return loads, a load at almost any price being preferable to the running of an empty vehicle. The railways at first complained that road
operators confined themselves almost entirely to the carriage of goods
in the more expensive categories of railway classification, and to routes
where density of traffic was high.

12. Nationalisation of inland transport

In 1947 an Act was passed to nationalise inland transport. This act
set up the British Transport Commission, whose work was distributed

---

[1] In the case of passenger services licences to operate had to be obtained from the Local
Authorities through whose areas the route lay.

among five executives covering: (*i*) railways, (*ii*) docks and inland waterways, (*iii*) road transport, (*iv*) London Transport and (*v*) hotels. On 1st January 1948 British Railways acquired the four main-line railways, British Waterways took over the inland waterways and docks, some of which had previously been owned by the railways and London Transport Executive took over London Transport.

Road haulage presented a more complicated problem, owing to the fact that over 20,000 firms were involved, many with only two or three vehicles. British Road Services were given power to acquire road-transport undertakings by individual bargaining with the firms concerned. Holders of "C" licences (that is, firms carrying their own goods) were exempt from nationalisation. The Road Haulage Executive had its headquarters in London, with eight regional divisions, further subdivided into thirty-one districts, each operational group comprising about 150 vehicles. Road transport was denationalised in 1953, but fear of renationalisation resulted in only 54 per cent of the vehicles being returned to private enterprise, the remainder having to be retained by British Road Services. Road passenger operation was not much affected by nationalisation on account of the delay caused by local interests being given an opportunity to put forward objections. The nationalisation of road passenger transport had to wait until 1968.

It was said that one advantage of nationalisation of all forms of inland transport was that it prepared the way for a degree of co-ordination not previously possible. One difficulty is the absence of a uniform system of calculating operational costs, without which comparison of the efficiency of different forms of transport is impossible. It may be that short-distance traffic, both passenger and goods, can best be left to road transport, and that long-distance traffic is more suited to the railway. It may be that fast traffic can best be dealt with by the railway, and road transport used for distribution from focal points on the railway system. Such decisions should depend primarily on economic factors, though social considerations, such as the congestion of town streets by through heavy traffic, ought to be taken into account.

The exemption from nationalisation of the "C" licence-holders, who together operate five times as many vehicles as the Road Haulage Executive, and the increasing number of private motor cars means that the nationalised industry was not free from outside competition. The problem of co-ordination of the various forms of inland transport was further complicated by the denationalisation of road transport.

13. Public transport today

An Act of 1963 transferred the functions and property of the Transport Commission to four boards—Railways (British Rail), London Transport, British Waterways and the British Transport Docks and the newly created Transport Holding Company, in which were vested shares in road haulage (British Road Services), many bus companies in England, Scotland and Wales, some shipping companies and travel agencies. Except for the haulage firms acquired by British Road Services, these companies continued to operate under their own names as, for example, Pickford's. Some decentralisation of the railway system was achieved by dividing the railways into six regions—Southern, Western, London Midland, Scottish, North-Eastern and Eastern—the work of the regional boards being co-ordinated by a central committee. Later the number of regions was reduced to five by combining the North-Eastern and the Eastern regions.

In their efforts to compete successfully against road operators British Rail tried to reduce its average costs by closing unremunerative branch lines, a policy accelerated under the Beeching Plan, 1963–5. Where services at regular intervals have been introduced, there has been some return of passenger traffic to the railways. Express goods services, too, have had some success. Though their local traffic has declined, the railways were still the main carriers of coal and their long-distance express passenger trains were usually well-filled.

The decline in passenger travel by railway is not confined to Great Britain. Two new competitors of both the railway and the bus have come into the field—the private motor car and the aeroplane. The huge increase in the number of privately owned motor cars in Great Britain has reduced the number of people using both the railways and suburban bus services. In 1975 there were nearly 14 million private cars in this country compared with 3 million twenty years earlier. The shortness of the distances between important towns has retarded the development of internal airlines in Great Britain, but in the United States 32 per cent of all travellers now go by air, 58 per cent in their own cars and only 10 per cent by bus or railway.

The Beeching Report (1963). This Report was the work of Dr (now Lord) Beeching, who was appointed by the Minister of Transport to study the problem of the railways. Its main recommendations, which came to be known as the Beeching Plan, were: (i) non-remunerative branch lines should be closed; (ii) on many routes stopping trains should be withdrawn; (iii) speedy, regular (liner) freight services should be introduced; (iv) main-line traffic should be concentrated on the most direct routes and some alternative routes closed. The aim was to use the railways for the traffic for which they were most suited, so that by 1970 it was calculated that the railway deficit would be wiped out, a forecast that was not realised.

Transport as a service. The increasing difficulty of profitably operating many railway and public road services, both in the case of rural districts and of commuter services to large cities, led to demands that transport should be regarded as a public service and provided whether it pays its way or not. If this view is accepted it becomes very difficult to decide how much of each service to provide, and excess capacity is likely to result. Once the profit motive is taken away it becomes difficult to test the efficiency of a service. Another argument for operating unremunerative railway services is to relieve traffic congestion on the roads, especially those leading into large cities. If it could be shown that the losses incurred on such services were offset by the reduced cost of urban road construction the argument would have economic as well as social support.

Transport Act (1968). This Act reorganised the administration of public transport in Great Britain. The various transport boards, set up in 1962, were brought directly under the control of the Ministry of Transport (by then a division of the Department of the Environment), as also were the newly created National Freight Corporation and the National Bus Company. The Act was in the nature of a compromise between a policy that required the cessation of all railway services that did not pay their way and the view that public transport should be operated as a service. The Act stated the Government's view that a transport system has both a social and an economic function to perform. It was held that the basic railway system should be regarded as a commercial undertaking and so should pay its way, but a number of specified lines regarded as of value to the community, and so socially necessary, should be subsidised. Many Local Authorities subsidised both bus and railway services in their areas which they considered should be retained. A National Freight Corporation was set up to provide an integrated road/rail system for goods traffic. For road passenger services a National Bus Company was established for England and Wales, with a separate company for Scotland. In each of the larger conurbations a single transport authority was set up, as in fact had been the case for London since 1933 when the London Transport Board was established. Where it considered necessary bus services were to be subsidised by the State. In spite of this, however, British Rail continued to show losses, with a deficit of £51 million in 1973 and £157 million in 1974. All hopes of making British Rail a viable commercial proposition seemed to end, even when "socially desirable" lines were subsidised.

RECOMMENDATIONS FOR FURTHER READING

G. C. Allen: *British Industries and their Organisation*, Chapters 3, 4, 8–11.
W. A. Robson: *Nationalised Industry and Public Ownership*, Chapters 1–5, 8.
G. Walker: *Road and Rail.*
M. R. Bonavia: *Economics of Transport.*
W. Hagenbuch: *Social Economics*, Chapters 9, 10.

QUESTIONS

1. "The pricing and investment policies of nationalised industries should be decided on commercial and profit-making lines." Do you agree? (Bournemouth)

2. "Nationalised industries rarely realise a net profit, and therefore are inefficient." Critically examine this statement. (Norwich)

3. Argue the case for and against a nationalised industry making a profit. (LC Com.)

4. What are the economic arguments for and against State ownership of industries? (CIS)

5. What are the economic criteria for deciding whether an industry should be nationalised? (CIS)

6. Examine, from the economic point of view, the expenditure by the State of large sums on "social services." (Exp.)

7. "Social security is a much larger issue than national insurance against particular risks." Discuss this statement. (IT)

8. "Economic planning is suited to backward countries but not to advanced ones." Discuss. (GCE)

9. Does economic theory indicate any rules which should govern the policies pursued by the nationalised industries? (CIS)

10. "Publicly owned undertakings should always be guided by the rule that price must be equated to marginal costs." Discuss. (Final Degree)

CHAPTER 29

FLUCTUATIONS IN EMPLOYMENT

I. CAUSES OF UNEMPLOYMENT

1. Unemployment

Unemployment is a hazard peculiar to an industrialised economic system. Primitive communities were usually self-sufficient and had no unemployment problems, though they had to accept a very low standard of living. The people shared the work that had to be done, and any spare time was enjoyed as leisure. There is still little unemployment in countries mainly engaged in the production of primary products, though these communities may suffer a general reduction in their standard of living if the prices of their products fall on the world market. Farm workers in industrialised nations are rarely out of work except perhaps in a prolonged period of bad weather. Industrialisation, with division of labour and specialisation, brought about a higher standard of living than had ever previously been enjoyed, but it also brought with it the risk of unemployment. In fact, some unemployment can be attributed directly to industrial progress. That is why it was the leading industrial nations that were the first to introduce schemes of social security.

There are a number of different causes of unemployment which it is necessary to consider before the problems of industrial fluctuations and full employment can be discussed. Clearly, before plans can be formulated for maintaining full employment, it is necessary to distinguish between these different causes, for only after an accurate diagnosis has been made can the appropriate remedy be applied.

2. Deficiency of demand

The feature of a trade depression is a general deficiency of demand. Consumers' wants may be as great as ever but they have not the means with which to satisfy them. The result is that nearly all industries are affected at the same time—though not all to the same extent—and so there is widespread mass unemployment. Unemployment arising from a general deficiency of demand is known as cyclical unemployment because of its association with the nineteenth century trade cycle.

During that period, however, neither boom nor depression lasted very long, and the level of unemployment once only—in 1879—exceeded 10 per cent.

The most serious example of mass unemployment occurred between the two World Wars, when there was a period of prolonged depression, during which unemployment among insured workers in Great Britain fell below 10 per cent only in 1927, when it was 9.7 per cent. In 1937, which marked the peak of recovery, 10.8 per cent of insured workers were still unemployed. In the inter-war period therefore unemployment was at a higher level in the best years, than it generally was in the worst years before 1914. In the worst of the depression years unemployment averaged 18.3 per cent, and in 1932 reached 21.9 per cent. It was not only the gravity of unemployment which characterised the Great Depression but the length of time it lasted. To achieve full employment, therefore, it will clearly be necessary to eradicate unemployment of this type.

3. Frictional unemployment

The economic development of a country frequently requires factors of production to be switched from one form of employment to another. If all factors, including labour, were non-specific transfer would be easier: it is mainly because this is not so that economic frictions occur, and factors become unemployed because the demand for their services in their present occupations has fallen off, although at the same time there may be a demand for labour in other occupations. This is the essential feature of frictional unemployment. Since so much labour is immobile, in both the geographical and the occupational senses, labour is particularly prone to this kind of unemployment. Economic friction arises from a variety of causes:

(i) *Change of demand.* This may occur for no other reason than a mere change of taste, as for example a preference for prepared breakfast cereals instead of oatmeal porridge. Or a change in demand may be the result of economic progress, some new commodity superseding an older one because it is superior to it in some way. The building of railways, for example, stimulated the demand for all kinds of railway equipment, but caused a fall in the demand for horse-drawn vehicles.

We have already seen that there are many causes of change in demand. At any time, therefore, there will be expanding industries and declining industries. A shift of demand from one commodity to another results in a fall in the demand for labour and other factors in one industry, and an increase in the demand for labour and other factors in another. If the labour could be easily transferred from the declining to the expanding industry no unemployment would occur. Labour, however, is not perfectly mobile, and even during the Great Depression there were expanding industries in some areas in which the level of unemployment was much lower than the average for the country as a whole. Where a declining industry is highly localised, unemployment in a trade depression will be above the average.

Unemployment due to a change in demand is called *structural unemployment* because it is caused by a change in the country's industrial structure, the switching from one kind of production to another. Such a change produces unemployment only because of the immobility of factors of production. It is possible, however, for structural unemployment to occur when an industry suffers a decline in the demand for its product without any compensating new demand arising. This is most likely to occur in the case of an industry manufacturing chiefly for export. It was largely because of the contraction of its export trade that the Lancashire cotton industry declined.

(ii) *Technical progress.* Frictional unemployment, too, may result from the invention of a new machine or an innovation which may reduce the demand for labour in the industry concerned. The invention of the automatic loom, for example, reduced the demand for weavers in both the cotton and woollen industries. The introduction of office machinery—typewriters, computers, book-keeping machines, etc.—has resulted in the employment of fewer clerks, except, of course, where for other reasons the volume of work has increased. We have already seen that, even if in the short run machines have displaced some labour in certain industries, a new and increased demand for labour generally arises in the long run elsewhere. Fewer people may be required in weaving, but more people perhaps will be wanted for the manufacture of looms. Fewer clerks may be needed, but instead there will be an increased demand for labour in industries making office machinery. The development of automation has resulted in fewer workers being required. Since then, economic progress often causes people to lose their jobs, it has been thought only equitable to give them compensation in the form of redundancy payments.

4. Other causes of unemployment

Two other types of unemployment may be noted:

(i) *Seasonal unemployment.* In outdoor occupations, such as building and road-making, bad weather often causes temporary unemployment.

Bad weather, too, may prevent a fishing fleet putting out to sea. Some occupations require labour only at certain periods of the year—hop-picking, potato-lifting, fruit-gathering, entertaining at holiday resorts, etc. Irregularity of employment at the docks led at one time to the amount of labour available often being greater than the amount required. Sometimes, however, seasonal occupations may be combined, as, for example, the raising of sugar beet in summer with working in the sugar factory in the winter.

(ii) *Residual unemployment.* This includes those people who, on account of physical or mental disability, are of so low a standard of efficiency that few occupations may be open to them. Payment of standard rates of wages, too, makes it more difficult for people so handicapped to find work. Even in a boom unemployment does not completely disappear because even in those conditions some people are regarded as unemployable. Then there always seem to be a few people who work as little as they can even if it means their having to accept a bare subsistence.

II. INDUSTRIAL FLUCTUATIONS BEFORE 1945

5. Types of fluctuations

Fluctuations in industrial production and employment in Great Britain fall into three well-defined periods:

(i) The trade cycle of the nineteenth century, with boom and depression following one another in regular succession, which began about 1792, that is, just before the opening of the century and lasted until just beyond the end of it to the outbreak of war in 1914.

(ii) The Great Depression of the inter-war years, when unemployment was exceptionally high throughout the entire period, reaching its peak during 1931–2.

(iii) The post-1945 period, which was characterised by a high level of employment with full employment for most of the time and only minor recessions until the more serious recession of 1974–6.

Figure 89 shows how the level of employment in this country has fluctuated during this century.

6. The pre-1914 trade cycle

Alternating periods of boom and depression, known as the trade or business cycle, were a characteristic feature of the industrial history of

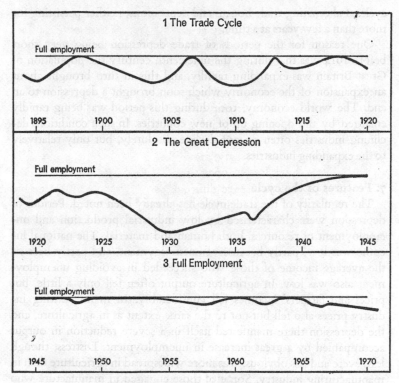

Fig. 89. The Level of Employment.

Great Britain in the nineteenth century and down to 1913. During this period boom and depression followed one another with great regularity. Lord Beveridge compiled a table to show the crests and troughs of business activity from 1792 to 1913.[1] During this period of 121 years the intervals between booms were as follows:

11, 7, 8, 7, 11, 9, 8, 7, 5, 9, 8, 7, 10, 7, 7 years.

Although this table shows a considerable variation in the time interval between one boom and the next, in eleven cases out of fifteen the intervals were of from seven to nine years, and the average interval for the whole period was eight years. Similarly, there was an average interval of eight years between one depression and the next. (See Fig. 80.) A feature, therefore, of the period 1792–1913 was a fairly regular

[1] W. H. Beveridge: *Full Employment in a Free Society*, p. 281.

cycle of alternating trade booms and depressions, neither persisting for more than a few years at a time.

One reason for the periods of trade depression being very short before 1914 was that during the nineteenth century the population of Great Britain was expanding rapidly, and this in turn brought about an expansion of the economy which soon brought a depression to an end. The world economy, too, during this period was being rapidly enlarged by the opening up of new countries. In such conditions declining industries often do not decline absolutely, but only relatively to the expanding industries.

7. Features of the cycle

The regularity of the trade cycle has already been noted. Periods of depression were characterised by low industrial production and unemployment of resources, both human and material. The national income was low, partly because of unemployment, and partly because the average income of those who succeeded in avoiding unemployment also was low. In agriculture output often fell only a little, but prices and farmers' incomes fell considerably. In manufacturing industry prices also fell but not to the same extent as in agriculture, and the depression there manifested itself in a severe reduction in output accompanied by a great increase in unemployment. Distress, though less severe and less obvious, was more widespread in agriculture than in manufacturing industry. Some of those engaged in manufacture who remained at work found that prices fell more than their wages, so that their *real* wages actually increased.

In the capital-goods industries, for example, production sometimes came almost to a standstill, the outlook often appearing so bleak that businessmen were not prepared to renew or extend their capital equipment. Just as the capital-producing industries were the first to feel the onset of a depression, so they were the first to benefit from recovery. Then, as production expanded and unemployment fell, wholesale prices began to rise, profit margins widened and recovery was further stimulated. The upswing of the cycle might be set in motion by increased demand due to an expanding population or by the development of new lines of investment. Recovery might be encouraged by a low rate of interest—though this generally had little effect at the very bottom of a depression—for an expansion of bank credit was characteristic of the upswing of the cycle, just as a contraction of credit was a feature of the down-swing. The stock exchange reflected the attitude of investors towards future business prospects, and the optimistic or pessimistic feelings engendered by movements of share prices tended to exaggerate these trends. Retail prices generally rose slowly until the later stages of a boom, but if full employment was reached with the boom unchecked, inflation was likely to ensue. In such a case, once the unsoundness of the position was realised, the boom would end in a crash and the return to depression could be precipitous. Prices would then fall, profit margins would be reduced or wiped out and the more cautious producers would curtail their output and unemployment would again become widespread throughout industry.

The nineteenth century trade cycle was not restricted to Great Britain. It was also experienced in varying degrees by other industrialised countries, and in a somewhat different way by those mainly dependent on primary production. With the development and expansion of international trade countries became more dependent on one another, so that both boom and depression spread from one country to others. Action taken in a country suffering from a depression was often harmful to the economies of others and this caused the depression to spread more widely.

8. The Great Depression

The rhythm of the trade cycle was completely upset by the First World War. As the war proceeded business activity soared to a higher level than ever before, full employment being reached for the first time since the Industrial Revolution. During 1919–25 the trade cycle appeared to be reasserting itself, as it did again in 1935–8, but the principal characteristic of the inter-war period was a world-wide trade depression of a severity, length and extent never previously experienced, and which affected not only manual workers but also many white collar workers.

In only one year—1927—during this period did unemployment in Great Britain fall below 10 per cent, and in the six years, 1930–5, it averaged 18.3 per cent, reaching a peak of 21.9 per cent in 1932 when nearly 3 million people were out of work. These rates of unemployment were averages for the country as a whole, but in many parts of the country there were very considerable divergences from the national average. For example, in South-east England (excluding London) the rate was only 6.2 per cent while the rate for London was 9.6 per cent, but in the "distressed areas" unemployment rates were very much higher—36.9 per cent for example in Glamorgan, 34.2 per cent in County Durham, 29.4 per cent on Clydeside and 21.1 per cent in Lancashire. Differences in rates of unemployment were even greater between individual towns. While some places in the South-east had only 2.0 per cent of their population unemployed, there were towns in South Wales and County Durham with over 50 per cent. Not only was the rate of unemployment exceptionally high in the worst years but it remained high even in the years of recovery. Another feature of unemployment during this period was that in some areas men were out of work for very long periods at a time, in some cases for several years at a stretch. Even when recovery at last occurred, the so-called boom of 1937 was accompanied by unemployment at a higher level than in any pre-1914 depression.

By modern standards it would appear that little was done by the Government of the day to try to bring the Great Depression to an end. One difficulty was that the depression was world-wide and, indeed, more severe in both Germany and the United States than in Great Britain, so that international trade dwindled to small proportions. Government action through the imposition of tariffs in 1932 protected a shrinking home market but could do nothing to assist exports. A depression of such length and severity had never previously been experienced. During the short depressions of the nineteenth-century trade cycle public works—usually road-building—were often undertaken to relieve distress among the unemployed, but in 1931 even work in progress on the roads was curtailed in order to reduce State expenditure in an attempt to balance the budget. The concept of a deliberately unbalanced budget for the purpose of stimulating demand was contrary to the economic thinking of those days, as was the whole idea that the State could do much to remedy the situation since the idea was still prevalent that supply creates its own demand, and therefore that Government intervention was useless.

Nevertheless, the Government attempted to assist the areas where unemployment was most severe by offering financial inducements to firms willing to set up in government-established trading estates in these "Special Areas". The Great Depression led many economists, both in Europe and North America, to study the trade cycle in the hope of explaining its causes (the better known theories are considered later in this chapter), but it was left to Lord Keynes and Lord Beveridge, the two architects of full employment, to show how the State could determine the level of employment, but Keynes's *General Theory of Employment, Interest and Money* was not published until 1936 and Beveridge's *Full Employment in a Free Society* not until 1944. The extent to which in face of a severe depression the State would have to stimulate demand is seen by the fact that it took over three years after the outbreak of war in 1939 to reach full employment.

III. THE DETERMINATION OF INCOME AND EMPLOYMENT

9. Saving and investment

Before the problem of full employment can be considered it is essential to know something of Keynes's theory which sought to show how the level of employment is determined. First, however, we must be quite clear what is meant by the two terms, *saving* and *investment*.

(*i*) *Saving*. As we have already seen, saving reduces the demand for consumers' goods and sets free resources for the production of producers' goods. That part of income not spent on consumers' goods can be said to be saved. Thus saving means refraining from consumption. The amount saved depends on several factors: the keenness of people to save (the propensity to save), the total income of the community and the way in which it is distributed. The marginal propensity to consume is the extra amount of consumption that takes place as a result of the smallest possible increase in income. When discussing the motives for saving it was seen that the rate of interest has much less influence on the rate of saving than was once thought. Of much greater importance than the rate of interest is the size of a person's income. The larger one's income, the larger the proportion of it one is likely to save.

(*ii*) *Investment*. By investment is meant the actual production of capital goods—the building of a railway, a motorway, a road bridge or a road tunnel, the erection of a new electric generating station, building up stocks of raw materials, the manufacture of machinery, etc. Investment is thus the amount of real capital produced during a period, some of this, of course, being required to make good depreciation. The volume of investment depends partly on the rate of interest and partly on the expectations of entrepreneurs regarding the trend of business in the immediate future. If it is thought that the rate of profit is likely to be less than the rate of interest, investment will not take place. If prices are rising, profit margins will also tend to rise and businessmen, taking an optimistic view of the future, will wish to increase their investment. But if prices are falling the reverse will happen, and however low the rate of interest, pessimism regarding the future will make businessmen generally unwilling to undertake investment.

Saving is carried out by the community at large—by individuals and corporate institutions; investment is partly undertaken by entrepreneurs in the private sector and partly by the State for the public sector. According to the supporters of the earlier theories of saving and investment, it was because saving was left to one group of people and investment to another that the equilibrium of the economic system was disturbed. Saving was a prerequisite of investment but, so it was thought, a given amount of saving did not guarantee an equal amount of investment. In other words, fluctuations in production occurred because sometimes saving exceeded investment, when there would be a tendency to curtail production, and because sometimes investment exceeded saving, with the probable development of a boom.

10. Investment, income and employment

Lord Keynes showed that the level of business activity and employment depends on the level of income, which also determines the extent of both saving and investment. Thus Saving, Investment and Income are mutually dependent on one another. The level of consumption too depends on Income. The main influence, however, is Investment, the extent of which is mainly responsible for the level of Income. Investment generates Income, and Income then determines the maximum extent of Saving and Consumption. The level of employment, therefore, is dependent partly on the production of capital goods (Investment) and partly on the production of consumers' goods (Consumption). A high level of Consumption, too, stimulates further Investment (*see* Fig. 90).

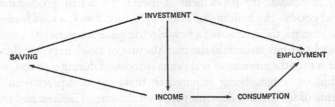

Fig. 90. Income Determination (1).

Equilibrium can occur at any level of employment, and so the objective becomes the achievement of equilibrium at full employment.

Keynes's psychological influences. Keynes stressed the importance of a number of psychological influences on saving, investment and consumption.

(i) *The propensity to consume,* that is, the keenness or otherwise of people to buy consumers' goods.

(ii) *The propensity to save,* that is, the keenness or otherwise of people to refrain from the purchase of consumers' goods.

(*iii*) *Liquidity-preference*. That is, the extent to which people prefer to hold money as distinct from investing it.

(*iv*) *Expectations*. Another psychological influence on the holding of money was considered by Keynes to be the speculative motive, this being dependent on expectation of future trends on the rate of interest. Thus, an important influence on the level of investment is the expectation of businessmen regarding the future level of business activity. This was not altogether a new idea, as A. C. Pigou had previously referred to businessmen being influenced by alternating waves of optimism and pessimism. Keynes, however, related expectations to the prospective yield of capital. The amount of investment undertaken in a period depends on whether entrepreneurs expect the yield from capital investment to exceed the rate of interest. This Keynes termed *the marginal efficiency of capital*, which he defined as the relation between the prospective yield of one more unit of capital and the cost of producing it.

Figure 91 summarises the situation:

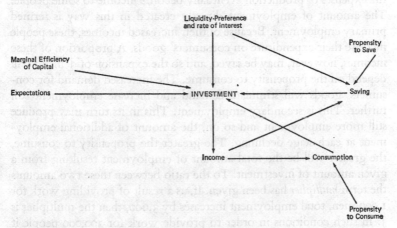

Fig. 91. Income Determination (2).

The diagram shows that there are five influences on investment—expectations, the marginal efficiency of capital, the rate of interest, saving and consumption. Three influences on saving are distinguished—income, the rate of interest and the propensity to save. Two factors are shown as influencing consumption—income and the propensity to consume.

Keynes developed his theories during the most severe trade depression ever experienced, his aim being to show how a high level of employment could be maintained. He refuted the argument of Say that supply creates its own demand, so that production itself stimulates a demand for what has been produced (the Law of Markets). To achieve the desired volume of production it would be necessary to ensure that the required amount of investment was undertaken. Though Keynes could be described as an under-consumptionist he did not favour directly increasing consumers' purchasing power, as did the exponents of the crude under-consumption theories, but this would follow from increased investment.

The concept of the multiplier. A given amount of investment, whether private or public, will create a greater amount of employment than that directly concerned with the actual production of the additional capital goods. For example, suppose that 1,000 men are employed upon a new Government project. Part of the expenditure is directly incurred in paying wages to these men, part is profit to the entrepreneur and part is devoted to the purchase of raw materials. Thus, all the expenses of production eventually become income to some people. The amount of employment directly created in this way is termed primary employment. Because of their increased incomes, these people increase their expenditure on consumers' goods. A proportion of these incomes, however, may be saved, and so the expansion of demand will depend on the propensity to consume. The increased demand for consumers' goods will stimulate demand and increase employment still further. This is secondary employment. This in its turn may produce still more employment and so on, the amount of additional employment at each stage declining. The greater the propensity to consume, the greater will be the total amount of employment resulting from a given amount of investment. To the ratio between these two amounts the term *multiplier* has been given. If, as a result of providing work for 1,000 men, total employment increases by 3,000, then the multiplier is 3. In such conditions in order to provide work for 300,000 people it would be necessary to initiate investment directly employing only 100,000. Thus the multiplier shows the effect of a given amount of investment on consumption in contrast to the acceleration principle, which shows the effect of consumption on investment.

11. Equality of saving and investment

Lord Keynes, in his most famous work, *The General Theory of Employment, Interest and Money*, declared that saving and investment are always equal. Consider his proof of this assertion. Personal income can either be spent or saved. Since, therefore, part of the total of personal incomes—the national income—will be spent on consumers' goods and part will be saved, it follows that:

$$\text{National income} = \frac{\text{Amount spent on}}{\text{consumers' goods}} + \frac{\text{Amount}}{\text{saved}}$$

that is:

$$\text{Income} = \text{Consumption} + \text{Saving}.$$

Therefore:

$$\text{Saving} = \text{Income} - \text{Consumption}.$$

Regarding national income now in real terms as the volume of production, which consists partly of consumers' goods and partly of producers' goods, we have the following equation:

$$\text{National income} = \frac{\text{Amount of con-}}{\text{sumers' goods}} + \frac{\text{Amount of pro-}}{\text{ducers' goods}}$$
$$\text{produced} \qquad \text{produced}$$

The production of producers' goods is known as investment, and so:

$$\text{Income} = \text{Consumption} + \text{Investment}.$$

Therefore:

$$\text{Investment} = \text{Income} - \text{Consumption}.$$

By the first line of reasoning Income—Consumption is equal to Saving, and by the second Income—Consumption is equal to Investment. Therefore:

$$\text{Saving} = \text{Investment}$$

In the case of a Robinson Crusoe, saving and investment would always be equal, because the two actions of saving and investment could be performed only at one and the same time. He would simply transfer his efforts from one form of production to the other. But in a modern society saving and investment are undertaken by different groups of people, and the factors that influence the propensity to save are not the same as those which influence the propensity of entrepreneurs to undertake investments.

Keynes, however, contended that if any new investment occurs there must be an equivalent amount of saving, for if people save, instead of spending stocks of goods (investment) will increase by exactly the same amount. If saving declines, investment will be similarly reduced, for stocks will not require to be replenished, and so production will be curtailed by the same amount as that by which saving has declined. If the money value of investment is reduced by a fall in prices the incomes of sellers will be reduced, and consequently saving also, since saving depends on income. Therefore it is through changes in income that equality of saving and investment is brought about.

The two opposing views, (i) that booms or slumps are the result of saving and investment not being equal, and (ii) that saving and investment are always equal, have been reconciled by the British economists, Sir Dennis Robertson and Sir Ralph Hawtrey, and Professor Ohlin of Sweden, by the so-called period analysis. Income received in one period becomes available for spending only in the next period. Therefore the amount of saving and consumption undertaken in one period both depend on the income generated by the investment of the previous period. Thus, though the saving of one period is equal to the investment of the previous period, saving and investment will rarely be equal to one another in the same period.

IV. FULL EMPLOYMENT

12. Full employment as a policy

There is not complete agreement as to what is meant by full employment. Lord Beveridge defined it as a situation where there are "more jobs than men" but other economists would consider this to be a state of "over-full" employment. A condition of full unemployment can be said to exist if the number of unfilled vacancies is equal to the number of people who are out of work. In such a case the reason why people are unemployed is to be found in the fact that labour is not perfectly mobile. The principal aim of a policy of full employment is to eradicate mass unemployment due to a general deficiency of demand. Other causes of unemployment are mainly frictional in character. As a result, full employment does not mean that there is work for everybody at all times. In such conditions, however, the volume of unemployment should be small only comprising an ever-changing group of people transferring from one kind of work to another.

In spite of the prolonged depression of the 1930s, it was not until 1944 that the State accepted responsibility for full employment. As we have seen, the classical doctrine that supply creates its own demand remained unshaken, in spite of the efforts of the under-consumptionists, until Keynes put forward the view that deficiency of demand was due to the level of investment being too low. He, therefore, took the view that the Government itself should undertake investment when private investment was insufficient to provide full employment.

In 1944 the Government published a White Paper on *Employment Policy*, in which it declared itself "prepared to accept future responsibility for taking action at the earliest possible stage to arrest a threatened slump."[1] Lord Beveridge described this declaration as "epoch-marking,"[2] for previously the British Treasury had always clung to the view that the State was powerless to increase permanently the volume of employment. A few days after the White Paper came the publication of Lord Beveridge's *Full Employment in a Free Society*, giving a comprehensive survey of the unemployment problem, together with proposals for maintaining full employment. Unemployment between the two wars was not a problem of cyclical fluctuations, but was, Beveridge says, "a problem of general and persistent weakness of demand for labour," the root of the trouble being the existence of "a chronic deficiency of demand."

Beveridge laid down four conditions for the maintenance of full employment:

(*i*) There must be adequate expenditure, public and private, in order to create sufficient total income to prevent a deficiency of demand. In a trade slump it may be necessary for the Government deliberately to unbalance the Budget in order to stimulate demand.

(*ii*) The location of industry must be controlled. Where industries are highly localised, changes in demand may cause structural unemployment of so severe a character as to produce pockets of mass unemployment. This danger is lessened the greater the diversity of industry in an area.

(*iii*) There must also be organised mobility of labour, for, in a progressive economy, there will always be some industries which are declining while others are expanding. A policy of full employment does not mean, therefore, that labour can be guaranteed employment in a particular job in a particular place. When frictional unemployment occurs it will be necessary to retrain for work in other occupations those who are unemployed on this account.

(*iv*) If inflation is to be avoided the trade unions must adopt a responsible attitude to the situation. Of Beveridge's four conditions for the maintenance of full employment this proved the most difficult to achieve.

Lord Beveridge did not aim merely at levelling out the ups and downs of the trade cycle. It was not enough for the Government to

[1] Cmd. 6527 (HMSO) § 41.
[2] Lord Beveridge: *Full Employment in a Free Society*, Postscript.

undertake public works in times of trade depression. What is required is a level of investment that will give full employment. Therefore if private investment proves to be insufficient to achieve this aim it must be supplemented by public investment. At the present day almost half the total investment in Great Britain comes from the public sector.

13. Problems of full employment

Experience has shown that the maintenance of full employment produces problems of its own:

(i) *The danger of inflation is increased.* There are two reasons for this:

(a) *Over-investment is likely to occur.* It is impossible to calculate exactly how much public investment is required to yield full employment, neither more nor less. In its anxiety to ensure full employment, a Government may be inclined to undertake too much investment, and so a condition of inflation will be induced, with the demand for labour greater than the supply.

(b) *The wages policy of the trade unions.* Full employment puts the trade unions in a strong bargaining position. In the past, in times of depression, trade unions have had to submit to some reduction in money wages, and had to wait for times of boom to secure wage increases for their members. If full employment is permanently maintained the situation becomes quite different—conditions are favourable to the trade unions all the time. If over-full employment exists, the problem will be intensified, for shortages of labour in many occupations will lead to proposals being put forward for raising wages in those occupations in order to attract more labour to them. Since in these conditions, however, labour can be drawn only from other occupations, wage increases will be demanded elsewhere as a means of retaining labour! Increased wages in one occupation lead to increased wages in others. In these conditions, costs can generally be passed on to consumers, and so rising wages are followed by rising prices, which in turn give rise to further demands for wage increases. In this way the inflationary spiral is kept in motion, and is difficult to arrest.

It was for this reason that on a number of occasions in recent years the British Government has tried to persuade the trade unions to agree to an "incomes policy," under which increases in wages might be related to the rate of increase in productivity. As yet no "incomes policy" has had more than a short temporary success.

(ii) *A maldistribution of resources may occur.* Another serious danger is that economic resources will not easily move from one occupation to another. Changing conditions may reduce the demand for factors in one employment and increase the demand for factors in another. Instead of a transfer of factors taking place there will be demands for the declining industry to be subsidised—especially if it happens to be a nationalised industry, such as the railways—or protected by a tariff if foreign competition is severe. If economic forces are not allowed to determine the distribution of factors among different occupations the assortment of goods produced will not be that which the community as a whole prefers.

(*iii*) *The quality of labour may fall.* There are three reasons for this: (*a*) the high demand for labour makes it possible for the least efficient workers to secure employment; (*b*) the removal of the fear of losing one's job may, often subconsciously, cause many workers to put forward less effort, and (*c*) labour turnover tends to increase as many workers find it easy to change jobs. In spite of all this, however, most countries in recent years found productivity rising as the result of the employment of more efficient capital.

(*iv*) *The international aspect of full employment.* The level of employment in a country such as Great Britain is to a large extent dependent on the prosperity of its export trade. In the past the trade cycle was an international phenomenon, and fluctuations in business activity in this country were generally accompanied by similar fluctuations in other parts of the world. Similarly the recession of 1974–6 affected all the western industrialised nations in varying degrees.

A decline in world trade is specially disadvantageous to Great Britain, for in addition to the loss of trade, there is also a decline in the income from the invisible items in the balance of payments. To be successful, therefore, a full employment policy needs to be international, and so all countries must strive towards this end. Like Great Britain, many other countries, including the United States, pledged themselves to maintain full employment. The danger is that at the onset of recession countries may be tempted to introduce measures to alleviate their own problems at the expense of others, perhaps by the imposition of export controls, as occurred during the Great Depression of the 1930s.

14. The maintenance of full employment

The years since 1945, at least until 1974, were characterised in Great Britain, the United States and most Western European countries by almost continuous boom conditions. For most of the time full employment was accompanied by inflation in varying degrees of intensity. In order to check inflation it was necessary on a number of occasions to damp down the expansion of credit. Thus, most of the recessions that occurred before 1974 were associated with curbs on credit following periods of severe inflationary pressure and difficulty with the balance of payments. In general, however, a disinflationary policy was reversed immediately unemployment began to increase. The effects of this "stop-go" policy, as it came to be called, were twofold: (i) inflation was only checked temporarily and not eradicated from the economy; and (ii) since disinflation had been allowed to proceed only a little way a reversal of policy was quickly followed by a rise in demand and a return to full or over-full employment. A more determined effort to put an end to inflation occurred during 1957–8, with the result that for the first time since the State accepted responsibility for full employment, an expansionist policy had to be adopted in 1958–9 to restore the situation. The success of this policy in restoring full employment gave hope that a recession could be overcome if action was taken in time.

For twenty-five years from 1945 a high level of employment was maintained. The average unemployment rate for the country as a whole for the twelve years to 1957 was only 1.2 per cent and in the recession of 1952 only 1.8 per cent.

After falling to 1.1 per cent in 1961 it rose to 3.5 per cent in the recession of 1963. Recovery was achieved only at the expense of a severe bout of inflation and a huge deficit in the balance of payments. From that point things took a somewhat different course. Difficulties with the balance of payments eventually resulted in the devaluation of sterling in 1967. In an effort to avoid devaluation a severe deflationary policy was adopted, as a result of which unemployment rose to 2.5 per cent in January 1968. This policy was continued until 1970. So far as the balance of payments was concerned the policy was highly successful but the effect on unemployment was extremely serious, the rate rising to nearly 3 per cent in 1970 and to 4 per cent in 1972 with a million people out of work. Full employment had been deliberately sacrificed to meet the needs of the external situation.

The successful recoveries that had been engineered to get out of earlier recessions made the monetary authorities confident that when the appropriate time came a reversal of policy would restore full employment. In spite, however, of tax reductions in 1971 unemployment continued to rise to the end of the year. Perhaps the reflationary measures were slow to take effect because the recession was more serious than any previous post-1945 recession, coupled with the fact that inflation was still rampant at the time they were introduced. Perhaps also unemployment due to deficiency of demand was less in evidence at this time than unemployment due to other causes which, therefore, aggravated the situation.

During 1974 unemployment again began to rise with the onset of the most serious world recession since the 1930s. The surprising feature of this recession was that it was accompanied in both Great Britain and the United States, and some other countries in Western Europe too, by inflation. This put the monetary authorities in a very difficult position: to check inflation required a deflationary policy, whereas the policy adopted since 1950 to reduce unemployment had been to stimulate demand through a reduction of taxation and an increase in the money supply, a policy which could only still further stimulate inflation. Table LXXIV shows the low level of unemployment down to 1970 and the rise in unemployment since that date:

Table LXXIV

Unemployment 1948–76

Year	Average number unemployed (thousands)	Total working population (thousands)	Percentage unemployed (5 years' average)
1950	274	22,954	1.3
1955	211	23,590	1.2
1960	305	24,526	1.4
1965	305	25,063	1.7
1970	555	25,293	2.3
1975	934	25,655	4.1
1976	1,303	25,740	5.1

V. SOME THEORIES OF THE TRADE CYCLE

(A) THEORIES BASED ON REAL CAUSES

15. The origin of the trade cycle

The late nineteenth-century economists—Jevons and Marshall for example—were aware of the swing of the pendulum of business activity, but it was the length and severity of the Great Depression of 1929–35 that focused the attention of economists on this problem. Much was written about it both by economists and others, the former group seeking to find a satisfactory explanation of the cycle, the latter more often looking round for a scapegoat to blame for its occurrence. Explanations of the trade cycle fall into three main groups: (*i*) those that attempt to explain it in terms of real causes; (*ii*) those that regard it mainly as a monetary phenomenon; and (*iii*) those that seek to explain it in psychological terms. The multiplicity of explanations put forward seems to show that there was not a single cause of the cycle but many. Therefore, though many different theories of the trade cycle were advanced, the acceptance of one theory does not necessarily imply a complete rejection of all others, for the most satisfactory explanation of the cycle is probably made up of elements from many theories.

16. Age distribution of capital

There appear to be inherent causes of fluctuations in industries producing capital goods because of the durability of such goods. If an industry making commodity A requires seventy units of capital B to produce it, and if each unit of B has a "life" of seven years a fixed stock

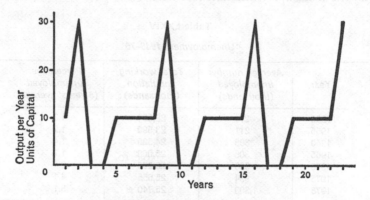

Fig. 92. Output of Capital Goods.

of this type of capital can be maintained if ten units of it are replaced each year. Provided that no change in demand takes place, production of capital B can be kept at a steady output of ten units per year, and in any given year, at the moment of replacement there will be ten units aged one year, ten aged two years, ten aged three years and so on, the oldest ten units being seven years old and due for renewal. To cover this replacement will require the production of ten units of capital B each year, and the provision of capital for the manufacture of commodity A can proceed smoothly. If, however, for any reason, this rhythm of production is upset a permanent wave of fluctuation may be set in motion. Such a disturbance could be caused by a temporary change of demand. Suppose that an expansion of demand occurs for commodity A, to produce which twenty additional units of capital B are required, and then suppose that the following year demand drops back to its former level. No new capital will be needed for two years, so that in future, instead of an equal amount of capital (*viz.* ten units) having to be renewed each year, there will be one year when thirty units have to be renewed and two years when no renewals take place.

Before this disturbance took place ten units of capital were produced each year; afterwards production varies from none to thirty units per year, and assuming no further disturbance occurs, production will then rise and fall in a regular cycle (Fig. 92). These fluctuations will be further exaggerated when transmitted to the industry making the machine tools to produce capital B—hence the term "acceleration principle". From such fluctuations in the production of durable capital goods some people believe that the trade cycle is born.

The greatest recent disturbances to the economic system have been the two World Wars. In time of war there is a tendency to live on capital, in order to concentrate production on the essentials of war, a combatant country hoping the war will end before failure to make good depreciation dislocates production. Capital goods are made to last longer, and no regular yearly renewals take place, so that immediately the war ends it is necessary to embark upon a big programme of capital replacement.

17. Fluctuations in agricultural output

Violent fluctuations in output are liable to occur in any industry where supply adjusts itself slowly to changes in demand, because a long period must elapse between the taking of the decision to produce, and the beginning of the flow of the product on to the market. The immediate effect of an increase in demand is a steep rise in price, because in the short period supply is fixed. This high price makes producers over-optimistic, so that they plan for a larger output than is justified by the change in demand. When this extra supply comes on to the market a steep fall in price occurs, and this then makes producers over-pessimistic, with the result that production is seriously curtailed. The rise in prices which follows sets the whole cycle of fluctuating production in motion again.

The fluctuations in output may have their origin in a temporary reduction of supply due perhaps to an exceptionally bad harvest. Price rises, and this encourages over-production, and price then falls, leading to a reduction of output and so on.

18. Irregularities of economic progress

In a progressive economy there will always be some forms of production that are declining while new forms are being developed. Such changes require resources—land, labour, capital and the entrepreneur—to be transferred from old to new occupations, and the more specific the factors of production, the more difficult the transfer becomes. It cannot be denied that this is a real cause of fluctuation in production, for economic development is irregular, periods of rapid and slow progress alternating with one another, although there has been a general tendency for technical progress to become increasingly rapid. There is, however, little to show that these fluctuations are cyclical.

It is clear, nevertheless, that there are a number of real causes why production and employment vary from year to year, some of which show a short-period cyclical trend. Jevons formulated a theory based on harvest fluctuations—sometimes called the "Sun-spot theory" because it was thought that harvests were influenced by sun-spots. He noticed that periodically there was a poor harvest, and he thought that when this occurred its influence was transmitted to other industries. There is no doubt that agricultural output due to vagaries of the weather is subject to wide unforeseen fluctuations from one year to another but as already noted, producers of commodities for which there is a fairly inelastic demand often enjoy larger incomes in a poor season, when supplies are small, than in a season of bumper harvest. That there are real causes of the trade cycle few people will deny, but no one today would try to explain the cycle solely in real terms. On the other hand, there are others who, attaching little importance to real causes, regard the trade cycle as a purely monetary phenomenon.

(B) OTHER THEORIES OF THE TRADE CYCLE

19. Purely monetary theories

Some writers stress the effect on business activity of changes in the money supply; others, though placing less emphasis on this, generally consider that monetary causes were at least contributory to the cycle. Few, however, believe that the pre-1914 cycle to have been a purely monetary phenomenon.

At the present time the principal kind of money is bank deposits which, as we have seen, are determined largely by the credit policy of the banks themselves and the monetary authorities. The upswing of the trade cycle was characterised by an expansion, and the downswing by a contraction, of bank credit. Some writers, therefore, sought to relate fluctuations in business activity to fluctuations in the volume of bank credit. Many businesses look to the banks to provide their working capital, so that when loans are relatively easy to obtain, such firms are able to finance a high level of production, but when bank credit is restricted many firms are unable to obtain the funds necessary for the purchase of raw materials or the payment of wages, and so are compelled to curtail production. It has been said that banks periodically tend to expand credit to excess, the fact that advances to customers are their most profitable activity often inducing them to do so. This tendency is encouraged by competition between different banks.

The principal instruments employed during the nineteenth century to influence credit expansion or contraction were varying the rate of interest and open-market operations. In a boom, however, optimism regarding the future trend of business may be so great that the rate of interest would have to be exceptionally high to discourage borrowers; in a depression, on the other hand, the outlook may appear so dark that businessmen will not borrow at any price. Credit contraction, however, could be supported by effective open-market operations and banks being more selective in their lending. In a depression open-market operations and a reduction in the rate of interest only make it possible for businessmen to borrow, but whether or not they do so depends on their assessment of the situation. Thus the monetary authorities could more easily terminate a boom than initiate recovery from a depression. Sir Ralph Hawtrey thinks, however, that the rate of interest made its influence felt through its effect on merchants rather than on manufacturers. To them even a slight change in the rate of interest affects the cost of financing the holding of stocks, and consequently their desire to borrow from banks. A rise in the rate of interest will cause the merchant to allow his stocks to run down, with the result that manufacturers suffer a reduction in orders; a fall in the rate of interest has the opposite effect, merchants building up their stocks, and their orders to manufacturers stimulating production. The effect is cumulative, and from small beginnings boom or depression results. It is only because there are limits to the creation of credit that the boom changes to depression, for the supply of cash is more rigidly fixed on the gold standard.

It is quite true that bank deposits are a fairly accurate barometer of business activity, rising as business improves and falling as it slackens, but this does not necessarily mean that there is a causal connection between them. According to Professor Sayers,[1] banks played a passive role

[1] R. S. Sayers: *Modern Banking*, Chapter IX.

in the trade cycle, for usually bank advances began to increase only after the upswing of the cycle had developed, and to decrease only after business activity had passed its peak.

20. Over-investment theories

The first industries to feel the effect of the onset of a boom or depression are industries making capital goods, and therefore the explanation of the trade cycle may perhaps be found in fluctuations in real investment. Members of the Austrian School of economists consider that monetary causes were only partly responsible for the cycle. Hayek starts from the influence of the rate of interest, but to him its principal effect is on the structure of production. If the rate is low this encourages a lengthening of the structure of production—that is, production becomes more specialised, more capitalistic or more "roundabout," because greater division of labour is introduced. The reduction in the rate of interest may be brought about by an increase in saving, voluntary or forced, the increased saving expanding the demand for producers' goods relatively to the demand for consumers' goods, thereby releasing factors of production for making producers' goods. At the lower rate of interest many lines of investment become profitable that were previously unprofitable. Over-investment, however, results, for there is a tendency for too many forms of investment to be undertaken and for the structure of production to be unduly lengthened, with the result that the stock of capital is greater than is required to produce the consumers' goods demanded. When the rate of interest rises it becomes necessary to shorten the structure of production, some intermediate stages being no longer profitable.

The demand for producers' goods, however, is derived from the demand for consumers' goods, and where the producers' goods are raw materials the two demands are even more closely related, since the demand for raw materials is directly related to the demand for the finished goods made from them. It is difficult to see, therefore, how an increased demand for consumers' goods can cause a fall in the demand for producers' goods.

21. Under-consumption theories

The notion that there is a tendency for purchasing power permanently to fall short of the amount required to purchase what has been produced is a feature of under-compensation theories. As a result of technological improvements and capital accumulation there is a tendency for production to expand but the volume of purchasing power fails to keep pace with it. The reason for this, it is said, is that some purchasing power is lost to the economic system because all costs of production do not return as purchasing power to consumers.

Purchasing power is lost, it is said, when producers purchase raw materials or new capital, when sums are put aside to cover depreciation, or when interest payments or repayments of loans are made to the banks. The fallacy of lost purchasing power can easily be demonstrated by the following diagram, showing the distribution of costs of production at various stages between payments for wages, rent and profits, and payments for raw materials:

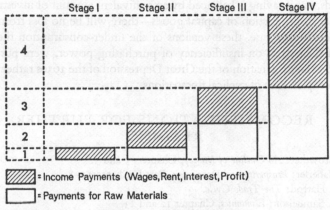

Fig. 93. Payments to Production.

Stage IV is the final stage in the process of production of some commodity—for example, worsted cloth. Stage I will, then, consist of the production of the raw material by sheep-farmers. In order to simplify the diagram, the many intermediate processes have been combined, and reduced to two—Stages II and III. At the final stage, as the underconsumptionists say, only part of the costs of production—wage payments, rents, interest and profits—become income to consumers. Costs incurred in the purchase of partly processed materials at Stage IV become revenue to the producers at Stage III, whose costs can again be divided between income payments to owners of factors of production and payments to partly processed goods. The payments made at every intermediate stage can be similarly analysed. At the primary stage (Stage I) in the production of any commodity in an extractive industry —mining, farming, lumbering, fishing, etc.—the costs of production may consist entirely of wage and other income payments.

It is clear, therefore, that the whole of the costs incurred in producing this piece of cloth have already become income to those who assisted in its manufacture. It will be remembered that it is just because this is so that the national income can be calculated either as the total volume of production or as the sum of all individual incomes.[1] It has been rightly said that every commodity is nothing more than a "bundle of services," the cost of each process in its manufacture being merely the price of a particular service. There is thus no loss of purchasing power because costs of production include payments for raw materials or partly processed goods. The greater the proportion of their income that consumers decide to save, the lower will be the demand for consumers' goods, but if saving is balanced by an equivalent amount of investment —that is, production of capital goods—there will be no loss from this source. In any case, these versions of the under-consumption theory, with their stress on insufficiency of purchasing power, were put forward as an explanation of the Great Depression of the 1930s rather than as an explanation of cyclical fluctuations.

RECOMMENDATIONS FOR FURTHER READING

G. Crowther: *An Outline of Money*, Chapters 3 and 5.
G. Haberler: *Prosperity and Depression*, Part I, Chapters 1–8.
R. F. Harrod: *The Trade Cycle*.
P. A. Samuelson: *Economics*, Chapter 12 and 13.
J. M. Keynes: *General Theory of Employment, Interest and Money*.
W. H. Beveridge: *Full Employment in a Free Society*.

QUESTIONS

1. What is meant by the "multiplier"? What factors influence the size of the multiplier in a country? (NC)

2. Is it possible to distinguish between different types of saving? Is saving ever undesirable from the point of view of the community? (City)

3. Analyse the causes of unemployment in the United Kingdom. Suggest appropriate remedies in the light of your analysis. (Yorks.)

4. What is meant by the trade cycle? Describe critically any one explanation of the phenomenon. (Exp.)

5. "At one period the individual does better service to the community by saving all the money he can: at another by spending all he can afford." Discuss the soundness of this view and what conditions warrant additional saving and what conditions warrant extra spending. Do you regard it as the social duty of

[1] See Chapter 16.

persons in England at the present time to save all they reasonably can or put their earnings into circulation so as to encourage extra production? (LC Com.)

6. Explain the meaning of (a) saving, and (b) investment, in modern economic theory. What consequences can be expected if investment exceeds saving during (a) a period of less full employment; (b) during full employment? (AIA)

7. "To secure at the same time a high average level of employment, rapidly expanding money rates (for work of given productivity) and a reasonable stability in the value of money passes the wit of man." (A. C. Pigou.)

Comment on this statement. (ACCA)

8. "Saving always equals investment." "It is because saving gets out of line with investment that variations in the level of national income occur." Discuss. (CIS)

9. Does a change in the rate of interest have a greater effect on liquidity-preference or the level of savings? (CIS)

10. Examine the meaning of full employment and the conditions for attaining it. (CIS)

11. What are the principal types of unemployment considered with reference to their major causes? (IB)

12. What is meant by redundancy of labour? Suggest ways of reducing it. (IB)

13. "The problem of unemployment in the United Kingdom is no longer a general, but a localised, one." Discuss. (GCE)

14. "By far the most important 'cause' of unemployment in a modern capitalist country is a deficiency in total expenditure." Duscuss. (GCE)

15. What do you understand by structural unemployment? Discuss possible remedies. (GCE)

16. What factors influence the level of investment in an economy? (GCE)

17. "Unemployment persists only because labour is immobile and trade unions refuse to accept cuts in money wages." Discuss. (GCE)

18. Outline the causes of unemployment. Which causes are particularly relevant today? (GCE)

19. "There may easily arise situations leading to unemployment, which the stabilisation of aggregate demand is unable itself to cure, although it may greatly ease whatever process of cure takes place."

Suggest some possible situations of this kind and some possible cures. (DPA)

20. Explain the meaning of the acceleration principle and discuss the conditions under which you would expect to find it operative. (Degree)

21. "Experience suggests that of the three objectives—full employment, stable prices and free collective bargaining—it is possible to have any two, but not all three simultaneously." Comment. (Degree)

22. Why have the severities of the pre-war trade cycle disappeared? (Degree)

CHAPTER 30

PUBLIC FINANCE

I. PURPOSES AND PRINCIPLES

1. Why taxation is necessary

Taxation is required to cover Government expenditure. For a long time Governments imposed taxes to raise revenue only to cover the cost of administration and defence, and in the case of despotic monarchs the personal expenditure of the ruler. It was recognised at quite an early date that some services, such as the maintenance of law and order at home and defence against external enemies could be provided more efficiently by the State than by individuals, and taxes raised to cover their cost could be regarded as payments for services provided by the State for the community as a whole.

During the nineteenth century Government expenditure in Great Britain began to increase as the field of State activity widened, but it was not until the twentieth century that Government expenditure really began to absorb a significant proportion of the national income—nearly two-thirds by 1972. Table LXXV (page 565) is taken from the Financial Statement laid before the House of Commons by the Chancellor of the Exchequer in April 1975. It shows that of estimated Government expenditure for 1975–6 of £28,729 million, defence was expected to require 16 per cent, social services (family allowances, national assistance, health, housing) 30 per cent, environmental services (including roads) 6 per cent and education, libraries and the arts 4 per cent. Some of these services—for example, education and roads—are only partly financed by the Exchequer, further sums being required from local rates. Subsidies to agriculture, primarily for the purpose of reducing food prices, are another important object of expenditure. Quite a considerable sum too is required to pay the interest on the national debt.

In real, as distinct from money terms, taxes are levied in order to curtail the demand (both of consumers and producers) in the private sector of the economy and thereby free factors of production, which are limited in supply, for the Government's requirements in the public sector. This is particularly obvious in the case of labour.

Table LXXV

Government Expenditure

£ million

Items of Expenditure	1975–6	197–[1]
CONSOLIDATED FUND (SUPPLY) SERVICES		
Civil Supply		
I. Defence	4,526	
II. Overseas Services . . .	686	
III. Law, Order, Protective Services .	753	
IV. Trade, Industry and Employment .	2,636	
V. Agriculture, Fisheries, Forestry .	957	
VI. Housing	1,518	
VII. Roads and Transport . . .	1,227	
VIII. Other Environmental Services . .	297	
IX. Health and Personal Social Services	4,015	
X. Social Security	3,144	
XI. Education, Libraries, Science, Arts .	1,132	
XII. Other Public Services . . .	759	
XIII. Common Services	759	
XIV. Northern Ireland	369	
XV. Rate Support Grant, etc. . . .	5,951	
Total	28,729	

[1] For the latest figures.

Nowadays, taxes are no longer imposed solely for the purpose of covering the unavoidable costs of administration, defence and the provision of certain services by the State, but also for the purpose of furthering social and economic policy.

Reasons for the imposition of taxes:

(*i*) To cover the cost of general administration, defence and the social services provided by the State.

(*ii*) To check the consumption of commodities regarded as harmful, at least if consumed to excess. It is for this reason that spirits and, to some extent, tobacco, are heavily taxed.

(*iii*) To redistribute labour. One aim of the Selective Employment Tax (SET), imposed during 1966–73, was to encourage labour to move from employments providing services to manufacturing industry.

(*iv*) To reduce inequality of incomes. In Great Britain inequality of incomes has been greatly reduced by a steeply progressive income tax, as a result of which it was necessary in 1975–6 for a married couple with two children to have a gross income of £10,000 a year in order to enjoy

£6,355 a year after payment of tax. (*See* Table LXXVIII on page 571.) Since 1971 family income supplements have been payable to families with low incomes and national assistance is available to others in need. The accumulation of large fortunes has been rendered difficult to achieve, partly because the ability to save has been reduced by income tax, and partly because of a progressive capital transfer tax, rising to 75 per cent of large estates, which has greatly reduced the amount that can be inherited. (*See* Table LXXX on page 572.) Inequality of income is still further reduced by the provision by the State of social services which, though available to rich and poor alike, are generally of most benefit to people in the lower-income groups.

Items mainly of a capital nature are shown in the National Loans Fund (Table LXXVII on page 567).

Table LXXVI

Government Revenue

£ million

	1975–6	197–[1]
TAXATION		
Inland Revenue		
Income Tax	14,093	
Corporation Tax	2,125	
Capital Gains Tax	325	
Capital Transfer Tax . . .	315	
Stamp Duties	220	
Total Inland Revenue	17,078	
Customs and Excise		
VAT (Value-added Tax) . . .	3,275	
Oil	1,550	
Tobacco	1,675	
Alcoholic Drink	1,475	
Betting and Gaming . . .	275	
Car Tax	170	
Protective Duties	530	
Other Duties	50	
Vehicle Excise Duties . . .	773	
Total Customs and Excise . .	9,773	
TOTAL TAXATION . .	26,851	
Broadcasting Receiving Licences .	234	
Miscellaneous Receipts . . .	1,025	
Total	28,110	

[1] For the latest figures.

2. Principles of taxation

To cover Government expenditure taxes have to be raised. Adam Smith enunciated four canons of taxation. In the first place, he said, the amounts people paid in taxes should be equal, by which in fact he meant proportional to their incomes. Secondly, he said that there should be certainty with regard to the amount to be paid, for it should not be a tax-gatherer's business to squeeze as much as possible from the taxpayer. Thirdly, there should be convenience of payment and collection. Fourthly, economy should be observed, so that taxes

Table LXXVII

National Loans Fund

	£ million	
	1975–6	*197–¹*
SERVICE OF THE NATIONAL DEBT		
Interest	3,570	
Management	80	
TOTAL	3,650	
CONSOLIDATED FUND DEFICIT		
LOANS (NET)	2,748	
To Nationalised industries² . . .	110	
To New Towns	283	
To Other Public Corporations . .	174	
To Local Authorities	1,235	
Others	83	
TOTAL LOANS	1,885	
Total	8,283	

¹ For the latest figures.
² From other sources nationalised industries also borrowed £847 million.

should not be imposed of a kind where the cost of collection was excessive. It has been estimated that in the case of some former taxes the expenses of collection absorbed more than 80 per cent of the yield. A serious objection to bringing small incomes within the orbit of income tax is the heavy cost of collection. The revenue required by a modern Government is too large, however, to be raised by taxing only the wealthy.

(*i*) *The proportional principle.* Under a proportional system of taxation, if a man with an annual income of £1,000 paid £100 in taxes, then a man with an income of £5,000 would pay £500. Adam

Smith supported the principle that taxation should be proportional to income, because he considered it to be the most equitable method of raising revenue open to the State. It was certainly more equitable than equality of payment—a fixed sum per head—as in the case of some poll taxes[1], and as may occur with taxes on necessary foodstuffs.

(ii) *The progressive principle.* Under a progressive system the amount of tax to be paid increases more than proportionately with income. A progressive system of taxation can be more closely related to the ability to pay, and so where great inequality of income exists it is generally regarded as being more equitable than the proportional system, for the Law of Diminishing Marginal Utility shows that the marginal utility of £1 of income is much greater to the man with an income of £350 than to one with an income of £5,000. Thus, on an income of £1,000 a year a tax of £80 might be paid (that is, 8 per cent), and on £2,000 a year perhaps £300 (15 per cent). The progressive principle would be easiest to carry out under a single tax system—that is, where each person was subject only to one tax based on his income. For reasons considered below, this is impracticable, and in Great Britain revenue is raised partly by taxes on income and partly by taxes on goods and services. As a result of taxation of commodities, the burden of taxation is more widely distributed, but some commodity taxes tend to be proportional to income, and some are even regressive. For example, a tax on necessary foodstuffs will result in a large family being more heavily taxed than a small one. The British income tax is now steeply progressive. This is achieved partly by granting tax-payers certain tax-free allowances and partly by taxing income above a certain level at increasingly higher rates (known until 1973 as surtax). The principal tax-free allowances are personal allowances for a single person, larger allowances for a married couple, allowances for children and dependent relatives and the married woman's earned income allowance.

On investment income over a certain amount there is an investment surcharge.

3. The Budget statement

Normally the Chancellor of the Exchequer presents his budget to the House of Commons in April. On an increasing number of occasions in recent years supplementary budgets have had to be presented, usually in the autumn. The financial statement accompanying it shows

---

[1] By the Poll Taxes of 1378–80 each person was not, however, equally taxed. A whole village was assessed at so much per head, but the rich paid more than the poor.

estimated Government expenditure for the next financial year (starting 6th April). In each case the previous year's estimate and outturn are shown. In some countries, for example Sweden, two separate budgets are presented, one covering current and the other capital expenditure. During 1949–64 the British budget was presented in two parts, with the object of distinguishing between current and capital expenditure, though this distinction between the two types of expenditure was not always clearly made. It will be noticed that the Financial Statement given above (Table LXXV, page 565) shows Government expenditure on what might be termed current account, while Table LXXVII (page 567) shows the servicing of the national debt together with loans made by the National Loans Fund to various bodies—nationalised industries, the New Towns, other public corporations and Local Authorities. Until recently the cost of servicing the national debt was included in Table LXXV as part of Government Ordinary expenditure, and it would seem that this is the most appropriate place for it. The distinction between current and capital expenditure is important because good accountancy practice would require current expenditure to be fully covered out of current revenue, but not necessarily capital expenditure of the kind shown in Table LXXVII, since loans will eventually be repaid. Comparison of Tables LXXV and LXXVI shows that in 1975–6 estimated revenue fell short of estimated current expenditure. Unbalanced budgets on this scale are one of the causes of inflation.

4. Government revenue

As Table LXXVI shows, Government revenue is derived almost entirely from receipts from taxation. Taxes are of two main types:

(i) *Direct taxes*. In this category are taxes on income (Income Tax), profits of companies (Corporation Tax), capital gains (Capital Gains Tax) and Capital Transfer Tax which in 1974 replaced Death Duties. These taxes are all levied directly on the person receiving the income (except tax payable at death) and paid by him direct to the Inland Revenue, although under the Pay As You Earn (PAYE) scheme introduced in 1943 most people in receipt of wages or salary have income tax deducted from their pay by their employers.

(ii) *Indirect taxes*. These are taxes on goods and services, and so they are known sometimes as outlay taxes, since they are paid only when particular purchases are made. Of this type are Value-added Tax (VAT), which, in 1973, replaced Purchase Tax, and Sales Taxes generally, as also are customs and excise duties on oil, tobacco, alcoholic drink, betting and gaming, and motor car road fund licences and some other licenses. In all these cases the tax is paid indirectly as part of the payment for a commodity or service, and very often the taxpayer is not aware of how much tax he is paying. How much a person pays in indirect taxes depends on the extent to which he uses taxed goods or services.

It will be seen from Table LXXVI that in the year in question direct taxes accounted for approximately £17,078 million out of a total revenue of £28,110; that is, about 60 per cent. In the nineteenth century less than a third of the British Government's revenue came from direct taxation. Since it can be more closely related to the ability to pay, direct taxation is generally regarded as being more equitable than indirect. By 1913 the yield from both groups of taxes was about the same. In the 1930s about 60 per cent of the State's revenue came from direct taxes, but the peak was not reached until 1945, when over 65 per cent of total revenue came from taxes of this kind. Since that date the tendency again has been for the proportion of indirect taxation to increase, as direct taxation appears to have a greater disincentive effect than indirect taxation both on the desire to work and on willingness to save.

Indirect taxation of necessaries would be regressive. The extent to which indirect taxes are regressive also depends to some degree on whether they are specific (as is the tax on petrol) or *ad valorem* (as is Value-added Tax). To the extent that the well-to-do buy more expensive things than other people, they will pay more tax if it is proportionate to the value of the goods. Upon what sort of things, then, should indirect taxes be imposed? Most people would agree that common necessaries of life should be excluded. Luxury goods therefore appear to be the things most suitable for taxation, but it is often very difficult to draw a sharp line of demarcation between luxuries and other things, and if luxury goods are rigidly defined the total yield from taxing them is not likely to be very great. The first principle of indirect taxation is to spread taxation over as wide a range of goods and services as possible, so that people of all tastes are brought within the net. Criticism may be levelled at the whole system of indirect taxation, but no one tax can be singled out for criticism. The smoker may ask why he has to pay more tax than the non-smoker; the beer-drinker wants to know why he pays more than the teetotaller; the motorist complains of the tax on petrol, different groups of consumers and shopkeepers complain of various other taxes and so on. The wider the range of

complaint, the more equitable probably is a system of indirect taxation!
It is sometimes said that indirect taxes, unlike direct, can be avoided by
forgetting the consumption of goods that are taxed, but this argument
is baseless if the tax net is widely spread, as is the case with VAT. Nevertheless, the taxation of a commodity is likely to reduce its consumption.
Goods in fairly inelastic demand, therefore, are those most suitable to
be taxed (*see* Para. 7).

5. Some taxes

(*i*) *Income tax*. First imposed by William Pitt in 1799 income tax
has become the most important direct tax. In 1975–6 taxes on income
accounted for £17,078 million out of total revenue of £26,851 million,
that is, 64 per cent. As noted in Para. 2. income tax in this country is
steeply progressive, as Table LXXVIII shows. Income tax falls more

Table LXXVIII

A Progressive Income Tax

For a married couple with two children

Annual income	1975–6		197–[1]	
	Amount of tax	Tax as percentage of income	Amount of tax	Tax as percentage of income
£	£	%	£	%
1,300	—	—		
1,400	6	0.4		
1,500	41	2.7		
1,600	76	4.7		
2,000	216	11		
2,500	391	19		
5,000	1,266	25		
10,000	3,645	36		
50,000	35,377	71		
100,000	76,877	77		

[1] For the latest figures.

heavily on the highest incomes in Great Britain than in many other
countries, though in 1971–2 it was less than it had been in earlier years.
Provided that it is not too steeply progressive, taxes on income are
probably the most equitable form of taxation. Some of its drawbacks
are considered below (Para. 8).

It may be of interest to compare income tax rates in the United

Kingdom with those prevailing in the leading EEC countries and the United States. Consider Table LXXIX:

Table LXXIX

Income Tax in the EEC and the USA

	Income	£5,000	£10,000
	(Tax as a percentage of income)		
UK		28	55
EEC { France . .		10	60
Germany . .		18	42
Netherlands .		20	50
USA		12	27

(*ii*) *Capital Transfer Tax.* This tax replaced Estate Duty (more often known as Death Duty) which had first been imposed in 1894. Capital Transfer Tax is levied not only on the estate of a deceased person but also on gifts (with minor exceptions) made during that person's lifetime. Transfers between husband and wife, however, whether made during their lifetime or at death, are free of tax.

Table LXXX

A Progressive Capital Transfer Tax

Value of estate	Tax (%)
On the first £15,000	Nil
On the next £5,000	25
,, ,, ,, £10,000	30
,, ,, ,, £10,000	35
,, ,, ,, £10,000	40
,, ,, ,, £10,000	45
,, ,, ,, £20,000	50
,, ,, ,, £20,000	55
,, ,, ,, £50,000	60
,, ,, ,, £50,000	65
,, ,, ,, £300,000	70
,, ,, ,, £500,000	75

Like income tax it is a progressive tax, each successive "slice" of the taxable amount being taxed at a higher rate. Table LXXX shows the rates of tax payable in 1975–6.

(*iii*) *Corporation tax.* This is a tax on the profits of companies. In calculating profits allowance is made for capital expenditure.

(iv) Capital gains tax. First imposed in Great Britain in 1962 this tax is levied on the increase in the value of certain kinds of property on its disposal as compared with its value at the time it was acquired. It is mainly applied to gains on stock exchange securities but it also applies to personal possessions with a value in excess of £1,000, though not to owner-occupied property. In an inflationary period, however, long-term gains may be more the result of the falling value of money than an increase in real value.

(v) Value-added tax (VAT). Many countries, including the members of the EEC, have adopted this type of tax on consumers' expenditure, and in Great Britain it replaced purchase tax, from which it differs in being imposed at each stage of production and distribution, whereas purchase tax was imposed only at the wholesale stage. With minor exemptions, VAT is usually applied over the whole field of consumer transactions, services as well as goods. This avoids its having directional effects on a limited range of goods, which was one of the drawbacks of Purchase Tax. On account of its wider spread it can be levied at a lower rate than Purchase Tax. When first imposed in the United Kingdom there was a single rate, but since 1974 there have been two rates for different classes of goods and services.

Two taxes no longer employed in Great Britain are:

(i) Purchase taxes. When first imposed in 1940 the aim was to curtail the demand for consumers' goods at a time when factors of production were required for war purposes. Varying rates of tax can be levied on different commodities, a high rate for example on luxury goods and a low rate on goods in more general demand. In 1973 it was replaced by value-added tax.

(ii) Selective employment tax (SET). This is a tax on labour imposed on employers. It was imposed in Great Britain (1966–73) to encourage labour to move from "service" to "productive" occupations, the tax being refunded in the case of manufacturing industry. It seems to have been overlooked that in an advanced economic system the proportion of workers in service occupations tends to increase.

Wealth tax. Many countries impose an annual tax on wealth. In 1974 it was proposed to introduce a wealth tax in the United Kingdom and a committee of inquiry was set up to consider what form it should take.

6. The Budget as an instrument of economic policy

In recent years two new practices have grown up in connection with the Budget. Shortly before Budget day a number of White Papers are published—the Economic Report, National Income and Expenditure and the Balance of Payments. These give details of the country's balance of payments, the national income and summaries of production of the basic industries—coal, iron and steel, textiles, agriculture—the distribution of labour among different industries, investment in various industries and personal expenditure on consumers' goods. For all these items comparison is made with the previous year, and prospects for the current year are considered. These surveys of the nation's economic position are very useful to a Chancellor of the Exchequer about to frame his Budget. Though the actual details of proposed changes in taxation or expenditure are kept a close secret until they are announced in Parliament, the general framework of the budget can often now be more clearly foreseen.

In recent years the budget has been regularly used as an instrument of economic policy:

(i) *To check inflation or an adverse balance of payments.* For much of the time during the past thirty years taxation has been maintained at a higher level than was necessary to cover Government expenditure in order to achieve a budget surplus, the aim being to reduce the amount of purchasing power in the hands of consumers. The first time this policy was attempted was in the interim budget of November 1947. A surplus has generally been achieved by increases in indirect taxes on account of the disincentive effect of direct taxation. It is extremely doubtful whether by itself this type of budget can be successful. Since the increased taxation falls on commodities it will raise their prices, thereby raising the cost of living and leading trade unions to make demands for higher wages. As a result, the inflationary spiral may be stimulated instead of being checked.

A similar policy has frequently been adopted to correct an adverse balance of payments, since this in itself is often a consequence of an inflationary domestic situation. During 1964–7 there was one budget after another of this kind, consumers' demand being curtailed to such an extent that serious unemployment was the result. Even so it did not save sterling from devaluation. Since 1971 there has been a succession of budget deficits.

(ii) *To stimulate recovery from a recession.* On a number of occasions in recent years the effect of a disinflationary budget has eventually been a rise in unemployment. Concern to maintain full employment has then led Governments to reverse their previous budget policy and try to stimulate demand by a reduction of taxation. In the minor recessions of this period this policy was usually sufficiently successful to make inflation again the problem of the day. As yet this policy has not been tested in the case of a depression or even a serious recession. In the later years of the Great Depression it was suggested that the budget should be deliberately unbalanced (a policy known as "deficit financing") in order to promote recovery. The serious recession which occurred during 1969–71 and budgetary policy on that occasion appeared to be slow to take effect.

II. EFFECTS OF TAXATION

7. The incidence of taxation

The incidence of a tax is upon the person who pays it. This is not quite so obvious as it appears at first sight. In the case of income tax the incidence is always on the person receiving the income, for income tax cannot be shifted to someone else, a person's income always being reduced by the full amount of the tax.

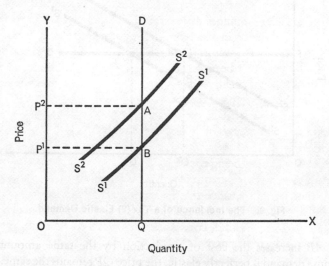

Fig. 94. The Incidence of a Tax (1) Inelastic Demand.

In the case of an indirect tax, however, one cannot be sure in advance whether the incidence of the tax will be on the buyer or on the seller of the commodity, or whether it will be divided between them. Suppose a specific tax of £2 is imposed on a commodity costing £10. If the price is immediately raised to £12 the incidence of the tax is clearly on the purchaser; for now he has to pay £2 more than previously for it— that is, the old price plus the full amount of the tax. If the demand for the commodity is perfectly inelastic the price will rise to £12 and the full incidence of the tax will then be on the buyer. This can be shown diagrammatically (Fig. 94). The tax *AB* increases the cost of production by that amount, and so the conditions of supply move from *S¹* to *S²*. The demand curve being perfectly inelastic, the price rises from *OP¹* to *OP²*, this increase being exactly equal to the amount of the tax *AB*.

If, however, the demand for the commodity is perfectly elastic the incidence of the tax will be entirely on the seller, since at any price above £10 sales will drop to zero. This is shown in Fig. 95. Again the

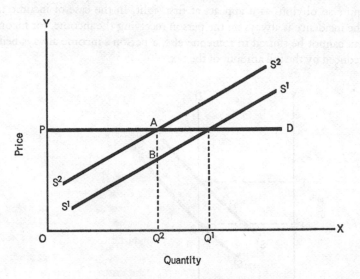

Fig. 95. The Incidence of a Tax (2) Elastic Demand.

tax *AB* increases the cost of production by the same amount, but because demand is perfectly elastic, the price *OP* remains the same.

Both these are extreme cases. If demand is moderately elastic, the quantity demanded will fall off as a result of the increase in price. In order to keep up sales, the price may have to be reduced to, say, £11. In such a case, buyer and seller each pay part of the tax so that the incidence of the tax is partly on the buyer and partly on the seller, as Fig. 96 shows.

From this it follows that the commodities most suitable for taxation (from the point of view of maximising revenue) will be those for which the demand is inelastic. Unfortunately, however, many of the com-

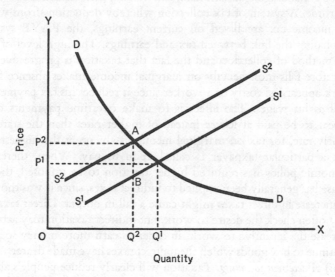

Fig. 96. The Incidence of a Tax (3) Moderately Elastic Demand.

modities for which there is a fairly inelastic demand are common necessaries of life, whereas for some luxury goods demand is inclined to be more elastic. Semi-luxuries, such as tobacco and alcoholic drink, have to bear an increasing burden of taxation because experience has shown the demand for them to be fairly inelastic.

A similar argument can be applied to the National Insurance contributions of employer and employee. To the employer these payments are, in effect, a payroll tax on the employment of labour. If the demand for labour was perfectly elastic wages might be expected to rise by an amount sufficient to cover fully the employee's contribution, this being equivalent therefore to the employer's paying both his own and the employee's contribution. This might occur in a time of over-full employment. On the other hand, if the demand for labour was perfectly elastic wages might be expected to fall by an amount equal to the employer's contribution, so that in such a case the employee would, in effect, be paying both his own and the employer's contribution. This might occur in a severe and prolonged depression.

8. Some economic effects of taxation

(*i*) *A deterrent to work.* Heavy direct taxation especially when closely linked to current earnings, can act as a serious check to production by encouraging absenteeism, and making men disinclined to work overtime. A system of tax collection whereby deductions from wages for income tax are based on current earnings, the PAYE system, emphasises the link between tax and earnings. The high level of tax, the method of collection and the fact that taxation is progressive and therefore falls most heavily on marginal income makes absence from work appear less costly to a worker since it reduces his tax payment as well as his wages. The effect is to make overtime payments often appear to be paid at lower instead of higher rates than the standard hourly rate, for tax on marginal income is always at the highest rate that a particular taxpayer is called upon to pay. When, therefore, economic policy has required higher taxation to be imposed, the increase has generally been applied to indirect taxes, since it was thought an increase in direct taxes might cause a fall in output. Direct taxation may often check the desire to work, but indirect taxation may actually increase the incentive to work, in order to earn more money so as to continue to buy goods which the indirect taxes have made dearer.

(*ii*) *A deterrent to saving.* Taxation will clearly reduce people's ability to save, since it leaves them with less money at their disposal. Taxation may therefore act as a deterrent to saving. However, this will not always be the case, as it will depend on the purpose for which people are saving. Just as a fall in the rate of interest may make some people strive even harder to save, when they are saving for a particular purpose, so increased taxation may make such people redouble their efforts in order to be able to save as much as before. Much personal saving was formerly for purposes for which provision is now made by social insurance—sickness, old age, etc.—covered by a compulsory deduction from income similar to a tax. More than half of total savings, however, is now provided by institutions such as insurance companies and by the undistributed profits of limited companies. In Great Britain at the present day profits are subject to Corporation Tax, and taxation of profits makes it more difficult for businesses to build up reserves to cover replacement of obsolete or worn-out capital.

(*iii*) *A deterrent to enterprise.* Those who regard profit as a reward for enterprise condemn taxes on profits because they consider that such taxes check enterprise. It is argued that businessmen will embark on risky undertakings only when there is a possiblity of earning large profits if they are successful. Heavy taxation of profits, it is said, robs them of their possible reward without providing any compensation in the case of failure. As a result, production is checked and economic progress hindered. It may be, however, that full employment provides conditions in which it is relatively easy for firms to make profits, and so there may be greater justification for taxation of profits in such conditions.

(iv) *Taxation may encourage inflation.* We have already seen that one of the methods used to fight inflation is to budget for a large surplus, the object being to reduce by increased taxation the amount of purchasing power in the hands of consumers. With full employment, however, increased indirect taxation will lead to demands for higher wages, thereby encouraging inflation. A general increase in indirect taxes pushes up the Index of Retail Prices, and so brings in its train demands for wage increases.

(v) *Diversion of economic resources.* Only if there are no hindrances to the free play of economic forces will resources be distributed among occupations in such a way as to yield that assortment of goods and services desired by consumers. Taxation of commodities is similar in effect to an increase in their cost of production. Thus, the influence of a change of supply has to be considered, the effect on price and output depending on the elasticity of demand for the commodity.

Differences in taxation may cause resources to move from the heavily taxed to more lightly taxed forms of production. This result may, of course, be desired on non-economic grounds. Where local rates are high, the establishment of new industry is discouraged, and new firms will seek sites where rates are lower. Similarly, in the international sphere taxes on imports will divert production from "low-cost" to "high-cost" areas, with the result that the total world output of goods will be less than it might have been.

9. Taxable capacity

Over the past hundred years the level of taxation has increased enormously in all countries, and time and time again there have been protests that the limit of taxable capacity has been reached. It is extremely difficult, however, to determine exactly the taxable capacity of a people. The limit must be the point beyond which the additional taxation would produce economically harmful results that outweigh the gain to the community from the use of the money raised by taxation. Everything, however, depends on what the State does with the revenue it raises. At the present day a great deal of it is returned to the people in the form of social services. The more the State does for its people, the greater the amount of taxation they are able to bear. Nevertheless, it must not be forgotten that taxation can be a deterrent both to work and to saving, and so above a certain level can be economically disadvantageous.

The extent of the increase in taxation in Great Britain can be seen from the fact that in 1913 taxation was equal to 10 per cent of the national income; a quarter of a century later it reached 20 per cent; and by 1975–6 it had risen to over 34 per cent.

III. THE NATIONAL DEBT

10. Public debt

Public debt. are of two main types, depending on the purpose for which the money was borrowed:

(i) *Reproductive debt.* When the purpose of a loan is to enable a public body to purchase a real asset, the debt thus incurred is said to be "reproductive". In Great Britain many Local Authorities formerly owned gas, electricity and tramway undertakings, the money for their acquisition or construction being borrowed. Most borrowing by Local Authorities is of this type, most recently mainly for housing. As already noted, a number of British industries have been nationalised, and the previous owners received compensation in the form of Government stock—Transport Stock, Electricity Stock, Gas Stock, etc. In this way the State increased its debt by the amount of the compensation paid, but it acquired in exchange real assets in the form of a number of industrial undertakings. All these stocks are known as guaranteed stocks, as both the interest paid on them and their redemption are guaranteed by the Government.

(ii) *Deadweight debt.* The second type of public debt is known as "deadweight" debt, because it is not covered by any real asset. Most of the British national debt is of this kind. The greater part of the debt has been accumulated in financing Great Britain's wars of the past 280 years, and consequently most of the money has been expended on materials which were dissipated at the time. Although no real asset exists to balance such debt, it might be regarded as the price the nation has paid for its freedom and independence. The British national debt had its origin in 1694 in William III's necessity to borrow in order to prosecute war against France. Each succeeding war in which Great Britain has been engaged has seen a large increase in the debt. In some of the intervals between wars it was slightly reduced, although in the half-century preceding the outbreak of war in South Africa in 1899 it had been reduced by one-quarter. During the First World War the debt increased by eleven times, to £7,800 million; at the end of the Second World War it had reached the colossal sum of £23,000 million. In Victorian days there were hopes that the debt would be completely paid off in the near future, but two costly world wars put an end to such plans. Indeed, the debt has considerably increased—by over £12,000 million—since the last war. In addition there is the external debt, mostly owing to the United States (under the Washington Loan Agreement of 1945) and to Canada. Repayment of the American loan by annual instalments began in 1952 and will continue to the year 2001. There were further heavy borrowings from central banks in 1965 and 1967 in an effort—unsuccessful, however—to save sterling from devaluation. During 1970 and 1971 much of this debt was repaid. Further borrowing from abroad, mainly from the International Monetary Fund, occurred in 1975 and 1976. In 1975 the external debt amounted to over £7,000 million.

Floating and Funded Debt. Most of the national debt is funded, that is, it exists in the form of unredeemable stocks such as Consols and War Loan or stocks redeemable at varying dates to well beyond the year 2000. The floating debt comprises Treasury bills and Ways and Means Advances and represents short-term borrowing.

In 1910 Treasury bills amounted to only £36 million, but in 1975 totalled over £7,522 million. Before 1914 the Floating Debt comprised only a small fraction of the total national debt, whereas in 1975 it formed 19 per cent of it. The funded portion of the debt has fallen from 94 per cent in 1910 to 56 per cent in 1975. The orthodox financiers of the pre-1914 period would have severely condemned such an expansion of the floating debt, which they considered should be kept to a minimum, since they thought that all long-term borrowing should be funded.

The national debt also includes over £4,000 million in national savings securities such as National Saving Certificates, British Savings Bonds, Premium Bonds. In addition to the national debt the total of public debt also comprises the debt of local authorities and of public corporations, excluding that part of the debt of these bodies which is owed to the central government.

The total debt of the public sector in 1975 was as in Table LXXXI.

11. The burden of the national debt

The extent of the burden on a nation of a public debt depends in the first place on whether it is an external or an internal debt. If one

Table LXXXI

The Debt of the Public Sector

	£ million
Foreign debt	7,137
Funded debt	26,250
National Savings	4,050
Floating debt	8,488
The National Debt	45,925
Debt of Local Authorities (net) . . .	22,740
Debt of Public Corporations (net) . .	23,100
Total	91,765

country obtains a loan from another it means that it can import from abroad goods and services to the value of the loan without at the time having to export anything in exchange. When interest on the loan has to be paid and the principal repaid these payments can be made only by exporting goods and services, without receiving any imports in exchange—"unrequited" exports as they are sometimes called. Thus the burden of the debt is thrown on to the balance of payments, which in consequence becomes more difficult to balance. If, however, the foreign loan is used for the economic development of the country, as were the nineteenth-century loans to the United States and present-day loans to the developing nations, the ultimate effect may be to increase productive capacity to such an extent that the loan can be easily repaid.

Internal debt is owed by the State chiefly to its own citizens, or to institutions such as banks and insurance companies or even to Government departments. Interest payments are raised from the taxation of the community, but are paid back to members of the same community. Such payments are said to be merely *transfer payments*, for the total wealth of the community as a whole is not affected, however great the total debt may be. People as a whole pay taxes to the State to enable the State to pay them interest, but the two groups—taxpayers and interest receivers—are not exactly the same, although those who pay most in taxes are likely to include those who receive most in interest. The size of the debt, however, will have an important effect on the amount of taxation to be levied. Whereas, in 1939 interest on the British national debt required taxation of about £234 million per year, in 1975–6 its cost to the Treasury came to about

£3,650 million, without in either case taking account of any repayment. However, a fall in the value of money as a result of inflation will reduce the burden of the debt, just as deflation would increase it.

The burden of the national debt to the community can be calculated in several ways. The cost of servicing it can be calculated (i) per head of the population, (ii) as a percentage of Government revenue or (iii) as a percentage of the national income.

Probably the best method is to relate the national debt to the national income. This shows the burden of the debt to be no greater today than it was in 1938.

Table LXXXII

Cost of Servicing the National Debt

(i) Per head of the population		(ii) Percentage of Government revenue		(iii) Percentage of National Income	
	£		%		%
1815	4	1938	22	1938	5
1914	0.50			1946	8
1938	5				
1975	6.60	1975	13	1975	5

12. The management of the national debt

The size of the national debt has made its management an important factor in monetary policy. Indeed, according to the *Radcliffe Report* (1959), the national debt "has come to be an integral part, even an indispensable part" of the British financial system, since the management of the debt provides the monetary authorities with an opportunity of influencing the economic system. Management of the national debt covers (i) the issue of new stocks and redemption of old stocks; (ii) operations in the open market securities by the Government broker; and (iii) the provision of capital when required for nationalised industries and local authorities. Holders of the debt are Government departments, including the Issue Department of the Bank of England, insurance companies, pension funds, commercial banks, trustee savings banks, merchant bankers, discount houses, building societies, overseas and foreign banks and private individuals.

The intervention of the Government broker in the securities market has resulted in the prices of Government stocks being largely determined by the Government itself. Usually the aim has been to influence the prevailing rate of interest in order to restrict the demand of both the public and private sectors of the economy for real resources to the available supply. A substantial part of the national debt—about 16 per cent—is held by Government departments. The Government broker intervenes in the market to buy up, a little at a time, stocks that are nearing their date of redemption, and on the issue of a new stock he buys what is not immediately taken up by other buyers and then gradually releases it to the market. To influence the short-term rate of interest operations in Treasury bills are undertaken by the Special Buyer (one of the smaller discount houses) acting on behalf of the Government. Thus, by dealings in Government securities the Government itself can influence both the long-term and the short-term rates of interest.

IV. LOCAL TAXATION

13. Local rates

The Central Government levies taxes; the Local Authorities levy rates. Since 1925 there has been a single rating authority in each area, but previous to that date different Local Authorities, often with overlapping boundaries, levied rates for different purposes.

Nowadays, Local Authorities provide many services on behalf of the State, the cost of which is met partly from local rates and partly by Government grants. The health and welfare services, education, police and road maintenance are provided for in this way. Only a portion of the rates is devoted to strictly local services, such as the provision of public parks, libraries and museums.

Rates are assessed on property, each house, shop, workshop, factory, etc., being given a rateable value, assessed according to its size, situation, etc. The owner or occupier of the property pays rates in proportion to its rateable value. For example, if a local authority imposes a rate of 80p in the pound the rates to be paid for a house of rateable value of £50 would be 50 × 80p—i.e. £40.

Serious objections have been raised to the basing of the assessment of rates on property. In the first place, a rate of, say, 80p in the pound will not produce the same sum in every local authority's area. Where most of the property consists of industrial premises and small dwelling-houses, as in some manufacturing towns, the yield per head will be much smaller than in an area where there is a high proportion of good property, as in many mainly residential towns. Differences in the burden of rates between one area and another have often influenced the location of industry. To some extent these differences have been lessened. The calculation of rateable values is now undertaken by the Department of Inland Revenue, and so assessments have been standardised, so far as is possible, throughout the country. Rate deficiency grants too, are now paid by the Government to places where the income from a one-penny rate is low. In spite of these reforms, however, the main objection still remains: ownership or occupation of property does not form a good basis for taxation, for it does not closely relate the amount to be paid to ability to pay. For example, a retired couple may pay the same amount in rates as their next-door neighbours with perhaps four or five times their income. As a result, therefore, local taxation tends to be regressive, as the *Allen Report* (1965) found. Since 1966 a little has been done also to assist ratepayers with low incomes or large families. Their rates have been reduced by a special discount, the cost being borne mainly by the Exchequer. For the really needy national assistance generally includes payment of the rates.

The increasing cost of Government services that have to be provided locally has drawn attention to the increasingly heavy burden of local rates. Reform of the method of assessment to bring it more into line with ability to pay—the basis of income tax—has so far found little favour. It had been suggested, however, that one way to alleviate the burden would be to transfer more expenditure from local Authorities to the Central Government. For example, to relieve Local Authorities of the cost of education would take from them their heaviest item of expenditure, which at present absorbs more than one-third of their total revenue.

RECOMMENDATIONS FOR FURTHER READING

H. Dalton: *Public Finance*.
U. K. Hicks: *Public Finance*.
A. R. Prest: *Public Finance*.

QUESTIONS

1. Compare the advantages and disadvantages of taxation on income and taxation on expenditure. (NC)
2. Discuss the merits and demerits of indirect taxation. (SE London)
3. Analyse the advantages and disadvantages of direct and indirect taxation in the economy of the United Kingdom. (UEI)

4. Local rates are frequently criticised. Examine critically the present rating system with reference to the alternative methods of raising revenue by local authorities. (Yorks.)

5. What is the Value-Added Tax? How does it differ from other forms of indirect taxation? (RSA)

6. Why should a good system of taxation include a variety of taxes? (AIA)

7. "The old theory of taxation has been killed by the double need to maintain incentive in the industrial system and to control private spending." Discuss this statement. (IB.)

8. Discuss the merits and demerits of indirect taxation. (Exp.)

9. "A tax on profits is ultimately a tax on consumers." Discuss this statement. (CIS)

10. It has often been claimed that indirect taxation is inequitable and that to the maximum possible extent taxation should be direct. Do you agree with this view? Illustrate your answer by reference to any current developments with which you are familiar. (CIS)

11. In what circumstances might the instrument of taxation be used other than for raising revenue? (IHA)

12. (a) Name Adam Smith's Canons of Taxation.

(b) Indicate, if you can, what modifications they require to adapt them to modern conditions. (ACCA)

13. Explain the statement: "Budgetary policy cannot now exist independently of monetary policy but must be integrated with it." (IMTA)

14. Discuss the advantages and disadvantages of high graduated death duties as a means of increasing revenue. (DPA)

15. Distinguish between direct and indirect taxation and discuss the relative merits of each type. (GCE)

16. Describe the main categories of government expenditure in the United Kingdom. What forces have determined the size of each category? (GCE)

17. What is the case for a high petrol tax in Britain? (GCE)

18. Discuss the arguments that have been put forward in support of the view that the size of the public debt is unimportant. (Degree)

19. "Since all taxation results in a transfer of income to the State, it matters little whether the transfer is effected directly by a tax on incomes, or indirectly by taxes on particular goods and services." Discuss. (Degree)

20. What considerations should the Chancellor bear in mind when deciding whether to tax income or outlay? (Degree)

ADDITIONAL EXAMINATION QUESTIONS

1. The Chancellor of the Exchequer's task in drawing up his budget is not only to raise enough in taxes to meet Government expenditure, but also to take into account other considerations. What are these other considerations? (Bolton)

2. "The growth in Government expenditure which has characterised advanced industrial countries this century has increased the need for efficiency in public expenditure whilst at the same time making control of expenditure in some ways more difficult." Comment on this statement. (Bournemouth)

3. "Economics is concerned with scarcity and choice." Discuss this statement and explain, giving appropriate examples, what is meant by "opportunity-cost." (Chesterfield)

4. "Increased spending by an individual does not make him richer. Similarly, increased spending by a Government does not make the country richer." Discuss. (City)

5. Trace the likely long-term consequences of the commercial exploitation of North Sea oil on the United Kingdom economy. (Huddersfield)

6. "The prices of primary products are subject to both large and more frequent price variations than are the prices of manufactured goods." With the aid of diagrams, illustrate whether you think this statement to be true or false. (Norwich)

7. What are the main causes of inequality of personal incomes in a country? (SE London)

8. Outline a suitable method for the evaluation of an investment project (*i*) by a large operation, (*ii*) by a local authority. (Southampton)

9. "Advertising is part of the cost of production in that it widens the market and helps to bring about the advantages of large-scale production." Discuss in relation to present-day advertising. (UEI)

10. How does the price mechanism solve the problem of allocating scarce resources to alternative uses in a free market economy? (ULCI)

11. In what ways, and to what extent, can the Government influence and control the economy of Great Britain? (Wales)

12. It is often said that one reason why the people of certain countries live in poverty is that the country is overcrowded. How can that be reconciled with the fact that the inhabitants of the world's three most densely populated countries, the Netherlands, Belgium and England, enjoy a high standard of living? (Yorks.)

13. "The market mechanism is the best way of allocating scarce resources." Explain and discuss this statement. (RSA)

14. Comment on the economic problems concerned with international trade that are likely to face (a) advanced nations, and (b) developing countries. (RSA)

15. There has been much talk about incentives to increase production. Which incentives would you place first, and why? (IT)

16. "We never find monopoly undiluted by competition and very rarely find competition undiluted by monopoly." Explain and illustrate this statement. (LC Com.)

17. "Capital goods are unquestionably productive—and nobody likes to part with his money. These two facts are sufficient to explain, and justify, the payment of interest on capital." Do you agree? Explain the point at issue. (LGB)

18. Compare the advantages and disadvantages which consumers may derive from production by a monopolist. How far would your arguments be modified if the monopolist were a public board? (IMTA)

19. Is it either possible or sensible to compare the national income of Britain with that of an under-developed economy? (CIS)

20. "A policy to boost productivity is more important than a policy to restrain incomes, because productivity always tends to rise more slowly than incomes." Do you agree? (CIS)

21. "Falling stock market prices are always the symptom and never the cause of a recession." Discuss this statement. (CIS)

22. Write notes on TWO of the following:

(a) oligopoly;
(b) marginal product;
(c) the employment Multiplier;
(d) elasticity of demand. (CIS)

23. On what grounds can state enterprise be justified as preferable to private enterprise? (IB)

24. Outline and discuss one major contribution to economic thinking made by either (a) Malthus, or (b) Ricardo. (IB)

25. "What is prudence in the conduct of every private family can scarce be folly in that of a great kingdom" (Adam Smith).

Do you accept that the income and expenditure policy of a government ought to be judged by analogy with that of a private family? (IB)

26. Write brief notes on THREE of the following:

(a) holding companies;
(b) the International Development Association;
(c) oligopoly;
(d) factor cost. (IB)

27. Are indirect taxes inflationary or deflationary? (GCE)

28. How can fiscal policy reduce aggregate unemployment? (GCE)

29. "Devaluation worsens the terms of trade and is therefore harmful." Discuss. (GCE)

30. Why do the prices of motor cars change less frequently and less markedly than the prices of ordinary shares in motor-manufacturing companies? (GCE)

31. Why do economists often disagree about whether a particular economic policy should be carried out? (GCE)

32. Outline the functions and importance of *either*

(*a*) the World Bank (the International Bank for Reconstruction and Development); *or*

(*b*) GATT (General Agreement on Tariffs and Trade). (GCE)

33. Why do some countries have a faster rate of economic growth than others? (GCE)

34. How can the Government influence the distribution of income? Refer in your answer to the actual conditions in the United Kingdom. (GCE)

35. Discuss the arguments for and against the levying of local rates upon industrial premises. (Degree)

36. Examine the case for and against short-time working as a means of dealing with redundant employees. (Degree)

INDEX

Details of some other Macdonald & Evans
publications on related subjects can be found on
the following pages.

For a full list of titles and prices write for the
FREE Macdonald & Evans Business Studies
catalogue, available from: Department E4,
Macdonald & Evans Ltd., Estover Road,
Plymouth PL6 7PZ

An Introduction to Economics: A Workbook and Study Guide L.B.CURZON

Though it may be difficult to agree on a satisfactory, concise definition of economics, its subject matter is beyond dispute. The continuing popularity of J. L. Hanson's *A Textbook of Economics* throughout the world bears testimony to the fact that its wide scope successfully encompasses this subject matter and confirms its position as one of the few standard textbooks in its field.

This *Workbook* is a study guide and a series of tests intended for students working through *A Textbook of Economics*, or similar textbooks. It includes introductory study notes keyed to each of Hanson's chapters, references to related reading, lists of concepts and definitions for study and additional questions for essays or discussions. The main part of the *Workbook* consists of a large number of self-examination questions, closely keyed to the text and based on the objective test method; this enables the student to check his progress when working through the textbook. Answers to the questions given in each chapter appear at the end of the book.

The author, L. B. Curzon, who was Chief Examiner in G.C.E. Economics for several years, is exceptionally well qualified to write this invaluable aid to students of economics.

An Introduction to
Applied Economics
J. L. HANSON
This book is primarily intended for students taking a course in applied economics for the HNC/D in Business Studies or Management Studies. It covers such topics as economic growth and the standard of living, the population problem, the European Community, the balance of payments and international monetary relations.

Economic Theory and
Organisation
ALFRED G. McARTHUR & JOHN W. LOVERIDGE
This textbook has been written with a view to the requirements of the Economics syllabuses of the B.I.M., I.W.M., I.B., H.N.C./D. in Business Studies, C.I.S., I.C.W.A., and A.C.C.A. ". . . a high quality product . . . deserves a good share of the market which is its concern." *Times Higher Education Supplement*

Dictionary of Economics
& Commerce
J. L. HANSON
Most of the entries in this dictionary refer to principles of economic theory and applied economics. They enable the reader quickly to find an explanation — not merely a definition — of some matter of economic interest without having to search a number of books for it.

English for Business Studies
L. GARTSIDE
This is a book for students preparing for, or engaged in, commercial or secretarial work. There are chapters on the essay, reported speech, comprehension, précis, writing, business letter writing and reports, covering the English Language requirements of most preliminary and intermediate examinations in Business Studies.

Geography for Business Studies
H. ROBINSON

This book caters primarily for students studying geography for the O.N.C. and O.N.D. examinations and the various papers in economic and commercial geography set by many professional bodies. Sixth-form students will also find it a comprehensive introduction to the subject.

Management and Business Studies
C. A. LEEDS & R. S. STAINTON

This is an introductory book for students of business studies and all those interested in management careers or an understanding of business. Among the wide range of subjects covered are industrial organisation, business law, finance and international trade. In addition the authors discuss marketing and production, management information and techniques, and macro-economics. A case study and business games are also included.

Mathematics for Economists
L. W. T. STAFFORD

The aim of this book is to help students of economics to handle the mathematical side of their work and to relate their mathematics to essential ideas of economic theory. Topics discussed include differential calculus, vectors and matrices, economic dynamics and the techniques of regression analysis. Worked answers to most of the test questions in the book are given in a special appendix.
M&E HANDBOOK series

Statistics for Business, Finance and Accounting
J. P. DICKINSON

This book is intended to provide a modern approach to the use of statistics. The emphasis throughout is on practical application and mathematical rigour is only introduced where essential for a proper understanding of the subject matter. The material covered meets the requirements of professional, polytechnic and university examinations in accounting and business studies.